Praise for

"Judging presidents by a deceptively simple metric—their impact on peace, prosperity, and liberty—leads Ivan Eland to reach radical conclusions about the rankings of presidents. Whether you agree that Coolidge was a good president and FDR a bad one, you'll never again glibly think to yourself that it's obvious which presidents are good and bad. It isn't—and Eland shows us why."
> —**Richard Shenkman**, Editor, History News Network; author, *Presidential Ambition* and *Legends, Lies, and Cherished Myths of American History*

"Independent Institute Senior Fellow Ivan Eland has his criteria ready. In *Recarving Rushmore: Ranking the Presidents on Peace, Prosperity, and Liberty*, he uses them to rank 40 previous presidents, yielding results that, he says, surprised him. Eland's assessment of each of the 40 is thoughtful and judicious. He neither obscures nor trumpets where he's coming from ideologically. He's for prudential foreign policy, free-market economics, and personal freedom. He's against entangling alliances, government aid programs, and second-class citizenship. Despite occasional dull wording, his writing provokes sober reflection about what a president ought to be. Reading him may be quite an adventure for an awful lot of citizens, including, perhaps, the first citizen." — ***Booklist***

"In the intriguing book, *Recarving Rushmore*, Ivan Eland reassesses the record of all U.S. Presidents based on the constitutional principles that each swore to uphold. While conventional accounts glorify the flagrant misdeeds of the 'Imperial Presidency,' this insightful and crucial book provides an inspiring vision for both conservatives and liberals on the crucial need to rein in White House power and restore peace, prosperity and liberty."
> —**Ron Paul**, former U.S. Congressman

"The majority view, that Lincoln was the best and Buchanan was the worst, results from shortcomings in the way US historians rate presidents, says Ivan Eland, author of *Recarving Rushmore*. Eland thinks presidential ratings are too easily swayed by charisma, activism and service during a crisis. In his book, he ranks the White House occupants according to how much they fulfilled the aims of the Founding Fathers to bring peace, prosperity and liberty to the country." — **BBC News Magazine**

"*Recarving Rushmore* is colorful, entertaining, and profound. Ivan Eland shatters the grand illusion that great presidents are those who wage war or deprive people of their liberty, either here or abroad. The new 'gold standard' for measuring presidential performance, this book upends what we 'know' about 'Great' presidents and will challenge your view of political history, one president at a time."
> —**Jonathan Bean**, Professor of History, Southern Illinois University

"Eland engagingly shows why the conventional wisdom on the American presidency is all wrong and why presidents like Van Buren, Arthur, and Harding in fact ably advanced the nation's interest, while iconic names like Lincoln, the two Roosevelts, and Wilson caused serious harm. *Recarving Rushmore* is must reading."
> —**Richard K. Vedder**, Distinguished Professor of Economics and Faculty Associate, Contemporary History Institute, Ohio University

"Eland calls into question our whole conception of presidential greatness. In this well-written book, Eland offers readers insightful surveys of every president from Washington to Obama. Along the way, he makes a compelling case that many of the so-called 'greats' were not so great after all when it came to preserving liberty, peace, and prosperity. Readers will never see the presidency the same way again."

—**David T. Beito**, Professor of History, University of Alabama

"According to American historians, the best presidents are the ones who get us into the biggest wars, impose the most interventionist economic policies, and trample civil liberties by expanding executive power beyond what the Constitution permits. The more European-style fascism the better seems to be their criterion. That's why Lincoln and FDR are always at the top of their lists. In **Recarving Rushmore** Ivan Eland makes a novel proposal: Why not rank presidents according to the traditional *American* values of peace, prosperity and liberty? Read this important new book and find out why John Tyler may be America's greatest president!"

—**Thomas DiLorenzo**, Professor of Economics, Loyola College in Maryland; author of *The Real Lincoln* and *Hamilton's Curse*

"No matter what party partisans say, no American president is perfect—to say the least. But when historians get around to ranking our greatest presidents, the top spots invariably go to the usual titans—Washington, Jefferson, Lincoln and the Roosevelts, Teddy and Franklin. Ivan Eland, a senior fellow at The Independent Institute and an expert on defense issues, begs to differ with the standard consensus—by about 180 degrees. In his book **Recarving Rushmore: Ranking the Presidents on Peace, Prosperity, and Liberty**, Eland doesn't rank our commanders in chief according to how many wars they won or how many new federal government social or regulatory agencies they fathered. He ranks them on how well they adhered to the principles of limited government as put down in the Constitution by our Founding Framers."   —**Pittsburgh Tribune-Review**

"**Recarving Rushmore** stands as a much-needed corrective to the history of America we are all taught in our schools. We are propagandized to adulate all American presidents simply by virtue of the office they held, regardless of what their record might have been. Indeed, it appears that the worse they trampled on civil liberties the higher the regard in which they are held. Dr. Eland has provided a far more accurate account of the actions of these men (and they are indeed men, not gods), pointing out the manner in which most abused their power and oppressed the nation. Historians who are dedicated to the truth are indebted to him for his efforts."   —**Ronald Hamowy**, Professor Emeritus of History, University of Alberta, Canada

"By focusing on peace, prosperity, and liberty, **Recarving Rushmore** moves us miles closer to a proper evaluation of America's presidents—especially those of the 20th century—than the hallowed (but misleading) Schlesinger poll of prominent historians. Eland makes an eloquent and persuasive case, for example, that Harding and Coolidge were better presidents than were FDR and LBJ."

—**Burton W. Folsom**, Charles F. Kline Chair in History, Hillsdale College; author, *New Deal or Raw Deal? How FDR's Economic Legacy Has Damaged America*

"Of the four presidents exalted in glory on Mount Rushmore, only George Washington deserves the honor, writes Ivan Eland, whose intriguing new book is appropriately titled *Recarving Rushmore*. The author argues that Theodore 'Teddy' Roosevelt was overrated by historians and scholars; Thomas Jefferson hypocritically violated his lofty rhetoric of liberty; and Abraham Lincoln provoked a civil war that achieved far less than believed. Mr. Eland's book profiles and ranks every U.S. president on the merits, including his oath to uphold the Constitution. Surprisingly, Dwight D. Eisenhower and Jimmy Carter are anointed the two best modern presidents, and Bill Clinton is declared in some respects more conservative than George W. Bush."   **—Washington Times**

"*Recarving Rushmore* is a 'very good' book of concise historical assessments of each U.S. presidential administration's domestic, defense and foreign policies regarding peace, national prosperity, and individual liberty. This book is 'better' in terms of the depth of the analysis of each administration's role in an evolving process of shaping the legacy of prior administrations for their successors. And the book is 'best' in the ways it provides insights into how a libertarian perspective on these issues is meaningful for the broader policy debates within U.S. society."   **—Edward A. Olsen**, Emeritus Professor of National Security Affairs, Naval Postgraduate School

"Well-written and fascinating, *Recarving Rushmore* provides a long-overdue reassessment of the actual record of all U.S. presidents. Thanks to Ivan Eland's efforts, the traditional classroom narrative of our 'great presidents' and their glorious deeds lies in well-deserved ruin."
                   —Thomas E. Woods, Jr., Senior Fellow, Ludwig von Mises Institute;
                   author, *The Politically Incorrect Guide to American History* and
                   33 Questions About American History You're Not Supposed to Ask

"*Recarving Rushmore* is a fine book, a thought-provoking study on national leadership in the United States from the perspective of a free society. Eland's rankings and rationales will provide provocative material for discussions of leadership where individual liberty is a priority. Avoiding the usual popularity contest of presidential rankings, Eland weighs practical realities of policies and accomplishments to come up with rankings that are sometimes surprising and always interesting."
                   —T. Hunt Tooley, Professor of History, Austin College

"With the righteous chisel of liberty, Ivan Eland chips away at the war-making, state-building 'great' presidents and sculpts an alternative gallery of America's finest chief executives—men of peace, of liberty, of a becoming modesty. Down with Wilson and the Bushes; hail to Grover Cleveland, Martin Van Buren, and John Tyler!"
                   —William Kauffman, former Associate Editor, *American
                   Enterprise*; author, *Ain't My America: The Long, Noble History of
                   Anti-War Conservatism and Middle American Anti-Imperialism*

"This provocative, profound and enlightening book by a respected scholar presents an intriguing and novel proposal on how to evaluate presidential effectiveness based on domestic, foreign and defense policies as they relate to peace, prosperity and individual liberty. Eland judges presidents not by who they were, how they led or how they governed, but by what they did. He explores the criteria that most political scientists, law professors and journalists use to evaluate presidential performance and points out why these do not accurately reflect a president's actual service to our country."   **—The Rocky Mount Telegram**

UPDATED RANKINGS FROM
GEORGE WASHINGTON TO BARACK OBAMA

★ ★ ★ ★ ★   ★ ★ ★ ★ ★

RECARVING RUSHMORE

RANKING THE PRESIDENTS ON PEACE, PROSPERITY, AND LIBERTY

IVAN ELAND

The INDEPENDENT INSTITUTE

Oakland, California

To my parents,
who have given me love, respect,
and a mind of my own

Recarving Rushmore: Ranking the Presidents on Peace, Prosperity, and Liberty

Updated edition © 2014 by The Independent Institute
Copyright © 2009 by The Independent Institute

The Independent Institute
100 Swan Way, Oakland, CA 94621-1428
Telephone: 510-632-1366 / Fax: 510-568-6040
E-mail: info@independent.org
Web site: www.independent.org

Library of Congress Cataloging-in-Publication Data

Eland, Ivan.
    Recarving Rushmore : ranking the presidents on peace, prosperity, and liberty / Ivan Eland.
        p. cm.
    Includes bibliographical references and index.
    ISBN: 978-1-59813-022-5 (hardcover: alk. paper)
    ISBN: 978-1-59813-129-1 (pbk: alk. paper)
    1. Presidents – Rating of – United States. 2. Presidents – United States – History. 3. United States – Politics and government. I. Title.
    E176.1.E43 2009
    973.09'9 – dc22   2008027839

Printed in the United States of America

11   10   09   08   07   06   05   04   03   02

Contents

Introduction

When historians, political scientists, law professors, journalists, and pundits rate the performance of presidents and their administrations, their analyses often focus on the men and their times. Presidents are often judged, for example, by personal charisma, intellect, communication skills, or management style. Their chances of being deemed a "great" president are significantly improved if they served during times of war and other crises. Bland men in boring times rarely achieve much note.

In addition, today's politics often permeate analyses of the past. As Anaïs Nin once said, "We see things not as they are but as we are."[1] For example, many analysts today prefer a nontraditional, militaristic, and interventionist U.S. foreign policy, and thus favorably rank Teddy Roosevelt and Woodrow Wilson, the men who started and personified it, and Harry Truman, who resurrected interventionism for presidents to use during the Cold War. Woodrow Wilson was roundly despised in the 1920s for leading the country into World War I but made a comeback among analysts because the United States, after World War II, adopted a bipartisan consensus around his ill-advised foreign policy. Harry Truman, unpopular when leaving office, garnered renewed standing after his interventionist version of containment was erroneously perceived to have "won" the Cold War.

Even when biases are openly discussed, it usually merely involves mudslinging between the left and the right. In most cases, commentators on the right label historians, political scientists, and journalists as having a leftist slant when looking at history. But the prejudices of such analysts are more complex than pro- or anti-left and right causes.

One bias, which this book can only partially address, is analysts' historical overemphasis on actions by the state — in particular, actions of the president. As James W. Loewen notes, this slant is especially inappropriate before Woodrow Wilson held office — a time when the state was much smaller and less important to American society than it is now. Wilson was a strong executive and the father of the permanent large federal government that now exists. Even after Wilson's time, analysts, either consciously or subconsciously glorifying the state, have focused too little on the accomplishments and important actions of private individuals and organizations in improving education, the environment, race relations, and other social issues during various administrations.[2] Given that this book is about our presidents, it may further contribute to this lack of balance. Throughout this book, however, readers will find constant reminders that the executive branch has vastly increased its power — more than what the nation's founders and the Constitution ever envisioned. Also, this book criticizes an activist government at home and abroad, which both liberals and conservatives have perpetrated.

The analysis in this book boldly takes a novel approach. It judges presidents not by who they were, how they led, or how they governed, but by what they did. In other words, it assesses their policies and how these enhanced or detracted from three conditions that almost anyone will agree are essential goals for any U.S. government: peace, prosperity, and liberty. The book provides a rank order of our presidents' success using "policy only" criteria and then undertakes an individual discussion of each president's performance.

In this introduction, I briefly explore the criteria that most historians, political scientists, law professors, and journalists use to evaluate presidential performance, and I point out why these may not accurately reflect a president's actual service to our country. Then I describe my own method, based on what the Constitution says a president should do—and *not* do. In other words, this book evaluates presidents as the Constitution's framers might have, had they been around to do it. I show how this method applies to each of the three criteria I use in assessing presidential performance. Finally, I reveal my rankings and compare them to other assessments.

Biases in Evaluating Presidents' Performance

Effectiveness Bias

Richard Neustadt's book *Presidential Power*, published in 1960 but still the most prominent study of the U.S. presidency, defines presidential success as the chief executive's effective use of power to make his policy choices a reality. Since World War II, presidential success has been defined using this "effectiveness" measure. An effective president, however, is not necessarily successful if he effectively implements policies that are bad for the country.

At the extreme of the effectiveness orientation is historian Steve Ambrose's curious observation in his book *Eisenhower: Soldier and President:*

To say that Eisenhower was right about this or wrong about that is to do little more than announce one's own political position. A more fruitful approach is to examine his years in the White House in his own terms, to make an assessment on the basis of how well he did in achieving the tasks and goals he set for himself at the time he took office.[3]

By Ambrose's criterion, any president with great political, tactical, or leadership skills who is able to get his program enacted, no matter how disastrous for the country, could be labeled a "great" chief executive. Thus, even leaders who caused their country great distress — in the extreme, Lenin, Stalin, and Mao — could have been deemed great if they had been U.S. presidents. In terms of U.S. chief executives, Woodrow Wilson, Franklin Roosevelt, Lyndon Johnson, Ronald Reagan, and even George W. Bush were reasonably effective in getting misguided policies promulgated.

The Siena Research Institute periodically asks history and political science professors to rank presidents on twenty characteristics, many of which are effectiveness-based — for example, party leadership, communication ability (speaking and writing), relationship with the Congress, ability to compromise, willingness to take risks, executive appointments, executive ability, leadership ability, and intelligence. Other criteria seem one step removed from effectiveness, such as imagination and background (family, education, and prior experiences).[4]

Similarly, Fred Greenstein, a professor emeritus of political science at Princeton University and author of the book *The Hidden-Hand Presidency*, has come up with six measures to evaluate the effectiveness of presidents, and the categories are typical and problematical: emotional intelligence, cognitive style, public communication, organizational capacity, political skill, and vision.[5] Analysts often dwell on the first four because personality characteristics are more fun to explore and write about than policies. Also, analysts claiming objectivity can stay away from implicitly commenting on current policy controversies by avoiding ranking the policies of past presidents.

This book will consider Greenstein's last two results-oriented measures, political skill and vision, asking the questions, "Did the president have an agenda that contributed to peace, prosperity, and liberty?" and "Was the president passably adept in getting that agenda implemented?" This could include deciding *not* to intervene domestically or overseas. Political skill is assessed only to the extent that it affected a president's ability to get his policies implemented, not as it applied to getting reelected.

Though Greenstein's first four measures are input measures that can influence a particular president's effectiveness in achieving the last two measures,
dwelling on them inhibits getting through both presidents' and analysts' smoke
and mirrors to ascertain the real effects that our presidents have had on the
United States and the world. Were their policies implemented, and did they
have positive or negative results?

Charisma Bias

In the typical election campaign, reporters focus on the candidates' personalities, background, strategy for winning the campaign, and performance in the
race. The average voter really has to dig to find the candidates' all-important
policy prescriptions. Written U.S. history is not quite as bad — historians do
discuss policies, but presidential personalities and charisma often get in the way
of their evaluating whether a president enhanced or eroded peace, prosperity,
and liberty in the United States.

Most human beings are suckers for someone with great charisma. Dull, drab,
or quiet presidents rarely are put in "good" or "great" categories. For example,
few historians would rank "Silent Cal" Coolidge as a good president — yet using
the criteria laid out in this book, he was "good." On the other hand, presidents
who have charisma, can deliver a good speech, and have memorable quotes or
good speechwriters have no trouble being put into top categories regardless of
their merit.

An excellent example of a president with such appeal is Theodore Roosevelt,
a man whose personal charisma and activism have led analysts to an excessive
fascination with and admiration for the man. He had a zest for life, and his
energy level was amazing. Although he came from a wealthy family, he served
in the Spanish-American War and became a war hero, he had been a cowboy, and he enjoyed macho sports, such as hunting and strenuous exercise.
The public loved this image at the time, and analysts still can't get enough
of this Rough Rider. Accompanying the rise of the neoconservatives during
the George W. Bush administration, Teddy Roosevelt's popularity soared to
even greater heights. Again, however, analysts have paid more attention to the
charisma than the record.

In fact, Teddy Roosevelt is less important as a president than William
McKinley, from whom he inherited the job after McKinley was assassinated.
Roosevelt was merely enhancing the already-expanded power of the presidency
pioneered by McKinley during the Spanish-American War. That war catapulted
the United States, long in possession of the largest economy in the world, into

being a global military power. During most of the nineteenth-century presidencies (with the exception of the Thomas Jefferson, Andrew Jackson, and Abraham Lincoln presidencies), the Congress was dominant and the presidency had a far more limited role than it has now — as the founders had intended in the original constitutional framework. The Spanish-American War, America's first overseas imperial excursion, consolidated more power in the president's hands. Compared to Teddy Roosevelt, McKinley doesn't get much attention from analysts — who like strong, active presidents — because the dull McKinley acquired power much less charismatically and ostentatiously. And McKinley, not Teddy Roosevelt, was the first president to travel the country, using the presidency as a "bully pulpit" to lead the country.

Teddy's cousin, Franklin Delano Roosevelt (FDR), is another example of a charismatic president. He was always upbeat and optimistic, which came in handy during the Great Depression. FDR was very persuasive as a communicator and public speaker, using language that the average person could understand, which translated into superb radio addresses and news conferences. He also had speechwriters who came up with memorable lines — for example, "The only thing we have to fear is fear itself."[6] Yet my assessment of FDR's record as president lands him in the "bad presidents" category.

Ronald Reagan, who modeled the way he operated (but not most of his policies) on FDR's presidency, also was an optimistic sort and gave polished public speeches in plain language that benefited from his training as an actor. In those addresses, he presented memorable lines written by his speechwriters, such as "Mr. Gorbachev, tear down this wall," and relied on carefully scripted made-for-television photo opportunities. Horses and cowboy hats added to his image as a macho man from the West, even though he was originally from Illinois. Yet Reagan is probably significantly overrated as president, although not as overrated as FDR.

Had the television show *Lifestyles of the Rich and Famous* existed in the 1950s and 1960s, John F. Kennedy (JFK) certainly would have been a subject of the show. He was what every American male wanted to be — a good-looking man from a rich family married to a beautiful, glamorous wife. Although John F. Kennedy wrote a Pulitzer Prize–winning book called *Profiles in Courage*,[7] his own biography should be included in the book *Profiles in Charisma*. He was the first president to maximize the effective use of television, and his speechwriter, Theodore Sorenson, gave him many memorable sound bites to use in speeches on the relatively new medium.

JFK mesmerized the American public and continues to do so decades after his death. But even analysts think JFK's effectiveness as president has been exaggerated. In 1988, some seventy-five historians and journalists deemed JFK the most overrated person in U.S. history.8 I agree and rank him even lower than most other analysts.

Abraham Lincoln wrote his own speeches and was quite good at it. Many choice tidbits from Lincoln's addresses are carved on the walls of the Lincoln Memorial. Even Edward Everett, the famous orator who was the main speaker at the dedication of the cemetery at Gettysburg,9 admitted that Lincoln's Gettysburg Address was a great speech. Unfortunately, the "government of the people, by the people, for the people" has all but perished from the earth, and Lincoln unfortunately had a role in making that happen.

Harry Truman and Andrew Jackson were charismatic in a way the common man could identify with. Truman, the "haberdasher from Missouri," was perceived as honest, plainspoken, and feisty.10 Andrew Jackson turned his lack of formal education into an asset with ordinary voters,11 and his status as a hero from the War of 1812 didn't hurt either. Yet I rank them both in the "bad presidents" category.

"Service during a Crisis" Bias

George Washington had a quieter charisma than these other men, but like Jackson and several others he came to the White House as a war hero. Having been a leader in defeating the powerful British, he won renown for life. Others would follow Washington's precedent of parlaying war-hero status into becoming president—Andrew Jackson, William Henry Harrison, Zachary Taylor, Ulysses S. Grant, Theodore Roosevelt, and Dwight D. Eisenhower—but none was as successful in maintaining such a revered status throughout his presidency. Washington's stature was so great that he was the only president to be elected unanimously by the electoral college, and he did it twice. Washington was always careful to stand above the fray and maintain his aloof and dignified presence. Like Teddy Roosevelt, FDR, and Reagan, he had a second-rate mind, but a first-rate temperament.

Washington is among three presidents—with Abraham Lincoln and FDR—whom historians and others rank as our greatest presidents in a remarkably consistent fashion. Only Washington was a war hero. What do these three presidents have in common, then? The answer: a crisis, especially war. The greatest crises in American history were the country's founding, the Civil War, and the Depression and World War II. Washington, Lincoln, and FDR, not coincidentally, were the presidents during these crises.

Being president during a lesser crisis also can elevate an individual's status, even if he does not make the "great" category, for example: John Adams served during the Quasi-War with France in 1798, Thomas Jefferson was president during U.S. disputes with the Barbary pirates and Britain over rights at sea, James Madison was president during the War of 1812, James Polk was in office during the Mexican War in 1846, William McKinley was president during the Spanish-American War of 1898, Woodrow Wilson served during World War I, and Harry Truman was president at the end of World War II and the beginning of the Cold War.

According to journalist Chris Wallace, author of *Character: Profiles in Presidential Courage*, presidents are often evaluated on how they reacted to crises rather than on whether they could have prevented them.[12] For example, Grant's presidency doesn't seem to have benefited from his decision to avoid war with Spain over a rebellion in Cuba in 1869 and 1870, whereas McKinley's tenure seems to have achieved "above average" stature for going to war against the same adversary for the same reason in 1898.

Similarly, according to Zachary Karabell, Chester Arthur's biographer, "Presidents who govern during a time of calm and prosperity often suffer the barbs of history. They are remembered, if at all, as bland."[13] Arthur ranks fifth in this book.

John Seigenthaler, biographer of James Polk, best summed up the way to achieving "greatness" status as combining personal charisma and being president during a crisis: "Presidential greatness is a term of elusive and elastic definition. It generally is conceded that presidents who combine a mesmeric personality with dynamic performance in times of crises are accorded the honorific. Their actions merge with their images to project an aura of public confidence, appreciation, and affection."[14]

The requirement of both having charisma and serving during a crisis to achieve high status is demonstrated by comparing analysts' evaluations of FDR and Woodrow Wilson, two liberal Democratic presidents who ended up on the winning side in the two biggest wars in U.S. history. Unlike FDR's "great" ranking, however, Woodrow Wilson usually gets a "good" or "above average" label. The difference is that FDR had personal magnetism and luck and Wilson had less of both. Charisma and popularity trump objective factors for most presidential analysts. FDR displayed confidence, exuberance, and reassurance.[15]

Activism Bias

Presidents who respond actively to crises are often rewarded by higher rankings than those who are less active. Princeton University political scientist Fred Greenstein notes that the bias in presidential assessments is toward strong activist presidents, unless the activism is doing the wrong thing — for example, Nixon participating in illegal and improper actions during Watergate.[16] Conservatives have concluded that activism automatically equates to a liberal bias among historians and analysts, but presidents can be active — for example, in warfare, law enforcement, drug interdiction, curtailing civil liberties, and restricting abortion and gay marriage — with conservative approval.

Also, as the presidencies of Ronald Reagan and George W. Bush show, big government is hardly the exclusive purview of liberals. However, it is true that FDR achieved "greatness" and LBJ "above-average" status by throwing federal dollars at social welfare programs without any strategic plan or conception of what would be effective in reaching the stated goal — ending the Great Depression or ending poverty, respectively. This method of operation resembles tossing spaghetti against the wall to see what sticks. FDR made the Great Depression worse using this approach, and LBJ probably made poverty worse using the same helter-skelter method. In contrast, the usually lower-ranked Martin Van Buren promoted recovery from the economic panic of 1837 by using restraint in government and by allowing the private market to naturally right itself. In this accounting, Van Buren is among the best and the others among the worst presidents.

Analysts have a bias toward activist methods instead of better outcomes. In fact, they rarely ask whether the president in office could have acted differently during a crisis to have avoided it or to have achieved a better result — or whether, in fact, he originally caused or aggravated the crisis he then resolved. For example, James Madison and William McKinley could have avoided needless wars in 1812 and 1898, respectively. If Lincoln had taken different actions, he might have avoided the Civil War, still the bloodiest conflict in U.S. history. Harry Truman could have countered the Soviets during the Cold War with less expense in the nation's blood and treasure. In 1846, James Polk clearly provoked a war with a weaker Mexico to grab its lands.

Allan Peskin, a professor emeritus of history at Cleveland State University and author of *Garfield: A Biography*, notes:

> The pantheon of presidential "greats" seems reserved for activists, which, in the nature of things, means those who dealt with major national crises.

Presidents with the good fortune to preside over quiet times seem doomed to obscurity.[17]

Similarly, John O. McGinnis, writing admiringly on Calvin Coolidge for a book on the presidents compiled by the hawkish *Wall Street Journal,* doesn't give Coolidge credit for keeping the U.S. at peace. McGinnis writes, "To be sure, Coolidge was not a truly great president, like Washington or Lincoln. While he successfully handled small foreign policy crises in China, Mexico, and Nicaragua without saddling the United States with permanent and expensive commitments, he was never tested by a substantial foreign war."[18] This passage shows the twisted logic of many analysts, which says that a president has to have served during a major war to be great — regardless of whether the president started the war or could have avoided it if he had adopted sounder policies.

Even a poll of an "ideologically balanced" group of professors of law, history, and political science, conducted by the *Wall Street Journal* and the conservative Federalist Society, ranked Coolidge twenty-fifth out of thirty-nine presidents ranked.[19] Silent Cal apparently had the misfortune to lack charisma, generally avoid governmental activism, and cherish peace — but he ranks tenth in this book.

Policies Leading to Peace, Prosperity, and Liberty

The framers of the U.S. Constitution, fed up with Europe's oppressive autocracies, envisioned a strictly limited role for the American federal government. The Tenth Amendment to the Constitution, now virtually moribund, states that powers not specifically delegated to the federal government, nor prohibited to the states, would reside with the states or the people. The framers also checked the executive's power by creating three independent branches of government, including a bicameral Congress. They originally intended that the Congress (the people's branch of government) and the states (governments closest to the people) would be the most important players in the federal system. Over time, however, the opposite happened: the Executive Branch and the unelected Supreme Court became the dominant players in the system.

This book uses the founders' conception of limited government, discerned by trying to determine their original intent in the Constitution, as a basis for evaluating presidential action in the areas of peace, prosperity, and liberty. The rankings of presidents here reflect the degree to which presidents upheld the founders' original vision of a limited federal government with an appropriately constrained executive. Throughout the book, readers will find constant reminders that the executive branch has vastly increased its power — more than the founders and the Constitution ever envisioned. This book criticizes an activist government at home and abroad, which is something both liberals and conservatives have perpetrated.

What about evolving standards over time? If the Constitution was amended formally — for example, by the Fourteenth Amendment, which, among other things, expects the federal government to prevent the state governments from abusing their citizens' rights — then this book will hold presidents accountable for executing and enforcing such amendments. Conversely, if a president informally amended the Constitution by his actions, he will be downgraded accordingly — for example, if he took the country into a conflict without a formal congressional declaration of war, as Truman did during the Korean War. And subsequent presidents will be evaluated on whether they followed the constitutional requirement to obtain congressional approval before they took the country to war. Changing the governmental system without formally amending the Constitution moves away from the all-important rule of law — the idea that no one is above the law. Without the rule of law, republics can quickly turn into autocracies.

This standard will disappoint some radical proponents of states' rights and fans of the Articles of Confederation, which assumed an even weaker role for the federal government. But all the presidents examined in this book have been sworn to preserve, protect, and defend the U.S. Constitution, not the Articles of Confederation. So this book will assess presidents on their record of upholding or violating the Constitution's original intent. In today's world, this means penalizing many presidents who have strayed outside the founders' intended constitutional limits on the federal government and the executive branch.

Because of the extra-constitutional expansion of government and the enlargement of executive power over the course of U.S. history, each president has to be evaluated at his point in time. Each president cannot be blamed for the size of government he inherited and the power he was expected to wield at the time he took office. The federal government cannot be rapidly shrunk, and the imperial presidency cannot be immediately made more modest overnight — to better conform to the founders' original vision. Laws, court precedents, and societal norms and expectations all would have to be revised against the tide of history. If a president came later in U.S. history — when the government had already become bigger — but tried to restrain the growth of governmental or presidential power (for example, Jimmy Carter), he gets a more positive ranking (number eight) than a president who served in the earlier years of the repub-lic — when the government and presidential power were more modest — but helped set precedents for their expansion (for example, James Monroe, number twenty-five).

Peace

The country's founders realized that the United States had a fairly secure posi-tion against most military threats — with weak neighbors and two large oceans as moats separating the nation from the great powers and from the principal overseas zones of conflict. This uniquely advantageous geostrategic situation continues to the present day, safeguarding the U.S. against conventional mil-itary threats, and has actually been enhanced by the acquisition of nuclear weapons, a deterrent to an enemy attack. A conventional military attack on or invasion of the United States is more unlikely than ever. This security tra-ditionally allowed the United States to stay out of most foreign wars and avoid maintaining a large standing army in peacetime, which often threatens civil liberties.

More recent presidents, however, have been more inclined to abandon this wise foreign policy for one of overseas interventionism. The new threat of terror-ism violating the traditional North American safe haven is generated by — and could be reduced dramatically by discarding — unneeded, counterproductive, and costly U.S. interventionism. An argument is often made that some wars are necessary, but this book will show that most wars in U.S. history were not — or at least could have been avoided using alternative policies. Wars have changed the social and economic fabric of the American nation, and almost never to the good.

While other assessments often reward presidents who serve in times of war — especially those who lead the nation to victory — this analysis gives presidents credit for avoiding wars and conducting only necessary wars of self-defense. Presidents receive demerits for conducting wars of choice — that is, most wars in U.S. history.

Prosperity

At the nation's founding, in the early years of the republic, and throughout the nineteenth century, the U.S. federal government accounted for only a small per-centage of the gross domestic product (GDP). The founders and their successors

generally believed that private markets, unfettered by government intervention and regulation, would lead to prosperity, and they built the nation's economy into the largest on earth on that principle. Unfortunately, presidents in
the twentieth century deviated from this philosophy and, over time, created a
monstrous federal government that now regularly sucks up 18 to 25 percent of
the nation's GDP. While other assessments often reward presidential activism
in domestic policy—FDR is the best example—this analysis deducts points for
activism that violated the founders' original ideas and rewards presidents who
encouraged the private sector to resolve problems with minimal government
intervention.

The effects of a president's economic policy are often delayed, with prosperity
or economic disaster occurring only after the chief executive has left office.
Even though the economy may have done poorly during the president's time in
office, if he adopted policies that led to an economic resurgence in a successor's
term, he might get high marks in this analysis. For example, Jimmy Carter experienced stagflation during his administration, which was primarily caused by
LBJ and Nixon's Vietnam War and their economic mismanagement. Yet Carter
fostered economic policies that eventually led to the prosperity of the Reagan
years and set a precedent for policies that led to renewed prosperity during the
Clinton years. Conversely, if the economy was strong during a president's tenure
but he adopted policies that caused problems down the road, he gets poor marks
here. For example, Nixon pumped up the economy to get reelected in 1972, but
the country had to endure the resulting stagflation for years after his reelection.

Liberty

The purpose of fighting the American Revolution and establishing the United
States was to guarantee that Americans had the liberties traditionally enjoyed
by Englishmen, which the British king and parliament were eroding. Some of
the most important of these liberties were enshrined in the U.S. Constitution,
as amended by the Bill of Rights.

Many presidents, especially those serving during a war or in the modern era,
have attempted—some successfully—to expand executive power past what
the founders intended. This vast inflation of presidential power has distorted the
founders' system of checks and balances at the expense of the other branches of
government and has resulted in the tyranny of the modern imperial presidency.
The imperial presidency, in turn, has eroded U.S. citizens' liberties; such freedoms make the United States unique among nations. Presidents often claim
that they are preserving liberty while, at the same time, they are taking actions

to subvert it. Only genuine acts promoting economic freedom (deregulation) and political liberty will be counted in the plus column in this analysis.

The Peace, Prosperity, and Liberty Rankings and a Summary Justification of Them

This section provides a summary of my ranking of presidencies, which reflects the degree to which presidents upheld the founders' original concept of a restrained foreign policy and a limited federal government with an appropriately constrained executive. Despite its perversion by many presidents, I maintain that this vision remains the best way to ensure peace, prosperity, and liberty for the American people.

Author's Ranking Compared to the Wall Street Journal and Siena Institute Analyses

Table 1, "Rankings of Presidential Success," divides the presidencies into five categories: excellent, good, average, poor, and bad. In the chapters that follow, in general, more text is devoted to the poor and bad presidents than to the good and excellent chief executives. There are two reasons for this. First, in U.S. history, presidential activism has proved pernicious for the republic. Thus, generally, the better presidents actually did less—and thus less prose is needed to describe their actions—and allowed the American people to flourish politically, economically, and socially with minimal government interference. Second, more text is required to explain why presidents who are titans in the minds of experts and the public weren't really good presidents at all. Only ten presidents are good or excellent in this analysis, and twenty-seven are either poor or bad, demonstrating that most presidents hurt peace, liberty, and prosperity more than they helped promote these goals.

The last two columns of Table 1 compare my rankings with those of the conservative Federalist Society/Wall Street Journal poll of eighty-five professors of history, law, political science, and economics taken in 200520 and the more liberal rankings of Siena Research Institute's survey of more than two hundred history and political science professors taken in 2002.21 Although the two surveys differ a little, their rankings generally track fairly closely. My rankings are

TABLE 1: RANKINGS OF PRESIDENTIAL SUCCESS

Ranking	Name	Party	Term	WSJ	Siena
Excellent					
1.	John Tyler	Whig	Apr.1841–Mar.1845	35	37
2.	Grover Cleveland	Democrat	Mar.1885–Mar.1889 & Mar.1893–Mar.1897	12	20
3.	Martin Van Buren	Democrat	Mar.1837–Mar.1841	27	24
4.	Rutherford B. Hayes	Republican	Mar.1877–Mar.1881 24	27	
Good					
5.	Chester A. Arthur	Republican	Sept.1881–Mar.1885	26	30
6.	Warren G. Harding	Republican	Mar.1921–Aug.1923	39	40
7.	George Washington	Federalist	Apr.1789–Mar.1797	1	4
8.	Jimmy Carter	Democrat	Jan.1977–Jan.1981	34	25
9.	Dwight D. Eisenhower	Republican	Jan.1953–Jan.1961	8	10
10.	Calvin Coolidge	Republican	Aug.1923–Mar.1929	23	29
Average					
11.	William J. Clinton	Democrat	Jan.1993–Jan.2001	22	18
12.	John Quincy Adams	Democrat	Mar.1825–Mar.1829	25	17
13.	Zachary Taylor	Whig	Mar.1849–July1850	33	34
14.	Millard Fillmore	Whig	July1850–Mar.1853	36	38
Poor					
15.	Benjamin Harrison	Republican	Mar.1889–Mar.1893	30	32
16.	Gerald R. Ford	Republican	Aug.1974–Jan.1977	28	28
17.	Andrew Johnso	Democrat	Apr.1865–Mar.1869	37	42
18.	Herbert Hoover	Republican	Mar.1929–Mar.1933	31	31
19.	Ulysses S. Grant	Republican	Mar.1869–Mar.1877	29	35
20.	William Taft	Republican	Mar.1909–Mar.1913	20	21
21.	Theodore Roosevelt	Republican	Sept.1901–Mar.1909	5	3
22.	John Adams	Federalist	Mar.1797–Mar.1801	13	12
23.	James Buchanan	Democrat	Mar.1857–Mar.1861	40	41
24.	Franklin Pierce	Democrat	Mar.1853–Mar.1857	38	39
Bad					
25.	James Monroe	Democrat	Mar.1817–Mar.1825	16	8
26.	Thomas Jefferson	Democrat	Mar.1801–Mar.1809	4	5
27.	Andrew Jackson	Democrat	Mar.1829–Mar.1837	10	13
28.	James Madison	Democrat	Mar.1809–Mar.1817	17	9
29.	Abraham Lincoln	Republican	Mar.1861–Apr.1865	2	2
30.	Richard M. Nixon	Republican	Jan.1969–Aug.1974	32	26
31.	Franklin D. Roosevelt	Democrat	Mar.1933–Apr.1945	3	1
32.	Lyndon B. Johnson	Democrat	Nov.1963–Jan.1969	18	15
33.	George H. W. Bush	Republican	Jan.1989–Jan.1993	21	22
34.	Barack Obama	Democrat	Jan. 2009–Present	–	–
35.	Ronald Reagan	Republican	Jan.1981–Jan.1989	6	16
36.	John F. Kennedy	Democrat	Jan.1961–Nov.1963	15	14
37.	George W. Bush	Republican	Jan.2001–Jan.2009	19	3
38.	James K. Polk	Democrat	Mar.1845–Mar.1849	9	11
39.	William McKinley	Republican	Mar.1897–Sept.1901	14	19
40.	Harry S Truman	Democrat	Apr.1945–Jan.1953	7	7
41.	Woodrow Wilson	Democrat	Mar.1913–Mar.1921	11	6

Note: The author and the *Wall Street Journal* survey of experts do not rank William Henry Harrison and James Garfield because both died after only short times in office. The Siena Research Institute ranks Harrison thirty-sixth and Garfield thirty-second out of all forty-two presidents ranked.

in dramatic contrast to those two surveys, indicating that both conservatives and liberals have a bias toward charismatic, activist presidents who promoted big government at home and abroad.

My rankings turn the standard assessments of presidencies on their heads. Some of the best presidents in the other two polls are in the poor or bad categories here, including Lincoln, Jefferson, Teddy Roosevelt, Franklin Roosevelt, Reagan, JFK, Madison, Truman, Wilson, Jackson, Monroe, and Polk. In contrast, I rank Tyler, Arthur, Harding, and Carter — presidents the other two surveys put in the doghouse — in the good or excellent categories. There is general agreement among the three assessments on only Washington, Eisenhower, Taft, and Nixon.

Author's Ranking Compared to "Short-Term Economics Only" Ranking

Table 2, "Peace, Prosperity, and Liberty (PP&L) Rankings Compared to Rankings of Presidents Based Only on Short-Term Economic Performance" compares my rankings of presidential success with rankings by Richard Vedder and Lowell Gallaway, two professors of economics at Ohio University who served on the Joint Economic Committee of Congress. In the first column, their rankings are based on the change in federal spending as a percentage of gross domestic product and the inflation rate during the presidency (weighted 50-50).

The rankings in Table 2 show a deviation between my overall presidential rankings and Vedder and Gallaway's composite presidential rankings on the change in federal spending as a proportion of gross domestic product (GDP) and the rate of inflation during each president's tenure.[22] Vedder and Gallaway's short-term economic rankings are a good but incomplete measure of presidential economic performance and overall success. First, the Vedder-Gallaway rankings neglect economic growth rates. Furthermore, as noted earlier, the effects of presidential economic policies are often delayed. For example, although short-term economic performance was not that good during Jimmy Carter's term, he appointed Paul Volcker as Chairman of the Federal Reserve, and Volcker's tight money policy laid the basis for prosperity for decades afterward.

The general success rankings in this book consider more than just short-term economic success. They also consider whether the president promoted peace, a restrained foreign policy, the rule of law, restraint of executive power, preservation of the checks and balances in the Constitution, and protection of individual rights and civil liberties. (Table 2 contains a break out of the general rankings on the basis of the peace, prosperity, and liberty subcomponents.)

TABLE 2: PEACE, PROSPERITY, AND LIBERTY (PP&L) RANKINGS COMPARED TO RANKINGS OF PRESIDENTS BASED ONLY ON SHORT-TERM ECONOMIC PERFORMANCE

Vedder and Gallaway's Economic Ranking		Eland Overall Ranking		*Specific Components of the Overall Rankings**			
Rank	*President*	*Rank*	*President*	Peace	Prosperity	Liberty	Total Score
1.	Warren G. Harding	1.	John Tyler	20	20	19	59
2.	Andrew Johnson	2.	Grover Cleveland	19	18	19	56
3.	Ulysses S. Grant	3.	Martin Van Buren	17	20	17	54
4.	James Monroe	4.	Rutherford B. Hayes	16	20	17	53
5.	Martin Van Buren	5.	Chester A. Arthur	14	18	18	50
6.	Zachary Taylor	6.	Warren G. Harding	20	16	13	49
7.	Thomas Jefferson	7.	George Washington	16	12	20	48
8.	Chester A. Arthur	8.	Jimmy Carter	17	15	14	46
9.	John Tyler	9.	Dwight D. Eisenhower	15	17	13	45
10.	John Quincy Adams	10.	Calvin Coolidge	18	14	12	44
11.	Rutherford B. Hayes	11.	William J. Clinton	14	15	12	41
12.	Grover Cleveland	12.	John Quincy Adams	18	11	11	40
13–14.	Calvin Coolidge	13.	Zachary Taylor	15	15	9	39
13–14.	Harry S Truman	14.	Millard Fillmore	17	14	7	38
15.	John Adams	15.	Benjamin Harrison	10	10	15	35
16–18.	James K. Polk	16.	Gerald R. Ford	15	11	8	34
16–18.	James Buchanan	17.	Andrew Johnson	9	17	7	33
16–18.	Herbert Hoover	18.	Herbert Hoover	20	4	8	32
19.	Dwight D. Eisenhower	19.	Ulysses S. Grant	10	16	5	31
20.	Millard Fillmore	20.	William Howard Taft	14	8	8	30
21.	Andrew Jackson	21.	Theodore Roosevelt	11	10	8	29
22.	George Washington	22.	John Adams	16	9	3	28
23.	Theodore Roosevelt	23.	James Buchanan	8	9	9	26
24.	William Howard Taft	24.	Franklin Pierce	8	10	7	25
25.	William McKinley	25.	James Monroe	4	10	8	22
26.	Benjamin Harrison	26.	Thomas Jefferson	12	7	2	21
27.	William J. Clinton	27.	Andrew Jackson	5	10	5	20
28.	James Madison	28.	James Madison	0	8	10	18
29.	Richard Nixon	29.	Abraham Lincoln	3	2	12	17
30–31.	Franklin Pierce	30.	Richard M. Nixon	8	4	4	16
30–31.	John F. Kennedy	31.	Franklin D. Roosevelt	4	0	10	14
32.	Ronald Reagan	32.	Lyndon B. Johnson	1	0	12	13
33.	Lyndon B. Johnson	33.	George H. W. Bush	2	1	8	11
34.	George H. W. Bush	34.	Barack Obama	3.5	3	4	10.5
35.	Franklin D. Roosevelt	35.	Ronald Reagan	2	5	3	10
36.	Jimmy Carter	36.	John F. Kennedy	1	2	5	8
37.	Gerald R. Ford	37.	George W. Bush	0	3	3	6
38.	Woodrow Wilson	38.	James K. Polk	0	2	3	5
39.	Abraham Lincoln	39.	William McKinley	0	1	3	4
		40.	Harry S Truman	0	1	2	3
		41.	Woodrow Wilson	0	1	1	2

Note: William Henry Harrison and James Garfield were not ranked by either the author or Vedder and Gallaway because they served too little time in office. George W. Bush and Barack Obama were ranked by the author, but not by Vedder and Gallaway.

*In each category, presidents were rated on a 0 to 20 scale, with 60 being a perfect score.

Many of these factors affect long-term economic performance and also may even exceed its importance. For example, although Grover Cleveland's composite short-term economic score from Vedder and Gallaway ranks him twelfth of thirty-nine presidents ranked, he set a very bad long-term economic and regulatory precedent by creating the Interstate Commerce Commission to regulate railroad rates, which Vedder and Gallaway's ranking did not take into account. That said, noneconomic considerations bump up Cleveland to number two of the forty-one presidents ranked in this volume. In general, Cleveland respected the limits of executive power, ran a noninterventionist foreign policy, and respected the rule of law.

James Monroe, who is ranked number four of thirty-nine presidents by Vedder and Gallaway's short-term economic ranking, is ranked only twenty-fifth of forty-one presidents in this volume. This lower ranking is given because Monroe began the long process of converting the Democratic-Republican (now the Democratic) Party and the nation from a small-government orientation into a big government mind-set—domestically, militarily, and in foreign policy. This bad precedent outweighs the good short-term economic performance during his term.

In the cases of Warren Harding, Martin Van Buren, Chester Arthur, John Tyler, and Rutherford B. Hayes, their good short-term economic performances more closely aligned with, but did not fully account for, the positive rankings given them in this volume. Similarly, in the cases of Abraham Lincoln, FDR, George H. W. Bush, LBJ, Ronald Reagan, JFK, Richard Nixon, James Madison, Benjamin Harrison, William McKinley, William Howard Taft, and Teddy Roosevelt, poor short-term economic performances paralleled, but did not totally account for, the poor rankings these presidents received in this volume.

Party Affiliations in the Rankings

As for party affiliation, the rankings here indicate that the Democratic Party (including its original Republican Party and Democratic-Republican Party antecedents) had most of the very best and worst presidents, while modern-day (Civil War and after) Republican Party presidents tend to be more numerous in the mid-ranges. This conclusion also holds among recent presidents.

Yet history shows that party affiliation is not necessarily a good indicator of what a particular president's policies will be. The parties have shifted policy positions over time. The Democrats, until Woodrow Wilson, were the party of small government, and the Republicans were the party of big government.

After Woodrow Wilson, the Democrats joined the Republicans in the big government camp. Overseas, for most of their existence in the nineteenth century, both parties propounded a restrained U.S. foreign policy. Now both parties are champions of U.S. interventionism worldwide. In addition, sometimes presidents who take stands against their party's tenets or their own ideological history have a greater chance of getting certain policies adopted—for example, anti-communist Richard Nixon opened diplomatic relations with China, hawkish Ronald Reagan achieved some arms control, Bill Clinton promoted welfare reform and free-trade agreements, and Whig John Tyler resisted big government policies.

In the end, the presidential rankings in this volume are surprising, even to me. But that's where the analysis led. Hopefully, readers will be convinced of the appropriateness of the rankings by the narrative for each chief executive.

Acknowledgments

I am grateful for each one who has assisted in the preparation of this book and in the tasks of reviewing, researching, writing, editing, designing, typesetting, marketing, and selling it. Colleagues at the Independent Institute that I would like to thank include: Anthony Gregory, first and foremost, for his ideas, suggestions, research, and constant support; David Theroux, President, for staying the course, in so many ways; Martin Buerger for overseeing the multiplicity of tasks; Alex Tabarrok, former Research Director, for his scholarly feedback and general assistance; Gail Saari, Publication Director, for her attention to all the details of the production process and her unflagging good cheer; Roland de Beque, former Production Manager, who labored away designing multiple covers and producing ancillary materials, all beyond the call of duty; Roy M. Carlisle, Acquisitions Director, for his editorial suggestions, marketing support, and general enthusiasm for the project; Wendy Honett, former Publicity Manager, for her lightning speed responses and ability to create buzz in the cacophony of the media world. Other professionals who contributed to this process include: Shirley Coe, freelance copyeditor, for her insightful comments and suggestions; Tom Hassett, for interminable proofreading tasks; Melody England, for producing a superb index; and, finally, the scholarly reviewers and professional colleagues who provided honest and challenging feedback, which made the book immeasurably better than it might have been.

Ultimately, of course, the rankings and opinions and ideas expressed in this book are my own and no one else can be blamed for lapses or lacunae. I do hope we can begin a new conversation in this country around these ideas and what it might mean to have a President and administration who take the Constitutional imperatives very seriously.

1

GEORGE WASHINGTON

A Precedent-Setting Presidency—
Both Good and Bad

PP&L* RANKING: 7
Category: Good

First president of the United States

Term: April 30, 1789, to March 3, 1797
Party: Federalist
Born: February 22, 1732, Westmoreland County,
    Colony of Virginia, British America
Died: December 14, 1799 (age sixty-seven), Mount Vernon, Virginia,
    United States
Spouse: Martha Dandridge Custis Washington
Education: Tutored and Self-taught
Occupation: Farmer and soldier
Religion: Anglican/Episcopalian

Analysts routinely rank George Washington as one of the three greatest American presidents, with Abraham Lincoln and Franklin Delano Roosevelt. So why is he ranked only seventh in this book — mid-range in the good category? Although Washington hated political parties and thus eschewed being labeled, by his second term he was clearly in the Federalist camp — as opposed to being in the Republican Party, which was the forerunner of the Democratic-Republican and Democratic designations. This meant that he had bought into Secretary of the Treasury Alexander Hamilton's vision of creating a strong executive and using government to the advantage of big business. In this book, Washington does not rank as one of the three greatest presidents because he

---

*PP&L = Peace, Prosperity, and Liberty.

expanded the president's power past what most signers of the Constitution had envisioned.

Yet Washington still gets better-than-average marks, despite his party's philosophy of expansive government, simply because he did not use his immense post–Revolutionary War prestige to become king — or at least not a democratic despot like Oliver Cromwell in Britain — and he did subject himself to some self-limitations. Thomas Jefferson believed that Washington's moderation prevented the American Revolution from ultimately destroying the freedoms it intended to enshrine.[1]

Washington also set dangerous precedents of presidential power by usurping control of foreign policy during his term, but the policy he practiced overseas was considerably restrained. At home, he used military force more readily and perhaps needlessly. Besides limiting himself to two terms as president, he made a critical contribution to liberty by suggesting that the Congress consider amending the Constitution to provide the revered Bill of Rights.

PEACE

Manhandled Domestic Incidents and Determined Foreign Policy

The Whiskey Rebellion of 1794 was not a revolt to overthrow the government but merely an anti-tax protest. Although no one was killed and Washington pardoned the rioters, he violated the Constitution by suppressing the rebellion, using military force even though the governor of Pennsylvania thought the issue could be settled in the courts. The Constitution requires that states have the discretion to call for federal intervention when domestic unrest occurs. Washington's action also set the bad precedent that the president — not the Congress, as implied in the Constitution — could approve the suppression of threats against domestic tranquility and the constitutional order. In a 1795 law, the Congress unconstitutionally formalized this alteration in the checks and balances system by delegating to the president its enumerated power of calling up the militia in emergencies.

Although Washington pledged to negotiate with the Indians over use of their territory, he aggressively used force to grab Indian land in what is now the Midwest.[2] During Washington's administration, fighting various Indian tribes consumed 80 percent of the federal budget. Although Washington previously had a high opinion of Native Americans, after fighting them in the Ohio War in 1790 he denounced the Ohio Indians as "having nothing human except the shape." Psychologists would later call this type of rationalization "blaming the victim."[3]

Curiously, in contrast to these belligerent actions, in 1793, before the Whiskey Rebellion, Washington refused a request to send troops to Georgia to defend against Indian attacks because he correctly believed that only the Congress could approve such a military deployment.[4]

Under Washington, the executive branch became the sole maker of U.S. foreign policy, a role that was not stipulated in the Constitution. Washington's desire to entrench the executive's dominance of foreign policy was so great that he proclaimed — without consulting the Congress — U.S. neutrality in the Franco-British war that broke out in 1793, a good policy that nevertheless undermined the Congress's constitutional power to start or refrain from initiating wars (the war power). Also, he refused congressional demands in 1792 for information about the ruinous war against the Indians and in 1796 for data on the negotiation of the Jay Treaty. In addition, he protested a House resolution in 1792 congratulating France on its new constitution.[5] The refusal to provide information to Congress on the Jay Treaty and the Indian war set a bad precedent for future presidents to withhold critical information from Congress. Modern pro-executive analysts have used these precedents to build support for the more recent constitutional myth of executive privilege.[6]

Washington, like many of the nation's founders, realized that the United States, with its geographical advantage of being far away from most of the world's centers of conflict, had the luxury of staying out of debilitating foreign wars and overseas alliances that could very well entangle the country in those faraway conflicts.

Demonstrating an avoidance of enduring alliances, Washington broke the U.S. alliance with France, left over from the American Revolution, when that nation declared war on Britain in 1793. Yet the United States did not adhere to strict neutrality in the conflict — ultimately signing the Jay Treaty in 1795, which was so favorable to Britain that it generated anti-U.S. hostility from the French. This enmity ultimately led to the naval Quasi-War with France during John Adams's administration. Meanwhile, the unresolved issues in the Jay Treaty with Britain ultimately led to the War of 1812.[7]

PROSPERITY

Inflated Executive Power Past the Constitutional Framers' Intentions

The Constitution — envisioning that the Congress would be the most dominant of the three branches of government — specified many more powers for that body, even in defense and foreign policy, than for the executive, which was to possess only vague powers in policy implementation, diplomacy, and command of the armed forces. Washington filled in the details of presidential responsibilities using an outlook of "energy in the executive." In contrast to the sentiment at the Constitutional Convention and among many presidents of the nineteenth century, Washington believed the president should legislate and execute rather than just administer.

Washington used Alexander Hamilton's economic proposals to insert the executive into Congress's constitutionally given sphere of creating legislation that governs fiscal and commercial policy. This intrusion into Congress's jurisdiction set a bad precedent, and executive powers in this arena were expanded later.

In economic policy, Hamilton, as secretary of the treasury, erected a protective tariff and established a national bank, which he argued could be created because the Constitution did not forbid the federal government from doing so. The Tenth Amendment to the Constitution, however, would say that all powers not specifically delegated to the federal government, nor prohibited to the states, would reside with the states or the people. The framers put this amendment into the Bill of Rights because they presciently feared that the federal government, and especially the president, would try to argue exactly what Hamilton was arguing — that if the Constitution didn't prohibit the federal government or the president from doing something, they had the inherent or implied power to do it.

Despite the ratification of the Bill of Rights in December 1791, almost three years into Washington's first term, Hamilton's pernicious doctrine of implied powers would continue to undermine the Tenth Amendment throughout U.S. history and eventually render it moribund. Ignoring the founders' attempt to block implied powers from leading to autocratic rule, Washington shaped an influential executive branch, which formulated most of the nation's domestic and foreign policies.[8] Washington inserted his power wherever the Constitution was silent or fuzzy in intent, a clear violation of the letter and spirit of the Tenth Amendment.

Hamilton also cut a deal with Thomas Jefferson and James Madison that would allow the federal government to assume the debts of the states, in exchange for a southern capital city in Washington, D.C. Hamilton hoped this deal would give the states no reason to impose taxes and every reason to wither away — leaving the federal government paramount. Yet Washington rejected the excesses of Hamilton's program — for example, providing assistance and subsidies to business and internal improvements (infrastructure projects, such as roads and canals).[9] Nevertheless, Vedder and Gallaway rank Washington mediocre — twenty-second out of thirty-nine presidents ranked — in promoting limited government and ensuring price stability.

Although the Federalist Party eventually went belly up, Hamilton's outlook later became the dominant political orientation in American history — unfortunately beating out Thomas Jefferson's competing philosophy of keeping government small to maximize liberty for the common man. During Washington's administration, Jefferson became so dissatisfied with government–business collusion and other activist administration policies that he quit his post of secretary of state, the most important cabinet position.[10]

LIBERTY

Set Precedents Limiting Presidential Powers

Despite Washington's enjoyment of fancy accessories and accommodations, he was committed to republican ideals and generally did respect the checks and balances system. For example, he deferred to Congress on most legislation and used the executive veto only when he believed domestic legislation was unconstitutional, a precedent that held for a while although it is not required by the Constitution.

In his first inaugural address, Washington recommended that Congress consider amending the Constitution to provide the Bill of Rights, a vital contribution to the republic.[11] In his Farewell Address, the former general and set a precedent and astutely warned against the United States entering permanent alliances and against maintaining a large standing army, a danger to liberty.

Perhaps one of the most critical actions that Washington ever took as president was to voluntarily leave office after two terms, even though he could have easily won a third term or even ruled for life, as some suggested he should do. He believed in rotation in office.[12] Washington's norm was so strong and important that it endured without any formal legal provision until Franklin Delano

Roosevelt abused it prior to World War II. Later, a constitutional amendment codified Washington's precedent.

In the modern era, many advocates of small government have disparaged Washington's presidency, but they forget that the victorious and immensely popular General Washington could have seized much more power in the new government than he did. If he had served in office until he died, it would have set an unbelievably bad precedent for the new country. Furthermore, according to Burns and Dunn, when Washington took office, the experiment of a republican government in a large nation — a unique historical event — was hanging in the balance, but when his term ended it had triumphed.[13] Washington needs to be given tremendous credit for just getting the new system through this critical and shaky first stage. And despite Washington's several bad precedents, without his magisterial presence, presidential power generally waned (except during the terms of Thomas Jefferson and Andrew Jackson, also a former general, who also had a strong personal aura) until the Civil War allowed Abraham Lincoln to augment it past anything the Constitution had ever envisioned.

CONCLUSION

Although George Washington did expand executive power past what the Constitution had envisioned, he also limited presidential power in certain ways, did not become a king, and ensured the survival of the new constitutional system. In addition, he realized that the United States' geographical advantages gave it the luxury of staying out of foreign alliances and conflicts. This earns him the rank of seven here. After Washington, with his strong presence, left the executive office, the presidency generally declined in power back toward what the framers originally had in mind.

2

JOHN ADAMS

Used the Quasi-War with France to Restrict Civil Liberties

PP&L* RANKING: 22
Category: Poor

Second president of the United States

Term: March 4, 1797, to March 4, 1801
Party: Federalist
Born: October 30, 1735, Quincy, Massachusetts
Died: July 4, 1826 (age ninety), Quincy, Massachusetts
Spouse: Abigail Smith Adams
Alma Mater: Harvard College
Occupation: Lawyer
Religion: Unitarian

Like Thomas Jefferson and James Madison, John Adams's exploits as a leader in the American Revolution before he became president were impressive, but his tenure as chief executive was much less so. He was, however, a better president (in the poor category) than either Jefferson or Madison (both in the bad presidents category).

In a time when the new nation's military force was weak, Adams steered a course away from involvement in conflict between France and Great Britain. His enforcement of the Alien and Sedition acts, with their repression of civil liberties, stands against him, as does his appointment of John Marshall as chief justice of the Supreme Court.

---

*PP&L = Peace, Prosperity, and Liberty.

PEACE

Avoided War with France

Wars involving France, during the revolutionary and Napoleonic governments, affected several presidencies. Britain and France were fighting, and U.S. maritime trade was being harmed in the process. Adams inherited this problem from the Washington administration, which had signed the British-friendly Jay Treaty. The treaty had infuriated France, a U.S. ally since the Revolutionary War days. Fearing that U.S. shipping was heading to Britain, the French navy began to seize American vessels in the Caribbean in what was called the Quasi-War, so named because of its limited naval combat.

In return, the Congress authorized Adams to seize ships sailing to French ports. Adams exceeded the congressional authorization by ordering the seizure of vessels sailing to or from French ports. When a U.S. ship seized a ship as it came out of a French port, the owners sued for damages in the U.S. courts. The Supreme Court, in the case *Little v. Barreme*, ruled in favor of them: the U.S. ship captain was liable because Adams's orders exceeded the authority Congress had given him as commander in chief.[1]

This ruling illustrates that in the early years of the republic, the Congress, not the chief executive, was expected to have primary war power, and the president's power as commander in chief was construed narrowly (that is, he had no "implied powers" to act independently of Congress). Unfortunately, during the Cold War and post–Cold War eras, the rise of an imperial presidency would allow the president to expand his role of commander in chief to the detriment of the people's branch, which the founders believed, in a republic, should be the branch to pass judgment about whether and under what circumstances the country went to war.

The young United States had little military strength to withstand a war with France.[2] Adams initially stirred up war fever, and the Congress, which was controlled by his own Federalist Party and which disliked France, would have voted for war if Adams had given them the nod. However, Adams — against the wishes of his own congressional supporters, most of his cabinet, and extremist members of his own party — sent a peace commission to France in 1799. He wisely and courageously avoided war with a much more powerful country. His peace initiative ensured a split in his party, his unpopularity in the face of the public's war fever, and his consequent political obituary.

In 1798, the threat of the French invading America diminished after British Admiral Horatio Nelson defeated the powerful French navy off the coast of

Egypt in the Battle of the Nile. Peace with France became much more likely, and a treaty was eventually signed.

Rather than rattle the saber against France and pay for the costly augmentation of armaments, Adams could have merely repudiated Washington's non-neutral Jay Treaty with Britain. The United States could not have expected its commerce to be treated neutrally by belligerents when it wasn't really neutral. Yet in the end, Adams did avoid a full-blown war with France.

Disbanded the Army to Prevent Hamilton's Coup

Adams built up the navy, created the Marine Corps, and separated the Department of the Navy from the War Department. Being suspicious of standing armies, Adams wisely disbanded the army after the naval hostilities were over because he feared that its de facto commander — his party rival, Alexander Hamilton — would stage a coup and lead the United States to rejoin the British Empire. Hamilton was secretly scheming to use the army, with help from the British navy, to conquer Florida, Louisiana, and maybe even all of Spanish America. Having no army is better than having a repressive and aggressive one.

PROSPERITY

Advocated Mediocre Economic Policies

Adams may have saved the country from Hamiltonian militarism, but he also had to create the first direct tax on the American people, a land tax, to pay for the military buildup.[3] In general, Adams's economic initiatives got him a slightly above average ranking from Vedder and Gallaway — fifteenth out of thirty-nine presidents ranked — on policies limiting government and fighting inflation. Given Adams's Federalist nature, this ranking might be a little high.

Made the Worst Supreme Court Appointment in U.S. History

In one of his last official acts, Adams appointed Federalist John Marshall as chief justice of the Supreme Court, which was one of his most consequential and unfortunate actions. Marshall served on the court for thirty-four years, and his more expansive vision of government, as enunciated in his many opinions, eventually had more influence on American history than Thomas Jefferson's philosophy of limited government.

Under Marshall, in the case *Marbury v. Madison*, for the first time the Supreme Court struck down as unconstitutional a law passed by the Congress and signed by the president. This precedent would eventually lead to recognizing the Supreme Court's power to review legislation created by the other branches — something not envisioned by the Constitution. Thus, the unelected Supreme Court eventually became much more powerful than the founders had intended. Before this case, each branch of government formed its own opinion on the constitutionality of laws.

LIBERTY

Threatened Constitutional Rights

Adams did not request passage of the Alien and Sedition acts of 1798, but he did use the new laws zealously. This was probably the second-worst compromise of America's unique and vital freedoms in the nation's history, exceeded in its severity only by Woodrow Wilson's crackdown on dissent during World War I. The Alien Act gave Adams the power to deport any foreigners he considered dangerous. The Sedition Act — even more insidious because it eviscerated the First Amendment's guarantee of free speech — banned insurrection, riot, and unlawful assembly and meted out fines and jail sentences for "false, scandalous, and malicious writing" about the president, Congress, or the nation.

Ostensibly, Adams's then-dominant Federalist Party passed this legislation as a "security" measure because the nation was engaged in a naval Quasi-War with France. In reality, however, the Federalists were aiming to stifle the Democratic-Republicans' opposition to their government. Several Democratic editors and one congressman were fined heavily and jailed.[4] This episode is a quintessential example of unnecessary war undermining the republic itself.

CONCLUSION

John Adams could have been ranked in the poor category solely for enthusiastically using the Alien and Sedition acts, creating one of the most dreadful threats to constitutionally guaranteed liberties in the history of the nation. But he also qualifies for inclusion in this category for nominating big government–loving John Marshall as chief justice of the U.S. Supreme Court. Combined, these sins were bad enough to have ranked him in the bad category, but Adams saved himself from this fate by sacrificing his political career to avoid war with powerful France, which the then-weak republic was unprepared to fight. So Adams is ranked twenty-two here.

In a vicious, mudslinging frenzy, Adams lost the election in 1800 to his vice president, Thomas Jefferson. During the campaign, Jefferson's Democratic-Republicans attacked Adams by spinning the yarn that Adams sent Charles Cotesworth Pinckney to England to get four young mistresses — two for Adams and two for Pinckney. Adams took it all in good stride, quipping, "If this be true, General Pinckney has kept them all for himself and cheated me out of my two."[5]

3

THOMAS JEFFERSON

A Hypocrite on Limited Government

PP&L* RANKING: 26
Category: Bad

Third president of the United States

Term: March 4, 1801, to March 4, 1809
Party: Democratic-Republican
Born: April 13, 1743, Shadwell, Virginia
Died: July 4, 1826 (age eighty-three), Charlottesville, Virginia
Spouse: Martha Wayles Skelton Jefferson
Alma Mater: The College of William and Mary
Occupation: Lawyer and farmer
Religion: Deist

Thomas Jefferson, our third president, was the most prominent proponent of limited government in U.S. history. Jefferson organized what would later become the Democratic Party (first going under the "Republican" and then the "Democratic-Republican" label), which championed more limited government than its opposing parties — the Federalists, the Whigs, and the latter-day Republicans — for more than a century, until Woodrow Wilson. The Democratic Party was one of Thomas Jefferson's greatest contributions to U.S. society.

In contrast to his republican philosophy, however, Jefferson wielded executive power with glee. From the nation's founding until the turn of the twentieth century, he was one of the three most powerful executives to sit in the White House, in the company of Andrew Jackson and Abraham Lincoln. While in terms of war he led a restrained foreign policy, he also unconstitutionally

---

*PP&L = Peace, Prosperity, and Liberty.

purchased the largest single addition of land to the United States. At home, his personal fiscal practices were austere, but he had no difficulty in drafting legislation for the Congress. The writer of the Declaration of Independence also engaged in gross violations of civil liberties. In sum, he was a fair-weather practitioner of his ideology of limited government.

PEACE

Advocated a Restrained Foreign Policy

In foreign policy, Jefferson adopted Federalist George Washington's caution against U.S. overseas interventionism, given in the first president's Farewell Address, and made it bipartisan policy. Jefferson said that the United States should have "peace, commerce, and honest friendship with all nations, entangling alliances with none."[1] In practice, Jefferson followed this maxim by avoiding war with Spain over Louisiana and by buying the territory from France — knowing that if France controlled the key port of New Orleans, the United States would be compelled to form an odious alliance with Britain.[2]

Although Jefferson surprisingly went to war in 1803 with the Barbary pirates, who had been demanding tribute from American ships traveling through North African waters for many years, it was a generally defensive action. Following a declaration of war by the Bey of Tripoli, Jefferson sent U.S. ships to the theater without a congressional declaration of war, but he ordered their commanders to wait for that congressional approval before taking offensive action.[3] Thus, although some might argue that Jefferson should have allowed private American ships to continue to assume the risk of international commerce — after all, they were getting the rewards — he did generally follow the founders' intention that the president, as commander in chief, could repel attacks, but first needed to get a declaration of war for offensive action.

Negotiated the Louisiana Purchase Unconstitutionally

Although Jefferson laudably resisted congressional pressure to take Florida and New Orleans by force, he knowingly violated the Constitution by buying Louisiana without first amending the document to permit the acquisition of land. Although Jefferson had objected to Alexander Hamilton's assertion of presidential primacy in foreign policy during the Washington administration, the first Democratic president issued what is now called an executive order to consummate the purchase with France.[4] Jefferson then chose to ram the purchase through Congress without saying much about such legal issues.

The Constitution gave the federal government only the powers it enumerated, and no provision existed for incorporating foreign lands into the United States. Jefferson, in a hurry to buy Louisiana before France changed its mind, later admitted that he "stretched the Constitution till it cracked."[5] This set a bad precedent for the subsequent incorporation of other new territories into the United States. Much later, in 1850, the Supreme Court ruled that only Congress had the power to annex territory into the United States.[6]

In reality, of course, Jefferson didn't buy Louisiana; rather he bought France's claim to the territory. The Indians, who lived in the enormous territory covered by the purchase, really owned the land, and the French didn't inform them about the deal. The purchase opened a gateway west for American settlers, who often slaughtered Indian residents and stole their land. Long after the United States paid Napoleon for Louisiana, the U.S. government had to pay and fight Indian tribes for the land. From 1819 to 1890, the U.S. Army fought fifty wars against the Indians on the land involved in the Louisiana Purchase.[7] Even worse, Jefferson condoned slavery in the massive Louisiana territory.

PROSPERITY

Advocated Limited Government and Restrained Executive Power

Unlike Federalists George Washington and John Adams, President Jefferson put the nation on a more republican trajectory and delayed the incorporation of Federalist big government policies into the nation's system of governance. Jefferson was frugal and persuaded Congress to: reduce government spending, including that for the army, navy, and diplomatic corps; pass a plan to eliminate the national debt; and abolish all internal taxes and the internal revenue service in charge of collecting them. These enlightened economic policies brought prosperity until Jefferson's imposition of a trade embargo in his second term.

The prosperity created a surplus of federal revenues, which Jefferson unfortunately wanted to use — only after authority was granted in a never-passed constitutional amendment — to provide public education; to improve roads, canals, and rivers; and to make any other internal improvements deemed necessary. In addition, Jefferson rightfully, but only rhetorically and futilely, opposed as unconstitutional Federalist Chief Justice John Marshall's creation of a powerful Supreme Court, which could unilaterally overturn laws approved by Congress and the executive branch.[8]

Yet some in his party thought that Jefferson, and Madison, had moved too far toward the Federalist line. Along with his Federalist predecessors, Jefferson set a bad precedent and expanded the president's authority beyond what the constitutional framers had envisioned. Only during the ensuing terms of James Madison through Grover Cleveland — that is, during most of the nineteenth century — did the system revert back to the congressionally dominated system intended by the founders. The powerful nineteenth-century presidencies of Jefferson, Andrew Jackson, and Abraham Lincoln were the only exceptions to this trend.

At a time when presidents were not expected to draft legislation, Jefferson and his cabinet did so in an effort to lead Congress as well as the executive branch.[9] On the other hand, Jefferson occasionally exhibited some executive restraint. Like George Washington he believed that the president should veto bills passed by Congress only when they violated the Constitution, not when the president just disagreed with the policy. Thus, he vetoed no bills during his eight-year tenure.

Even though substantial pressure was exerted on him to run for a third term, he declined because he was afraid that if the Constitution or presidential practice did not limit the president to two terms, it would become an office for life. Jefferson should be given credit for following George Washington's important informal precedent and turning the nation away from an early path toward potential dictatorship.

Drastically Curtailed Economic Liberties

Undoubtedly the most atrocious action of the Jefferson presidency was the draconian embargo he placed on U.S. international commerce and coastal U.S. trade in response to British and French violations of U.S. neutrality in the Napoleonic wars. British warships were stopping U.S. merchant ships, inspecting and seizing the ships and cargo, and then searching the ships for British deserters and impressing them back into the royal navy. Sometimes Americans were also seized because of shortages of British naval manpower; the United States was partially at fault by making it easy for deserting British sailors to get U.S. citizenship papers and enlist on American ships. Also, goods from the French West Indies were being laundered in the United States into neutral goods bound for France, and the French were seizing American ships and cargo arriving in France through Britain.

Jefferson felt pressure to do something about these affronts to U.S. honor but was trying to avoid a war with Britain, so he chose to end all U.S. foreign trade in late 1807. Jefferson's embargo, which ultimately failed to change British policy, caused pressure for even more drastic action and eventually led to a declaration of war by the unprepared United States against the British superpower in 1812 during the subsequent Madison administration. Chris Wallace claims that Jefferson's embargo bought time for the United States to augment its military to defend against British attacks in the War of 1812. Even as late as 1812, however, the United States was still militarily unready for a war it was first to declare, and it was much poorer — and therefore weaker — as a result of Jefferson's embargo.[10] Finally, U.S. industry could have used some of those embargoed imports to build armaments.

The embargo was devastating for the U.S. economy but had minimal effect on its British and French targets. The British developed new manufacturing industries to replace imported American goods and opened new markets in Spain for their previous exports to the United States. Even after the embargo was lifted, the British kept stopping U.S. ships and impressing sailors. And the chief U.S. diplomat in France reported little economic effect there. Conversely, in a year, U.S. exports plummeted 80 percent, and imports dropped 60 percent. Massive U.S. unemployment ensued, and the banning of U.S. coastal trade led to starvation in the U.S. agricultural paradise.[11]

Under few U.S. presidential administrations have people starved due to deliberate government policy. (Even during the Great Depression, the Hoover and FDR administrations were trying to end starvation when they inadvertently made it worse.) This fact alone should qualify Jefferson as one of the worst presidents in American history. Although Vedder and Gallaway give Jefferson a high ranking — seventh among thirty-nine presidents ranked — on policies that promoted limited government and fought inflation, this ranking shows the limitations of their ranking system. Although Jefferson's other economic policies may have fulfilled their criteria, they obviously did not give enough weight to the effects of his severe curtailment of U.S. foreign trade.

LIBERTY

Enforced Near-Martial Law

Going from bad to worse, in an attempt to stop the rampant efforts to smuggle goods in violation of the embargo, Jefferson adopted increasingly oppressive enforcement measures that violated citizens' civil liberties.[12] For example, Jefferson extended the embargo to prohibit hauling of goods by "carts, wagons, and sleds," modes of transportation that could be used to take goods across borders and onto vessels, but this ban had much wider effects.[13]

Congress complied with Jefferson's request for greater enforcement powers by giving him unprecedented control over individual citizens' economic activities.[14] According to Senator Samuel White of Delaware, the Embargo Act placed "the whole country under military law" and allowed search, seizure, and arrest without warrants and with the slightest suspicion that the party had the goal of exporting goods. Historian Leonard Levy opined, "To this day," the embargo "remains the most repressive and unconstitutional legislation ever enacted by Congress in time of peace."[15]

Without warrants, such searches, seizures, and arrests were blatantly unconstitutional and characteristic of a police state, not a republic. Jefferson even implicitly admitted the embargo was a failure by signing, in late 1808 just before exiting the presidency, Congress's repeal of it.

The man who ended the persecution of free speech under the Alien and Sedition acts, enacted during the Adams administration, and who pardoned those convicted under it, committed many other violations of civil liberties under his own watch. When Jefferson experienced unfavorable press coverage, he urged selective prosecutions of unfriendly editors for libel under state laws so that it wouldn't look like general persecution. Yet even after his apparent approval of the Pennsylvania governor's prosecution of an editor for seditious libel, Jefferson hypocritically proclaimed in his second inaugural address, "Since truth and reason have maintained their ground against false opinions in league with false facts, the press, confined to truth, needs no other legal restraint."[16] Apparently, unfriendly editors didn't tell the "truth" and had to be legally restrained. In fact, during the Jefferson administration, more people were prosecuted for sedition than during the Adams administration under the Alien and Sedition Acts.

Similarly, Jefferson accused Supreme Court Justice Samuel Chase, who had conducted trials of Jefferson-friendly editors in 1800 under the now-defunct Sedition Act, of seditious conduct against the Constitution and a state's proceedings. Chase had engaged in a political rant to a grand jury, and Jefferson implied that he should be impeached. Members of Jefferson's own party, however, realized that Chase's actions were wrong but believed they didn't rise to the standard needed for removal from office — that of "high crimes and misdemeanors." Thus, the Senate acquitted Chase.[17]

Jefferson violated the constitutional separation of powers by meddling in the treason trial of Aaron Burr, his former vice president and political rival. Even though a court under Jefferson's other nemesis, Chief Justice John Marshall, eventually acquitted Burr, Jefferson opined, before the verdict was rendered, that Burr was guilty.

Set a Bad Precedent on Indian Policy

In addition to violating Indians' rights in the purchase of Louisiana, President Jefferson came up with the general idea that if Native Americans would not assimilate into white society and were in the way of white westward settlement, they were to be moved to less desirable "empty" land farther west. In his mind, the Indians were too disorganized to put up much of a fight. Jefferson wanted to domesticate the Indians, thus requiring them to give up their land and culture.

This policy was not implemented on a grand scale until the Andrew Jackson and Martin Van Buren administrations in the 1830s, but Jefferson set the bad precedent.[18] This policy is one of Jefferson's most unpublicized and heinous legacies and does a great deal to put him in the category of bad presidents.

CONCLUSION

The long period of Democratic rule after 1800 vaulted the Declaration of Independence and Jefferson, its principal author, into legendary status, even though the document had only a modest influence in the nation's early years. Jefferson lifted most of the key passages of the Declaration from George Mason's Virginia Declaration of Rights and admitted that they weren't original thoughts.[19] The Declaration of Independence, however, did eventually become a powerful symbol of human rights around the world. The document was also an important admonition that governments derived their just powers from the consent of the governed and had a duty to secure their people's rights — not take them away. Yet in practice, as president, Jefferson often used the government to do just what he railed against: abscond with people's rights.

Jefferson sometimes used his executive power for disastrous purposes, especially when he implemented the harshly enforced embargo that usurped American freedoms and resulted in economic devastation and even starvation. Jefferson's idea to force Native Americans onto less desirable land farther west was a horrible precedent that had terrible long-term human consequences.

Although James Monroe set more policies in place that would slowly harm the country over time, Jefferson's immediate and disastrous embargo and enormously bad precedent in Indian policy are alone sufficient to rank him below Monroe. To those bad policies must be added Jefferson's execution of the Louisiana Purchase without amending the Constitution, which set a bad precedent for the government acquiring future territories and severely undermined that jurisprudential bedrock. Thomas Jefferson is ranked twenty-six here.

4

JAMES MADISON

Started an Unneeded War
That Got the U.S. Capital Burned

PP&L* RANKING: 28
Category: Bad

Fourth president of the United States

Term: March 4, 1809, to March 4, 1817
Party: Democratic-Republican
Born: March 16, 1751, Port Conway, Virginia
Died: June 28, 1836 (age eighty-five), Montpelier, Virginia
Spouse: Dolley Todd Madison
Alma Mater: Princeton University
Occupation: Lawyer
Religion: Episcopalian

Like Thomas Jefferson, James Madison is a titan in American history for what he did prior to being chief executive, but he was one of the country's worst presidents. Similar to Jefferson's principal authorship of the Declaration of Independence, Madison's creation of the template for the U.S. Constitution made world history. Unlike the British system, which has only an unwritten constitution, the new American republic would have a written one. Although that document has been severely twisted over time and is really no longer strictly observed when policy is made, it still has some influence and has worked to constrain the growth of government over the centuries that it has been in effect. So Madison should be credited with this achievement, but not for his record as president.

---

*PP&L = Peace, Prosperity, and Liberty.

PEACE

Decided to Fight

Madison is one of the nation's worst presidents because he gave up his republican principles when he decided to take a new, weak nation into an unnecessary and avoidable war with the British naval superpower. The war resulted in the only foreign invasion of the republic in its 230-year history and the burning of Washington, D.C., its capital city. When the war was done, little was solved with Britain because the status quo ante (the way things were before) reigned.

Ironically, Madison's horrendous bungling is best summed up by Lynne Cheney — wife of war hawk Vice President Dick Cheney, the prime mover behind the U.S.'s disastrous invasion of Iraq, which also left the U.S. worse off than before starting a conflict — in a piece she wrote on Madison for a book on the presidents published by the *Wall Street Journal:*

> Madison was not a forceful president.... The War Hawks in Congress, led by Henry Clay, ran roughshod over him and propelled the country into the War of 1812, a conflict that resulted in the burning of both the Capitol and the White House and ended in a peace treaty that left the situation after the war unchanged from what it had been before.[1]

Actually, although the war hawks pressured Madison by threatening to desert him in his bid for a second term if he did not declare war, Cheney gives Madison too much credit. Rather than being passively dragged into the conflict, as Cheney argues, Madison stoked war fever in the U.S. and didn't undertake available policy options that were viable alternatives to war.

Most American history books focus on the principal cause of the war as being Britain's impressments of U.S. sailors to fight in the British navy. Indications are that this was not the principal reason for the U.S. declaring war against a reluctant Britain. A desire by the war hawks in the U.S. Congress to grab Canada and western Indian lands, perhaps along with anger over British abuse of U.S. neutral trading rights during the Napoleonic Wars, seem to be bigger causes of the war. Even the impressments issue was more complex than most American history books claim.

From 1799, when Napoleon took power in France, until 1815, Britain and other nations in Europe were locked in a titanic struggle against France. Although the French had provided critical armies, navies, weapons, and money in the American colonies' fight for independence from England, the new nation declined to help Revolutionary France against Britain and other powers in Europe in the 1790s. The United States even got into an unofficial naval war — called the "Quasi-War" — with France in the late 1790s during the Adams administration. In the first two decades of the 1800s, during the Napoleonic Wars, the United States initially assumed a posture of neutrality, as both Britain and France ruthlessly tried to cut off trade with their adversary; U.S. neutral rights at sea suffered, as ships and cargo were commandeered.

By the time Madison became president in 1809, both Britain and France had been violating U.S. neutral shipping rights for years. The United States was not blameless. U.S. vessels were laundering goods from the French West Indies through U.S. ports to France, which Britain did not appreciate. In addition, British sailors were deserting their ships to avoid the war — obtaining U.S. naturalization papers easily through forgery or hasty action by the U.S. government — and serving aboard American vessels. Desperate to retain naval personnel during a major war, the British navy began boarding American ships, liberally taking off anyone thought to have deserted, and impressing them into service in the royal fleet.

Curiously, however, New England, the region of the United States most adversely affected by violations of U.S. neutral rights and British impressments, was against the War of 1812 because of a correct belief that American slaveholders were using the war to appropriate Native American lands.[2] The war hawks — members of Congress who wanted Canada and Indian lands in the West — were from the southern and western regions. Britain's maritime laws had been in force since 1807, and they caused no war with the United States until after the frontier states sent war hawks to Congress in 1810.

John Calhoun and Henry Clay led the hawks.[3] Under political pressure from the hawks, Madison became determined to declare war on Britain if it didn't recognize U.S. rights as a neutral nation. The primacy of the goal to snatch Canada and western Indian lands was demonstrated by a rapid U.S. invasion of Canada after the U.S. declared war on Britain. As for the western areas, the Americans had the legitimate complaint that the British were stirring up Indian uprisings there. Britain wanted an Indian buffer zone between the United States and British Canada.

In 1809, British and American officials reached an agreement to settle the neutral rights issue. The United States had been trying for fifteen years to get Britain to agree that neutral rights would not be sacrificed when one belligerent was trying to harm another. The British, temporarily weakened by U.S. economic sanctions and Napoleon's victories in Spain, finally agreed to this proposition.[4] Without waiting to see whether the British government would stand behind the agreement reached by its minister, Madison immediately released six hundred ships full of cargo to England. Had he submitted the agreement to Congress for ratification, as he was required to do under the Constitution, he wouldn't have undertaken this rash act.

As it turned out, the British saw that the U.S. ships now on their way would satisfy the demand for American goods years into the future. Also, they felt that the anti-British Madison, in a message, had egregiously and unnecessarily insulted the British king, which provoked the king's refusal to ratify the agreement.[5] This insult was disastrous in the long term, because it ruined a fleeting opportunity to solve the crisis that would lead eventually to the War of 1812.

Declared War

Ironically, the U.S. had already gotten what it wanted from Britain but didn't know about it when Madison asked for the declaration of war on June 1, 1812. Two days earlier, the British had revoked the Orders in Council — which commanded the British navy to stop and search neutral ships suspected of transporting contraband — that had ostensibly provoked the U.S. declaration. But word of the British action didn't arrive in the United States until after Congress had declared war, and U.S. war fever was raging. Even if Madison had originally stoked war fever in the United States merely to try to negotiate from a position of strength, it was a very dangerous strategy. The weak United States was ill prepared for war with a superpower. If Madison had waited and built up the U.S. military for the probable upcoming conflict, no war might have occurred because word would have arrived of the British accommodation.

The U.S. declaration of war surprised the British because U.S. Secretary of State Robert Smith had undercut Madison's pro-war posture by telling foreign representatives that influential people in the United States didn't support it. Thus, the British originally thought that they could maintain the peace, which they wanted to do, without making any concessions.

After the U.S. declaration of war, the British made attempts to avert war. But whereas the Orders in Council were originally and ostensibly the U.S.'s major gripe with Britain, once war was declared, Madison refused British peace overtures because they were absent a deal to stop British impressments of sailors. He was afraid that British peace feelers were designed to sap the U.S. public's enthusiasm for war and thus deny the U.S. military any advantage of swift action.[6] Such advantages would have been greater, however, if the design was to invade Canada and take Indian lands, rather than merely defend U.S. soil. If

Madison had not been so eager for war and instead had spent more time wisely undertaking badly needed preparations for a potential conflict, he could have delayed the war while negotiating an agreement to halt British impressments. Madison knew that because the British didn't want war, those negotiations might have borne fruit.

Madison had several better alternatives to a destructive war on U.S. soil that would solve nothing. The Treaty of Ghent, which ended the war, merely reaffirmed the status quo ante.

One alternative Madison could have tried would have been to smooth things over with Britain by making it harder for defecting British sailors to get U.S. naturalization papers and by stopping the laundering of French trade through U.S. ports. Britain might then have had less cause to impress sailors aboard U.S. ships and violate U.S. neutral shipping rights. Also, Madison could have used French belligerence — seizures of American ships in French ports and interference with U.S. neutrality rights by attacking and burning American vessels — to avoid war with Britain. He could have said publicly that Britain was doing nothing more to the United States than France was. Instead, fearing the French activities would make war with England more difficult to justify, he threatened war with France through diplomatic channels. Madison's reckless foreign policy could have put the weak United States at war with the two greatest powers on earth simultaneously.

Still another alternative would have been to use the French violations of U.S. neutrality to form a temporary alliance with Britain. Britain would have changed its policy toward the United States if the U.S. had agreed not to trade with France, but only with Britain. Britain was the stronger nation at sea — having defeated the French fleet at the Battle of Trafalgar in 1805 and driven French commerce from the oceans — and was therefore the only one of the two powers that could effectively threaten the faraway United States. Sometimes weak nations have to make pragmatic accommodations to stay secure. But Madison's Democratic-Republican Party generally hated Britain and liked France. In addition, the war hawks wanted an excuse to seize Canada — a possession of Britain and not France. In contrast, the opposition Federalist Party, in its New England stronghold, was almost in open revolt against the federal government over the prospect of a U.S. war with Britain, because it would impede New England's commerce. Also, the Northeast was suspicious of the South's wish to grab Florida and the West's coveting of Indian lands.[7] Ultimately, New England refused to provide soldiers to fight the British and almost seceded from the United States because of the war.

Madison selected none of these better options and instead took the divided and unprepared United States to war against the British naval superpower. Although the United States had only one-third of an authorized ten-thousand-man army and a rotting and unready navy one-sixth the size of the British North American fleet,[8] Madison believed that the same factors that made the U.S. victorious in its war of independence would allow a U.S. victory in the War of 1812. The United States would have the advantage of fighting on home territory, a vast expanse that would be hard to subdue, and the war would be fought far away from the British home islands, resulting in long supply lines for the British and short ones for U.S. forces. These factors ultimately made the British settle the war, but the status quo ante was achieved only after a destructive British invasion and the burning of Washington, D.C.

Although not settled in the Treaty of Ghent, which ended the War of 1812, violations of U.S. neutrality rights and British impressments went away as issues when the Napoleonic Wars ended in 1815. Had those been the real reasons for the U.S. declaring war against the British, Madison should have calculated that he could have waited for the European war to run its course, instead of starting his own war with the British. But, as noted earlier, it is unlikely that they were the real causes.

If the United States had lost the risky war, the nation probably would have become a British vassal or broken up, with New England separating from the rest of the country. Although Madison had requested that Congress fund an increase in the army's authorized strength from ten thousand to twenty thousand men and an effort to make the fleet seaworthy, the legislative body had — with the help of Albert Gallatin, Madison's secretary of the treasury — cut the military budget rather than hiking it. But Madison bears some of the blame for the lack of readiness for war by his only lukewarm support for augmenting the nation's defenses.[9]

Madison was more to blame for the inadequate defenses of Washington, D.C. By 1814, Napoleon had been defeated and was in exile, leaving the British free to concentrate on the ongoing war with the United States. Madison's secretary of war and the general he assigned to defend the capital city were incompetent. Madison correctly realized that in the early 1800s, Baltimore was a more strategic city than Washington, but he did hold ten thousand militiamen in reserve to defend the capital. In addition, one hundred thousand militiamen were available from neighboring states, but Secretary of War John Armstrong and General William Winder sat passively by, not calling them up, organizing them, or training them. Madison let week after week pass without overriding such bad military decisions, because he was reluctant to get involved in military planning.

Even when the British fleet sailed up the Chesapeake Bay and landed near Washington, Armstrong refused to plan a defense — believing that the British would attack Baltimore — and impeded the efforts of those who wanted to mount one. Armstrong didn't listen to warnings from Virginians that the Chesapeake region was vulnerable, and he wouldn't bring in weapons and militia from surrounding areas to fortify Washington.

The British were slow to march from their landing spot to Washington, but no U.S. militia were there to harass their journey. Madison eventually fired Armstrong and tried to organize a last-minute defense of the capital, but his efforts were too little, too late. The British burned the public buildings in Washington in retaliation for the American burning of public buildings in Toronto during the earlier U.S. invasion of Canada. The only mitigating factor was that in the decentralized United States of the day, Washington was a far less important city than it is now.

Madison had deviated from republican philosophy by not avoiding war against a vastly superior power and by supporting conscription and a national bank to finance war debt. War requires central control and frequently leads to a concentration of government power that remains long after the war is over. Madison cannot be criticized severely for assuming such strict control, for vastly and permanently increasing the size of government, or for suppressing civil liberties (he allowed the Federalists to be very critical of the war), but the United States came dangerously close to losing the war.

In short, Madison failed as commander in chief. After burning Washington, the British moved on to Baltimore, where their fleet was held off the peninsula by Fort McHenry cannon and militia sharpshooters. The British failure to take Baltimore and the U.S. victory at the battle of Plattsburgh in New York improved the U.S. negotiating position at the peace talks in Ghent, Belgium. On December 24, 1814, the armistice-like Treaty of Ghent was signed, which returned the two nations to the status quo ante without solving the problems of U.S. neutral rights and the British impressments of U.S. sailors. At the end of the war, the "rally around the flag" effect reigned in the United States, as it does with most countries that have been invaded, and Canada was more loyal to the British crown than ever.[10]

Fortunately for the American version of history and Madison's political fortunes, General Andrew Jackson defeated the British at New Orleans after the war was supposed to be over. As with the start of the war, the slowness of communications during that day and age caused unnecessary violence to occur. Word of the peace treaty did not reach the United States until the Battle of New Orleans was over. Jackson's victory rescued Madison from the political doghouse and gave American settlers free use of the Mississippi. Yet the Treaty of Ghent already recognized American rights to the Mississippi — so Jackson's "glorious" military victory was not needed to achieve this end.

Most U.S. analysts like to see the war as a draw, or even a U.S. victory, but this is a stretch. The War of 1812 was really undertaken for reasons of U.S. pride and territorial aggrandizement, could have been avoided in several ways, saw the only invasion of the homeland in U.S. history, and didn't change anything in U.S. relations with Britain. A U.S. loss might have led to recriminations with the Federalist stronghold in New England and civil war or the conversion of the United States into a client state of Britain.

The most important outcome of the war was that the British quit supporting Native Americans in exchange for the United States keeping its hands off Canada. Without this European support, the Native Americans were at a disadvantage militarily against the technologically superior American whites in the Indian Wars during the remainder of the nineteenth century. In short, the War of 1812 ensured that American whites would be able to steal Indian land in the American West successfully.[11]

Enlarged the Military

Madison also adopted the un-republican idea of enlarging the regular army, bringing the state militias under greater federal control, and drafting men into the militia. Madison tried to enhance federal power at the expense of its counterweight in the state militias.[12] Congress thankfully rejected increased federal control and conscription. Congress also rejected Secretary of War James Monroe's proposed larger army of twenty thousand and cut it back to prewar levels of a ten-thousand-troop ceiling, but let him add some coastal fortifications. Even after a British invasion, the refusal of Congress to create a large standing army is a remarkable testament to the entrenchment of republican ideals at this time in U.S. history

Congress, less concerned about a navy's threat to the republic, endorsed Madison's necessary efforts to expand the fleet. In Madison's last year, the legislative body decided to spend one million dollars per year over an eight-year period to build nine ships of the line, twelve frigates, and three steam batteries.[13]

Invaded Florida

Even before the War of 1812, Madison had acted aggressively toward foreign powers. At the time, Florida was divided into east and west sections, with the west region stretching to New Orleans. The U.S. asserted, without much credibility, that West Florida was part of its Louisiana Purchase. The Spanish military still occupied it, but 80 percent of the settlers were Americans. Madison was cocksure that if American settlement continued, the U.S. would eventually wrest possession from the weakened Spanish Empire by default, occupation, or purchase. The U.S. government had been conducting covert operations in Florida.[14]

To prevent French and British encroachment and avoid so-called anarchy among U.S. settlers, Madison wanted American settlers to request a U.S. occupation. He also feared that the Spanish government would sell land in western Florida to private American speculators, and he wanted to keep the lands in the public realm. U.S. settlers, with Madison's backing, seized a Spanish fort at Baton Rouge and requested that Florida enter the United States. Madison ordered the governor of the Orleans territory, under the jurisdiction of the United States, to invade western Florida with armed forces and establish a government without attacking any other Spanish forts.

Madison's aggressive move was an act of war, unauthorized by Congress, which could have provoked three foreign powers into hostile retaliation. His action was another rejection of republican principles; Madison admitted it was a "transgression" but felt that the executive should have the power to act rapidly to react to unplanned circumstances or crises.[15] In the debates on the Constitution in 1787, however, the founders meant to grant the executive the power to respond to unforeseen developments, but only when it was necessary to defend the United States — not when invading another country to seize territory.

Later, in early 1811, Madison did only a little better with eastern Florida. He got Congress to pass a law allowing him to invade eastern Florida if local authorities asked for help or if foreign nations threatened to take the territory by armed force.

PROSPERITY

Advocated Policies Leading to Bigger Government

The War of 1812, like most wars, led to increased taxes and government borrowing as the nation's fiscal condition deteriorated. Although the

Democratic-Republican Congress did not usually like raising taxes, the body approved new taxes on licenses, stamps, salt, sugar, spirits, carriages, and land. After the war, many of these taxes were retained, illustrating the ratchet effect of wars on the permanent size of government.

During the war, Congress began to balk at approving more taxes, so the government had to begin heavy borrowing to finance the war. As a result of war financing, Madison abandoned republican principles to re-create a national bank. As Andrew Jackson said when he later opposed the recharter of this bank, nothing in the Constitution permitted the national government to form such an institution and perform banking functions. Although Madison, in principle, wanted to reduce the national debt, the war caused the debt to triple. Not until Andrew Jackson's administration would the debt be expunged.

The war also led to the expansion of government powers over the people, especially in the form of the stamp tax, which required people to pay for a government stamp on all official documents. In the lead-up to the American Revolution, the hated British stamp tax increased hostilities between England the colonists. The American people had rejected a stamp tax proposed by the Federalists in 1790. Yet the War of 1812 allowed the U.S. government to get away with imposing a similar stamp tax. In addition, Madison signed a bill for mildly protective tariffs.

The war also caused Madison to begin abandoning his opposition to the national government's funding of internal improvements — that is, the building of roads, canals, and so on. In late 1811, with war imminent, Gouverneur Morris and De Witt Clinton, the mayor of New York City, on national security grounds, convinced Madison to back their plan to build a canal from Lake Erie to the Hudson River, even though Madison had constitutional qualms about the project. In 1817, after the war ended, Madison vetoed a bill to federally fund the building of roads and canals. Like Jefferson before him, he thought the national government should do these types of projects, but he could find nothing in the Constitution that allowed it. Therefore, Madison wanted a constitutional amendment that would allow the national government to undertake such projects. Yet Madison's and Jefferson's philosophical support for the national government's role in doing these projects helped later presidents federally fund them without first passing a constitutional amendment.

In addition, Madison advocated that a national university be set up in Washington, D.C., so that graduates could spread feelings of nationalism when they went back to their home states. Of course, the Constitution didn't say that education was the federal government's role either.

Although Federalist opposition to a "successful" war was one of the factors that led to the party's demise, the war caused the "small government" Democratic-Republicans to begin to adopt the Federalist vision of a bigger government and implant it into the American social fabric — where it would metastasize throughout American history. Higher taxes, a protective tariff, heavy borrowing, a national bank, and government funding of internal improvements were all in the Federalist program that Madison essentially adopted because of the war. In fact, Madison, author of the Virginia Resolutions that championed states' rights, now pilloried them as undermining the Constitution. Thus, despite his label as a proponent of small government, Madison got a poor ranking from Vedder and Gallaway on policies that promoted limited government and fought inflation — twenty-eighth out of thirty-nine presidents ranked.

As for positive accomplishments, an economic boom followed the war, but this prosperity was mainly explained by the industriousness of the American people and the now-open trade channels to the rest of the world, not by Madison's actions.

LIBERTY

Did Not Restrict Civil Liberties during War

Even bad presidents usually attempt or accomplish a few good things. In Madison's case, the universe of these positive accomplishments was small. As noted earlier, Madison did not restrict civil liberties during the War of 1812 — a rarity in American history during wars. Of course, doing the right thing as a corollary to a monstrous blunder — starting a war — shouldn't merit too much praise.

CONCLUSION

It is difficult to find something positive to say about Madison. When the social skills of his vivacious and well-loved wife, Dolley, were the highlight of his administration, it demonstrates just how badly Madison performed in office. Madison's aggressive foreign policy resulted in a U.S. invasion of Spanish Florida and the only foreign invasion of the United States in its history. It is faint praise to observe that at least Madison's War of 1812 was less destructive to the U.S. homeland than the titanic Civil War Lincoln unleashed on the republic almost a half-century later.

Perhaps it is better to focus on Madison's masterful accomplishment prior to ascending to the presidency — creating the blueprint for the U.S. Constitution. James Madison is an example of the Peter Principle at work. The principle argues that people who are promoted for their accomplishments at lower-level jobs are often incompetent in a different job at a higher level. Historians need to avoid being blinded by the aura of Madison's prior achievement and downgrade him for his abysmal presidency. Accordingly James Madison is ranked twenty-eighth there.

5

JAMES MONROE

The First Wisps of Permanent Government Expansion

PP&L* RANKING: 25

Category: Bad

Fifth president of the United States

Term: March 4, 1817, to March 4, 1825
Party: Democratic-Republican
Born: April 28, 1758, Westmoreland County, Virginia
Died: July 4, 1831 (age seventy-three), New York City, New York
Spouse: Elizabeth Kortright Monroe
Alma Mater: The College of William and Mary
Occupation: Farmer (planter)
Religion: Episcopalian

James Monroe was the fifth president of the United States. Coming to office after two eight-year, two-term presidents, Thomas Jefferson and James Madison, Monroe slowly began to move away from their theoretical republicanism and toward a new view of the federal government. He began to incorporate the big government principles of the dying Federalist Party into his now-dominant Democratic-Republican Party. His actions increased federal involvement in the U.S. economy via tariffs and funding for internal improvements. Monroe helped ensure that advocacy of an energetic federal government would eventually become the most influential paradigm in American governance — in direct

---

*PP&L = Peace, Prosperity, and Liberty.

contravention of the founders' intention in the Constitution and especially in the Tenth Amendment.

Monroe also drifted away from Jeffersonian and Madisonian republicanism by augmenting the nation's military and laying the first seedlings of an eventual American empire. He is best known for the Monroe Doctrine, in which the United States promised to stay out of European affairs if Europe would stay out of the New World, with the exception of already-established colonies. Other presidents would elaborate that policy over the years, and it would provide the grounds for America's expansion of influence, first within its own hemisphere, and later across the world. As a result, according to one analyst, Monroe's administration was one of the six or so presidencies that were most important in defining America's role in the world.[1]

Monroe was also the first president to "triangulate" (adopt part of the other party's program) and hand out government goodies to win support from nontraditional Democratic constituencies — many decades before Franklin D. Roosevelt and Bill Clinton would use the same strategy — even though the opposition big government Federalist Party was so sickly that Monroe ran unopposed for reelection in 1820.

PEACE

Sponsored the Monroe Doctrine

In foreign policy, Monroe's presidency had momentous ill effects, but these would not manifest themselves for many decades. The most serious external threats to America had ended with the termination of the Napoleonic Wars in 1815, which included the inconclusive War of 1812 between the United States and Great Britain. Nevertheless, Monroe believed that the United States had achieved an elevated status among nations. He was afraid that European powers would try to reverse the republican revolutions happening in Latin America, that they would try to create new colonies there, and that Russia was encroaching on the northwestern part of the North American continent.

As a result, Monroe issued a declaration, without congressional legislation or approval, which came to be known as the Monroe Doctrine. The doctrine left existing European colonial possessions in the New World alone and promised that the United States would not interfere in European affairs; on the other hand, the United States expected that the Europeans would not colonize new areas or reinsert themselves into newly independent countries in the Western Hemisphere.

Over time, U.S. presidents managed to forget the part about staying out of Europe's quarrels and focused solely on keeping Europeans out of the Western Hemisphere. The distorted surviving part of the doctrine was the forerunner of a uniquely "morality-driven" interventionist U.S. foreign policy that began to take shape at the turn of the twentieth century and accelerated in the later part of that century after World War II.[2] The surviving remnant of the doctrine — when combined with Theodore Roosevelt's corollary that the United States also would intervene if countries in the Western Hemisphere became unstable or unruly for any reason — has been used to make Latin America a playground for U.S. military action up until the present day. In one instance, U.S. escalation of the Cuban missile crisis could have turned into a global nuclear war.

When Monroe promulgated the original doctrine in 1823, however, the United States had little military power to back up its claim to the dominant role in the Western Hemisphere. Monroe, in the wake of the British invasion of the United States during the War of 1812 and the burning of Washington, D.C., understandably wanted to increase U.S. coastal defenses. But at a time when most threats, foreign and domestic, had receded, he took the unneeded action of proposing an increase in defense spending, expanding the U.S. naval presence into the Pacific, and he was alone among his party in advocating an expanded standing army in peacetime — all concomitant with what he believed was the United States' new rank among nations. Using questionable military logic, Monroe believed that the growing country could no longer be defended by a small standing army until state militias could be called up.[3] In reality, a larger territory would allow the small regular army to fall back and conduct a defense in depth to give the militias more time to mobilize.[4]

While the Congress gave Monroe the coastal fortifications he requested, it gutted his expansion of the military in the wake of the economic panic of 1819–1820. Congress cut the defense budget by about half, from $9 million a year in 1818 to less than $5 million per year from 1821 to 1824, and actually reduced the size of the standing army. The navy fared a little better because it had the legitimate mission of protecting commerce. The shipbuilding program started at the end of the Madison administration was continued, but the budget for it was cut in half.

Mishandled Other Foreign Initiatives

Another demerit for Monroe is his administration's ordering, without a declaration of war, General Andrew Jackson's invasion of Florida, which was then controlled by a weakened Spain. John Quincy Adams, Monroe's secretary of state and a future president, set a precedent, using what became known in modern times as the "failed state" argument. This argument attempted to justify U.S. imperial conquests when instability and turmoil in another country allegedly necessitated U.S. intervention.[5] Jackson chased runaway slaves who were living among the Seminole Indians in Florida and ruthlessly burned Native American villages to the ground in what came to be known as the First Seminole War.

Following Jackson's invasion, the United States forced Spain to sign the Adams-Otis Treaty, which ceded Florida to the United States and settled the boundary of the Louisiana territory.[6] This acquisition was the culmination of covert U.S. meddling in Florida over several administrations.[7]

Monroe's recognition, under congressional pressure, of the new governments of Chile and Argentina also undermined Spanish influence in the Western Hemisphere. These new countries had declared their independence from the declining Spanish empire.[8]

PROSPERITY

Moved toward Big Government

Monroe managed to continue Madison's post–War of 1812 economic boom. This boom was marred by the panic of 1819 and 1820,[9] but Monroe's economic policies helped steer the country out of that depression and again into prosperity for the rest of his administration. Overall, the generally prosperous times helped Monroe reduce the national debt. These achievements contribute to Vedder and Gallaway's very high ranking of Monroe on policies limiting government and fighting inflation — fourth out of thirty-nine presidents ranked.

Yet the Monroe presidency shows that even when a chief executive's policies bear fruit during his term, he can set bad precedents that have deleterious effects on the country for decades, and even centuries, into the future. In moving away from Jeffersonian and Madisonian small-government policies by advocating increased defense spending and by incrementally moving toward greater domestic activism, he started America down the long, but slippery, slope toward big government.

Monroe repeatedly approved increases in tariffs,[10] didn't attempt to get rid of the national bank, the Second Bank of the United States, and tried to circumvent the lack of authority in the Constitution for federal funding of internal improvement projects.[11]

LIBERTY

Continued Jefferson's Policy of Ethnically Cleansing Native Americans

Although Monroe was rhetorically committed to rescuing the Indians from aggressive white expansion, he adopted Jefferson's idea of moving them outside the western boundaries of the United States and giving them what was supposedly equally fertile land. Today, if this happened in Bosnia or Darfur, we would call it ethnic cleansing. Monroe seemed to say that rescuing the Indians entailed stealing their land — which was their traditional home and which they considered sacred in some cases — and transferring them somewhere else involuntarily. Besides, Monroe was a big proponent of U.S. western expansion, which had led to the Indians' plight in the first place. Whites eventually stole the Indians' land and slaughtered them or confined them to undesirable reservations.

CONCLUSION

The tragedy of the top four presidents in the bad category — James Monroe, Thomas Jefferson, Andrew Jackson, and James Madison — is that philosophically, at least, they all were for limited government (with the exception of retaining tariffs).[12] But some of their important actions deviated so dramatically from their philosophy that they have to be severely downgraded.

Democratic-Republican Monroe is put in the bad category, ranking number twenty-five here, because he planted the seedlings of big government at home by adopting the dying Federalist Party's notions of a more active federal government. He did the same abroad by promulgating the Monroe Doctrine, advocating increased defense spending, and pushing for a large standing army during peacetime — all without any major threat existing to the nation's security.

6

JOHN QUINCY ADAMS

A Federalist Wearing a Democrat's Clothes

PP&L* RANKING: 12
Category: Average

Sixth president of the United States

Term: March 4, 1825, to March 4, 1829
Party: Federalist, Democratic-Republican,
    National Republican, Anti-Masonic, and Whig
Born: July 11, 1767, Braintree, Massachusetts
Died: February 23, 1848 (age eighty), Washington, D.C.
Spouse: Louisa Catherine Johnson Adams
Alma Mater: Harvard College
Occupation: Lawyer
Religion: Unitarian

John Quincy Adams, the son of President John Adams — the only other father-son presidents in U.S. history were the two George Bushes — was an average president who never did anything too spectacularly good or too spectacularly awful. Some of the explanation lies in how he came to the office, lacking any public mandate to lead.

The election of 1824 was a four-way race among Adams, General Andrew Jackson, Congressman Henry Clay, and Secretary of the Treasury W. H. Crawford. Andrew Jackson had a significant lead over the others in popular and electoral votes, but no majority in either. When the election was thrown into the House of Representatives, Henry Clay shifted his support behind the ideologically compatible John Quincy Adams; Adams won, becoming the first man to win the presidency but lose both the popular and electoral vote to

---

*PP&L = Peace, Prosperity, and Liberty.

his opponent.[1] After the president-elect announced that Henry Clay would be secretary of state, the Jacksonians accused Adams and Clay of a "corrupt bargain." With little support in Congress, Adams's one term as president was a rough one.

PEACE

Lightly Meddled in Latin America

In general, Adams's foreign policy was fairly benign. However, Adams and Clay, both of whom rhetorically supported the liberation of Latin America from colonialism, delayed Cuban independence by blocking Colombia and Mexico from taking Cuba and Puerto Rico from Spain. Spain had opened Cuba and Puerto Rico to U.S. trade, and the U.S. government wanted to ensure that the commerce kept flowing. Thus, Adams put mercantilism over nonintervention and Cuban and Puerto Rican independence.

By accepting the invitation to participate in the Panama Congress, which included freed blacks from Haiti, Adams angered U.S. southerners, violated the Senate's power to ratify treaties, promoted the hegemonic Monroe Doctrine, and weakened George Washington's original noninterventionist foreign policy. Andrew Jackson claimed that Adams had eroded the constitutional checks and balances.[2] These protests about the president's mere acceptance of an invitation to an international conference as a violation of the Constitution show how far from that document our modern-day foreign policy has strayed.

PROSPERITY

Proposed an Antebellum New Deal and High Tariffs

Although Adams had broken with his father's Federalist Party in 1807 during the Jefferson administration and had joined Jefferson's Democratic-Republican Party, the forerunner of the modern Democratic Party, he remained a Federalist at heart. In his first message to Congress, Adams proposed what Richard Norton Smith has called an antebellum New Deal. Adams wanted ambitious federal funding of interstate canals and roads, scientific expeditions, a naval academy, aid to education, a national astronomical observatory, and an Interior Department to regulate the use of natural resources.

Clay, who would later push a similar program under the heading of the "American System," cautioned Adams that the American people weren't yet ready to move from Jeffersonian limited government to Adams's planned economy. Also, Jacksonian Democrats, proponents of small government, were vehemently opposed to Adams's program, which he made very little effort to get enacted.[3] Many people correctly believed that the Constitution didn't specifically mention these internal improvements as legitimate for the federal government to undertake.

Adams's proposed navigational survey of the entire East Coast, along with his proposed national university and naval academy, were voted down in Congress, at least in part to uphold the Constitution's intentions. However, illustrating that Congress doesn't always act on principle alone, Adams did get congressional approval for federal funding of the first passenger railroad, an extension of the National Road from western Virginia to Ohio, and subsidized local canals and navigational surveys of ports.[4] In spite of the Congress's constitutional concerns, outlays for these internal improvement projects during Adams's single four-year term almost equaled such expenditures for the previous five presidential administrations combined.[5] Also, Adams wanted to fund a larger navy and an around-the-world voyage for the fleet.

Always gunning for Adams, the Jacksonians introduced the Tariff of 1812, which southerners, hardest hit by it, called the "Tariff of Abominations." Surprisingly, it passed Congress by a narrow margin. Adams foolishly signed it because he had to pay for his internal improvements and wanted to protect industrial sectors that might support him for reelection. The Jacksonians were gleeful that the tariff had lost the president what support he had in the South.[6]

In addition, Adams wanted to force Britain, which had closed its ports to American ships, to open itself to U.S. trade, so he retaliated by closing American ports to British ships coming from ports that were closed to American ships. Essentially, this disastrously closed American ports to trade with British colonies.[7]

Significantly, Vedder and Gallaway rank Adams tenth out of thirty-nine presidents based on his limiting government and fighting inflation. Part of this excessively high ranking, however, may be attributed to Congress's refusal to pass some of his internal improvements projects. Although Adams had raised tariffs, he reached several commercial agreements with European and Latin American nations. Also, he refused to hand out spoils to fellow party members and appointed people to federal positions on the basis of merit.

LIBERTY

Held Enlightened Views on Indian Policy, but Maintained the Usual Bad Reality

Adams was against slavery and had relatively enlightened views toward the Indians. He wanted to guarantee Native Americans rights and land in the West. However, many presidents between George Washington and the closing of the western frontier in 1890 had theoretically benevolent policies toward the Indians that were not borne out in reality. In Adams's case, the Jacksonians did not like this Adams policy, and Congress rejected it.

The preceding Monroe administration had negotiated the Treaty of Indian Springs, which gave the Creek Indians less than two years to leave their land in Georgia. The anti-Indian governor of Georgia, however, wanted whites to have immediate access to the land, which was valuable for growing cotton, and so he ordered a survey of Creek lands. The Adams administration threatened to use military force against Georgia if the state began the surveying, which violated the treaty and thus federal law. Adams was convinced that the original treaty had been signed fraudulently. But he pressured the Creeks to give up even more of their land in the Treaty of Washington. Yet Georgians still were not satisfied — they didn't get all Creek lands within the state's borders. Congress refused to ratify the new treaty as it was written, amending it to make the Creeks cede nearly all of their lands in Georgia. Thus the Treaty of Washingon took more Indian land than the Treaty of Indian Springs, and then Congress enlarged Indian forfeiture under the Treaty of Washington to take even more land than that.

Even so, Georgia refused to recognize the expanded Treaty of Washington. The Creeks had to sign the Treaty of Fort Mitchell, which sold all their remaining land in Georgia. Although Adams avoided a civil war with Georgia, he did eventually come to concur with the state that the Indians had to be evicted. Thus, Adams was no different from many other presidents who exhibited benevolent rhetoric and intentions on Indian policy but, in the end, acquiesced to white aggression against Native Americans.[8]

After Adams's term was over, all pretense of benevolence to Native Americans was dropped. Andrew Jackson, Adams's successor, had been an Indian fighter and had very harsh policies toward the Indians that resulted in them being either exterminated or removed from their land.[9]

CONCLUSION

Because two-thirds of the American people didn't want Adams to be president in the first place, Andrew Jackson was able to comfortably defeat Adams in his 1828 reelection bid. America was not yet ready for Adams's nationalist central planning. Continuing to serve in politics, John Quincy Adams was the only former president to become a House member after serving in the White House. He served for eighteen years and fought the gag rule that pigeonholed antislavery petitions.

Although Adams's foreign policy was fairly benign, almost nothing of what Adams proposed as president was enacted — except for some internal improvement pork projects and the Tariff of Abominations. Congress acted wisely in disapproving most of this antebellum New Deal but should not have rejected his somewhat more benevolent policy toward Indians. Thus, Adams was both an ineffective and average president, ranking twelve here.

7

ANDREW JACKSON

Aggressive against Indians and Southerners

PP&L* RANKING: 27

Category: Bad

Seventh president of the United States

Term: March 4, 1829, to March 4, 1837
Party: Democratic-Republican and Democratic
Born: March 15, 1767, Lancaster County,
    South Carolina
Died: June 8, 1845 (age seventy-eight), Nashville, Tennessee
Spouse: Rachel Donelson Robards Jackson (died);
    niece Emily Donelson Jackson and daughter-in-law
    Sarah Yorke Jackson were first ladies.
Education: Studied law for admission to the North Carolina State Bar
Occupation: Prosecutor, judge, farmer (planter), soldier (general)
Religion: Presbyterian

Andrew Jackson was one of the three most powerful presidents of the nine-teenth century, along with Thomas Jefferson and Abraham Lincoln. Indeed, historian Clinton Rossiter has argued that Jackson was second only to George Washington in molding the presidency. While Washington's effect on the pres-idency had both positive and negative aspects, Jackson's impact was mostly negative. After a period when executive power had diminished vis-à-vis the Congress—more toward what the framers of the Constitution had in mind—Jackson dramatically reexpanded the presidency's power over American society and the economy, a precedent that Lincoln eventually used to augment the office even further during the Civil War.[1]

---

*PP&L = Peace, Prosperity, and Liberty.

Jackson came to the presidency as a military hero, and his posture as president was often bellicose. Although he didn't involve the United States in foreign wars, his use of military coercion against a state that was threatening to secede set a precedent for the Civil War that came three decades later. He used the executive veto to establish power over Congress and began to build a true executive branch that went beyond the president and his cabinet. His harsh treatment of Native Americans is also a large blot on his record.

PEACE

Responded Belligerently to the Nullification Crisis

As Michael Farquhar has noted, Andrew Jackson, throughout his career, exhibited "marked homicidal tendencies," which were "coupled with a hair-trigger temper and an overheated sense of personal honor." He was the king of dueling and had much lead rattling around in his body to prove it. He fought most of his duels over the honor of his pipe-smoking wife, Rachel, whose reputation had been sullied by the fact that she began seeing Jackson while she was separated from her first husband and may have been a bigamist when she married Jackson in 1791.

A more important example of Jackson's aggressive nature[2] and use of presidential power occurred when his first-term vice president, John Calhoun, and other South Carolinians favored nullification of a federal tariff law and threatened secession if Congress authorized force against them. These events are referred to as the nullification crisis of 1832. Although Jackson was a southerner who favored slavery and states' rights, he threatened to use force against the nullifiers if any bloodshed resulted from their opposition to U.S. law. He also issued a proclamation stating that states had no right to invalidate federal law. Jackson sent federal agents to protect federal officials and property and to arrest the leaders of the nullification movement. He also dispatched two warships to patrol the South Carolina coast, fortified the federal forts in Charleston's harbor, made very visible preparations to send an army to the state, and threatened to hang the nullifiers.

South Carolina hoped to get support from neighboring states, but Jackson threatened to arrest the governors of those states if they helped South Carolina. At the same time, he gave South Carolina a face-saving way out of the crisis by offering a compromise tariff and allowing that he had no constitutional power to call out the militia to put down an insurrection unless South Carolina first used or assembled military forces. Congress passed the compromise bill at about the time that it expanded Jackson's authority as commander in chief to use military power to enforce federal laws. South Carolina then revoked its nullification law, and both sides claimed victory. In reality, Jackson's intimidation had worked, and his idea of a federal union triumphed.[3]

In fact, however, the Constitution didn't clearly delineate whether it created a confederation or a federation — in other words, whether member states retained the right to remove themselves at will. When the Constitution was being ratified, some states — including Virginia, New York, and Rhode Island — reserved the right to secede, supporting the idea that the new arrangement was a confederation. The preceding Articles of Confederation were essentially a treaty among sovereign states, and the articles claimed they were permanent. The Constitution clearly created a stronger national government, as was indicated by the phrase "to form a more perfect union" in the preamble. This phrase originated from the union of England and Scotland in 1707, which was intended to be everlasting. Also, the Constitutional Convention adopted a letter to the Congress — the only official explanation by the Constitution's framers about the document's meaning — that spoke about the "consolidation of our Union" and asserted that, practically speaking, states would need to give up a share of liberty to preserve the union.

Federalist 40 — one of a series of articles written by Alexander Hamilton, James Madison, and John Jay — notes that the Constitutional Convention's purpose was "to establish in these States a firm national government," which would be "adequate to the exigencies of government and preservation of the Union."[4] In addition, in the absence of a breach, all parties to any contract must foreswear it to make it a dead letter. Thus the Constitution can be thought of as a type of contract or compact.

Even under the more centralized Constitution, the founders limited federal power to certain severely circumscribed areas, but the Supremacy Clause was to preempt state laws in those realms. The document gave the federal government powers in clearly defined and limited areas, such as commerce, levying taxes, and relations with nations overseas.[5] The Constitution said that tariffs, to which South Carolina objected, were clearly in the purview of the federal government.

Also, even during the period when the Articles of Confederation were in force, when every state had just one vote in Congress, decisions made by the majority of states were binding on all the rest, at least in the few areas where the national government then held sway. Under the Constitution, majorities in both the Senate and House of Representatives would be required to make decisions that bound the states, at least in the somewhat expanded realm of the federal government (compared to its jurisdiction under the Articles of Confederation). In addition, the Constitution could be amended and all the states held to the amendment by only a two-thirds majority in both legislative chambers and the ratification of the amendment by only three-quarters of the states.

Under either the Articles or the Constitution, state nullification of nationally passed laws would have undermined any national governance. Of course, this effect is much more severe under the more centralized Constitution than under the decentralized Articles of Confederation. Secession is nullification writ large — that is, a state nullifying all national laws. As for the legality of secession by a state or states, a greater case can be made for it in the Articles, under which the states were clearly more sovereign, than in the Constitution, which split sovereignty between the states and the federal government. The threat of nullification or secession would effectively replace national majority rule with consensus decision-making among states — reversing what the abandonment of the Articles and replacement of them with the Constitution had intended to do.[6]

Although what the framers of the Constitution intended is somewhat ambiguous, Jackson was probably right that the document was not meant to allow nullification or secession, and he was also probably correct that the president did not have the right to suppress an insurrection by force until acts of violence were committed by a state, such as South Carolina, or its militia was assembled to do so. In addition, Article III, Section 3 provides that treason is committed against the United States when war is conducted against the federal government.

Under this reasoning, both Jackson and later Lincoln had a legal right to put down by force any insurrection aimed at secession and to ensure that federal laws were enforced, but only when violence was imminent or had already broken out. In fact, Jackson's proclamation during the nullification crisis later helped make Lincoln's somewhat convincing argument for an eternal union, one which could be preserved by using military means. Although, at the Constitutional Convention, Madison defeated a measure to allow the federal government to coerce a state, this de facto ban on coercion appears to apply only in the absence of insurrection. Also, Madison quoted Jefferson as saying that no right of coercion need be explicitly found because such a right was inherent in any compact — that is, enforcement is permitted in any contract.

Yet while such coercion may very well have been legal under the Constitution, such actions violate the spirit of self-determination embodied in the

American Revolution and enshrined in the Declaration of Independence. After all, if a group of people no longer want to be a part of an exercise in self-government, don't they have a moral right to secede and isn't it ill-advised to try to coerce them into "living free"? That is, coercing states to remain in a "free" national government severely erodes that freedom.

Although Jackson aggressively coerced South Carolina over a mere economic issue — unlike the moral ill of slavery that Lincoln faced — Jackson is ranked more highly than Lincoln because he avoided a massive civil war by giving South Carolina a face-saving way out of the dispute, and he did not commit the egregious violations of the Constitution and civil liberties that Lincoln perpetrated. Furthermore, Lincoln's Civil War was the most terrible war in U.S. history and did not ultimately better greatly the conditions faced by African Americans. Jackson's aggressive actions in the nullification crisis, however, served as a bad precedent for Lincoln's later provocation of the Civil War.

Jackson set another bad precedent for Lincoln during the Civil War. According to the Constitution, Congress was supposed to call out the militia to suppress insurrections, not the president. Congress, in laws passed during the late 1700s and early 1800s, delegated its authority to call up the militia to the president, but this delegation was of dubious constitutionality. Although Jackson, like Lincoln later, eventually obtained questionable congressional support for increased authority as commander in chief to enforce federal laws, it was only after he already had employed coercion against the recalcitrant party.

Asserted Military Power

Surprisingly, given his past as an aggressive general, President Jackson didn't involve the United States in a major war, but he did assertively employ the military on occasion. He prepared for military action to help acquire Texas and to garner French debt repayment from the Napoleonic Wars.

In Texas's war for independence in 1836, Sam Houston tried to lure General Santa Anna's Mexican army across the disputed U.S.-Mexican border, where the U.S. Army, deployed by Jackson, was waiting to pounce. But Houston's Texans got eager and defeated the Mexicans without the aid of the U.S. Army.[7] In March 1837, just before leaving office, Jackson provided de facto recognition of Texas's independence, thus beginning the journey toward his dream of acquiring that large piece of land for the United States.[8]

In addition, in 1835 and 1836, because France hadn't paid for its destruction of U.S. ships during the Napoleonic Wars, Jackson made military preparations, threatened to seize French ships, and asked Congress for more funds for the

Navy. France then paid up.[9] But this minor grievance didn't merit the risk of starting a war with a powerful nation.

PROSPERITY

Expanded Executive Power

Jackson's expansive views on presidential power were the root of the modern-day unitary executive theory — used to justify a hyper-imperial presidency — later adopted by George W. Bush and his vice president, Dick Cheney.

Unlike Washington and Jefferson, who believed that the presidential veto should be used only when Congress passed a bill that was unconstitutional, Jackson used the veto aggressively to block bills that didn't comport with his policy views. Jackson's twelve vetoes were more than the vetoes of all the previous presidents combined. He did veto some bad legislation — for example, the recharter of the Second Bank of the United States and federal funding of internal improvements as stipulated in the Maysville Road bill — but these congressional actions were clearly unconstitutional.[10] In general, although the founders did give the president the power to veto bills, Jackson's expansion of the criteria justifying such action probably set a bad precedent for the ballooning of executive power.

Furthermore, Jackson expanded the spoils system, whereby a significant number of federal officials were thrown out and replaced with Jacksonian loyalists. Also, Jackson began to formalize and bureaucratize the previously informal executive branch. These two developments allowed Jackson to increase executive dominance over the federal bureaucracies, achieving a greater degree of control than was exerted by his predecessors. He also enhanced presidential power by gaining unprecedented independence from Congress and achieving predominance over his cabinet.[11]

Opposed Renewing the National Bank

Congress had authorized a national bank in 1791, disapproved it in 1811, and reapproved it in 1816.[12] Jackson hated the Second Bank of the United States, which was largely a private bank that had been given a sweet deal by the government. The bank, by controlling the nation's money supply, had great power over the economy, gave its wealthy owners a large return with very little risk, and was involved in corruption, such as bribing government officials and making sweetheart deals with congressmen and newspaper editors.[13] Jackson appropriately vetoed the bill rechartering the bank. He also removed the federal government's money and stored it in private banks chartered by the states.

Although in 1819 the Supreme Court, under Federalist Chief Justice John Marshall, had deemed the bank to be constitutional, Jackson disputed this ruling, saying that the federal government didn't have the power to charter a bank outside Washington, D.C. One senator properly wanted to know where in the Constitution chartering a national bank was authorized at all.[14] Jackson also thought the bank was a collusion between government and business that enriched the few at the cost of the general population.[15]

Actually, despite his constitutional rationale, Jackson may have disapproved of the bank for the wrong reasons. He didn't care that much about the bank until his archrival, Henry Clay, supported it; then he opposed it. Jackson didn't like a single private bank controlling the nation's money and would have supported a substitute government agency.[16] Also, Jackson was censured by the Senate for transferring federal monies to state-chartered private banks without congressional approval, which stretched presidential power under the Constitution.[17] If he had gotten congressional approval, Jackson's solution would have been preferable to what eventually did happen, the concentration of federal financial power in an Independent Treasury—subsequently created by Martin Van Buren and resurrected by James Polk—and much later in a quasi-central bank called the Federal Reserve Board.

In an effort to ensure the national bank's survival, Nicholas Biddle, the bank's chief, tried to starve the economy of money, but cash began to flow again when federal money went to state-chartered banks. The economy hummed for a time. Because of the prosperity, Jackson was thus able to pay off the national debt for the first time in the nation's history.[18]

Jackson wanted not only to store federal funds in state-chartered private banks (a good idea), but also to give federal aid to state governments (a bad idea). The flow of the federal budget surplus to the states may have eventually caused the Panic of 1837—a severe economic downturn—just after Martin Van Buren, Jackson's successor, was sworn into office. Jackson was against Henry Clay's American System, which included federal funding of internal improvements (such as canals and roads), but Jackson wanted to fund those projects by having the federal government share revenue with state governments. Thus, Van Buren inherited an excessively turbocharged economy with excessive monetary expansion, credit and inflation.[19] All in all, Vedder and Gallaway probably

were too generous when they gave Jackson a mediocre ranking for his policies to limit government and fight inflation — ranking him twenty-first out
of thirty-nine presidents ranked. This example demonstrates the limitations of
Vedder and Gallaway's rankings. Some of the economic policies adopted during
Jackson's administration, which ensured short-term prosperity, led to economic
catastrophe in the longer term during Van Buren's administration.

LIBERTY

Treated Native Americans Harshly

Georgia unconstitutionally nullified a federal treaty that guaranteed land in that
state to the Cherokee Indian tribe. As happened so many times in American
history, gold was discovered on Indian lands, and whites wanted it. Georgia
even passed a law that made it illegal for Indians to mine gold on their own
land.[20] The Cherokees had given up war, were cooperative with the whites,
and were trying to blend in with American society by creating self-government.
Georgia evicted the Cherokees, and instead of making war, the Indians took
the case to court. Ultimately the Supreme Court ruled in their favor. Jackson
urged Georgia to ignore the Supreme Court ruling.[21]

Jackson didn't think that whites and Indians could live peacefully near each
other. Self-servingly, he believed that the Indians had to be pushed west of the
Mississippi or white settlers would exterminate them.[22] But Jackson didn't like
the Indians, and this faux concern for their safety was merely his excuse for
standing by while whites brutally pushed the Indians off their land.

Jackson argued that whites had left their homes to travel to new far-flung
destinations and the Indians were just being asked to do the same. Of course,
Jackson missed the obvious fact that the whites did so willingly, and the Indians had their land stolen forcibly and were coerced and terrorized into pulling
up stakes. Also, whites were seeking better opportunities in the West, and
the Indians were forced to give up their sacred homelands for poor land in
Oklahoma.

Nevertheless, although Jackson was willing to send troops to South Carolina
to suppress the nullification of federal tariff law, he did not send troops to protect Indians from whites in Georgia when Georgians nullified a federal treaty
and threw the Indians out.[23] In fact, in 1830 Jackson got Congress to pass an
Indian Removal Act to drive Indian tribes off the land that had been guaranteed to them by more than ninety treaties, and he used state militia to evict the

Indians from their homes.[24] The act fulfilled Thomas Jefferson's idea of ethnically cleansing Indians from their land within existing states, which whites coveted, and pushing them into vacant western territories. Jackson ordered the U.S. Army to begin removing the Cherokees and other tribes in what would be called the Trail of Tears, as thousands of Indians died en route to their new western homes.

Less passive than the Cherokee, the Seminoles refused to be moved from promised reservations in Florida to west of the Mississippi River. During Jackson's second term, the longest Indian War in U.S. history — the Second Seminole War — began, with the Indians using guerrilla tactics to kill as many as two thousand U.S. troops. The violence attenuated only after Osceola, the Seminoles' chief, was captured in an underhanded fashion while negotiating an agreed truce under Van Buren. Most Seminole Indians eventually agreed to move peaceably to lands in the west, but the ones that remained in Florida had their crops burned and bounties put on their heads. Jackson began this horrific saga.

The Sauk and Fox Indians of Illinois, led by Chief Black Hawk, had been driven off their land in Illinois into Iowa. In 1832, Black Hawk decided to move his men, women, and children back into Illinois in a non-warlike move to attempt to resist white encroachment. U.S. troops and Illinois militia pursued them, and Black Hawk attacked. He then retreated to Bad Axe River in Wisconsin, where most of the Sauk and Fox were massacred. The savagery of the war led most Native Americans to flee west, leaving most of the Northwest Territory (now the Midwest) open to white settlement.[25]

In sum, Jackson had an awful record in his dealings with the Indians. He brutally pushed them west and did not honor even the treaties he personally negotiated with them.[26]

CONCLUSION

Andrew Jackson is ranked below Monroe and Jefferson in the bad category for three reasons: (1) his dramatic expansion of executive power past what the founders had intended, (2) his overly belligerent response to South Carolina's nullification of increased federal tariffs and threatened secession from the union, and (3) his harsh treatment of Native Americans.

Although he correctly opposed a recharter of the Second Bank of the United States, he probably did so for the wrong reasons and acted unconstitutionally while doing so. Thus, opposing the bank helps his ranking only to some extent. Although supposedly a proponent of limited government, his economic policies were poor and he greatly expanded presidential power, both of which lessen this ostensible plus and lower his ranking — bringing Jackson to number twenty-seven here.

8

MARTIN VAN BUREN

Practiced What He Preached

PP&L* RANKING: 3
Category: Excellent

Eighth president of the United States

Term: March 4, 1837, to March 4, 1841
Party: Democratic-Republican, Democratic, and Free Soil
Born: December 5, 1782, Kinderhook, New York
Died: July 24, 1862 (age seventy-nine), Kinderhook, New York
Spouse: Hannah Hoes Van Buren (died); daughter-in-law
Angelica Van Buren was first lady
Education: : Kinderhook Academy and studied law for admission to the New York State Bar
Occupation: Lawyer
Religion: Dutch Reformed

Martin Van Buren, a Democrat whose four years in office preceded the William Henry Harrison/John Tyler term, was an advocate of restraining federal authority, maintaining states' authority, and limiting the president's power. According to historian Jeffrey Rogers Hummel, Van Buren admired Thomas Jefferson and his mentor, Andrew Jackson. But Van Buren was actually a better president than these "champions of liberty" by my criteria. Hummel notes that Van Buren didn't impose a disastrous embargo or unconstitutionally purchase Louisiana, as Jefferson did, nor did he coerce South Carolina to stay in the union during the nullification crisis of 1832, as Andrew Jackson did.[1]

Van Buren refused to intervene in a severe economic downturn, thus shortening its length. Also, he established what may have been the best banking

---

*PP&L = Peace, Prosperity, and Liberty.

system in U.S. history. Despite challenges from American's northern and southern neighbors, Van Buren kept the nation out of potential border wars. Within the nation, however, Van Buren sustained costly and, in retrospect, unconscionable wars against Native Americans, as did my number four–ranked president, Rutherford B. Hayes. Were it not for their excessive policies against native tribes, Van Buren and Hayes would have been listed first and second in this ranking of presidents.

PEACE

Avoided Several Potential Wars

In foreign policy, Van Buren was impressive. He declared his opposition to foreign alliances. In addition, he defused a potential dustup with Britain over Canada in 1837. The British sent the Canadian militia to burn the American ship *Caroline*, which was carrying illegal weapons to Canadian rebels who were being supported by many New Yorkers, even though the ship was in U.S. waters. In retaliation, in 1838, Americans burned a Canadian ship on the St. Lawrence River. Van Buren chose to avoid war by issuing a neutrality proclamation, then asked northern state governors to help him soothe tempers and sent General Winfield Scott to mediate the dispute. He then disarmed the American radicals, who were making one of the many attempts in U.S. history to grab Canada.[2]

Also in 1838, Van Buren settled a boundary dispute between Maine and New Brunswick, Canada — the Aroostook War — that could have led to a full-blown conflict between Britain and the United States. The governor of Maine riled the lieutenant governor of New Brunswick by sending a militia into a disputed border area to clear out what he deemed to be Canadian intruders. Canadian and U.S. militias then squared off across the border. Van Buren supported Maine's claim but warned its governor that the U.S. government would not be dragged into the fray. In 1839, Van Buren again sent General Scott to successfully mediate the crisis. The British and American governments then agreed to withdraw all troops from the border area.

In addition, Van Buren avoided a war with Mexico. The United States had monetary claims against the Mexican government, which the aggressive Andrew Jackson had pursued vigorously. Far less anxious for war, Van Buren adroitly got the Mexican government to accept arbitration by a commission, thus avoiding conflict. Also, Van Buren refused Texas's bid to be annexed by the United States after it became an independent republic in 1836, following a separatist war with Mexico. He correctly feared that admitting Texas would exacerbate sectional fissures in the United States by bringing in a slave state, while also worsening friction with Mexico and fracturing the Democratic Party. James Polk later started a war with Mexico — which Van Buren had avoided[3] — aimed at stealing the weaker nation's land.

Unfortunately, Van Buren did not hesitate to "show the flag" abroad via U.S. naval power. President John Quincy Adams had initiated the United States Exploring Expedition, and Van Buren pushed the exploration and power projection mission over the U.S. Navy's opposition to it. The voyage, lasting from 1838 until 1842, was the last circumnavigation of the world by an all-sail naval squadron (and a precedent for the world cruise of the steamships of the Great White Fleet during Theodore Roosevelt's administration). It not only explored but also projected U.S. forces into the unknown Southern Hemisphere (Antarctica) and the farthest reaches of the Pacific Ocean.[4]

Set Shameful Policies toward Indians and Blacks

Van Buren is placed third in this ranking of presidents, behind Tyler and Cleveland, because he continued Andrew Jackson's harsh policies toward the Indians, yet told Congress that the government's treatment of Native Americans was "directed by the best feelings of humanity."[5]

Jackson had already sent most of the Indians in the Southwest to the arid and unappealing Indian Territory, which is now Oklahoma. The Cherokees were able to delay their deportation, but the U.S. Army "escorted" them over a thousand miles to their desolate new homeland. The march in the winter of 1838 and 1839, under Van Buren, was the worst the Cherokee Nation experienced. Insufficient government funding for the move and inclement weather caused thousands of members of the tribe to die of hunger, disease, or exposure on the Trail of Tears. This episode alone reduces Van Buren's stature in the presidential rankings.

About the same time, the Seminole Indians were resisting eviction from their promised reservation in Florida to lands west of the Mississippi River. The vicious Second Seminole War was already underway when Van Buren took office, and it was still raging when he left the presidency four years later. Van Buren could have settled the lengthiest and costliest Indian war in U.S. history and let several hundred Seminoles remain on the reservation, as John Tyler eventually did. Van Buren, however, opted to keep fighting a war in which as many as two thousand U.S. troops and many more Indians were killed. Osceola, the Seminole chief, was captured using the underhanded technique of waving a fraudulent flag of truce — contrary to the laws of war. The war and Indian removals led to an increase in the size of the U.S. Army by 50 percent and the establishment of new forts.[6]

PROSPERITY

Demonstrated Restraint in an Economic Crisis

The Panic of 1837 was caused by excessive monetary expansion, resultant rampant economic growth, and speculation during Andrew Jackson's administration. The monetary expansion led businesses to overinvest, and such excessive investments eventually had to be liquidated, thus causing a recession. The panic arrived, however, shortly after Van Buren took office. Prices rose, many financial institutions failed, bankruptcies were epidemic, massive unemployment ensued, significant numbers of people perished from starvation, and the ill effects spread around the world.

Facing the panic, Van Buren resisted pressure for Jacksonian government activism and generally advocated a "hard money" policy, in which bank notes were redeemable only in gold. This restricted the money supply, dampened inflation, and thus made the economic decisions of the private sector more predictable. In the 1930s, the Great Depression was exacerbated by the policies of Herbert Hoover and FDR, who didn't let wages and prices fall so that the market could reestablish equilibrium quickly. In contrast, Van Buren's laissez-faire policies allowed the market to readjust fairly rapidly.[7] Van Buren reduced public spending, balanced the budget, and railed against the creation of national debt.[8] Vedder and Gallaway gave Van Buren a very high ranking — number five of thirty-nine presidents ranked — for policies that limited government and promoted price stability (the reduction of inflation).

After Andrew Jackson got rid of the national bank, Van Buren advocated for and eventually won the opportunity to establish an independent federal treasury to replace Jackson's federal deposits in state-chartered private ("pet") banks. Initially, Van Buren tried and failed to formally separate the failing state-chartered private banking sector from the federal government, but he achieved this goal informally by making the government follow a hard-money policy (paying in gold, not printed money). Later, he established the Independent Treasury, a storehouse for federal funds, which led to much-needed national financial deregulation in the near and medium term. Van Buren then supervised the dismantling of much of Alexander Hamilton's centralized financial apparatus.[9]

No nationally chartered bank existed, and the Independent Treasury avoided dealing with the state-chartered private banks. After Van Buren left office, the Independent Treasury was repealed, but later James Polk got it reinstated.

According to Jeffrey Hummel, Van Buren's laissez-faire banking system was the best in U.S. history. Not surprisingly, bankers did not like Van Buren. Hummel notes that the losses to banknote holders from fraud, insolvency, or speculation were less than the potential losses from inflation caused by more regulation. Yet in the long term, Van Buren's Independent Treasury had the effect of gradually centralizing financial power in the federal government, culminating in the creation of the Federal Reserve System — a quasi-central bank. Thus, Jackson's scheme to store federal funds in state-chartered private banks was probably superior to the Independent Treasury, if Jackson had not unconstitutionally circumvented Congress's need to approve it. That said, Van Buren's banking system was superior to others that came in its wake.

Staunchly Advocated Limiting Federal and Executive Power

To his credit, Van Buren got Congress to stop distributing federal aid to state governments and substantially cut real federal spending on internal improvements such as roads and canals. Van Buren opposed federal funding of this sort of infrastructure on the grounds that the Constitution did not strictly authorize it — in accordance with the Tenth Amendment, which stated that all powers not specifically given to the federal government would reside with the states or the people. In reality, the private sector could and did provide private roads, canals, and infrastructure. Not so desirable was Van Buren's decision during the Panic of 1837 to undertake government attempts to improve working conditions. For example, in 1840 he issued an executive order that limited work in the federal government to a ten-hour day. According to Frederick Jackson, an eminent historian, these initiatives were the first whisperings of the progressive movement of the early twentieth century.[10] Much of the regulation created during that movement ended up hurting those it was intended to help.

LIBERTY

Generally Acquiesced to Slave Owners' Demands

Van Buren's record on bettering the lot of African Americans was one of political temporizing. Like many earlier and later northern politicians, Van Buren knew that his policies would be doomed without southern support; in Van Buren's case, this meant his economic program, the potential to recover from the Panic of 1837, and his reelection chances. Thus, his policies on slavery left a lot to be desired.

In 1839, slaves owned by Spaniards rose up and took control of the slave ship *Amistad* off the coast of Cuba in order to return to Africa. When they ended up landing on Long Island and being imprisoned in Connecticut, Van Buren issued an executive order that the slaves should be taken to a naval vessel to speed their return to their owners. In 1841, former President John Quincy Adams eloquently argued the slaves' case before the Supreme Court and won their freedom.[11]

Also, Van Buren resisted abolishing slavery in the District of Columbia and threatened to veto congressional restrictions on slavery in Florida as a condition for its admission to the union. In 1840, Van Buren did, however, rule that blacks' testimony could be used in a naval court-martial case.

CONCLUSION

Unlike Thomas Jefferson, James Madison, and his mentor, Andrew Jackson, who all embraced limited government in all facets of public policy, but only in theory, Van Buren was a superior president because he actually practiced what they preached. Van Buren also limited government involvement in conflict by avoiding several wars with other white nations. But his major failing was that he exhibited no such limits on coercion of Indians and African Americans, and he has been downgraded in these rankings as a result. Martin Van Buren is number three here.

9

WILLIAM HENRY HARRISON

Served for Thirty-One Days

NOT RATED

Ninth president of the United States

Term: March 4, 1841, to April 4, 1841
Party: Whig
Born: February 9, 1773, Charles City County,
Colony of Virginia
Died: April 4, 1841 (age sixty-eight),
Washington, D.C.
Spouse: Anna Symmes Harrison
Alma Mater: University of Pennsylvania
Occupation: Soldier
Religion: Episcopal

When Harrison took office in 1841 at the age of sixty-eight, he was the oldest man to become President — a record that stood for 140 years, until Ronald Reagan was inaugurated in 1981 at the age of sixty-nine. Harrison died thirty-one days into his term — the briefest presidency in the history of the office. He was also the first U.S. President to die while in office. His death threw the country into a constitutional crisis.

10

JOHN TYLER

"...and Tyler Too!"

PP&L* RANKING: I
Category: Excellent

Tenth president of the United States

Term: April 4, 1841, to March 4, 1845
Party: Democrat and Whig
Born: March 29, 1790, Charles City County, Virginia
Died: January 18, 1862 (age seventy-one), Richmond, Virginia
Spouse: Letitia Christian Tyler (first wife); Julia Gardiner Tyler
    (second wife)
Alma Mater: The College of William and Mary
Occupation: Lawyer
Religion: Episcopalian (possibly a Deist)

War hero William Henry Harrison was elected president in 1841 under the Whig Party banner and died in office after serving only one month, the shortest term as president in U.S. history. It was the first time a president had died in office. In that national crisis, John Tyler asserted that a vice president was not a mere caretaker in such circumstances; rather, he held all of the powers given to the president by the Constitution. With this assertion, he set an important precedent for vice presidential successors.

The Constitution then said that the responsibilities of a deceased president would "devolve on the Vice President," but it did not say that the number two man could then be called "president" and serve out the president's term.[1] Nevertheless, Tyler had a judge swear him in, and he moved into the White House.[2] Normally, powers not specifically mentioned in the Constitution should not be assumed, but in this case the Constitution did not provide an alternative

---

*PP&L = Peace, Prosperity, and Liberty.

77

course of action — for example, establishing an explicit caretaker status for the vice president and calling for a special election to choose a new president. It is not clear that remaining an "acting president" in title and action would have served the country well for almost four years. Thus, although increasing executive powers generally earns demerits in my calculations, Tyler gets only a few for the precedent that he set in this case. Indeed, in the context of his times, his assumption of presidential powers served to promote what I see as the most praiseworthy presidential agenda in U.S. history.

Having been elected with Harrison as a Whig Party candidate, most people expected John Tyler to promote his party's platform. The Whigs were primarily a polyglot party formed by people who believed Andrew Jackson had grabbed too much power as president. In general, however, the Whigs believed in high tariffs and a strong national bank, both of these in order to federally fund internal improvements (infrastructure projects, such as roads and canals).

Tyler had rightly fallen out with Jackson over Jackson's belligerent response in 1832 to South Carolina's refusal to accept a federal tariff (the nullification crisis). Although John Tyler was a Whig in name, he was an ex-Democrat, and he remained a Democrat in philosophy. Back then, Democrats laudably believed in limited government and the traditional U.S. foreign policy of staying out of other countries' business.

Tyler stood against the Whig Party and its agenda on several important issues and suffered the consequences. After Tyler vetoed the revival of the national bank in his first year in office, his party expelled him, and almost his entire cabinet quit, leaving him as an unelected president without a party. When Tyler vetoed a Whig bill to raise tariffs, he was also the first president to endure an impeachment attempt, which his own party instigated. The impeachment attempt failed.

Tyler, as an unelected president, exhibited tremendous political courage in defying his own party on the national bank, high tariffs, and federal funding of internal infrastructure improvements. He also exercised great restraint in dealing with threats at home and abroad. The result was that the best president who ever held office, by my account, lacked the party support he needed to be reelected.

PEACE

Ended the Worst Indian War in U.S. History

To his credit, Tyler ended the longest and bloodiest Indian war in U.S. history — the Second Seminole War — by allowing several hundred Seminoles to stay on their reservation in Florida instead of being sent to lands west of the Mississippi River. Martin Van Buren, his predecessor, had rejected this settlement and had pursued a harsher Indian policy. After the war ended, Tyler cut the number of troops in the U.S. Army by 33 percent — from twelve thousand to slightly more than eight thousand.[3]

Responded with Restraint to Internal Rebellion

Tyler also used restraint when Thomas Dorr's rebellion erupted in Rhode Island in 1841.[4] At the time, only 6 percent of Rhode Islanders were allowed to vote, leading Dorr and his followers to form an alternative system of government without the state's sanction. The governor of Rhode Island asked for military forces to quell violence, but Tyler was reluctant to send forces when, in his view, no insurrection yet existed.

After Dorr's rebels tried to take over state government buildings, the governor imposed martial law and again requested troops. Tyler sent his secretary of war on a fact-finding mission and agreed to call out the Connecticut and Massachusetts militias if needed (the Constitution gave Congress the authority to call out the militia, but Congress had delegated that power to the president by laws passed in the late 1700s and early 1800s, a mistake in my view). Dorr was arrested, convicted, and released. His action managed to spur Rhode Island to adopt universal voting eligibility for white males.[5]

Tyler's restraint helped create the best possible outcome — an improvement over the status quo without more violence. The use of restraint proved wise because no general insurrection resulted from the short-lived Dorr rebellion, and the reckless use of federal troops could have actually spurred one in defiance.

Responded with Restraint to an International Dispute

Martin Van Buren's restraint had avoided a war over a border dispute between New Brunswick, Canada, and Maine. Van Buren had supported Maine's territorial claim but insisted that the state not drag the federal government into war with Britain. Tyler eventually got Maine and Britain to agree on a compromise that gave both New Brunswick and Maine swaths of territory of identical size and allowed Maine residents to use the Saint John River to get their agricultural and forest products to market.

Also, Tyler, a man with southern sympathies, reached an agreement with Britain to jointly enforce a ban on the slave trade; the agreement was ratified in both countries.[6]

Annexed Texas and Contributed to the Eventual War with Mexico

Tyler violated his own belief in the narrow construction of the Constitution by annexing Texas into the United States without obtaining the constitutionally required two-thirds vote in the Senate for a treaty with a separate nation. He couldn't get a two-thirds majority so instead relied on only a majority in both houses of Congress.[7]

At a Texas convention in July 1844, Texans voted to accept annexation. Since the annexation was consensual between the independent nation of Texas and the United States, the assimilation of the population was not forced (at least for the white population, since Texas was made a slave state); thus U.S. troop deployment for the defense of the new land was technically permissible. Tyler ordered General Zachary Taylor's troops into Texas at Corpus Christi — a provocative act in the eyes of a war-ready Mexico, which had never relinquished its claim to Texas despite the 1836 rebellion making it an independent state.

The more belligerent James K. Polk succeeded Tyler in March 1845. The Mexicans seemed, by early 1846, less likely to oppose with force Texas's annexation to the U.S. Polk sent General Taylor's forces farther south into a disputed area on the Texas-Mexican border. His action had less to do with Texas or its border and more to do with making a blatant attempt to start a war with a weaker country and grab its territory: what is now the southwestern United States, including the prize of California.[8]

Although Tyler didn't provoke a war with Mexico, sending General Taylor and the U.S. Army to Texas in the first place laid the groundwork for Polk's later war of territorial aggrandizement, which began in 1846. Thus, Tyler played only a minor role in the disputes that led to the Mexican War. Although the main purpose of the U.S. annexing Texas was territorial expansion, it also brought a slave state into the union, which was then closely divided, North and South, on whether slavery should expand into the American West.

Extended the Monroe Doctrine

Tyler regrettably sent a message to Congress that extended the Monroe Doctrine to cover Hawaii. The Monroe Doctrine was a unilateral proclamation that the United States would stay out of European affairs if Europe's powers would not establish new colonies in the Western Hemisphere. Hawaii was not even a possession of the United States at the time of Tyler's message, and his action began to extend U.S. hegemony into the Pacific theater, eventually leading to colonialism, interventionism, several wars, and an informal U.S. Pacific empire.

PROSPERITY

Opposed Big Government

Most Whigs believed in a national bank and high tariffs to provide federal funds for internal improvements — that is, the building of infrastructure projects such as roads and canals. Such a program does not promote prosperity because tariffs, taxes that raise the price of imports, interfere with free trade across national boundaries. Free trade allows both the buyer and the seller to benefit from lower prices, specialization in production, and the resulting economic efficiency.

Tyler, however, used the presidential veto extensively to obstruct his own party's program and to protect the states' powers from the federal Congress's intervention. On constitutional grounds, he vetoed bills to recharter the national bank and to distribute federal aid to states. The Constitution did not provide for a national bank, and the one that had temporarily existed had interfered with free financial markets by overregulation; it also had been corrupt.

There was no need for the government to subsidize, at taxpayer expense, infrastructure projects that the private sector would have undertaken anyway. In the nineteenth century, private roads and canals were common. Like railroads, then and into the twentieth and twenty-first centuries, owners of these thoroughfares charged a fee for their use.

Tyler also favored a tight monetary policy based on sound paper currency backed by gold and silver. Vedder and Gallaway, two free-market economists, rank Tyler ninth out of thirty-nine presidents rated on their composite indicator, which measures promotion of small government and price stability (low inflation).

Responded to Dropping Federal Revenue

Scheduled decreases in rates under a compromise tariff were draining the federal treasury. To raise federal revenue, Tyler reluctantly advocated suspending tariff reduction and also demanded that Congress end federal distribution of funds to states generated by selling federal land. Congress passed a tariff increase in 1842, which Tyler signed, but continued the distribution of land proceeds to states, which Tyler pocket-vetoed (held unsigned until Congress adjourned).

Instead of raising revenue, Tyler could have balanced the budget by cutting defense spending. Tyler had cut the army but had given the navy some new funding for ships, facilities, and coastal forts, which could have been canceled.

LIBERTY

Expanded Executive Privilege

Tyler, like George Washington, claimed a crude form of executive privilege to avoid turning over information to Congress: for example, on correspondence related to treaty negotiations with Britain over the boundary between Canada and Maine, on the names of members of Congress applying for office, and on negotiations over the investigation of a Cherokee land-fraud scandal. Although Tyler claimed presidential discretion over the data, not absolute executive control over information, such instances of proto-executive privilege seem questionable.[9] Nothing about such a privilege is found in the Constitution. In general, however, Tyler's record on preserving liberty was very good.

CONCLUSION

Tyler exhibited restraint in dealing with an internal rebellion, a bloody Indian war, and a boundary dispute with Canada. He supported a sound policy of limiting the money supply, and he generally opposed high tariffs, a national bank, and federal welfare to the states. In sum, John Tyler gets the number one ranking here not only because he favored limited government, but because he fought members of his own party to preserve it — thereby torpedoing his chances for a second term.

11

JAMES K. POLK

War for Land to Carry Out
Aggressive Manifest Destiny

PP&L* RANKING: 38
Category: Bad

Eleventh president of the United States

Term: March 4, 1845, to March 4, 1849
Party: Democratic
Born: November 2, 1795, Pineville, North Carolina
Died: June 15, 1849 (age fifty-three), Nashville,
   Tennessee
Spouse: Sarah Childress Polk
Alma Mater: University of North Carolina at Chapel Hill
Occupation: Lawyer, farmer (planter)
Religion: Methodist

James Polk is the classic example of an effective president who was not a successful one. He achieved his enhanced power by dominating the executive branch, including the cabinet, the federal bureaucracy, the patronage system, the budget, and the military. The Mexican War, as with most wars, allowed him to expand such domination and consolidate executive power.[1] Polk should be praised, though, for keeping his pledge to serve only one term. However, despite his status as a built-in lame duck, he managed to snatch a lot of land and power and get much done — most all of it bad for the country.

   Predictably, most analysts, who tend to be kind to bold chief executives and those who increase the presidency's power, regularly rank Polk in the "near great" category. This ranking comes from his policies of aggressive land and

---

*PP&L = Peace, Prosperity, and Liberty.

power grabbing, not from his charisma. Polk was rigid, puritanical, self-righteous, dishonest, secretive, and unlovable.[2]

PEACE

Started a War with a Weaker Country to Snatch Its Land

Polk, a strict Calvinist protestant, believed that the United States' manifest destiny was to extend from the Atlantic shore to the Pacific coast. Such preordained territorial expansionism was a common ideology at this time in American history. Even before Polk took office, he endorsed a joint congressional resolution, signed by Tyler in the last days of his administration, to annex Texas. Although Texas had been an independent nation since 1836, following a secessionist war with Mexico, Mexico had not psychologically accepted the loss of the territory.

The Mexicans believed that Americans had come from the east and stolen their land. After Texan Sam Houston defeated Mexican General Santa Anna at the battle of San Jacinto in 1835, Santa Anna was captured and agreed, during captivity, that the Rio Grande River would be the southern border of an independent Texas. The Mexican Congress later repudiated this coerced agreement, thus staking Mexico's claim that the southern border of Texas was north of the Rio Grande at the Nueces River.

In early 1845, after his inauguration, Polk tried to buy California and New Mexico from Mexico, but the Mexicans, incensed by Congress passing a resolution to annex Texas, refused to negotiate and broke off diplomatic relations with the United States. After the United States formally annexed Texas in December 1845, the Mexicans mobilized for war.[3] Yet by early 1846, the Mexicans seemed less inclined to oppose the annexation forcefully.[4]

Because Polk had had no luck in buying California and New Mexico, he decided to initiate a conflict with Mexico and win those lands in the peace settlement. He sent General Zachary Taylor and his army into the disputed border area between the Rio Grande and Nueces rivers. The subsequent Mexican raid into disputed territory north of the Rio Grande claimed only eleven U.S. lives, but Polk already had ordered Taylor to invade Mexico if the Mexicans crossed the river. Although some histories of the war mention this U.S. provocation and the subsequent Mexican raid on Taylor's scouting group just north of the Rio Grande, they rarely mention the prior U.S. blockade of the Rio Grande River, which cut off supplies to the Mexican town of Matamoras. Blockades are recognized as international acts of war. Thus, the United States didn't just provoke the Mexicans to start the Mexican War, the U.S. Army actually started the war by taking the first hostile action.

Although the Mexican raid was actually just north of the Rio Grande River in disputed territory, Polk falsely claimed that it was north of the Nueces River, clearly in U.S. territory. After the Mexican raid, in May 1846 Congress declared war, but even before that Mexican attack, Polk had already drafted a message to Congress to ask for such a declaration. The raid merely provided a pretext for sending it.[5]

Taylor successfully invaded northern Mexico, winning several key battles, and Major General Winfield Scott launched an amphibious assault on Veracruz and marched overland to capture Mexico City. In response to Mexican guerrilla warfare, Scott ordered bombardments that minimized U.S. military casualties at the cost of increased casualties among Mexican civilians.[6] In battles with the Mexicans in California, San Francisco was captured.[7] The Mexican War was the first of many successful U.S. offensive wars on foreign soil and the first occupation of an enemy capital.[8]

Because of the military success in 1846, some Americans wanted to annex all of Mexico, but a growing number of people in the United States condemned an aggressive, offensive war aimed at grabbing a weak opponent's territory. Antiwar sentiment started to build as the war dragged on without conclusion. In 1848, the House passed a resolution that censured Polk for a war "unnecessarily and unconstitutionally begun by the President of the United States."[9] Polk decided to limit his territorial aspirations. He lopped off the northern part of Mexico and left the rest. Polk even paid the Mexicans for the land taken by force to ensure that a viable peace was achieved.[10]

Polk really wanted a transcontinental nation and especially the protected West Coast port of San Francisco. The first successful offensive U.S. war extended the United States' undisputed southern border to the Rio Grande and added the present southwestern part of the country, including California. Polk had perpetrated the second-largest land grab in U.S. history — eclipsed only by the Louisiana Purchase of 1803.

Expanded Presidential Power

In the process of his belligerent land grabbing, Polk expanded presidential power past what the founding fathers had envisioned. According to Professor Edward S. Corwin, an authority on the U.S. Constitution, Polk was one of the top ten expanders of presidential power[11] and the only powerful executive between Andrew Jackson and Abraham Lincoln — Congress overshadowed the rest.[12]

Polk was determined, even as a man without any military experience, to have the final say on military issues, setting precedents for future presidents. He used this power to effectively remove the power to declare war from Congress. Polk deployed, without prior congressional approval, U.S military forces in disputed territory against a Mexican government that was inclined toward war and blockaded the Rio Grande River — an act of war. When the U.S. forces were attacked, Congress was confronted with a fait accompli and was forced to recognize an already existing state of war. Congress declared war but censured Polk for exceeding his authority.

Without congressional approval, Polk ordered U.S. military commanders in Mexico to collect duties on imports entering U.S-controlled Mexican ports. This usurped Congress's constitutional role of collecting duties and regulating commerce and used conquest to reap plunder from war. The war also allowed Polk to create many new federal patronage jobs and then fill them with his Democratic cronies.[13]

Like Jefferson, Madison, and Jackson, Polk, in theory, championed a restricted role for the federal government but significantly deviated from that philosophy in practice. The deviation was so great that, like Jefferson, Madison, and Jackson, he has to be grouped with the bad presidents.

Risked Starting Two Wars Simultaneously

At the same time that Polk was being antagonistic toward Mexico, he pursued a policy of reckless brinksmanship in an effort to grab sole possession of the Oregon Territory from the British — even though a U.S.-British treaty, signed in 1818, provided for sharing the vast territory that extended into what is now Canada. President Tyler, a Whig, had proposed that Oregon be split between the United States and Britain at the forty-ninth parallel, roughly the present border between Washington State and Canada; Polk and the Democratic Party had run in the 1844 election on the slogan, "Fifty-four forty or fight!" They wanted all of Oregon up to the 54 degrees 40 minutes north latitude, which marked the border of Oregon with Russian-controlled Alaska. In contrast, the British wanted the U.S.-Canada border to be the Columbia River, the current boundary between the states of Oregon and Washington.

When Polk declared that the British should relinquish shared control of the territory and that the U.S. government would safeguard the security of American settlers there, the British regarded this as an implied threat. Polk's secretary of state and a future president, James Buchanan, told Polk that if he demanded territory north of the forty-ninth parallel, there would be war, and the American people probably wouldn't support him. Buchanan also thought it unwise to engage in behavior that might trigger simultaneous wars with Britain (over Oregon) and Mexico (over Texas). Polk disagreed and told Buchanan to be tough with the British. Polk withdrew from the 1818 treaty.

What saved Polk was that the British preferred negotiation over warfare. The British proposed the forty-ninth parallel as the border — Tyler's original proposal — and the issue was settled. The Oregon Territory — comprising present-day Oregon, Washington, and parts of Idaho and Wyoming — became U.S. soil.[14]

Created a Monroe Doctrine on Steroids

What might be called the "Polk Doctrine" exceeded the hubris of even the Monroe Doctrine. Polk's manifesto prohibited European *diplomatic* intervention in the Western Hemisphere, not just military meddling and colonization by European powers. Polk also barred the transfer of any territory in the Western Hemisphere to a European power, even if the people of the territory approved of it. In 1848, white inhabitants in Yucatán, Mexico, were fighting with the Indians there. Yucatán wanted to sell itself to Spain or Britain to get cash to fight the Indians. To prevent the sale, Polk, in accordance with his doctrine, asked Congress to approve aid and military forces for Yucatán. But before the U.S. meddling occurred, the whites in Yucatán made peace with the local Indians.

In 1847, Polk signed a treaty that gave the United States the right-of-way across Panama for a future railroad or canal.[15] This treaty eventually allowed the U.S. to use the right-of-way to construct both, and it made the Canal Zone a virtual U.S. colony, with future heavy U.S. intervention in Panamanian politics.

PROSPERITY

Opposed Whig Big Government Programs

To his credit, Democrat Polk, like Andrew Jackson, opposed Whig Henry Clay's American System of using high tariffs (protecting industries) and a central bank to fund the building of roads and canals (internal improvements), actions that served to subsidize big business. Polk was called "Young Hickory" for carrying out the principles of "Old Hickory" Jackson.

Polk believed that the American System was unconstitutional because the Constitution didn't specifically give the federal government the power to do the things the system called for. In addition, he astutely believed, as most Democrats did at the time, that such government intervention helped the few at the expense of the many.[16] Today, many Democrats believe, usually incorrectly according to public choice economics, that government intervention helps the masses at the expense of the rich few.

Polk stuck to the Constitution when he said that tariffs should be used only to raise revenues for the government and not to protect industries. He believed burdening one part of the economy to benefit another was unfair, especially when tariffs tended to be regressive taxes that benefited the rich at the expense of the poor. Luxuries tended to be taxed at a lower rate than necessities.[17] Polk's Walker tariff of 1846 substantially reduced the high tariff levels of 1842 and ushered in a period of low duties until the Republicans became dominant, starting with the Civil War. The low tariffs helped end the repeated depressions of the 1830s.[18] Also, Polk vetoed a huge bill to federally subsidize harbor and river projects.

Thus, Vedder and Gallaway justifiably gave Polk a slightly above-par ranking — tied for the sixteenth to eighteenth rankings with James Buchanan and Herbert Hoover out of thirty-nine presidents ranked — for policies that promoted limited government and fought inflation.

Polk also had a mixed record on the central bank issue. Although he, Jackson, and Van Buren had correctly opposed the crony capitalism of the Bank of the United States, Van Buren and Polk's solution — the Independent Treasury — was less than optimal. The Bank of the United States had a few government officials on the board of directors, but private interests, given a sweet deal by the government, mainly ran it. Jackson — unconstitutionally without asking Congress — took federal money out of the national bank and deposited it in state-chartered private ("pet") banks. Van Buren came along and took money out of the state-chartered banks and created an Independent Treasury. This scheme met its demise during the Tyler administration.

Polk revived Van Buren's Independent Treasury under the slogan "Constitutional Treasury." Because of potential corruption, Polk wanted government money to be secured in its own vault, not in those of private state-chartered banks.[19] Polk's Constitutional Treasury lasted until 1913, when the even more powerful Federal Reserve took its place.[20] Actually, the Constitutional Treasury was no more constitutional than the Bank of the United States. Nowhere in the Constitution is the federal government allowed to amass such financial power.

Jackson's distribution of federal money to state-chartered private banks was probably the right solution, if only he had obtained congressional approval before having done it. Under Jackson's vision, the corruption in the decentralized, private system would have been less dangerous than the precedent of creating powerful and unconstitutional federal financial machinery. The dangers of a centralized federal banking authority that eventually evolved to the Federal Reserve, a quasi-central bank, were realized, for example, in its contribution to the Great Depression (see the chapters on Wilson, Harding, Coolidge, and Hoover).

Thus Polk permanently returned the United States to a road that eventually led toward centralized governmental financial power. Yet, despite the fact that Polk had planted the seeds of centralization, the banking system continued to remain fairly deregulated for more than sixty years, until the Federal Reserve was created.

Expanded Domestic Powers

Since the republic began, the president's role in suggesting legislation has been unclear. Polk not only proposed legislation, he pressured Congress to act by exhortation and threats to directly appeal to the public (something that was then taboo). This legislative activism set a precedent and expanded presidential influence.

Polk also created the first unified executive budget. Previously, executive branch departments individually requested their funding from Congress without the president's prior review, but Polk now demanded that all departments request funding through him. In effect, he became the nation's first budget director. Although Polk's precedent increased presidential power, a lesser positive effect may have been an added counterweight, in some cases, to the cozy iron triangles that develop between government departments, congressional committees, and narrow constituencies, which tend to inflate federal spending. Polk's unified executive budget did not last, but it helped Warren Harding to permanently achieve that change in the next century.

LIBERTY

War Booty Raised the Issues of Black and Indian Rights

Polk's primary blind spot — as with many small-government conservatives today — was his failure to see that war is the primary cause of big government and of erosion of the separation of powers as described in the Constitution. The Mexican War — like all wars — strengthened the presidency vis-à-vis the other branches of government and distorted the governmental system that the nation's founders had envisioned. For example, the war created a vast ballooning of federal patronage, with most of the new positions going to Democratic hacks. Congress also violated the Constitution during the war by calling up the state militias to fight in Mexico. The Constitution provides that Congress can call forth the militia to enforce domestic laws, suppress insurrections, and repel invasions, but it doesn't say anything about sending the militia overseas to fight a war that the U.S. initiated.

The end of the Mexican War brought up the question of whether the new states arising from the war would be slave states or free states. The issue was not whether slavery would exist to any real extent in these new states, because they were largely comprised of mountains and deserts — not good for growing the crops that were farmed with slave labor. The issue was voting power in Congress. By 1846, northern interests had a majority in the House of Representatives. The South looked to the Senate, where rural states were overrepresented, to block antislavery measures.

The creation of states from the Louisiana Purchase threatened to tip even the Senate to the antislavery side. Thus Polk, a pro-slavery president, accepted a proposal that might have eventually turned Texas into five states, dramatically increasing slavery's power in the upper chamber.[21] In 1846, Congressman David Wilmot, an abolitionist from Pennsylvania, tried to abolish slavery in any new territory conquered during the Mexican War. Polk's efforts helped kill the amendment.

Polk could have come out against slavery, but he didn't.[22] Polk did, however, moderate his pro-slavery stance on occasion. In 1848, Congress was establishing governments for Oregon, California, and New Mexico. Polk didn't like a bill that banned slavery in Oregon in accordance with the Missouri Compromise of 1820, which prohibited slavery above a certain latitude, but he signed it anyway. For California, Polk supported the state making its own decision on slavery, rather than the federal government. As long as the Congress didn't interfere with slavery below that latitude line, Polk accepted that California would probably choose to be a free state.

Polk also indirectly trampled on Indian rights by announcing in December 1848 that an "abundance of gold" had been discovered in California, which led to a stampede of white settlers to the new territory in the gold rush of 1849.

Over one hundred thousand Indians were killed in California alone and their land stolen following the discovery of gold.

CONCLUSION

Although Polk gets a slightly above-par ranking for promoting policies that limited government and fought inflation during his term, his presidency demonstrates the inadequacy of that ranking for determining overall rankings of presidential success. He started the Mexican War just to steal territory from a weaker country. Polk's Mexican War and other aggressive land-grabbing policies led to a significant expansion of executive power, which would lead ultimately to big government in the future. James K. Polk is ranked number thirty-seven here.

12

ZACHARY TAYLOR

Risked Civil War Years before It Happened

PP&L* RANKING: 13
Category: Average

Twelfth president of the United States

Term: March 4, 1849, to July 9, 1850
Party: Whig
Born: November 24, 1784, Barboursville, Virginia
Died: July 9, 1850 (age sixty-five), Washington, D.C.
Spouse: Margaret Smith Taylor
Education: Privately tutored
Occupation: Soldier (general)
Religion: Episcopalian

Zachary Taylor, a Whig, served as president for only sixteen months after his March 1849 inauguration and had a generally good economic policy, despite increasing tariffs and subsidizing business. Taylor, a southerner, owned slaves but was so ashamed of the fact that he hid his slaves in the White House attic;[1] he was thus a moderate on the issue. As a former general in the Mexican War, he had to deal with the fruits of his battlefield victories, and these led to his decisions that are historically noteworthy.

PEACE

Risked a Likely Smaller Civil War in 1850

Texas had entered the union as a slave state in 1846, and in 1850 the state was threatening to use force to spread slavery by claiming part of New Mexico, which

---

*PP&L = Peace, Prosperity, and Liberty.

had been won in the Mexican War. In 1847, David Wilmot, a Pennsylvania Democrat, had formulated the Wilmot Proviso, which banned slavery in any territory gained from Mexico during the war. The proviso — which passed in the House but failed in the Senate — became a key indicator of politicians' true colors.

At this time in the country's history, every new free state admitted to the union had the perceived potential to alter the balance between slave and free states, a situation that would continue as the North gained industry and population compared to the southern slave states. Southerners believed that growing northern political power — if not arrested by the addition of more slave states — would eventually doom slavery in existing southern states. Taylor believed that California and New Mexico should decide for themselves whether they wanted to be slave states or free states, and his expectation was that they would elect to be free states. In response to Texas's threats of force against New Mexico, Taylor tried to circumvent Congress and the Wilmot Proviso by secretly planning to bring both California and New Mexico into the nation before Congress had time to vote on the matter.

Although Taylor was leery of Congress regulating slavery, the Constitution said that Congress may admit new states and make the rules and regulations governing U.S. territory.[2] Generally, Congress could and did let new states determine whether they wanted to be free or slave states. Nevertheless, Taylor, like other moderate southerners, wanted to limit slavery's expansion but guarantee the status quo in states where slavery was already permitted. This tack alarmed many conservatives in the South, who felt that if slavery were contained, it would die.

California applied for statehood, but Taylor's plan was dashed when New Mexico was given the status of a territory.[3] Not only did Taylor's scheme undermine the constitutional system of checks and balances and aggravate sectional tensions, it also fractured Taylor's Whig Party, which eventually dissolved.

Taylor did manage to dissuade Texas from forcibly grabbing New Mexico and imposing slavery there, but only by issuing threats and then occupying New Mexico with federal troops. The federal government had coercively purchased New Mexico from Mexico as a result of the Mexican War, and Taylor felt it should administer the territory for the time being. Such federal occupation was probably needed since Texas was trying to grab New Mexico by force, and southern leaders threatened to throw federal troops out of New Mexico.

In the end, senators Daniel Webster, Henry Clay, and John Calhoun came up with the Compromise of 1850, a series of laws designed to appease politicians in both the North and South and thus provide a temporary solution to the problem of slavery. The compromise, among other things, brought California into the union with self-determination on the slavery issue — which meant it would be a free state — and created territorial governments for New Mexico and the Mormon land of Deseret, now Utah (also allowing them self-determination on slavery, which undermined the Missouri Compromise of 1820 by allowing the possibility of slavery north of the 36 degrees 30 minutes north latitude line). Also, the settlement drew the boundary between Texas and New Mexico east of where Texas would have liked.[4] Finally, the compromise contained the Fugitive Slave Act, which required that escaped slaves be returned to their owners.

Taylor did not like the legislation, and, had his death not intervened, he likely would have vetoed the measure. The compromise was later signed during the succeeding Millard Fillmore administration. Webster, a fellow Whig, believed that if Taylor had not died, a civil war would have started in 1850.[5] Any civil war at this time probably would have been smaller and shorter, but that might not have prevented an even bigger war later. Yet the Compromise of 1850 began to erode the Missouri Compromise of 1820, which had restricted slavery to below the latitude of 36 degrees 30 minutes north and had thus prevented civil war for decades.

Laid the Groundwork for the Panama Canal

In foreign affairs, Taylor laid the basis for the later excavation of a canal across Central America. The British had interests in the area, and so any canal route had to be made neutral before digging could commence. The Clayton-Bulwer Treaty, signed during the Taylor administration, guaranteed that any future canal route would be neutral.[6] The canal was not completed until more than a half-century later, and the treaty was later modified so that the United States could entirely control the Canal Zone.

PROSPERITY

Pursued Whiggish Policies of High Tariffs and Subsidies

The expenses of the Mexican War and the costs of coercively buying California and New Mexico from Mexico had increased the national debt. To reduce that debt and to protect industry, Taylor asked Congress for a hike in tariffs. Taylor wanted not only to subsidize industry but also to hand out more goodies to farmers; he also wanted to create an agricultural bureau in the Interior Department to administer the welfare program.

In addition, Taylor wanted to subsidize a transcontinental railroad. He fore-saw that California's mineral wealth and its harbors, good for trade with the Asia/Pacific region, would eventually lead to the growth of cities on the nation's West Coast. Taylor wanted the government to do a study on the feasibility and cost of creating a transcontinental railway to link the Atlantic and the Pacific and to examine whether the government should build the railroad, or allow the private sector to do so with government aid.[7]

Note that the best alternative of letting the private sector fund the project entirely on its own did not seem to be an option. Later, private railroads did spring up and continue to this day, showing that the extensive government subsidies that were eventually provided were not needed.

LIBERTY

Ignored the Continued Murdering of Indians

The gold rush in California, which was in progress during Taylor's presidency, caused whites to shamefully murder two-thirds of California's Indian popula-tion — a hundred thousand people — and evict the rest from their lands.[8] Taylor did nothing to alleviate this situation.

CONCLUSION

Although Taylor wasn't a good president during his brief time in office, he didn't do anything that would qualify him as poor. He risked a smaller civil war when he occupied New Mexico with federal troops and disagreed with the Compro-mise of 1850. However, Taylor was probably right to resist the compromise, which included the pernicious and divisive Fugitive Slave Act. The slaughter of California's Indian population and his Whiggish increase in tariffs and sub-sidization of industry and agriculture earn him a low ranking in the average category. But he is saved from the poor group by Vedder and Gallaway's rel-atively high ranking on economic policy — sixth out of thirty-nine presidents ranked. Here, Zachary Taylor is ranked thirteen.

13

MILLARD FILLMORE

Avoided an Earlier Civil War, but at a Cost

PP&L* RANKING: 14
Category: Average

Thirteenth president of the United States

Term: July 9, 1850, to March 4, 1853
Party: Anti-Masonic, Whig, and American
Born: January 7, 1800, Summerhill, New York
Died: March 8, 1874 (age seventy-four), Buffalo, New York

Spouse: Abigail Powers Fillmore (first wife); Caroline Carmichael McIntosh Fillmore (second wife)
Alma Mater: New Hope Academy
Occupation: Lawyer
Religion: Unitarian

Millard Fillmore succeeded Zachary Taylor when the latter died suddenly. While his predecessor likely would have vetoed the Compromise of 1850, Fillmore signed it. That action may have averted an earlier start to the Civil War, but an onerous component, the Fugitive Slave Act, increased the federal government's role in sustaining the institution of slavery.

In other ways, Fillmore's administration was a continuation of Taylor's policies. Fillmore provided heavy subsidies to create a national railroad, for example. He had a mixed record in foreign policy, which included the coerced opening of the Japanese market, using U.S. naval power.

---

*PP&L = Peace, Prosperity, and Liberty.

PEACE

Signed the Compromise of 1850

After the United States snatched California and New Mexico in the Mexican War, Texas tried to grab part of New Mexico in order to extend slave territory, almost igniting a civil war in 1850. The heavy migration to California, which had accompanied the gold rush of the late 1840s and early 1850s, led to demands for statehood there.

At issue was the balance of free versus slave power in Congress as western territories were made states and brought into the union. Northerners did not want to ban slavery in the South, but they wanted to confine it to that area and admit only free states into the union. This, combined with the North's more rapid industrialization and increasing population, scared the southerners into thinking they would lose their traditional dominance in the Congress and face an eventual ban on slavery in the South.

The Compromise of 1850 — five laws proposed by senators Henry Clay, Daniel Webster, and John Calhoun — allowed California's entry into the union as a free state; permitted New Mexico and Utah to determine whether they were to be slave states or free states (allowing the possibility of slavery north of the 36 degrees 30 minutes north latitude line, in opposition to the Missouri Compromise of 1820, which had kept the nation from civil war for decades); demarcated the Texas–New Mexico border east of where Texas would have liked it; made slave trade but not slave owning illegal in the District of Columbia; and enacted a fugitive slave law, which required people to return escaped slaves to their owners, usually in slave states.

Thus, the Civil War was put off for eleven years, but the compromise allowed the slavery issue to fester and become more inflammatory during that period and explode into a large war — still the worst in U.S. history.

Coerced Foreign Policy

In 1852, Fillmore ordered Commodore Matthew Perry to take his heavily armed naval flotilla to Japan, which was then largely isolated from the rest of the world, to intimidate the Japanese into a trading relationship with the United States. Coerced trade is merely a form of mercantilism, or government subsidization and favoritism for business, using taxpayer dollars. Although Perry didn't get to Japan until Fillmore was out of office, Fillmore usually gets "credit" for this sorry "opening" of Japan. Trade is mutually beneficial to countries so engaged, but the use of force to compel it is usually not cost-effective, is a form of regressive taxation — the taxpayer pays for military power used in the furtherance of wealthy U.S. business interests — and is always unethical.

In 1849, before Fillmore took office, Napoleon III of France seized Honolulu, and the United States protested. The French withdrew, but pressure grew for U.S. annexation of Hawaii. To his credit, Fillmore resisted the pressure. In 1851, however, the French made a list of demands on the Hawaiian king that would have established a de facto French protectorate. Fillmore enforced the Monroe Doctrine with regard to Hawaii when he told the French to stay away. The French meddled no more in Hawaii. Although Fillmore shooed another power away from Hawaii, he resisted the temptation to annex the islands — but apparently only because Hawaii would have been a free rather than a slave state.

On the positive side of the ledger, Fillmore tried to patch up relations with Latin America, which James Polk had frayed by strengthening the Monroe Doctrine. Fillmore instituted a good-neighbor policy toward that region of the world. He improved relations with Mexico and insisted that U.S. businessmen buy prized Peruvian dung for fertilizer rather than commandeer it through force. When the Spanish executed two U.S. citizens for attempting to overthrow the Spanish colonial government in Cuba, Fillmore wisely avoided retaliation and a potential conflict.[1]

PROSPERITY

Whiggish Subsidies and Lackluster Economic Policies

Fillmore heavily subsidized railroad construction in the West. The existence of private railroads shows that this welfare was unneeded and was merely a redistribution of wealth from taxpayers to rich railroad barons. Vedder and Gallaway give Fillmore a slightly below average ranking in limiting government and fighting inflation — twentieth out of thirty-nine presidents ranked. This ranking generally agrees with this volume's more comprehensive ranking of Fillmore as low in the average category of presidents.

Reneged on a Self-Imposed Term Limit

On the day he became chief executive, Fillmore admirably announced that he would not seek a second term, but then he broke the promise by having his name considered for nomination at the 1852 Whig convention. His party did not renominate him.

LIBERTY

Delayed Civil War at the Expense of Liberty

Like Zachary Taylor, his predecessor, Fillmore was leery of Congress regulating slavery, but the Constitution said that Congress may admit new states and make the rules and regulations governing U.S. territory.[2] Thus Congress, acting constitutionally, could have banned slavery in the new territories. As the territories became states, the balance of power in Congress would have shifted to the free states. But political forces in the Congress prevented such an outcome.

The main problem with Fillmore's caving in to southern slave interests by signing the Compromise of 1850 — and it was a whopper — was the pernicious Fugitive Slave Act. The act caused opinion on slavery in the nation to become even more divided and motivated Harriet Beecher Stowe to write *Uncle Tom's Cabin*, which fanned the antislavery flames in the North. Fillmore used federal agents to enforce the act strictly, much to the chagrin of abolitionists.[3] Mobs attacked these federal marshals in order to free runaway slaves that the lawmen had apprehended.

Federal enforcement of the Fugitive Slave Act was unconstitutional because the national government was returning slaves to their owners; the Constitution clearly did not give the federal government such law enforcement powers. Fillmore threatened to send troops to the North to uphold the law and did send troops to the South to stop a threatened insurrection. The Act spurred the creation of the Underground Railway, which clandestinely transported slaves to freedom in violation of the law.[4]

Thus, if an enforced slave provision had been avoided, a haven for slaves could have been created openly in the North, which could have, over time, depleted the South of slaves.

CONCLUSION

In sum, signing the Compromise of 1850, Fillmore's most important action, was a mixed bag. In order to avoid a small civil war, Fillmore's capitulation to slave interests by accepting and unconstitutionally enforcing the Fugitive Slave Act hardened attitudes on slavery in both the North and the South.

This appeasement ensured that when the Civil War did break out eleven years later, it was cataclysmic. If an enforced provision could have been avoided, slaves might have fled from the South, perhaps eroding or eliminating this horrendous practice without a major conflict. Also, Fillmore unconscionably coerced Japan into trade with the United States. The one positive thing that Millard Fillmore did in his almost three years as president was to mend fences with Latin America. Thus, he earns a ranking of average, coming in at number fourteen.

14

FRANKLIN PIERCE

Made Civil War More Likely

PP&L* RANKING: 24
Category: Poor

Fourteenth president of the United States

Term: March 4, 1853, to March 4, 1857
Party: Democratic
Born: November 23, 1804, Hillsborough,
New Hampshire
Died: October 8, 1869 (age sixty-four), Concord,
New Hampshire
Spouse: Jane Appleton Pierce
Alma Mater: Bowdoin College
Occupation: Lawyer
Religion: Episcopalian

In the 1852 election, Democrat Franklin Pierce ran against Whig Winfield Scott, one of the heroes and chief generals of the Mexican War. As a brigadier general under Scott during that war, Pierce had a service record so undistinguished that the Whigs sarcastically distributed a book one inch tall and a half-inch wide entitled *The Military Services of General Pierce*. According to historian David K. E. Bruce, in his first skirmish of the war Pierce fell from his horse and fainted, "being injured in that portion of a man's anatomy that is least tolerant of suffering." Making reference to Pierce's well-known enjoyment of alcohol, the Whigs named him the "hero of many a well-fought bottle." Yet the charismatic Pierce won the election against war hero Scott handily.[1]

---

*PP&L = Peace, Prosperity, and Liberty.

This election proves that in American politics, charisma is so important that sometimes it can even triumph over heroism in war. Pierce was the first of many charismatic presidents who weren't the sharpest knives in the drawer — for example, Warren G. Harding, Franklin D. Roosevelt, John F. Kennedy, Ronald Reagan, and George W. Bush. In all but Harding's case, such presidents were failures. Pierce followed the general trend.

Pierce's administration is known for a Kansas policy that led to the Civil War, but he was also an interventionist enforcer of the Monroe Doctrine.

PEACE

Barely Made a Positive Contribution to Foreign Policy

In foreign affairs, Pierce signed the Canadian Reciprocity Treaty, which settled a long-time dispute with Canada over fishing rights, better delineated the border between the two nations, and eliminated tariffs on some products traded between the two countries.[2] It was his only positive foreign policy contribution.

Initiated Slave-Based Diplomacy

In 1854, Pierce bought, from Mexico, the Gadsden Purchase, tracts of land in southern Arizona and New Mexico. Although the avowed purpose was to provide land for a rail route to the Pacific Ocean, Pierce's decisions about land acquisition were often motivated by the goal of expanding areas where slaves were held or inhibiting antislave power in Congress.

A plan to acquire Cuba was also related to slavery. The southern states feared that the Spanish were about to free their slaves in Cuba, which might lead to slave uprisings in the United States. Pierce tried unsuccessfully to threaten the Spanish so they would give up Cuba, which could then have been admitted to the union as a slave state. This would have increased southern voting power and removed another potential area of free blacks that might have acted as a beacon of liberty to southern slaves. Naturally northerners, unlike most southerners, were opposed to acquiring Cuba by either purchase or use of force, and thus it did not happen. Conversely, when Hawaii — a likely free state — applied for entry into the United States as a state, Pierce refused.

Supported Commerce at Gunpoint

Pierce supported the coerced trade deal with Japan in 1854, which came about because Millard Fillmore, before he left office, had ordered Commodore

Matthew Perry and his fleet to intimidate Japan into signing it. Also, under Pierce, the U.S. Navy indiscriminately shelled, and thus razed and burned, Greytown (now San Juan) on the coast of Nicaragua — a clear war crime, even though no deaths resulted — and used an early antecedent of the modern failed-state argument (that instability and turmoil in another country necessitated U.S. intervention) to justify this U.S. military intervention.[3] Pierce recognized the questionable Nicaraguan government of William Walker, a proslave American adventure seeker who had started a rebellion and made himself president of the country.

Approved the Kansas-Nebraska Act and Opened the Door to Civil War

While his foreign policy record was grim, Pierce's principal — and negative — impact as president had to do with his policies that tended to promote eventual civil war at home. Like James Buchanan who followed him, Pierce was a doughface — a northerner who stuck up for the South and slavery. Pierce pledged to strictly enforce the Compromise of 1850 and endorsed the catastrophic Kansas-Nebraska Act of 1854 — both of which effectively repealed the Missouri Compromise of 1820, which had held the country together by prohibiting slavery above the latitude of 36 degrees 30 minutes north.

The Compromise of 1850 admitted California as a free state but potentially opened the Utah and New Mexico territories to slavery. The Kansas-Nebraska Act of 1854, which Pierce signed, allowed those two vast territories — north of the 36 degrees 30 minutes north latitude line — to determine whether they would be free or slave states, thus also making them potential slave states. Like his predecessor, Millard Fillmore, Pierce doubted that Congress should regulate slavery, but the Constitution said that Congress may admit new states and make the rules and regulations governing U.S. territory.[4]

Besides endorsing the 1854 legislation, Pierce tried to pervert the territories' decision-making process by allowing pro-slavery border ruffians to cross into Kansas from Missouri and set up a pro-slavery government, which he recognized.[5] He repeatedly appointed pro-slavery governors in the Kansas and Nebraska territories. These actions angered the antislave majorities in those territories, triggering a mini civil war in Kansas ("bloody Kansas") years before the Civil War began. The small war in Kansas helped cause that major conflagration by making slavery a greater national issue than ever before and by leading to the creation of the antislavery Republican Party.

Also, Pierce used federal troops to enforce the Fugitive Slave Act, which Millard Fillmore, his predecessor, had only threatened to do.[6] Instead Fillmore enforced the Act with federal agents. Federal enforcement of the Fugitive Slave Act was unconstitutional because the Constitution gave no law enforcement role to the federal government in rounding up escaped slaves. The idea that the federal government should enforce this act was actually a figment of the constitutional imaginations of nationalist northern jurists.[7] Had it not been enforced, however, the North would have been a potential refuge for runaway slaves; the goal of the legislation was to eliminate such a haven.

PROSPERITY

Endorsed Lackluster Economic Policies

Like most Democrats of the day, Pierce did not believe that the Constitution allowed public funds to be spent on internal improvements such as roads and canals. The money he saved by not endorsing these projects enabled Pierce to reduce the national debt by 83 percent.

He did, however, make exceptions by giving land grants to railroads and federally subsidizing the Atlantic cable for communications with Europe. Surprisingly, Vedder and Gallaway gave Pierce a fairly low ranking — tied for thirtieth and thirty-first place with John F. Kennedy out of thirty-nine presidents ranked — on policies promoting limited government and fighting inflation. This ranking may be too severe.

LIBERTY

Continued to Steal Land from Indians

During Pierce's presidency, from 1853 to 1856, the U.S. government "negotiated" fifty-two treaties with Native Americans, essentially stealing an area the size of Texas from the tribes.[8]

CONCLUSION

The signature of Pierce's administration is the disastrous Kansas-Nebraska Act, which repealed the Missouri Compromise of 1820, which had previously prevented an internecine conflict in the United States. The act elevated slavery's importance as an issue and caused a precursor civil war in the Kansas territory between pro- and antislavery forces. In short, Pierce's signature of this act pushed the country toward a massive civil war six years later. Pierce cannot be blamed solely for a war that had been on the horizon for some time, but he and James Buchanan, his Democratic successor, both took actions in Kansas to help the pro-slavery minority that helped propel the country into the internally ruinous struggle. For those actions, they are both ranked low in the poor category. Franklin Pierce comes in at number twenty-four.

15

JAMES BUCHANAN
Should Have Let the South Go in Peace

PP&L* RANKING: 23
Category: Poor

Fifteenth president of the United States

Term: March 4, 1857, to March 4, 1861
Party: Democratic
Born: April 23, 1791, Mercersburg, Pennsylvania
Died: June 1, 1868 (age seventy-seven),
Lancaster, Pennsylvania
Spouse: None (bachelor)
Alma Mater: Dickinson College
Occupation: Lawyer, diplomat
Religion: Presbyterian

James Buchanan is often blamed for starting the Civil War, which began just as his single term in office was ending. Although sectional divides as old as the republic caused the war, Buchanan did help bring it about by splitting the Democratic Party by avidly and illegitimately supporting the pro-slavery minority in Kansas. Then, when secession became inevitable, he didn't carry his pro-South sentiments to their natural conclusion and let the South secede in peace. He merely went halfway and allowed the South critically needed time to arm itself, take over federal arsenals and forts, and recruit and train forces for the upcoming titanic Civil War. By trying to temporize, stall, and dump the massive sectional dispute on his successor, Buchanan created the worst of all situations for the country. This was not his sole indiscretion. Abroad, Buchanan was one of the most bellicose and interventionist presidents in American history.

---

*PP&L = Peace, Prosperity, and Liberty.

PEACE

Helped to Bring About the Civil War

Beginning in 1820 with the Missouri Compromise, presidents and political parties sought to avoid a final disposition of the slavery issue. Buchanan and his predecessors are often called "northern men with southern principles," since they sought to take a moderate course. Yet Buchanan, a northern Democrat from Pennsylvania, actually went well beyond moderation and supported the South. Although he personally opposed slavery, he believed that northerners who wanted to abolish slavery were to blame for the sectional strife that gripped the nation.[1] Further, Buchanan supported the South for political reasons. In the 1856 presidential election, most of his votes came from the South, while the Republicans captured the Northeast.

Although Buchanan prided himself on being a strict constructionist — that is, interpreting the Constitution as the founders had intended it — he deviated from this view in his inaugural address when he endorsed slave codes. Jefferson Davis and other prominent southerners, normally advocates of states' rights, increasingly wanted the federal government to protect slave ownership, even in territories north of the 36 degrees 30 minutes north latitude line, which the Missouri Compromise had disallowed. On inauguration day, Buchanan threw his support behind them.

At the time of Buchanan's inauguration, the Supreme Court was considering the case of a slave named Dred Scott, who had sued for his freedom because his master had temporarily relocated from the slave state of Missouri to the free state of Illinois and the free Wisconsin territory. Although Buchanan, in his inaugural address, pledged to abide by whatever the court decided, he already knew the outcome. Violating the spirit of the constitutional separation of powers that his strict constructionist view so admirably exalted,[2] he, as president-elect, had improperly lobbied the court's members in order to raise the vote total in favor of the ruling against the Missouri Compromise of 1820 — to make it carry more legal and political weight.

The Supreme Court ruled that the Missouri Compromise's stipulation — that all territories north of the 36 degrees 30 minutes north latitude line should be free — was unconstitutional. Only when the territories became states could they opt for prohibition of slavery, the court ruled. Congress could not prohibit slavery in the territories it had created.

The Supreme Court made a grievous error in the Dred Scott case. The court's ruling declared that Congress had no power to keep slavery out of the new western territories. Yet the Northwest Ordinance, governing the first land the United States acquired after the thirteen colonies — which the much weaker Confederation Congress passed under the Articles of Confederation government in July 1787, even before the Constitution was signed and ratified — banned slavery within that new territory.[3]

Not only did nothing in the Constitution contradict this precedent, the document reinforced it explicitly. Although the Constitution generally limited federal power, Article IV, Section 3 states, "The Congress shall have Power to dispose of and make all needful Rules and Regulations respecting the Territory or other Property belonging to the United States."[4] Until statehood, the territories belonged to the United States. Therefore, within those territories, the Congress did have a right to legislate on slavery. Thus, contrary to the Supreme Court's Dred Scott decision, the Missouri Compromise should have been deemed constitutional. A different court ruling might have preserved the Union longer.

Divided Democrats

Buchanan's strident support for the South divided the Democratic Party, then the only national party in the United States, and resulted in the election of Abraham Lincoln in 1860 from the largely regional Republican Party — the spark that ignited the Civil War. Creating this fissure in his party is the biggest knock on the Buchanan presidency, and it is quite a big one indeed.

From the beginning of his administration, Buchanan made no attempt to heal sectional divides in the Democratic Party or the country. In fact, he exacerbated them. For his cabinet, he picked all Democrats from the same wing of the party: four men from the South and three northern "doughfaces" who, like Buchanan, agreed with the South. Buchanan selected none of Stephen Douglas's Free-Soil northern Democrats for the cabinet or even for lower administration positions. Also, he removed a large number of northern Democrats from federal positions — some for no reason — while retaining most of the southern Democrats.[5]

But Buchanan's most divisive act, affecting his party and the nation, was his policy toward Kansas, which was key because Kansas's location between the North and the South was critical for spreading slavery to the West. The Civil War started not because of slavery per se but because of the question of expanding slavery into the new western territories. Because the antislavery camp outnumbered the pro-slavery group in Kansas by three or four to one, Buchanan, Douglas, and Franklin Pierce, Buchanan's predecessor, all believed that Kansas would enter the union as a free state. Any legitimate constitutional process would have produced a Kansas constitution that banned slavery.

In 1857, however, the pro-slavery faction controlled Congress and thus all territorial appointments. This congressional group manipulated delegates to the Kansas constitutional convention. A pro-slavery conclave in Lecompton, Kansas, formulated a constitution that allowed slavery. Moreover, Kansans accepted the Lecompton government's pro-slavery constitution only because less than a quarter of the population could vote; proponents of a free state were excluded from voting, while pro-slavery residents of neighboring Missouri were encouraged to vote illegally in Kansas. Also, the Lecompton government adopted a slave code that allowed only proponents of slavery to be officeholders, made criticism of slavery a felony, and mandated capital punishment for assisting a fugitive slave. Free-Soilers, outraged by this perversion of democratic processes, set up an alternative government in Topeka.

Rather than choosing a more neutral approach and restarting the electoral process in search of some legitimacy, the Buchanan administration predictably recognized the illegitimate pro-slavery government at Lecompton. Buchanan did pledge, however, not to use force against the rival Topeka government unless it violated the Constitution and law. Buchanan broke a promise to the governor of Kansas that a referendum would be held on the proposed state constitution. Instead, Buchanan allowed Kansans to vote only on slavery. The Lecompton-organized election was marred by fraud and a boycott by Free-Soilers, who organized their own referendum and impressively voted down the Lecompton constitution.

Ignoring Kansas's popular will and sovereignty, Buchanan continued to support the Lecompton constitution and sent it to Congress to be approved. There he used bribes — cash, commissions, patronage jobs, mail routes, shipbuilding contracts, and even prostitutes — and threats, such as removing congressmen's relatives from patronage jobs, to attempt to win congressional approval. The Senate passed the Lecompton constitution, but the House voted it down. Northern House Democrats broke from Buchanan and voted against it — foreshadowing the most catastrophic party split in U.S. history.

Still refusing to order a new constitutional convention in Kansas, Buchanan tried to bribe Kansans into adopting the Lecompton constitution by a promise to get them statehood quickly. Kansans just said "no," voting overwhelmingly against the Lecompton document. They held a new constitutional convention that adopted the antislavery Wyandotte Constitution and entered the union as a free state in January 1861.[6]

After the Lecompton fight, the Democratic Party split into the southern pro-slavery Democrats and northern Free-Soil Democrats. Buchanan, by taking the South's side and trying to ram through the admission of Kansas as a slave state against the wishes of its own people, had made northern Democrats apoplectic.[7] He had taken the risk of splitting the Democratic Party, although he knew it was one of the few remaining bonds holding the nation together.

Radical southerners foresaw the northerners pulling out of the Democratic Party, predicted the resultant Republican win in the presidential election of 1860, and saw that as a justification for creating a separate southern confederacy.[8] True to their predictions, the northern Democrats split off, held their own convention, and fielded their own candidate for president. In early November 1860, Republican Abraham Lincoln won a four-way race for the presidency, with less than a majority of the total vote. The states of the Deep South seceded from the union, beginning in late December 1860, before Lincoln was inaugurated in early March 1861.

Should Have Let the South Secede Peacefully

Although Buchanan is correctly pilloried for siding with the South and helping to cause the Civil War, he is unfairly criticized for not strong-arming the seceding states into staying in the union, as Andrew Jackson had done with South Carolina during the nullification crisis in the 1830s. Although southerners appreciated Buchanan's support, they were dismayed when he said — probably correctly — that they had no constitutional right to secede. He argued that "a deliberate, palpable, and dangerous exercise of powers not granted by the Constitution" had to occur before rebellion was justified. He didn't think the election of the Republican Lincoln qualified.[9]

As it turned out, southerners were probably excessively alarmed by what Lincoln and the Republicans would have done on the slavery issue. Lincoln was a moderate on the issue. Had the South stayed in the union, the Congress wasn't much of a threat either. With the South still in the union and a high number of third-party members, the Republicans would not have controlled either congressional chamber. Furthermore, from the country's inception, white southerners were grossly overrepresented in Congress. In 1858, whites in the South made up less than 20 percent of the U.S. population but had at least 32 percent of the seats in the House and 34 percent of the seats in the Senate.

Historian Jean H. Baker says that the United States was a contradiction: a democracy with majority rule, but effectively controlled by a minority from the South.[10] This undermines the southern view that the Civil War was caused primarily by high tariffs, because the tariff level was whatever the southern-dominated Congress said it was. Rather, the Civil War was mainly caused by southerners seeing their political dominance eroded by increasing populations in the northern states and the addition of new western states, which were reducing the proportion of slave states in the nation and the fraction of the country's population in those slave states.

Buchanan believed — probably correctly — that the slavery problem would eventually solve itself by expiring in the West, where the climate made it un-economical (since it was not good for growing the crops that were farmed with slave labor). Lincoln also thought that slavery, if confined to the South, would eventually die out. But he more actively wanted to isolate it in the South by restricting slavery in the western territories. Perhaps the South saw the writing on the wall, but southerners also had the irrational fear that Lincoln would stoke slave rebellions in their states. In any event, slavery's demise in the North came about because industrialization demanded free labor for wages rather than the less-efficient compulsion of slave labor. As the South industrialized, slavery most likely would have eventually collapsed there, too. Slavery was already declining in the border states and upper South, though it was growing in the backward Deep South.[11] It is a dreadful shame that six hundred thousand Americans had to die in a brutal Civil War that did not significantly better the lot of African Americans for many decades, especially since slavery would have probably ended naturally. Unfortunately, American society, North and South, would not be ready to give blacks equal rights until a century later.

Although Buchanan didn't believe the South had a constitutional right to secede, he also argued that there was no enumerated power in the Constitution that allowed the federal government to coerce a state to stay in the union by force of arms. Also, Buchanan argued that such strong-arm tactics were not "necessary and proper for carrying into execution" any of the federal government's enumerated powers. Yet Lincoln was probably right that Article I, Section 8 of the Constitution did explicitly permit the federal government to call forth the militia to put down insurrections and carry out the laws of the union (for example, delivering the mail, collecting taxes, and controlling and defending federal forts and arsenals) and to suspend habeas corpus in times of invasion or rebellion. The problem was that the Constitution gave *Congress* these powers, not the president. Lincoln, in dictatorial moves, acted on his own while Congress was out of session. He later got Congress to approve both actions retroactively.

Although Buchanan conveniently based his avoidance of coercion on the rationale that the Constitution didn't allow it, he ultimately had more common sense than Lincoln. Even if the secession by numerous states was illegal and the president had a right to put it down with force, the most important question was whether it was moral or smart to do so. On both counts, the answer was a resounding "no." The states founded the republic in the spirit of self-determination, and if some states no longer wanted to stay in the union, they should have been allowed to go in peace. More practically, the most horrendous conflict in U.S. history resulted in the North winning the war but the South eventually winning the peace (for more on this, see the chapter on Ulysses S. Grant).

Buchanan should have acted on his belief that the South could go in peace. If, between the secession of South Carolina and six other states starting in late December 1860 and Lincoln's inaugural in early March 1861, Buchanan had recognized southern secession and withdrawn U.S. forces from federal installations in the seceding states, he then could have petitioned the rump Congress (made up of members from only the non-seceding states) to repeal the fugitive slave provision. The representatives and senators from the remaining northern states most assuredly would have done so. Had this provision been rescinded, over time, slaves would have made their way to the northern safe haven. Thus, southern slavery would have been severely undermined and might have even collapsed. At the time, abolitionists were essentially arguing for this two-nation strategy, which would turn out to be the most astute avenue that could have been pursued.

Unfortunately, Buchanan did nothing but stall so that the crisis and possible war were dumped into the lap of Republican Lincoln, who would prove to be much more belligerent to the South. Buchanan even rejected a "peace convention," planned by loyal southerners to try to halt the secessionist movement.

Moreover, when it looked like Lincoln was going to win the 1860 election, Major General Winfield Scott, the top general in the army, urged Buchanan to reinforce federal forts in the South to prevent southerners from launching surprise attacks against them; Buchanan did nothing. His idleness allowed southerners to buy time in order to take over federal forts and arsenals, receive arms indirectly from members of Buchanan's southern-sympathizing cabinet, and train and equip their army. Thus Buchanan's actions, or lack thereof, set up the worst of all worlds: a more heavily armed South that had undertaken unrecognized secession and a new northern president who made the catastrophic decision to repress southern self-determination.

Was Aggressive in Foreign Policy

Buchanan signed a treaty with Mexico that would allow U.S. military forces to put down any threat to the Mexican government. Buchanan wanted Congress to give him authority to gather a military force for a preventive invasion of Mexico and to set up a U.S. protectorate in the northwest part of that country, which would have housed U.S. military posts in Mexico across the border from Arizona. Not only Republicans and northern Democrats, but also some southerners, opposed Buchanan's aggressive policies. Congress avoided approving any such crass expansionism, including the treaty with Mexico.

Buchanan tried unsuccessfully to buy Alaska from Russia. But Buchanan's foreign adventures, like his domestic policy, favored southern interests. Any southern expansion had the potential of adding to the power of pro-slavery factions in Congress. Buchanan wanted to buy Cuba, even though Spain had never made known its desire to part with the real estate.[12]

Buchanan strengthened the Monroe Doctrine by reinterpreting the Clayton-Bulwer Treaty, which limited British influence in Central America. Buchanan felt that this treaty excessively restricted U.S. hegemony over any future trans-isthmus canal. He negotiated a treaty with Nicaragua that would have allowed the United States to dispatch military forces to protect transportation routes across the isthmus, but the Senate rejected the pact.

A confrontation with Britain arose over an international treaty that had ended the trade in slaves. Taking advantage of U.S. lethargy in implementing the pact, slave traders in the Caribbean flew the U.S. flag. When the British navy started boarding and searching U.S. ships to try to find slaves, Buchanan protested and readied the U.S. Navy. The British decided they didn't want a fight over this issue and ordered their fleet home from the Caribbean. Also, Buchanan sent troops to the Pacific Northwest over a border disagreement with the British, but the dispute was eventually settled peacefully.

PROSPERITY

Was Not Frugal

Buchanan's administration was fiscally irresponsible and was among the most corrupt in U.S. history. During his four years, federal expenditures increased 15 percent, and he left Lincoln with a significant budget deficit, even before the massive expenses required to fight the Civil War were incurred.[13]

Buchanan deviated from his strict constructionist philosophy, which limited both federal and executive power, when it suited him — mainly to help the South and to demand preventive war authority from the Congress — but his ideology did serve to restrain his behavior in some cases. For example, Buchanan responded in only a limited way to the economic panic of 1857. Because he took office in March of that year, the downturn was caused by the policies of Franklin Pierce, his predecessor. In the 1800s, the public perceptively expected the federal government to do much less about economic slowdowns than it does now. Buchanan said that the federal government was "without the power to extend relief." He did take limited actions that were, for the most part, constructive and conducive to letting the private sector be the engine of recovery. He urged the redemption of the public debt in gold and thus tried to reduce the amount of paper currency (money supply). Also, he refrained from starting new "make work" public works programs that would have exacerbated the federal deficit.

Also, Buchanan vetoed the Homestead Act, a Republican bill that gave 160 acres of publicly owned land to each settler after five years. Buchanan maintained that the bill was unfair to previous settlers in older states because they didn't get land. He concluded that the government didn't have the constitutional authority to give such land away. In fact, the government probably had no constitutional right to acquire the land in the first place, either through transactions with other nations, such as the Louisiana Purchase, or through the use of military force, such as the land grabbed from Mexico during the Mexican War or from Native Americans. On constitutional grounds, Buchanan correctly vetoed another Republican favorite: using public lands to create public land-grant agricultural colleges. Nothing in the Constitution talks about a role for the federal government in education, at the college level or otherwise.[14]

But probably because Buchanan irresponsibly increased the federal budget by 15 percent during his four years, Vedder and Gallaway gave Buchanan only a slightly above average ranking on policies limiting government and fighting inflation — tied with James Polk and Herbert Hoover for sixteenth through eighteenth place out of thirty-nine presidents ranked.

LIBERTY

Was Willing to Use Force against the Mormons

Buchanan's behavior toward the Mormon government in the Utah territory, which he believed to be in revolt, cast doubt on whether Buchanan actually believed he had no constitutional authority to put down southern secession. Brigham Young's government had little reverence for the federal government, had continually tormented federal judges and agents, and had even assassinated one federal official. Non-Mormon settlers and even travelers were discouraged within the territory's borders.

In 1857, Buchanan sent a federal governor to replace Young as the head of Utah's government and a 2,500-man army to enforce federal law. Mormons, with the aid of Indians, harassed those troops and massacred 125 civilians en route to California. A friend of both the Mormons and Buchanan mediated the crisis, and the Mormons accepted the new federal governor. Buchanan hated Mormons and loved the South, which was demonstrated by his ready use of force against the former and avoidance of the same against the latter.

CONCLUSION

Buchanan believed that two terms was too long a service for presidents, and before his inauguration, he had decided to not seek reelection to a second term. This self-limiting of power and ambition is rare and should be commended. Analysts roundly regard James Buchanan as one of the worst presidents in U.S. history, if not the worst. For example, an October 2000 poll of professors of law, history, and political science conducted by the *Wall Street Journal* and the Federalist Society ranked him dead last out of thirty-nine presidents ranked.[15]

Analysts usually criticize Buchanan for not preventing the Civil War and for actually helping to cause it. Both charges have some validity. However, Buchanan gets disproportionate blame for a sectional crisis that had been brewing since the beginning of the republic, simply because he was the last president before it exploded. In short, Buchanan wasn't that good a president, but he wasn't as awful as many analysts argue. This volume ranks James Buchanan number twenty-three, next to last in the poor category — just above Franklin Pierce, his predecessor.

16

ABRAHAM LINCOLN

Provoked a Catastrophic Civil War
That Achieved Far Less Than Believed

PP&L* RANKING: 29
Category: Bad

Sixteenth president of the United States

Term: March 4, 1861, to April 15, 1865
Party: Whig (1832–1854), Republican (1854–
1864), and National Union (1864–1865)
Born: February 12, 1809, Hardin County, Kentucky
Died: April 15, 1865 (age fifty-six), Washington, D.C.
Spouse: Mary Todd Lincoln
Education: Self-taught for admission to the Illinois State Bar
Occupation: Lawyer
Religion: Attended churches but never officially acquired
membership in a church

Abraham Lincoln has one of the most prominent monuments in Washington, D.C., and he has attained an almost mythological status. Yet a close study of his presidency shows that there is much less greatness to him than meets the eye. At the time he took office, Lincoln had virtually no military, diplomatic, or executive experience, had no formal education, and had not held public office in more than a decade — and then only as an unremarkable congressman.[1] His presidential record, then, is perhaps not surprising.

Lincoln was very passive on issues unrelated to the Civil War. He let Congress initiate the pernicious first national income tax, raise tariffs, establish land-grant colleges, create a new Department of Agriculture, and build the legal framework

---

*PP&L = Peace, Prosperity, and Liberty.

116

for a transcontinental railroad. Lincoln merely signed all these unnecessary legislative actions. More favorably, he did sign the Homestead Act, which gave public lands to private settlers.

On anything related to the Civil War, however, Lincoln was an activist. Without congressional authorization, he spent government money on private military recruiters, and without getting a constitutional amendment, he freed the slaves with a largely bogus emancipation proclamation. Later, he supported the Thirteenth Amendment, which actually freed the slaves in a more constitutional manner. In addition, he unilaterally suspended the writ of habeas corpus for people detained, when, under the Constitution, only Congress had the power to do so.[2]

Although he signed some bad non-war-related legislation, Lincoln is not ranked lower because he still retained some executive restraint in those areas. Also, most of his war-related executive power grab did not become permanent, because Congress reasserted dominance after the war was over.

PEACE

Provoked the Civil War

Overreacting to the election of a Republican president, seven southern states seceded and formed the Confederate States of America even before Lincoln was inaugurated on March 4, 1861. At the time, the Republicans were a regional party in the North that had snared the presidency only because the national Democratic Party had split over slavery into northern and southern wings. In a four-man presidential race in 1860, Lincoln won with less than 40 percent of the vote, almost a record low in U.S. history. The Republicans wanted to prohibit slavery in the new territories in the West, not to abolish slavery where it already existed in the South. Yet the South feared that this stand masked a move toward total abolition; southerners also worried that, in a country expanding by adding free states, their disproportionate representation, and thus influence, in the Congress would erode. According to Crenson and Ginsberg, experts on presidential power, Unionists from all sections of the country tried to extract some statement from President-elect Lincoln that would lower southern anxieties about the future of slavery, but got none.[3]

Lincoln's inaugural address was firm, but conciliatory to the South — promising no violence unless the South resorted to arms first (like Andrew Jackson did during the nullification crisis of 1832 with South Carolina) and pledging support for an enhanced Fugitive Slave Act. Rather than insisting that the South stay in the republic, he suggested a Constitutional Convention as the best forum for solving the North–South problem. In the meantime, he would enforce the current Constitution, he said.[4] The South, however, saw this as a declaration of war.

Lincoln's inaugural statements all could have been rhetoric, for his later behavior seemed to be setting up the Confederacy to take the blame for starting the war. But the Confederates were guilty of overreacting to Lincoln's statements and potential policy initiatives.

By the time of Lincoln's first day on the job, rebels threatened Fort Sumter in Charleston, South Carolina, which was the last federal fort remaining in the South and was running low on supplies. According to Jay Winik, author of *April 1865: The Month That Saved America,* Lincoln had four options: (1) force a showdown, (2) reinforce the fort, (3) try diplomacy, or (4) give up the fort. Major General Winfield Scott, Lincoln's top military advisor, Gideon Welles, Secretary of the Navy, and William Seward, Secretary of State, all thought the fort was militarily insignificant and should be abandoned, mirroring national opinion in much of the country at the time. Seward knew that any assertive actions by Lincoln would start a civil war and felt that abandoning the fort would buy time for Unionists to strengthen themselves throughout the South. Unbeknownst to Lincoln, Seward had even assured southerners that the fort would be given up.[5]

Lincoln himself had promised he would not reinforce the fort. Yet it is fairly clear that Lincoln wanted to maneuver the South into starting the war. At a peace conference of twenty-one states at the Willard Hotel in Washington, D.C., shortly before his inauguration, Lincoln spoke against a proposed constitutional amendment to perpetually retain slavery in order to preserve the union.[6] In March 1861, he refused to meet with Confederate peace commissioners offering to pay for federal property on southern soil and the southern portion of the national debt.[7] Had Lincoln wanted to avoid war, he could have withdrawn federal forces from Fort Sumter and claimed that he had negotiated a good deal with the South for compensation for that fort, other federal installations, and the southern share of the national debt.

The day after Lincoln's inauguration, the commander of Fort Sumter sent word that the installation was running low on supplies. Lincoln mulled the matter over for a month and then decided to send food, but not weapons or men. Next to abandoning the fort, this action was the least provocative measure he could have taken, but his military advisors told him that even this option might provoke an attack by South Carolinians.

Lincoln was also sending men into a potential combat situation with no prior congressional approval. Yet in this defensive situation, with Congress then out of session, the framers probably would have been content with the subsequent congressional post-event blessing of Lincoln's action.

The smart thing to do militarily was to attempt a secret reprovisioning of the fort, but Lincoln alerted the enemy of the food-only resupply, perhaps purposefully to draw fire. Lincoln knew that South Carolinians had fired on a ship that President Buchanan had sent to reprovision the fort and had reason to believe that they would likely do so again. This time the Confederates fired on the fort, as well as the supply ship, and caused the facility's surrender.

Historians Bruce Catton and Shelby Foote believe that Lincoln maneuvered the South into starting the war. According to Catton, Captain Gustavus Fox, the federal naval commander on the scene in Charleston, said Lincoln seemed to think it was very important that South Carolina "should stand before the civilized world as having fired upon bread." Lincoln's personal secretaries and northern newspapers also agreed that Lincoln was trying to put the Confederacy in the "wrong."[8] Lincoln had even said, "The tug has to come and better now than any time hereafter."[9] As with many overconfident politicians throughout the course of history, however, Lincoln believed that the war into which he was leading the country would be short.

Acted Constitutionally, but Not Wisely

If the war was fought to preserve the union, Lincoln probably had a constitutional right to put down the South's insurrection, aimed at secession, once it turned violent — as long as Congress approved, which it later did. Furthermore, the Constitution implies a right to control and defend federal property — and Fort Sumter qualified.

Many modern southern sympathizers talk about the northern "invasion" of the South — as if no prior southern provocation had occurred. Yet Lincoln's calling up the northern militia; occupying the border states of Maryland, Kentucky, and Missouri; creating a naval blockade of southern ports; and attacking Manassas and other points in southern states happened only after the Confederate attack on Fort Sumter. The original states in the Deep South — including South Carolina, home of the fort — officially seceded because of Lincoln's perceived threat to slavery. (There was also the secondary issue of the South paying more than half of all federal taxes — because of rising tariffs on imports of foreign manufactured goods — even though the South's population was less than half of the North's and most federal spending benefited the North. But the

South had long dominated Congress, and the tariffs were ones agreed to by that legislative body.)

The northern tier of southern states (Arkansas, North Carolina, Tennessee, and Virginia), however, would not have seceded if Lincoln had not occupied the border states (Maryland, Kentucky, Missouri, Delaware, and what is now West Virginia) and called forth the militia. Washington, D.C., was under threat, and Lincoln mobilizing the militia, later approved by Congress, was understandable given the circumstances. Even a normally offensive federal naval blockade of southern ports could be justified as defensive, because Jefferson Davis, president of the Confederacy, had encouraged southern privateers (government-sanctioned pirates) to plunder federal commercial shipping. Although Lincoln is guilty of provoking the original attack on Fort Sumter, the Confederates didn't have to fire first on mere food supplies, and unfortunately were foolish enough to oblige Lincoln's provocation.

Thomas DiLorenzo, a prominent critic of Lincoln, would disagree about whether Lincoln's actions were constitutional, but he does not believe that is the main issue.

> The vital issue is whether Lincoln was justified in having the Federal army kill 300,000 fellow citizens, cripple tens of thousands more for life, destroy their economy, burn entire Southern towns to the ground, abolish civil liberties in the North, and inflict all the other costs of war . . . to prevent them from leaving the Union.[10]
>
> For a "free" government that is based on self-determination, using force to compel people to continue to live under that government severely undermines their freedom and self-determination. Such self-determination was the basis for the Declaration of Independence. Thus, there was a rationale to let the states choose to leave the union. In 1848, Lincoln seemed to agree with the Declaration's claim of a right to rise up against an unwanted government, when he said, "Any people anywhere, being inclined and having the power, have the right to rise up and shake off the existing government, and form a new one that suits them better." He deemed this "a most valuable — a most sacred right — a right, which we hope and believe is to liberate the world."[11]

By 1861, Lincoln seemed to be relying on the Constitution's implied legalistic language as a justification for him to maneuver the South into attacking Sumter, rather than focusing on the Declaration's spirit of self-determination, which he venerated. In contrast, southerners, implicitly acknowledging the validity of

Lincoln's position in invoking the Constitution to put down secession, more commonly invoked the right to secede contained in the Declaration.[12]

If the goal of the war was to end slavery, Lincoln had other better options than unleashing the unpredictable dogs of war. If he also wanted to preserve the union, prior to the commencement of hostilities he could have offered southern slave owners compensation for a gradual emancipation of slaves. Many other countries that had ended slavery peacefully during the earlier part of the 1800s had adopted such measures and, earlier in his career, Lincoln himself had made such proposals. The cost of compensated emancipation would have been far less than the mammoth human and financial costs of the American Civil War. The Civil War killed more than six hundred thousand Americans, about thirty-eight thousand of whom were African American soldiers.

If a faster end to slavery was the main goal, Lincoln could have urged the free states to secede from the rest of the nation and then proposed that Congress repeal the Fugitive Slave Act, which prosecuted those who did not return escaped slaves to their owners. The hard-core abolitionists who had made this proposal realized that a haven for escaped slaves near the slave states would cause a large increase in escape attempts and rapidly empty the South of slaves.

By the time of the U.S. Civil War, all European nations and most American countries had abolished slavery. For example, the British Empire eliminated slavery during the 1833–1838 period, and the comparatively backward Mexico did away with slavery in 1829.[13] Walter Williams, an African American economist, notes that in most countries, slavery was eliminated without resorting to bloody wars.[14] Slavery in the South likely would have eventually become as uneconomical as it had in the North when that region had become more industrial and urban. Slave labor is less efficient than free labor because there are few incentives to improve skills and productivity. Prior to the war, in the border states of Maryland, Kentucky, Missouri, Delaware, and what is now West Virginia, the percentage of slaves in the population had already declined because of these economic factors.[15]

In fairness to Lincoln, these economic indicators portending the demise of slavery may not have been obvious at the time. As noted earlier, the Civil War actually was caused by attempts to expand slavery to new lands in the middle and western United States. The first signs of the erosion of the "peculiar institution" of slavery were camouflaged by the march from earlier compromises to create a slave state/free state balance to allowing state choice (free or slave) in the northern territories in the Kansas-Nebraska Act of 1854 to the Supreme

Court's Dred Scott decision contending that slavery could not be outlawed anywhere and the South's insistence on slave codes guaranteeing slavery. Slavery was actually expanding in the Deep South, and southern rhetoric had changed from slavery being a necessary evil to being a positive force for good. But even as the South eliminated the political and legal obstacles to the westward expansion of slavery, the economics of industrialization was eroding the vile institution in the border states and upper South.

Managed the Civil War in an Incompetent, Brutal, and Dictatorial Way

Lincoln's management of the war effort was less stellar than many analysts have claimed, and this led to many unnecessary casualties. According to General Josiah Bunting III, a biographer of Ulysses S. Grant, few American presidents made as many blatantly political appointments to the senior ranks of the army as Lincoln did.[16]

For example, Lincoln was unimpressed (correctly) by General Joe Hooker's military abilities but appointed him commander of the crucial Army of the Potomac in the eastern war theater because he had no political aspirations and thus would not run for president against Lincoln in the 1864 election.[17] Lincoln is often portrayed as valiantly holding the Union together until he found a competent general — that is, Ulysses S. Grant — to lead the Union war effort. But the problems Lincoln experienced with his generals for much of the war were largely of his own making.

Bungling Union generals failed to take advantage of a flawed southern strategy and vast northern advantages in resources and manpower in order to end the war sooner, thus costing tens or even hundreds of thousands of lives on both sides. Lincoln should have fired some of his generals — for example, the obviously incompetent George McClellan — far sooner than he did. In addition, unnecessary casualties mounted because, during the war, Lincoln rebuffed several Confederate offers to hold a peace conference.

Analysts who have elevated Lincoln to near godlike status also cover up the war crimes over which he presided. Lincoln, ruthlessly and incompetently, micromanaged the war effort. In 1864, the Union war effort was flagging, opposition to the draft was growing, war exhaustion was rampant in the North, and Lincoln was up for reelection. At this time, Lincoln approved total war against the South.[18] The ruthless General William Tecumseh Sherman unleashed his brutal March to the Sea, and General Philip Sheridan burned the Shenandoah

Valley in Virginia. These generals bombarded southern towns and cities with artillery, burned them to the ground, and looted and pillaged the rest — all in violation of acceptable conduct in war as enshrined in the 1863 Geneva Convention. Sherman ordered houses to be burned and Confederate civilians to be killed in retaliation for Confederate troops attacking Union soldiers. Sherman wrote to his wife that the war's objective was "extermination, not of soldiers alone, that is the least part of the trouble, but the people." In addition, the North's Anaconda plan, the effort to suffocate the South's economy with a naval blockade along southern coasts, adversely affected civilians and did not even allow medicine to pass through.[19]

Lincoln often gets credit for his generous words to the South as the war eventually wound down — "with malice toward none and charity for all" — but his total war policy against the states in the Southeast was hardly magnanimous. The modern-day equivalent is burning down people's houses and then demonstrating compassion by promising them a place in a homeless shelter. In fact, Lincoln's scorched-earth wartime policy caused hard feelings in the South, which were compounded by the harsh reconstruction measures imposed by subsequent presidents. These hard feelings later manifested themselves in attacks on freed blacks after the war.

Thomas DiLorenzo says that "quite a few" Lincoln scholars have called the wartime president a "dictator."[20] Lincoln's drastic executive acts were unusual because of the general weakening of the presidency vis-à-vis Congress from Thomas Jefferson to James Buchanan (with the possible exception of the Jackson and Polk years). Even Lincoln admitted that he would take unconstitutional actions:[21] "These rebels are violating the Constitution to destroy the Union; I will violate the Constitution, if necessary, to save the Union."[22] He did so in a major way.

Lincoln even acknowledged that his unilateral executive orders expanding the regular army and calling for volunteers to serve an extra three years — all without congressional approval — were questionable. He claimed, however, that the public was clamoring for those actions and that he had reason to believe that Congress would ratify them when they came into session.

He decided by himself, however, that southern secession was illegal, that he would use force to defend federal property, and that he would effectively declare war by calling up the militia and instituting a naval blockade on the South.[23] Although these unilateral decisions could be justified as defensive measures (in the wake of the Confederate attack on Fort Sumter) taken when Congress was out of session, Congress had little choice but to later approve Lincoln's drastic actions.

Lincoln invented implied presidential war powers, which were not "discovered" by other presidents during the War of 1812 or the Mexican War.[24] In 1863, in the Prize cases, the Supreme Court properly rejected Lincoln's broad, extra-constitutional conception of executive war power as being inherent in his role as commander in chief of the armed forces. It did, however, validate his initial unilateral order to blockade southern ports, citing Congress's delegation to the president, in laws passed in 1795 and 1807, of its authority to call up the militia and use the military to suppress insurrections. The Supreme Court also noted the chief executive's responsibility to defend against attacks and invasions.[25] Confederate maritime raiders were using southern ports to attack U.S shipping, thus justifying the Union blockade of those ports — at least constitutionally, if not morally.

Lincoln's invented war powers continue to haunt the republic and its civil liberties to the present day. For example, George W. Bush claimed inherent presidential power, during the "war on terror," to conduct spying on Americans without a constitutionally guaranteed warrant and in violation of existing law. Even pro-Lincoln scholars such as Daniel Farber acknowledge that some of Lincoln's actions were illegal and unconstitutional. He admits that "the great question during the war was whether the rule of law could survive the effort to defend it." Farber mentions as suspect Lincoln's unauthorized expansion of the army and his executive order that used government money, without congressional approval, to hire private individuals to further the war effort.

Lincoln's illusory Emancipation Proclamation — which freed slaves only in areas of rebellion and changed the North's main war objective from saving the Union to getting rid of slavery — has been regarded by many analysts as a stroke of political wizardry that prevented the slavery-averse British and French governments from recognizing the slaveholding South. But its incredibly searing domestic consequences have been underanalyzed. The proclamation caused enlistments in the North's army to evaporate.

Therefore, Lincoln, for the first time in U.S. history, instituted a military draft. This bad precedent caused large draft riots in New York and other northern cities. Lincoln had to send ten thousand soldiers from the battlefront to New York City to keep the peace. Lincoln also used the conscription act to arrest dissenters and hold them without trial — thus dramatically increasing opposition to the war among northern Democrats.[26]

PROSPERITY

Was the Father of Big Government in the United States

Lincoln was the father of big government in the United States. The "American System," invented by Federalist Alexander Hamilton and named and promoted by the Whig Henry Clay, made little progress in America during the first seventy years of the republic but was brought to fruition by Lincoln during the Civil War. The program consisted of providing government subsidies — which were financed by high tariffs and a nationalized banking system that printed money — to businesses for making internal improvements throughout the country.

In spite of internal improvements' failure at the state level, Lincoln wholeheartedly embraced them at the national level. Prior to Lincoln's taking office, the federal government had little connection with the banking system because there was no central bank. The nation's currency was state-chartered banknotes that could be exchanged immediately for gold and silver. Needing money for the war, Lincoln ran state-chartered banks out of the note-issuing business and created nationally chartered banks that could issue greenbacks that weren't immediately redeemable for gold and silver. This increase in the money supply created substantial inflation.

The war also necessitated the first income tax and the first internal revenue bureaucracy designed to collect it. The tax was eliminated in 1872, but the precedent was set for its reemergence in the twentieth century. Thus Vedder and Gallaway justifiably give Lincoln the worst ranking of any president — thirty-ninth of thirty-nine presidents ranked — in limiting government and fighting inflation.

In short, the Civil War allowed Lincoln to originate a burdensome government. By 1860, the limited federal government that the founders had set up had actually withered into a tiny presence in the nation. But Lincoln's corporate welfare, national banking system, protectionism, income tax, and large standing army created the seeds of big government in America.[27] Fortunately much of the wartime big government didn't remain after the war, but Lincoln's usurpation of power did serve as a precedent for future presidents during wartime.

Then why is Lincoln ranked toward the top of the worst presidents category? Although he created big government, this situation again receded — although not to the tiny presence it had in 1860 — until the Spanish-American War and World War I. The instigators of those two later wars — William McKinley and Woodrow Wilson, respectively — are ranked toward the bottom of the bad category because they permanently enshrined big government in the American psyche.

LIBERTY

Freed the Slaves

The permanency of state bureaucracy, or lack thereof, is not the only reason that Lincoln is ranked as highly as he is. Although Lincoln probably could have and should have avoided the massive war that resulted in a horrible loss of life, property, and liberty and only nominally freed the slaves, he did have the constitutional right to put down the insurrection. Proponents of liberty and small government oftentimes go overboard in vilifying Lincoln's constitutional suppression of an insurrection and defense of federal facilities, in overemphasizing states' rights in the Constitution, and in holding up the Confederacy as an icon of freedom and minimal government.

It is true that Lincoln probably should have acted in the spirit of the Declaration of Independence and pushed harder for a new Constitutional Convention or even let the South peacefully secede, but he probably did have the authority under the mildly centralizing Constitution to put down the southern insurrection. (For a more detailed discussion of this important point, see the chapter on Andrew Jackson, which elaborates on Jackson's snuffing out the similar, but much smaller, nullification rebellion of 1832.)

Protecting slavery, not safeguarding states' rights, was most of the South's primary goal in secession, although not for some "outer" southern states, such as Virginia, North Carolina, Tennessee, and Arkansas. Before and during the Civil War, the South's dubious party line was that the northern states had violated the constitutional contract by not adequately enforcing the provision to return fugitive slaves.[28] In fact, the Constitution gave the federal government no role in enforcing such a law. After the Civil War, southerners revised history to falsely assert that states' rights, not slavery, was the primary reason for the South's secession from the union.[29]

Moreover, when states' rights interfered with maintaining slavery (a gross violation of individual rights), the South became an advocate of federal power. For example, the South was ecstatic when the Supreme Court ruled, in the Dred Scott decision of 1857, that territories had no right to choose to ban slavery. Also, in 1858, slaveholders pressured then-President Buchanan to use federal power to allow slavery in Kansas. Jefferson Davis, the Confederate president, attacked the states' rights doctrine as destructive to the Confederacy. Historically, whatever faction did not control the federal government's machinery championed states' rights. Only after the South no longer had a friendly executive branch — after Lincoln's election in 1860 — did southerners emphasize states' rights.[30]

More philosophically, individual rights should never be given up to ensure the rights of state governments. A state government is still a government and can abuse the rights of its citizens. The Fourteenth Amendment, ratified after the Civil War, allows the federal government to step in to protect individuals from abusive state governments, but this should be done as prudently as possible. An example of a positive use of this amendment was when African Americans were protected from abusive state governments during the civil rights movement in the 1950s and 1960s.

Indeed, the South was hardly a bastion of political and economic freedom. The Confederacy was a one-party state that enacted conscription and committed violations of free speech against people opposing slavery. Jefferson Davis, its president, suspended habeas corpus. Economically, the South had many nationalized industries. The Confederacy overreacted to Lincoln's election and is responsible for igniting the tragic Civil War by attacking Fort Sumter. Most important, the South practiced the abominable practice of human slavery — a fact that should horrify any friend of liberty to the greatest degree. Thus, historians friendly to the South tend to overlook these glaring southern problems and also overvilify Lincoln's motives (even though his actions were often excessively belligerent, incompetent, or dictatorial).

Although Lincoln was assassinated before Reconstruction began, evidence exists that he favored lenient policies toward a defeated South, which his Democratic successor, Andrew Johnson, unsuccessfully tried to continue in opposition to the Radical Republicans controlling the rump Congress. For example, after the 1864 elections, Lincoln failed to win Louisiana's reentry into the union on its own terms. Congress had the right to readmit members from the Confederate states and simply refused Lincoln's initiative. In fact, if the Radical Republican policies toward the South were too harsh, the Lincoln and Johnson policies were probably too lenient — with insufficient safeguards for the rights of the newly freed African Americans.

Although the seven states of the Deep South seceded primarily because they thought Lincoln posed a threat to slavery, he actually was a moderate on the issue and at first was more concerned with saving the Union than with freeing slaves. In fact, throughout his political career, Lincoln made it clear that he thought blacks were inferior, could not live in peace with whites if freed, and should be deported back to recolonize Africa or Latin America.

Lincoln implicitly admitted that his famous Emancipation Proclamation, which freed only the slaves in areas occupied by Confederate armies, was a political gimmick. He calculated that northerners would be more motivated to fight for freedom than for merely keeping people in the union who no longer wanted to remain there. As noted earlier, quite the opposite happened — Union enlistments dried up and a divisive new draft law was needed.

Also, because the war's purpose evolved from saving the union to ending slavery, Britain and France, which had already ended slavery, were discouraged from recognizing the South as a separate nation. Lincoln's unilateral executive order freeing the slaves without congressional approval was probably unconstitutional. But it did commit the North to freeing the slaves. Later, the Thirteenth Amendment, which won Lincoln's support, constitutionally freed slaves everywhere.

In the end, America's most horrendous conflict left African Americans in the South little better off after being "freed" than before. For a few years after the war, blacks were allowed to vote and hold office. After Union occupation forces eventually left the South, however, blacks were subjected to discriminatory Jim Crow laws and "black codes" that tied them to the land they once had worked as slaves, making life almost as bad as during slavery. Northern "total war" tactics and harsh reconstruction measures led to Southern white resentment, manifesting itself by violent Southern reprisals against blacks by the Ku Klux Klan and other racist militias. African Americans really didn't begin to become free until southern society changed enough to permit the civil rights movement of the 1950s and 1960s to take hold. As the country has experienced in recent failed U.S. efforts to "build democracy" in Iraq and other countries, an outside power trying to change the culture of a large region and population using a temporary military occupation is often unsuccessful. No matter how many white southerners Union armies killed and how much southern property they destroyed, the Union was bound to lose the peace in the South after the war was over because the white southern culture was not yet ready to accommodate African Americans as equals. Moreover, in this futile "nation-building" effort, about 38,000 black soldiers died.

Rampantly Violated Civil Liberties

During the Civil War, Lincoln justified draconian usurpations of civil liberties — many of them unnecessary to winning the war — as deriving from his role as commander in chief and his duty to "take care that the laws be faithfully executed."

The writ of habeas corpus makes it illegal for governments to confine people in jail without their being able to challenge that detention. Ignoring Supreme Court Chief Justice Robert Taney's order that Congress, not the president, had the authority to suspend habeas corpus in wartime, Lincoln unilaterally suspended it anyway. Lincoln then retroactively requested and received congressional support for his action. Lincoln also created military tribunals to try civilians who had discouraged people from enlisting in Union armies. The Constitution promises a jury trial for civilians, and these civilians were merely exercising their First Amendment rights.

Conveniently after the war was over, in 1866, the Supreme Court, in the case of *Ex parte Milligan*, rejected Lincoln's claim, as commander in chief, that he held emergency powers during wartime that were outside the law or Constitution. Justice Davis, for the Supreme Court, stated, "The Constitution of the United States is a law for rulers and people, equally in war and peace. No doctrine, involving more pernicious consequences, was ever invented by the wit of man than that any of its provisions can be suspended during any of the great exigencies of government."[31]

Lincoln also flagrantly violated the First Amendment by shutting down newspapers, closing the mail to publications that opposed his war policies, arresting newspaper publishers, deporting an opposing congressman, and physically attacking and eliminating a peace movement. He nationalized railroads, used Union troops to win elections by intimidating Democratic voters, threw northern civilians in military prison camps for opposing his policies without giving them constitutionally guaranteed warrants and trials, and seized and destroyed southern property without the compensation required by the "takings" clause of the Constitution. Congress later approved most of Lincoln's unconstitutional actions.

CONCLUSION

In many analyses, Lincoln is named as one of the three best presidents in U.S. history; this assessment views him as one of the worst chief executives. Although the South probably didn't have the right to secede from the union and Lincoln probably did have the right to put down the violent insurrection, the massive loss of life, liberty, and property with only nominal freedom won for blacks made war a disastrous choice. Rarely do wars greatly enhance genuine freedom, and they usually undermine it; the Civil War was generally no exception. Instead of choosing war, Lincoln should have let the South go in peace, as the abolitionists advocated, or, prior to the conflict, offered southerners compensated emancipation of slaves. Under the first option, industrialization and rising moral objections likely would have peaceably eliminated slavery in the South — as they did in most other places in the world — helped out by a slave haven in the free North. Without war, the 600,000 deaths, the rise of a large, intrusive federal government and an excessively powerful executive branch could have been prevented. In sum, a close study of Lincoln's presidency leads to thoughts of tearing down the Lincoln Memorial. Abraham Lincoln is ranked twenty-nine here.

17

ANDREW JOHNSON

Uncompromising Attitude Led to Harsh Reconstruction Policies

PP&L* RANKING: 17
Category: Poor

Seventeenth president of the United States

Term: April 15, 1865, to March 4, 1869
Party: Democratic
Born: December 29, 1808, Raleigh, North Carolina
Died: July 31, 1875 (age sixty-six), Greeneville,
    Tennessee
Spouse: Eliza McCardle Johnson
Education: Self-taught and tutored
Occupation: Tailor
Religion: Christian (no denomination; attended Catholic and
    Methodist services)

Analysts regularly rank Andrew Johnson's presidency an abject failure. For example, the poll of professors done by the *Wall Street Journal* and the Federalist Society ranked him thirty-sixth of thirty-nine presidents ranked.[1] This judgment is too harsh and probably stems from Johnson being one of only two presidents who were impeached. If Bill Clinton's impeachment was questionable because his lying under oath over a sex scandal did not rise to the level of a high crime or misdemeanor *against the state*, then Andrew Johnson's was totally unjustified because he was merely trying to defend the Constitution.

Andrew Johnson's impeachment arose out of continued jousting between the Democratic president and the rump Congress of northern states, which was

---

*PP&L = Peace, Prosperity, and Liberty.

dominated by Radical Republicans, over how severe the government's Reconstruction policies should be toward a South defeated in the Civil War. In the end, radical Reconstruction was approved, and it failed, even after a bloody Civil War, because the South was simply not ready for dramatic change and harsh northern military occupation could not force lasting reforms on an unwilling southern white population. The North won the war, but the South won the peace.

It is questionable whether the deaths of more than six hundred thousand Americans, more than thirty-eight thousand of them black soldiers, in what is still the bloodiest U.S. war, was worth only marginal immediate improvements in the daily lives of African Americans and a brutal backlash against them in the South. Besides, if freeing the slaves was the war's real goal, the North could have seceded from the union and repudiated the Fugitive Slave Act, thus creating a haven for slaves and likely emptying the South of them, or simply compensated southern slave owners for freeing their slaves. Although it was growing in the Deep South, slavery was already on the wane in the border states and the upper South[2] because industrialization made slavery much less efficient than free labor (see a more detailed discussion in the chapter on Abraham Lincoln).

PEACE

Advocated Benevolently Reintegrating the Nation

Republican Abraham Lincoln chose the Democratic Tennessean — the most prominent southerner (and the only southern senator) who had remained loyal to the Union during the war — as his vice president on a national unity ticket in 1864. At Lincoln's second inaugural ceremony, Vice President Andrew Johnson showed up drunk and went on a tirade against Lincoln's cabinet, a harbinger of his dealings with those same men during his future presidency.

After Lincoln was assassinated and Johnson became president, Radical Republicans thought that they could finally push through their harsh Reconstruction policies, because they believed Johnson to be weaker than Lincoln and noted that Johnson had been at odds with the southern aristocracy. Johnson, however, was no pushover, and he was determined to carry out the benevolent Reconstruction desires of his now-deceased running mate.

As historian David Whitney puts it, Johnson "believed the South should be treated more as a wayward friend than as a conquered enemy."[3] Johnson, like Lincoln, wanted to welcome the defeated southerners back into the union with as few requirements and punishments as possible. After the 1864 elections, Lincoln had failed to convince Congress to readmit Louisiana into the union on the state's own terms. After Lincoln died, Johnson pushed for easy reentry for all southern states. Johnson thought it more important to reintegrate the South back into the nation than to integrate blacks, whom he thought unfit for full citizenship, into southern society. Johnson wanted to disenfranchise only the white Confederate leadership, turn over southern state governments to whites, and allow them to decide whether blacks should vote.

On the other side of the battle lines, Radical Republicans wanted to socially reengineer and transform a South that was not yet ready for appreciable change. To get votes and win elections in the South, which was overwhelmingly Democratic, and to keep control of the federal government, the minority Republicans realized that they needed to enfranchise former slaves — who would likely vote Republican — and bar most former Confederates from running for office. They correctly realized that to ensure that slaves were freed and blacks were allowed to vote, a northern presence in the South was needed. Instead of approving a civilian presence, as Johnson wanted, however, the Radical Republican Congress approved a harsh, unconstitutional military occupation.

This unwise "nation building at gunpoint" ultimately failed, as it has done so many times since when the United States has tried it overseas — Vietnam being a prominent example. The South, like North Vietnam did with America, simply waited for the North to become exhausted and go home.

Given that the Civil War happened, however, perhaps a more moderate and better solution to its aftermath lay somewhere between Lincoln's and Johnson's benevolence to the South and the severity of radical Reconstruction. Such a moderate course perhaps could have brought gradual change in the South without a backlash against southern African Americans. If southern states had respected the repeal of slavery, black voting rights, and civilian federal officials carrying out federal functions in the South, they could have been restored to representation in Congress. Universal pardons, with rare exceptions for war atrocities, could have been given to Confederate rebels. However, draconian military rule, social reengineering of the South, and attempts at confiscation of southern land and property should have been avoided. Instead of confiscating the land belonging to southerners, both presidents Johnson and Grant should have identified the considerable amount of unowned land in the South and distributed it to African Americans.

Although the Radical Republicans never had a majority even in their own party, Johnson was unwilling to compromise with moderate Republicans; they turned against him and voted with the Radicals.[4] This made a two-thirds, veto-proof majority hostile to Johnson and his excessively pro-southern policies.

In foreign policy, Johnson was also aggressive. For example, he sent fifty thousand troops to the U.S.-Mexican border to encourage the French to withdraw from that country, and he also grabbed Midway Island in the Pacific. His more significant battles, however, were with Congress.

Wielded Presidential Power Excessively

Although Andrew Johnson felt he was sticking up for the Constitution against the onslaught of the Radical Republicans, he sometimes wielded excessive and unconstitutional executive power in doing so. Although Johnson's numerous vetoes of legislation passed by the Radical Republican rump Congress — most of them overridden — were constitutional, he also resorted to questionable uses of unilateral executive power. He declined to enforce laws passed by Congress, refused to spend money it appropriated, used patronage power to intimidate politicians across the country to support his mild view of Reconstruction, and even threatened to use military force against the Congress. Also, after the Civil War ended, Johnson didn't immediately rescind Lincoln's unconstitutional suspension of habeas corpus. Because he couldn't win legislative battles in the rump Congress, Johnson resorted to making policy by writing unconstitutional executive orders and engaging in bureaucratic chicanery — a forerunner of the modern presidency.

Endured Excessive Congressional Power

Before the Civil War, the South's representation in Congress was based on its white population and three-fifths of its slave population. After the war, the slaves had been freed and would have been counted as whole persons; therefore southern representation would have actually increased, with the whites controlling the representation because of blacks still being disenfranchised. Thus, even after losing the war the South would have been stronger in Congress. As a result, in December 1865, Congress refused to seat its elected southern members.

Early the next year, the legislative body passed a law instituting military governments in the South and extending the Freedmen's Bureau, which aided distressed war refugees and assisted emancipated slaves. Johnson vetoed this measure, and the Congress initially failed to override it. Later, military rule and another Freedmen's bill were enacted over Johnson's veto.

In the spring of 1867, Congress passed a series of severe Reconstruction laws that replaced the South's elected governments with military rule. The military could overrule local government and even make decisions on voter eligibility. The laws also said states could be readmitted to the union if they generated new constitutions, ratified the Fourteenth Amendment, and gave voting rights to blacks while taking them away from Confederate leaders. Johnson concurred with the Supreme Court decision *Ex parte Milligan*, in 1866, which said military rule during peacetime was unconstitutional, and he vetoed the legislation. The unconstitutionality of it all didn't seem to bother Congress, as they overrode Johnson's veto in every case.[5] Some of the requirements for readmission were needed — such as ratification of the Fourteenth Amendment and acceptance of black voting rights — but military rule was too harsh.

In March 1867, Congress passed the Army Appropriations Act, which undermined Johnson's authority as commander in chief of the armed forces by requiring that military orders go through General Ulysses S. Grant, the nation's top military officer, who was sympathetic to the Congress. Johnson should have vetoed this violation of the checks and balances, but instead he signed it.[6] Of course, if a president threatens unconstitutional military action against the Congress, which Johnson did, then he should expect an unconstitutional pushback from the legislative body.

Opposed the Tenure of Office Act

In the spring of 1867, the Radical Republicans overrode another of Johnson's vetoes, his veto of the Tenure of Office Act. The law prohibited the president from firing, without the Senate's approval, any appointee whom the Senate had confirmed. The Radical Republicans passed this law because they were afraid Johnson would fire Secretary of War Edwin Stanton, their spy and ally in Johnson's cabinet.[7]

Johnson argued convincingly that the Tenure of Office Act was unconstitutional, using precedents going back to 1789. The Supreme Court eventually vindicated Johnson's reasoning in a 1926 ruling.[8] The Constitution says that a president needs the Senate's advice and consent when appointing officials but makes no mention of that when firing them. Although the unconstitutional augmentation of executive power at the expense of the Congress, as U.S. history has progressed, is of grave concern, in this instance the Constitution was on the president's side. As a check on presidential power, the Senate should approve presidential appointees, but presidents should be able to fire officeholders if their performance is inadequate. Presidents need to have people in office they believe will carry out their policies well. In this unique case, Johnson protected the president's legitimate powers in the checks and balances system from an ascendant Congress.

Johnson also said that the Tenure of Office Act did not apply to Secretary of War Stanton, whom he did fire. The act protected officials only during the term of the president who appointed them, and Lincoln had appointed Stanton.

Faced Impeachment

In late February 1868, the House of Representatives voted to impeach Johnson on eleven counts. The most important count was violation of the Tenure of Office Act for firing Stanton, but there were also counts charging disrespect for congressional authority, anti-Congress speeches, and intent to overturn Congress's wishes on command of the army and Reconstruction. Johnson convincingly argued that he was not defiant of legislative authority because he signed much legislation and that he had free-speech rights and authority as president to comment on public affairs.

In reality, as in the impeachment of Bill Clinton 130 years later, the congressional Republicans were primarily trying to lessen an obstacle to their political program — in Johnson's case, his opposition to Congress's harsh Reconstruction policies. In Johnson's Senate trial, impeachment failed on several of the counts by only one vote. The closeness on multiple votes and the willingness of certain senators to change their vote if conviction were likely indicate that Congress orchestrated the trial to intimidate Johnson without actually removing him from office. In both the Clinton and Johnson cases, thankfully for the constitutional system of checks and balances, impeachment on primarily political grounds, instead of for crimes against the state, failed.

PROSPERITY

Was Good on Economic Policy

National productivity climbed during Johnson's presidency. Part of this prosperity was the post–Civil War transfer of resources from the government back to the much more productive private sector. Nonetheless, Vedder and Gallaway credit Johnson with promulgating policies that limited government and fought inflation. They ranked him second out of thirty-nine presidents ranked on these criteria.

Except where presidential powers were concerned, Johnson was for limited government, but he deviated from this ideal to assist, via government financing, the building of railroads and mining of gold and sliver. Johnson's purchase of Alaska for $7.2 million — nicknamed "Seward's folly" after his secretary of state — resembled that of the Louisiana Purchase, which even Thomas Jefferson thought was probably unconstitutional.

Johnson commendably signed the extension of the Homestead Act of 1862 to Louisiana, Arkansas, Mississippi, Alabama, and Florida. The act gave public land to white and black settlers, thus privatizing it, and prohibited discrimination against African Americans in so doing.

LIBERTY

Opposed Congress's Excesses against Southern Whites, but Was Insufficiently Concerned with Black Rights

Johnson opposed some of Congress's excesses. For example, although Johnson unnecessarily and unconstitutionally approved the trial of Lincoln's assassins in the harshness of a military court, he opposed the use of unconstitutional military tribunals in the South during peacetime, arguing that the civil courts were operable. Nevertheless, military tribunals were used for several years after the Civil War.[9]

As early as June 1865, Johnson proclaimed a general amnesty for southerners. Johnson's declaration of amnesty differed little from Lincoln's offer to the South in 1863. Johnson also issued an order that allowed the southern states to commence setting up elected white governments. By the time Congress convened in December 1865, the states had done so and ratified the Thirteenth Amendment, abolishing slavery, but they enacted a new form of it by passing the "black codes," which tied freed slaves to the land they had worked while in bondage.[10]

In the spring of 1866, Congress passed and Johnson vetoed a civil rights bill providing citizenship to African Americans. Johnson cared more about continuing Lincoln's policy of benevolence to southern whites — not necessarily a bad goal in itself — than about safeguarding the rights of newly freed blacks. In June of 1866, Congress passed the critical Fourteenth Amendment. The amendment, among other things, prevented the states from abusing individual rights or denying equal protection of all citizens under the law. Although he could not veto the amendment, Johnson unconscionably advised the states not to ratify it.

Although Johnson was an avid racist, blacks probably would have experienced a diminished backlash from southern whites if Congress had followed Johnson's preference of using federal civilian officials to protect them, rather than authorizing ruthless military rule. Also, northerners imported to the South (carpetbaggers), their southern collaborators (scalawags), and freed slaves teamed up to grab control of the legislatures of southern states. Such Reconstruction southern legislatures were corrupt and imposed high taxes, driving many scalawag landowners over to the Democrats and eroding support for the Reconstruction governments.

Johnson warned, and was correct, that the harshness of northern military rule in the South would cause a backlash against southern blacks. Resentful of the grinding northern military occupation, southerners developed a terrorist organization called the Ku Klux Klan to harass, attack, and kill blacks in the South. Ironically and tragically, northern Reconstruction policies may have made southern blacks less safe. Furthermore, freed blacks were gradually disenfranchised from voting and subjected to "black codes" and discriminatory Jim Crow laws. Much of this ill treatment did not end until almost one hundred years later in the 1960s.

CONCLUSION

Although Johnson tried to be a counterweight to Radical Republicans, who wanted to impose ruthless military rule on the South, his failure to compromise with moderate Republicans in Congress alienated them and caused draconian measures to be enacted over his veto. Instead of reaching a moderate compromise, winning the limited rights for blacks that southern society was willing to give them at the time, Johnson's intransigence merely led to the very severe Reconstruction policies he abhorred. Despite a horrific Civil War, blacks were little better off than they were before the conflict. Southern society, and American society, would not be ready to give blacks full rights for another century. Throughout American history, using military force to try to change deeply held cultural and societal norms and practices rarely has been successful. Although Johnson tried to oppose the Republicans' unforgiving Reconstruction policies, he failed miserably, did not care much about black civil rights, and should thus be ranked only high in the poor category of presidents. Andrew Johnson is number seventeen here.

18

ULYSSES S. GRANT

Better Than Expected, but Still Poor

PP&L* RANKING: 19
Category: Poor

Eighteenth president of the United States

Term: March 4, 1869, to March 4, 1877
Party: Republican
Born: April 27, 1822, Point Pleasant, Ohio
Died: July 23, 1885 (age sixty-three),
    Mount McGregor, New York
Spouse: Julia Dent Grant
Alma Mater: U.S. Military Academy at West Point
Occupation: General in chief
Religion: Methodist

Ulysses S. Grant, taking office in early 1869, inherited the wreckage of the cataclysmic Civil War. According to Josiah Bunting III, one of the most recognized authorities on Grant's presidency, Grant faced a landscape that was more challenging than that of all incoming presidents except Lincoln and Franklin D. Roosevelt.[1] Grant's dilemma was that he wanted to conciliate with the South and heal the nation's wounds — as Republican Abraham Lincoln had advocated before his death and Andrew Johnson, his Democratic successor, had tried to do — but he also felt obligated to guarantee the new rights of African Americans enshrined in the Fourteenth and Fifteenth amendments. As a result, he used military power to enforce a harsh Reconstruction in the South, with unintended negative results for the nation and for the African Americans he had hoped to help. Thus, although the North won the war militarily in 1865 and the union stayed together geographically, the South eventually won the peace.

---

*PP&L = Peace, Prosperity, and Liberty.

While Grant's foreign policy was relatively restrained, his treatment of Native Americans, both in battle and on the reservations, was disastrous. Grant has been blamed for the corruption that marked his administration, but he was not directly responsible for this, and indeed he brought sound fiscal policy to the federal government.

PEACE

Generally Ran a Restrained Foreign Policy

Grant, like most presidents who had been generals, was a closet moderate. Grant avoided an unneeded war with Spain over a Cuban insurgency, which William McKinley would initiate thirty years later. In 1869, two unfortunate American tourists found themselves on board a ship bound for Cuba with guns and rebel fighters supplied by wealthy Cubans in America — a violation of U.S. law. The Spanish, in violation of a treaty with the United States, shot the two men when the ship got to Cuba. This development angered Grant — who, along with most Americans, supported the Cuban rebel cause — because the Spanish had already arrested Americans in Cuba without cause and had commandeered American ships on the high seas.

Pressure mounted on Grant from the media and public to intervene in the Cuban conflict, and the House passed a resolution that supported any intervention Grant wanted to prosecute. U.S. recognition of the Cuban insurgency meant war with Spain, which had a large fleet in the Caribbean. The United States had demobilized after the Civil War and had only a small army, which was preoccupied with occupying the Reconstruction South and battling Indians in the West.

The Civil War made Grant want to avoid future wars, and as a result he would not be pressured into recognizing the Cuban rebellion. A famous former soldier advocating peace had great influence and won the day.[2] Grant should be given credit for this courageous stand.

Grant also set a precedent by solving other international disputes peacefully, agreeing for the first time to use binding arbitration to settle a disagreement with another nation. The Washington Treaty that he signed with Britain has been deemed an important watershed in diplomatic history. In the treaty, the British accepted blame for building the Confederate ship *Alabama*, which sank Union ships during the Civil War, and referred the dispute to a tribunal in Geneva for arbitration. The tribunal awarded the United States damages of

$15.5 million. The treaty also removed one of the last obstacles to developing a lasting friendship with Britain, which had been a principal rival of the United States since the American Revolution.

On the negative side, Grant, like many of his predecessors and contemporaries, such as Thomas Jefferson and Abraham Lincoln, did not feel blacks were equal to whites, seemed skeptical that they could live together with whites, and hoped that they could be exported overseas. These beliefs led Grant into an ill-fated foreign adventure. Buenaventura Baez, president of Santo Domingo, the modern-day Dominican Republic, was trying to sell his country for a profit. To the horror of Hamilton Fish, Grant's secretary of state, Grant wanted to annex the country because its great harbor was perceived to have a strategic location in the middle of the Caribbean, because of its potential use as a navy coaling station, and because it could serve as a place to which America's entire African American population could emigrate. Grant sent U.S. warships to protect Baez's life from threats. Fortunately, the Senate rejected the proposed treaty of annexation.[3]

Promoted a Draconian Reconstruction That Did Little to Help Blacks in the Long Term

Grant was prepared to be more ambitious than his predecessor, Andrew Johnson, in enforcing the rump Congress's makeover of the defeated South, including implementing the harsh Reconstruction Acts. Grant reluctantly used the military to enforce African American rights in the South through occupation and martial law. Such federal coercion was not only unconstitutional (the Constitution provides that the federal government will provide protection against domestic violence only when states request it) but also unlikely to work on a southern white population that was not yet ready to give up unequal and oppressive treatment of African Americans.

Grant's rigorous enforcement of the Reconstruction acts led to guerrilla warfare in the South.[4] The Ku Klux Klan (KKK) and related groups stepped up their activities and savagely attacked blacks. Southern law enforcement either collaborated with the Klan or was intimidated into acquiescing to its violence.[5]

In the Enforcement Acts (including the KKK Act) of 1871, Congress outlawed the KKK and allowed Grant to impose martial law and suspend habeas corpus in the South. Unlike Lincoln's unilateral suspension of habeas corpus during the Civil War, this action might have been constitutional because Congress can suspend the writ in times of invasion or rebellion. Under the act, thousands of people were arrested and turned over to federal authorities, thus circumventing southern courts and juries; this part of the act was likely unconstitutional.[6] Grant had finally smashed the Klan,[7] which he unintentionally had a hand in strengthening in the first place, but its members fought on under different organizational banners.

Josiah Bunting III cogently compares the North's military occupation of the South to U.S. entanglement in Vietnam. Both episodes involved a powerful outside actor attempting to impose its will on people who didn't share the same culture or customs. Both southerners and the North Vietnamese knew that if they kept resisting, thus slowing progress, the democratic foreign occupier — responding to public pressure to withdraw troops — would get exhausted, lose patience, and go home.

Politics figured heavily in Reconstruction. Using military power, Republicans were sustaining unrepresentative governments of northern carpetbaggers and their southern collaborators, called scalawags. Guaranteeing the black vote with military power was bound to help the Republican Party make inroads into a solidly Democratic South, because, at the time, blacks overwhelmingly were likely to vote Republican — the party of emancipation. Grant's policy was criticized for vacillating between harshness and reconciliation, using armed force to make political hay rather than to respond to severe local conditions.[8] For example, Grant decided on whether to send troops to Mississippi based on how the decision was likely to affect the Republican candidate's prospects in the Ohio governor's race.

The turning point in Reconstruction came when the money ran out, as the Panic of 1873 led to an economic depression. In 1874, the depression, combined with voter vexation with Reconstruction, led to a Democratic takeover of Congress; Reconstruction was effectively dead. U.S. military forces, however, were not removed from the South until Rutherford B. Hayes assumed the presidency in 1877. As can be concluded from a look at history, U.S. nation-building missions have rarely worked, whether they be in Vietnam, Haiti, Somalia, Iraq, or right here at home. Imposing values, customs, and laws on people who are not interested in adopting them almost never works, no matter how bad their transgressions — and oppressing African Americans was a very bad transgression.

Instead of enforcing unconstitutional military rule against the South, Grant should have pleaded with Congress to lift military rule, and he should have used only federal civilian officials to guarantee the black rights enshrined in the new Fourteenth Amendment. Avoiding the southern backlash to military rule actually might have made things safer for African Americans in the South.

A more moderate solution to the Civil War's aftermath might have been something between Lincoln's and Johnson's excessive benevolence to the South and Congress's failed severe Reconstruction, which Grant accepted and enforced militarily. If the southern states had respected the repeal of slavery, black voting rights, and civilian federal officials carrying out federal functions in the South, their representation in Congress could have been restored. Universal pardons, with rare exceptions only for war atrocities, could have been given to Confederate rebels. However, draconian military rule, the social reengineering of the South, and attempts at confiscating southern land and property should have been avoided. Instead of confiscating land belonging to southerners, both presidents Johnson and Grant should have found and distributed unowned land in the South — much of the land in that region — to African Americans.

Employed Harsh Policies toward Native Americans

The army did not follow Grant's benevolent, yet condescending, Indian policy. Whenever an Indian raid took place during this period, the army responded with a disproportionate slaughter of Indians. To avenge an Indian raid in Montana in 1870, for example, the army massacred warriors' families. In another case, General Edward Canby and an Indian agent, both unarmed, were murdered during a meeting with the Modoc Indians in northern California, which was held to settle a standoff between the Native Americans and military forces that were herding them onto reservations. In a reprisal, General William Tecumseh Sherman instructed his forces, "You will be fully justified in their extermination." The bloodthirsty Sherman was Grant's right-hand man during the Civil War, when he waged total warfare against the southern population by burning his way to the sea after capturing Atlanta, and his chief general during the Indian Wars.

George Custer's deliberate exaggeration of gold discoveries in the Black Hills Indian lands of the Dakota Territory led to his eventual debacle at the Little Bighorn in 1876. Custer's embellishment caused the desired gold rush, as well as government violations of the Second Treaty of Fort Laramie. Purportedly protecting the Indians from white gold-seekers — but actually doing the reverse — Grant ordered General Philip Sheridan to force the Indians onto a portion of the reservation and keep them under surveillance, while white prospectors stole their gold.[9]

Sheridan was to surround the Indians with three large armies coming from the east, south, and west. The ruthless Custer, commanding the force coming from the east, had little intelligence about where the Indians were and became isolated from the other two armies. There were no survivors among his Seventh Cavalry after Crazy Horse's ambush at the Little Bighorn in Montana in June 1876. One cannot say that Custer and the army didn't richly deserve this ambush and defeat. However, that defeat ended Grant's nominal peace policy with Indians.

PROSPERITY

Restrained Executive Power and Ran Austere Fiscal and Monetary Policies

Grant intervened in the gold market in 1869 to prevent two financiers from trying to corner it and raise the price of gold. Grant's effort to sell government gold into the market, and thus reduce its price, was designed to stanch the erosion of an already inflation-depreciated currency. Despite this unfortunate intervention in the market, however, Grant generally pursued a sound monetary policy.

The nation's debt had risen from $64 million at the beginning of the Civil War to $3 billion when Grant's first term commenced in 1869. Lincoln had financed the war by printing greenbacks, which caused runaway inflation. In contrast, Grant believed the national debt should be paid down in gold at the earliest possible time. Grant got Congress to pass the Public Credit Act, which required the administration to pay all holders of government bonds in gold and to begin to redeem greenbacks. By 1873, Grant had reduced the number of greenbacks in circulation and thus the money supply.

The Panic of 1873, however, caused much pressure, especially from farmers and westerners who were political supporters of the president, to print more greenbacks. Congress passed a bill to print greenbacks in 1874 and expected Grant to sign it, assuming that a veto would be the Republican Party's death knell in the West. Courageously, Grant vetoed the bill and had his veto sustained. As a result of Grant's winning the showdown, Congress then passed the Specie Resumption Act, which stipulated that government payments would be in gold and that greenbacks must be out of circulation by 1879.

This goal was accomplished, and the United States prospered with a hard-money (gold, not greenbacks) policy for decades.[10] Reversing Lincoln's disastrous "easy money" policy was Grant's greatest accomplishment as president. As a result of Grant's fiscal austerity and tight money policies, Vedder and Gallaway correctly rank Grant third among thirty-nine presidents ranked on limiting government and fighting inflation.

In addition, like many presidents of the 1800s, Grant correctly interpreted the Constitution to authorize only the limited executive role of administering the laws as passed by the people's elected representatives in Congress.

Was Overly Faulted for the Effects of Corruption

Grant's performance as president is below par, but not because of his administration's corruption, for which he is so often blamed. Although Grant's Reconstruction and Indian policies had bad effects and qualify Grant in the poor category, Grant's culpability for the corruption during his administration and the concomitant ill effects have been overstated. Although certainly not good, corruption based on personal greed, as exhibited in the Grant and Harding administrations, is not as bad as corruption that perverts the constitutional system, such as that of Reagan's Iran-Contra and Nixon's Watergate scandals. Corruption by personal greed — even when substantial, as during the Grant administration — is less pernicious to the millions of citizens in the republic than unconstitutional, illegal, or just plain ruinous policies on the part of presidents.

Most historians credit Grant with being an honest man but one who had excessive loyalty to his friends. For example, Grant had little to do with the most famous scandal during his administration. The board of directors of the Union Pacific Company used Crédit Mobilier, a dummy company, to build a railroad. The directors paid themselves well, using government subsidies. To prevent trouble in Congress if the scheme were discovered, one congressman distributed free Crédit Mobilier stock to Grant's former and current vice presidents and members of the House and Senate, starting before Grant took office. As a result, the House censured a congressman and one of his colleagues, and one senator was expelled from the Senate. So most of the beneficiaries of Crédit Mobilier's largesse were members of Congress, rather than officials of Grant's administration.

Worse than Crédit Mobilier was the Indian Trading Scandal, the only scandal that directly tainted a principal Grant political appointee. Secretary of War William Belknap's wife convinced him to give a monopoly trading post at Fort Sill, Oklahoma, to her friend Caleb Marsh. Marsh found that the current trader at the post didn't want to leave, so Marsh said that he could stay if he paid a kickback to him. Marsh then split the kickback with the secretary and Mrs. Belknap and actually made payments to the secretary himself. Trying to prevent impeachment by the House, Belknap raced to the White House and resigned.

Grant accepted his resignation, and, after the House impeached Belknap anyway, the Grant administration unsuccessfully tried to undermine the House investigating committee's case by dragging it into court. In his Senate impeachment trial, Belknap had to be acquitted because he was no longer an officeholder.[11] Although Grant seemed to be protecting Belknap, the entire patronage system of political appointments to lucrative monopoly positions was also to blame for encouraging kickbacks to public officials. Eliminating the government-backed monopoly positions in favor of free and private competition would have eliminated the potential for corruption.

Another scandal involved Secretary of the Treasury William Richardson, who signed off on a contract that allowed John Sanborn to collect back taxes owed the government in exchange for half the take. There was collusion between Treasury officials and Sanborn. Most of the four hundred thousand dollars Sanborn collected would have been collected by the Internal Revenue Department anyway. In 1874, a House committee investigated, and Grant forestalled the committee from introducing a "no confidence" resolution on Richardson. No criminal blame was proved, but Grant fired Richardson anyway.[12] Grant had little to do with this scandal.

The Whiskey Ring was yet another scandal involving the Treasury Department. For many years prior to the Grant administration, the Treasury Department's revenue agents had taken kickbacks to lower the taxes on whiskey distillers. In turn, the distillers gave some of their tax savings to Republican campaigns. Grant was unenthusiastic about previous entreaties to bust the ring, perhaps because he wanted the lucrative campaign contributions to continue. A federal investigator was sent to St. Louis but was muzzled after he returned to the nation's capital. Grant and his aide, Orville Babcock, also went to St. Louis, where they were guests of General John McDonald, Grant's revenue supervisor for the Midwest, who later was exposed as the Whiskey Ring's leader. Grant and Babcock had accepted a team of horses from McDonald as a gift.

The new secretary of the treasury, Benjamin Bristow, then began to investigate the tax scheme, but Grant believed that Bristow's real target was him since Bristow wanted the 1876 Republican presidential nomination. Bristow informed the president that General McDonald was the head of the Whiskey Ring and that Babcock had allegedly taken a bribe from the ring to have the investigation quashed. Grant told Bristow to prosecute without partiality and rejected a more lenient military trial for Babcock, even though Grant believed Babcock was innocent. Babcock was acquitted on the president's testimony, but resigned.

In sum, two members of Grant's cabinet resigned to avoid being impeached for fraud and bribery. Five federal judges also resigned.[13] Grant did, however, ultimately insist on full investigations of his aide, Babcock, and Secretary of War Belknap.

Corruption pervaded the government and the two parties at this point in history because of the patronage system, whereby politicians could give their cronies cushy government jobs or exclusive rights to some lucrative business. Grant recognized the problem and proposed civil service reform. In 1871, Congress approved the Civil Service Commission, which recommended that examinations be given for all jobs except very high politically appointed positions, that each department have its own examining board, and that politicians could not fleece bureaucrats for campaign contributions.

Grant wanted to implement the recommendations, but the Congress declined to authorize them and discontinued funding for the commission after three years. Civil service reform eventually occurred during Chester Arthur's administration in 1883.

LIBERTY

Defended Black Rights

The Thirteenth Amendment abolished slavery, the Fourteenth Amendment prohibited states from violating the rights of any U.S. citizen, and the Fifteenth amendment gave African Americans the right to vote. Although southerners could no longer own slaves, most of them did their best to deny all the rights in the Fourteenth and Fifteenth amendments to African Americans. In the end, they succeeded in establishing Jim Crow laws, which severely discriminated against African Americans and which lasted until the 1960s. Furthermore, after the Civil War, under the "black codes," African Americans were required to work for meager wages, in a state of near slavery, for the men who had been their masters before the war. Eric Foner, a historian, quotes a freed black: "The whole South — every state in the South — has got [back] into the hands of the very men that held us as slaves."[14]

Although Grant supported the Civil Rights Act of 1875 and was the greatest champion of black civil rights in the next eighty years — for which he should be commended — the rest of society, especially in the South, wasn't there yet. By trying to pass and militarily enforce stringent laws to guarantee blacks' newly won voting and other rights, Grant and Congress may have unintentionally made things worse for the intended beneficiaries. With the backlash in the South and the resultant rise of the KKK and similar organizations, African Americans had to worry not only about being disenfranchised at the polls, but also about being killed or maimed by the Klan. "In the end," concludes historian David C. Whitney, "Radical Reconstruction proved a failure and left a bitter legacy to future generations."[15]

Failed at a "Benevolent" Indian Policy

Grant's Indian policy, also pregnant with good intentions, failed. In 1869, when Grant took office, 370 treaties with Indians had been violated, and there had been recent massacres of Indians by whites, including George Armstrong Custer's ruthless massacre of the Washita Indians in 1868. Grant believed that whites deserved most of the blame for the fighting between settlers and Native Americans. He also condescendingly believed that white superiority should lead to leniency toward the Indians, which essentially meant affording them equal treatment with whites.

After a peace commission recommended that Native Americans be moved to and "domesticated" on reservations — learning to be farmers, artisans, and so on and sending their children to government-provided schools — Grant adopted this policy and demanded that Congress provide funding for such programs. In a harbinger of George W. Bush's faith-based initiative almost a century and a half later, Grant recruited Quakers and other church people to replace corrupt public officials as Indian agents.[16]

Although Grant's creation of the reservation system was an effort to prevent the total annihilation of the Indians, reservation land was often not good for hunting or farming, and the Native Americans became dependent on the fickle U.S. government for food and provisions. Instead of creating an abysmal existence for the Indians on reservations, Grant should have concentrated on preventing whites from stealing Native American land.

In sum, Grant moved Indians to reservations — what would now be called "ethnic cleansing" — and tried to make them live like whites. Then when their reservation land became valuable, he used the army to allow whites to steal it. Finally, Grant allowed General Sheridan to begin a harsh policy of retribution for the army's defeat at Little Bighorn.

CONCLUSION

The Federalist Society and the *Wall Street Journal* poll of professors of law, history, and political science ranked Grant thirty-second among the thirty-nine presidents they assessed,[17] due mostly to the corruption surrounding his administration. Over time, his star has risen slightly because of his efforts to promote black rights in the South after the Civil War. Demonstrating this slight ascension in the rankings, the above poll should be compared to Arthur Schlesinger's famous 1948 poll of historians for *Life* magazine, which ranked Grant the second-worst president ever.[18]

Here, Ulysses S. Grant is ranked nineteenth of forty presidents ranked, in the poor category. In sum, Grant's severe and counterproductive policies toward Native Americans and toward the South during Reconstruction probably render his presidency below par, but he should get credit for his hard-money policy, his avoidance of war with Spain over Cuba, and his precedent for settling disputes through international arbitration. Although most historians focus on the scandals during his administration, this emphasis is misplaced because the scandals did not directly taint Grant, and Grant had little involvement in the most famous one. More important, petty corruption is less dangerous to the republic than constitutional perversion or even bad policy.

After leaving office, the destitute, dying, and cocaine-addicted Grant wrote one of the best memoirs in U.S. history and earned big money for his family.

19

RUTHERFORD B. HAYES

Practiced Military Restraint, Except with Indians

PP&L* RANKING: 4
Category: Excellent

Nineteenth president of the United States

Term: March 4, 1877, to March 4, 1881
Party: Republican
Born: October 4, 1822, Delaware, Ohio
Died: January 17, 1893 (age seventy), Fremont,
    Ohio

Spouse: Lucy Webb Hayes
Alma Mater: Harvard Law School
Occupation: Lawyer
Religion: Methodist

Rutherford B. Hayes, ranked number four in this analysis, did not get reelected because he did not seek it. Hayes believed that presidents performed better if they term-limited themselves, and so he pledged, in his campaign for president, not to seek reelection. He kept his promise. Very few presidents have self-limited their duration in office and therefore their power. Hayes's action is important and should be commended.

Although Hayes usually gets blamed or credited with ending Reconstruction in the South, it was effectively over when he took office. President Grant had withdrawn federal troops from all southern states except Louisiana and South Carolina. However, Hayes can take credit for demonstrating considerable restraint in the use of military force at home and abroad, except in

---

*PP&L = Peace, Prosperity, and Liberty.

the case of the Indian wars. His continued pursuit of previous policies against Native Americans dropped his rank in this accounting from number two to number four.

In economic policies, Hayes pursued a hard-money (referring to gold coins instead of paper money) agenda and refused to get involved in strife between employers and workers. He also took steps to eliminate political corruption from government employment, beginning the move toward a nonpartisan civil service. Like all presidents of his time, he was unable to help newly freed African Americans to achieve true equality. Hayes's other demerits include strengthening the presidency (vis-à-vis Congress) from what the Constitution had envisioned.[1] He did not defer to Congress on proposing legislation and used the veto frequently.

PEACE

Pursued Restraint in Foreign Policy

Adopting a largely noninterventionist foreign policy, Hayes used arbitration to settle international disputes.

Hayes ordered U.S. forces to hunt down marauding Mexican bandits — who were entering the United States and stealing livestock — having the troops engage in hot pursuit across the border into Mexico. Although the Diaz government in Mexico was not happy about the hot pursuit policy, Hayes resisted going to war over the issue. Hayes recognized the Diaz government, restored order to the border, eventually revoked his hot pursuit order, and developed trade and rail service links with Mexico during the ensuing peace.[2]

His only major deviation from a noninterventionist stance occurred when he became alarmed over a French businessman's preparations to build a canal in Central America. Overreacting, he opposed this effort as a European threat to the Western Hemisphere and a violation of the Monroe Doctrine. Declaring that any canal in Central America would be under the U.S. shield, he sent U.S. warships into the Caribbean and unsuccessfully lobbied Congress to set up coaling bases in that region.[3] These actions set a precedent for an expanded Monroe Doctrine and foreshadowed Teddy Roosevelt's later, more formal corollary to the principle. Both Hayes and Roosevelt believed activities short of foreign military intervention in Latin America could trigger U.S. military intervention there.

Advocated Bad Indian Policy

Although Hayes prevented the War Department from taking over the Indian Bureau, he authorized the use of force to put down several Indian uprisings. This suppression is the biggest blemish on Hayes's presidency, and it is a significant one.

The bloodthirsty George Armstrong Custer and his men were killed at the battle of the Little Bighorn, an Indian retaliation to the army helping gold seekers steal Indian lands in the Black Hills and the U.S. government violating other treaty provisos. The white public nevertheless demanded retribution against the Native Americans. Under President Ulysses S. Grant, and continuing under Hayes, the U.S. Army forcibly returned the Sioux and Cheyenne to reservations.

With the Sioux, the Cheyenne had defeated Custer, but they were later forced to capitulate. The tribe wanted to join their kinsmen in Montana, but the government sent them to the undesirable Indian Territory in what is now Oklahoma, with the understanding that they could return to their homeland in the Black Hills if they didn't like Indian Territory. In Indian Territory, they found starvation and malaria. When the Cheyenne asked to return to the Black Hills, the federal Indian agent broke the government's promise and refused their request. The tribe then surreptitiously left the reservation and went north.

In 1878, the Cheyenne were captured, and they asked again to go to the Black Hills, but General Philip Sheridan said that the whole reservation system would be undermined if the Cheyenne were not taken back to Indian Territory. When they refused to go back, the army surrounded them. On January 9, 1879, when the Cheyenne tried to break out, the army massacred most of them, including women and children.

The Nez Perce Indians, led by Chief Joseph, did not want to follow President Grant's orders to be removed from the Wallowa Valley in Oregon. During the Hayes administration, gold was discovered on the Indians' land in Oregon, and General Otis Howard was ordered to force the Nez Perce off their holdings. The Native Americans, avenging the deaths of their tribe members, murdered some innocent white victims, which triggered a war with the U.S. Army. Pursued, the Nez Perce retreated into Montana and Wyoming, losing men, women, and children because the army had ordered that no prisoners be taken.

Although they were trying to reach the sanctuary of Canada, the Nez Perce entered Yellowstone Park, astonishing tourists on vacation and embarrassing the federal government. The ruthless General William Tecumseh Sherman ordered a "no holds barred" attempt to stop the tribe. General Nelson Miles called for a council with Chief Joseph and unethically captured him when he arrived. Miles promised the Indians that if they surrendered, they would be sent to a reservation in Idaho. This promise was not kept, and they were confined as prisoners of war. Many died of disease during confinement.

When the Ponca Indians were removed from their land in northeastern Nebraska and southeastern Dakota Territory, the Hayes administration finally tried to stop the removal policy. This attempt obviously didn't work because the tribe finally had to settle on the Arkansas River.

Similarly, Hayes announced that any whites attempting to settle in Indian Territory would be evicted. When Captain David L. Payne led white settlers into the territory, Hayes had him prosecuted. Yet eviction did not stop whites from stealing Native American land; whites simply returned to the territory and settled it anyway. In 1889, Congress officially opened Indian Territory to white settlement, and Hayes went along with their action.

PROSPERITY

Set Enlightened Economic Policies

Ambitious government expansion of the money supply causes inflation and ultimately recession — excessive investments, caused by the money-induced illusion of enhanced prosperity, have to be liquidated. When Congress passed a law effectively expanding the money supply by authorizing limited silver coinage (the Bland-Allison Act), Hayes vetoed it, but Congress overrode the veto. Nevertheless, Hayes minimized its effect and then sensibly returned the United States to the anti-inflationary gold standard. Hayes's hard-money policy restored financial confidence and helped bring the United States out of one of its worst recessions. Hayes also paid U.S. debts, restored the nation's credit, and reduced the tax albatross around America's neck.[4] Vedder and Gallaway gave Hayes a high ranking — number eleven out of thirty-nine presidents ranked — for promoting limited government and promulgating anti-inflationary policies.

Despite Republican Party rhetoric during certain periods in American history, the organization has never had much of an actual affinity for small government. The vast majority of Republicans in Hayes's day supported high tariffs, large veterans benefits, and substantial pork-barrel spending (unneeded government spending benefiting narrow special interests) for GOP constituencies. Yet Hayes was a fiscal conservative. As will become apparent throughout this book, party labels don't always predict actual policies adopted during presidential terms.

Provided an Appropriate Model to Deal with Labor Unrest

In 1877, state and local officials asked Hayes to send troops to scatter violent railroad strikers during the worst strike, to that date, in American history. However, he correctly believed violent strikes to be the purview of governors and mayors, not the federal government. While he fulfilled his constitutional requirement to protect states against domestic violence if they requested federal troops (Article IV, Section 4), he generally refused to use troops to break the strike or to operate the railroads — deeming those responses to be unconstitutional.

Federal troops did not suppress rioters or kill or wound even one person. The troops were used only to guard federal installations, thus promoting law and order in a nonviolent way. Later, when dealing with a strike against the company that made Pullman railroad cars, Grover Cleveland could have opted for the same nonviolent response but chose to use federal power to break the strike.

In other developments with economic implications, Hayes vetoed a law passed by Congress to throw out parts of the Burlingame Treaty of 1868, which guaranteed unrestricted immigration from China. Then, however, he negotiated an agreement with China to reduce immigration,[5] which traditionally had been the life's blood of the American economy, providing new ideas, skills, and workers to do the jobs that Americans couldn't or wouldn't do.[6] Having people from different backgrounds and cultures also made the country more cosmopolitan and more competitive economically, as ideas from different cultures were combined and products and services were improved.

Tried to Take Politics out of the Civil Service and Pardons

Hayes was careful not to inject too much political bias into the civil service or the issuance of pardons. In 1877, he ordered that civil servants stay out of politics and political campaigns and that politicians be prohibited from charging federal employees a certain percentage of their salaries (called "assessments") to be used to fund election campaigns. In 1878, Hayes suspended future president and fellow Republican Chester Arthur and other Republicans from the New York Custom House and imposed nonpartisan regulations. He later implemented these standards in other government offices.

These were the first steps toward converting a partisan civil service into a nonpartisan one. Lacking congressional support for legislation, however, Hayes could not make such reforms permanent. Although the best route to reducing such partisan corruption is to reduce the size and functions of the civil service, the next best tack is to convert it to a nonpartisan bureaucracy. Hayes's reforms were good, but his successor Chester Arthur went beyond this elimination of politics from government positions and began to give civil servants excessive job protection, eventually making the civil service immune from the popular will.

In addition, Hayes was judicious in his use of the presidential pardon. His informal guidelines included issuing no rapid pardons, consulting the prosecutor and judge in each case, and not pardoning anyone who did not have a job upon release and a friend to retrieve him from prison.

LIBERTY

Advocated Black Voting Rights

Although Hayes advocated black voting rights and equal civil and political rights for all, he knew that Reconstruction, which had treated the South as a conquered territory under military rule, was a failure. He also recognized that continued intervention in southern affairs had little support in the North. Hayes's predecessors had wrongly believed that military force could quickly change a deep-rooted contempt for blacks in southern culture into acceptance overnight. Hayes realized that military force in the South had failed blacks and was counterproductive by propping up unrepresentative Republican governments in that region.[7]

Knowing that the chances for continued black voting rights without federal military occupation were remote, he withdrew federal troops from the two remaining beachheads of federal control in the South. Using troop withdrawal as a bargaining chip, he got pledges from the de facto Democratic governors of the two states to honor black civil and voting rights, but these were not kept. Hayes successfully vetoed the Democratic Congress's legislation to block enforcement of the Fourteenth and Fifteenth amendments. The legislation would have obliterated even the theoretical possibility that the federal government could have ensured that southern elections were peaceful and fair. Constitutionally, Hayes had an obligation to try to protect black voting rights in the South, but he knew that military occupation could never have achieved this end anyway. He did the best he could under the circumstances.

Treated Native Americans Badly

Besides using military force to push Native Americans onto reservations, Hayes promoted additional policies that took from them the rights accorded to other U.S. citizens. At the end of 1877, no Native Americans were living on their traditional tribal lands. They were all on reservations selected by the U.S. government, and a new phase in their relationship with federal authorities began. The government wanted to "civilize" them and prod them to go from a hunting to a farming lifestyle. Indians were forced to abandon their tribes and settle down on individual plots like white farmers ("detribalization"), thus destroying Indian culture.[8] Native Americans were given land that was too dry and plots that were small to provide a living at farming.

Also, culturally, whites converted preexisting Indian property systems, some of which were matrilineal or individual, to exclusively patrilineal systems of ownership.[9] In sum, reservations proved to be abysmal for Indians — with no buffalo and little employment, food, or medical care.[10]

CONCLUSION

Both Van Buren and Hayes are docked substantially because of their horrible Indian policies. Hayes is placed after Van Buren because of his non-Indian transgressions — reduction in Chinese immigration and a needlessly militaristic response in the Caribbean. Throughout U.S. history, wars have been the principal cause of government expansion; they result in government spending increases, even in nonsecurity areas, and in growing government penetration of the private-sector economy. Thus, presidents who take excessive military action or expand U.S. overseas commitments or the armed forces — to make the needless use of force a temptation for later presidents — get hefty numbers of demerits here for doing so. Hayes gets demerits for expanding the Monroe Doctrine. In general, however, he was a very good president because he ended useless inflammatory military occupation of the South, pursued good economic policies, and generally used restraint in foreign policy and in dealing with labor unrest. This assessment ranks Rutherford B. Hayes as number four.

20

JAMES A. GARFIELD

Served for Six Months

NOT RATED

Twentieth president of the United States

Term: March 4, 1881, to September 19, 1881
Party: Republican
Born: November 19, 1831, Moreland Hills, Ohio
Died: September 19, 1881 (age forty-nine),
     Elberon (Long Branch), New Jersey
Spouse: Lucretia Rudolph Garfield
Alma Mater: Williams College
Occupation: Lawyer, educator, minister
Religion: Disciples of Christ

James Abram Garfield was the twentieth president of the United States and, as a result of his assassination, served only six months in that office — the second shortest administration in United States history.

21

CHESTER A. ARTHUR

Promoted Limited Government and Fought Inflation

PP&L* RANKING: 5
Category: Good

Twenty-first president of the United States

Term: September 19, 1881, to March 4, 1885
Party: Republican
Born: October 5, 1829, Fairfield, Vermont
Died: November 18, 1886 (age fifty-seven),
New York, New York
Spouse: Ellen Lewis Herndon Arthur
Alma Mater: Union College, Schenectady, New York
Occupation: Lawyer, civil servant, educator (teacher)
Religion: Episcopalian

Chester A. Arthur may have been the best-dressed American president — he was always decked out in the finest clothes. He also confessed to being a "night person." In fact, he may have been dressed well enough at night to entice both a wife and a mistress. Before becoming president, when Arthur was confronted with rumors that he had a mistress, he sputtered, "This is worse than assassination."[1]

Arthur took over after James Garfield was assassinated within a few months after taking office in 1881. Though Arthur turned out to be one of the best presidents ever, his party did not nominate him to run for a second term.

The number five ranking puts Arthur at the top of the good presidents list; he would have been in the excellent category if it were not for his unnecessary

---

*PP&L = Peace, Prosperity, and Liberty.

and significant attempt to expand the army, the navy, and the United States' coercive role in the world. Other than that, he advocated limited government and an anti-inflationary hard-money policy, while opposing pork-barrel spending (which benefited particular constituents at the expense of the general population). As a former political crony himself during a postal scandal, Arthur was careful to support the removal and prosecution of wrongdoers, even his own appointees. Arthur's civil service reforms, however, although well intentioned, may have inadvertently set the stage for the eventual dramatic expansion of federal bureaucracy. Also, Arthur's rather passive policy toward Indian land rights and his restrictions on Chinese immigration earn major demerits in this assessment.

PEACE

Expanded the Navy to Run a More Ambitious Foreign Policy

In the early 1880s during Arthur's presidency, Congress apparently still wisely harbored the founders' fear that standing armies were a threat to liberty and refused Arthur's effort to expand the army to thirty thousand men. Less afraid of the navy's threat to freedom, however, the legislature allowed Arthur to begin converting the largely defensive navy into one that possessed offensive capabilities. Arthur has been called the "Father of the U.S. Navy."[2]

Up until this time, the U.S. government thought of the navy as a force for defensive warfare. With the absence of an ongoing war and no maritime threats to speak of — no nation in the Western Hemisphere challenged U.S. superiority, and European navies were focused on colonialism in other distant parts of the world — Arthur had to justify increasing the fleet size in peacetime by appealing to nationalistic notions of strength and pride. Arthur wanted an expanded navy to protect the far-flung economic interests of U.S. businessmen, in a form of mercantilism, and to run a nontraditional coercive foreign policy abroad. Without Arthur's efforts, William McKinley might not have had a strong navy to attack the Spanish in 1898, and later still, Teddy Roosevelt would have been unable to run a more muscular foreign policy.

An example of the overseas economic interests Arthur hoped to protect was the possibility of building a canal between the Atlantic and Pacific oceans. In a treaty with Nicaragua, Arthur attained U.S. co-ownership of a strip of Nicaraguan territory that could have been used to dig such a transoceanic canal, but

Grover Cleveland, his successor, withdrew the pact from Senate consideration. On the positive side of his foreign policy, Arthur did avoid intervening militarily in faraway Madagascar against the French, who were trying to snatch parts of that country.

PROSPERITY

Set Good Economic Policies

Arthur is ranked highly because he advocated limited government and good economic policies. Although ignored by Congress, he opposed (unusual for a Republican) pork-barrel infrastructure projects (which would benefit the businessmen running the projects) such as improvements to rivers and harbors; favored an anti-inflationary hard-money policy; and unsuccessfully proposed the abolishment of most internal taxes. Thus, Vedder and Gallaway ranked him highly on their composite ranking of policies that promoted limited government and fought inflation — eighth out of thirty-nine presidents ranked.

In the case of pork-barrel infrastructure projects, the possibility of a federal budget surplus derived from a rise in tariffs was too tempting for politicians in Congress. In 1882, the legislative body passed the Great Divide, the most horrendous pork-barrel legislation since the country's inception. Arthur generally was against infrastructure largesse.[3]

However, Arthur unsuccessfully pressed for increased regulation of interstate commerce and signed only meager tariff reductions (the Mongrel Tariff of 1883). Tariff reductions lessen the barriers to freer international trade, which benefits both the buyer and seller by taking advantage of specialization in production.

Enacted Civil Service Reform

The Pendleton Act of 1883 — which Arthur promoted and signed because of earlier having been a political crony that President Hayes suspended from heading the lucrative New York Customs House — created a commission to hire civil servants on merit rather than continuing the practice of hiring whomever the ruling party proposed, regardless of qualifications. The act also safeguarded their salaries. Prior to passage of the law, the ruling party would harvest "assessments" — a percentage of patronage employees' salaries — to fund election campaigns. In addition, the act gave civil servants job security and thus immunity from political winds.

The act was designed to clean up cronyism and foster "good government," but it affected only a small portion of federal employees. Nevertheless, it effectively set a precedent that would lead to the rise of a modern bureaucratic state largely immune from public pressure.[4]

Because the Pendleton Act no longer allowed politicians to use assessments to fund their electoral campaigns, they began to depend more heavily on business interests for campaign contributions, leading to the major influence that special interests have on U.S. society to this day. The only way to effectively end that stranglehold is to end the unnecessary government programs that give the interests clout.

In fairness to Arthur, if unnecessary government programs do exist — and they do by the truckload — it may be well advised to have egregious party cronyism removed from them and instead hire civil servants on the basis of merit. However, unlike Hayes's laudable effort to keep civil servants out of politics, Arthur's more ambitious provision of excessive job security for bureaucrats tended to make them more slothful, inefficient, and unresponsive to the public, congressional, and presidential will — tendencies that became more dangerous over time as the executive bureaucracies expanded exponentially in size. Thus, Arthur's well-meaning, but in the end somewhat counterproductive, civil service reform caused a good president to be rejected by his own party machinery for renomination.[5]

LIBERTY

Had a Poor Record on Policies toward Minorities

Although Arthur promulgated some restrictions on white settlement of Indian lands, he passively allowed settlers to ignore them. In one case, he even opened the Crow Creek Indian reservation to white settlers, but later Grover Cleveland wisely revoked this policy. Arthur should have been more proactive in preventing whites from stealing lands the federal government had promised to Indians. In addition, Arthur boosted funding for the federal government's education of Indians, but this effort failed to teach Native Americans many useful skills for their new reservation life.

In policy concerning another minority, Arthur vetoed one bill excluding Chinese immigration for twenty years and denying such immigrants citizenship, but then he signed a bill providing for a ten-year period of exclusion and again blocking citizenship.[6]

CONCLUSION

In sum, Arthur rises to the top of the good category for his efforts to promote limited government and fight inflation. His policy failures include starting the U.S. offensive naval buildup of the late 1800s that led to a more coercive U.S. foreign policy, introducing somewhat unproductive civil service reform, making meager tariff reductions, passively permitting bad Indian policies, and restricting Chinese immigration. Chester A. Arthur is ranked five in this assessment.

22

GROVER CLEVELAND

Exemplar of Honesty and Limited Government

PP&L* RANKING: 2
Category: Excellent

Twenty-second president of the United States
Term: March 4, 1885, to March 4, 1889

Twenty-fourth president of the United States
Term: March 4, 1893, to March 4, 1897

Party: Democratic
Born: March 18, 1837, Caldwell, New Jersey
Died: June 24, 1908 (age seventy-one), Princeton, New Jersey
Spouse: Frances Folsom Cleveland
Education: Self-taught for admission to the New York State Bar
Occupation: Lawyer
Religion: Presbyterian

Grover Cleveland, ranked number two here, was one of the few scrupulously honest presidents. For example, in the campaign of 1884, leading to Cleveland's first term, the then-bachelor candidate was accused of producing a child out of wedlock. Haunted by the mocking slogan, "Ma, Ma, where's my pa? Gone to the White House, Ha, Ha, Ha." Cleveland did an unheard-of thing: he admitted that the story was true, but that he had conscientiously met the obligations of parenthood.[1] But Cleveland's honesty is not why he earned the number two ranking. Honesty is to be admired, but, as will become apparent later, many presidential policies are worse than being dishonest or tolerating petty corruption in an administration.

---

*PP&L = Peace, Prosperity, and Liberty.

Cleveland was an ardent proponent of limited and devolved government. Cleveland believed that the president should be a referee who ensured that nobody was shorn of their rights or granted special privileges — that is, the president should do just what the Constitution had envisioned and nothing more.[2] He believed, as the founders had, that the president was an executor of the laws passed by Congress, rather than a legislator. Addressing an entreaty for presidential initiative, Cleveland once said, "I did not come here to legislate."[3] He also conducted a largely restrained foreign policy in spite of his efforts to enforce the Monroe Doctrine.

In some ways, Cleveland strengthened the presidency vis-à-vis the Congress. For example, he resisted attempts by Congress to seize executive branch documents. Congress feared that a Democratic president would remove Republicans from patronage positions in the U.S. Post Office without Senate approval, as required by Tenure of Office Act, which was later ruled unconstitutional and repealed. (Congress had earlier impeached Andrew Johnson for allegedly violating this act.)[4] Cleveland did not want to create executive branch dominance, but he did want to stop what he considered to be unconstitutional congressional aggrandizement.[5]

Cleveland was ultimately proved correct about his right to fire government political appointees. Yet his equivalent to the modern-day claim of executive privilege to withhold information from Congress was not in the Constitution. Also, Cleveland admirably vetoed more bills — mostly legislation that benefited special interests at the expense of the general taxpayers — than all previous presidents combined.[6] After Cleveland's vice president died, Cleveland urged that something should be done to cover this eventuality, and Congress passed the Presidential Succession Act to deal with the problem.

PEACE

Practiced a Restrained Foreign Policy

In foreign policy, Cleveland — in his second term — courageously withdrew and squelched the treaty that annexed Hawaii, which his predecessor, Benjamin Harrison, had sent to the Senate for ratification. American businessmen in Hawaii and those who wanted to "civilize backward peoples" were pushing the treaty. But Cleveland, from an older anticolonial generation, knew that most Hawaiians didn't agree with the U.S.-assisted coup there and didn't want to be part of the United States. He believed the treaty was unscrupulously obtained and contravened the right of true self-determination as explicated in the Declaration of Independence.[7]

In 1896, Cleveland — unlike his successor, William McKinley — resisted congressional and public pressure for interventionism by avoiding war with Spain over the rebellion in Cuba against its empire. Cleveland could have profited politically from such a war — because it would have taken the American public's mind off the economic downturn in the 1890s — but he instead bore the substantial costs of doing the right thing. He also tried to avoid conflict with Britain over the rights of U.S. fishermen in Canada, but the Senate rejected his proposed treaty, which would have created a commission to determine boundaries.

Finally Cleveland withdrew the Frelinghuysen-Zavala Treaty from Senate consideration; signed in 1884 before he took office, the treaty allowed the United States to construct a canal through Nicaragua. Both countries would have owned this canal. Cleveland believed the treaty would require the United States to defend Nicaragua, thus violating the American tradition of avoiding "entangling alliances."[8] Later, however, in the mid-1890s during Cleveland's second term, when the new leader of Nicaragua threatened to revoke the U.S. canal concession, Cleveland unfortunately had a change of heart and landed the U.S. Marines to eradicate British influence in that country.

Built Up the Navy to Enforce the Monroe Doctrine

Cleveland continued Chester Arthur's buildup of the U.S. Navy. Although Cleveland supported staying out of other countries' business, he thought an enhanced navy was needed for coastal defense. When military assets are created, however, an overwhelming temptation exists to use them. Cleveland got into a naval standoff with Germany over Samoa, but a huge storm sank both sides' ships. William McKinley later used the augmented navy to meddle in Cuban and Philippine affairs by starting and winning America's first colonial conflict, the Spanish-American War.

With the exception of the withdrawal of the Nicaraguan canal treaty, Cleveland's policies toward Latin America were driven by U.S. bankers eager to displace Britain, which had been dominant in the region, and thus win export markets and investment opportunities that they could finance. Although Cleveland was generally a noninterventionist, he believed in strongly enforcing the Monroe Doctrine against European activities in Latin America.

In 1895, Cleveland eagerly pounced on a forty-year-old border dispute between Venezuela and British Guiana. The Venezuelans had shrewdly dragged the United States into this obscure imbroglio by granting concessions to Americans in the goldfields within the disputed border region. Richard Olney, Cleveland's secretary of state, sent Britain an insulting and arrogant message on the dispute. When the British rejected the "diplomatic" note, Cleveland gave what amounted to a war message to Congress.

Luckily, Britain was preoccupied with Germany's rising power and with difficulties with the Boers in South Africa. The British decided to compromise on the border dispute and give over dominance of Latin America to the United States. Unfortunately, Cleveland's belligerence had cemented acceptance, in the American popular mind, of the Monroe Doctrine as a lasting principle in U.S. foreign policy. After this dustup, however, Cleveland backed the Olney-Pauncefote Treaty, which created an arbitration panel to solve future U.S.-British disputes.[9] After the British essentially ceded domination of Latin America to the United States, the once-fierce rivals began a friendly relationship that enmeshed the United States in two world wars.

The Cleveland administration also engaged in several minor naval shows of force to enforce the Monroe Doctrine. In 1894, the United States illegally broke a blockade of Rio de Janeiro by British-supported rebels trying to bring back the Brazilian monarchy. In a demonstration of mercantilism at its finest, the United States sent a warship to Santo Domingo (now the Dominican Republic) to intimidate the French, who were threatening to use force to get reparations for the murder of a French citizen. The reparations would have come from Dominican customs revenues, which New York bankers were tapping to pay the debt owed them by the island nation. In 1885, Cleveland sent a small number of marines to quell one of the perennial revolts by the province of Panama against its Colombian overlords.

PROSPERITY

Advocated a Hard-Money Policy

In his first term (1885 to 1889), Cleveland was opposed to the Bland-Allison Act, originally passed during the Hayes administration over Hayes's veto, which compelled the government to buy and coin all the silver that could be dug up — thus increasing the money supply. Cleveland, however, believed the executive branch should have limited power and did not actively pursue alternative legislation. He chose not to violate the constitutional separation of powers and meddle in congressional debates, but he asserted his right to veto any bill he opposed.

As a result, the Bland-Allison Act remained the law during both of Cleveland's stints as chief executive, with negative impacts.[10] Because limiting executive power is so key to maintaining the checks and balances implied in the Constitution, the bad as well as the good arising from efforts to do so must be accepted — with the expectation that the good will outstrip the bad. Thus, Cleveland shouldn't be criticized too severely for not trying to overturn the easy-money policy imbedded in the Bland-Allison Act.

In his second term, from 1893 to 1897 (Cleveland was the only president to serve two nonconsecutive terms as president), the second-worst depression in U.S. history — exceeded only by the Great Depression in the 1930s — settled in. This depression was primarily caused not by Cleveland but by the high tariffs, profligate federal spending, and loose monetary policies of Republican Benjamin Harrison, who served as chief executive between Cleveland's two terms. This is a classic example of bad economic policies by one president causing trouble in a future president's term.

Increasing the money supply usually causes inflation, which in turn can eventually cause a recession because the market must correct for inflation-induced overinvestment. Excessive federal spending can require government borrowing, which crowds out, because of limited funds available, more productive private borrowing — thus slowing the economy. High tariffs increase the prices of imports to consumers and decrease their buying power, cause a rise in economically inefficient domestic production, and cause U.S. exports to decline as other countries retaliate with tariffs of their own — all harming economic growth.

Cleveland attempted to lift the nation out of the Panic of 1893 by restoring confidence in the currency, this trust having been shaken by Congress's legislation to base the national currency on silver and gold. He restored the gold standard, a strict monetary policy, and the nation's faith in its currency. In order to stop the drainage of gold from the Treasury's reserves and restore the gold standard, Cleveland successfully urged repeal of the Sherman Silver Purchase Act, vetoed Congress's inflationary proposal to compel the Treasury to convert its silver stock into coins, and engineered a deal by which J. P. Morgan and other Wall Street financiers would buy U.S. bonds with gold.

According to economist Robert Higgs, the latter deal worked — confidence was restored in the government's capability to sustain the gold standard, and no gold flowed from the Treasury. Higgs also concluded that the public ideology of the times didn't allow a depression to lead to New Deal–style central planning, which would have made the depression worse.[11] Thus, Vedder and Gallaway gave Cleveland a rank of 12 out of 39 presidents ranked on policies limiting government and fighting inflation — a fairly good ranking.

Advocated Tariff Reductions and Spending Restraint

Cleveland tried to spur economic expansion by cutting tariffs, which he felt were a tax on the common folk (making their imported goods more expensive) that would generate profits for the few (wealthy industries that were protected from foreign competition). Because the Treasury had a surplus in 1887, Cleveland tried during his first term — albeit unsuccessfully — to lower tariffs on necessities rather than to reduce taxes on luxury items, such as tobacco and whiskey.

In 1894, during his second term, Cleveland got a reduction in tariffs, but at a steep price. Congress acted to offset the lowering of tariffs by bringing back the income tax on the wealthy. (Lincoln was the first to impose such a tax, initiating it during the Civil War, but the tax was repealed after the war.) Cleveland should be faulted here because he could have successfully vetoed this measure, which was found to be unconstitutional in 1895.[12] The income tax dragged down the economy and was one of the worst taxes in terms of giving the government access to information on people's private lives and finances in order to enforce payment of the tax.

To reduce excessive federal spending, Cleveland, who had paid to get out of fighting as a soldier in the Civil War, courageously vetoed excessive Civil War veterans benefits and other veterans benefits he thought could be abused. One bill gave money to any person who had served at least ninety days in uniform, and another bill provided federal support for all veterans with disabilities, whether or not they were disabled by war injuries.

Opposed Welfare

Cleveland correctly saw no constitutional basis for welfare and famously said, "Though the people support the government, the government should not support the people." Although he vetoed a relief bill for Texas farmers affected by drought, he saw subsidized Department of Agriculture research, along with dissemination of such information, as within the "general welfare" clause of the Constitution's preamble. When the founders stated that the Constitution should "promote the general welfare," they didn't mean giving out subsidies or creating welfare programs for specific groups in society. For example, most of them didn't believe the Constitution permitted federal subsidies for building roads and canals. It is clear that at the time, the founders meant that the "general welfare" clause simply should indicate that the Constitution had the purpose of allowing progress in U.S. society as a whole.

Enlarged Bureaucracy

Cleveland raised the Department of Agriculture (previously the Bureau of Agriculture) to cabinet rank in 1889 and created the Department of Labor in 1888.[13] Both of these agencies would become unwieldy bureaucracies that advocated for and aided special interests.

LIBERTY

Promoted Heavy-Handed Policies toward Labor

Despite the Illinois governor's statement that federal troops were not needed during the violent railroad strike against the Pullman Car Company in Chicago in 1894, Cleveland, without consulting him, declared martial law and ordered federal troops to take violent action against the strike. The Constitution specifically gives Congress, not the president, the power to call forth the militia to execute the laws of the union (in the late 1700s and early 1800s, Congress passed laws of questionable constitutional validity that delegated this enumerated power to the president), and it allows the federal government to protect a state from domestic violence only when requested by the state legislature or governor.[14] So Cleveland's action violated the Constitution. In a similar situation, Rutherford B. Hayes had reluctantly used requested troops to protect federal facilities and deter violence but had avoided using them to bust the strike or operate the railroads — correctly believing these latter functions to be unconstitutional.

Advocated Benevolent Policies for Indians but Not African Americans

Cleveland tried to protect Native American land in Indian Territory (now Oklahoma) from white settlers, only somewhat successfully. He also gave Indians U.S. citizenship and doled out reservation land for individual Indians to farm under the auspices of the Dawes Act. Unfortunately, although Cleveland may have meant well, the act eventually allowed whites to get control of millions of acres of Indian land — reducing Native American holdings by 67 percent.[15]

Although Cleveland had a relatively benevolent policy toward the Indians, he signed legislation revoking the remaining federal enforcement laws that at least nominally prevented southern efforts to deny blacks the right to vote. Yet the Fourteenth Amendment requires the federal government to ensure that states don't violate the rights of citizens and the Fifteenth Amendment guarantees everyone's right to vote.[16] Mitigating his action, however, was the fact that after oppressive, exhausting and unsuccessful Reconstruction efforts, federal enforcement of black voting rights in the South wasn't going to happen anyway, since there was no longer support in the North for using coercion to that end. Regrettably, Cleveland also backed segregation as constitutional and didn't oppose the South's discriminatory Jim Crow laws.

Promoted Federal Activism with Long-Term Effects

Probably most important economically for future generations, Cleveland signed the Interstate Commerce Act, which regulated the rates that railroads charged to haul goods and limited state authority over a nationwide industry. The act created the Interstate Commerce Commission, the first regulatory commission in U.S. history. The law was a precedent for federal regulation of private economic behavior, which would expand dramatically over the next century.[17] Cleveland thus provided the underpinning for the Progressive movement, which would, in the name of progress, advocate further usurpation of individual economic and political rights — to the detriment of those it was trying to help.[18]

CONCLUSION

Historians ranked Grover Cleveland as a "near great" president until small government fell out of favor in the profession. Michael Farquhar's comment about Cleveland demonstrates historians' modern-day bias for activism during crises: "He was a good guy and a hard worker who might well have been a great president had anything at all important occurred during his tenure. Alas, it didn't, so he is not particularly noteworthy."[19] The phrase "anything at all important" should be taken to mean a crisis.

Cleveland believed in limited government, a restrained executive branch, tight money, letting the economy right itself naturally from depression, anti-colonialism, and a noninterventionist foreign policy — making him a very good president. But he set a bad precedent by creating new bureaucracies for regulating private economic behavior; he also brought back the income tax, smashed the Pullman strike with the unconstitutional use of military force, continued the naval buildup, and was too eager to enforce the Monroe Doctrine, thereby risking war with Britain over a minor Venezuelan border dispute. For these transgressions, Cleveland has to be ranked second behind John Tyler.

23

BENJAMIN HARRISON

Bad Economics and the Use of Coercion at Home and Abroad

PP&L* RANKING: 15
Category: Poor

Twenty-third president of the United States

Term: March 4, 1889, to March 4, 1893
Party: Republican
Born: August 20, 1833, North Bend, Ohio
Died: March 13, 1901 (age sixty-seven), Indianapolis, Indiana
Spouse: Caroline Scott Harrison (first wife); Mary Scott Lord Dimmick Harrison (second wife)
Alma Mater: Miami University, Oxford, Ohio
Occupation: Lawyer
Religion: Presbyterian

Although Benjamin Harrison correctly thought that Congress should be the dominant branch of government — as the founders had intended — and accordingly restrained his actions as chief executive, he went along with several congressionally passed policy disasters. Harrison's support of the high McKinley tariff and the Sherman Silver Purchase Act helped to cause the second-worst economic depression in U.S. history. His support of the Sherman Antitrust Act allowed future administrations to meddle in the market instead of letting the market ultimately take care of industrial concentration (the extent to which a small number of firms dominate an industry), which it ultimately does. In fact,

---

*PP&L = Peace, Prosperity, and Liberty.

Harrison actually fostered industrial concentration by protecting industry from foreign competition through high tariffs.

Harrison's naval buildup and expansive foreign policy were precedents for and harbingers of far worse interventionist U.S. foreign policy to come. Although no catastrophic wars occurred during Harrison's term, he almost ensnared the United States in two needless conflicts. By comparison, Harrison's accomplishments were paltry. Even his laudable successes in achieving greater rights for African Americans were limited. Harrison thus achieves only a poor ranking.

Harrison refused to court the party bosses and was only lukewarm on the spoils system — that is, the choosing of officials based on party loyalty, not competence. These stances contributed to his electoral defeat against Grover Cleveland in the 1892 election.

PEACE

Used International Arbitration, but Continued to Build Up the Navy

Harrison used international arbitration to avoid conflicts with Chile, Italy, Britain, and Germany. He also held the first Pan-American Conference, which led to better relations with Latin America. Otherwise, his foreign policy record was not good.

Harrison enlarged the navy, subsidized steamship construction, and favored exorbitant Civil War pensions, which Grover Cleveland, his predecessor, had vetoed.[1] Although Chester Arthur had started the U.S. naval buildup in the early 1880s, it had been erratic; Harrison took it to the next level. In doing so, Harrison made the navy strong enough to tempt policymakers to use the fleet in the first U.S. imperial foray, the Spanish-American War of 1898. Seven of the ten modern navy ships used during that war were authorized during Harrison's administration.[2] As for excessive veterans benefits, any Civil War veteran who could not work received a pension, even if his injury was not caused by the war.

Was Aggressive Overseas

In foreign policy, Harrison enlarged the U.S. presence overseas and aggressively pursued U.S. claims in the Pacific. He was influenced by the imperialistic Alfred Thayer Mahan's *The Influence of Sea Power Upon History, 1600–1783* and pressed for a canal in Central America, navy coaling stations in the Caribbean, and the annexation of Hawaii.

Though the U.S. representative had a role in overthrowing the Hawaiian government to further U.S. business interests, Harrison swept this under the rug and submitted a treaty to annex Hawaii to Congress, just before he left office. He also sent U.S. forces to Hawaii to "protect American lives and property." The Democratic Senate delayed acting on the treaty, and Democratic President Grover Cleveland, Republican Harrison's successor as well as predecessor, withdrew the treaty of annexation from consideration because he rightly felt that it had been dishonorably obtained.

Further, Harrison almost embroiled the United States in a naval war with Germany over U.S. claims to Samoa[3] and what would have been an inane war with Chile over a demanded apology from the Chilean government concerning a saloon brawl involving U.S. sailors on leave in Valparaiso.

Continued the War on Native Americans

Harrison, like so many presidents, allowed the U.S. military to pursue harsh policies against Native Americans, but the butchery at Wounded Knee, South Dakota, in December 1890 was especially egregious. Authorities had shot Chief Sitting Bull, and his supporters had joined another Sioux chief — Big Foot — in the Badlands, causing the government to become concerned. The U.S. military was sent to bring Big Foot back to the Sioux reservation. Big Foot sought protection at the Pine Ridge Reservation in South Dakota, and camped near Wounded Knee Creek. The military surrounded the Indian camp and aggressively searched the camp for weapons. When outraged Sioux youth shot a trooper, the U.S. Army massacred most of the tribe — men, women, and children.[4]

PROSPERITY

Set Bad Fiscal and Monetary Policies

Harrison supported the tariff bill authored by future president William McKinley, which hiked import duties to historical highs. This increase in taxes dragged down the economy. The law also gave the president the power to negotiate reciprocal tariff reductions with other countries.

In addition, Harrison supported the Sherman Silver Purchase Act, which increased the money supply and depleted the nation's gold reserves. It allowed the government to purchase silver with dollars that were redeemable in gold. The money supply increased moderately with the extra infusion of dollars into the economy, which many people then cashed in to get gold from the government's gold supply. The McKinley tariff and the silver purchases combined to help throw the country into the second-worst depression in U.S. history.

At the same time that Harrison was fostering industrial concentration by reducing foreign competition through high tariffs, he supported the Sherman Antitrust Act, which prosecuted such concentration. The act increased presidential power and set a powerful precedent, which allowed the government to interfere in the market in an effort to achieve the perfect industrial structure — attempts that would ultimately prove to do much more harm than good. In the long term, the international market will undermine domestic business concentration and monopoly through changes in technology and increased competition. Domestic antitrust laws merely reduce the size, and therefore competitiveness, of U.S. companies internationally. Harrison did not rigorously enforce the Sherman Antitrust Act, but future presidents would use it to go after big companies that could have been better constrained by competition in the world marketplace.

Harrison allowed Congress to spend money lavishly on pork-barrel projects and excessive veterans benefits. Thus, Vedder and Gallaway rank Harrison twenty-sixth out of thirty-nine presidents ranked in their measure of presidential policies limiting government and stanching inflation.

LIBERTY

Inconsistently Supported Citizens' Liberties

Harrison called for unneeded and discriminatory restrictions on immigration from Asia, though immigration has always been the life's blood of the U.S. economy — infusing new ideas and skills into the American market. On the other hand, he enforced the Fourteenth Amendment, which allowed the federal government to guarantee individual rights when state governments failed to do so. He deplored lynchings of African Americans and requested legislation to give him the authority to stop them.[5] To improve the Republican Party's performance in the South, he unsuccessfully pressed for federal guarantees of black voting rights and appointed black postmasters in southern cities whenever he could.[6]

CONCLUSION

All in all, according to historian Louis W. Koenig, Harrison did the most of any president in the half century between Lincoln and the progressive administrations of Teddy Roosevelt and Woodrow Wilson.[7] This statement betrays the activist bias of most analysts. As has been demonstrated, activism is often bad, as all of these presidents proved, including Harrison. Like the others mentioned, Harrison's failures exceeded his accomplishments, but he did not quite have the extreme negative impact of the really bad presidents. Benjamin Harrison is number fifteen here.

24

GROVER CLEVELAND

Served a Second, Nonconsecutive Term

PP&L* RANKING: 2
Category: Excellent

Twenty-second president of the United States
Term: March 4, 1885, to March 4, 1889

Twenty-fourth president of the United States
Term: March 4, 1893, to March 4, 1897

Party: Democratic
Born: March 18, 1837, Caldwell, New Jersey
Died: June 24, 1908 (age seventy-one), Princeton, New Jersey
Spouse: Frances Folsom Cleveland
Education: Self-taught for admission to the New York State Bar
Occupation: Lawyer
Religion: Presbyterian

Grover Cleveland was the only president to serve two nonconsecutive terms. See chapter 22 for a composite analysis of both of his terms.

---

*PP&L = Peace, Prosperity, and Liberty.

25

WILLIAM MCKINLEY

The First Modern President, with Imperialist Aspirations

PP&L* RANKING: 39
Category: Bad

Twenty-fifth president of the United States

Term: March 4, 1897, to September 14, 1901
Party: Republican
Born: January 29, 1843, Niles, Ohio
Died: September 14, 1901 (age fifty-eight), Buffalo,
New York
Spouse: Ida Saxton McKinley
Alma Mater: Albany Law School
Occupation: Lawyer
Religion: Methodist

William McKinley — not Theodore Roosevelt, as commonly believed — laid the basis for the strong modern presidency, using the Spanish-American War to set the United States on the road to empire in the Western Hemisphere and the Pacific, and trampling the liberty of people there. When foreign policy, especially a war, is most important in the public mind, the president can increase his powers. McKinley made the executive branch the center of power in Washington, D.C. His domestic policies laid the foundation for progressivism, and his reluctant return to the gold standard was his only positive contribution to the economy. He was very close to the nation's worst president, exceeded only by Harry Truman and Woodrow Wilson.

---

*PP&L = Peace, Prosperity, and Liberty.

PEACE

Started the Spanish-American War —
A Small War with Large Implications

McKinley's "little" war had huge implications for the U.S. and the world. Presidents Grant and Cleveland had skillfully avoided involvement in Cuban revolts against Spain in 1869–1870 and 1895, respectively. Some say that the jingoist (belligerently nationalistic) press and public figures dragged an unwilling and irresolute McKinley into just another one of the many revolutions in Cuba. Jackson Lears, a professor of cultural history at Rutgers University, ranked McKinley as the seventh worst president in U.S. history because he "allowed [Theodore Roosevelt] et al to push him into a savage and unjustified war in the Philippines."[1] Another author, Michael Farquhar, wrote that McKinley was so chained to public opinion that he essentially allowed a newspaper to declare war on Cuba. Farquhar quoted the then–Speaker of the House as saying that McKinley kept his ear so close to the ground "it was full of grasshoppers."[2] In contrast, still others note that the wily McKinley usually let others think they were driving policy when they were actually doing his bidding.

The Spanish-American War began when Cuban rebels attacked the Spanish government in Cuba, destroying American and other civilian property to provoke U.S. entry into the conflict. In response, the Spanish put Cubans into prison camps. The rebels organized a public relations offensive that exaggerated Spanish atrocities and minimized their own. Their successful appeal to anticolonial American sentiment was reflected in the American "yellow" (sensationalist) press of William Randolph Hearst and Joseph Pulitzer, which clamored for U.S. military intervention.[3]

In 1898, the Spanish empire was declining and the United States wanted to snatch pieces of it. Some authors note that McKinley did not rush to war and instead tried diplomacy for a year — offering to buy Cuba or to mediate between the two sides. The Spanish refused both of these proposals.[4] McKinley was criticized in Congress for not rushing to war after the U.S. battleship U.S.S. *Maine* blew up in Havana harbor. McKinley's slow advance to war, however, may have been a clever ruse to build public and congressional support for the coming conflict in a nation not used to such foreign adventures.

Even if he was being railroaded into a war, McKinley had the powerful means to "just say no" to a war over Cuba (after all, presidents Grant and Cleveland had done so). It had no relevance to U.S. security or the Monroe Doctrine, which did not apply to preexisting European colonial possessions.

Under steady U.S. pressure, Spain promised to close the detention camps, give amnesty to political prisoners, free U.S. citizens from Spanish jails, suspend fighting against the rebels, give Cuba self-government, and send the hard-line Spanish military commander in Cuba home to Spain.[5] McKinley could have resisted the push toward war by citing these concessions and observing that the explosion of the *Maine,* rather than being sabotage, might have been an accident, as many important Americans — including the ship's commanding officer — believed at the time and evidence has since supported.

The business community and congressional leaders initially were unenthusiastic about military intervention and feared the effects of war on a recovering economy. If McKinley didn't support them, it may have been due to worrying that William Jennings Bryan and the Democrats would play on rampant public jingoism and use a "Free Cuba" campaign to win the 1898 and 1900 elections.[6]

McKinley later maintained that Congress would have declared war on Spain without him calling for it. Thus McKinley claimed that he reluctantly, on April 25, 1898, requested war, feeling that he had done all he could to avoid conflict.[7] Yet he could have waited for Congress to declare war and then vetoed it.

McKinley had not used the year of diplomatic tensions prior to the war to make enough military preparations. The navy, however, was well prepared because of a gradual buildup and modernization stretching back to Chester Arthur's administration in the early 1880s. In 1890, the U.S. Navy was twelfth in the world; in 1900, it was sixth (after the war, McKinley greatly expanded it); and by 1906, it was second only to the British fleet. The navy disposed of the Spanish fleets in the Caribbean and Philippines handily. Unfortunately the army was too small and had to hurry unready volunteers into the fray.[8]

McKinley, who had military experience during the Civil War, was an activist commander in chief who kept in touch with his field commanders by telegraph and was not shy about interfering with their military decisions. McKinley's secretaries of state and war were incompetent, so he did the work of three men.

Fought a Precedent-Setting War

The United States, which had once been a colonial possession and traditionally and wisely had stayed out of most of the Old World's disputes, now entered the race among the Europeans and Japanese for colonies, markets, and influence abroad. After crushing the Spanish, the U.S. became a world military power for the first time and acquired Cuba, Puerto Rico, the Philippines, and even Hawaii. The Spanish-American War set the precedent for military interventions in Latin America — the U.S. sphere of influence — during the early part of the twentieth century, the U.S. interventions in World Wars I and II, and the creation of a permanent informal global empire during and after the Cold War.

At the turn of the twentieth century, European powers were carving up China, and the U.S. wanted to make sure that there was an "open door" for other nations — read: the United States. In 1900, the Boxers, revolutionaries in China, wanted to kick out all foreign colonial powers. Without a declaration of war, McKinley sent U.S. Marines to China as part of an eight-nation international "relief" mission. In reality, the United States helped suppress an indigenous movement that opposed coerced Chinese trade with the West and the U.S. open-door policy. The foreign armies conquered China's capital and made China pay a war indemnity.

Ironically, the erroneous U.S. rationale for building an empire — for example, taking the Philippines and Hawaii and helping Europeans forcibly intimidate China to keep its markets open — corresponded exactly with Lenin's crackpot theory of imperialism, which he had adopted from John Hobson, an English economist. The American imperialists and Lenin both bought into the fallacy that capitalist economies produced more than they could consume (underconsumption or overproduction) and thus needed to open overseas markets for their goods. The implication was that if they couldn't access foreign markets, their home economies would deteriorate and domestic unrest would ensue. So the United States began using its military to coerce the opening of foreign markets. Coerced trade is unethical and rarely cost-effective, given the price of developing, operating, and maintaining the large military forces required to do so. Even unilateral free trade is less costly and more efficient than coerced trade.

If long-term overproduction or under-consumption does exist in an economy, it's usually because of government intervention in the market via tariffs. When prices are artificially raised on imported goods via tariffs, domestic businesses produce excess goods, while at the same time consumers' demand for those same goods is reduced.[9] This phenomenon is another example of the government causing the problem in the first place and then using further intervention to ride to the rescue — in this case, undertaking military coercion to open markets to sell the excess goods.

McKinley's policies also laid the basis for U.S. involvement in World War I. For most of the 1800s, the U.S.'s relationship with Britain was tense, especially after British tacit support for the South during the Civil War. Britain's increasing rivalry with Germany, however, helped McKinley improve ties with the British and begin the long-standing special relationship between the two countries that endures today. That relationship helped draw the United States into two world wars. Also, the British fleet was dominant in Europe, Asia, and Africa but had to give way to growing U.S. dominance in the Western Hemisphere.

Was the First Modern President, Not Teddy Roosevelt

The modern presidency began under McKinley, who turned the White House into the powerful bully pulpit that it has become. McKinley had congressional experience and lobbied Congress heavily. He probably violated the separation of powers in the Constitution by using commissions that included members of Congress and experts to research issues and sell McKinley's policies to Congress. But he also knew that he could be very effective in going over Congress's head directly to the people. The people would then pressure their government to pass McKinley's agenda. McKinley went directly to the people by giving speeches nationwide and cultivating an excellent relationship with the media. Prior to McKinley, there was a taboo against the president speaking directly to the people, except on ceremonial occasions. But numerous routine speeches made McKinley a popular and powerful president.

Following McKinley's precedent, Teddy Roosevelt and Woodrow Wilson also launched presidential speaking tours around the nation to win support for their policies.[10] The rise of large publications, such as the Hearst and Pulitzer newspapers, as well as national wire services, created a national media market, which the president could better take advantage of than the many members of Congress who were from localized regions of the country.[11]

McKinley was able to wage war with a freer hand than even Lincoln had. At the start of the Spanish-American War, Congress passed the Volunteer Army Act, which gave the president, rather than governors, the power to appoint generals and their staffs of militia (now called National Guard) units. Because the Constitution specified that the states would choose the officers of the militia, the law was really unconstitutional. The new statute increased the president's power over the militia and eroded the states' traditional control over it.[12]

Furthermore, McKinley demanded money for the war with no congressional debate and complete freedom to spend it as he saw fit. The Congress gave McKinley carte blanche to run the war, the postwar occupation, and the counterinsurgency conflict in the Philippines.[13]

In contrast to Lincoln's increase in power solely in the military realm, McKinley expanded the role of the presidency in other areas too. Also, unlike Lincoln's increase in presidential power, which proved to be mostly temporary, McKinley's became permanent. McKinley created the institutional structure for the modern presidency. He expanded the White House staff and the size of government.

PROSPERITY

Increased Taxes and the Size of Government

McKinley increased taxes — including inheritance taxes, excise taxes, and a stamp tax on public documents (similar to the British tax that enraged the American colonists) — to fund this bigger government and the Spanish-American War. Vedder and Gallaway gave McKinley a relatively poor ranking on economic policies that promoted limited government and fought inflation — twenty-fifth out of thirty-nine presidents ranked — undoubtedly because he increased tariffs, taxes, and the size of government.

Kevin Phillips, a McKinley biographer, argues that McKinley, not Teddy Roosevelt, started progressivism. Phillips argues that although McKinley is seen as a conservative by historians, he created the political organization, the Republican cohort of political operatives that served for twenty-five years, the expert investigations, the anti-machine spirit in politics, the commitment to economic and popular democracy, the leadership while Teddy Roosevelt was still maturing, and the political realignment that made the Republicans the dominant party for thirty years.[14] In other words, Roosevelt used the tools McKinley gave him to begin enacting his progressive policies, such as trust-busting.

Used Government to Help Business

Ironically, while coercing other countries to open their markets, McKinley and the Republicans were famous for closing off U.S. markets to imports, thus restricting foreign competition for the benefit of American industry. In fact, McKinley raised tariffs shortly after taking office in 1897. Giant business combinations proliferated in the late 1890s, partly because of the higher tariff protection. McKinley didn't attempt to bust the huge trusts, but he did threaten them with prosecution and put special taxes on them.

America had become the strongest industrial power on earth. McKinley knew that the United States could not simply use its military to forcibly open all markets, so he negotiated reciprocal trade agreements with other nations. Since U.S. tariffs were not only for enhancing government revenues but also for protecting U.S. industries, he believed that they could be lowered on imports in exchange for the reduction of foreign tariffs on U.S. manufacturing exports. For

McKinley, a famous protectionist, to adopt this reciprocal trade policy was like Richard Nixon going to China.[15] Of course, unilateral free trade is the best and most efficient policy for the United States, but at least, over time, McKinley made some advances in his thinking on tariffs.

Reluctantly Put the Nation on the Gold Standard

Reluctantly putting the nation on the gold standard was McKinley's finest achievement. Early in his term, McKinley tried, without success, to negotiate a system of international currency based on gold *and* silver with Britain, France, and Germany. The purpose was to mildly inflate the money supply by adding silver to the international currency system. Britain, the dominant trading nation, had created a club of countries that adhered to the gold standard, and 80 to 90 percent of U.S. trade was with those countries. Thus, the U.S. had no choice but to be part of the club.

Although U.S. attempts to add silver to the currency system failed, world gold production, during the years of economic recovery from 1897 to 1902, increased greatly because of gold finds in the Yukon, Australia, and South Africa. According to Milton Friedman, this caused the U.S. money supply to rise 80 percent. Therefore, silver was not needed to increase the money supply, and the United States was able to go on the gold standard in 1900.

U.S. paper money was redeemed only for gold. This action ended twenty-five years of strife in the U.S. about whether the currency should be based on only gold or on gold and silver. More important, going on the gold standard created sound money with tame inflation and ended frequent drastic economic recessions. Overall, McKinley's policies created an economic boom that lasted from 1897 until 1907, long after his presidency ended (1901).[16]

LIBERTY

Suppressed Freedoms Abroad

In his request for war, McKinley listed humanitarian concerns as foremost among his reasons for the coming conflict. Ironically the Spanish-American War was supposed to have been motivated by U.S. opposition to the Spanish repression of the Cuban independence movement. Yet in the postwar Philippines, the United States responded to a Filipino guerrilla independence movement with atrocities against the Philippine people. From 1898 to 1902, about two hundred thousand Filipinos died in the colonial counterinsurgency war that followed Admiral Dewey's smashing of the Spanish fleet in Manila Bay. McKinley defended U.S. repression by saying that if the U.S. had not inserted itself into the Philippine void after defeating the Spanish, America's first colony could have fallen into less benevolent hands — such as those of Kaiser Wilhelm II's Germany.[17] With the atrocities that the U.S. military committed and the huge numbers of Filipinos who died in the counterinsurgency war, however, it is unclear whether the Wilhelmine Germans could have done any worse to the Philippines.

Before the war, few Americans had heard about the faraway Philippines, and McKinley had to search for them on a globe. McKinley was so ignorant about the Philippines that he said, "I walked the floor of the White House night after night until... it came to me... that there was nothing left for us to do but to take them all, and to educate the Filipinos, and uplift them and civilize and Christianize them."[18] The nagging fact was that most Filipinos were already Catholic. But advocates of projecting U.S naval power around the world to build an empire were less ignorant about the potential of using the Philippines as a coaling station for maritime operations around China.

As noted earlier, in 1900, a couple of years after the United States took control of the Philippines, to preserve its policy of an "open door" to coerced trade with China, the United States helped the Europeans subdue the Boxer Rebellion there.

After the U.S. military occupation ended after a year, Cuba was given independence only in name. The United States was worried about German designs on the island. Congress's Platt Amendment of 1901, which the United States coerced a Cuban constitutional convention into adopting, prohibited Cuba from impairing its "independence" by entering into a treaty with a foreign power and allowed the United States to intervene "for the preservation of Cuban independence and the maintenance of stable government."[19] Through U.S. force of arms, Cuba won its future compulsory independence from European powers, but not from America's meddling if the U.S. government didn't like what was going on in Cuba. As usual, everyone attributes such policies, which McKinley actually initiated, to the more charismatic Teddy Roosevelt. In the case of Cuba, even before Roosevelt formalized it, McKinley actually practiced the Roosevelt corollary to the Monroe Doctrine. The corollary was that the United States would intervene in the Western Hemisphere, not only to curb the influence of the European powers, but also to stabilize Latin American states that were having internal problems.

Also, the war allowed the annexation of Hawaii. The islands were in a strategic location in the middle of the Pacific Ocean; they already contained a coaling station and a repair facility for the U.S. fleet, and they were the gateway to increasing U.S. trade in the Pacific. Now that the United States was a military power with a two-ocean navy, bringing Hawaii under U.S. control before the Japanese grabbed it was regarded as important. In early 1893, Americans in Hawaii overthrew the Hawaiian monarch, and there had been a prior unsuccessful move to annex the islands to the United States. McKinley tried too. When McKinley could not muster the two-thirds vote in the Senate to ratify the treaty, he merely circumvented the Constitution and got simple majorities in each house to pass a joint resolution that made Hawaii a U.S. territory.[20]

CONCLUSION

Like James Polk and Abraham Lincoln, William McKinley used a war to greatly strengthen the presidency. And if Polk's Mexican War laid the basis for the United States becoming a transcontinental nation, McKinley's Spanish-American War began America's quest for a trans-world empire. Thus McKinley is a much more important president than the charismatic Teddy Roosevelt.

Reluctantly going on the gold standard was McKinley's only unadulterated achievement, but it was a significant one and is the only thing that prevents him from being the worst president in U.S. history. McKinley's bad precedents were monumental — planting the seeds for an eventual U.S. international empire, for an excessively strong modern presidency, and for a permanently expanded role for the federal government. McKinley is ranked lower than Lincoln because, although Lincoln became a near dictator during the Civil War and wasted many more lives in war than McKinley, the slaves were eventually freed because of Lincoln's actions and much of the larger government he instituted did not become permanent.

On a personal basis, McKinley, like Harry Truman, was a nice man and was well liked by almost everyone. Even after he was mortally wounded by an assassin, McKinley said, "Don't let them hurt him."[21] But, also similar to Truman, McKinley's policies ultimately led to the deaths of hundreds of thousands of innocent people. McKinley is number thirty-eight here.

26

THEODORE ROOSEVELT

Overrated in Accomplishments and Significance

PP&L* RANKING: 21
Category: Poor

Twenty-sixth president of the United States

Term: September 14, 1901, to March 4, 1909
Party: Republican
Born: October 27, 1858, New York, New York
Died: January 6, 1919 (age sixty), Oyster Bay,
New York
Spouse: Alice Hathaway Lee Roosevelt (first wife);
Edith Kermit Carow Roosevelt (second wife)
Alma Mater: Columbia Law School; dropped out; Harvard College
Occupation: Polymath, author, historian, conservationist,
civil servant
Religion: Dutch Reformed

Theodore Roosevelt's powerful personality and charisma often lead to an inflated assessment of his presidency. In fact, Roosevelt merely expanded, with more gusto and verve, the already-enlarged presidential powers that McKinley accrued during the Spanish-American War. Roosevelt expanded the president's role in foreign affairs, federal patronage, the mediation of disputes between labor and business, and the busting of trusts.

He also enlarged the U.S. military and engaged in at least six incidents of gunboat diplomacy, some of them risking unnecessary wars over unimportant issues or countries. He encouraged a rebellion in the Panamanian province of Colombia and supported it with U.S. military force in order to steal a swath of

---

*PP&L = Peace, Prosperity, and Liberty.

territory for a future Panama Canal. Also, Roosevelt condoned atrocities by the U.S. military in the Philippines, a U.S. colonial possession.

At a time of increasing competition and economic growth, Roosevelt fostered protectionist trade policies that helped create large industrial enterprises, while he also made at least some effort to dismember and regulate them using government power. In short, in keeping with the history of the Republican Party, Roosevelt loved a powerful government that helped big business — even when it was ostensibly regulating commerce. He also took the unprecedented step of conducting federal meddling in domestic labor–business disputes. Because Roosevelt was a big government conservative, which may be why he was admired by George W. Bush, he increased the number of government employees by a whopping 50 percent.

PEACE

Maintained a Muscular Foreign Policy

Because Roosevelt was a sickly child, had a high voice, and had a father who never served in a war, he became a lover of macho activities, such as hunting, mountain climbing, and war. During the 1912 presidential campaign, he was shot by a would-be assassin and insisted on going ahead with his planned speech while bleeding. As assistant secretary of the navy before becoming president, Roosevelt glorified war and plotted to get the United States into a war with Spain. One soldier wrote that during the Spanish-American War, Roosevelt — despite having no previous military experience — led U.S. volunteers on the charge up Kettle Hill at San Juan Heights, Cuba, "just reveling in the victory and gore."[1] Jackson Lears, a professor of cultural history at Rutgers University, ranks Roosevelt the sixth-worst president in U.S. history because he was the only president "who celebrated the regenerative effects of military violence."[2]

Roosevelt, like McKinley, believed in national greatness and a muscular foreign policy, backed by military power, which would export America's values and civilization to the world. Roosevelt continued McKinley's effort to make the United States a world military power by projecting military influence far from U.S. shores. In a sense, McKinley and Roosevelt were prototypical of what would be called "neoconservatives" during the Reagan and George W. Bush administrations. Despite their less multilateral orientation and greater concern for "national greatness," this camp is very similar to the idealistic and militaristic liberal foreign policy first practiced by Woodrow Wilson and later adopted by

Bill Clinton. Both camps, in recent times, have replaced Christian evangelism in U.S. foreign policy with the spread of a strangely more politically correct secular faith: democracy at gunpoint.

To further his muscular foreign policy, Roosevelt expanded the U.S. Army, and his shipbuilding program increased the U.S. Navy's rank from fifth in the world to second only to Britain. Roosevelt's U.S. naval expansion was rendered somewhat obsolete, however, as the British and then the Japanese began to get dreadnought battleships — ships that were a quantum leap ahead of existing U.S. naval vessels. Following this development, Roosevelt asked Congress to authorize the construction of a battleship of unlimited size and heavy armaments, which it did.

Challenged the Kaiser in Venezuela

In 1902 and 1903, the first and most dangerous episode of gunboat diplomacy during Roosevelt's presidency was a confrontation with Germany over Venezuela. Venezuela hadn't paid its debt to a British-German consortium, and the governments of those two countries threatened a naval blockade until the money was paid. Both Britain and Germany made it clear to the United States — with the Monroe Doctrine in mind — that they just wanted debt repayment and not a permanent toehold in Latin America. Roosevelt concluded that the recently signed Hay-Pauncefote Treaty with Britain (superseding the Clayton-Bulwer Treaty, which had limited British influence in Central America) meant that the British had no ulterior ambitions in the Western Hemisphere. On the other hand, Germany had said that it would consider a temporary occupation of Venezuela's ports and imposition of duties there. Roosevelt knew that the Germans had made a "temporary" acquisition of Kiauchow, China, which would last ninety-nine years.

At the time of this incident, the British and Germans had larger fleets, but the United States had local superiority in the Caribbean, with fifty-three U.S. ships compared to only twenty-nine for Britain and Germany combined. Commodore Dewey could beat the German flotilla, and Roosevelt was eager to brandish the Monroe Doctrine. The United States did large-scale naval exercises in the area of the Anglo-German blockade of Venezuela.

That blockade eventually escalated, and the offshore British-German fleet seized and sank Venezuelan gunboats and shelled Venezuela. After Roosevelt accused Germany of threatening war, the British and Germans agreed to hold talks in Washington that could be the basis for arbitration in The Hague. Eventually, the Germans compromised, joining Britain in accepting a nominal settlement, and the blockade was lifted. In keeping with his famous slogan "Speak softly and carry a big stick," Roosevelt wisely avoided crowing about Germany's capitulation.

Roosevelt had risked starting a major conflagration with Britain and Germany over the mere possibility that Germany could establish, in the worst case, a small toehold in the vast Western Hemisphere. Also, Roosevelt sent U.S. military forces on an offensive mission that could have led to war without seeking congressional approval.

Roosevelt confronted Germany again in 1904 over debt repayment owed by the Dominican Republic. This time, Germany didn't send its fleet into America's backyard, but Roosevelt ordered naval maneuvers in the area anyway and put the Dominican Republic into U.S. receivership. To ensure Latin American countries paid their debts in order to keep European powers out of the Western Hemisphere, he had U.S. officials commandeer the Dominican Republic's customs office, collect taxes, and repay the country's loans — without the consent of Congress.

Expanded the Monroe Doctrine

Roosevelt then formalized two corollaries to the Monroe Doctrine. The first was that Latin American countries could not stand behind a U.S. shield in order to avoid paying their debts, although in fact U.S. intervention in the Venezuelan dispute seemed to demonstrate that they could do just that. Thus, Roosevelt implicitly promised the Europeans that he would see that Latin American countries paid their debts, obviating any excuse for the Europeans to use debt as a pretext for intervention.

The other corollary, which vastly expanded U.S. intervention in Latin America, was that the United States would intervene in the internal affairs of any country in the Western Hemisphere to stanch any wrongdoing, instability, or weakness that could become an excuse for foreign intervention. These vague criteria meant that the United States could intervene south of the border any time Latin American nations were not following U.S. wishes. The United States didn't have to wait for a European nation to try to intervene in the Western Hemisphere.

When promulgated, the Monroe Doctrine said that the United States would stay out of European affairs if Europeans would generally stay out of the Western Hemisphere. The distortion of the original doctrine, by eventually dropping the prohibition on U.S. interventions in Europe, and an excessive U.S. sensitivity to any foreign activity in the Western Hemisphere, led to many unneeded and counterproductive U.S. interventions in Latin America. Roosevelt's expansion of the doctrine further set up the profligate U.S. interventions of the twentieth century, including those of Woodrow Wilson, who ran hog wild in the region.

Launched the Great White Fleet

Labor unions in San Francisco didn't like competition from Japanese immigrant workers, and they pressured the San Francisco Board of Education to segregate Japanese children in the public schools, which it did. The Japanese pledged to clamp down on exit permits for their citizens if San Francisco schools were reintegrated. Roosevelt persuaded the San Francisco mayor to let Japanese children back into the city's schools, but anti-immigrant rallies then commenced in the city.

In response, Japan did nothing to halt the flow of Japanese immigrants into Hawaii and even began making preparations for war with the United States. Roosevelt sent the U.S. fleet from the Atlantic to the Pacific to intimidate the Japanese — over a minor immigration and integration issue. The issue wasn't worth risking war with a great power, especially when the United States was on the wrong side of the segregation issue.

Roosevelt then decided to send the Great White Fleet, four squadrons of battleships, around the world. The Great White Fleet's voyage was more famous than the near-conflagration with Germany over Venezuela, but actually less important. Although many historians bill the voyage as the coming-out party for the U.S. as a world power, Admiral Dewey's convincing defeat of the Spanish fleet in Manila Bay in the Spanish-American War during the McKinley administration had already put the United States on the map as a military power and as a member of the imperial club. More significant than the flashy naval voyage was how it all started: in a dispute with Japan, also a potent rising power, that began in the San Francisco public schools.

When Congress balked at paying for the Great White Fleet's voyage, Roosevelt noted that he had enough money and coal to sail the fleet to the western Pacific and that it was fine if the Congress wanted to leave it there. Without consulting Congress, Roosevelt gave the fleet commander secret orders to stay in the Pacific for a time and then sail back home through the Indian Ocean and Suez Canal — all without consulting Congress. In a forerunner to George W. Bush's argument, Roosevelt erroneously claimed that the decision to sail the fleet was solely his as commander in chief.[3] The Constitution says that the Congress has the authority to regulate the armed forces and provide and maintain a navy, giving it the authority to order — or stop — any naval operation and its funding.

Stole the Panama Canal Zone

Gunboat diplomacy also resulted in one of Roosevelt's most celebrated accomplishments: stealing the Panama Canal Zone. Roosevelt began by supporting revolutionaries in Panama, which was then part of Colombia, in contravention of U.S. treaty obligations to Colombia. The treaty said that in return for railroad rights across the isthmus, the United States would defend Colombia's integrity; the United States had already defended Colombia from outside attackers and internal rebellion on many previous occasions. Roosevelt knew that the Panamanian rebels would most likely give a canal zone to the Americans for a share of any canal's profits and U.S. support for their break with Colombia.

Instead of giving the Colombians what they took to be an ultimatum, the United States could have merely stoked the competition by negotiating with Nicaragua for canal rights, which probably would have brought around the Colombians quickly. After the U.S. threats and refusal to increase the price for canal rights, however, the Colombian senate voted down a treaty providing the United States with such rights.

Roosevelt then gave the wink and nod to Frenchman Philippe Bunau-Varilla — a former chief engineer on France's failed Panama Canal digging project and a man with many investments in Panama — who got the message that if he fomented a rebellion against Colombia in Panama, Roosevelt would support him. Secretary of State John Hay told Bunau-Varilla that the United States would deploy a flotilla of ships off the isthmus. Bunau-Varilla then gave the Panamanian rebels a military strategy, a declaration of independence from Colombia, and a constitution; he even began to design a flag for them. Bunau-Varilla also gave the rebels money in exchange for being appointed their minister (ambassador) in Washington.

The U.S. military prevented Colombian forces, who arrived to put down the rebellion, from using their own railroad to get across the country. The U.S. commander then threatened the Colombian troop ship that brought the soldiers, stranding the Colombian forces that had already landed. An altercation between U.S. and Colombian forces was avoided by paying the Colombian commander off, and another ship was hired to take the Colombian soldiers home.

Roosevelt thought that rapid U.S. recognition of Panama's independence might dissuade Colombia from sending a larger force to put down the Panamanian revolt. Also, Bunau-Varilla believed that negotiations for a canal treaty would have to proceed quickly because another Panamanian delegation was already on its way to Washington to negotiate a treaty in his place. Bunau-Varilla quickly signed a treaty and presented the fait accompli to an astounded and disgusted Panamanian delegation when it arrived in the city. The Panamanians reluctantly accepted the treaty — which gave the U.S. perpetual control over a chunk of Panama that would be used to dig the canal — and the U.S. Senate ratified it.

The United States had concluded the most costly real estate deal in its history to date and was ready to sink millions of taxpayer dollars into a hugely expensive project to connect two oceans. Instead of letting another government or private interests spend money on the project, the U.S. government did it for the glory and to further its growing informal empire.

Yet even Roosevelt's advisors felt guilty about the way the Canal Zone was obtained and made sarcastic comments to that effect. Attorney General Philander Knox ribbed Roosevelt that "it would be better to keep your action free from any taint of legality." Secretary of War Elihu Root told Roosevelt, "You have shown that you were accused of seduction, and you have conclusively proved that you were guilty of rape." More seriously, former Secretary of State Richard Olney lamented, "For the first time in my life I have to confess that I am ashamed of my country." The anti-imperialists were more blunt, calling the grabbing of the canal zone a "sleek and underhanded piece of national bank robbery."[4] Years later, Senator Samuel Hayakawa summarized the U.S. acquisition of the canal zone by saying, "We stole it, fair and square."[5]

Instigated Other Gunboat Episodes

Other adventures in gunboat diplomacy were done for downright ludicrous reasons and show how truly aggressive Roosevelt was as president. In Turkey, the sultan refused to grant U.S. missionaries the same privileges that competing European missionaries received. Roosevelt sent navy ships to show the U.S. flag. The sultan quickly agreed that the unequal treatment would end.

In 1904, someone claiming to be a U.S. citizen living in Morocco was kidnapped by a man called Raisuli, who demanded a huge ransom from the sultan in charge of Morocco. Roosevelt diverted the U.S. fleet to intimidate the sultan into negotiating with Raisuli for the hostage's release. Today we would call this tactic pressuring for negotiations with a criminal or terrorist. As the negotiations went forward, the State Department learned that the kidnapped person was actually a Greek, and U.S. Secretary of State John Hay wanted Roosevelt to back off. Since Raisuli still believed the man was a U.S. citizen, however, Roosevelt believed the kidnapper was still insulting the United States and ordered yet another warning to both the sultan and Raisuli.[6]

A final episode of gunboat diplomacy involved Cuba, an island the United States had won from Spain in the Spanish-American War of 1898. Although Roosevelt should be given credit for being reluctant to act militarily and for trying to limit the ultimate incursion, he still intervened — and without Congress's prior approval.

In 1904, a treaty of "independence" for Cuba was ratified, reducing U.S. tariffs on Cuban exports in exchange for a continued U.S. military base at Guantanamo. Cuba was forced to amend its constitution in ways that gave the United States continued dominance at the expense of Cuban sovereignty. When an insurrection broke out in 1906, both sides in the conflict requested U.S. intervention. Roosevelt reluctantly sent U.S. ships and marines but tried to avoid a full-blown U.S. intervention. He pleaded with Cubans to settle their differences peacefully and sent U.S. officials to try to negotiate a cease-fire between the two sides.

When a U.S. senator reminded Roosevelt that the U.S.-Cuban treaty gave the United States, not the president, the right to intervene and demanded that Roosevelt seek congressional approval before committing U.S. troops, Roosevelt said that he would depend on Congress to set long-term policy and reserved the right to intervene in the short run. He said that he didn't summon Congress to discuss the Cuban situation because it was evolving too rapidly. He also admitted that he purposefully didn't consult Congress in order to expand the president's role in foreign affairs.

Cuban president Tomas Estrada resigned, and Roosevelt launched a full-blown U.S. intervention. U.S. troops protected the Cuban treasury and policed the towns and cities. William Howard Taft became the administrator for Cuba, and he appointed a U.S. governor for the island. The insurgents agreed to stop fighting pending elections.[7]

The U.S. Constitutional Convention made clear that the founders allowed for short-term presidential military actions without congressional approval only when the nation was defending itself from attack. In this case, the threat to U.S. security was hardly dire, and the mission was an imperial offensive to bring stability to a country in the Western Hemisphere so that foreign powers could not use instability as an excuse to get a toehold there. Thus Roosevelt's intervention without consulting Congress was clearly unconstitutional.

Tried to Whitewash Oppression in the Philippines

When Roosevelt took office, a long guerrilla war was winding down in the Philippines, another conquered area won during the Spanish-American War. Edmund Morris, a Roosevelt biographer, said this about the U.S. "liberation" of the Philippines from Spain:

> Filipinos seemed ungrateful. Rebellion had been raging on the archipelago for almost two years; [Secretary of War Elihu] Root needed a seventy-thousand man army to control it. Some measure of peace had at last been achieved.... But neither Roosevelt nor Root cared to speculate what nice, clean-cut American boys were doing to keep that peace.[8]

Root wrote a letter to Congress saying that U.S. troops were conducting themselves humanely and that atrocities were isolated. But Nelson Miles, the chief general of the army, had a report from the U.S. military governor of a Philippine province, saying that U.S. soldiers had been vicious in the villages. The report was met by a public firestorm in the United States. The Anti-Imperialist League then published the comments of a U.S. officer, who admitted that General Jacob H. Smith had ordered him to burn villages and kill all Filipinos down to the age of ten who could bear arms. The officer directly quoted General Smith's order, which stated, "The interior of Samar must be made a howling wilderness." Many witnesses came forward with stories of U.S. use of torture, including simulated drowning. Also, U.S. troops burned, whipped, and hung up Filipinos by their thumbs.

Roosevelt publicly demanded the truth from the army and punishment for the guilty, as well as a court-martial for General Jacob H. Smith. But Roosevelt had known about Smith's orders to slaughter Filipino boys — which Smith had admitted — for four months and had done nothing about it. Roosevelt and Root had allowed military commanders to end the guerrilla war in any way they could and had asked few questions.

At General Smith's court-martial, his military colleagues found him guilty only of excessive fervor and urged him to change his habits. Because Smith had condoned the slaughter of Philippine women and children, however, Roosevelt felt he had to at least cashier him from service. Smith should have been indicted for war crimes.

The Democrats called for Philippine independence, but Roosevelt refused for strategic reasons. Congressman Cordell Hull talked about the ten thousand U.S dead and wounded, the hundreds of millions of dollars wasted, the scorched Philippine territory, the slaughter of people the United States was supposedly trying to help, and the atrocities. Roosevelt answered that Americans were fighting in the Philippines to impose "orderly freedom" on the fractious nation, while keeping with rules of "just severity" sanctioned by Abraham Lincoln. The U.S. government had "liberated" and then brutally pacified the Philippines — with the counterinsurgency war causing roughly two hundred thousand Filipino deaths from atrocities, combat, disease, and starvation.

Solved Some International Disputes Peaceably

In 1905, Roosevelt mediated both the Russo-Japanese War in East Asia and the European competition over Morocco. One could argue that the United States should stay out of mediating disputes among other nations, especially great powers. If such mild intercession can avoid a large war in which the United States could get enmeshed, however, it is probably acceptable to do so. Roosevelt was probably justified in mediating both of these disputes.

The Russians had occupied Manchuria and had a lust for Korea, too. Japan could not let this stand and smashed the Russian fleet at Port Arthur in 1904. Despite the fact that Japan was winning the war, the Japanese approached the United States, which had declared its neutrality, to mediate a peace conference. Roosevelt's proposed terms to resolve the crisis were incorporated into the Treaty of Portsmouth, which ended the war. Ironically, the jingoistic, bellicose, and imperial Roosevelt won the Nobel Prize in 1906 for these peacemaking efforts.

The downside of Roosevelt's peacemaking efforts was a stamp of approval for a Japanese sphere of influence in East Asia[9] — an outcome, however, that was probably inevitable given Japan's rising power. When the Japanese attempted to establish their protectorate over Korea, the Koreans tried to invoke an 1882 treaty with the United States to save them from Japan. But Roosevelt wisely avoided a risky confrontation with Japan over this issue.[10]

Roosevelt also avoided getting dragged into the European conflict over Morocco. Rather, he helped settle a dispute that could have triggered World War I nine years earlier, when Germany was at the height of its power. Germany's Kaiser Wilhelm II hoped to join with the United States and force France to abandon its monopoly trading position in Morocco and create an open-door trading policy in North Africa. Roosevelt said he wouldn't agree to any international meeting on Morocco without French approval. At the Algeciras Conference in Spain, Roosevelt proposed a compromise that allowed the kaiser to back down while saving face.[11]

Roosevelt was also willing to submit U.S. disputes for international settlement. The United States and Mexico were the first countries to submit a legal disagreement to The Hague for settlement. Later, the United States and Britain submitted a border dispute to a neutral international panel for resolution.

In-house, Secretary of War Elihu Root conducted a much-needed reform of the U.S. military command structure to establish more civilian control. At the time, the top general commanded and the secretary of war administered the army, and they were essentially equals. Root's reform created a vertical structure, with the secretary in charge; promoted military personnel on merit rather than seniority; and eliminated the commanding general's position, instead establishing an army general staff, with the army chief of staff at its head and under the secretary.[12]

Expanded Presidential Powers

Ignoring the founders' intent at the Constitutional Convention, Roosevelt believed that the president's power "is limited only by specific restrictions and prohibitions appearing in the Constitution or imposed by the Congress under its Constitutional powers."[13] Roosevelt's repeated efforts to expand presidential power contradicted the spirit of the Tenth Amendment to the Constitution, which states that powers not specifically delegated to the federal government, nor prohibited to the states, are reserved for the states or the people. This strict limiting of federal authority to what the Constitution specifically enumerates clearly applies to the powers of the executive branch, which the founders meant to play second fiddle to the people's branch — the legislature.

After breaking away from a constitutional monarchy, the founders clearly would not have accepted Roosevelt's basic assertion that if the Constitution did not prohibit the president from doing something, he could do it. The founders would have feared that this interpretation would have meant an unlimited and unacceptable expansion of executive power. In fact, they did not intend for the chief executive to add to the rather short list of specific presidential powers mentioned in the document. Joe Cannon, the Republican speaker of the house who was frequently at odds with Roosevelt, best summed up Roosevelt's disregard for the founders' intent when he said that Roosevelt had "no more use for the Constitution than a tomcat has for a marriage license."

PROSPERITY

Developed "Progressive" Policies That Were Harmful to the Country

Roosevelt came into office when the progressive movement was in full force. The Progressives wanted to increase government regulation of business, claiming that this would help consumers and workers. In the end, government intervention into the marketplace mainly helped the industrialists who were being regulated.[14] Since Roosevelt's time, public-choice theory has done much to debunk the idea that government can act to balance big business. The theory basically says that rich businesses are better organized politically than the average consumer, worker, or taxpayer and can use government intervention to further increase their wealth by restricting competitors, obtaining government subsidies, or getting preferential tax treatment. Thus, counterintuitively, consumers, workers, and taxpayers are better off with a marketplace unfettered by government involvement. Thomas Jefferson realized this truth when the republic was young and before he became president. Alexander Hamilton, his nemesis, believed that the government should help business. In American history, Jefferson's conception largely defeated Hamilton's up until the twentieth century.

Roosevelt, a progressive Republican and an advocate of aggressively using government power, may have, in some instances, even believed that he was curbing the power of big business[15] when the effects of his policies had the opposite effect. For example, Upton Sinclair's novel *The Jungle*, which highlighted unsanitary conditions in Chicago's meatpacking houses, enabled Roosevelt to regulate the food industry. U.S. meatpackers actually wanted federal meat inspection because European countries were banning the importation of American meats due to insufficient U.S. government regulation. Also, other large firms and trade associations that were to be regulated — such as the Brewers Association and the Wholesale and Retail Grocers' Association — were big supporters of Roosevelt's Pure Food and Drug Act of 1906.[16]

Big business also wanted to create a department of commerce and labor to replace a myriad of state regulations with uniform national regulations. Roosevelt envisioned a cooperative rather than an adversarial relationship between government and business. Legislation authorized a new Bureau of Corporations. Roosevelt named James R. Garfield, the son of President James Garfield and a friend of business, to be the chief of the new bureau, but Roosevelt directly controlled the office. Garfield's proposal to federally license corporations was popular with big business because it was thought to limit state regulation.[17] Also, it was a way for businesses to limit competition. Corporate disclosure of accounting data to the Bureau of Corporations — for government monitoring of firms — was voluntary. Roosevelt had discretion over publication of the data and thought that he might curb trusts by publicizing such information.

Roosevelt was the first president to endorse an antitrust program, but it was modest and discretionary. His policy for controlling trusts was tolerance, mild regulation, and making public their accounting data. To some extent, to satisfy public pressure, he was creating only the facade of going after the trusts. Yet Roosevelt set a bad precedent that would ultimately get the government more actively involved in the economically counterproductive trust-busting business. Instead of increasing competition, antitrust laws usually allow politically well-connected companies to break up or keep out large potential competitors from a particular market.

Taking over after McKinley was assassinated, Roosevelt was slow to bust the large-business trusts. After his record landslide election over Alton Parker, winning a full term in 1904, Roosevelt was very popular and also had a bipartisan progressive majority in the House that was pro-regulation. So he stepped up his "assault" on business.

Even before Andrew Carnegie created the biggest trust of the time by combining ten steel companies, big-business trusts accounted for 65 percent of the nation's wealth. Presidents Grover Cleveland, Benjamin Harrison, and William McKinley had thought that combining firms was a natural economic phenomenon. They sued the trusts to some extent, but not voluntarily and not with Roosevelt's zeal. Although Roosevelt has been called the preeminent "trust buster," William Howard Taft, his successor, prosecuted twice as many trusts in his one term as Roosevelt did in almost two full terms.[18]

Even Roosevelt had to admit that the economy did better and ran more efficiently when big business operated most of it. For example, because of the giant Standard Oil's operations, the price of kerosene had been declining for thirty years. As Roosevelt began to regulate trusts, the trend toward industrial combination was slowing and competition and the economy were flourishing — making the need to regulate trusts questionable.

Also, with the advance of technology, the development of substitute products, and overseas competition, the market usually eventually eliminates monopolies. In contrast, the government is often responsible for fostering industrial concentration. Typical of inconsistent government policy, Roosevelt was prosecuting trusts at the same time that he and his party advocated high tariffs, which impeded foreign competition and helped foster the larger trusts he was trying to break up. Roosevelt once hinted at tariff reduction but backed off in the face of objections from conservative Republicans.

In the Northern Securities Company railroad trust case, the Supreme Court ruled for the government by a non-precedent-setting five-to-four vote. The decision affirmed national control of business, broke up the world's second-largest trust, and gave Roosevelt his inflated reputation as a trust buster. Roosevelt knew, however, that he could not restrain the growth of industrial combinations via slow prosecutions under the Sherman Antitrust Act. Therefore Roosevelt wanted, and Congress passed, the Expedition Act, which gave the government the power to obtain faster antitrust trials and provided public monies for such prosecutions.

As with anything the government does, politics and favoritism crept into Roosevelt's trust busting. For example, Roosevelt prosecuted trusts in the sugar, beef, coal, and railroad industries, but not in the steel industry. Yet the steel industry's trust was even bigger than the Northern Securities railroad trust. Roosevelt reached gentlemen's agreements with both U.S. Steel and International Harvester, which were given preferential treatment and allowed to open their books. Then only Roosevelt would make the decision on whether the government would pursue antitrust proceedings against the two companies.

In 1903, Roosevelt asked for, and Congress enacted, the Elkins Act, banning railroad rebates to large industrial companies. Under the act, railroad companies, in charging for their services, could not stray from the published rate schedule. Roosevelt believed such rebates were price discrimination against smaller companies that also used the railroads. Economists would say, however, that price discrimination is a standard business practice — for example, even the small guy gets discounts for buying in bulk. More philosophically, don't businesses have a right to charge a particular customer anything they want? Roosevelt prosecuted John D. Rockefeller's Standard Oil Company for violating the anti-rebate law.

Roosevelt went overboard on regulating railroads. Because he believed that the Sherman Antitrust Act and the Elkins anti-rebate bill were insufficient, he wanted to use the Interstate Commerce Commission (ICC) to regulate railroad rates. This regulation interfered with the ability of businesses to set their own prices in the marketplace; Roosevelt felt the ICC should be able to set maximum rates to be charged when the market rates were unfair. Of course, government determination of what is unfair is subjective and arbitrary.

In 1906, the Hepburn Act gave the ICC the power to set "just and reasonable" rates.[19] It was the most important piece of domestic legislation during Roosevelt's tenure because of its far-reaching interference in the marketplace. The Hepburn Act, when combined with other government regulations, blocked rate increases that the rail companies needed to make and led to the eventual collapse of the system of privately owned railroads in the United States.

Jitters over a potentially bad future business environment created by Roosevelt's prosecution of the Northern Securities antitrust case contributed to a crash on Wall Street in 1903. Roosevelt thought that the government should intervene to help with the crisis, but Congress's Joe Cannon rejected the idea because he correctly believed that a turbocharged market needed a slump to move back to equilibrium. Similarly, excessive railroad regulation in 1906 contributed heavily to a depression and stock market panic in 1907.

J. P. Morgan, a rich banker, raised funds from the heads of America's wealthy corporations to bail out certain failing trusts, New York City, and the New York Stock Exchange, which was in danger of closing. Secretary of the Treasury George Cortelyou also provided assistance by depositing public funds in banks and floating government bond issues. Cortelyou's initiative preempted additional large contributions from large private financiers. Despite their help in the economic crisis, Roosevelt kept up his wildly popular rhetoric against Wall Street financiers — at one point calling them "criminals of great wealth."

In 1908, Roosevelt erroneously believed that the tumble of railroad stocks and the panic of 1907 were caused by the insufficiency of the Hepburn Act to regulate railroad rates, not by its passage in the first place. He proposed a debilitating expansion of the ICC's powers to full financial supervision of the railroads, physical control of interstate railroad operations, and even the scheduling of rail deliveries.[20]

These episodes are classic examples of disastrous effects of government intervention creating a crisis and thus a demand for even more government action. This strange and debilitating cycle has happened many times in American history.

Established National Parks

Roosevelt is also known for placing 230 million acres of land into public trust. He often used unconstitutional executive orders, sometimes against the congressional will, to create numerous national monuments, parks, forests, bird refuges, and game preserves from this acreage.[21] For example, in 1907, Congress passed legislation that would have prevented Roosevelt from creating parks or wilderness areas in six western states. Before signing the measure, Roosevelt flouted the congressional will by issuing executive orders, with no statutory basis, that created and expanded forest reserves in those states.[22]

In 1902, Roosevelt got the National Reclamation Act passed. The act was a scheme to irrigate arid lands — one-third of U.S. territory — and then sell the land, deposit- and interest-free, to small ranchers and farmers. They would then pay back the government with earnings from their crops. Congress then enacted unenforceable public land laws, allowing a water monopoly to take hold in the American West. In effect, this scheme irrigated speculative tracts of land at the expense of established communities.[23] The program resulted in virtually all of the West's rivers being dammed up. Roosevelt, in effect, subsidized western farmers and ranchers — mainly Republican constituents — living on marginal lands. People usually assume that government involvement will improve the environment. This program is an example of conservation going awry. Before the government got involved on a massive scale, private and local irrigation projects had been successful.

LIBERTY

Set Precedents for Federal Coercion

Roosevelt set precedents for government meddling in disputes between private business and labor. In 1902, the United Mine Workers union went on strike against the anthracite (hard) coal industry. Violence erupted in Pennsylvania, but the governor said that no federal assistance was needed. Although Roosevelt admitted that he had no "right or duty to intervene in this way upon legal grounds," politics made him enter the dispute.

Fearing that, because of high coal prices, the Democrats could win New England in that year's election, Roosevelt set a precedent by being the first president to mediate between labor and business when he called both parties to Washington. Then, despite a constitutional requirement that a governor must request federal military assistance, Roosevelt threatened the union leader with use of the army to stop any future violence. Going even further, Roosevelt gave orders to an army general to be ready to use force to halt the strike, throw out the coal operators, and seize and operate the mines.

A shocked James E. Watson, the House Republican whip, asked, "What about the Constitution of the United States? What about seizing private property without due process of law?" Roosevelt became so agitated that he clutched

Watson's shoulder and yelled, "The Constitution was made for the people and not the people for the Constitution."[24] In reality, Roosevelt was remaking the Constitution for his own ends. In the end, his coerced mediation was better than Grover Cleveland's blunt use of force against strikers, but it set a precedent for the federal government's involvement in a new realm — using intimidation to mediate labor disputes.

Roosevelt's threat of force was good politics for the 1904 presidential election. J. P. Morgan bailed out Roosevelt, not for the last time, and came up with an agreement for Roosevelt to establish a coal strike commission that settled the strike. Letting the coal market eventually settle the strike without threats of force would not have been as wildly popular and would not have portrayed Roosevelt as a decisive and activist leader in his bid to win a full term on his own in 1904.

Roosevelt's authoritarian instincts were not limited to using intimidation in labor disputes. Rumors swirled that Roosevelt had been using the Secret Service to gather intelligence on political opponents and to harass opposition politicians. There was some substance to these accusations. Senator Joseph Foraker purportedly had a "journalist" spying on him, and his mail was opened. Also arousing suspicions was Roosevelt's opposition when Congress wanted to restrict the Secret Service's role to guarding the president and investigating counterfeit money. Eventually, Roosevelt created the Federal Bureau of Investigation in 1908; it is questionable whether the founders envisioned a powerful federal investigative agency that usurped the authority of state and local law enforcement.

Had a Mixed Record on Race Relations

Roosevelt's record on race relations and civil rights was mixed at best. He took small symbolic actions, but then retreated under public pressure. In one instance, Roosevelt actually was guilty of persecuting blacks.

Roosevelt believed that African Americans were inferior to whites because of blacks' "natural limitations." But Roosevelt infuriated the South by inviting Booker T. Washington — a prominent black author, educator, and political figure — to the White House for dinner. With this action, Roosevelt became the first president to entertain an African American at the White House. Yet after the tempest over Booker T. Washington's White House dinner, Roosevelt snubbed him at a Yale graduation ceremony.

Roosevelt's most atrocious act in race relations was requiring black soldiers to prove their innocence to avoid dishonorable discharges from the military for allegedly shooting up Brownsville, Texas, and killing one man and injuring another. The consensus among the press was that the government's case against the black soldiers was weak and that the only evidence found seemed to show that they had been framed. Yet in contradiction to the American tradition of innocence until proof of guilt, Roosevelt said that if none of the African American soldiers admitted to shooting up the town, they would all be assumed guilty and dishonorably discharged. None did, and he discharged them.

Trying to smother a Senate debate and investigation of whether he exceeded his authority by firing the soldiers, Roosevelt agreed to reinstate any soldier who could prove his innocence. Roosevelt admitted that many innocent soldiers had been labeled as criminals by their dishonorable discharges, yet he stuck by his unfair decision, and the Senate Committee on Military Affairs said that he had justifiably discharged the soldiers. Needless to say, after this travesty of justice, Roosevelt's popularity in the black community sank like a rock.[25]

CONCLUSION

The charismatic Theodore Roosevelt was a less important president than William McKinley, and his performance has been vastly overrated. Roosevelt's continuation of McKinley's expanded use of military power abroad, and the con-comitant unconstitutional augmentation of presidential power at home, make Roosevelt a poor president. Keeping Roosevelt out of the bad category of pres-idents was his avoidance of a major war, despite his aggressive use of threats overseas; his mediation of international disputes that could have turned into global wars; and his assertion of civilian control over the military. Unfortu-nately, he took the United States farther down the road to a mixed capitalist economy and away from the laissez-faire system that had served the United States so well and built the world's largest and most dynamic economy. Thus Vedder and Gallaway rank Roosevelt twenty-third out of thirty-nine presidents ranked on policies promoting limited government and fighting inflation — not a good score.

Although the positive side of the ledger is much smaller than the negative side for Roosevelt's presidency, he did do a few good things during his seven-and-a-half years as president. Most important, he decided to count his three-and-a-half years spent filling in for the assassinated McKinley as a full term and did not seek the Republican nomination for an unprecedented third term in the 1908 election. However, four years later, after William Howard Taft's presidency, he changed his mind and ran as a candidate for the Progressive, or Bull Moose, third party. The good news for the country was that, stripped of a major party label, Roosevelt did not win an unprecedented third term. The bad news was that Roosevelt's third-party candidacy split the Republican vote, leading to the election of Woodrow Wilson, the worst president in U.S. history. Theodore Roosevelt comes in at number twenty-one.

27

WILLIAM HOWARD TAFT

Not a Hefty Policy Innovator

PP&L* RANKING: 20
Category: Poor

Twenty-seventh president of the United States

Term: March 4, 1909, to March 4, 1913
Party: Republican
Born: September 15, 1857, Cincinnati, Ohio
Died: March 8, 1930 (age seventy-two),
　　　　 Washington, D.C.
Spouse: Helen Herron Taft
Alma Mater: Yale University, University of Cincinnati
Occupation: Lawyer, jurist
Religion: Unitarian

William Howard Taft was the largest president, weighing in at 332 pounds at the time of his inauguration. Taft was so heavy and lethargic that he fell asleep almost anywhere — even at state funerals and White House dinners. Before becoming president, when he was governor general of the new U.S. colony in the Philippines, he sent a telegram to Secretary of War Elihu Root, saying, "Took a long horseback ride today; feeling fine." Root cabled back: "How is the horse?"[1]

Taft was not, however, a heavyweight in policy innovation. During his term, Progressives regarded Taft as a post–Teddy Roosevelt conservative disappointment, but he generally continued, consolidated, and codified his mentor's activist policies. This mythical laissez-faire image of Taft's presidency has continued to this day. In this volume, Taft gets a slightly higher ranking than Roosevelt because he was less bellicose in foreign policy and somewhat less active in most other policy areas.

---

*PP&L = Peace, Prosperity, and Liberty.

Nevertheless, he won the passage of a constitutional amendment that allowed an income tax and initiated a large number of antitrust lawsuits, among other ill-advised initiatives, to regulate business.

PEACE

Projected U.S. Influence: Less Military Power and More Dollar Diplomacy

Although Taft was less aggressive in foreign policy than Teddy Roosevelt, in 1912 alone he intervened in Cuba, Nicaragua, and the Dominican Republic. Taft was naively blatant in imitating what McKinley and Roosevelt had done — using U.S. diplomacy to champion business overseas. This policy was called "dollar diplomacy." Conversely, Taft also tried to use U.S. businesses to foster U.S. diplomatic objectives. For example, to reduce Japanese influence in China, Taft proposed that U.S. bankers finance railway construction in the Middle Kingdom (China). The blatantly neomercantilist dollar diplomacy backfired and brought criticism from Democrats, liberal Republicans, and nationalists.[2] The U.S. government should be reluctant to mess with the neutral market — that is, to regulate, subsidize, help, or enlist the help of business for its own purposes.

In positive actions, Taft tried to create an international framework in which countries could arbitrate disputes that otherwise might lead to war. In 1911, he signed treaties with France and Britain that would take any future disagreements with those countries to an international body, such as The Hague Court of Arbitration. In the Senate debate on ratification of the treaties, however, Republican senators attached reservations that allowed the Senate to approve of whether the president could submit a particular dispute for international arbitration.[3] Exhibiting perhaps too much intransigence, Taft then rejected the treaties. The Senate was just exercising its constitutional right to share authority in foreign policy matters.

PROSPERITY

Was a Surreptitious Economic Activist

The years of the Taft presidency (early 1909 to early 1913) saw a steady recovery from the Roosevelt-induced economic panic of 1907. Although Taft's policies were about as progressive as Roosevelt's, his reputation was one of a quiet conservative, which did not scare the business community into panics, as did Roosevelt's bombastic verbal attacks on wealthy capitalists in 1903 and 1907. Nevertheless, Taft's activism produced some far-reaching negative results.

Reinstated the Income Tax and Approved High Tariffs

The worst thing that Taft did was to propose, and get enacted, the Sixteenth Amendment, which allowed the reinstitution of the income tax. The tax was first introduced during the Lincoln administration, in an effort to finance the Civil War. The tax was abolished afterward, then reinstated by Grover Cleveland, and then found to be unconstitutional. The Sixteenth Amendment was not fully ratified until 1913, and it took effect during the Wilson administration. Taft is not docked as much for the tax as he could have been because he did not set the precedent for it — Lincoln did. Significantly, however, Taft did overcome the tax's unconstitutionality by amending the Constitution.

The income tax is especially pernicious for two reasons. The first is that this type of tax penalizes people for being successful and earning money, whether directly or through interest or dividends. Instead, especially in the modern era of profligate consumption, the federal government should probably tax such spending. Second, the income tax requires taxpayers to open their entire lives to the government to make sure that they are not hiding income. The taxpayer must submit detailed information to the large Treasury Department bureaucracy, which audits the information and enforces the tax. This information is regularly shared with law enforcement agencies, thus violating the privacy of U.S. citizens.

Because the income tax is currently so complex, vested interests can get hidden tax breaks, and the government can charge exorbitant taxes without protest from the victims, especially when taxpayers never see some of the income because it is now withheld in advance by the government. The income tax has become so convoluted that some taxpayers have trouble filling out the forms, and others cannot discern what the forms actually mean in terms of tax policy. All of these problems are lessened with a sales or consumption tax, which you simply pay when buying something at the store. Thus, Taft's constitutional amendment has had many deleterious effects.

Taft also levied a 2 percent tax on non-bank corporations, which helped not only to reduce the federal deficit but also to offset revenue losses from his proposed tariff reductions. Lowering tariffs was not part of the historical position of Republicans, including his mentor Teddy Roosevelt. Taft acted principally to lower tariffs with the United States' Philippine colony in order to help it economically.[4] But Taft's good intentions on tariffs were not very deep. When the Republican Congress passed the Payne-Aldrich Act, which actually kept tariffs high, Taft signed it.[5] So America got the worst of both worlds: new taxes and high protectionist tariffs.

Was Aggressive in Antitrust Policies and Business Regulation

Taft actually outdid the progressive Roosevelt in the important area of antitrust initiatives. Although Roosevelt developed the first government antitrust policy and has been labeled by historians as the "trust buster," Taft initiated almost double the number of antitrust suits against businesses in his one four-year term as Roosevelt did in his almost two terms. Also, Taft brought the dissolution suit, the broadest single antitrust initiative, which affected more than one hundred companies. Even Roosevelt thought this action was excessive. Taft's antitrust policy, however, was fairer and conformed more to the rule of law than Roosevelt's inconsistent and arbitrary prosecuting of certain trusts while leaving others alone.

Taft increased other regulations on business as well. He strengthened the Interstate Commerce Commission's regulatory powers by signing the Mann-Elkins Act of 1910, which allowed the ICC to regulate the communications sector and gave it greater power to regulate transportation rates. In addition, Taft gave the Department of Labor cabinet rank, to further meddle in labor relations. Setting up this new bureaucracy was a natural outgrowth of Roosevelt's unprecedented and unconstitutional heavy-handed intervention in business–labor disputes.

Taft withdrew almost as many acres of land from commerce for conservation as Roosevelt had. Unlike Roosevelt, however, he did not sneak around Congress using executive orders but instead obtained the legislative body's approval for the withdrawals.[6]

Increased Presidential Power and Tried to Consolidate the Executive Budget

In general, Taft, like Roosevelt, took the self-serving stance of many modern presidents — that a strong presidency is good for the country — but even he was troubled by Roosevelt's energetic use of executive power. In the election of 1912, in which Republican incumbent Taft ran against Democrat Woodrow Wilson and the Progressive former president, Taft assailed Roosevelt for undermining the Constitution with his alarmingly militant views of executive power:

"I have got to win, not for myself, but to prevent this attack on the indepen-dence of the judiciary and to prevent the triumph of a dangerous demagogue." This strong statement reflects the falling out between mentor and protégé, which had led an infuriated Roosevelt to run as a third-party candidate in order to (successfully) deny Taft a second term.

Yet despite Taft's anti-Roosevelt rhetoric, he tried to augment presidential power vis-à-vis Congress by trying to create a consolidated executive budget for the entire government.[7] In those days, congressional committees had more control over federal spending by the executive branch because they dealt with each executive agency individually. A consolidated executive budget might have been needed to see the totality of government expenditures. The creation of a consolidated budget, however, ultimately contributed further to the trend since William McKinley of increasing presidential power vis-à-vis Congress, which the Constitution never intended. House Speaker Joe Cannon, who regarded the congressional responsibility for spending as a firebreak against executive authority, stopped Taft's attempt to get authority for a consolidated executive budget. Warren Harding later got this authority.

In another move that promised to strengthen executive power, Taft proposed clearly unconstitutional legislation that would have given cabinet members a nonvoting seat in each house of Congress so that they could have involved them-selves in congressional debate in their areas of jurisdiction.[8] The nation's founders, by creating the Constitution's separation of powers, categorically rejected and broke free from the parliamentary model, which commingles the executive and legislative functions by allowing members of parliament to serve in the cabinet.

Continuing the democratization of the republic, which had been going on since the time of Andrew Jackson, and weakening the power of state govern-ments vis-à-vis the federal government, the Congress passed the Seventeenth Amendment, authorizing the residents of each state to directly elect U.S. sen-ators instead of having them be selected by state legislatures. By the Civil War, the vast majority of states had passed legislation providing for such direct election, but this much later constitutional amendment made it universal.

LIBERTY

Made Transparent Campaign Contributions

Taft's income tax amendment increased the government's ability to snoop into the private affairs of its citizens, but he also made a good move in the area of private citizen rights. Taft proposed and got enacted the Publicity Act, which allowed the public to examine records of donors to campaigns for public candidates to the House of Representatives. Enacting sunshine laws is a much better approach to keeping campaigns aboveboard than regulating campaign contributions, as the recent McCain-Feingold law does. Modern laws limiting contributions are frequently evaded, distort the funding of campaigns, and usually work to the advantage of the incumbents who write them. Contribution limits work to the detriment of challengers, who need more money to compete with the advantages of incumbents. Taft took the right approach by requiring the illumination of such contributions to the public and media, which helped to fight corruption and backroom dealing.

CONCLUSION

Despite the myth that Taft took a laissez-faire approach to economic policy, he actually continued Roosevelt's interventionist antitrust, environmental, and dollar-diplomacy policies. He also permanently reinstated the intrusive and pernicious income tax. Thus, Vedder and Gallaway correctly rank Taft twenty-fourth out of thirty-nine presidents ranked on promoting limited government and fighting inflation. They rank Teddy Roosevelt only slightly better — twenty-third out of thirty-nine presidents ranked.

In this volume, however, William Taft, who is ranked twentieth out of forty presidents, scores slightly better than Roosevelt, who is ranked twenty-first, both of them being in the category of poor presidents. Taft presided over prosperity, was much less bellicose in foreign policy than Roosevelt, and was less of a policy innovator than his mentor in the antitrust, environmental, and dollar-diplomacy areas. Taft was the only president to later become the chief justice of the Supreme Court, a position he enjoyed more and was better at than being chief executive.

28

WOODROW WILSON

Made the World Safe for War, Autocracy, and Colonialism

PP&L* RANKING: 41
Category: Bad

Twenty-eighth president of the United States

Term: March 4, 1913, to March 4, 1921
Party: Democratic
Born: December 28, 1856, Staunton, Virginia
Died: February 3, 1924 (age sixty-seven),
　　　Washington, D.C.

Spouse: Ellen Axson Wilson (first wife); Edith Galt Wilson
　　(second wife)
Alma Mater: Princeton, University of Virginia
Occupation: Academic (political scientist), lawyer
Religion: Presbyterian

World War I was the single most important event of the twentieth century and only appeared to be a victory for the United States.[1] Woodrow Wilson entangled the United States in the war, which altered its likely outcome, and made missteps at the Paris Peace Conference; thus, he helped indirectly cause the Russian revolution, the even more cataclysmic next World War II, and eventually the Cold War with the Soviet Union. In these and other actions, Wilson took the U.S. down the road to an informal overseas empire in the twentieth century. Therefore, in foreign policy, he was the most influential U.S. president during that century.

"Wilsonianism," derived from many U.S. Christian missionaries proselytizing overseas, made the promotion of American ideals overseas the focus of U.S.

---

foreign policy. In other words, selling secular American values — read: democracy — overseas was substituted for peddling Christianity abroad. In addition, ironically, Wilson, like his Republican predecessors, believed in the crackpot Leninist view that capitalist economies needed to enlarge markets overseas for their expanding industries — by using force, if necessary — or face economic stagnation and social unrest at home.[2] Wilson's liberal imperialism was applied especially to Latin America, where he wanted to "teach the South American republics to elect good men."

Even before World War I, however, Wilson had dramatically changed the Democratic Party from a Jeffersonian party of small government and military restraint overseas into a party of big government and profligate armed intervention abroad. The war also allowed Wilson to engineer an unprecedented government takeover of the domestic U.S. economy — a model that was later repeated during other crises, such as the Great Depression and World War II.[3] Although the beginnings of big government in the U.S. occurred in the Lincoln administration during the Civil War, in the McKinley administration during the Spanish-American War and in Teddy Roosevelt's terms in its aftermath, the father of the permanent big government is Wilson, not FDR.[4]

As a graduate student, Wilson wrote a widely known book called *Congressional Government*, which derided the president's traditionally constricted role and Congress's dominance in government. He instead praised the parliamentary model, in which the prime minister had more power.[5] When in office, Wilson practiced what he preached and made the executive more powerful. He believed the president should act like a prime minister and propose legislation to the Congress. He and LBJ may have been the most effective "legislative" presidents in history. The long road toward an imperial presidency, which Wilson helped pioneer, has worried many historians and political scientists because it has permanently distorted the balance of power between branches of government as envisioned in the Constitution.

PEACE

Decided to Enter World War I

In 1916, Wilson ran for reelection on the slogan, "He kept us out of war," but in April 1917, shortly after his narrow reelection and second inauguration, he asked Congress to declare war on Germany.[6]

The United States had little strategic stake in the outcome of the ongoing war in Europe. U.S. territory was not threatened by an attack from Germany or the weak empires of the Austro-Hungarians or the Ottomans. Those armies were tied down on the European continent by Allied armies on the eastern (Russia) and western (England and France) fronts. Colonel Edward House, Wilson's closest advisor, thought that if Germany gained control over Europe, it could challenge Britain and its benevolent command of the seas, which he believed was responsible for the security the United States enjoyed.[7] The problem with this line of reasoning was that up until the very late 1800s, British power, on land and at sea, had not been benevolent to the United States and sometimes had posed a security threat. Thus, U.S. security depended more on its vast distance from Europe than on an unchallenged British fleet. Instead of getting involved in World War I, the United States could have further built up its fleet to promote security.

At any rate, this fear is more applicable to Nazi Germany's rapid conquests in World War II than to the stalemated battlefield that Wilson saw in April 1917 when he asked for a declaration of war. Even if Germany had won World War I, it would have been by a fifteen-round decision rather than by a knockout. Both sides would have been exhausted from more than four years of unprecedented carnage. The likely negotiated settlement would have shifted borders only somewhat in the victor's favor — as they had in so many other European wars that the U.S. had avoided. In sum, as British historian Niall Ferguson has pointed out, German domination of Central Europe eventually occurred anyway — as German preeminence in the modern-day European Union shows — but it would have occurred at a far lower cost if it had been allowed to begin in 1918.[8]

In fact, as early as December 1916, the Germans desired peace talks, while wanting to keep the land they occupied in Belgium and France. But because Britain and France expected that U.S. entry into the war was likely and would turn the tide in their favor, they rejected this settlement. If the United States had stayed out, the French and British would have been forced to take this settlement and end the war.[9]

Chose Sides Early

The U.S. government was on Britain's side long before the U.S. officially entered the war. As early as 1915, two years before U.S. entry into a war that had been going on since 1914, Colonel Edward House, Wilson's alter ego, assured France and Britain that the United States would not allow them to lose the war.

With the advent of World War I, Britain became more of a market for American loans and goods, giving the United States an interest in a British victory over Germany. The United States could not have expected Germany to treat the United States as neutral when it was shipping large quantities of war materiel to German enemies.[10] Eventually, Germany, realizing that the United States would enter the war on the British, French, and Russian side, resumed unrestricted submarine warfare in an attempt to knock England out of the war before the United States entered. That resumption, in early February 1917, was a major spark that eventually triggered U.S. entry into the war.[11]

The Zimmerman telegram, released by Wilson in early March 1917, was a secret diplomatic cable from the German Foreign Minister Arthur Zimmerman to his ambassador in Mexico, which the British had intercepted. The ambassador was instructed to offer Mexico financial assistance and the return of the American Southwest if — should the U.S. declare war on Germany — Mexico went to war with the United States. The Mexican leader maintained that the Germans never actually offered this deal and thus that Mexico didn't respond to Zimmerman.[12] In any event, Mexico was selling the British navy most of its oil and so had little incentive to take Germany up on any such offer.

Even the telegram did not convince most Americans that war with Germany was needed, and Congress still refused to approve the arming of U.S. merchant ships. After his second inauguration, Wilson then took the step of ordering that merchant ships be armed anyway,[13] which usurped Congress's constitutional power "to provide and maintain a navy." After the Germans sank three armed U.S. merchant ships with no warning on March 18, 1917, Wilson asked for a declaration of war on Germany on April 1, 1917.[14]

As in the War of 1812, however, both sides in the European war had violated U.S. neutrality, but the U.S. chose to go to war with only one side — in this case, Germany. In contrast to his admonition to Americans staying in Mexico during its civil war that they did so at their own risk, Wilson astonishingly maintained — against the advice of Secretary of State William Jennings Bryan and in the wake of his resignation over the issue — that U.S. citizens had the right to travel on armed merchant ships of belligerent nations (England) through the European war zone around Britain.[15] When a German U-boat torpedoed and sank the armed British ship *Lusitania*, transporting arms and ammunition in its hold, America and Wilson were outraged at the killing of 128 Americans riding aboard. Wilson maintained that U-boats should surface before attacking and warn such ships that they were about to be attacked. Of course, this demand was not neutral because U-boats on the surface are very vulnerable to attack, and British merchant ships were under orders to ram any U-boat that surfaced to give warning. Needless to say, the Germans would not comply with Wilson's demand. Although Wilson complained bitterly about German U-boat attacks on British and American commerce, he did not comment on the British naval blockade of Germany, which was causing starvation, was against international law, and was not lifted even when the eventual armistice was signed. The hunger blockade was certainly a war crime.[16] Jim Powell, author of *Wilson's War*, persuasively argues that if the U.S. had remained truly neutral early in the war, the Germans wouldn't have attacked U.S. ships because, with the British blockade in force, they needed all the friends they could get.[17]

Although not perfect, Germany, the enemy, had democratic tendencies — providing freedom of the press except under extreme conditions, the liberty to criticize the kaiser, the broadest voting franchise in Europe (including that of Britain), the rule of law, and due legal process if arrested. The German kaiser had less power than the American president, and Germans had more leeway to criticize the war than their American counterparts. Also, the Germans, in their much more limited empire, did not use the harsh repression of the French and Belgian empires. Before the war, Germany was regarded as a liberal society; only during and after the war was the "enemy" portrayed as a society run by an autocratic king.

Wilson engaged in a war of choice without first preparing the country to fight it. After declaring war in April 1917, it took more than a year to get sizeable U.S. forces to Europe. Once they got there, they did turn the tide of the war. In the spring of 1918, the Germans had made a series of offensives that almost won the war. But in June 1918, U.S. forces helped to halt the German advance at Château-Thierry and Belleau Wood and heavily contributed to the counteroffensives thereafter against the exhausted German forces. These counteroffensives won the war for the allies.[18] One reason they were successful was that U.S. entry into the war had shattered German morale.

Negotiated a Peace

Because the U.S. had tipped the balance of a stalemated battlefield in favor of the allies in the war, it should have had immense negotiating power at the postwar Paris Peace Conference. To get his ultimately unsuccessful League of Nations, however, Wilson allowed France and Britain to impose a harsh peace on Germany. Wilson went along with their imposition on Germany of a "war guilt" clause, even though both sides could have been blamed for starting the war. Also, the German Rhineland was occupied, and heavy war reparations were demanded.[19]

The Republicans, who won control of Congress in 1918 because of disillusionment over the carnage Americans had experienced during the war, wanted to make sure that Wilson's League of Nations did not automatically drag the U.S. into future wars to preserve all international boundaries — as the Treaty of Versailles suggested. Led by Henry Cabot Lodge and supported by many Americans, the Republicans sought amendments to ensure that the United States would not be obligated to enter unnecessary wars or to have its army policing the world. Wilson refused any such sensible amendments and ordered Democrats to vote down the amended treaty in the Senate twice. In 1921, Wilson's successor, President Warren Harding, won congressional support for a separate peace treaty with Germany that did not provide U.S. security guarantees for Britain and France.[20]

Made the World Safe for Colonial Expansion

Wilson originally said in his request for a declaration of war that the United States would be fighting for self-government, democracy, and the rights of small nations. After the Bolsheviks took power in Russia in 1917, however, they published secret treaties between the British, French, and Czarist Russia, indicating that the U.S. allies actually had been fighting to divide up the spoils in Europe and elsewhere.[21] Embarrassed, Wilson said that the United States was not fighting for the sordid goals of Britain and France and claimed that the U.S. wanted "peace without victory" based on his fourteen idealistic points.

Among the fourteen points was national self-determination, open instead of secret treaties, and what was to become the League of Nations. Despite Wilson's pledges in the fourteen points of open treaties and self-determination, the Germans were left out of secret negotiations leading to the Versailles peace treaty, and the French and British divided up German colonies between them and grabbed lands in the Middle East from the collapsed Ottoman Empire. In other words, instead of fighting to "make the world safe for democracy," as Wilson claimed, the United States had fought so that its allies could expand their colonial oppression of foreign peoples.

Apparently Wilson's principle of self-determination did not apply to the French and British Empires.[22] For example, the British had promised independence to the Arabs in Palestine if they helped the British fight the Ottoman Empire. Instead, the Arabs got a British occupation designed to control Middle Eastern oil. Even worse for them, the Balfour Declaration of 1917, a British promise, gave some of the Arab lands to Jews returning to Palestine after almost two millennia of absence — as a "homeland" (not a state). Promising the same land to two peoples inevitably led to the never-ending Israeli–Arab conflict and the later senseless U.S. entanglement in it.[23]

Instigated Decades of Aftermath

On his national whirlwind tour to build support for the Treaty of Versailles and create the League of Nations, Wilson contradicted his earlier promise that World War I would be the "war to end all wars" by predicting that U.S. involvement in another huge war would be needed to reach nirvana. Wilson stated:

> There will come sometime ... another struggle in which, not a few hundred thousand fine men from America will have to die, but many millions ... to accomplish the final freedom of the peoples of the world.[24]

Little did Wilson know that he would be largely responsible for causing the largest war in world history, which was only twenty years in the future. In addition, World War I brought to power three monstrous dictators — Hitler, Lenin, and Stalin.[25]

Illustrating the often severe, unpredictable, and unintended consequences of war, German resentment over the unjust war-guilt clause and other humiliations, as well as economic pain caused by the war and exorbitant reparations, led to the rise of Adolf Hitler and the even more cataclysmic World War II. In the interwar years, the large reparations gave the Germans reason to inflate their currency to pay their debts in devalued marks, thus creating a hyperinflation that was worse than in other nations. Also, the British hunger blockade, which was starving the German population, continued even after the fighting had long stopped. The continuing blockade, designed to increase British leverage during the peace negotiations, was clearly a war crime. In addition, Wilson pushed for the abdication of Kaiser Wilhelm II, removing a huge obstacle in Hitler's path to power. Also, Hitler's popularity fed off German national humiliation and economic problems.

Wilson also played a role in triggering the Russian Revolution and then meddled in the ensuing Russian civil war — that is, he inadvertently helped the communists take power initially in Russia and then made them hate the United States, thus paving the way for a Cold War that lasted more than forty years.

Wilson had nothing to do with the first uprising in the Russian Revolution — which led to the czar's abdication on March 15, 1917, and the installation of the

Provisional Government, eventually headed by Alexander Kerensky. After the U.S. entered World War I, however, Wilson offered the Provisional Government $325 million ($4 billion in today's dollars) in credits to remain in the war, adding to the extensive pressure on Kerensky's regime to continue to support the allied cause. With U.S. involvement, the Provisional Government had hope that Germany actually could be defeated. The outcome was the so-called Grand Offensive against the Germans: about four hundred thousand Russians died — bringing the Russian wartime death total to 1.7 million — and hundreds of thousands more deserted.

The disastrous offensive motivated most of the Russian army to sympathize with the Bolsheviks, the only Russian party that wanted Russia to immediately withdraw from the hugely unpopular war. After an ensuing summer crisis, the Russian army collapsed, and the Provisional Government couldn't have been defended even if the military had desired to do so. The Bolsheviks, benefiting from the radicalization of the population, came to power in the fall of 1917. Lenin noted, "Our revolution was born of the war." According to Jim Powell, if the allies had not pressured the Provisional Government into staying in the war and Wilson had not bribed it to do so, that government might have survived and Lenin would have been a forgotten man.

Powell is not the only one taking this line. Diplomat George Kennan, an expert on Russia and the creator of the U.S. Cold War doctrine of containment, said:

> It may be questioned whether the United States government, in company with other western Allies, did not actually hasten and facilitate the failure of the Provisional Government by insisting that Russia should continue the war effort, and by making this demand the criterion for its support. In asking the leaders of the Provisional Government simultaneously to consolidate their political power and to revive and continue participation in the war, the Allies were asking the impossible.[26]

After the Russian Revolution, from 1918 to 1920, the Western powers intervened in the great civil war that erupted in Russia between the Bolsheviks (the Reds) and anti-Bolshevik forces (the Whites). Wilson helped to impose a naval blockade on the Soviet Union, provided monetary assistance to the Whites, and secretly sent thousands of U.S. troops to Russia, without congressional approval, in a failed attempt to help the Whites overturn the Bolshevik revolution. The Bolsheviks had nationalized oil interests, and Standard Oil of New Jersey prodded the U.S. government to take action on behalf of the Whites. After the Bolsheviks won the civil war, Lenin, not surprisingly, felt bitter toward the United States.[27]

The Russian Revolution, when it came, had horrific implications. According to conservative historian Richard Pipes, "Had it not been for the Russian Revolution, there very likely would have been no National Socialism; probably no Second World War and no decolonization; and certainly no Cold War." Wilson helped, in one way or another, to cause all of these monstrous calamities.[28] Thus, he is ranked as the worst president in U.S. history.

Was the Most Interventionist President in U.S. History

Wilson's most catastrophic intervention was World War I, but it was not his only one. In fact, Max Boot notes that Wilson was the most interventionist president in U.S. history. The American mainland has rarely been attacked with ground forces. Only in the Madison administration during the War of 1812 and in the Wilson administration did this occur — in both cases because the U.S. first started hostilities with an adversary, who later attacked the American homeland. Wilson's snafu was on a far smaller scale than Madison's, but it was a blunder nonetheless. Wilson turned a minor incident into a U.S. military intervention that ultimately caused Mexican guerrillas to attack a U.S. town near the Mexican border, which in turn spurred a U.S. invasion of Mexico.

In 1914, eight U.S. sailors went ashore in Mexico to get gasoline. A Mexican colonel ordered their arrest. He soon realized the political implications and released them. A Mexican general then arrested the colonel and apologized to the U.S. ship's commanding officer. Unbelievably, the U.S. officer demanded a formal apology, assurance that the colonel would be punished, and a twenty-one-gun salute to the U.S. naval vessel. The matter was escalated to the top of both the U.S. and Mexican governments.

General Victoriano Huerta, the president of Mexico, offered to apologize, but refused the twenty-one-gun salute. Wilson demanded that Huerta order the salute. U.S. marines went ashore at the Mexican port of Veracruz. Although Wilson was told there would be no resistance, the infuriated Mexicans caused twenty-four American casualties, so Wilson sent more than five thousand troops to Veracruz and installed an American mayor in the city. The U.S. intervention spawned anti-American demonstrations throughout Latin America and rioting in Baja California. Wilson declared that he would accept no settlement to the crisis that didn't oust Huerta. Venustiano Carranza, a rebel leader, defeated Huerta's forces and was ready to attack Mexico City, the capital. When Huerta abruptly resigned, Carranza became president.

The United States withdrew after occupying Veracruz for seven months. However, the U.S. continued to back Carranza against his rebelling commanders and initiated an arms embargo against them. Pancho Villa, one of these commanders, was enraged at Wilson for backing Carranza. Villa and his men conducted raids along the U.S.-Mexican border, including the famous raid on Columbus, New Mexico, in 1916.[29] That raid killed seventeen Americans.

After Villa raided Columbus, Wilson sent General John "Black Jack" Pershing and ten thousand U.S. troops to invade Mexico and get Villa. Pershing's mission was ultimately unsuccessful, and he almost caused a war with Mexico.[30]

Wilson's adventures in Mexico weren't his only U.S. interventions in Latin America. During Wilson's presidency, the United States intervened militarily in Latin America more frequently than at any other time in its history. Contrary to Wilson's always-idealistic rhetoric, these invasions were designed to protect U.S. economic interests or to assert U.S. power over the Western Hemisphere under the Monroe Doctrine — not to promote self-determination or democracy in the affected nations.

In addition to invading Mexico in 1914 and 1916, Wilson ordered U.S. forces to invade Nicaragua in 1914, Haiti in 1915, the Dominican Republic in 1916, Cuba in 1917, Panama in 1918, and Mexico nine other times. In Nicaragua, the U.S. military chose the country's president and extorted privileges to build an Atlantic-to-Pacific canal. The occupation of Haiti lasted nineteen years, was motivated by pressure from a U.S. bank, killed thousands of Haitians, and made the country less democratic. The occupation of the Dominican Republic lasted eight years and created a local centralized military force that future dictators would use to suppress their people.

According to former Marine Corps General Smedley Butler, "I helped make Mexico safe for American oil interests in 1914. I helped make Haiti and Cuba a decent place for the National City Bank boys to collect revenue in. I helped purify Nicaragua for the internal banking house of Brown Brothers . . . I brought light to the D.R. for American sugar interests in 1916."[31]

Most of Wilson's neocolonial invasions caused outrage at home and abroad. The outcry at home finally caused Wilson to withdraw forces from Mexico. Furthermore, although many of Wilson's profligate foreign adventures were counterproductive debacles, historians have since spruced up Wilson's tarnished image because he was one of the pioneers of the interventionist foreign policy that took the nation's fancy permanently after World War II. The present regularly colors how analysts perceive the past.[32]

PROSPERITY

Promoted Prewar Economic Interventions

Even before Wilson mobilized the entire economy to fight World War I, he was pursuing an activist domestic agenda contrary to the history of the Democratic Party, which had been a bastion of small government. Like Wilson's faith-based foreign policy, which included total war, religion also fueled his missionary ardor for the progressive movement at home.[33] Along with FDR and LBJ, Wilson is among the three most legislatively active presidents of the twentieth century. Analysts with a bias toward activism generally give these three presidents credit for this legislative activity, but many of the results have been negative.

In Wilson's case, decades after the idea of a national bank was buried, his New Freedom legislative agenda created the Federal Reserve System, which Nobel Prize–winning economist Milton Friedman later showed to be the cause of the Great Depression, as it excessively expanded the money supply in the 1920s. Prior to 1913, when Wilson created the Federal Reserve System, the nation's seven thousand banks operated with only the very effective coordination of private bank clearinghouse associations.[34] The United States had no standard currency, instead having a polyglot of greenbacks, certificates, and gold and silver coins.[35] Despite this decentralized banking system, the country got along fine.

Wilson, however, wanted the government to rule the banking system and did not want banks to dominate entrepreneurs and businessmen. The new Federal Reserve System acted as a central bank, and its board of governors had the power to regulate the money supply and interest rates. The system took monetary policy away from Congress. Wilson wanted an easy-money policy.[36] The country got that, and the massive depression that it eventually caused during the 1930s. Analysts have long claimed the Federal Reserve System to be Wilson's most important domestic achievement. Even after Friedman's research, however, few are willing to acknowledge its contribution to the Depression.[37]

In 1913, the Sixteenth Amendment to the Constitution was ratified, which allowed the return of the income tax. Wilson was happy to oblige under his New Freedom agenda. The tax was 1 percent of taxable incomes above three thousand dollars — at the time, it affected only rich people. Later, in 1916, during a second wave of New Freedom legislation, Wilson got more sharply graduated income and inheritance taxes passed. In a classic example of the "ratchet effect" (going up but not back down), some of the high taxes on incomes and corporate profits were retained after the war ended.

The income tax was later expanded by subsequent administrations to tax most strata of society and at much higher rates. Of all government taxes, the income tax is probably the most pernicious. It discourages people from being productive and making more money — unlike consumption taxes — and it allows the government to snoop heavily into people's lives and financial dealings.

Wilson's agenda also strengthened U.S. antitrust laws. Despite the renewed use of the Sherman Antitrust Act under Theodore Roosevelt and William Howard Taft, progressives in both parties craved a stronger law to control big business and fight monopolies. In 1914, Wilson got Congress to pass the comprehensive Clayton Antitrust Act, which became the bedrock federal statute to attack monopolies and fortified the government's ability to prevent them. Under another statute, the Federal Trade Commission, with the support of business interests, was created to oversee business.[38]

Although the idea that big government should counter big business is widespread among modern liberals, public-choice economic theory shows that the moneyed power of big business usually co-opts government regulators into creating regulations that benefit the regulated. Antitrust regulation is no exception. The government has created more monopolies through tariff protection, regulation, or direct or indirect government subsidization than it has broken up using antitrust legislation. If the free market is allowed to work with no government intrusion, monopolies tend to be temporary — as technological advances and new products, as well as international competition, tend to erode even the dominant positions of big companies.

In 1919, spurred by World War I and by religion-infused government, the Eighteenth Amendment to the Constitution was ratified, prohibiting the production, sale, or transportation of alcohol. During the war, as a precursor for prohibition and for the ostensible purpose of conserving grain, the Congress passed a law and Wilson issued an executive order restricting the use of foodstuffs in the manufacture of alcohol.[39] There was rampant evasion of prohibition, and thus organized crime, with its concomitant violence, expanded dramatically during this time. The Twenty-First Amendment later ended this failed social experiment, but the precedent was set for the government to intrude on decisions best made by individuals, not the state.

Laid the Groundwork for Expanded Government

After World War I, the U.S. economy was never the same. Many conservatives blame Franklin D. Roosevelt for creating a permanent big government in the

United States, and he certainly did contribute to it, but Wilson laid the ground-work by intervening in the economy during World War I on an unprecedented scale. For example, Wilson appointed William Gibbs McAdoo to run the rail-roads, Bernard Baruch to supervise industrial production, and Herbert Hoover to manage food production.[40]

The National Defense acts of 1916 and 1917 gave Wilson the power to procure military armaments by any means needed, and the Lever Food and Fuel Control Act of 1917 allowed Wilson to fix prices, commandeer needed materials for war, seize and operate industrial plants, and regulate production, mining, transportation, and storage of items needed for the war.[41] The Trading with the Enemy Act of 1917 authorized Wilson to declare a state of national emergency and control transactions in which any foreign nation had an interest. The blanket law covered censoring all communications with foreign nations, property seizures, suspension of the gold standard, and even conscription.[42]

The Overman Act allowed Wilson to reorganize the responsibilities of ex-ecutive agencies without congressional approval, which bestowed on Wilson near-dictatorial powers. Under the act, Wilson unilaterally created new agencies not related to the military or combat — for example, the Food and Drug Admin-istration and the Fuel Administration, which rationed food and fuel respectively. Wilson also created the Railroad Administration, which seized railroads and operated them until 1920 — well after the war was over. These are costly and inefficient methods; even during wartime, the market is still the best at allo-cating goods and services. In one of the most severe government interventions into the marketplace in U.S. history, Wilson's War Industries Board was given immense power to regulate the economy by fixing prices in key industries.[43]

Although Wilson was usually careful to get a delegation of authority from Congress for his broad newfound powers during the war (the principal excep-tion was setting up a new propaganda agency to sell the war to the American public), it is unlikely that the founders intended even the Congress to have such great power over the economy. Yet the courts, in violation of the Consti-tution, validated Congress's emergency legislation during the war and almost all of Wilson's repression of political, economic, and civil rights. After the war, however, Congress overruled Wilson when he tried to prevent it from taking most of his wartime powers away.

During the Great Depression, FDR merely brought back many of the wartime agencies and renamed them. He even used some of Wilson's people to manage them. Thus, Vedder and Gallaway, free market economists, gave Wilson a dismal ranking on policies that promoted limited government and fought inflation —

thirty-eighth out of thirty-nine presidents ranked. Only Lincoln during the Civil War was worse.

World War I, like all wars, increased the size of government at home — but the difference this time was that the massive government penetration of civil society was lasting. Although the government had grown in size during prior wars — the Civil War under Lincoln and the Spanish-American War under McKinley — it was either reduced to a great extent after the war (Civil War) or the war was small enough that the increase in government power was less pronounced (Spanish-American War). Thus Wilson, not FDR, is the father of modern permanent big government. He did not create the massive peacetime welfare state, but he made it possible for Hoover and FDR to do so later.

LIBERTY

Undermined Constitutional Checks and Balances

Wilson used World War I to vastly enlarge the president's powers. Under the National Defense Act of 1916, Wilson could appoint all commissioned and noncommissioned officers of the National Guard. Previously, William McKinley had won the right to appoint the general officers of such units. Both of these encroachments subverted the states' constitutional right to appoint the officers of the militia. The law also created national military reserves, which began to replace the state-based National Guard in filling out active military units in time of war.[44] This act effectively increased the president's authority over the military and undermined the Constitution's provisions for ensuring some state control over militia as a counterweight to federal power.

Eroded Civil Liberties

In U.S. history, World War I and its aftermath were probably the worst times for the erosion of precious and unique American civil liberties. First of all, conscription, a form of involuntary slavery, was resurrected from the Civil War. The Congress passed the Selective Service Act of 1917, which authorized Wilson to draft men against their will to fight in a distant war — that is, to "fight for freedom" by losing their own liberty.

Second, James W. Loewen, author of *Lies My Teacher Told Me: Everything Your American History Textbook Got Wrong*, notes that the Espionage Act of

1917 (which made discouragement of military recruitment illegal) and the Sedition Act of 1918 were "probably the most serious attacks on the civil liberties of Americans since the short-lived Alien and Sedition acts of 1798" during the administration of John Adams. Yet the Supreme Court upheld convictions under these unconstitutional World War I–era laws. Loewen says of the Wilson administration's crackdown on civil liberties during and after World War I, "Neither before nor since these campaigns has the United States come closer to being a police state."[45]

Wilson tried to erase dissent against his war policy by using the U.S. Post Office and the Justice Department to suppress free speech. He ordered the War Department to censor all telegraph and telephone traffic. Wilson arrested, convicted, and imprisoned thousands of socialists under the Espionage Act and refused to pardon socialist leader Eugene Debs for opposing the war. (President Warren Harding later freed Debs and had a cordial meeting with him at the White House.) Robert Goldstein was sentenced to ten years in prison for producing a film on the American Revolution called *The Spirit of 1776*, which depicted the now-allied British in an unflattering light.[46] Wilson's unconstitutional actions helped ignite wartime panic in the United States, which lasted into the postwar years. One man in Lansing, Michigan, was sentenced to twenty years in prison and a ten thousand-dollar fine for criticizing the war.[47]

In 1920, two years after the war had ended, Wilson vetoed the repeal of the Espionage and Sedition acts — illustrating that big government created by war is hard to reduce or eliminate.[48] In fact, in the postwar period, the Wilson administration accelerated its attacks on civil liberties at home. After the war and the resultant Bolshevik revolution and because of them, anti-immigrant sentiments and a Red scare ensued in the United States.

Some anarchists and socialists had refused to fight in the war, and that had enraged the general U.S. population. In addition, strikes swept the nation and many thought that communists were behind them. An anarchist bomb plot targeting prominent people was uncovered. A. Mitchell Palmer, Wilson's attorney general, who had presidential aspirations, conducted the Palmer raids to stamp out "subversive" activity. As many as five thousand resident aliens were arrested, using brutal techniques without proper warrants, a right to counsel, information about the charges against them, or a right to appeal their deportation. But as is usually the case when hysteria reigns, few real subversives or weapons were found. Michael Farquhar concluded that "with his [Wilson's] Gestapo tactics he spit on the Bill of Rights and reduced the U.S. government to the status of a second-rate police state."[49]

Another example of the anti-immigrant and "antisubversive" sentiments emanating from Wilson's war occurred in 1921, after Wilson had left office. Nicola Sacco and Bartolomeo Vanzetti, both anarchist immigrants, were convicted on scant evidence and later executed for murder.

Set Bad Policies toward Blacks and Women

To Wilson, some racial groups were more equal than others. A Democrat originally from the South and a blatant white supremacist, Wilson sought unsuccessfully to get Congress to pass legislation to restrict the civil liberties of African Americans. He also put whites in jobs that his Republican predecessors had given to blacks and allowed some of his southern cabinet members to try to reinstitute strict racial segregation into federal agencies.[50] Wilson opposed a statement on racial equality in the document that governed his prized League of Nations.

During and after Wilson's administration, racial violence spiked, in some measure, because of the racist tone Wilson had set. The results were lynchings, anti-black race riots, and the emergence of the second Ku Klux Klan (KKK) to dominate the Democratic Party in the southern and western states. The Klan also dominated the Republican Party in Ohio and was strong in New Jersey and the Midwest. When the most intense anti-black race riots in the nation's history broke out during Wilson's second term, J. Edgar Hoover, Wilson's law-enforcement leader, spied on blacks, not the KKK.[51]

Similarly, Wilson had women suffragists arrested, but later, under their continuing pressure, he campaigned for the Nineteenth Amendment, which passed in 1920 and gave women the right to vote.

CONCLUSION

As mentioned in the introduction to this book, those who assess the quality of presidents are often impressed by communication skills and charisma. Both of these characteristics may help to account for Wilson's standing in many lists of great presidents. Wilson expanded the president's role in public speaking started by William McKinley and Teddy Roosevelt. Prior to McKinley, it was considered unseemly for the president to do any public speaking. Wilson went on a national speaking sojourn to sell the League of Nations and took public speaking a step further by being the first president since John Adams to address Congress in person. Presidents before Wilson had shied away from such events because of unfavorable similarities to the king's speeches before parliament in Britain and because of the perceived symbolic erosion of the constitutional separation of powers. Wilson also invented the presidential press conference, which dramatically expanded the chief executive's "bully pulpit" and eventually led to the media's excessive coverage of the president at the expense of the other branches of government.

Like Lincoln, FDR, and JFK, Wilson was a charismatic orator, and this attribute helped him take the nation to war and get his legislative agenda passed. But Wilson, like other presidents, should be judged not on charisma, but on how his policies affected the nation. They were catastrophic.

It can be argued that Wilson screwed up the entire twentieth century and beyond. U.S. involvement in World War I was instrumental in causing a violent twentieth century for the world. As a result of the two world wars, the Russian and Chinese revolutions, and civil wars and conflicts spawned by the Cold War — most of which can be traced to U.S. entry into World War I — the twentieth century was by far the bloodiest in world history. Approximately 110 million people lost their lives in war in that century.

Even in the twenty-first century, people are still losing their lives in conflicts (for example, in Iraq) indirectly generated by the United States entry into World War I. Max Boot, a dedicated advocate of U.S. overseas intervention, has admitted that Wilson's help in creating the artificial states of Yugoslavia and Czechoslovakia, containing ethnic groups that didn't want to live together, contributed to their eventual unraveling in the 1990s — the former with a bloody civil war. Boot also has acknowledged that Iraq, an artificial state created by the victorious British after World War I, may yet join the ranks of failed states. Had the Germans and their Ottoman allies won World War I, no such countries probably would ever have existed.

Such U.S. meddling overseas led to permanent big government at home. Wilson's only positive accomplishments were his reluctant support for women's suffrage and tariff reduction. Wilson's achievements pale in comparison to the pain and loss of freedom he inflicted on Americans and the rest of the world.

In 1919, as Wilson campaigned around the United States for ratification of the Treaty of Versailles, he collapsed and returned to Washington. When he got back to the nation's capital, he had a debilitating stroke in early October of that year. He became confined to his bed or a wheelchair. Yet instead of allowing the vice president to finish the rest of Wilson's second term, his wife, Edith, chose to hide the seriousness of Wilson's condition. During the eighteen-month period from October 1919 until Warren Harding was inaugurated as the new president in March 1921, Edith Wilson was effectively the first woman president of the United States. Given Woodrow Wilson's abominable track record as president, this incapacitation and substitution might have been a blessing in disguise for the country, except that his wife's covert governance was as bad or maybe worse than his.[52] Woodrow Wilson is ranked last here, at number forty.

29

WARREN G. HARDING

Scandals Masked a Good Presidency

PP&L* RANKING: 6
Category: Good

Twenty-ninth president of the United States

Term: March 4, 1921, to August 2, 1923
Party: Republican
Born: November 2, 1865, near Blooming Grove, Ohio
Died: August 2, 1923 (age fifty-seven), San Francisco, California
Spouse: Florence Kling Harding
Alma Mater: Ohio Central College
Occupation: Businessman (newspapers)
Religion: Baptist

Readers may do a double take when looking at the second president in the good category (sixth in overall ranking here). Harding is often listed among the nation's worst presidents, and this view usually comes as a result of the corruption associated with the Teapot Dome and other scandals during his administration. Such analyses place too much emphasis on the venal activities of Harding's underlings.[1] In this volume, Harding is docked for the scandals, but not as much as if they had been constitutional scandals of the Iran-Contra and Watergate variety.

Some of Harding's bad reputation, however, has to do with his avoidance of government activism. For example, H. L. Mencken claimed that Harding was a "do nothing" president. Yet the strength of America is in its vibrant society and economy, and the government usually just gets in the way. With all presidents,

---

*PP&L = Peace, Prosperity, and Liberty.

the physicians' motto, "First, do no harm," might be the best standard to govern by, a standard that the vast majority of presidents did not meet; but Harding did. His lack of charisma and formal education also led to criticisms. Even Harding said, "I am not fit for this office and should never have been here."[2] Harding was much too hard on himself.

All of these negative assessments overlook Harding's considerable impact on the war-ravaged U.S. economy, reviving it with tax cuts and an actual reduction in federal spending. His astute foreign policy regarding Europe was designed to avoid unnecessary entanglements there; he reached a path-breaking arms control agreement; and his record on civil rights and other liberty-related issues was sound.

Overly Faulted for the Scandals during His Administration

Harding's secretary of the interior, Albert B. Fall, took bribes from oil company executives in return for the companies' access to government oil reserves, including the Teapot Dome reserve in Wyoming.[3] Ohio political boss Harry Daugherty, Harding's main benefactor and later attorney general, created an influence-peddling scheme at the Department of Justice and was indicted for malfeasance.[4] He believed Harding to be a dimwit and admitted that he had backed him for chief executive only because "he looked like a president."

Like Ulysses S. Grant, Harding was not personally implicated in any of the scandals and did what he could to oust the guilty individuals; he died before some of the scandals became known. Also, as with the Grant scandals, corruption by Harding's presidential appointees had to do with money-grubbing greed, not administrations' constitutional mischief such as the much more serious Iran-Contra scandal during the Reagan administration and the Watergate affair during the Nixon years. Both Harding and Grant were ultimately responsible for appointing some dishonest men. In Harding's case, however, he also appointed many ethical and capable men — for example, Herbert Hoover, Andrew Mellon, and Charles Evans Hughes.

Harding was famous for saying, "I have no trouble with my enemies," but noted that his friends "keep me walking the floor nights."[5] However, the amount of money pocketed by dishonest individuals during his administration was minuscule compared to the money the government wasted on legal pork-barrel spending and special interests. Both Harding and Grant have been overly tainted by such scandals, but Harding was a much better president than Grant, even when these episodes are seen in their proper light.

PEACE

Advocated a Very Restrained Foreign Policy

In foreign policy, Harding had an exceptional record. After Woodrow Wilson's term ended, even some Republicans wanted some form of U.S. involvement in the League of Nations, an organization that required automatic international sanctions in the face of "aggression." Harding said no to U.S. participation in the League and reached a separate peace with defeated Germany.

Harding, in the fine American tradition, did not want to become entangled in every European dispute and lose U.S. sovereignty to an international organization. Interventionist critics of this policy have claimed, without much evidence, that U.S. participation in the League and continued U.S. involvement in Europe during the 1920s and 1930s would have prevented Adolf Hitler's rise. In fact, they ignore that the U.S. rescue of the French and British colonial powers during World War I resulted in their harsh postwar treatment of Germany, leading directly to Hitler's ascension.

In addition, Harding led the negotiations for the Washington Naval Treaty of 1921, the first significant arms control agreement in U.S. history. Harding reversed Wilson's post–World War I naval buildup because he knew that if the United States didn't cut back its warships by a greater number, Britain and Japan wouldn't cut back theirs. The reductions led to a 5–5–3 ratio in battleship tonnage among the U.S., Britain, and Japan, respectively, and it saved all three nations much money over a twelve-year period. Because Harding had been smarter than Wilson was with the League of Nations treaty — involving senators in the negotiations — the Washington Naval Treaty was confirmed unanimously.[6]

PROSPERITY

Generally Set Good Economic Policies

Woodrow Wilson's legacy to Harding was an economy and a social fabric that had been damaged by U.S. involvement in World War I. Regardless, Harding started an economic boom that lasted through the 1920s by cutting taxes, which increased investment, and by becoming the only postwar president in U.S. history to slash federal expenditures below prewar levels.[7] For example, during an election year, he vetoed excessive benefits for World War I veterans, which were very popular.[8] Vedder and Gallaway acknowledge Harding's excellent laissez-faire economic policies by ranking him number one out of thirty-nine presidents ranked on promotion of limited government and price stability.

Harding's administration did play a minor role in causing the Great Depression in the 1930s. The economic slowdown was initially caused by the rapid expansion of the money supply in the 1920s — especially ballooning credit to businesses — and was exacerbated by the imposition of high tariffs and government policy interventions that did not allow market forces to correct the downturn. In capitalist economies, periodic recessions are needed when forces of supply and demand get out of balance. When the economy overheats — usually caused by government expansion of the money stock leading to over-investment — products supplied eventually outrun the demand for them. Then prices and wages need to be allowed to decline, with a resulting recession, to bring the system into balance.

Unfortunately, higher tariffs were a mainstay of the Republican platform under Harding, Coolidge, and Hoover. Contrary to his philosophy, Harding pressured federal, state, and local governments to initiate public works programs to alleviate unemployment, thus keeping wages artificially high.

The root cause of the Great Depression was a surge in the U.S. money supply during the 1920s, which followed Woodrow Wilson's creation of the Federal Reserve System in 1913. The money supply increased a whopping 61.8 percent from mid-1921 to mid-1929 — an average annual rate of 7.7 percent.[9] During this period, four major spurts of monetary expansion occurred, only one of which was during Harding's presidency. In addition, Harding was president less than two and half years during this period, and Coolidge was the chief executive for more than five and a half years. Of the three Republican presidents, however, Harding was the least culpable in creating the conditions for the Great Depression.

Increased Presidential Powers

In 1921, Harding fought for and won the authority to develop a consolidated budget for the executive branch. Previously, each federal department would negotiate its budget with the appropriate congressional committees, which allowed the committees to effectively control the various federal bureaucracies. President William Howard Taft had failed to get Congress to allow him to create such a consolidated budget. After Harding did so, Congress gradually lost power over the government's spending and began to use the president's budget document as a starting point for setting taxing and spending priorities.[10]

This development eventually eroded Congress's most important constitutional authority, the power of the purse. Today, the Congress makes only incremental changes to the president's massive yearly budget submission. Over U.S. history, the president has encroached on Congress's constitutional powers in two crucial areas: warfare and control over the federal budget. President Harry Truman was the culprit in beginning the unconstitutional expansion of executive war powers. Harding, despite his good presidency, began the long process of executive usurpation of the congressional power over federal spending.

Promoted Subsidies and Government Coercion

Harding also called for a new Department of Public Welfare and wasteful internal improvement projects for conservation. Unfortunately, Harding subsidized farmers and instituted pro-business regulations that benefited the agricultural, radio, and transcontinental cable communications sectors. He also argued for unneeded federal promotion of highways, aviation, and the merchant marine. Although most of these policies were pro-business, they were not free-market policies.

In addition, he restricted immigration, offered federal troops to governors to put down coal and railroad strikes, intimidated labor and management to end strikes, and coerced management to reduce the steel industry's twelve-hour workday.[11] The government should refrain from getting involved in private labor–management disputes.

LIBERTY

Tried to Heal the Domestic Wounds from World War I

To heal the wounds opened by World War I, laissez-faire Republican Harding freed most of the labor union chiefs and socialists incarcerated during the Red Scare of 1919 and threw in a pardon for antiwar socialist leader Eugene Debs, a very unpopular move. He even invited Debs to visit the White House and hosted him there. Also, Harding had a good civil rights record compared to his virulently racist predecessor — the "liberal" Woodrow Wilson.[12]

CONCLUSION

In a famous 1948 poll of historians for *Life* magazine by Arthur Schlesinger Sr., Harding was ranked as one of the ten worst presidents in U.S. history.[13] Even a tabulation by conservatives James Taranto and Leonard Leo, who chose an "ideologically balanced" group of analysts to survey, ranked him the second-worst president in history (he came in thirty-eighth in a field of thirty-nine presidents).[14] Only occasionally — for example, in Paul Johnson's work — do analysts mount a defense of the Harding and Coolidge administrations.[15]

Harding was much better than most analysts give him credit for being. For some policy transgressions (for example, the consolidated executive budget) and his scandals — not for his frequent, but irrelevant, womanizing — Harding fails to make the excellent presidents category. However, he was still good — for his rejection of the League of Nations, his restrained foreign policy, his success in arms control, and his relatively laissez-faire economic policies. Warren G. Harding is number six in this assessment.

30

CALVIN COOLIDGE

Silent Cal's Presidency
Should Silence the Critics

PP&L* RANKING: 10
Category: Good

Thirtieth president of the United States

Term: August 2, 1923, to March 4, 1929
Party: Republican
Born: July 4, 1872, Plymouth, Vermont
Died: January 5, 1933 (age sixty), Northampton,
    Massachusetts
Spouse: Grace Goodhue Coolidge
Alma Mater: Amherst College
Occupation: Lawyer and politician
Religion: Congregationalist

Calvin Coolidge once said that the United States had an excessive number of laws "and we would be better off if we didn't have any more [sic].... The greatest duty and opportunity of government is not to embark on any new ventures."[1] Like so many presidents advocating limited government and tight money policies, Coolidge didn't always quite measure up to his own rhetoric. In fact, Coolidge was less a supporter of limited government than Warren Harding, his predecessor. Harding died after two scandal-plagued years in office, and Coolidge succeeded him. As a result, Harding is remembered less fondly among modern-day Republicans than is "Silent Cal."

While Coolidge's tight fiscal policy generated the prosperity of the Roaring Twenties, his monetary policy — expanding the supply of money significantly —

---

*PP&L = Peace, Prosperity, and Liberty.

236

contributed to the Great Depression that followed his term in office. Commendably, like Harding, he used restraint in foreign policy. Coolidge was a hybrid between conservative Republicans like Harding and progressive Republicans like Theodore Roosevelt. For example, Coolidge supported women's right to vote and government strictures limiting work hours for women and children. Thus, John O. McGinnis, a professor of law at Northwestern University who wrote a piece on Calvin Coolidge for a *Wall Street Journal* book on the presidents, said that Coolidge was the original "compassionate conservative."[2] Using this term for Coolidge implicitly compares him with George W. Bush, thus admitting that Coolidge sometimes strayed from the small-government line.

PEACE

Endorsed Foreign Policy Fiascos

At the end of World War I, Germany owed $2.5 billion in reparations to France and Britain, who in turn owed $2.5 billion in war debt to the United States. The Germans couldn't pay the steep reparations to the allies, and because of high U.S. tariffs that Coolidge supported, France and Britain didn't have the surplus dollars from exports to pay the United States. Coolidge was unwilling to cancel the allies' debt or reduce the tariffs. Under the Dawes Plan, therefore, the United States loaned $2.5 billion to Germany to cover reparations to France and Britain, which then paid the $2.5 billion to the United States.[3] Although this "pay yourself" scheme seems ridiculous, it was politically beneficial to Coolidge. The U.S. loans to Germany came from the taxpayer, but the loan payments from France and Britain went to private banks, and the retained tariffs protected U.S. industry. Thus, in this sleight of hand, wealth was transferred from the average taxpayer to U.S. economic elites.

Also, Coolidge endorsed the United States' dubious entry into the Permanent Court of International Justice, an initiative also supported by Harding. The United States was blocked from entering, however, because the League of Nations objected to U.S. reservations about the Versailles treaty. This outcome was actually favorable, because international courts — even today — rarely have the procedural safeguards that U.S. citizens, who might come before them, enjoy in their domestic judicial system.

In addition, the Coolidge administration, with excessive idealism, led the negotiations for and signed the Kellogg-Briand Pact, a treaty that outlawed war. Sixty-two nations signed the treaty, but it had no enforcement mechanism, which probably would have required war.

In 1927, more realistically and concretely, Coolidge made a laudable, but unsuccessful, attempt to convene a conference of naval powers to restrain the growth of navies. A similar conference during the Harding administration, which signed the Washington Naval Treaty of 1921, had been successful.

Exercised Military Restraint

Following Woodrow Wilson's numerous military interventions in the Western Hemisphere, Coolidge continued Harding's policy of military restraint in Latin America. He helped bring U.S. forces home and, like Harding, stayed out of unneeded foreign wars. Yet McGinnis doesn't give Coolidge credit for keeping the United States at peace. McGinnis writes, "Coolidge was not a truly great president, like Washington or Lincoln. While he successfully handled small foreign policy crises in China, Mexico, and Nicaragua without saddling the United States with permanent and expensive commitments, he was never tested by a substantial foreign war." This passage shows the twisted logic of many analysts, which says that a president has to serve during a major war to be great — no matter if the president started the war or could have avoided it if he had adopted sounder policies.

PROSPERITY

Practiced Fiscal Restraint, Though Pro-Business

In 1924, in keeping with his policy of fiscal austerity, Coolidge vetoed benefits — called a "bonus bill" — for veterans of World War I, but Congress overrode his veto. Another of his vetoes was sustained, however, when Congress attempted to increase pensions for veterans of all wars. He also twice vetoed relief for the farm economy, which was experiencing a depression that contrasted with the general prosperity of the 1920s. These bills would have had the government buy up farmers' crops and send them overseas.[4]

Coolidge deserves a lot of credit for vetoing a Republican Congress's attempts to spend the budget surplus on untested programs and pork-barrel projects, for example, farm price supports; he instead reduced the federal budget, debt, and taxes on gifts and for the nonrich. He also relaxed regulations on business.[5]

Yet rather than being a strict adherent of small government and free markets, Coolidge instead could be characterized as pro-business. In fact, Coolidge said,

"The business of America is business."[6] He was so pro-business that, like Ronald Reagan and George W. Bush, he maintained comparatively high tariffs to protect industrial concerns.

Pursued Unnecessary Monetary Expansion, Helping to Cause the Great Depression

Because Coolidge continued Harding's fiscal austerity, the U.S. economy also continued its prosperity during Coolidge's one-and-a-half terms as president from 1923 until early 1929. At the end of the decade, when the U.S. stock market was hyperactive, Coolidge correctly believed that New York, not the federal government, should regulate the New York Stock Exchange. Much of the excessive speculation in the market was driven by excessive brokers' loans to investors.

The underlying problem, however, was the government's excessive expansion of the money supply, and it caused the Great Depression. The government's expansion of credit to business (that is, the money supply) during Coolidge's and Harding's terms resulted from Woodrow Wilson creating the Federal Reserve System in 1913. Such excess money usually causes businesses to miscalculate and overinvest in long-term projects. When consumers eventually get the money, however, they will consume as they always did — thus keeping their consumption-to-saving ratios constant. In other words, even though savings (the supply of capital) has increased, investment (the demand for capital) has increased more. Because savings provide the funds for business investment, there will be insufficient savings for such investment. So some long-term projects of business will have to be canceled and liquidated.

This state of affairs is called a recession or a depression. Contraction is the natural companion of expansion. The liquidation of projects causes unemployment, but it will be temporary unless wages are not allowed to fall in order to increase the demand for labor. A secondary effect also usually occurs — a contraction of credit. This causes prices to fall. Thus, the system goes back to equilibrium automatically, and the recession or depression comes to an end. The Hoover and FDR administrations' activist policies actually prevented the market from clearing and eliminating the economic downturn.

The money supply increased 61.8 percent from mid-1921 to mid-1929.[7] Thus the average annual increase was 7.7 percent. Major increases in the money supply occurred from 1922 to 1923 under Harding and in late 1924, late 1925, and 1927 under Coolidge. Over the eight-year period — most of it under Coolidge's leadership — uncovered dollars (those not supported by gold) in circulation increased 63.4 percent, whereas gold reserves increased only 15 percent.

Coolidge should bear some of the blame for causing the largest economic disaster in U.S. history; yet from the stock market crash in 1929, the first year of Hoover's presidency, until 1931, the economic downturn was merely a typical recession (less severe than the recession of 1921). Had Hoover and Franklin Roosevelt allowed market forces to restore prosperity, the downturn might have been shorter and less serious. Thus Coolidge should get blamed for causing the economic downturn, while Hoover and FDR should be held culpable for not allowing recovery and even exacerbating the situation into the Great Depression.

Nevertheless, although Coolidge generally supported limited government, he is downgraded significantly in these presidential rankings principally because his reckless monetary expansion ultimately led to the greatest economic collapse in American history. Surprisingly, Vedder and Gallaway rank Coolidge tied for thirteenth and fourteenth of thirty-nine presidents ranked on limiting government and fighting inflation (tied with Harry Truman), but this ranking is high considering Coolidge's transgressions.

LIBERTY

Was Uneven on Civil Rights and Cleaned Up after the Harding Scandals

Despite his support for an anti-lynching law and a civil rights stance that was better than the openly racist Woodrow Wilson and other progressive Democrats, Coolidge didn't always rush to protect the rights of African Americans.[8]

Although he cleaned up the scandals of the Harding administration after Harding died in office, Coolidge was slow to fire people. After the Teapot Dome scandal became known, Coolidge ordered up a special prosecutor, who convicted Albert Fall, the secretary of the interior, on bribery charges. When the Senate demanded that Secretary of the Navy Edwin Denby resign, however, Coolidge declined to fire him until he was given proof of guilt. When Attorney General Harry Daugherty obstructed the prosecution of other Harding administration corruption scandals, Coolidge confronted him and decided he should be fired but didn't actually sack him until he refused to let Senate investigators examine his department's records.[9]

In 1924, Congress passed a law that stopped any new Japanese immigration to the United States. The legislation undermined Coolidge's diplomatic initiative in Southeast Asia and caused increased anti-Americanism in Japan.

CONCLUSION

According to John O. McGinnis's excessive praise for both men, Calvin Coolidge provided the best defense of limited government in the twentieth century until the presidency of Ronald Reagan. McGinnis further notes that Coolidge performed this defense when intellectuals of the day almost universally favored ambitious government. Thus McGinnis, like many conservative Republicans today, feels Coolidge was underrated.[10] Paul Johnson and Thomas B. Silver are also examples of the few analysts defending the Harding and Coolidge administrations.[11]

Coolidge's fiscal austerity — cutting spending, taxes, and the national debt — contributed to the prosperity of the Roaring Twenties because the government just stayed out of the people's way and let them prosper, the model for good government. Unfortunately, Coolidge's excessive monetary expansion during the 1920s eventually caused an economic downturn. Also, he created an environment for the eventual crash of the stock market in 1929 by making overly optimistic statements that fueled excessive investor optimism and speculation, despite his private view that stockbrokers were making too many loans to investors. In this assessment Coolidge is number ten.

31

HERBERT HOOVER

Sucked the Economy into the Great Depression

PP&L* RANKING: 18
Category: Poor

Thirty-first president of the United States

Term: March 4, 1929, to March 4, 1933
Party: Republican
Born: August 10, 1874, West Branch, Iowa
Died: October 20, 1964 (age ninety), New York,
New York

Spouse: Lou Henry Hoover
Alma Mater: Stanford University
Occupation: Engineer (mining), businessman, humanitarian
Religion: Quaker

Herbert Hoover was a Republican who had supported Teddy Roosevelt's Progressive Party candidacy in 1912 and Democrat Woodrow Wilson's progressive campaign in 1916. In contrast to his Republican predecessors, Warren Harding and Calvin Coolidge, Hoover had a progressive agenda.[1] With its activist approach, the Hoover presidency converted a run-of-the-mill recession into the Great Depression and set the precedent for FDR's New Deal, which was only an expansion of the policies of the late Hoover administration and had the same goals: relief, recovery, and reform.

According to John D. Hicks, a historian specializing in the Republican dominance of the 1920s, it was Hoover "who first accepted as a governmental responsibility the task of defeating the depression."[2] By doing so, Hoover set a bad precedent. Previously, American society did not expect the government to take an active role in restoring prosperity in bad economic times. Astutely, the

---

*PP&L = Peace, Prosperity, and Liberty.

American people had believed that the market would eventually correct itself. For this colossal misstep, Hoover deserves his poor ranking.

PEACE

Eschewed Foreign Intervention

Like Woodrow Wilson, on whose war effort he had worked as food administrator, Hoover was a committed interventionist and believed in an activist U.S. government overseas.[3] Yet, with the massive carnage of World War I still vivid in the American public's mind, Hoover was forced to be restrained in his foreign policy.

When Japan invaded Manchuria in 1931, Hoover's Secretary of State Henry Stimson advocated imposing economic sanctions and threatening or actually using force against Japan. Hoover, however, decided to limit his response to a verbal condemnation. Some would argue that if he had taken action then, the Japanese attack on Pearl Harbor would not have taken place ten years later. Delaying war for ten years, however, was not a bad thing, especially when the American people, in the absence of any Japanese attack on the United States, would not have supported a war with Japan in 1931.

In reaction to Woodrow Wilson's profligate U.S. interventions in Latin America, Hoover, like his Republican predecessors Harding and Coolidge, eschewed such adventures in the Western Hemisphere.

PROSPERITY

Practiced Activist Government, Which Aggravated Economic Malaise

Hoover was not a proponent of laissez-faire economic policies, even before assuming the presidency. Hoover believed that Americans should have "ordered freedom"; that government money might be spent on public works, scientific research, or anything with "some great major purpose"; and that federal funds could even subsidize business, if it enhanced the "public good."

Hoover's rhetoric promoted individualism and was more pro-freedom, and his activism subtler, than that of FDR, which may be why some historians have given him the "do nothing" moniker. His stated vision was a society of self-regulating industrial trade associations, labor organizations, and agricultural cooperatives voluntarily coordinating with each other — that is, voluntary corporatism.[4] But his actual policies led down the road to government coercion, regulation, and subsidization. For example, instead of mandatory controls on businesses, he asked them to accept voluntary controls. Of course, the implication was that if they didn't adopt them, compulsory controls would be imposed. Another example was Hoover's advocacy of government loans to aid farmers, whereas Congress wanted to provide outright subsidies.

Hoover also set direct precedents for FDR's activism, as in the creation of the Reconstruction Finance Corporation (RFC), itself an outgrowth of the War Finance Corporation during World War I, which loaned money to railroads, financial institutions, agricultural cooperatives,[5] and states for relief efforts. The RFC was continued under the New Deal. Hoover also gave the country the Emergency Relief and Construction Act (ERCA) of 1932, which increased the federal government's authority to lend money to states for aiding the unemployed. Hoover believed that direct federal aid to the unemployed was unconstitutional and that such assistance was a state and local responsibility. Yet ERCA set a precedent for the federal government taking responsibility for the unemployed and was a precursor to FDR's Works Progress Administration, Civil Works Administration, and Federal Emergency Relief Act, which provided grants to states aiding the unemployed and may have had wider effects than any other New Deal program.[6] Hoover's Farm Board was the precedent for FDR's Agricultural Adjustment Act.

At the end of his term in 1932, some criticized Hoover for not doing enough about the Depression, and others blamed him for doing too much. Unfortunately, both activist presidents — Hoover and FDR — did too much and thus turned a typical recession into the Great Depression, the worst economic calamity in U.S. history. Although Hoover set the precedent for government activism, FDR is ranked lower than Hoover because FDR took unnecessary and counterproductive government intervention in society to staggering new levels, and that role has never diminished.

Deepened the Economic Downturn

After the 1929 stock market crash, Andrew Mellon, Hoover's secretary of the treasury, advocated initiating laissez-faire policies that had led to recovery in previous recessions and depressions. These policies would have entailed slashing government spending and allowing businesses to liquidate unprofitable investments, thus letting the market clear itself. This liquidation would have caused unemployment, but it would have been temporary as long as wages and prices were allowed to fall, thus increasing the demand for labor. Instead, activist Hoover subtly coerced businesses to maintain wages and employment levels, avoid liquidating their investments, and even expand them. Businessmen across industries agreed to refrain from cutting wages and also pledged to increase the construction of new facilities. In other words, businessmen invested in new production capacity while the demand for their products was falling — creating a government-driven, artificially induced expansion that exacerbated the eventual Depression.

In addition, Hoover artificially caused the prices of farm commodities to rise. He created government-encouraged cartels in the grain, bean, pecan, livestock, wool, and cotton markets. Other government programs stabilized the prices of grapes, butter, and dairy products. In addition to prolonging and deepening the economic downturn by not allowing prices to fall back to equilibrium, Hoover's action was morally questionable, as the rising prices of such necessities benefited certain narrow groups, when most people had far less money to buy them during an economic downturn.

Hoover also expanded federal public works programs and encouraged states to do the same. Although initially Hoover had been skeptical of public works spending, businesses seeking contracts supported such programs. Hoover's public works programs were a precursor to FDR's Civilian Conservation Corps and other artificial make-work programs. Moreover, because Americans didn't want competition for scarce jobs in a time of depression, Hoover used his administrative powers to stop immigration into the country. A lack of immigration, however, can also slow economic growth by blocking new ideas and skills from entering the economy.

Shortly after the October 1929 stock market crash, Hoover used a tax cut to try to spur business expansion and increase consumer spending, but in December 1931 he proposed and Congress enacted one of the largest peacetime tax hikes in U.S. history. The package included doubling the estate tax; restoring the terminated gift tax; establishing new taxes on bank checks, securities transfers, and radio, phone, and telegraph messages; bringing back excise taxes from World War I on a wide variety of products; and increasing personal and corporate income taxes. Raising taxes during a depression tends to slow economic growth rates even further.

Hoover recklessly responded to excess credit with more excess credit, which eventually worsened the economic slump. Although the money supply remained fairly constant, he increased the federal government's reserve currency holding.

The Glass-Steagall Act of 1933 was good for big banks because it expanded the Federal Reserve System's lending power.

In addition, Hoover provided federal government loans to specific groups — homeowners, farmers, railroads, financial institutions, and, indirectly, the unemployed — further expanding credit. Overall, Hoover was less reluctant to provide federal assistance to business interests than to unemployed individuals.[7] Thus Hoover gets an average ranking from Vedder and Gallaway on whether his policies limited government and fought inflation — he was tied for places sixteen to eighteen (with James Polk and James Buchanan) out of thirty-nine presidents ranked. This ranking is much too high because Hoover converted a run-of-the-mill recession into the Great Depression.

Set Bad International Economic Policies

The disintegration of Austria's largest bank had the same depressive effect on the economies of Europe that the stock market crash had on the U.S. economy. As a result, Hoover realized that payment of war reparations and debts would not happen, and he proposed a one-year moratorium on all international debt payments. This moratorium included German reparations for World War I to the French and British and the repayment of war debt by those two nations to the United States. The French delayed their assent to Hoover's proposal, and all German banks failed. Yet suspending debt repayment is unhelpful to the international financial system, no matter what the economic conditions, because it rewards countries for shirking their responsibilities and will thus produce more deadbeat borrowers in the future.

In 1930, against the advice of virtually all economists, Hoover signed the Smoot-Hawley Tariff Act, which raised tariffs to their highest level in American history. According to Richard Hofstadter, this action was "a virtual declaration of economic war on the rest of the world."[8] The act triggered worldwide retaliation in higher tariffs. The closing of foreign markets hurt U.S. exporters, including farmers. Imports needed for U.S. industries rose in price. Thus protectionism, such as the Smoot-Hawley trade bill, deepened the world's economic downturn.

Vetoed the Huge Tennessee Valley Authority Pork-Barrel Project

One bright episode in Hoover's presidency was his veto of the proposed Tennessee Valley Authority — a massive government project intended to generate electricity and public works jobs — because it would put the government in competition with its own citizens. The veto of this project demonstrates that although Hoover was an activist, he paled in comparison to FDR. The Tennessee Valley Authority was eventually enacted during FDR's administration, as were countless other big government programs under the New Deal.

LIBERTY

Grossly Violated Privacy; No Friend of Liberty

In a gross violation of privacy, Hoover ordered the Treasury Department to publish the names of taxpayers who got large tax refunds from the government and instructed the Justice Department to publish the names of those who had lobbied for the appointment of federal judges. Hoover's regulatory lust also led him to zealously enforce the ongoing prohibition on the production and sale of alcohol, which had started in 1920 and lasted until it was recognized as a failure in 1933 during FDR's administration.

In February 1931, Congress enacted, over Hoover's veto, the Bonus Act, which gave substantial subsidies to the veterans of World War I.[9] These benefits were not the first given to World War I veterans. In the spring of 1932, when the veterans — the "bonus army" — weren't satisfied with these expanded benefits and camped in the nation's capital to campaign for early pension distribution, Hoover brutally and unconscionably repressed them, using the military under the command of Douglas MacArthur.

CONCLUSION

Although Hoover's activism didn't allow the market to correct the economy back into prosperity and actually aggravated a typical recession into the Great Depression, FDR's hyper-activist agenda sunk the nation further into a dependence on big government programs and exacerbated the situation even further. Herbert Hoover is ranked a poor president, not because he did too little about the deepening Depression, as the conventional wisdom holds, but because he took actions that interfered with the economy's tendency to right itself naturally. Hoover is number eighteen in this assessment.

32

FRANKLIN D. ROOSEVELT

Lied the Nation into War and Expanded Government

PP&L* RANKING: 31
Category: Bad

Thirty-second president of the United States

Term: March 4, 1933, to April 12, 1945
Party: Democratic
Born: January 30, 1882, Hyde Park, New York
Died: April 12, 1945 (age sixty-three),
Warm Springs, Georgia

Spouse: Eleanor Roosevelt
Alma Mater: Harvard University
Occupation: Lawyer (corporate)
Religion: Episcopalian

Franklin Delano Roosevelt is often ranked among the three greatest presidents, largely because of the crises he faced during his term. The conventional wisdom is that he brought the nation out of the Great Depression and guided America through its greatest and most justified war, which vanquished the evil autocratic dictators in Germany, Italy, and Japan.

In reality, FDR exacerbated and prolonged the Great Depression, while in the process enlarging government bureaucracy and creating welfare programs that haunt us to this day. He lied America into a war that might have been avoided, and although he won a victory, some of his means might be classified as war crimes. Both at home and abroad, he greatly expanded the roles of both the

---

*PP&L = Peace, Prosperity, and Liberty.

248

presidency and government beyond what the Constitution's framers originally intended.

FDR had John Adams's quotation as president — "May none but honest and wise men ever rule under this roof" — carved into the mantel of the White House State Dining Room.[1] The problem is FDR was neither honest nor wise. According to Turner Catledge, the *New York Times* White House correspondent during FDR's administration, "Roosevelt's first instinct was always to lie, but halfway through an answer the president realized he could tell the truth and get away with it, so he would shift gears and something true would trickle out."[2]

What FDR had was mesmerizing charisma — an amazing presence on the radio and at news conferences, ebullient optimism and tranquility through major crises, a way to turn a phrase (for example, "The only thing we have to fear is fear itself"), and thus popularity — which he used to indirectly pressure Congress to legislate. Since FDR, presidents have been evaluated more and more on their persona — to the country's detriment.

PEACE

Maintained a Deceitful and Aggressive Foreign Policy prior to World War II

FDR's lying to enmesh America in World War II has been justified by what was later deemed as the glorious and total Allied victory over brutal Nazi Germany, fascist Italy, and Imperial Japan. Yet this interpretation has been written after the fact. Just prior to the U.S. entering World War II, most Americans still wanted to avoid getting into the war. About 70 percent of the public believed that U.S. involvement in World War I was a catastrophe and did not want to repeat it.

As Europe moved toward war, public opposition in the United States to American participation was strong, and it continued even as Hitler invaded Poland in September 1939, prompting France and Britain to declare war, and later as German troops overran Norway, Denmark, the Netherlands, Belgium, and France in the spring of 1940. Neither did Japan's invasion of Manchuria, China, and French Indochina alter public opinion.[3] From 1935 to 1939, Congress enacted four neutrality laws to keep FDR from getting the United States involved in a Pacific or European conflict.

Because U.S. public opinion was still receptive to the traditional U.S. foreign policy of military restraint overseas, FDR had to sneak the United States into the war. Sometime in the 1930s, FDR concluded that the United States could not live with Hitler, yet he kept even his closest aides guessing about his plans.

Even before World War II started, FDR signed a 1938 executive order that allowed the U.S. Army to sell older weapons to private contractors, who then could sell them overseas — to the British. After Hitler invaded Poland in September 1939, FDR successfully lobbied Congress to amend the Neutrality Act of 1935 and sell weapons to countries if they paid cash and transported them on their own vessels ("cash and carry"). The law also banned American ships from entering areas under naval blockade.[4] Of course, because the British controlled the seas and the Nazis didn't, the arms sales only went to the United Kingdom. In the summer of 1940, Congress passed and FDR signed the first peacetime draft in U.S. history — forcing young men to fight for a "free" society. Conscription faced fierce opposition, which FDR attempted to deflect by saying that the draft was necessary to keep the United States out of war[5] and that draftees would only be used to defend the United States and would never be deployed beyond the Western Hemisphere. None of these promises were borne out.

In September 1940, without congressional approval, FDR, unconstitutionally and in violation of the Neutrality Act of 1935 and other laws, traded fifty U.S. destroyers for access to British bases in the Caribbean.[6] In March 1941, after he had been reelected for a first-ever third term, he asked Congress to lease weapons to Britain with virtually no requirement for repayment.[7] FDR justified all these actions as steps to keep the United States out of the war, even though the U.S. military argued that he was severely eroding U.S. preparedness for war — a fact that became glaringly obvious when the country later entered the war.

At the same time, FDR engaged in provocative acts against both the Nazis and the Japanese. According to Republican columnist Michael Barone, "Roosevelt could say that World War II was not a war of choice. Yet the choices he made before Pearl Harbor certainly helped to provoke an attack."[8] In April 1941, after the presidential election of 1940 was conveniently over and almost nine months before the Japanese attack on Pearl Harbor, the United States entered World War II. FDR expanded the U.S. security zone to encompass a vast area in the western Atlantic and ordered U.S. warships and aircraft to assist the British in finding German U-boats. He told aides and Winston Churchill that he hoped to provoke an incident with Germany that would make Americans receptive to U.S. warships protecting British convoys in the Atlantic. In the spring of 1941, FDR took advantage of a minor altercation between a U-boat and the USS *Greer* to effectively order, without congressional approval, U.S.

protection of British convoys, the arming of U.S. merchant ships transporting allied cargo, and shoot-on-sight orders against German submarines. Those actions were a flagrant violation of the founders' intention that Congress should decide whether, with whom, and when the nation went to war. Also in the spring of 1941, FDR, without congressional authorization, sent U.S troops to protect Iceland and Greenland from the Nazis.

On the Pacific front, U.S.-Japanese relations had remained stable through Japan's invasions of Manchuria (1931) and China (1937). Japan was seeking a Western-style empire such as those of the British and French. In July 1940, however, to deter further Japanese acquisitions, the United States fortified the Philippines, transferred the Pacific Fleet to Pearl Harbor, increased aid to China, and imposed severe economic sanctions on the Japanese. The embargo included a ban on exports of scrap metal and aviation fuel. U.S. sanctions may have spurred the Japanese to form an alliance with Italy and Germany. In July 1941, retaliating for Japan's invasion of southern Indochina, FDR froze all Japanese assets in the United States and slapped a ban on oil exports to that nation.

According to Patrick Maney, a friendly FDR biographer, the oil embargo was a provocation rather than a deterrent. The Japanese started eying British Singapore and the oil-rich Dutch East Indies. Desperate in the face of diminishing oil supplies, the Japanese vowed that unless the United States resumed oil exports and gave them a green light in China, they would wage war to conquer oil and raw materials. During negotiations, the United States demanded that Japan get out of China and Indochina and rescind its alliance with Germany and Italy or the oil spigot would not be turned back on. In August 1941, the Japanese proposed that FDR and the Japanese premier meet for talks, but FDR declined. The Japanese also offered to withdraw from Indochina.

Maney asserts that FDR was taking what he felt were the lessons of Chamberlain's concessions to Hitler at Munich and transplanting them to East Asia, thus adopting a hawkish stance against the Japanese. Maney admits, however, that a more conciliatory attitude by FDR toward Japan — that is, a relaxation of the oil embargo, other U.S. concessions, or a willingness to meet with their premier — might have convinced the Japanese to delay or avoid war with America.[9] FDR had little to lose by trying this more conciliatory approach — other than forgoing a back door to war against the Nazis, which he had been stymied from by his own "stay out of the war" rhetoric and Hitler's unwillingness to oblige U.S. provocations in the Atlantic.

The Philippines stood in the way of Japanese oil supply lines from the Dutch East Indies. The Japanese believed that an attack on the U.S.-fortified Philippine islands would trigger an unwinnable war with the economically more powerful United States, but if they could knock out the U.S. fleet at Pearl Harbor, they hoped the United States would be demoralized and not fight. At minimum, knocking out the U.S. fleet for six months would allow Japan to take the Philippines, Malaya, and the Dutch East Indies and form a defense perimeter in the Pacific in an attempt to withstand a U.S. counteroffensive.

Much debate has occurred about whether FDR knew about the planned Japanese attack on Pearl Harbor and let it happen to draw the "isolationist" American public into wars against Japan and Germany. What is undisputed about FDR's behavior is damning enough. FDR imposed the provocative oil embargo against the Japanese, which he had to know would make them desperate for oil. FDR and the U.S. military knew that war was imminent and that the Japanese were probably going to attack somewhere. In both the Pacific and Atlantic theaters, FDR's strategy was the same: undertake provocative acts and then let the enemy attack the United States first. Of course, this dishonest and provocative "defensive" strategy ended up costing almost 2,500 lives at Pearl Harbor.

Before Pearl Harbor, advocates of the traditional U.S. foreign policy of military restraint, with the support of most of the American people, made at least a credible case for staying out of World War II. Traditionalists supported strong U.S. defenses, abhorred Japan and Germany, and didn't mind assisting Britain as long as it didn't involve the United States in the war. They reasoned that although some German bombers could hit certain points in the Western Hemisphere, even in the worst case — Hitler's conquest of all of Europe — Germany had nowhere near the naval power or logistics to invade the United States over the vast Atlantic Ocean. Besides, many of Hitler's forces would be tied down occupying the large European territory. If the United States maintained adequate defenses, the traditionalists argued that the United States would be safe from Hitler.[10]

FDR feared that if Germany defeated the British and gained access to the powerful British fleet, the Germans could isolate the United States. Prior to World War II, FDR had engaged in a naval buildup, and further augmentation of the U.S. fleet was a viable policy alternative to jumping into the European war against Hitler. If Germany didn't beat Britain, or if the losing British scuttled their fleet as they had promised, Hitler had only a second-rate navy, which was less capable than the German fleet during World War I, and had to rely primarily on U-boats. Submarines were an instrument to deny other nations control of the sea rather than a tool for asserting that control.

cities.[14] The United States and Britain continued the deliberate massive bombing of German and Japanese cities long after it was obvious that Germany and Japan were going to lose the war — for example, the horrific firebombing of Dresden in February 1945, just a few months before Germany was overrun by Allied ground forces.

The bombing was designed to target enemy civilian populations to get them to put pressure on their governments to change course (surrender) — a strategy the world now calls "terrorism" when groups like al Qaeda commit such acts. Not only was this unconscionable, the bombing of civilians was actually counterproductive — enraging the enemy and making him fight harder.

Although Allied atrocities were not in the same league as those of Hitler, Mussolini, and the Imperial Japanese government, they were war crimes nonetheless. FDR countenanced such intentional attacking of civilians, and Truman, after FDR's death, continued that policy, which culminated in the dropping of two atomic bombs on Japan even after U.S. officials knew that the country was about to surrender.

Obtained Victory, at Least

FDR had few positive accomplishments, but winning World War II was a big one. Although he tried to provoke adversaries and lie the United States into a war that some maintained should not have concerned the country, he did win it. Although FDR can be accused of provoking an attack by Japan and a subsequent sympathetic declaration of war by its ally, Nazi Germany, Japan could have sidestepped U.S. provocations, as Nazi Germany did in the Atlantic. Although U.S. sanctions on oil did hurt Japan's economy, the Japanese didn't have to fall into the mercantilist view that they had to conquer the Dutch East Indies to grab alternative supplies of oil. Taking a lesson from Scottish and English classical economists of yore, it would have been cheaper to buy the oil from the Dutch East Indies, other suppliers, or the black market. Because there was no U.S. naval blockade of Japan, oil could have been imported from somewhere, albeit at above the market price. Thus, Japan could have ignored the U.S. provocation and refrained from starting a war it was likely to lose. This situation is analogous to the U.S. Civil War, in which the South was provoked by Lincoln into attacking Fort Sumter. Thus FDR, like Lincoln, had a right to respond when attacked.

Because of the geographic advantages of the United States and because FDR skillfully delayed the cross-channel Allied invasion of Europe so that the Soviets took most of the casualties against the Nazis, America was the only great power to come out of World War II relatively unscathed. Also, unlike Abraham Lincoln, FDR selected good generals; but because the United States had so much industrial power, it might have beaten the Axis powers with lesser men. Since the American Civil War, the first modern conflict, every major conventional war has been won by the nation or nations with the greatest economic power.

Was Deceitful about the Yalta Agreement Governing the Post–World War II World

Painting Stalin as a lover of liberty and human rights during the war made it necessary for FDR to keep lying after the war, when he secretly allowed Stalin to set up friendly — read: communist — regimes in Eastern Europe. This region was a critical buffer zone against another devastating attack on Russia from the West. When "Uncle Joe" did install such communist regimes, the disillusionment in the West helped cause the Cold War. Similar to Woodrow Wilson's making excessive concessions after World War I to get the ineffective League of Nations, FDR got only a vague promise from Stalin to include some noncommunist Poles in a provisional Polish government, and FDR had to approve a secret British–Soviet agreement to divide up Europe — all in order to get what turned out to be a feckless United Nations.

To be fair to FDR, the Soviets already occupied Eastern Europe with the Red Army in February 1945, when the Yalta conference convened. To prevent any future invasions of their territory, the Soviets' only nonnegotiable item on the postwar scene was that they be allowed to establish friendly regimes between the USSR and Germany, with the invasion corridor through Poland being the most vital. The United States and Britain didn't consult the USSR on the armistice in Italy in 1943, and the Soviets allowed the United States to have a free hand in the occupation of postwar Japan. In World War II, the Soviet Union had vastly more casualties than any other nation; with twenty-seven million dead, the Soviets had achieved the most costly victory in human history.

FDR did not follow the advice of George Kennan, a diplomat in the U.S. embassy in Moscow, who wanted FDR to be honest with the American public about the reality that the Soviets had borne the brunt of Nazi aggression and weren't about to give up control over the buffer zone of Eastern Europe between them and Germany, their traditional rival. FDR's refusal to be honest led to American disillusionment with Soviet actions during the Truman and subsequent administrations and was at least one of the causes of the ensuing Cold War.

PROSPERITY

Expanded the Welfare State[15]

FDR limited the economic freedom of Americans by expanding the welfare state. This strategy began with his New Deal in the 1930s. During the New Deal, federal intervention in the marketplace expanded to include heavy government involvement in retirement and unemployment payments; labor–management relations; wages, hours, and working conditions; securities and investments; and the regulation of specific economic sectors, such as radio broadcasting, agriculture, trucking, airlines, and oil and coal marketing.[16]

In 1933, Congress modified the Trading with the Enemy Act, passed during World War I, to expand to peacetime the president's authority to declare a state of national emergency. That same year, FDR used the broadened authority to declare a "bank holiday," which suspended banking across the nation during the run on banks in the Great Depression.[17]

Passage of the National Industrial Recovery Act, the centerpiece of the New Deal, compelled industries to form cartels, or "code authorities," which had the authority to regulate production, quality, wages, prices, and distribution channels.[18] To accomplish this, FDR suspended antitrust statutes that prohibited such collusive industrial arrangements. This example illustrates that government intervention more often benefits, rather than harms, those being regulated. Companies shielded from competition in cooperative cartels could then charge more for their products. In fact, the NIRA resembled proposals for government–business partnerships put forth by the U.S. Chamber of Commerce, the lobby for big business. Such business–government cooperation had been used for the first time during World War I, and this precedent was used to justify the NIRA. The industrial cartels were modeled after fascist Italy's "corporatives," which were industrial trade associations that planned production, quality, prices, distribution, and labor standards and were regulated by the Italian government.[19]

After the Supreme Court ruled the law unconstitutional because it inserted the federal government into intrastate commerce, NIRA's central planning approach gave way to a somewhat more competitive economy, which the government still regulated.[20] In a time of economic slowdown and declining income for the average consumer, it would have been disastrous and immoral to restrict production and competition — through the creation of industrial cartels — thereby excessively driving up prices and corporate profits. The court's ruling undermined but did not completely defeat anticompetitive forces in the economy.

The Agricultural Adjustment Act took a similar approach to the agriculture industry. It controlled farm production (initially by burning crops and slaughtering livestock and later by paying farmers to restrict output of both), licensed producers, and allowed restrictive marketing agreements — thus reducing supplies of food and raising prices for people who were already going hungry. FDR's somewhat fuzzy goal was to raise farm prices, get people to move from the cities to the countryside by sponsoring a public jobs program called the Civilian Conservation Corps (CCC), and let the increased purchasing power of the agricultural quarter of the population increase the demand for the output of business — thus driving the U.S. economy out of depression.

But the Agricultural Adjustment Act (AAA) mainly benefited large landowners and hurt poor sharecroppers and tenant farmers, who were thrown off the soil so rich landlords could get subsidies for not producing on that land. Thus government intervention helped those with political power — the farm groups who negotiated with the government for the competition-restricting law — at the expense of the poor. Once again, however, the Supreme Court ruled a centerpiece of the New Deal unconstitutional.

Although the NIRA and AAA were the two linchpins of the New Deal, they were only part of FDR's program. After taking office in 1933, FDR called Congress into a special session, which passed fifteen initiatives that either tried to help the economy recover or provided assistance to the unemployed. In June 1935, FDR again nudged Congress by declaring that members should not adjourn until they passed a second New Deal, which they did. After the Supreme Court had struck down the AAA and NIRA, FDR got the Third New Deal passed in 1937 and 1938.

Expanded Government Services

In large part, FDR was not responsible for the copious legislative record with which he is credited. Lyndon Johnson always admired FDR's legislative acumen, but LBJ really possessed far more himself. LBJ had a more direct role as president in getting the Great Society programs through Congress than FDR had in getting the New Deal passed. Congress generated most of the New Deal, not FDR, who had poor skills as a legislative president. Yet FDR signed the legislation Congress passed and should be held partially responsible for substantially expanding unnecessary government control over the U.S. economy and society. Like LBJ later, FDR was less concerned with the specifics of the experimental government programs created than with the fact that some sort of legislative program was being enacted. FDR was under pressure to "do something" about the Depression.

Driven by the Spanish-American War and World War I, the government had been expanding its penetration into the economy since the turn of the twentieth century. During the New Deal, however, defunct government agencies were resurrected from the World War I period and renamed. Even some of the same people were brought back to run them.

Although the public thought that FDR had a master plan or blueprint for the New Deal, there was no overall economic philosophy. FDR did not buy readily into Keynesianism — the theory by which increased government spending expands aggregate demand and thus economic growth — and, when he first took office, he had conservative tendencies about excessive federal spending and balancing the budget. He didn't act on those tendencies, however;[21] he became more receptive to Keynesianism only later in his presidency.

The New Deal was a series of expensive experiments that wasted billions of taxpayer dollars at a time when the average American did not have much cash to spare. The New Deal's programs were duplicative and sometimes worked against each other. Despite conventional wisdom today, many times, the New Deal's programs gave a disproportionate amount of benefits to the "haves" rather than the "have-nots."

For example, the New Deal gave the American public the Securities and Exchange Commission, which benefited the securities industries; the minimum wage, which benefited people who had jobs but reduced business's demand for labor, thus throwing poor unskilled workers out of jobs; public housing, which benefited homebuilders; and the Federal Deposit Insurance Corporation (FDIC), which subsidized banks by insuring bank patrons' deposits, thus bringing more money into those financial institutions. This measure was part of a trend toward governmental rescue of unsound banks, thus encouraging further irresponsible behavior on their part and allowing them to escape their legal obligations.[22]

Although FDR did not believe that large public-works spending would revive the economy, he ended up creating a dizzying array of redundant agencies to do just that — the Civilian Conservation Corps (CCC), the Works Progress Administration (WPA), the Public Works Administration (PWA), and the Civil Works Administration (CWA).

All in all, during his long tenure, FDR created sixty-five new federal agencies to provide public works, subsidies for banks, loans for homes, securities regulation, and farm credit. During his presidency, employment in the federal government increased by a factor of five.[23]

Contrary to popular belief, however, FDR did not pioneer the federal welfare state — Republican Herbert Hoover did when he signed the Emergency Relief and Construction Act in 1932 to give federal loans to states for providing aid to the unemployed. This law set a major precedent in creating a federal responsibility for taking care of the unemployed.[24] FDR's administration merely went further in the Federal Emergency Relief Act, providing federal grants to states for relief to the unemployed.[25]

But in 1935, during the Second New Deal, a major expansion of the welfare state commenced when Social Security was inaugurated. FDR purposefully funded the retirement system with a regressive payroll tax, paid by those least able to do so, rather than through increases in the progressive income tax. His thought was that no politicians could ever abolish a retirement system that was funded by the workers themselves. The fatal problem with the system is that workers do not save for their own retirement. Current workers fund current retirees. Since the U.S. population is aging, there are fewer workers to support more and more retirees. The system is prone to such demographic time bombs. Social Security has turned out to be a mammoth entitlement program that grows automatically and will eventually be bankrupt.

After the Supreme Court struck down the NIRA and AAA, FDR could see that Social Security and the Wagner Act, which gave designated unions monopolies over collective bargaining,[26] would be next. In one of the most momentous decisions of his presidency, he tried to add friendly justices to the Supreme Court by increasing the number of Supreme Court justices from nine to fifteen. Doing so required only simple majorities in both houses of Congress, but FDR made Congress angry by failing to consult them on the matter. The national legislature voted down his bid to pack the court.

Also contributing to the defeat of FDR's court-packing initiative was the Supreme Court's fear of the consequences of being too far outside of mainstream opinion. In the spring of 1937, instead of upholding the original intent of the Constitution by throwing out more New Deal legislation, the court ran for the hills by ruling that Social Security, the Wagner Act, and a state minimum-wage law (almost identical to a bill it previously had ruled unconstitutional) were constitutional. Later, FDR bragged that he had lost the battle and won the war.

According to Maney, one of FDR's most important deeds was changing the way people thought about the role of the federal government. He enshrined

a new mentality of making the federal government responsible for the economic well-being of its citizens, a concept Hoover had introduced. Earlier, the
American people believed that they were responsible for their own economic
lot in life.

Myths surrounding the Great Depression conclude that either FDR came to
the rescue with his New Deal policies or that Hitler and the Japanese brought
the United States out of the long period of economic hard times by starting
World War II. Neither is true. In fact, FDR's policies prolonged and deepened
the Depression, and the economic downturn continued until the end of the war.

Fiscally, FDR did not fulfill his 1932 campaign pledge to balance the budget,
and his director of the budget resigned because of that failure. The New Deal
raised taxes during a time of depression. In 1935, 1936, and 1937, FDR asked
for tax increases, thus further dragging down a stagnant economy. Also, FDR
and Congress enacted many programs that threatened private property rights.
Because investors were uneasy about the economic climate, capital investment
in the economy did not rebound.

Monetarily, although FDR avoided extreme measures that were advocated
to increase the money supply, he did remove the United States from the gold
standard, a tight money policy that had served the nation well by restraining
inflation.[27] Exacerbating the Depression, FDR's heavy regulation and extensive
management of business led to reduced output and employment and higher
prices.[28]

Neither Hoover nor FDR allowed natural market forces to reestablish economic equilibrium after rapid increases in the money supply during the 1920s,
which caused a typical recession in 1929. Their activist policies converted
this recession into the worst economic disaster in American history. All in
all, Vedder and Gallaway correctly give FDR an abysmal ranking for policies promoting limited government and fighting inflation — thirty-fifth out of
thirty-nine presidents ranked.

Advocated Wartime Economic Intervention

During World War II, following the model of World War I, Congress abdicated its constitutional jurisdiction over interstate commerce and gave FDR
the expansive power to mobilize the entire economy for war. In May 1941,
even before the Japanese attacked Pearl Harbor, FDR declared a state of emergency and seized factories threatened by strikes. Congress later ratified such
seizures by passing the War Labor Disputes Act, which allowed the president
to commandeer plants used to produce war materiel.

The Depression-era Reconstruction Finance Corporation (RFC) was expanded to make loans and investments for defense goods and to engage in government (socialized) provision of certain items deemed key for the war effort — for example, petroleum distribution, rubber production, and insurance underwriting.[29] FDR had the authority to commandeer private resources, tell factories what to produce, disregard private contracts, and control prices and rents.[30] To fund the war, many new taxes were instituted; the income tax was expanded from the wealthy to everyone and was repeatedly hiked; and the pernicious mandatory and automatic withholding of personal income for tax purposes was initiated.

If government interference and regulation had prolonged and exacerbated the Great Depression, even more government intrusion into the economy during World War II made the Depression last through the conflict. This depression was masked by massive war production, which actually led to labor and material shortages. If defense production is excluded, the civilian economy during the war had lower growth rates than during the prewar depression years. It did not turn around until after the war, when resources were converted from the public sphere back to the private sector and from war consumption to productive investment.

Expanded Presidential Power

The Great Depression and World War II allowed FDR to expand federal — especially executive — power. Although FDR did not create the modern presidency — which can be ascribed to William McKinley, Teddy Roosevelt, and Woodrow Wilson — and had not yet attained the power of the "imperial presidency," which evolved during the Cold War and thereafter, he took the presidency to a "first among equals" status among the branches of government. This outcome contravened the founders' intention that the Congress and the states would be the most powerful players in the U.S. federal system.

FDR's serving over twelve years in the presidency allowed him to accumulate power. He used the dark international outlook in 1940 to win an unprecedented third term and the ongoing war to win a fourth in 1944. One of the worst things that FDR did was to run for a third term with no hot war raging in 1940. Fortunately, FDR's actions eventually led to a constitutional amendment to limit the president to two terms in office. FDR's aggressive accumulation of presidential power undermined the republic and was one of his greatest failures.

The War Powers Act allowed FDR some power to reorganize the federal bureaucracy, regulate international financial transactions, and censor all communications with foreign lands. FDR also issued an executive order that authorized government seizure of private businesses for defense production. During a war, Congress had little choice but to ratify this violation of one of the bedrocks of a free society: private property.[31]

Congress sometimes stymied FDR's expansive attempt to pass legislation that increased presidential power. He was unsuccessful in acquiring new authority to administer and reorganize the federal government, in terminating the autonomy of independent agencies, and in expanding the White House staff. Yet in 1939, Congress agreed to a compromise that gave him some additional staff members and temporary power to reorganize the government. FDR made quick use of the ephemeral new power and issued an executive order establishing the Executive Office of the President (EOP) — an "epoch-making event in the history of American institutions," according to Luther Gulick, a public administration specialist. FDR relocated the Bureau of the Budget from the Treasury Department into the EOP and began using it to clear all legislative proposals from federal agencies, as well as proposed executive orders, vetoes, and presidential proclamations. Since the Harding administration, presidents had used the bureau to clear only spending legislation. The bureau, later changing its name to the Office of Management and Budget (OMB), would become a powerful instrument of presidential control over the expanding federal bureaucracy.[32]

During World War II, under the same 1939 executive order and his claimed authority as commander in chief, FDR created entire government agencies via executive order — for example, the Office of Censorship, the Office of Production Management, the Office of War Mobilization, the Office of Civilian Defense, the War Food Administration, the Office of Price Administration, and the National War Labor Board.

In sum, although Lincoln and Wilson got Congress to approve their aggrandizement of power during the Civil War and World War I, respectively, FDR, for an even greater expansion of presidential power than in those two prior large wars, used executive orders to fill in powers that Congress did not legislate.[33]

LIBERTY

Didn't Rescue the Jews

Retrospectively, the Nazi threat to the United States has been magnified by Hitler's horrendous treatment of the Jews, and ending that enormous tragedy is often put forward as a justification for the war. At the time, however, FDR did little about such persecution — one of the greatest failings of his presidency. The mass extermination of Jews — the Holocaust — did not start until 1942, but Nazi persecution and insidious intentions toward the Jews were becoming obvious during the 1930s. Yet FDR did very little to change restrictive American rules, which kept out many Jews who wanted to come to the United States.

In 1942, the U.S. government learned of Nazi intentions to exterminate the Jews at specific camps. But FDR accepted the advice of his military officers not to bomb the rail lines to the camps and did little to rescue the Jews from the gas chambers.[34] Even during the war, he could have proposed to Hitler that the United States would accept all of them as refugees.

Unenthusiastic about Civil Rights and Incarcerated the Japanese

FDR was unenthusiastic about providing civil rights for blacks — even though his wife, Eleanor, was a champion of such liberties and even though the United States was fighting Hitler, at least in part, for his policies of white supremacy. Although FDR did sign an executive order to end discrimination in government hiring, he acquiesced to a revolt by the Pentagon against desegregating the military and let an anti-lynching bill be defeated.

FDR had assembled and held together a new disparate coalition of groups under the Democratic umbrella, which had replaced the Republicans as the majority party. One of the keys to the new coalition was its expansion among white southerners. Promoting civil rights for blacks would have instantly smashed that electoral coalition and endangered his New Deal legislative program. So FDR avoided the civil rights issue like the plague.

Also, FDR issued an executive order that threw seventy thousand Japanese-Americans and tens of thousands of resident Japanese aliens into crowded prison camps without charges or trials just because of their ethnic heritage — not because they were accused of spying or sabotage.[35] In fact, no charges were ever brought against any individual in these groups for espionage, sabotage, or treason.

The irrationality of locking up almost all Japanese Americans and Japanese aliens on the U.S. mainland was shown by the government's different behavior toward local Japanese in Hawaii, the U.S. territory that had actually been attacked by the Japanese military. Although martial law was declared in Hawaii, only "suspicious" Japanese were locked up[36] — thus creating a more lenient policy toward Japanese in the war zone than on the home front. In neither

Hawaii nor the western United States, where almost all of the Japanese lived, did the State Department find a security problem with this population. Racial bias undoubtedly played a role in FDR's executive order for such unconstitutional detention, because German Americans and Italian Americans were not detained, and Japanese aliens were detained in greater numbers than German and Italian aliens.

During wartime, the Supreme Court upheld the constitutionality of FDR's actions, saying that it could not question a president's state of military emergency or the actions taken under it.[37] Apparently, the court forgot its earlier *Ex parte Milligan* ruling in 1866 that said the Constitution could not be suspended in time of war. The Supreme Court would not nullify FDR's internment of Japanese Americans or his unconstitutional creation of extrajudicial military commissions to try German saboteurs, including one U.S. citizen, caught on U.S. soil.

In *Ex parte Milligan*, the Supreme Court had ruled that the president, even during wartime, could not create military commissions in areas that were not a theater of war and where civilian courts could still operate. The civilian courts were functioning fine during World War II and could have heard the cases. But in the 1942 case *Ex parte Quirin*, the court inexplicably allowed FDR to set up military commissions to try the Germans as enemy combatants.[38] This bad precedent allowed George W. Bush to create similar unconstitutional military commissions after the 9/11 attacks. The Constitution requires civilian trials for all but U.S. military personnel, who receive military courts-martial.

Violated Civil Liberties

Although during World War II, FDR's conscientious Attorney General Francis Biddle wanted to avoid repeating the excessive violations of civil liberties that had occurred in World War I, FDR kept belittling him at cabinet meetings for not prosecuting the "seditionists." Biddle reported that FDR wasn't much interested in the theory of sedition or First Amendment rights, but just wanted to halt visible opposition to the war.

To get around U.S. trepidations on restricting civil liberties, FDR and the executive branch cooperated with British government agents sent to the United States to help drag a reluctant America into World War II. The British agents tapped phones, intercepted mail, cracked safes, kidnapped people, started rumors, and smeared "isolationists."[39]

The U.S. government also censored radio programs and newspapers, some of which were banned. The government prosecuted fascist sympathizers under the Espionage Act of 1917, which was still on the books, for their views rather than for spying. Congress passed the Alien Registration Act of 1940, also known as the Smith Act, which required that all resident aliens register, made deportation of people easier, and prohibited persons from advocating the overthrow of the U.S. government.[40] Also, federal authorities suppressed war dissidents, including members of the Jehovah's Witnesses religious group, who were imprisoned and denied hearings on writs of habeas corpus merely because of their opposition to conscription.

CONCLUSION

FDR's massive, unnecessary, and wasteful expansion of the government during the Great Depression (worsening and prolonging the economic downturn) and his lying and provocative behavior in the lead-up to World War II qualify him as one of the worst presidents. Although FDR lied the country into World War II and some analysts think that U.S. involvement in the conflict could have been avoided, FDR helped to oversee the overwhelming Allied victory over aggressive autocratic regimes. Yet he began to deliberately, unnecessarily, and counterproductively bomb enemy cities even after decrying this practice before the U.S. entered the war.

FDR's New Deal and his wartime expansion of the presidency and the state still haunt the United States. FDR is ranked below Lincoln in these rankings because much of Lincoln's expansion of the presidency and government withered after the Civil War. But FDR is not ranked last among presidents, and he is not the father of permanent big government in the U.S. — that would be Woodrow Wilson. By ensnaring the U.S. in World War I, Wilson contributed greatly to the causes of World War II and set a bad precedent for government mobilization of the entire economy for war — which became the model for FDR's New Deal and intrusive management of the economy during World War II.

FDR is not the first modern president — that would be William McKinley — nor the first imperial president — that would be FDR's successor, Harry Truman. One could say, however, that FDR did make the presidency the "first among equals" of the branches of government, but not the crushingly dominant branch that it became after his tenure. A period of permanent war — the Cold War — was needed for the creation of the imperial presidency. Franklin D. Roosevelt comes in at number thirty-one.

33

HARRY S TRUMAN
The First Imperial President

PP&L* RANKING: 40
Category: Bad

Thirty-third president of the United States

Term: April 12, 1945, to January 20, 1953
Party: Democratic
Born: May 8, 1884, Lamar, Missouri
Died: December 26, 1972 (age eighty-eight),
Kansas City, Missouri
Spouse: Bess Wallace Truman
Education: Attended Kansas City Law School for two years
Occupation: Small businessman (haberdasher), farmer
Religion: Baptist

When Harry Truman left office, the vast majority of Americans thought he had done an abysmal job. Although his reputation has been restored recently, sometimes first impressions are the most illuminating. Truman's greatest transgression was changing the traditional U.S. foreign policy of military restraint into one of an informal global empire. Although McKinley and Woodrow Wilson began the transition to empire and military interventionism, the U.S. demobilized its military after World War I and went back to military restraint during the interwar period in the 1920s and 1930s, even restraining from intervening in Latin America. Such demobilization occurred after World War II but was short-lived because a return to military restraint did not happen. Under Truman, the United States got involved in the Cold War, which eventually led to the first large permanent peacetime military in U.S. history.

---

*PP&L = Peace, Prosperity, and Liberty.

Even if the Cold War was a given because of the antagonism between the capitalist and communist systems, the United States would have been smarter to conduct it in a more limited way, rather than creating a globe-girdling empire of its own. Truman's beginning of the permanent U.S. empire was more important than his dropping the atomic bomb and the possibility that he — not the Soviets — started the Cold War.

PEACE

Was the Father of the Permanent U.S. Empire

Truman began the informal U.S. empire of armed interventions, alliances, and foreign aid and military bases, in part, as an activist response to the Soviet Union. This activist peacetime foreign policy set a revolutionary precedent for other presidents and lasted through the Cold War and down to the present. Yet the Soviet threat to the United States was substantially overstated, because the Soviet economy was never more than half that of the United States and was burdened with complete state ownership and planning embedded in a nonviable communist system. The Soviet Union was sometimes called "the Upper Volta with missiles." In the late 1940s, when Truman initiated his policy of containing the Soviet Union globally, the Soviets had no way to attack the United States, either conventionally or with nuclear weapons. They had no surface navy, no atomic bomb, and no way to deliver an attack with a long-range bomber force or intercontinental ballistic missiles. Finally, they had no way to damage the U.S. economy.[1]

At the end of World War II, the U.S. had half the world's economic capacity and two-thirds of its industrial production. The Soviet Union was in ruins physically and economically, like the rest of Europe. The Soviets were in no position to challenge the United States for world primacy — in fact, the threat they posed was always overrated — and after just enduring the worst fighting in world history on their soil, they were in no mood for a hot war with the United States over Western Europe.

Nevertheless, to shore up Western Europe against the Soviets and to avoid an economic collapse there, which U.S. policymakers believed could cause renewed depression in the United States, the U.S. created the Marshall Plan, which infused billions of dollars into this region.[2]

The claim that the U.S. single-handedly rescued its former bitter enemies from economic ruin, however, is exaggerated.[3] The recovery of modern, first-world economies was inevitable. The Germans provided 80 percent of the capital and 100 percent of the labor for reconstructioning their economy. In addition, the West German and Japanese governments evaded or minimized most of the U.S. rehabilitation programs in Germany and Japan, which were generally ineffective.

In 1947, when Truman began to aid Turkey and Greece[4] in the battle against communist insurgencies, he was making a momentous change in U.S. foreign policy by meddling in European affairs during peacetime. This new policy contravened the original Monroe Doctrine, which resisted new European intervention in the Western Hemisphere and, in turn, pledged U.S. restraint from intervening in European affairs.

Actually, Truman went even further, turning local rebellions (the Soviets had agreed not to give Greek rebels aid)[5] in a backwater region of Eurasia into a global effort to "support free peoples who are resisting attempted subjugation by armed minorities or by outside pressures." (Propping up the rightist Greek dictatorship was hardly supporting "free peoples.") Prominent foreign policy advisors — including Secretary of State George Marshall and even George Kennan, author of the expansive policy of containing the Soviet Union — thought Truman's vision was too ambitious.[6] But Republican Senator Arthur Vandenberg had told Truman that he had to "scare the hell out of 'em" regarding the Soviet threat, and Truman did. Truman's Secretary of State Dean Acheson later admitted that the administration had exaggerated the Soviet threat.

George Kennan's original policy prescription entailed containing the USSR politically, economically, and militarily until the Soviet system buckled because of its internal contradictions, but over time, his doctrine was perverted into primarily a policy of military containment. Truman knew that the Soviet system was a house of cards, and he shouldn't have exaggerated the Soviet threat to the point of turning a regional crisis into a worldwide, militarized crusade against communism. Truman and the United States should have had more confidence that the vastly superior U.S. political and economic system would have ultimately won out, even if such a U.S. armed crusade was not undertaken.

Future presidents would pick up on Truman's broadly based defense of the world from communism. Since Truman abandoned previous presidents' noninterventionism, the United States has intervened nearly eighty times overseas in the sixty or so years since 1945, mostly in minor countries — an average of an intervention every nine months.[7]

Truman began the long line of imperial presidents by institutionalizing presidential power — adding the National Security Council (NSC) and the Council of Economic Advisors to the Executive Office of the President. The National Security Act of 1947 created not only the National Security Council but also the Central Intelligence Agency, which could intervene in the affairs of other countries without public or congressional scrutiny. The law also gave the president more control over the military by fusing the Navy and War departments, along with the new air force, into a new Department of Defense.

Through this new bureaucracy, Truman began to govern by secret executive orders and executive agreements with foreign countries — some of the latter requiring only a majority vote in each of two houses of Congress, instead of the more demanding constitutional requirement of a two-thirds vote in the Senate for treaties. Other agreements were not sent to Congress at all. NSC-68, a secret executive order, established the U.S. containment policy toward the Soviet Union during the Cold War.[8]

The rationale for the post–World War II expansion of executive powers was the rapidity with which the nation might need to respond to the threat of a Soviet nuclear attack, with no time to consult Congress. The traditional reading of the Constitution, however, certainly allowed the president to act if the nation was under direct attack by any means, so the expansion of executive powers was unneeded.

The United States should have helped Japan and Western Europe with security until these nations got on their feet economically after the war and were able to be the first line of defense against the Soviet Union. The original purpose of the containment policy was to do just that, but it was perverted into a worldwide imperial policy of encouraging allies to do only so much for their defenses so that they would have to depend on the U.S. protective umbrella.

Entered the Korean Debacle

In January 1949, Truman withdrew the last troops from South Korea and recognized that nation. Despite the Joint Chiefs of Staff writing off Korea as likely to fall under communist influence because of its proximity to the communist giants of the Soviet Union and China and Dean Acheson's exclusion of South Korea from the U.S. defense perimeter, North Korea's invasion of South Korea in 1950 spurred a frantic U.S. response. Truman's policy was the worst of all worlds. If the U.S. had decided before the fact that saving the then-poor South Korea from communism was vital to U.S. interests (which it was not), then Acheson should not have ruined deterrence by implying that the United States would not defend that nation. The North Koreans obviously read Acheson's words and decided the U.S. wouldn't do anything about the North's invasion of the South. Despite Korea's lack of strategic significance, Truman, fearing the consequences of "appeasement," falling dominoes, and a diminution of U.S. prestige (a frequent worry of empires), decided after the fact that the United States had to come to the rescue. Yet the widespread assumption at the time was that the United States would do nothing about the North Korean invasion. Thus Truman could have let this then-backwater nation go communist without much public criticism.

But Truman and the Democrats had endured much opprobrium for "losing" the larger and more important China to communism the year before. After World War II, the United States had sunk billions to help Chiang Kai-shek stay in power, and there was nothing more Truman could have done to stop Mao Tse-tung's victory, except exercising the unappealing option of sending U.S. troops into the Chinese civil war. He should be given credit for not having done so. But when North Korea invaded South Korea, Truman was likely afraid of a repeat of such criticism. This time, he sent the U.S. troops.

Although the Korean War resulted in thirty-seven thousand American deaths, compared to the fifty-eight thousand American deaths during the Vietnam War, the Korean War was much more important. Many analysts mark the Cold War as starting with the U.S.'s precedent-setting peacetime meddling in European affairs with aid to Greece and Turkey in 1947, but the Korean War showed that the United States was willing to commit large numbers of U.S. combat troops on the ground to battle communism in unimportant areas of the developing world. Moreover, the Korean War inaugurated drastic changes in U.S. foreign policy, which moved the country from its traditional and wise policy of military restraint to a permanent policy of interventionism and global empire.

Truman also decided not to ask Congress for a declaration of war, an action that stripped from the people's branch one of its major responsibilities — the war power. Shockingly, congressional leaders abdicated one of Congress's main powers and allowed Truman to act on his authority as commander in chief, which the founders had not intended to apply to situations other than direct defense of the United States. Truman began the tradition — followed by George H. W. Bush in Desert Shield and Desert Storm and Bill Clinton in Haiti — of getting U.N. approval for a war and then presenting Congress with a fait accompli[9] — one of the worst things he did while in office. Today, based on Truman's precedent of widening the commander in chief's role, presidents send military forces into combat without Congress's authorization (for example,

Clinton bombed Kosovo without congressional approval) or maintain that asking for congressional approval is only a presidential courtesy (both Bushes used this argument prior to the Gulf Wars).

Truman committed the nation to fight a war that it was not ready to fight. In addition, he approved risky wartime military actions. Indications are that Truman, from the start, intended to use the North Korean invasion of South Korea to defeat the North Korean army and invade North Korea. Initially, Truman approved only air and naval support for South Korean forces and said no U.S. military action was approved north of the thirty-eighth parallel separating North and South Korea — adding "not yet."

The North Koreans had overrun all of South Korea except the toehold around Pusan, which was on the southern tip of the Korean peninsula. The Joint Chiefs of Staff wanted to delay Douglas MacArthur's reckless plan to conduct an amphibious assault against Inchon, near Seoul, until they were sure the Pusan perimeter could be defended successfully. But Truman overruled the military chiefs and turned the swashbuckling MacArthur loose. MacArthur was successful and soon was trundling his army into North Korea.

The Chinese warned the United States that if U.N. forces crossed the thirty-eighth parallel, they would send forces to help the North Koreans, a warning the United States regarded as a bluff. It wasn't. When U.S. forces got near the Chinese–North Korean border, the Chinese sent two hundred and sixty thousand troops into North Korea and pushed the U.N. forces back into South Korea. Unbelievably, MacArthur wanted to widen the war with U.S. reinforcements, the use of Taiwanese troops, and thirty to fifty nuclear weapons to be used against Chinese cities.

Fortunately, after recklessly expanding the war aims to allow MacArthur to invade North Korea, Truman prudently decided that he didn't want a wider war that could bring in the newly nuclear-armed USSR. Also, Truman was advised that the United States could not defeat the Chinese in Korea because their proximity to the theater of battle allowed them to insert more troops than the United States could muster. General Matthew Ridgway, however, was able to overcome being outnumbered three hundred and sixty thousand to four hundred and eighty thousand and fight his way back to the thirty-eighth parallel, where the front stagnated.

Despite warnings, MacArthur had repeatedly taken actions or made comments that contradicted or criticized Truman's more moderate policies relating to the war. Truman believed that MacArthur had challenged his Constitutional authority as commander in chief. Although Truman's popularity was only at

26 percent, he did take the courageous act of firing MacArthur. In the public fury that followed, almost 70 percent of Americans supported MacArthur. But at later congressional hearings, MacArthur couldn't answer questions about what would have happened if his proposed provocative strategy against China had brought a nuclear-armed Soviet Union into the conflict. Decisively, the Joint Chiefs of Staff backed Truman and said that they had never supported MacArthur's widening of the war against China.

Policies Led to Military-Industrial Complex and Large Peacetime Military

Truman's recklessness ended his political career. By late 1951, the Korean War was so unpopular that Truman's job approval rating was only 23 percent, and as a result he didn't run for reelection in 1952.

The Korean War brought a reversal of the post–World War II military drawdown (including Secretary of Defense Louis Johnson's naval cuts), a massive increase in defense spending, a doubling in size of the armed forces, an expansion of the U.S. nuclear arsenal, an extension and expansion of involuntary military service that had begun in 1948, and increased taxes to pay for it all.[10] In 1952, defense spending had increased twentyfold over its level in 1940 and approached that of World War II.[11]

Helping to drive these huge defense budgets and the interventionist foreign policy that justified them is what President Eisenhower later derided as a dangerous "military-industrial complex." Truman had inadvertently invented it. In most prior wars in U.S. history, civilian industries changed to war production and then converted back to civilian production after a conflict ended. This time Truman had created a dedicated defense industry, and postwar industrial reconversion did not happen after the Korean War. After the Korean War, for the first time in U.S. history, high defense spending and large military forces were maintained during peacetime in the long Cold War.

During World Wars I and II, the president was given the power to dictate what the private sector produced and even to commandeer its resources and seize and operate its production facilities. Instead of commanding industry to meet defense requirements, Truman came up with the idea of giving lucrative military contracts to industry. With peacetime defense spending so high for so long during the Cold War, some companies became permanent wards of the state — doing little else but defense production.[12] This peacetime military-industrial complex, every bit as dangerous as Ike predicted, continues to push successfully for foreign interventions to justify the high defense budgets, which in turn make such military adventurism possible.

Intentionally Dropped Bombs on Civilians

The much-hyped dispute over whether Truman should have dropped an atomic bomb on Japan is less important than meets the eye.

Truman should have refrained from using the weapon. Because the U.S. had broken the Japanese written code, Truman knew that Japan was searching for a way to surrender and save face by retaining the emperor. Japan's home islands were surrounded and cut off by a vastly superior enemy force. Most wars don't end with utter destruction of the enemy and instead conclude with a negotiated settlement. The U.S. tradition of decisive military victory and unconditional surrender, which began with Ulysses S. Grant's victory in the Civil War, is actually an aberration in world history. With a negotiated peace, the United States could have avoided many of the expenses associated with occupying and administering Japan.

The Japanese interpreted the unconditional surrender demand to mean that the revered emperor would be dethroned. Suspiciously, after the two A-bombs were dropped, Truman dropped this demand — allowing the Japanese to keep their emperor — and the Japanese surrendered with this condition.[13]

A U.S. intelligence study, completed after the war, concluded that Soviet entry into the war in the Pacific — which occurred between the dropping of the first and second A-bombs on August 6 and August 9, respectively — would have caused a Japanese surrender even if the super bombs had not been used.[14]

Thus, some have said that the major audience for the bomb was the Soviet Union, not Japan.[15] Suspiciously, Truman kept delaying the Potsdam Conference with Stalin and Churchill until the A-bomb was ready to test; thus Truman may have been keen to threaten Stalin with the new device by telling him about the successful test, which curiously happened during the conference. At the conference, Secretary of War Stimson noted that the United States wore the A-bomb "rather ostentatiously on our hip."[16]

Knowing that the Japanese had made overtures to the Soviet Union to surrender — three weeks before the first A-bomb was dropped on Hiroshima on August 6, 1945 — Truman should not have used nuclear weapons. His decision to do so was against the advice of most of his military leaders. In making the decision, Truman claimed that he was concerned only with U.S. casualties during any invasion of the Japanese home islands, but no one had made a serious study of what those likely casualties would have been. Also, it is questionable ethically to intentionally bomb enemy civilians to reduce casualties among friendly military forces. Yet Truman explicitly acknowledged that he was willing to make that trade-off, saying, "A quarter of a million of the flower of our young manhood were worth a couple of Japanese cities, and I still think they were and are."[17]

Furthermore, a U.S. invasion probably would have been unnecessary to achieve a Japanese surrender. The United States already had undertaken a crippling naval blockade of Japan's island economy, and this maritime strangulation undoubtedly would have eventually forced the Japanese to sue for peace even without a massive U.S. invasion. The blockade could have allowed the passage of some food and medicine, so as not to have been inhumane.

Clearly purposefully targeting civilians, no matter how noble the end goal, is terrorism or a war crime. But Truman did not begin the U.S. policy of intentionally targeting German and Japanese civilians during World War II bombing raids; FDR did. Truman merely made the practice more efficient by doing it with fewer, more powerful atomic bombs. Actually, the many conventional and incendiary bombs caused at least as many Japanese casualties as did the two atomic bombs. At minimum, late in the war when at least some kind of U.S. victory was assured, Truman could have reversed FDR's policy of intentionally bombing Japanese civilians, but he didn't. Perhaps the debate should be about whether the mass aerial slaughter of civilians was effective or moral, not about whether or not it should have been done with a couple of atomic weapons; thus the importance of the debate on the dropping of the A-bomb may be overstated.

Although Truman merely continued FDR's policy of intentionally targeting civilians en masse, he did inaugurate the atomic age. However, the mere creation of nuclear weapons, which FDR was also responsible for initiating, would have done this anyway.

Some have argued that Truman's use of the A-bomb was a blessing in disguise because it showed the world how dangerous nuclear weapons were — thus making nations so cautious about their use that the world has not seen a repeat performance. Yet this same stunning effect could have been achieved by a secret demonstration of the weapon on an uninhabited desert island, which could have been photographed and presented to the Japanese.

Similarly, although most analysts have deemed Truman's Korean conflict a limited war, a U.S. firebombing campaign against North Korean cities, similar to that inflicted on Japanese cities in World War II, leveled half or more of eighteen of twenty-two major cities and much of everything in northern and central Korea, compelling the surviving population to live in caves.[18] The United States deliberately bombed North Korean dams so that the resulting flood would wipe out North Korean crops and cause starvation. In the case of remote and poor North Korea, the U.S. government did not even have the excuse that a dire threat required such draconian measures.

Helped Start the Cold War

Historians debate who started the Cold War — with the conventional wisdom arguing that the Soviets were at fault and the revisionists focusing blame on the United States. Much of this debate hinges on when the Cold War started. The two nations, with very different ideologies and economic and political systems, were bound to be suspicious of each other. According to revisionist Eric Alterman, the Cold War may have occurred anyway for such reasons, but he says the immediate cause was Truman's failure to live up to FDR's acquiescence at Yalta in February 1945 to a Soviet sphere of influence in Eastern Europe. Historically, Russia had been invaded through Eastern Europe, and the Soviets were not going to take any chances with having unfriendly governments in Eastern Europe, especially in Poland. The flat geography of Poland had presented an especially attractive route for foreign invaders.

FDR didn't tell Truman or anyone else that he had tacitly approved the Soviet sphere of influence in Eastern Europe. Truman — after becoming president upon FDR's death — bluntly told Soviet Foreign Minister Vyacheslav Molotov that Stalin needed to keep his pledge at Yalta to get rid of the Soviet-backed Lublin government in Poland and hold free elections there; he implied that U.S. aid might be cut off if the Soviets failed to live up to their agreements. Yet the Soviets had not promised at Yalta to get rid of the Lublin government, but merely had agreed to reorganize that government on a broader democratic basis by including democratic leaders within and without Poland (without mentioning the West-favored London Poles per se). Thus, according to Alterman, Stalin correctly charged that the United States was violating the Yalta accords. Even people in Truman's administration, including Secretary of State James Byrnes, and the British ambassador to Moscow read the Yalta accords as the Soviets did. Some revisionists argue that the Truman confrontation with Molotov on April 23, 1945, was the beginning of the Cold War.

By the summer of 1945, Truman knew what had really transpired at Yalta, yet he directed the U.S. to undermine negotiations between China and the Soviet Union and ordered the U.S. military to prevent the Soviet military from seizing lands in Manchuria, which FDR had also promised the Soviet Union. At the subsequent Potsdam Conference, Truman again told the Soviets that they had not faithfully carried out the Yalta accords by helping to establish democratic governments in Eastern Europe via free elections. In addition, the U.S. reneged on a provisional agreement for German reparations to the USSR.

According to Alterman, Truman's actions fueled Stalin's paranoia and irreparably harmed U.S.-Soviet relations, thus leading to the Cold War. Stalin told a high-ranking U.S. official that he couldn't grasp why the United States wanted to throw Yalta in the trash over Poland and why the U.S. couldn't understand that the Soviets needed a friendly neighbor in the invasion corridor.[19]

FDR and Truman should have been honest about what could have been obtained with the Red Army sitting in Eastern Europe. They could have acknowledged Soviet apprehension about having unfriendly governments in the invasion corridor to their homeland and showcased Stalin's losses elsewhere. Stalin didn't get four-power control over the industrial Ruhr Valley in western Germany — which was occupied by Allied troops — did not get a coveted naval base on the Bosporus Strait, and didn't get to be a trustee over Italy's former colonies in Africa.[20] The Soviets also gave the U.S. unhindered rule over Japan, allowed U.S. troops in South Korea, largely accepted U.S. primacy in China, and acquiesced to U.S. influence over the western and most prosperous parts of Europe. Stalin also honored the October 1944 deal he made with Winston Churchill to divide up Europe. Stalin allowed British suppression of Greek communists, pulled out Bulgarian forces from Macedonia and Thrace, withdrew forces from northern Norway, didn't meddle at all in Finland, allowed fair elections in Hungary and Czechoslovakia, and didn't exploit his military advantage when challenged in Iran.[21]

However, Truman did not start the Cold War all by himself. In February 1946, Stalin gave a speech arguing that war was inevitable between the incompatible socioeconomic systems of capitalism and communism. He tripled the resources for Soviet defense and made the manufacture of consumer goods a lower priority.[22] He may have made this speech because he was bitter that the U.S. had cut off aid so fast after the war and had violated the Yalta agreements. Stalin was one of the most bloodthirsty tyrants in world history, but Truman and the U.S. also had some role in starting the Cold War.

As part of his strategy to contain the Soviet Union, Truman created the North Atlantic Treaty Organization (NATO) in 1949. It was the first major permanent and entangling peacetime alliance created in the long history of the United States. By the 1960s, even though principal U.S. allies had recovered from the devastation of World War II and were prospering, the United States was still providing security for countries financially capable of being the first line of defense in Europe and East Asia.

The road to the creation of the NATO alliance in 1949 began in early 1948 with the Soviet-supported communist coup in Czechoslovakia, which the Soviets believed was in their FDR-approved European sphere of influence. In response, Truman asked for rapid passage of Marshall Plan aid to Europe, a "temporary" resumption of the draft, and universal military training. Also, the United States, Britain, and France announced that the western zones of Germany would be merged into the new nation of West Germany.

This action brought instant Soviet hostility, in the form of threats to access routes to the isolated enclave of West Berlin in the heart of communist-controlled eastern Germany. The Soviets cut off supplies of electricity, coal, vegetables, and milk to West Berlin and halted water, rail, and road traffic to the city in an attempt to starve it. This blockade was an act of war intended to stop the creation of West Germany, to halt the introduction of the new deutsche mark currency, and maybe even to push the allies out of West Berlin for good.[23]

Truman gets credit for dismissing advice that the United States should force its way into West Berlin with an armored convoy. This provocative strategy might have triggered a war with long odds of the United States winning.

Even though the United States had nuclear weapons and the Soviets would not get them until the next year, there were only 6,500 allied troops in West Berlin compared to 18,000 Soviet forces in East Berlin and 300,000 more forces in the eastern part of Germany. For this reason, Truman had to resist pressure from most of his military advisors to abandon West Berlin. They said that risking war over Berlin was "neither militarily prudent nor strategically sound."[24] They also believed that an airlift was unsustainable without weakening other security commitments.

In an election year in which no one thought he had a prayer of beating Republican Thomas Dewey, Truman ordered a full-scale airlift to resupply Berlin, daring the Soviets to fire the first shot. If he had abandoned Berlin, he could have kissed good-bye to any hope of getting reelected. In early 1949, after a fourteen-month blockade, Stalin lifted restrictions on water, rail, and road access to West Berlin without attaining any of his goals. Allied nations created West Germany, made the deutsche mark its currency, and formed the NATO alliance.

Once again, although Truman acted with some moderation during the crisis and did defend the international agreement that guaranteed Western access to West Berlin, he helped cause the crisis in the first place by leading the allies in announcing the plan to combine their zones of control to create West Germany and issue the deutsche mark as its currency. These moves hardened the division of Germany into stone and left the Soviets alone among the wartime allies on the other side of the dividing line.

The Cold War, in which the United States and the Soviet Union confronted each other on virtually every continent, had begun. The United States could have saved many lives and much treasure by being more selective in countering the communist threat — leaving to the Soviets economically backward places such as Korea, Vietnam, Angola, Afghanistan, and Nicaragua. The Soviet Union would have had to spend so much money stabilizing and controlling such nonstrategic economic basket cases that that empire likely would have become overextended and collapsed earlier than it did. And the United States could have helped defend only Japan and Western Europe — the world's regions of high technology and economic power — until they recovered economically from the devastation of World War II. After such recovery, the United States could have become the second line of defense (or balancer of last resort) instead of being the primary guarantor of security for those now-prosperous regions.

Analysts have rehabilitated Truman's legacy because the Cold War was eventually "won" and because a bipartisan consensus has formed around the post–World War II interventionist foreign policy, which Truman pioneered. He must take responsibility, however, for the resulting developments, including the assault on the U.S. Constitution.

Contributed to War in the Middle East

To come from behind in the 1948 election, Truman also helped spur confrontation in the Middle East. Although the allies probably should have carved off a section of Germany, the perpetrator of the Holocaust, for a Jewish homeland or state, European Jewish survivors preferred to go to Palestine, the Biblical "promised land." Until the late nineteenth and early twentieth centuries, significant numbers of Jews had not lived in Palestine for almost two millennia.

At the beginning of World War II, the land then known as Palestine was a League of Nations protectorate governed by Britain and home to a preponderance of Arabs and a much smaller number of Jews. Following the war, Britain was shrinking its empire, and Palestine was offered as a homeland for the Jews — not as a state. But the British had also promised Palestine to the Arabs. The U.S. preference was for immediate independence for Palestine, which would have been partitioned into Jewish and Arabic states with an economic union. The United States also supported massive Jewish emigration to the new Jewish homeland.

Jews all over the world favored partition, but the Arabs opposed it. Presciently, the State Department knew that the Arabs would never accept a partition, that they would fight it using armed forces, and that any conflict would allow the Soviets to come to their aid and get a foothold in the Middle East. The Arabs even said in advance that partition would mean war. They believed the British had given the Jews Arabic land as compensation for the Holocaust.

But the Democratic Party in the United States depended on the votes and, even more important, the campaign contributions of American Jews. In his uphill battle against Thomas Dewey in 1948, Truman desperately needed to win New York, and the Jewish vote was critical. Advisors told Truman success hinged on creating the state of Israel. When U.S. diplomats transmitted the Arab point of view to Truman, he responded that he had few Arabs among his constituents.[25]

The United Nations voted narrowly for partition, and Clark Clifford said that the measure had passed because of Truman's support. Prior to British withdrawal, even as war became likely, Truman recognized Israel a mere eleven minutes after it provocatively announced statehood.[26] Israel's announcement triggered an immediate Arab attack and contributed significantly to the chronic future climate of violence there that continues to this day.

Prior to the 1948 war, over the previous fifty years, Jews had purchased about 7 percent of Palestine, mostly from absentee Arab landholders. Using force during the war, Jews expelled Arabs from their land and expanded Jewish holdings to 79 percent of Palestine. After the war, the Israelis expropriated even more Arab lands. Thus the land of Israel was created primarily by the use of armed force, not land purchases.[27]

PROSPERITY

Increased Government Meddling Domestically

Responding to popular demand, Truman cut back the government and rapidly demobilized the massive armed forces after World War II. Government spending as a portion of the gross national product (GNP) had soared to significantly more than 40 percent during World War II — still a record. The demobilization cut that back, but not below prewar levels. The rapid conversion of resources from military production to civilian industry avoided a postwar recession. Truman and the Democratic Congress should be given credit for this substantial cutback in the government and the record rises in incomes, standards of living, and levels of education it produced, but they should have gone even further in their shrinkage of the state — back to the level of the interwar years or even lower.

When Truman took office, the conventional wisdom was that he would be a proponent of more limited government, but he outdid even the New Deal with the agenda of government activism he laid before Congress. He wanted strengthened antitrust laws, national compulsory health insurance funded by payroll deductions, a minimum wage, unemployment benefits, meddling in labor–management relations, subsidies for farmers, aid to veterans, mandatory universal military training, federal aid to education, federal homebuilding, aid for housing, and redevelopment of blighted urban areas for all income groups. He also wanted to implement a tax cut and balance the budget. It's very hard to balance the budget when trying to cut taxes and enact many new federal programs that need to be funded somehow. All of these programs were bad ideas for various reasons. A coalition of southern Democrats and Republicans blocked much of this program.

After his election victory, Truman repackaged his program as the "Fair Deal." Congress did pass the Housing Act of 1949, which created public housing projects, and the Employment Act, which pledged the government's efforts to foster maximum employment and prosperity — the first time in American history that the government had been given these official responsibilities. But the coalition of Republicans and southern Democrats did not do as much on public housing as he would have liked and once again nixed the national health insurance program and federal aid to education. They did, however, pass the GI Bill, which provided educational benefits for veterans.[28]

Intervened in Labor Disputes

Organized labor was unhappy that Truman extended wartime wage and price controls after the war ended and wanted them removed. Labor was now unencumbered by wartime "no strike" laws and wanted to test right-to-strike laws passed in the 1930s. Thus a rash of strikes occurred in 1945 and 1946.[29] After the coal and rail strikes began, Truman seized the coal mines and railroads and had the government operate them. He also called on railroad workers to go back to work and threatened to use the army to break the strike. Truman's cabinet was shocked when he threatened to draft striking railroad workers into the military. Truman's attorney general objected in writing that the president was overstepping his constitutional authority. But Truman said, "We'll draft them and think about the law later." As he was giving the speech before Congress asking for the authority to draft workers, a note was passed to him that settled the strike on his terms. Ultimately, the requested legislation was passed by the House, but rejected by the Senate.[30] The threat to draft striking workers was very dangerous, because it would set a precedent that the president could severely punish anyone who didn't agree with him on any issue, thus stifling private action, civic protests, and even debate.

In a 1952 steel strike, Truman seized the steel mills under his alleged "inherent power" as commander in chief, supposedly to prevent a paralysis of the national economy and using the rationale that soldiers in the Korean War needed weapons and ammunition.

A public uproar ensued, and the press asked him if his inherent power as commander in chief would also allow him to seize radio stations and newspapers. A federal district judge ruled against Truman, saying that a steel strike was less injurious to the republic than judicial validation of unbridled presidential authority. By a wide margin, in the case *Youngstown Sheet & Tube Co. v. Sawyer*, the Supreme Court struck down Truman's executive order to seize the mills because it had no statutory or constitutional basis. Truman was the commander in chief of the U.S. armed forces, not the country.

Although Truman did few positive things during his almost eight years in the White House, he made some contribution to the record prosperity in America. If Truman had had his druthers, however, he would have demobilized the U.S. military more slowly after World War II and so reduced the abnormally large size of government (more than 40 percent of the GNP) less. But it was precisely this return of resources from the inefficient government to the efficient private sector that caused the postwar economic prosperity. Thus Truman contributed to the economic good times, but only under public pressure to do so. Seen in this light, Vedder and Gallaway's relatively high ranking for Truman on policies limiting government and fighting inflation — ranked tied for thirteenth and fourteenth with Calvin Coolidge out of thirty-nine presidents ranked — is probably too high.

LIBERTY

Did a Little "Red Baiting"

Domestically, the Korean War and Cold War brought the usual erosion of civil liberties so common in wartime throughout American history. Red scares in the 1940s and 1950s were common. Believing that J. Edgar Hoover's FBI was becoming a secret police, Truman thought the fear of communism to be inflated and was generally uncomfortable with Hoover and the organization — except when he wanted domestic surveillance done for him on possible political troublemakers.

In 1946, with the Red scare rising, Truman continued wartime surveillance to protect national security, but Attorney General Thomas Clark didn't tell Truman that FDR's surveillance during World War II applied only to aliens. So domestic surveillance was worse during the Cold War than during World War II. The attorney general also told Truman that the number of disloyal government workers was likely to be low. Instead of standing up to the Republicans, Truman instituted, by executive order, a loyalty program for government employees. There had been such a program during World War II, but Truman's was the first during a period of peace — another bad precedent of pernicious government activism in war hanging over into peacetime.

Clark Clifford, a close Truman advisor, later admitted that the loyalty program had been instituted for political, not security reasons. The statistics bore that out. By 1951, 3,000,000 government employees had been investigated and exonerated by the Civil Service Commission and another 14,000 by the FBI. More than 1,000 workers quit, but only 212 were dismissed for suspect loyalty. No evidence of spying was ever found, and no one was ever prosecuted. Truman later, in a private letter, said the program was a terrible error.

Yet following a staff memo arguing that the American people back their president during a crisis, Truman manufactured the War Scare of 1948 in his uphill battle for reelection. As part of that scare, he gave speeches on the urgency of the Soviet threat and accelerated the loyalty program. Although the Soviet Union continued to suffer from its wartime trauma, Truman made the Soviet Union seem like an imminent threat. It was not Joe McCarthy and the Republicans, but the liberal Democratic Truman administration that initiated Justice Department prosecutions of alleged communists, thus heightening the country's anticommunist fervor.[31] Although Truman eventually denounced McCarthy, the president, for selfish political reasons, had contributed to the atmosphere that allowed McCarthyism to flourish.[32]

In the longer term, the Cold War brought about a permanent war footing during peacetime. Unlike the hot wars of American history, which were of limited duration, the Cold War lasted for more than forty years and was probably even more detrimental to the constitutionally mandated balance of powers between government branches. This long "armed peace" turned FDR's "first among equals" presidency, based on political acumen and charisma, into an institutional and imperial one — at the expense of congressional power. Because Truman helped begin the Cold War and started prosecuting it in an interventionist — rather than a much smarter minimalist — manner, he was indirectly responsible for this erosion of the constitutional checks and balances.

Expanded Rights for Some

The one unadulterated accomplishment that Truman achieved was progress on increasing the rights for African Americans. In 1946, at the Lincoln Memorial in Washington, D.C., Truman gave the strongest speech on civil rights since Lincoln. He called for, among other things, taking action against lynching, ending the caste system based on race, and terminating the poll tax, which discouraged many African Americans from voting. Although Truman's advisors told him that the work of his Committee on Civil Rights would be political suicide, he created the panel in 1946.

During the next twenty years, many of the committee's recommendations became policy and shaped the policy debate on civil rights — for example, in 1964, the Twenty-fourth Amendment to the Constitution prohibited the poll tax and the Civil Rights Act banned those receiving federal money from discriminating based on race. In 1948, Truman banned discrimination in the armed forces and guaranteed equal opportunity in government civil service jobs. At the Supreme Court, Truman's Justice Department supported parties that challenged segregation. Truman also appealed to Congress to satisfy claims made by Japanese Americans who were unfairly imprisoned in camps during World War II only because of their race. Years later, Truman's proposal was finally adopted.

CONCLUSION

All in all, Truman is one of the worst presidents ever because of his over-the-top reaction to the Soviet Union and his initiating of a long-term activist Cold War posture; his pioneering of a nontraditional interventionist foreign policy during peacetime; his institution of the military-industrial complex, which helped lead to a large peacetime standing army for the first time in the republic's history; his precedent-setting refusal to get a declaration of war in the unnecessary Korean War that disturbed the constitutional system of checks and balances;

his commencement of the institutional imperial presidency; his laying the seeds of Middle East wars; his scary threat to draft striking workers; and his unconstitutional seizure of private industries. His modest achievements in civil rights didn't come close to balancing out his horrendous revolutionary trailblazing in these other policy areas. Harry S Truman comes in at number thirty-nine.

34

DWIGHT D. EISENHOWER
Overt Dove and Covert Hawk

PP&L* RANKING: 9
Category: Good

Thirty-fourth president of the United States

Term: January 20, 1953, to January 20, 1961
Party: Republican
Born: October 14, 1890, Denison, Texas
Died: March 28, 1969 (age seventy-eight),
Washington, D.C.
Spouse: Mamie Doud Eisenhower
Alma Mater: U.S. Military Academy at West Point
Occupation: Soldier (army general)
Religion: Presbyterian

Dwight Eisenhower generally presided over peace and prosperity, with one of the best decades in the twentieth century. During his eight-year presidency, the gross national product increased by 45 percent, personal income increased by 48 percent, and savings and capital investment soared, while inflation was restrained.[1] Some of this economic growth, however, was the inevitable boom created after World War II by resources being returned to the more efficient private sector from the inefficient government sector.

Eisenhower ended the Korean War, warned about the military-industrial complex, was fiscally conscious, reduced defense costs, cut taxes, balanced the budget, lowered inflation, and was able to keep tariffs low. Philosophically, Ike was a Democrat from the 1800s, suspicious of federal government spending, budget deficits, and activism in all areas — in defense, foreign policy, and the domestic social and economic spheres. In the end, Ike didn't retreat, didn't

---

*PP&L = Peace, Prosperity, and Liberty.

start a nuclear war, and wasn't bullied to increase military spending.[2] Yet Eisenhower didn't try to roll back the foray into unneeded domestic big government by Hoover, FDR, and Truman, and Ike even enlarged the government.

PEACE

Ended the Korean War

Looking back on the Korean War, many people conclude that the Eisenhower administration had no choice but to accept a negotiated settlement arising from the stalemated battlefield situation. Syngman Rhee, the South Korean president, and U.S. General Mark Clark, however, both wanted to invade the north again and drive the Chinese back to the Yalu River, thus unifying Korea. Eisenhower, thinking these plans mad in the face of formidable Chinese and North Korean defenses, refused to even review their plans. According to Stephen Ambrose, Eisenhower, the general who accepted unconditional surrender from Nazi Germany, realized that unlimited war in the new nuclear age was unfathomable and that limited war was unwinnable.

Eisenhower thus had the choice of continuing to negotiate for an armistice or continuing to fight while accepting a military stalemate. Despite the advice of nearly all his advisors, Republicans, and most Democrats, Eisenhower wisely believed that continuing to take significant casualties on a locked-up battlefield was idiotic. Despite his campaign rhetoric of liberating communist countries, rather than merely containing communism, he opted for pursuing a negotiated peace. South Korea was then underdeveloped and has never been strategic to the United States; the United States should have avoided sending its own forces in the first place. Eisenhower's move was a wise one.[3]

On the negative side, Eisenhower may have discreetly threatened North Korea with nuclear war unless a settlement to the stalemated Korean conflict was reached.[4] This act set a bad precedent for Richard Nixon doing the same thing to the North Vietnamese during the negotiations to end the Vietnam War. Also, to get the aggressive Rhee and the South Koreans to give up their quixotic desire to grab all of Korea, Eisenhower agreed to a security guarantee for South Korea and continuing U.S. assistance for the Rhee regime — ensuring continued U.S. entanglement on the peninsula that endures to this day.

Nevertheless, one of Eisenhower's greatest accomplishments while in office was realizing that the price of winning the war in Korea was prohibitive. By negotiating the United States out of the costly conflict, he saved many lives on both sides of a bitter, stalemated, and strategically unimportant conflict.

Defended Europe

Eisenhower favored more political, economic, and military integration in Europe as a bulwark against Soviet expansion. The last could be achieved, he felt, by European ratification of a signed treaty to create the European Defense Community (EDC), which would build a European army and make Europe pay most of the cost of its own defense. The Soviet Union, because of its much closer proximity to Europe, was a bigger threat to the Europeans than it was to the more distant United States. Thus Eisenhower correctly felt that the Europeans should pick up most of their own defense burden, thus allowing the United States to decrease its defense spending.

In the end, the French defeated the European Defense Community, West Germany was rearmed under the U.S.-dominated NATO alliance, and U.S. defense spending remained high during and after the Cold War. Ike's idea of a "United States of Europe" became largely economic; thus he did father the creation of the European Union.

Pleading that they could not afford more spending on defense, the European allies suggested that the United States deploy more of its nuclear weapons to Europe.[5] If the Soviets did attack Europe, the launch of such U.S.-Euro nukes against them probably would have guaranteed escalation to a general nuclear war between the superpowers. Thus, in effect, by agreeing, the United States was holding itself hostage to defend Europe. Although a Soviet invasion of Europe would not have been a good thing, it would not have been as bad as getting U.S. cities incinerated in a nuclear war. The United States was betting, however, that the prospect of a general nuclear war would deter the Soviets from attacking Europe in the first place. That was a very dangerous bet. This illogical and dangerous policy stood for the duration of the Cold War.

Eisenhower wanted to rely on European ground forces and U.S. nuclear weapons to defend Europe; he never intended to keep U.S. forces in Europe permanently and eventually wanted to completely withdraw them, but would not do so cold turkey because of the likely European reaction. He did withdraw some U.S. forces stationed in Germany, Japan, and elsewhere. He also wanted to pull the U.S. Sixth Fleet out of the Mediterranean because he felt that sea was a British and French responsibility. But he and the presidents who followed him refused to take the radical actions needed to spur the Europeans to do more for their own defense. The United States could have conducted the Cold

War much less expensively if the Europeans were not chronic deadbeats in the security realm.

Although Ike reluctantly decided that the United States had to stay in Europe and assisted nonstrategic countries around the world in staving off communism, he agreed to create a neutral Austria and meddled only indirectly in the Soviet sphere of influence in Eastern Europe.

Attempted Relations with the Soviet Union

Unlike Truman before him and other Cold War presidents who came after him, Eisenhower did not overstate the Soviet threat. Even as a military man, he realized what other Cold War presidents refused to acknowledge: that the basis of all national power — military, cultural, and diplomatic — is a large and thriving economy. Because the Soviet Union had a dysfunctional state-owned (communist) economy, the United States would always be, by far, the more powerful of the two superpowers.

In 1956, after Nikita Khrushchev's denunciation of Joseph Stalin at the Twentieth Party Congress of the Communist Party in the Soviet Union, rebellions broke out in Eastern Europe. Protests in Hungary restored Imre Nagy as prime minister after having been dumped by the Soviets in 1955, but the violence continued. In an unconscionable act, the United States had encouraged the uprising by radio broadcasts and CIA-sponsored underground cells in Eastern Europe. The Soviets then sent troops to crush the Hungarian rebellion. With Hungary almost totally surrounded by Eastern Bloc nations, Eisenhower could do little about a nuclear superpower policing its own sphere of influence, and he thus refused to send troops to help the rebels. Ike even turned down a CIA request to airdrop weapons and provisions to the rebels, but he did push to accept more Hungarian refugees.[6] The United States should not have encouraged rebellion in the first place because it could do little to save the rebels.

Overall, during Eisenhower's administration, the liberation of peoples from communism, as promised in his 1952 campaign, did not go well. Ike signed an armistice that left North Korea communist, went along with the Geneva Accords that divided Vietnam and made the northern part communist after the French defeat at Dien Bien Phu, and acquiesced and even contributed to Cuba going communist. All of these areas, however, were poor, nonstrategic backwater areas that were not worth expending U.S. lives and money to defend or liberate.

More positively, Eisenhower tried heroically to get an arms control agreement with the Soviet Union, which was a major goal of his presidency. He proposed to end nuclear weapons testing in the atmosphere, but a treaty that did so was not signed until the Kennedy administration. Ike did get the United States, the Soviet Union, and Britain — the only nuclear powers at the time — to adopt a voluntary moratorium on atmospheric testing. Ike also proposed the Atoms for Peace program, which would have taken fissionable bomb-making material from U.S., Soviet, and British nuclear stockpiles and given it to a new International Atomic Energy Agency to do research on peaceful uses for nuclear power. The Soviets declined.

After this rejection, Ike toughened his stance toward the Soviet Union. He did, however, propose the Open Skies initiative, which would have opened up both Soviet and U.S. territory to aerial reconnaissance, provided airfields in each other's country from which the opposing side's spy planes could be launched, and required exchange of blueprints of military organizations and facilities. Khrushchev, the Soviet leader, dismissed Ike's initiative as a ploy to gain intelligence on the closed USSR — which it was.

Although Ike wanted an arms-control agreement, he reluctantly allowed the U.S. military to keep building thousands of nuclear weapons and new delivery systems, such as the Polaris submarine, which fired nuclear ballistic missiles. As a famous hero of World War II, Eisenhower was the only man with the stature to unilaterally stop this unneeded nuclear arms buildup, but he did not do so. One reason Ike wanted to build more nuclear weapons and missiles and an expanded strategic air force was so that he could reduce more expensive conventional weapons on land and at sea, thus reducing the overall U.S. defense budget.[7] This New Look military strategy, however, helped trigger an arms race in dangerous nuclear weapons with the Soviet Union.

What Ike should have done was reduce conventional forces, cut atomic forces to the minimum level for nuclear deterrence, and reformulate a more modest U.S. national security strategy. This strategy would have made the United States a second line of defense in Europe and Japan, the centers of world economic and technological power outside North America, instead of an interventionist superpower.

Avoided Overt Military Intervention

Laudably, Eisenhower was very restrained in his use of conventional military power. On six occasions or more, Ike rejected the virtually unanimous opinion of his senior advisors to go to war: over the Korean armistice negotiations in 1953; Dien Bien Phu in Vietnam in 1954; the Quemoy and Matsu islands in the Strait of Formosa in 1955; the Soviet invasion of Hungary in 1956; the Israeli,

British, and French attack on Egypt in 1956; Berlin in 1959; and the downing of the U-2 spy plane in 1960. Presidents never get credit for avoiding wars, and Eisenhower deserves much praise for his peaceable intentions. He boasted that during his administration, not even one soldier had been lost.[8]

Eisenhower's greatest strength was managing crises and dampening hawkish pressures to act by simply denying that a crisis existed. One instance of this occurred when Nikita Khrushchev set a deadline of May 1959 for the Western allies to start talks to withdraw their forces from Berlin or he would sign a separate peace treaty with East Germany, which could have limited allied access to West Berlin. Ike allowed Khrushchev room to retreat from what Ike believed was a bluff and, while remaining firm on Berlin, offered to negotiate and made new concessions on a nuclear test ban.

The only exception to Ike's policy of military restraint in his eight years in office was the dispatch of U.S. forces, without congressional authorization, to Lebanon in 1958. He did so at the request of Lebanon's Christian president to put down a Muslim rebellion and to carry out the Eisenhower Doctrine, which stated that the United States would aid, financially and militarily, any country in the Middle East threatened by any communist nation.[9] The United States had helped the Christians fix the 1957 parliamentary election in their favor. Because the Muslims were denied a fair shake in the voting, they rebelled. Eisenhower sent in U.S. Marines to save the illegitimate Christian government. The reasons for this intervention were murky at best. Lebanon was never vital to U.S. strategic interests and was under no real threat from the Soviets or Egypt's President Gamal Abdel Nasser.

Eisenhower was more concerned with Nasser's Arab nationalism in the Middle East than he was with communism there. Nasser was stirring up the populations of the conservative monarchies of Jordan, Iraq, and Saudi Arabia to overthrow their rulers. Pro-Nasser forces did overthrow the monarchy and assassinate the Hashemite king in Iraq, but there was no evidence of Nasser's direct involvement. King Hussein was also targeted in Jordan. The Saudi ruler was scared and demanded that the United States send troops to the region or he would throw in his lot with Nasser. When President Chamoun of Lebanon requested British and American military help, the United States put marines ashore in Lebanon for about three months, and the British sent paratroopers to Jordan. The biggest reason for Ike's intervention in Lebanon may have been to intimidate Nasser with an imperial show of force.[10] The irony of the U.S. invading Lebanon in 1958, after stopping the Israeli, British, and French attack on Egypt two years earlier in 1956, was not lost on the Arab world.

Used Too Much Covert Action

Unfortunately, although Eisenhower used overt military force sparingly, he relied heavily on CIA covert action and foreign aid as substitutes — providing a bad precedent for other Cold War presidents. Ike believed that nuclear war was incomprehensible, limited wars could not be won, and stalemate with the communists was undesirable, so he fell back on CIA covert action. Also, the use of secret action freed him from persuading Congress and the public that it was needed, thus allowing the president to perilously usurp power.[11] This evasion of the checks and balances in the Constitution and lack of openness in a republic are dangerous for the system. Often, the enemy knew more about U.S. covert operations than the American public did.

Eisenhower's attention focused on preventing developing countries from becoming communist. It would have been better to allow these backwater areas to become communist and make the Soviet Union overextend itself by paying the costs of administering and providing assistance to these nations. Eisenhower, however, got trapped in the Cold War mentality of falling dominoes. According to this thinking, if one country became communist, it would be used as a base for destabilizing its neighbors, and so on and so on, until the developing world was a disastrous sea of red. U.S. policymakers never stopped to realize that losing such economic basket cases to the Soviets might have been a godsend. A more minimalist U.S. strategy during the Cold War actually would have hastened the eventual collapse of the USSR's rickety economic system, but Eisenhower and most other cold warriors didn't see it that way and meddled heavily, using the CIA in the developing world.

For example, Eisenhower supported coups to overthrow democratic leaders in Iran and Guatemala and, after the French failed to beat the Vietnamese guerrillas, sent aid and the first U.S. military advisors to Vietnam, which eventually resulted in the tragic escalation of an unnecessary war. In Iran, Eisenhower's overthrow of the popularly elected Mohammed Mossadegh and restoration of the despotic shah in 1953 demonstrated that post–World War II U.S. foreign policy preferred friendly governments over democratic ones. When Mossadegh nationalized the British oil company there, the CIA bribed Iranian army officers to depose him. The United States then negotiated with the shah to get 40 percent of Iranian oil for American companies. This CIA-sponsored coup is an example of the neo-mercantilist use of government to promote the interests of big business.

Similarly, in Guatemala in 1954, the United Fruit Company benefited from the overthrow of Jacobo Arbenz Guzmán, whose elected government had threatened the U.S.-based United Fruit Company by advocating land reform and planning a highway and railroad that might have broken up the U.S. monopoly on trade. In both Iran and Guatemala, the United States falsely labeled such uncooperative democratic leaders as communists.

In Vietnam, the United States gave France 75 percent of the funding for its colonial fight against the rebels. The United States also provided ten bombers and 220 U.S. personnel for them. Before and after the French garrison at Dien Bien Phu surrendered to the Vietnamese guerrillas, Ike's senior advisors in Washington pressured him to deepen U.S. involvement in Vietnam by means of air strikes against the guerrillas, including the use of nuclear weapons. To his credit, Eisenhower resisted this pressure.

After Dien Bien Phu, the Geneva Accords established a cease-fire, partitioned Vietnam into the communist north and the autocratic south, called for nationwide elections in 1956, and prohibited the export of new armaments from foreign nations into either section of the country. Ike was embarrassed by the loss of North Vietnam to the communists, so the United States did not sign the agreements but pledged not to use force to upset them.[12] In the end, the United States did not honor the Geneva Accords. Nationwide elections in Vietnam were not held because the United States knew that communist Ho Chi Minh would win them. The United States sent arms to the South Vietnamese and used force in Vietnam. Ike also organized the Southeast Asia Treaty Organization, SEATO, to protect what was left of Southeast Asia — Laos, Cambodia, and South Vietnam — from communism. JFK's and LBJ's later escalation of the war rested, in part, on the perceived need to honor this alliance.

Ike also contributed to decades of problems in U.S.-Cuba relations. When Castro overthrew the corrupt Batista regime in early 1959, the United States recognized his government. At the time, he was a utopian socialist, not a communist, and he appointed liberals to the high echelons of his government. After Castro's first premier quit because Castro was executing Batista supporters and using anti-U.S. rhetoric, Ike withdrew recognition of Castro's government. The Eisenhower administration declined to send in the marines to take out the Castro government but did hatch the disastrous CIA plan for the Bay of Pigs invasion using Cuban exiles, which took place during his successor's term. After the Bay of Pigs fiasco, U.S.-Cuban relations went into a deep freeze from which they have never recovered.

Generally, Eisenhower's admirable inclination was to remain aloof from the Middle East, but he also wanted to keep the Soviets out. He refused to sell weapons to Israel or the Arabs, but he maintained relatively good relations with the Arabs despite U.S. support for Israel. Inadvertently, however, Ike helped trigger a major crisis in the region. Because he wanted good relations with Egypt, the most populous and powerful Arab state, he promised money and technical assistance to its leader, Nasser, for the Aswan Dam project. When Nasser bought weapons from Czechoslovakia and recognized communist China, Ike pulled the plug on aid. Nasser then nationalized the Suez Canal and said he was using the revenue to pay for the dam.

To grab the canal, Israel, Britain, and France then colluded to attack Egypt in the 1956 Middle East war. They believed that the United States would have to accept their fait accompli to get the Jewish vote in an election year in the United States and because Britain and France were U.S. allies in NATO. To his credit, Ike resisted these pressures and supported Egypt diplomatically. When the Soviets threatened to use force against Britain, France, and Israel, however, the United States threatened to use force against the Soviets. Britain then accepted a cease-fire, British and French troops evacuated their invasion forces from the Suez Canal, and Israel withdrew its forces from the adjacent Sinai Peninsula.

In East Asia, Eisenhower laid the seeds for future U.S. tension with China. Truman and Ike had both instructed the U.S. Navy to stop a Chinese communist attack on the Chinese nationalist island bastion of Formosa, now called Taiwan, but there was no formal treaty requiring the United States to do so. In 1954, after the Chinese began shelling the two small offshore islands of Quemoy and Matsu, controlled by the nationalists, Ike resisted bombing the mainland with nuclear weapons — as advocated by almost all of his senior security advisors. He did, however, sign an ill-advised formal agreement in December 1954 to defend Formosa. Eisenhower then took the unprecedented step of asking Congress for advance approval of a blank check for military action at a time and under conditions of his own choosing.[13] At the time, Formosa was a small poor island with little strategic value to the United States but of great importance to China because Chiang Kai-shek, the autocratic ruler of Formosa and loser of the Chinese civil war, wanted to reinvade China from the island.

Another kind of overt intervention involved Ike's belief that U.S. economic assistance to the Third World would act as a bulwark against communist subversion and lead to economic development, democracy, stability, and humanitarian relief. It never bore much fruit. Even today, only a small portion of foreign aid goes for emergency assistance to people in crisis. The majority still goes to politically important nations to buy their cooperation in foreign policy (for example, Egypt), to pay for military bases on their soil (for example, central Asian republics), or to satisfy the countries' influential friends in the United States (for example, Israel and Armenia). Furthermore, long-term structural economic aid distorts the recipient's economy, shields it from pressures to make market reforms, and often props up and enriches corrupt political regimes. Foreign aid is also a hidden subsidy for U.S. business; recipient nations are often required to spend the money on U.S. weapons or commercial goods and services. Although Ike campaigned fearlessly for foreign aid, Congress cut his requests for this waste of taxpayers' money.

PROSPERITY

Restrained Spending

In the last two and a half years of the Truman administration — during the Korean War — the U.S. defense budget had increased more than 300 percent, and Eisenhower, an enlightened former general, wanted it reduced; he accomplished that goal. Eisenhower wisely believed that there could be no real security without a strong economy, which he believed required a balanced budget.[14] He also noted that public spending on defense had an opportunity cost of important private consumer items foregone: "Every gun that is made, every warship launched, every rocket fired, signifies, in the final sense, a theft from those who hunger and are not fed, those who are cold and are not clothed." He added, "We pay for a single fighter plane with a half-million bushels of wheat. We pay for a single destroyer with new homes that could have housed more than eight thousand people."[15]

As a former general with immense prestige, only Eisenhower could hold the line on defense spending and reject a federal program to build fallout shelters, all in the wake of the hysteria that followed the Soviet Union launch of *Sputnik,* the first satellite, into space. Ike believed that the communists followed Lenin's strategy — to bankrupt the capitalist world with high defense spending. He put a second nuclear-powered aircraft carrier on hold, canceled the B-70 bomber for being outdated in the missile age, and cut the military budget.

In his farewell address, his most famous speech, Ike warned of a military-industrial complex that would usurp American liberty. The root cause was the creation of huge and permanent U.S. peacetime military and armaments industry after World War II to conduct the Cold War. Before that, in U.S. history, industries would make civilian goods in peacetime, convert to war production during a conflict, and then convert back to commercial production when peace was restored. Eisenhower warned: "In the councils of government, we must guard against the acquisition of unwarranted influence, whether sought or un-sought, by the military-industrial complex. The potential for the disastrous rise of misplaced power exists and will persist." He concluded that the complex should not be permitted to "endanger our liberties or democratic processes."[16]

After *Sputnik,* however, Eisenhower did have to retreat in the face of over-whelming congressional pressure and create the National Aeronautics and Space Administration (NASA), which would become part of the military-industrial complex. Ike was firmly against a moon shot, which he thought the new civilian space agency would champion. He correctly judged that a moon program would be undertaken only for reasons of national prestige, not real science. Yet Ike could be politically courageous at times, vetoing a farm bill and alienating an important Republican constituency shortly before the 1958 election. His veto of a housing and urban renewal bill was not overridden.

Enlarged the Activist Government

Yet Eisenhower made no attempt to rescind the big government domestic policies of the Republican Hoover and the Democratic FDR and Truman ad-ministrations. The absence of such a rollback initiative was remarkable, given Ike's repeated public criticism of the welfare state. In fact, Eisenhower added to the welfare state by providing subsidies to the private health insurance industry. The Social Security rolls doubled, and benefits were increased; the middle class was subsidized by student loans under the National Defense Education Act of 1958; and a new federal bureaucracy — the Department of Health, Education, and Welfare — was created to oversee such programs.[17]

Social Security became entrenched under Ike, and the federal government began to intervene more in education and other areas of social policy. Ike also raised the minimum wage, which throws the poorest and least skilled workers out of jobs by increasing the cost of labor for business, and then expanded the universe of people who could receive unemployment benefits from the government.

In an attempt to dampen the peaks and valleys of unemployment caused by the business cycle, Ike undertook the biggest public works project in his-tory, dwarfing those of the Roosevelt and Truman administrations, by spending massive amounts of federal dollars to create the interstate highway system. This gargantuan program was the natural extension and culmination of earlier unconstitutional federal spending on internal improvements by Whigs and Re-publicans, such as Abraham Lincoln.[18] Even though private roads and other infrastructure had been common in the eighteenth and nineteenth centuries, that had long been forgotten by Ike's time. Because of all this, Ike gets only an average ranking from Vedder and Gallaway — nineteenth out of thirty-nine presidents ranked — on limiting government and contributing to price stability.

LIBERTY

Avoided Civil Rights Issues

Like John F. Kennedy, his successor, Ike didn't realize that society was ready for more civil rights for African Americans and tried to duck the issue. He believed that racial desegregation should proceed slowly to avoid aggressive southern pushback. Eisenhower did take the minor steps of desegregating public facilities in Washington, D.C., and on military bases and put forth a timid civil rights bill, which Congress watered down greatly.

More important, he thought that the Supreme Court's *Brown v. Topeka Board of Education* ruling, which said racial segregation in public schools was unconstitutional, was wrong and refused to support it publicly. Before the ruling, Ike even invited Chief Justice Earl Warren to a White House dinner at which he and segregationist guests subtly and improperly lobbied him on the case. Eisenhower was happy, however, that in the *Brown* decision the Supreme Court said that school desegregation had to be achieved gradually.

The Fourteenth Amendment to the Constitution holds that the federal government will prevent the states from infringing on their citizens' rights. If the president had openly endorsed the *Brown* ruling, he might not have had to send federal troops to desegregate schools when the Arkansas governor refused to recognize that same Supreme Court ruling, and white mobs threatened the desegregation effort.[19] Many thought — and the segregationists said — that Ike's silence made the racists bolder in their violent opposition to implementing desegregation. Ike, however, did appoint Earl Warren, who was a driving force behind progress in civil rights, as chief justice of the Supreme Court.

Also, unlike Truman, Eisenhower never denounced Senator Joe McCarthy's witch hunt for communists and actually fired people to appease the senator. McCarthy came into his own as an anticommunist demagogue during 1950, the year the Korean War started, thus illustrating how war causes the erosion of civil liberties.

Eisenhower believed McCarthy controlled seven or eight votes in the Senate, felt he needed his support, and led himself to believe that the best way to combat the publicity-hungry McCarthy was to ignore him. Eisenhower turned out to be right in his belief that McCarthy would eventually hang himself politically. Early presidential opprobrium of a fellow Republican, however, might have led to McCarthy's demise sooner, thus saving many people's reputations and careers.

Created "Executive Privilege"

Ike's only opposition to McCarthy took the form of the modern concept of "executive privilege" — nonexistent in the Constitution — to shield internal executive branch deliberations from McCarthy's congressional committee. Eisenhower was able to invent executive privilege because McCarthy had discredited congressional investigations.[20] Herbert Brownell, Ike's attorney general, could find no credible precedent for the doctrine. Despite George Washington's original precedent of withholding information from Congress, presidents had traditionally been reluctant to withhold data or witnesses from the nation's legislative body. Unfortunately, subsequent presidents have used Ike's executive privilege to obstruct congressional investigations.

CONCLUSION

Eisenhower's fiscally responsible policies, including restrained defense spending, his attack on the military-industrial complex, and his decision to end the Korean War contributed to a period of peace and economic growth. But Eisenhower threatened to use nuclear weapons in an effort to spur negotiations to end that stalemated brushfire war, launched coups against democratic governments, and supported corrupt regimes around the world in the name of fighting communism.

Also, he ratified the New Deal and big government as the norm, only grudgingly safeguarded civil rights, and was timid in the face of McCarthyism. Ike's creation of the modern-day doctrine of executive privilege and his emphasis on CIA operations that were largely kept secret from Congress and the public further enhanced the power of an already too potent executive branch. These poor policies somewhat mitigated his accomplishments and caused him to be ranked second behind Carter in terms of the best post–World War II presidents. He is ranked ninth behind the eighth-ranked Carter in terms of all presidents. Dwight D. Eisenhower has been put in the good category because his two administrations contributed to an era of general peace and prosperity.

35

JOHN F. KENNEDY

Almost Incinerated the World
So as Not to Appear Weak

PP&L* RANKING: 36
Category: Bad

Thirty-fifth president of the United States

Term: January 20, 1961, to November 22, 1963
Party: Democratic
Born: May 29, 1917, Brookline, Massachusetts
Died: November 22, 1963 (age forty-six),
  Dallas, Texas
Spouse: Jacqueline Lee Bouvier Kennedy
Alma Mater: Harvard College
Occupation: Senator
Religion: Roman Catholic

John Fitzgerald Kennedy (JFK) was the first president to benefit from the relatively new medium of television. JFK was young, charming, and good-looking, had an attractive wife and kids, and was from a famous well-to-do family — making him a charismatic and telegenic celebrity, equaled only by Ronald Reagan. His inaugural address, shaped by adroit speechwriters and coining such phrases as "ask not what your country can do for you — ask what you can do for your country," was regarded as one of the most stirring of the twentieth century and on par with FDR's first inaugural speech.

Although JFK barely squeaked out an election victory over Richard Nixon, his performances at press conferences covered by television and radio caused his popularity to skyrocket above 70 percent after inauguration. Yet, as with

---

*PP&L = Peace, Prosperity, and Liberty.

Reagan, charismatic television images hid dire policy failures — JFK's being even worse than Reagan's.

JFK's charisma and untimely death by assassination have made him a folk hero among the public. He is consistently ranked by popular opinion as one of the five greatest presidents, but analysts believe his presidency has been vastly overrated. Analysts complain about his meager legislative accomplishments, his timidity on civil rights, and his mixed foreign policy record. They cite his handling of the Cuban Missile Crisis and signing of the partial nuclear test ban treaty on the plus side of the ledger and his driving Cuba further into Soviet hands and increasing involvement in the Vietnam conflict on the negative side. In fact, in 1988, seventy-five historians and journalists voted JFK as the most overrated person in U.S. history.[1]

The analysts are correct about his unwise policies on Vietnam and civil rights, but even their assessment is too kind. JFK's policies toward Cuba and the Soviet Union almost caused a needless cataclysmic nuclear war, just so he wouldn't appear weak when elections came around.

PEACE

Mishandled the Bay of Pigs

The Cuban Missile Crisis was, by far, the most significant event of JFK's presidency and maybe one of the most important events in human history to date. The world looked into the abyss of strategic thermonuclear destruction, and JFK did more to cause this confrontation than his Soviet adversaries. The only reason that JFK is not ranked the worst president in U.S. history in this assessment is because after his policies caused an atomic showdown, he realized the immense danger and rejected the hawkish options offered by his advisors, which clearly would have led to a nuclear war.

The origins of the Cuban Missile Crisis of late 1962 came in the form of the botched invasion of the Bay of Pigs in Cuba in 1961 — a plan the CIA concocted under Eisenhower that awaited the young, inexperienced president when he arrived in office. Although some of JFK's advisors opposed the scheme, Allan Dulles, the CIA director, told him that it would be a "military cakewalk" and convinced him to go ahead with it.[2]

The CIA's plan was implausible from the beginning: how would a force of 1,500 Cuban exiles defeat a much larger Cuban opposition force, which JFK estimated at a whopping 25,000?[3] In addition, the press had been reporting for months, and thus Fidel Castro knew in advance, that the CIA was training Cuban exiles in Guatemala for an invasion of Cuba.

Before the invasion, JFK had warned the Cuban exiles that he would not support them with U.S. air strikes because he wanted the military action to seem like an internal uprising. Although JFK was reluctant to let the exiles' air force support their outnumbered troops during the initial assault for fear of revealing U.S. involvement, he allowed their planes to bomb the Cuban air force on the ground before the assault, with the erroneous intelligence coming back that the exiles had destroyed 80 percent of Castro's aircraft.

Castro, given plenty of warning of the invasion, ordered an air strike with his large remaining air force and amassed an overwhelmingly superior ground force to meet the attack. The CIA and the exiles had believed that if the exiles began to lose the fight, JFK would be forced to intervene with U.S. aircraft.[4] He didn't and, reprehensibly, let the exiles die or be captured on the beach.

The CIA also erroneously assumed that the invasion of exiles would cause a massive uprising on the part of the Cuban people, overthrowing Castro and putting in a new government. Yet this assumption flew in the face of reports beforehand by returning U.S. observers that Castro was popular in Cuba. As a result of the botched U.S. attempt at sponsoring an invasion, Castro was able to consolidate power, and in December 1961 he declared himself to be a communist and allied with China and the Soviet Union.

Even after the Bay of Pigs fiasco, the U.S. government made numerous attempts to assassinate Castro or sabotage his regime (Operation Mongoose), and planned to launch an invasion by U.S. forces — of which the Soviets became aware. The Joint Chiefs of Staff, in Operation Northwoods, formally proposed that the U.S. government should commit acts of lethal terrorism against American citizens in U.S. cities, international air traffic, and even their own military hardware and personnel. The unbelievable scheme was designed to frame Castro for the crimes, thus justifying a U.S. invasion of the island.[5] Civilians in the Kennedy administration rejected the Operation Northwoods proposal but not much of the other anti-Castro skullduggery of the time.

Although Cuba was only ninety miles from the United States, it was a small, poor nation that, by itself, was not a great threat to U.S. security. Rationally, the United States could have lived with Castro's utopian socialism, or even his later communism. But the Monroe Doctrine, and the U.S. government's irrational fear of any form of leftist government, motivated the attempt to remove the Castro regime. In fact, over the decades, the Bay of Pigs invasion and assassination attempts, economic sanctions, and diplomatic quarantine helped to generate Cuban support for Castro and gave him someone else to blame for the poor performance of his dysfunctional centrally planned economic system. Ironically, Castro probably would have been long overthrown by Cubans themselves if the United States had instead established commercial ties with Cuba and exported products, technology, and ideas into the island.

Confronted the Soviets in Berlin

In the summer of 1961, the Soviets had threatened to block Western access to Berlin, which was guaranteed by a treaty. Kennedy rattled the nuclear saber a bit, sent U.S. troops to Germany, and vowed that the United States would not be ejected from Berlin. When Khrushchev began erecting the Berlin Wall, Kennedy responded calmly that the Western position in and access to Berlin had not been compromised. He realized that the Soviets weren't planning to attack West Berlin if they were putting up a wall, which was designed to stem the flow of Germans from communist East Germany and East Berlin into West Berlin.

JFK took the symbolic actions of reinforcing West Berlin and delivering a letter of support to its mayor. Although there were threats from both sides, a confrontation of tanks at the boundary between East and West Berlin, and a U.S. armed convoy that tested passage from West Germany through East Germany to West Berlin, Kennedy responded fairly moderately and made evident his desire to negotiate. The Berlin Wall was built, but it did not deny Western access to West Berlin and became a powerful symbol of communist oppression during the Cold War.[6]

In 1963, JFK visited West Berlin and was, unsurprisingly, welcomed as a hero. The confused crowd even applauded when Kennedy meant to say, "I am a Berliner and stand with the citizens of Berlin" (*"Ich bin Berliner"*), but instead mistakenly said, "I am a jelly doughnut" (*"Ich bin ein Berliner"*).

Mishandled the Cuban Missile Crisis

One unfortunate consequence of the Bay of Pigs was that JFK, with egg on his face after refusing to provide U.S. air power for the 1961 invasion, felt he had to do something to appear stronger with the midterm elections coming up in 1962. Despite the fact that during JFK's term in office, the Soviet gross national product was less than 40 percent of America's, and both U.S. parties had grossly overstated the Soviet threat, fierce anticommunism was a must for any U.S. politician. JFK had used Castro's takeover of Cuba in 1959 against

Richard Nixon in the 1960 election campaign. After taking office, Kennedy had responded moderately to Khrushchev's blustering at the Vienna summit, done nothing while the Soviets built the Berlin Wall, and accepted a coalition government with the communists in Laos. Although all of these were actually smart moves, JFK was concerned about looking weak to the home audience.

In 1962, a year after the Bay of Pigs invasion, JFK faced a far more dangerous confrontation with the Soviets; under pressure to look tough, his actions were less measured. Nikita Khrushchev, the Soviet leader, had decided to put long-range surface-to-surface nuclear missiles in Cuba primarily because of his fears in mid-1962 that the United States would invade his ally. The American public, however, was led to believe that the Soviets had placed missiles in Cuba to threaten the United States and alter the nuclear balance of power.

Khrushchev had double-crossed Kennedy by previously assuring him that he would do nothing to disrupt U.S.-Soviet relations before the U.S. elections. Even before the nature of the Soviet involvement in Cuba was known, however, JFK made a tough-talking public declaration that in the event of such a missile deployment "the gravest issues would arise" and the United States would do whatever was necessary to protect its security.[7] JFK privately admitted during the height of the Cuban Missile Crisis that if he had refrained from these bellicose statements, he would not have had to do anything about the missiles.

He told General Maxwell Taylor, "We weren't going to [allow the deployment of Soviet missiles in Cuba]. Last month I should have said that we don't care. But when we said we're not going to [allow the missile deployment] and then they go ahead and do it, and then we do nothing, then I would think that our risks increase. . . . What difference does it make? They've got enough to blow us up now anyway." Kennedy added, "After all, this is a political struggle as much as military."[8] Secretary of Defense Robert McNamara too regarded the missiles in Cuba as "a domestic political problem" caused by JFK's tough rhetoric, not a strategic threat to U.S. security.[9] John Kenneth Galbraith, Kennedy's ambassador to India, later said that JFK's political needs motivated him to take almost any risk to get the Soviet missiles out of Cuba.[10] In other words, JFK was risking thermonuclear Armageddon merely to save face and demonstrate U.S. dominance to look stronger for the 1962 midterm elections.

As Eric Alterman noted, JFK could have just dismissed the military threat to the world's greatest superpower from the tiny island nation and saved the world from the brink of nuclear disaster.[11] Jackson Lears, a professor of cultural history at Rutgers University, generally agreed, ranking JFK as the fifth-worst president because he "put the whole world under the shadow of nuclear war."[12]

Both JFK and McNamara knew then and privately stated that the Soviet missiles in Cuba didn't significantly change the strategic nuclear balance between the superpowers. In the 1960s, the United States still had a vast nuclear superiority over the USSR, and Soviet missiles in Cuba would have only added a few more warheads that could hit the United States, which even General Maxwell Taylor admitted. At the time, the United States had about 3,000 strategic nuclear warheads and the Soviets had about 250 such warheads, the latter being sufficient to incinerate most of the United States.

Khrushchev had a number of motives in deploying long-range nuclear missiles in Cuba, beyond preventing another U.S. invasion against his Cuban ally. He also wanted to give the U.S. a dose of its own medicine for installing nuclear missiles near Soviet borders in Turkey, Japan, and Italy and to gain leverage in the superpower dispute over Berlin. And in the summer of 1962, Attorney General Bobby Kennedy had subtly threatened that the U.S. might launch a nuclear first strike against the Soviets.[13] Although JFK had ordered the removal of the missiles in Turkey before the Cuban Missile Crisis occurred, he had not followed through to get it done.

According to historian Barton Bernstein, JFK — with his risky and aggressive Bay of Pigs invasion, his continued efforts to threaten Castro, his buildup of nuclear weapons well above Soviet levels, and his acquiescence to the deployment of U.S. Jupiter missiles in Turkey — can be faulted for giving Khrushchev reasons to deploy Soviet nuclear missiles in Cuba[14] and creating a needless public showdown over a nonstrategic issue that could have been solved quietly and more easily behind the scenes.

Once the crisis was underway, however, JFK realized the gravity of the situation. While almost all of his military and civilian advisors advised him to order an air strike or an invasion to remove the Soviet missiles, JFK opted for a naval quarantine to prevent further Soviet missiles from arriving.

In retrospect, the choice of a blockade was fortunate because the situation was even more dangerous than JFK or his advisors perceived at the time. The Soviets already had shorter-range battlefield tactical nuclear weapons in Cuba to guard the long-range nuclear missiles, and any U.S. invasion could very well have triggered an escalation to all-out nuclear war.

After the naval quarantine was put in place, the Soviet ships carrying more long-range missiles turned around without trying to run the U.S. gauntlet, but the United States still had to get the Soviets to remove the existing long-range missiles in Cuba. To do this, JFK publicly agreed not to invade Cuba in exchange for a removal of the Soviet missiles. In private, he also pledged to remove U.S.

missiles from Turkey after a short time had elapsed but demanded that this promise be kept secret. Khrushchev accepted the entire deal.

The public aspects of the deal led the world to believe that JFK had "won" and that Khrushchev had blinked, thereby agreeing to remove all Soviet missiles from Cuba. But when all aspects of the arrangement, both open and secret, are examined, Khrushchev could have claimed that he had won. He traded a withdrawal of U.S. missiles from Turkey for a removal of his missiles from Cuba and got a U.S. pledge not to invade Cuba to boot.

JFK usually gets credit for giving Khrushchev a face-saving way out of the Cuban Missile Crisis. But as a result of the Soviets being perceived as having "lost" the Cuban missile showdown, JFK's secret deal indirectly led the Soviets to go all out to reach parity with the United States in nuclear weapons — thus creating a full-blown nuclear arms race.[15]

The Cuban Missile Crisis scared both superpowers and the entire world and changed the nature of the Cold War. Only after both superpowers had looked nuclear Armageddon in the eye could the United States negotiate with the USSR without risking another Yalta.[16] The two superpowers installed a hotline and took other confidence-building measures to reduce the risk of nuclear war. They also began arms control talks that led to a commendable ban on explosive nuclear tests in the atmosphere, in the sea, and in space. The partial test ban treaty, signed in 1963, permitted only underground nuclear tests.

Intervened in Southeast Asia and the Third World during the Cold War

In March 1961, JFK clandestinely allowed U.S. combat aircraft to fight North Vietnamese planes over South Vietnam. Also, Americans secretly piloted some South Vietnamese aircraft. JFK wanted to keep the U.S. air campaign under wraps because it was a violation of the 1954 Geneva Accords, which banned outside military forces from Vietnam. In addition, Kennedy didn't want the U.S. air war to provoke increased communist aid to the Viet Cong.

Rather than commit large U.S. land combat forces, JFK preferred diplomacy, economic aid to South Vietnam, and the use of South Vietnam's forces, U.S. air and naval power, and a small U.S. ground force. When the press queried JFK on whether U.S. ground forces were fighting in Vietnam, he lied and said "no." He had not consulted Congress before dispatching the U.S. Special Forces and air power to Vietnam. Thus, JFK was fighting a secret undeclared war in violation of the Constitution.

JFK seemed reluctant to make an unambiguous commitment to defend South Vietnam, yet he feared that presiding over a communist takeover of South Vietnam would make him and the United States appear weak and lead to cries from the Right that he had lost Southeast Asia. (Again, the Democrats were scared of a repeat of being blamed for losing China. LBJ would also have this fear.) JFK did begin the U.S. air war over Vietnam and dramatically increased the number of U.S. advisors to the South Vietnamese military from seven hundred to tens of thousands, thus beginning the escalation process. JFK hoped for a negotiated settlement that would maintain an independent South Vietnam tied to the United States.

Early in his administration, JFK had negotiated a neutral coalition government for neighboring Laos and had accepted that the U.S. should not use force in Laos even if the country was likely to fall to the communists. One wonders why the Kennedy and Johnson administrations couldn't have accepted a communist Vietnam as well. Although slightly more important than Laos, Vietnam was still a backwater country of no strategic significance to the United States.

Then-Senate Majority Leader Mike Mansfield later recalled a conversation in which Kennedy had said that he agreed with Mansfield's call for a complete U.S. pullout from Vietnam but couldn't make that move until after the 1964 election. Like Nixon in 1972, Kennedy was willing to let U.S. military people continue to die for a questionable cause merely to win an election. In May of 1963, JFK made public a plan to withdraw one thousand U.S. advisors from Vietnam by the end of 1963.

Then, in August, Kennedy suggested to Henry Cabot Lodge, the U.S. Ambassador to South Vietnam, that the U.S. support a coup to topple South Vietnamese President Ngo Dinh Diem. Lodge agreed. Michael Barone terms the Diem coup the "critical moment of escalation" of the Vietnam War. He notes that it effectively made the United States responsible for developments in South Vietnam from then on.[17] Others have argued that the Diem coup was when the United States lost the Vietnam War. Future dictators of South Vietnam had no popular legitimacy at all.

So at roughly the same time that he began a small withdrawal of American advisors, Kennedy — in sponsoring the coup that would forever lay responsibility for Vietnam at the U.S. doorstep — made it harder for him, or his successors, to completely withdraw U.S. forces from Vietnam.

Although his foreign policies on Cuba and Vietnam had the most negative impact during his administration, Kennedy also sponsored covert interventions in Haiti, Peru, and Brazil under the cover of the innocuous-sounding Alliance for Progress — allegedly a program for economic development and self-determination. In the newly independent Congo (Zaire), violence broke out, and the CIA pushed successfully for the assassination of President Patrice Lumumba in 1961. The CIA then helped Joseph (Sese Seko) Mobutu into power. The autocratic Mobutu, a staunch U.S. ally during the Cold War, grew rich by siphoning off the African nation's wealth and making it an economic wasteland.

Changed Military Doctrine and Increased Defense Spending

In March 1961, shortly after taking office, Kennedy increased the U.S. defense budget — with increases in Polaris missile submarines and their nuclear missiles, in the number of land-based intercontinental ballistic missiles, and in the number of strategic nuclear bombers on alert. Those actions reinforced Soviet inferiority and spurred Khrushchev to threaten to increase defense spending. As a result of the Berlin crisis, both the Soviets and the Americans further hiked defense expenditures. Kennedy also used the crisis to expand the army, navy, and air force and civil defense efforts.

Later in his administration, however, JFK began to challenge the military by attempting to cut costly, ineffective, or obsolete weapons — for example, the B-70 bomber, the Nike Zeus missile defense system, and the Skybolt air-to-surface missile.

JFK wanted to scrap Eisenhower's doctrine of massive nuclear retaliation in response to a Soviet attack on Western Europe and instead beef up U.S. conventional forces to defend Europe (flexible response). This plan was expensive because conventional forces cost much more than nuclear forces. Instead, JFK should have encouraged U.S. European allies, now fully recovered from World War II and wealthy, to increase their own conventional forces to defend against any Soviet attack. After U.S. allies became rich, the United States should have become the second line of defense (balancer of last resort) against a Soviet attack, not the first line of defense. To maintain its informal empire, the United States eagerly paid to provide allied security and discouraged its allies from developing military capabilities that might make them competing powers. JFK's "flexible response" doctrine and discouragement of French and German efforts to increase their own defense capabilities were costly and unwise policies.

PROSPERITY

Could Not Get His Keynesian Domestic Program through Congress

JFK's legislative record was especially bad. Although the Democrats had an eighty-eight-seat advantage in the House and a twenty-nine-seat edge in the Senate, conservative Democratic committee chairmen tied up Kennedy's legislative agenda. Congress put a hold on JFK's proposed limited tax cut (tied to tax increases), the creation of Medicare, federal aid to education, a new housing department, and a war on poverty. The only major piece of legislation Kennedy got passed was the Redevelopment Act, which attempted to ameliorate unemployment in West Virginia and nine other regions of the country.

More important, even though he had been a senator, JFK had never liked the collaborative efforts needed to pass legislation. Instead of using Vice President Johnson, the former majority leader of the Senate, who had some of the best legislative skills in American history, he turned over legislative efforts to inexperienced aides. Kennedy was afraid of being overshadowed by LBJ, who later used Kennedy's death to get all of the dead president's initiatives — and more — through Congress.

Although Keynesian — believing that increased government spending expands aggregate demand and thus economic growth — JFK was interested in restraining inflation so the Treasury Department, the Federal Reserve, and conservatives would not oppose his tax cut in 1962. He wanted this tax cut to pump up the economy so that it would be humming during the election year of 1964. JFK sought to pair his increased spending with proposed cuts in personal and corporate tax rates. Yet, he, like the Republican "conservative" supply-siders of today (who believe large tax cuts will greatly spur economic growth, thus limiting government revenue losses, and tend to neglect the need for government spending cuts), disagreed with the conventional thinking that deficits caused inflation. Instead, Kennedy believed that public and private debt could spur economic growth.

To reduce inflation, Kennedy believed that steel was key to the U.S. manufacturing sector and that higher steel prices could adversely affect the entire economy. Therefore, he concentrated on holding down steel price increases, taking the government where it should not have gone — into negotiations between the steel companies and their unions.

The companies let JFK pressure the unions into a no-wage-increase contract, and then they hiked steel prices by 3.5 percent anyway. Kennedy was so furious that he had the FBI and the antitrust division of the Justice Department investigate the steel companies for price fixing and collusion. The companies' executives had their expense accounts and tax returns scrutinized and their phones tapped. The Department of Defense redirected contracts to smaller steel producers who were playing ball by restraining prices. The larger steel companies got the message and rolled back prices.

As result of JFK's bad economic policies, Vedder and Gallaway gave him a fairly low ranking on policies that promoted limited government and fought inflation — tied for thirtieth and thirty-first place with Franklin Pierce out of thirty-nine presidents ranked.

Although JFK's creation of the Peace Corps and his goal of putting a man on the moon before the end of the decade seemed to have little in common, their real purposes were the same and had nothing to do with helping poverty-stricken nations or expanding humankind's reach into space. Rather, they were designed to win propaganda wars with the Soviet Union in the Third World over whether capitalism or communism was the better socioeconomic system.

The Peace Corps, recruiting inexperienced U.S. college students to help people on a small scale, is an inefficient and wasteful way to help the poor of the developing world. The program continues to garner political support, principally because it subsidizes middle-class college students in their efforts to see the world. Eisenhower had dubbed going to the moon a stunt and said that spending $40 billion on the project was "just nuts." JFK's science and budget advisors worried about the costs, and scientists were especially critical because they believed a moon mission took money and effort away from meaningful space science. But JFK told NASA administrator Jim Webb, "Everything we do ought to really be tied in to getting on to the moon ahead of the Russians. Otherwise we shouldn't be spending that kind of money, because I'm not interested in space." Although the Apollo space program eventually provided electrifying television pictures of men on the moon, it crowded out other more useful space research. In the long run, government efforts in space probably have superseded private ventures that would have been more efficient and productive.

LIBERTY

Was Timid on Civil Rights

JFK was a northern Democrat who had to depend on southern Democrats to get his legislative program passed. Like FDR, JFK had higher legislative priorities than civil rights. But JFK's problem was even worse than FDR's because he had won the 1960 election by only a razor-thin margin. Thus, the Democratic Congress was not excited about passing his policy program anyway. Because he needed every vote, he didn't want to rile powerful southern committee chairmen by pushing civil rights.

LBJ, a southerner, was more ardent about and better equipped to push for civil rights than Kennedy. He also realized something JFK didn't understand — that the movement had tremendous moral and political power and that the time was ripe for change. LBJ's commitment to civil rights was so great that he pushed for it despite his realization that it would destroy the Democratic Party in the South, which over time it did. But LBJ also realized that pushing for civil rights would enhance his legacy.

JFK began to realize the power of the movement after the racial violence that took place in Birmingham, Alabama, in April 1963. Martin Luther King and other civil rights leaders strategically decided to lead nonviolent civil rights protests in cities where they expected to get a violent response from local authorities, thus generating sympathetic media coverage. The civil rights leaders believed that the spectacle of white racist police beating up peaceful black demonstrators, including young students, would bring pressure for action by the federal government. In Birmingham, Alabama, King's protest got more than he bargained for.

The anticipated thuggish repression by white authorities met black violence — one of the first times in twentieth-century American history that this occurred. JFK feared that black violence in more cities would sink his presidency, and belatedly, in June 1963, he introduced legislation designed to desegregate public accommodations and ensure black voting rights. But then Kennedy watered down the bill at the first hint of opposition.

Although JFK won approval of two civil-rights-friendly appointees to replace two conservatives on the Civil Rights Commission, he was afraid to ask Congress for legislation to formally renew the commission's mandate. Instead, he kept it alive by an executive order, which was probably unconstitutional. Also, only after the 1962 election was safely over did JFK belatedly promulgate an executive order to desegregate federally financed housing.

To get southern support for creating Medicare and providing federal aid to education, JFK nominated five racists to fill federal judicial spots. In the end, however, he didn't get southern support for either measure. In addition, he refused to see "freedom riders" — blacks who intentionally violated the law by sitting in sections of buses in which they were prohibited from riding — at the White House, urged them to end their activities, and declined to issue a statement condemning segregated transportation. Finally, JFK discouraged, as provocative to Congress, the civil rights march on Washington in August 1963, which culminated in Martin Luther King's "I have a dream" speech.[18]

Arthur Schlesinger, Jr., a former Kennedy administration official, admitted that "the best spirit of Kennedy was largely absent from the racial deliberations of his presidency."[19] Robert Dallek, a friendly biographer of JFK, argued that Kennedy should have taken a moral stand on an issue that could have been sold as defending basic American values. Polls showed that while most of the public didn't want blacks living next door, they supported legislation upholding constitutional principles. Civil rights legislation would have to wait for the much better legislative skills of JFK's successor, LBJ.

CONCLUSION

Almost incinerating the world during the Cuban Missile Crisis, so as not to appear weak, really sends JFK's presidential ranking plummeting. His reckless attempt to invade Cuba with an exile army at the Bay of Pigs was a significant cause of the missile crisis in the first place. Furthermore, JFK deepened U.S. involvement in Vietnam and supported the coup against the Diem government, which then made the new illegitimate South Vietnamese government a U.S. ward and probably lost the war even before LBJ even escalated it. In addition, JFK was timid on civil rights. All of theses bad policies make John F. Kennedy one of the worst presidents ever, ranked number thirty-five here.

36

LYNDON B. JOHNSON

A Failure with Both Guns and Butter

PP&L* RANKING: 32
Category: Bad

Thirty-sixth president of the United States

Term: November 22, 1963, to January 20, 1969
Party: Democratic
Born: August 27, 1908, Stonewall, Texas
Died: January 22, 1973 (age sixty-four), Stonewall,
Texas

Spouse: Claudia Taylor (Lady Bird) Johnson
Alma Mater: Southwest Texas State Teachers College
Occupation: Teacher, career politician
Religion: Disciples of Christ

LBJ's top priority was to expand the federal government to help better the American community and uplift the poor, thus finishing FDR's revolution. To fulfill these goals, the former Senate majority leader, probably the most successful legislative leader of any president, engineered passage of the ambitious Great Society and War on Poverty programs. Unlike FDR — who has a reputation for being a great legislator but was not — LBJ schemed in detail about how to get the hundred bills of his program through Congress, wheeling and dealing along the way. LBJ had grown up in rural poverty in Texas and felt a kinship with the downtrodden. Yet most of his programs, once enacted, were abysmal failures. An effective leader doing the wrong things is the worst possible situation.

LBJ, like Richard Nixon, was a liberal president characterized by lawlessness and honesty. Whereas Nixon wished domestic policy would go away so that he could spend all of his time on foreign policy, LBJ had no training in

---

*PP&L = Peace, Prosperity, and Liberty.

foreign policy and wished it would evaporate so that he could pass his domestic agenda. Unsurprisingly, it was a domestic event — Watergate — that brought Nixon down and the foreign policy debacle in Vietnam that ruined LBJ's presidency. This war defined LBJ's administration, even affecting his ambitious Great Society and War on Poverty programs.

PEACE

Escalated the War in Vietnam

U.S. involvement in Vietnam actually started when Truman gave assistance to the French and their Vietnamese allies to fight the communists. This U.S. attempt to help France recolonize Indochina failed and should have given the United States pause before directly trying to pacify Vietnam with armed force. After the crushing communist victory over the French at the battle of Dien Bien Phu in 1954, a conference of nineteen nations chopped up French Indochina into Laos, Cambodia, North Vietnam, and South Vietnam. The Geneva conference barred foreign military intervention there and called for free elections that would reunite Vietnam.

Eisenhower, who endorsed but did not sign the Geneva Accords, knew that communist Ho Chi Minh, the leader of North Vietnam, would win any Vietnam-wide election.[1] He promised Ngo Dinh Diem, South Vietnam's premier, that the United States would help him create a separate state that could resist any aggression or subversion from North Vietnam. South Vietnam, however, was an artificial country, run by an oligarchy and military that had little popular support.

When Eisenhower left office in 1960, less than one thousand U.S. advisors were in South Vietnam. JFK increased this total to tens of thousands, which also prompted an increase in Viet Cong guerrillas there.[2] JFK also hiked arms shipments to South Vietnam and approved the military coup that toppled and assassinated Diem, but he refused multiple requests from U.S. military brass to send U.S. troops to fight, not just advise.

LBJ feared that Vietnam would be a quagmire, even before the Gulf of Tonkin incidents — in which North Vietnamese patrol boats allegedly attacked U.S. ships twice — triggered U.S. escalation. He griped to McGeorge Bundy, advisor to LBJ and JFK:

> It looks to me like we're getting into another Korea. . . . I don't think that we can fight them 10,000 miles away from home. . . . I don't think it's

worth fighting for and I don't think we can get out. It's just the biggest damn mess that I ever saw.[3]

Why did LBJ go against his instincts, then, and make a bad decision to escalate this brushfire war?

LBJ believed the domino theory: if South Vietnam fell, the communists could use it as a base to subvert the whole of Southeast Asia. It obviously didn't occur to him that Southeast Asia was a remote backwater with little economic power and strategic value to the United States. LBJ also thought imperially and believed that U.S. prestige and power throughout the world would be tarnished if South Vietnam were to fall to the communists. LBJ didn't foresee that the nation's prestige and power would be undermined even more if a ragtag guerrilla force defeated the superpower, showing the world how to most effectively bloody the colossus's nose.

Most important, LBJ feared that the Republican Right would harangue him for losing Vietnam — as Truman had been criticized for losing China — and that another McCarthy might arise out of Vietnam's loss. He also feared that Robert F. Kennedy would try to reclaim the throne for the Kennedy family, attacking him for selling out JFK's commitment to South Vietnam. Yet LBJ could easily have withdrawn from Vietnam in early 1965 after thrashing Barry Goldwater and the Republican Right in one of the most lopsided elections in U.S. history in 1964. After the landslide, his advisors told him that he could carry public opinion with him, whatever he decided about the war. The 1968 election was a long way off and voters would have forgotten about a communist victory in the small, obscure country of Vietnam.

LBJ's Goal in Vietnam Was Not Victory

LBJ never tried for an outright military victory in Vietnam. Rather, he wanted to use U.S. military power to drive the North Vietnamese into signing a negotiated settlement. LBJ bombed North Vietnam in a graduated campaign called Rolling Thunder, meant to signal to the North Vietnamese that they had better negotiate. LBJ feared that bombing too indiscriminately or invading North Vietnam could bring a replay of the Korean War, thus igniting a war with China or the Soviet Union. Richard Nixon, LBJ's successor, was more indiscriminate in his bombing of North Vietnam.

Military men later claimed that LBJ overly constrained them from "winning" the war. His decision to conduct a limited, calibrated war, however, makes more sense if the goal was not to win but to drive the North Vietnamese to the negotiating table, while avoiding a wider, possibly even nuclear, war with China or the Soviet Union. A more legitimate criticism of LBJ is very basic: he secretly escalated a brushfire war that even he feared would be unwinnable and bog down the United States.

The secret escalation was based on the flimsy Gulf of Tonkin Resolution rather than on a formal declaration of war against North Vietnam. The resolution allowed the president to take "all necessary measures to repel any armed attacks against forces of the United States and to prevent further aggression." This appeared to permit LBJ to authorize U.S. forces to defend themselves and take preventive military strikes against North Vietnamese patrol boat bases to prevent future attacks. It certainly was not meant to authorize a massive escalation of U.S. involvement in Vietnam — indeed LBJ had promised not to do so. But that is exactly how LBJ used the resolution.

There is still debate about whether LBJ had deliberately tried to provoke a North Vietnamese attack in the Gulf of Tonkin to escalate U.S. involvement in the war or merely took advantage of circumstances that occurred. However, LBJ was ready to escalate the war and to ask Congress for a resolution approving it, even before the alleged North Vietnamese attacks.

LBJ knew that the French had been defeated in Vietnam, that guerrillas were hard to fight with regular forces, that the North Vietnamese were fighting for their homeland and thus would be tenacious foes, that the American people would tire of a war costly in casualties and money, and that his Great Society would be undermined by the costs of the war. But his fear of criticism from the Right for "losing" Vietnam and the perceived worldwide implications for U.S. power and prestige of a communist victory pushed him into a war he feared that he could not win.[4]

Before the 1964 election, LBJ promised, "We don't want our American boys to do the fighting for Asian boys. We don't want to get ... tied down in a land war in Asia."[5] After the election, in 1965, LBJ kept the escalation from Congress and the public, contrary to the advice of his advisors, because Congress was not yet done passing his Great Society program; passage was completed in October 1965.

Even as LBJ secretly escalated the war in June 1965, he was pessimistic about winning it. He confided to Secretary of Defense Robert McNamara that he was "very depressed about it because I see no program from either Defense or State that gives me much hope of doing anything, except just praying and gasping to hold on ... and hope they'll quit. I don't believe they're ever going to quit. And I don't see ... any ... plan for victory, militarily or diplomatically."[6]

According to Robert Dallek, a biographer of LBJ, he could have proclaimed victory after the Vietnamese election in 1967 and withdrawn U.S. forces. The communists would have taken three to five years to overrun Vietnam, and that interval might have been enough to absolve the superpower of responsibility for the defeat. Dallek argues that once deeply involved in Vietnam, however, LBJ could not let the centerpiece of his presidency fail.[7]

In 1968, the Viet Cong and North Vietnamese launched the massive Tet Offensive into South Vietnam. The offensive was a military disaster for them — 30,795 enemy soldiers died versus only 973 U.S. troops and 2,119 South Vietnamese forces — but it was a more consequential political disaster for the U.S. war effort. The Tet Offensive became the turning point in the war because the administration had told Americans that the United States and South Vietnam were winning handily and that a negotiated settlement was imminent, only to be confronted with a massive enemy invasion of South Vietnam. The Joint Chiefs of Staff shocked the nation's capital by asking for a call-up of 100,000 added reservists to be sent to Vietnam. The national debate was on.

In October 1968, a month before U.S. elections, negotiations with North Vietnam actually appeared to offer the promise of a deal — peace for an end to the U.S. bombing of North Vietnam. But the Nixon campaign, in an act bordering on treason, secretly convinced the South Vietnamese government to balk at the talks by offering them a better deal during a Nixon administration. Without an eleventh-hour peace deal to help Vice President Humphrey's campaign, Nixon narrowly defeated him in the election.

The war in Southeast Asia was fought mainly to insulate LBJ from conservative attacks in his bid for another term in 1968 and to maintain U.S. hegemonic prestige in the world. It had the opposite effect on both counts. The war became so unpopular that LBJ withdrew from the presidential race in 1968, and, after the war, U.S. prestige was at its lowest worldwide until the second Iraq War after the turn of the millennium.

The ramifications of the Vietnam War were significant. During LBJ's tenure, U.S. forces engaged in war crimes in Southeast Asia. The United States established free-fire zones in which all civilians in the areas were considered to be the enemy. General William Westmoreland, commander of U.S. forces in Vietnam, demonstrated the U.S. military's cavalier attitude about civilian casualties when he said, "It does deprive the enemy of the population, doesn't it?"

The war cost hundreds of billions of dollars, tens of thousands of American lives, and millions of Vietnamese lives. Although LBJ achieved five years of economic growth, the Vietnamese conflict generated inflation and contributed to the stagflation (slow economic growth combined with high inflation) of the 1970s in the United States; it contributed to urban unrest and riots all over the United States, as well. The war also torpedoed an informal U.S.-Soviet arrangement to reduce defense budgets, which would have reduced the chance of cataclysmic war and probably improved both countries' economic performance.[8]

Intervened Militarily in the Dominican Republic

In late 1962, left-of-center Juan Bosch was popularly elected in the Dominican Republic, only to be replaced seven months later in a coup by a military junta. In April 1965, the United States feared that a constitutionalist countercoup, then underway, would restore Bosch. To justify a U.S. invasion, LBJ overstated both the need to protect American lives and the possibility of a communist takeover. In June 1966, with U.S. troops occupying the country, Joaquin Belaguer beat Bosch in an election, but Bosch's forces claimed their voters had been intimidated.[9]

The U.S. invasion was done purely to enforce the Monroe Doctrine, which in this case involved ensuring that a ruler friendlier to the United States replaced a popularly elected leader. Despite post–World War II U.S. rhetoric about exporting democracy, LBJ's invasion of the Dominican Republic is an example of U.S. policymakers routinely choosing friendly governments in developing countries at the expense of ones that have been democratically elected.

Pursued Arms Control and Antiballistic Missile Systems

U.S. superiority in long-range, offensive strategic nuclear weapons led to Soviet deployment of a crude and limited antiballistic missile (ABM) defense system. The Soviet ABM system then spurred the U.S. to work on its own ABM and develop multiple independently targeted reentry vehicles (MIRVs) — multiple nuclear warheads on the same offensive missile — to overcome the Soviet defenses. LBJ thought that U.S. pursuit of a limited ABM system to use against China's offensive missiles would cause the Soviets to negotiate away their ABM systems. He was right, and negotiations to eliminate ABMs were started in the summer of 1968.[10]

Building systems to negotiate them away merely wasted resources. All the United States needed during the Cold War was a minimum survivable nuclear force to deter other nations from attacking it conventionally or with nuclear weapons. A better approach would have been to unilaterally scrap the U.S. ABM system, limit U.S. offensive nuclear warheads to a level needed to survive any Soviet preemptive strike and overcome the existing crude Soviet defense system, and let the Soviet Union strain its economy by engaging in an arms race with itself.

Demonstrated Occasional Military Restraint

Although LBJ escalated the Vietnam War and invaded the Dominican Republic, he also, in a few instances, exhibited military restraint overseas. Fidel Castro demanded the return of Guantanamo, a U.S. base on Cuban soil, and turned off the base's water. LBJ, instead of invading Cuba, ordered the base to make its own water. Castro eventually gave up and turned the water back on. Of course, the United States, later when not under pressure, should have returned the Cuban base to Cuba — but at least LBJ didn't go to war over the issue. Similarly, in 1968, when North Korea captured the spy ship *Pueblo* off its coast, LBJ did not start a war over the incident.[11]

Though LBJ considered bombing the nuclear installations of Maoist China, a radical communist country getting nuclear weapons in the 1960s, he astutely decided against it. He avoided an ill-advised preventive war that could have been more disastrous than George W. Bush's invasion of Iraq.

Instead of using military force to stop the spread of nuclear weapons, LBJ supported the Nuclear Non-Proliferation Treaty, which was signed in 1968. The pact committed nuclear powers to arms control and eventual disarmament and nonnuclear countries to eschew nuclear weapons in exchange for receiving peaceful nuclear technology. The treaty's net effect has been to slow proliferation, but the nuclear powers never really intended to get rid of their nuclear weapons, and some nonnuclear nations have used peaceful nuclear technology to make weapons. LBJ also reached an agreement to ban weapons of mass destruction in space.

PROSPERITY

Expanded Government Domestically

Like FDR during the New Deal, LBJ cared less about the content of domestic legislation and more about getting Congress to pass many audacious, "visionary" programs. LBJ figured that once the programs were in place, Congress would probably not terminate them, even the ones that failed. Thus they could be adjusted over time. With this irresponsible approach, the New Deal, the Great Society, and the War on Poverty have resulted in trillions of wasted dollars.

LBJ had no idea how to end poverty, nor did anyone else in the U.S. government. Trying to capitalize on JFK's martyrdom, LBJ supplied the martyr's cause. He appointed Sargent Shriver, JFK's Peace Corps director, to lead the War on Poverty, although Shriver privately asked sarcastically, "Now you tell me how I abolish poverty."[12]

Harry McPherson, the president's counselor, admonished LBJ, "There is no real agreement on how to go about improving the job situation, or education, or family incomes in the slums. I think we have about all the social programs we need — already authorized. We may have too many. . . . You need to ask: What is this program trying to accomplish? How well has it done? What should we be trying to accomplish in this area?"[13] Most of these questions should have been asked before the programs were enacted and funded.

Aided Education

An example of LBJ's penchant for throwing money at programs not backed up by research was a fourfold hike in federal funding for an education initiative, the highest priority in his Great Society. Traditionally, in America, education was a state and local responsibility. LBJ believed that education was the road out of poverty, even though social research found that a lack of education had less to do with poverty than did family upbringing and social environment.

The math and science programs in LBJ's Elementary and Secondary Education Act (ESEA) helped kids in the short term, but in the long term it left enrollees only marginally ahead of non-enrollees.[14] In addition, ESEA was not quite the antipoverty program it was sold to be; a 1977 study showed that greater than 50 percent of the students enrolled were not underachievers, two-thirds were not poor, and 40 percent were neither. In 1989, a National Institute of Education study estimated that half the money spent on the program went to people who weren't poor.[15]

This program is a typical example of government attempts to help the poor. Often such programs give the wealthy and middle class an avenue to acquire government subsidies, while assuaging their guilt as long as the poor get some table scraps. Instead of giving to private charity, politically powerful classes merely use the taxpayers' money for themselves and get the satisfaction of doing at least a little for the poor. The crafty LBJ designed many Great Society and War on Poverty programs to benefit the middle class or key groups so that they were politically unassailable once enacted. The poor have minimal political clout in Washington.

Another example was the Higher Education Act of 1965, which, among other things, included Title Four programs to provide student loans, scholarships, and work-study programs. By 1970, however, one in four college students in the United States was receiving some form of financial aid through this law. Since fewer poor children go to college, this high percentage of students getting benefits indicates that many non-poor kids were being subsidized.

Other projects had the same outcome. LBJ's public housing programs benefited housing contractors and left poor people with dwellings that were decrepit. His expansion of food stamps was great for agricultural interests but restricted poor recipients to buying food when perhaps they had a greater need for clothing or shelter. Rich farmers receive far more agricultural subsidies than poor ones.

The poor did receive some of the additional federal spending, and the proportion of poor people in the U.S. population declined from 22 to 17 percent. The question is whether the former had anything to do with the latter. General prosperity reigned in the 1950s and 1960s, which pulled many people out of poverty.

LBJ's programs created a permanent underclass, dependent on the government for its livelihood. There is also some evidence that state and local governments, instead of using their own money to help the disadvantaged, applied for federal funding. This makes assistance programs less responsive to the local needs of the people they are trying to help. Also, state and local programs displace the contributions of private charities. Instead of creating or expanding inefficient and intrusive federal bureaucracies to help the poor, it might have been better if the government had just given the people the money and let them decide how best to spend it on their needs.

Supported Medicare and Other Social Welfare Programs

One of the bigger programs enacted under the Great Society banner was Medicare, which in 1965 extended Social Security to cover basic health care for senior citizens. As usual, the program lacked means testing, so that no one needed to be poor to receive benefits. Yet income figures show that older people are the wealthiest group in society because they have had more years to accumulate assets.

In addition to subsidizing many people who didn't need to be subsidized, Medicare helped cause a monstrous increase in U.S. health care costs. Because LBJ wanted to ensure that hospitals and doctors went along with the program, it favored them. Hospitals could be reimbursed for reasonable costs, which they defined. Doctors were reimbursed their customary fees, which they raised because the government was paying, not the patient. Societal medical costs more than doubled as a portion of the GNP over a period of about thirty years — soaring from 6 percent in 1965 to 13.5 percent in 1997. Medicare spending soared from $1 billion in 1965 to $237 billion by 2001 because the program had no method for controlling costs and was overused by patients because they were subsidized.[16]

Other Great Society initiatives included Medicaid, the National Endowment for the Arts and Humanities (a subsidy for the middle class and wealthy), two new massive bureaucracies for transportation and housing and urban development, and a morass of regulations on business that were supposed to improve the environment and protect consumers and worker safety. The Great Society also established National Public Radio and the Public Broadcasting System. The government of a free society controlling radio and TV stations seems innocuous in the short term, but it may not be in the long term if those stations begin supporting the government's message.

LBJ used JFK's death to pass the supply-side tax cut that had been part of Kennedy's stalled New Frontier legislative program. The profligate spending on the Vietnam War, the Great Society, and the War on Poverty, however, necessitated later tax increases. Tax cuts with no concomitant spending cuts are a sham and come at a great price to the economy. Thus, Vedder and Gallaway gave LBJ an abysmal ranking for policies that promoted limited government and fought inflation — thirty-third out of thirty-nine presidents ranked.

LIBERTY

Was the Titan of Civil Rights

LBJ's major accomplishment was civil rights. In those days, Democratic presidents needed the votes of southern whites to win elections and pass legislation. LBJ understood that if the Democrats were responsible for civil rights legislation, the South would eventually go Republican. So he believed that he was sacrificing his party's future in the South in exchange for his own place in history by pressing for the Civil Rights Act of 1964, which required the long-overdue integration of public facilities. The bill was stronger than anything JFK could have or would have gotten passed.

LBJ was more reluctant to support the Voting Rights Act of 1965, which, among other things, abolished the requirement of passing a literacy test to become registered to vote. Martin Luther King attempted to get LBJ's support by attracting a violent response from city and state officials in Selma, Alabama, the most oppressive city in the South, when blacks peacefully petitioned for the right to vote. City and state law enforcement obliged King and attacked the protesters, which got national media coverage. After this episode, LBJ worked very hard to get the critical Voting Rights Act passed, personally going before Congress to give the greatest speech of his career. With the passage of the act, by the end of 1966 there were only four states in the old South where fewer than 50 percent of the African American citizens were registered to vote. The Fourteenth Amendment to the Constitution required the federal government to ensure that state and local governments do not abuse their citizens' rights. The Civil Rights Act of 1964 and the Voting Rights Act of 1965 worked toward fulfilling this mandate.

Backed Wartime Abuses

As all wars do, the Vietnam War led to government abuses of civil liberties at home. LBJ believed that communists were behind the organization of antiwar protests, and he had government agencies — such as the CIA, the National Security Agency, and the army — spy on domestic antiwar protesters. The FBI infiltrated student antiwar groups and secretly funded friendly groups. FBI agents, posing as antiwar protesters, incited demonstrators to violence for purposes of legal entrapment and to further the administration's political objectives.

LBJ bugged extensively, rivaling what was done during Watergate in the Nixon administration. He had the FBI make recordings of his opponents' telephone calls at the 1964 Democratic convention; placed bugs at embassies and businesses to monitor Nixon's 1968 presidential campaign; tapped his vice president's line because he suspected Hubert Humphrey was going to publicly declare against the war in 1968; and had William Fulbright, Chairman of the Senate Foreign Relations Committee, put under surveillance after he held hearings in February 1966 to allow the antiwar camp to speak. LBJ also recorded his own telephone calls and White House meetings, unbeknownst to other participants.[17]

CONCLUSION

Because LBJ obtained passage of the Civil Rights Act of 1964 and the Voting Rights Act of 1965 at great cost to his party in the South, occasionally exhibited restraint in foreign policy, and had some success in arms control, he is ranked above the presidents who did nothing constructive during their terms. But his wholesale and needless expansion of government at home and his escalation of what turned into the Vietnam quagmire nevertheless leave him in the category of bad presidents.

Although FDR and LBJ spent billions both abroad and at home, FDR is ranked above LBJ largely because of his successful management of war against the Axis powers. Although the need for the United States to fight World War II can be debated, the Vietnam War, which LBJ escalated, has been universally regarded as a debacle. LBJ, however, did not massively bomb civilians as FDR and Nixon did, but lesser war crimes were committed in Vietnam during his watch. Lyndon B. Johnson is ranked number thirty-two here.

37

RICHARD M. NIXON

Undermined the Republic at Home; Had a Mixed Record Abroad

PP&L* RANKING: 30
Category: Bad

Thirty-seventh president of the United States

Term: January 20, 1969, to August 9, 1974
Party: Republican
Born: January 9, 1913, Yorba Linda, California
Died: April 22, 1994 (age eighty-one), New York City
Spouse: Thelma Catherine "Pat" Ryan Nixon
Alma Mater: Whittier College, Duke University School of Law
Occupation: Lawyer
Religion: Quaker

Richard M. Nixon is remembered primarily for Watergate, the scandal that involved significant violations of the laws and the Constitution and ended his presidency prematurely. However, there are other reasons — perhaps equally compelling — for considering him one of America's worst presidents. Largely for political reasons, he sustained U.S. involvement in an unwinnable war in Vietnam, ordering actions against North Vietnam that should be considered war crimes. His monetary policies, ending the last remnants of the gold standard, were disastrous for the United States, and his fiscal policies were not much better. As the last liberal president, he continued an unreasonable expansion of federal involvement in everything from social welfare to the environment. Yet Nixon also began reducing the only existential threat to the United States (and much of the world) that has ever arisen. He did this by attempting to ease

---

*PP&L = Peace, Prosperity, and Liberty.

relations with the nuclear-armed nations of the Soviet Union and China and by pursuing the first treaty to limit nuclear arsenals with the USSR.

PEACE

Killed Many by Prolonging War in Southeast Asia to Attain "Peace with Honor"

In the 1968 presidential campaign, Nixon pledged to end the war in Vietnam. Then he needlessly spent four years and twenty-two thousand additional American lives (out of about fifty-eight thousand total U.S. deaths) to get the same settlement he could have gotten in 1969, shortly after taking office.

At the same time that he was publicly withdrawing U.S. forces and turning the war over to the South Vietnamese military to reduce antiwar sentiment at home, he was secretly escalating the war in Southeast Asia in other respects. Nixon was afraid that the communists' use of Laos and Cambodia as sanctuaries from which to attack South Vietnam would ruin "Vietnamization," the effort to help South Vietnam stand on its own feet. So he bombed Cambodia with U.S. aircraft and invaded with U.S. forces. In Laos, he used U.S. air power to support a South Vietnamese invasion and inflicted heavy casualties on civilians. Both actions were conducted secretly and unconstitutionally, without the approval of either Congress or the American public.

In response to North Vietnam's Easter Offensive in the spring of 1972, Nixon, in the Linebacker air offensive, resumed heavy bombing of North Vietnam and mining of Haiphong, the harbor where the North Vietnamese received supplies from the Soviet Union. To bring the reluctant North Vietnamese to the peace table, Nixon threatened the use of nuclear weapons and unleashed the Linebacker II bombing campaign, which included bombing civilian areas in North Vietnam. The Linebacker II campaign was the heaviest bombing in human history, and its indiscriminate nature could be classified as a war crime. It did, however, eventually cause the North Vietnamese to reach a peace agreement.

As a demonstration that Nixon didn't care about civilian casualties in Southeast Asia, he was heard on the White House tapes telling advisor Henry Kissinger, "You're so goddamned concerned about the civilians, and I don't give a damn. I don't care."[1]

The slow U.S. retreat from Southeast Asia was necessitated by politics. In December 1970, Nixon began to talk about ending U.S. involvement in the war by spring 1971. But Kissinger convinced him that if the South Vietnamese started losing the war after U.S. forces left, this debacle would occur in 1972, the year Nixon would be trying to get reelected. Kissinger favored continuing to wind the war down slowly, with a final U.S. pullout during the fall of 1972, so any unfavorable developments after the U.S. withdrawal would occur subsequent to the U.S. election.[2] Nixon's Linebacker II air offensive in the spring of 1972 had the desired effect — it played to the hard-line sentiments of many American voters and kept the North Vietnamese Easter Offensive on the ground from causing the South Vietnamese regime to collapse during an election year. The unconscionable political delay in ending the war, however, led to the deaths of more U.S. soldiers and Vietnamese on both sides in what was already known among U.S. policymakers to be a lost cause.

After the 1972 election, Nixon reached a peace agreement with the North Vietnamese that was unfavorable to the South Vietnamese government and that he knew the North Vietnamese would violate. If the South Vietnamese continued to refuse to sign the agreement, Nixon threatened to cut off aid to South Vietnam and implied that its President Thieu could meet the same fate as the assassinated South Vietnamese President Ngo Dinh Diem did in 1963. Nixon told Thieu that if the North Vietnamese violated the agreement he would bomb them from Guam, but Nixon knew at the time that the incoming Congress would likely cut off money for the war effort. Congress did and Nixon agreed to the termination.

All told, the Vietnam War had killed 58,000 Americans and 2.1 million Vietnamese soldiers and civilians on both sides. Furthermore, the United States had dumped $138 billion in military aid and $8.5 billion in economic assistance into the country.[3] And all in a futile attempt to prevent an autocratic and corrupt government in a backwater country from being taken over by another form of despotism.

Congress — alarmed about Nixon's commencement of secret, unconstitutional wars without congressional or public consent[4] — passed the War Powers Resolution of 1973, which requires executive consultation with Congress before any military action begins and after-the-fact congressional approval of any belligerent activities. But even this law did not reassert the Congress's constitutional power to declare war before a president achieves a fait accompli by having U.S. military forces already in combat. Even with the War Powers Resolution, once U.S. forces are engaged in fighting, it is difficult for Congress to disapprove the military mission without facing criticism that the legislative body is failing to support the troops when they are under fire. Thus, because the resolution undermines prior congressional approval of armed hostilities, it is probably unconstitutional for a reason opposite those given by recent presidents: that the law erodes "inherent" presidential authority in foreign policy and as commander in chief. No such inherent authority for national belligerence exists in the absence of a declaration of war — with the exception of an immediate need for self-defense of the country. Also, the founders meant the president's commander in chief authority to be taken narrowly — that is, commanding troops on the battlefield once war was declared.

The meager War Powers Resolution shows how much the post–World War II imperial presidency has usurped the vital congressional war powers that the framers envisioned. Even worse, subsequent presidents have flouted the resolution — even the weak requirement to consult Congress before initiating hostilities.

In the end, Nixon kept U.S. forces way too long in Southeast Asia in a vain attempt to achieve "peace with honor," but the longer he stayed, the more U.S. prestige and credibility were tarnished in the eyes of the world.

Demonstrated a Slightly More Humble U.S. Foreign Policy after the Debacle in Vietnam

In foreign policy, Nixon and Kissinger believed that the United States was declining in relative power. After the Cuban Missile Crisis, the Soviets built up their conventional forces and reached general parity with the United States in strategic nuclear forces. In 1969, relations between China and the Soviet Union, badly strained since the late 1950s, became so bad that a border war broke out between the two giants. Nixon decided to take advantage of the situation in an effort to keep the two communist powers apart. Although China was the more radical of the two communist powers — still in the tumult of the Cultural Revolution — the anticommunist Nixon, always a realist, believed in supporting this weaker power against the stronger Soviet Union.

His dramatic visit to China and the improved U.S. relations with that power caused the Soviets also to want better relations with the United States. Nixon cleverly played off one communist power against the other one. The Soviets signed arms-control agreements with the United States that limited offensive nuclear weapons and antiballistic missile systems. This agreement was the first ever between the superpowers to limit nuclear weapons and saved both countries much money. Although China and the USSR were supporting U.S. enemies in the Vietnam War, Nixon was nevertheless able to improve relations with both nuclear-armed nations, thus reducing the chances of having an atomic Armageddon — the only real existential threat to the United States in its history.

Because of the malaise in the United States induced by the Vietnam War, Nixon astutely scaled back the ambitious Truman Doctrine — designed to contain the Soviet Union and amplified by JFK's unrealistic "pay any price, bear any burden" speech. The Nixon Doctrine was designed to reduce U.S. commitments around the world, except in the Middle East. The doctrine avoided rushing U.S. troops into any conflict in the third world. If an internal revolt broke out in a country, the government of that nation would be responsible for battling it. If the Soviets sent aid to the rebel movement, the United States would send assistance to the threatened government. Sending U.S. troops was no longer at the top of the list of executive responses, as it had been in Vietnam.

Nixon did avoid confrontation with North Korea over its downing of a U.S. Navy reconnaissance plane and with the Soviets over alleged strategic nuclear ballistic missile submarine pens being built in Cuba. This latter episode calls into question JFK's aggressive response to Soviet land-based nuclear missiles in Cuba in 1962.

Although the Vietnam malaise prompted the adoption of the Nixon Doctrine, a slightly more humble U.S. foreign policy than previously, the Nixon administration did not completely end needless U.S. interventionism, which had become the norm after World War II. In the early 1970s, at the prodding of large U.S. corporations afraid that their lucrative investments in Chile would be nationalized, Nixon and Kissinger ordered the CIA to organize the destabilization and overthrow of the freely elected Marxist President Salvador Allende. This pressure came even though all major U.S. security agencies concluded that the United States had no vital interests in Chile, that Allende would pose no threat to peace in the region, and that the world balance of military power would not be affected by Allende's victory. Yet Kissinger declared privately, "I don't see why we need to stand by and watch a country go Communist due to the irresponsibility of its people."

In 1973, the Chilean military blasted Allende's office with aircraft and tanks and declared that he had committed suicide.[5] Despite periodic rhetoric about the United States promoting democracy in the world, this is an example of the U.S. government's usual desire for friendly governments rather than democratic ones.

An action in Nixon's favor was that he ended the draft, which eliminated the contradiction in a free society of compelling people of a certain age group and gender, against their will, to enter a dangerous occupation for little pay. In addition, Nixon agreed to destroy U.S. biological and chemical weapons.

PROSPERITY

The Last Liberal President; Set Bad Economic Policies and Expanded Government

Nixon promulgated bad economic policies. Despite his philosophical opposition to wage and price controls, he instituted such measures to contain inflation, which was caused, in part, by the Vietnam War. The disastrous measures distorted the economy and did not hold back inflation, which surged after the controls were taken off. The main reason for Nixon's adopting the controls was that he hoped to steal a campaign issue away from the Democrats.[6]

Also, the Nixon administration believed that wage and price controls were needed to restrain the inflation caused by the ultimate U.S. abandonment of fixed international exchange rates, which pegged foreign currencies to the U.S. dollar and gold. Profligate spending on Lyndon Johnson's Great Society programs, which Nixon didn't try to rescind, and the Vietnam War had undermined the dollar's position relative to other currencies.[7] Fearing a run on U.S. gold reserves — as foreign actors exchanged the undermined dollar for other currencies, and foreign banks, in turn, exchanged the received dollars for U.S. gold — Nixon allowed the dollar to float. The United States would no longer exchange its gold for dollars at thirty-five dollars an ounce.[8] That is, the value of the dollar was no longer fixed to gold and ultimately was unhooked from the value of other currencies. This action essentially devalued the dollar and raised the price of U.S. imports.[9] The Nixon administration further increased the price of imports by imposing a 10 percent tax on them. The disastrous wage and price controls were instituted to counteract these other bad government economic policies.

Flexible exchange rates are better than fixed ones because each currency can find its own natural value, but U.S. abandonment of what was left of the gold standard (only enough gold existed in U.S. reserves to back 25 percent of the dollars in circulation worldwide) caused great amounts of inflation over the long term. Also causing inflation was Nixon's blatant political pressure on Federal Reserve Chairman Arthur Burns to rapidly expand the money supply — artificially pumping up the economy so that Nixon could be reelected in 1972. The high inflation caused by this monetary expansion, of course, did not hit the

American people until the election was long over. The public got inflation, high interest rates, and burgeoning unemployment — called "stagflation" — which lasted through the Carter administration. All in all, Nixon's monetary policies, for the most part, were unprincipled and bad for the country.

Nixon's fiscal policies weren't much better. He could not have cared less about domestic policy. He was only interested in foreign policy and the politics needed to get him reelected.[10] Nixon traded his continuance of most of LBJ's Great Society programs for Democratic support of, or tempered opposition to, his attempt to remake the world by U.S. foreign policy. Such a bargain also occurred during the Reagan administration, with Reagan offering his support for a Democratic Congress's exorbitant domestic spending in exchange for its backing of his profligate and unneeded military buildup. This "warfare state leads to welfare state" logrolling has taken place numerous times in American history.

Federal spending on social programs increased greatly during the first half of the 1970s. Nixon proposed universal medical insurance and declared himself to be a Keynesian (he believed hiked government spending led to increased aggregate demand for goods and services, thus promoting economic growth) in economic policy (something even FDR did not do), calling for federal deficits in times of recession.[11] Thus, he is accurately referred to as the "last liberal president."[12] Vedder and Gallaway give Nixon a low ranking on policies limiting government and fighting inflation — twenty-ninth out of thirty-nine presidents ranked.

Like fellow Republicans Ronald Reagan and George W. Bush, Nixon paid lip service to free trade, but was unwilling to reduce trade barriers and would increase them whenever political gain might result — for example, increasing tariffs on textiles to win votes in the South.[13]

In a liberal frenzy, Nixon created the Environmental Protection Agency by executive order, the Occupational Safety and Health Administration (OSHA), the Consumer Product Safety Commission, Amtrak, and a war on cancer; he also substantially increased federal subsidization of the arts. In addition, Nixon wasted a lot of money ramping up the government's "war on crime," which, like other government wars on society's maladies, failed. Nixon strengthened penalties for drug use,[14] a "crime" that hurts only the user. Drug arrests and seizures soared.

Finding that environmental issues were popular with the public, Nixon created the National Oceanic and Atmospheric Administration in the Commerce Department, forced carmakers to reduce emissions under the Clean Air Act

Extension of 1970, signed the Endangered Species Act, and expanded the national parks.[15]

Warren Harding had assigned the Bureau of the Budget to review agency budgets and compile a unified executive budget, and FDR had transferred the bureau into the executive office of the president and had given it the power to review agency legislative proposals; Nixon renamed the bureau the Office of Management and Budget (OMB) and also gave it the power to review agency regulations and undertake rulemaking without involving Congress. This effectively centralized the approval of regulations in the Executive Office of the President.

Nixon gave elderly Americans, the wealthiest group in society, an increase in Social Security benefits and indexed them to inflation one month before the election, but he delayed the payroll tax increase to pay for it until after the voting.[16]

Nixon tried in 1969 to weaken the Voting Rights Act and encouraged the Department of Health, Education, and Welfare and the civil rights division at the Justice Department to go slow on enforcing civil rights legislation passed during LBJ's administration.[17]

Nixon proposed — although not too seriously — a negative income tax or guaranteed annual income for the poor. Many conservatives would object to the government just giving poor people cash, but Nixon wanted to do so as a substitute for the government dispensing welfare services. In other words, if coupled with the termination of all categorical welfare programs — such as the Food Stamp Program and Aid to Families with Dependent Children (AFDC) — a negative income tax would have eliminated all the grossly inefficient federal welfare bureaucracies and instead would have allowed poor people to decide what they wanted to spend the money on. That combination would have been a step in the right direction. Unfortunately, Nixon's proposal didn't terminate all categorical welfare programs and actually added people to the welfare rolls. On balance, during his presidency, Nixon enhanced the federal role in welfare.

Nixon also wanted to end categorical federal aid to the states for specific projects — for example, road construction, vocational education, and slum clearance — and just give states the money to be used as they saw fit, including possibly returning some to the taxpayers. This New Federalism, based on "revenue sharing" by the national government to the states, aimed at reversing what Nixon saw as the federal government grabbing all the choice sources of revenue.[18] This devolution of decision making to the states was progress, but cuts in federal aid and federal taxes would have been preferable.

LIBERTY

Involved in Watergate

The other major catastrophe during Nixon's presidency was his own corruption, including Watergate. Unlike the petty corruption for money in the Grant and Harding administrations — in which neither president had any direct role — Watergate and related corruption during Nixon's administration cut to the heart of the political system and raised legal and constitutional issues. In addition, the president was directly involved in the scandal.

Nixon, paranoid by nature, believed his enemies were out to get him, thus necessitating, in his mind, the use of illegal means to spy on them and to wage political warfare to get them first.[19] The tax returns of political opponents were audited, Democratic events were disrupted, and Vietnam protesters were illegally spied upon and manhandled.

Nixon's aides established a "plumbers" unit to do illegal acts that the CIA and FBI refused to do without presidential authorization. Although Nixon did not specifically order the Watergate burglary and wiretapping of the Democratic national headquarters (he had ordered or discussed with his staff other break-ins, including that of antiwar dissenter Daniel Ellsberg's psychiatrist's office and the liberal Brookings Institution), he had directed that an aggressive and illegal intelligence campaign be conducted against his political opponents — of which the Watergate break-in was a part.

The creation of the plumbers unit and the surveillance of political opponents, in turn, grew out of the wiretapping of journalists and White House staff members to find out who had leaked his secret bombing of Cambodia to the press. This illegal domestic surveillance is another example, which recurs throughout American history, of overseas war leading to the erosion of civil liberties at home.

Once the Watergate burglary became known, Nixon ordered the CIA to claim that it was a national security operation. This effort was an unsuccessful attempt to obstruct a criminal investigation. Nixon also ordered that hush money be paid to the Watergate burglars to ensure their silence.

Congress began investigating the Watergate affair. When it was disclosed that Nixon had a White House taping system that might incriminate him in the cover-up, congressional committees wanted the tapes. Nixon pleaded that the tapes were protected by executive privilege — something that was never mentioned in the Constitution but has been invoked by presidents since Dwight Eisenhower. The Supreme Court ruled that the concept was not absolute and did not shield material relevant in a criminal inquiry. Yet, as the founders envisioned the original checks and balances system, Nixon could have disagreed with the Supreme Court and refused to turn over the tapes, which many thought that he would do. To his credit, Nixon turned over the damning tapes, which revealed his complicity in the cover-up.

Nevertheless, despite not letting Nixon invoke executive privilege in these specific circumstances, the court validated the questionable concept; subsequent presidents would use it broadly at later dates.

The Judiciary Committee reported a resolution to the House of Representatives that impeached Nixon for obstructing justice, being in contempt of Congress for his thwarting of congressional subpoenas,[20] and abusing power and violating the presidential oath of office. Nixon resigned and was later pardoned by Gerald Ford, his vice president turned president.

In all, convictions of officials in the Nixon administration included Vice President Spiro Agnew, three cabinet officers, the president's top White House aides, and many other government officials and campaign contributors.[21] Nixon himself was listed as an "unindicted coconspirator" in a conspiracy to defraud the United States and to obstruct justice.[22]

Ironically, the campaign illegalities and dirty tricks that brought paranoiac Nixon down were unnecessary. In June 1972, at the time of the Watergate burglary, Nixon's likely opponent was George McGovern, a weak challenger. Nixon ultimately won the greatest electoral landslide in U.S. history, garnering a whopping 60.7 percent of the vote.[23]

Watergate was serious because the U.S. political system was undermined by the use of illegal dirty tricks in the 1972 election, by the chief executive trying to misuse U.S. security agencies, by the president illegally obstructing justice in an attempt to cover up crimes, and by enshrinement of the legally unconstitutional concept of executive privilege.

CONCLUSION

Nixon's accomplishments — improved relations with China and the Soviet Union and a more restrained post-Vietnam Cold War foreign policy — did not make up for the unnecessary deaths and war crimes arising out of the needlessly prolonged war for a "lost cause" in Vietnam and for the substantial harm that Watergate did to the U.S. political system.

But the scandal probably was less serious constitutionally than Ronald Reagan's Iran-Contra scandal. Reagan is ranked below Nixon in the standings here because he had fewer ameliorating accomplishments than Nixon, needlessly increased the existential nuclear threat by reversing Nixon's policy of détente with the Soviet Union, knowingly authorized illegal sales of arms to a state sponsor of terrorism, and then used the proceeds to flout congressional prohibitions on funding the Nicaraguan Contra movement. Reagan secretly tried to circumvent Congress's most important, but already eroded, constitutional power — to approve or disapprove funding for federal initiatives — thus undermining the heart of the Constitution's system of checks and balances. Yet Nixon's cover-up and obstruction of justice, abuse of government power, and attempts to misuse U.S. security agencies during Watergate harmed the rule of law significantly. Reagan was saved from impeachment and disgrace only by being more popular, by benefiting from better economic conditions, and by finally making his scandal public rather than covering it up, as Nixon had attempted to do. Richard M. Nixon, is number thirty here.

38

GERALD R. FORD

Pardon Me!

PP&L* RANKING: 16
Category: Poor

Thirty-eighth president of the United States

Term: August 9, 1974, to January 20, 1977
Party: Republican
Born: July 14, 1913, Omaha, Nebraska
Died: December 26, 2006 (age ninety-three),
    Rancho Mirage, California
Spouse: Elizabeth Bloomer Warren Ford
Alma Mater: University of Michigan
Occupation: Lawyer
Religion: Episcopalian

Gerald Ford was the only president who was never elected either as president or vice president. Richard Nixon appointed him vice president when Spiro Agnew resigned after pleading "no contest" to income-tax violations to avoid bribery charges. When Watergate activities forced Nixon's resignation, Ford succeeded him. Thus Ford took office in a historically weak position — unelected and leading a nation that was disillusioned by Nixon's and Lyndon Johnson's administrations; these were two very bad presidents, who together gave the United States Vietnam, Watergate, poor economic policies, and rampant inflation.

Ford, nevertheless, managed to make things even worse. Although he had one of the most restrained foreign policies of any modern president, he still got into trouble with a few interventionist moves, and his financial policy further weakened the American economy. In addition, his pardon of Nixon undermined the rule of law that is the foundation of American liberties.

---

*PP&L = Peace, Prosperity, and Liberty.

PEACE

Had a Restrained Foreign Policy

During World War II, Ford changed from advocating military restraint overseas into being an interventionist. While assistant football coach at Yale University, Ford was a founding member of the America First Committee, which was leery of U.S. entry into World War II. But he resigned from the organization when he feared membership might adversely affect his job.

Nevertheless, as president, he still was rather peaceable in comparison to other recent chief executives. Ford did engage in overseas activism in a couple of instances and had hawkish advisors — such as Donald Rumsfeld, Dick Cheney, and Henry Kissinger — who years later advised George W. Bush. However, Ford was better than Bush at overriding their usually bad advice. Ford's only missteps in foreign policy were authorizing the botched *Mayaguez* rescue attempt and giving the green light to Suharto slaughtering numerous people in East Timor; the latter episode was particularly reprehensible.

Conversely, Ford took Kissinger's good advice and maintained Nixon's détente policy with the Soviet Union and China. With Soviet party chief Leonid Brezhnev and the leaders of thirty-three other countries, Ford signed the Helsinki agreements. These agreements finally recognized the post–World War II borders in Europe and called for the respect of human rights in all nations of Europe, including the free movement of people and ideas. Conservatives criticized Ford for recognizing Soviet domination of Eastern Europe, but this state of affairs was a reality backed up by the occupation of the then-large Soviet Red Army. Even Thomas J. Bray, writing in the conservative *Wall Street Journal* book *Presidential Leadership*, admits that the Helsinki accords' emphasis on human rights helped undermine the moral authority of the Soviet Union.[1] Separately, Ford admirably removed U.S. support from the racist governments of South Africa and Rhodesia.

Failed in Arms Control and Increased Defense Spending

In 1975, when communist North Vietnam invaded South Vietnam — having waited a "decent interval" after the U.S. military's withdrawal in 1973 — Ford asked Congress to fund emergency aid to South Vietnam. Fortunately, the Congress refused to get the United States re-entangled in a lost cause and voted down the money. Ford did not attempt to flout the will of the Congress and the

American people on this issue. Ford and the Congress commendably agreed to resettle 130,000 Vietnamese refugees in the United States.

Congress also cut off CIA aid to anticommunist, but thuggish, forces in Angola — where Ford had deepened U.S. involvement in a backwater country that was strategically unimportant. Angola was a classic example of overreach in the U.S. policy of containing the Soviet Union.

Despite the winding down of the Vietnam War, Ford pushed through Congress the first defense spending hike in a number of years. This waste of taxpayer dollars likely was an attempt by politicians to demonstrate toughness in the wake of the final failure of three decades of needless and futile U.S. meddling in Southeast Asia.

In late 1974, Ford and the Soviets reached an accord on the framework for a SALT (Strategic Arms Limitation Talks) II treaty, which would limit the production and deployment of strategic nuclear arms. Both Ford and the Soviets, however, cooled on the idea, and a treaty was not signed until Jimmy Carter's administration. Ford succumbed to conservative pressure, and the Soviets realized that Ford would probably not be reelected and thought they might get a better deal from Carter.

Was Overly Aggressive in the Mayaguez *Incident*

Two weeks after the North Vietnamese overran Saigon in 1975, the new communist government in Cambodia captured the U.S. merchant ship SS *Mayaguez,* which was hauling supplies for the U.S. military, eight miles off an island claimed by Cambodia. Instead of downplaying the seizure and using diplomacy to effect the release of the captives, Ford declared it an act of piracy, demanded the ship's release, and attempted to use the opportunity, after the loss of Vietnam, to show that the United States could not be pushed around. The bungled military rescue he ordered resulted in the deaths of more Americans than if the Cambodians had killed all the members of the *Mayaguez*'s crew, whom they eventually freed.

The U.S. military erroneously believed that the thirty-nine *Mayaguez* crew members were being held on a small, but heavily defended, Cambodian island. In the course of their assault, the marines recovered the empty ship. During the operation, however, the Cambodian government released the captives, who had been held elsewhere. While it might be argued that the release was prompted by the marines' attack, the U.S. Merchant Marine Web site says that the cause of the prisoner release is still unknown but may have come about because of intervention by the Chinese or Israeli governments. Meanwhile, the

U.S. assault resulted in forty-one Americans dead and fifty more wounded.[2] Even putting aside the question of whether the United States had violated Cambodian territorial waters, Ford should have used diplomacy and delayed the military operation, because the captives probably would have been freed without the loss of forty-one U.S. servicemen.

U.S. forces attempting to free the *Mayaguez*'s crew operated from bases in Thailand, and the Thais were outraged that the United States did not seek their approval before using those bases to attack a neighboring nation. They forced the United States to withdraw its remaining fifty-thousand-man military presence from their country, the last U.S. presence on the Southeast Asian mainland.[3]

The only bright spot in the entire *Mayaguez* affair was Ford's scrupulous following of the 1973 War Powers Resolution, which required the president to notify Congress before any military action and get congressional approval of an operation lasting more than ninety days. This instance was the only time a president has fully followed this statute.[4]

In another episode of Ford's activism in foreign policy, his hawkish advisors convinced him to give the wink and nod to Suharto, Indonesia's strongman, to invade then-independent East Timor in 1975. Suharto killed one-third of the local population, two hundred thousand people, and annexed the territory.

PROSPERITY

Set Bad Economic Policies

When Nixon resigned, prices were climbing at a rate higher than at any time since right after World War II. Ford blamed the quadrupling of oil prices in 1974 for the problem. But if consumers have constant budgets, a price increase in one item won't cause inflation — the upward movement of all prices — because people will have less money to spend on other items, thus depressing those prices.

Wars, however, always produce inflation. Inflation is usually defined as too much money chasing too few goods. In wartime, resources are transferred from producing goods for private consumption into manufacturing the public implements of war. Thus consumers have too few private goods to spend their money on and bid up prices for the limited number of items available. In addition, politicians often eschew bad and obvious forms of funding wars — higher taxes or borrowing — for a worse and hidden method of financing — printing money. Printing money can cause severe inflation. In the Vietnam War, all three methods were used. That war caused much inflation, which lingered after American troops left Vietnam in 1973. In addition, Nixon pumped up the money supply, and thus the economy, so that he could get reelected in 1972, leaving the nation to suffer the inflation in his second term.

Ford inherited this mess but then aggravated the situation. To reduce inflation, he called for consumers to save more and buy less and asked Congress to pass a tax hike — a 5 percent surtax on incomes — to take money away from consumers. His WIN (Whip Inflation Now) exhortation became the butt of jokes for comedians and citizens alike. Consumers did reduce their consumption, which cut inflation from 12 to 7.8 percent, but Ford's actions also caused a deep recession by 1975. The stock market dropped 50 percent, and unemployment surged to almost 9 percent, the highest level since 1941. The nation then experienced stagflation, a combination of inflation and recession that the then-dominant Keynesian school of economics could not explain.

A former football player, Ford then had to reverse field and propose immediate tax cuts in an attempt to revive the economy, which the opposition Democrats had already been advocating. Ford's policy reversal on taxes came only three months after he had proposed tax increases. As a Republican following the dubious Keynesian model, he also tried to cure the unemployment problem by creating new useless government make-work public jobs and running a federal deficit. The Democratic Congress, also mostly Keynesians, obliged him on all counts. Thus the country was in recession for most of the two-and-a-half years of Ford's presidency. And the worst of it was that inflation only went down because of Ford's recession. Vedder and Gallaway give Ford an abysmal ranking — thirty-seventh out of thirty-nine presidents ranked — in promoting limited government and fighting inflation.

Ford's flip-flop from a tax increase to a tax cut was linked to demands for spending cuts. Holding tax cuts hostage to spending cuts was admirable and quite contrary to usual Republican policy. Although Ford kept all of Nixon's existing programs going — and Nixon had maintained the vast majority of Lyndon Johnson's Great Society programs — Ford used the veto more than any other president, for a record sixty-six times in eighteen months. For example, he rejected the Democratic Congress's excess spending in the health, education, and social service areas. Some of Ford's vetoes were overridden, but they resulted in the lowest average yearly spending increases of any president since Eisenhower.[5] Spending restraint caused the moribund economy to surge but then level off before the 1976 election.[6] But perhaps such efforts to cut spending make Vedder and Gallaway's very low economic ranking too harsh.

Interfered with the Oil Market

Following Ford's lead, blaming inflation on rising oil prices became a favorite of future presidents and, unfortunately, seared itself into the public imagination — along with the gas lines caused by government oil-price controls. Responding to the inflation, Ford proposed a plan in 1975 to make the U.S. independent of foreign energy imports,[7] an impossible and even undesirable goal, according to many economists. If anything, this would increase the price Americans would pay for energy.

Ford further interfered with the workings of the oil market by signing the Omnibus Energy Bill, which tightened controls on oil and gas prices but allowed the president to decontrol prices gradually over a long period. The bill also required car makers to improve the fuel efficiency of their new autos. Ford further distorted the market by allowing the government to buy oil and store it for emergencies in a billion-barrel Strategic Petroleum Reserve — again tending to increase the oil price.

The oil market works, and modern economies can withstand high oil price increases while still humming along. The German economy endured an increase in oil prices of 211 percent from the fourth quarter of 1998 to the third quarter of 2000 and yet sustained economic growth with falling unemployment and inflation.[8] In 2006 through 2008, the U.S. economy experienced record high oil prices and did not collapse. Many countries that export oil sell little else abroad. They need to export the oil as much or more than the United States needs to buy it.

LIBERTY

Pardoned Nixon Unconstitutionally

Although Ford was a genteel man who boasted, in his final State of the Union address on January 12, 1977, that "I am proud of the part I have had in rebuilding confidence in the presidency, confidence in our free system, and confidence in our future," he did nothing of the sort. Within a month of taking office after Richard Nixon resigned in disgrace, Ford pardoned Nixon before the former president could even be charged with any crime. The Constitution says that the president "shall have Power to grant Reprieves and Pardons for Offences against the United States." To have a pardonable offense, the accused first has to have been tried and convicted of something, which Nixon had not yet been. As a result, Ford's action was unconstitutional.[9]

It also severely undermined the rule of law and further contributed to the rising power of the imperial presidency. Nixon had allegedly committed illegal acts and abuses of power as chief executive and was in legal jeopardy because the Watergate prosecutors had named him an unindicted coconspirator.

Some historians are convinced, probably by Ford's prior image of being an honest politician, that he told the truth when he said he had cut no deal to pardon Nixon in exchange for the presidency. Ford was also, however, a very ambitious politician and a wheeler-dealer. Ford purposefully never asked Nixon whether he was guilty of covering up the Watergate break-in, and White House aides protected Ford, as vice president, from the Watergate scandal by deleting his remarks from transcripts of meetings or marking them "unintelligible."[10]

Nixon nominated Ford to be vice president on October 12, 1973. By then the gale of the Watergate scandal was in full force, and Nixon knew full well in advance that his presidency might eventually go down because of the severity of the Watergate illegalities and other related dirty tricks. Ford might have agreed to give the embattled Nixon a future pardon in exchange for being named vice president. Journalist Evan Thomas, however, claims that Ford, as House minority leader, received the vice presidency as a reward for quashing, at Nixon's request, a House Banking and Currency Committee investigation on the source of newly printed hundred-dollar bills found on the Watergate burglars when they were arrested.[11] Or perhaps Ford was already vice president when he agreed to give Nixon clemency so that he would resign and make Ford president. Alexander Haig, Nixon's then–chief of staff, denied that he offered such a deal to Ford, but Ford reported the offer at the time to a close aide and claimed that he had not accepted it.

Circumstantial evidence, however, might belie Ford's claim that there was no deal. Ford moved in secret to orchestrate the pardon. His closest advisors had tried to talk him out of it.[12] Nixon had resigned on August 9, 1974, and Ford waited only a month before pardoning him, most likely to allow as much time as possible for the public to forget it by Ford's election run in 1976. On a sleepy Sunday morning, when only a skeleton press crew was at the White House, Ford announced the unconditional pardon. This is a tried-and-true technique in Washington to minimize press coverage of an unpleasant or embarrassing news development. Ford had not consulted members of Congress, congressional party leaders, the special Watergate prosecutor, or the public about the pardon or given any hint that he was going to take this dramatic action. Simultaneously,

Ford announced that Nixon would be allowed to destroy the tapes of Oval Office conversations that had led to his downfall. Congress later stopped this arrangement to destroy history.

The reaction to the pardon was a tsunami of disapproval. J. F. ter Horst, Ford's press secretary, resigned in disgust. Ter Horst felt that his credibility had been undermined; he had told reporters that Ford would stand behind his statement in the 1973 vice presidential confirmation hearing that "I do not think the public would stand for [the pardon]." Indeed, the White House was inundated by messages of public outrage. Senators and representatives were angered about the pardon and about not being consulted in advance. Congressional leaders called the decision a "misuse of power," which is an impeachable offense.

The media were outraged that Nixon would go free but that more junior men carrying out his crimes and abuses would go to prison. Ford, however, intended to take care of that problem, too. A few days after the Nixon pardon, the Senate got wind that Ford was planning to pardon everyone involved in the Watergate scandal. The chamber overwhelmingly passed a resolution indicating that the president should not pardon anyone before conviction.

The term "rule of law," which is even more important than democracy in the American system, simply means that everyone is treated equally under the law. In other words, no one gets special treatment. Gerald Ford said it best on August 9, 1974, the day Nixon resigned: "Our great Republic is a government of laws and not of men."[13] Yet Ford's pardon gave Nixon, as a former president, special treatment that the average person would not have received. Nixon was spared the further humiliation of a trial, likely conviction, and jail time. Even if Nixon had been tried and convicted, he should not have been pardoned. Nixon's crimes and abuse of executive power surrounding the Watergate burglary and cover-up seriously harmed American society, dwarfing the seriousness of any run-of-the-mill burglary and obstruction of justice.

Ford justified the pardon by saying that he wanted to spare the scandal-exhausted nation the trauma of a long trial of Nixon, which he asserted would have been more harmful than the pardon.[14] He was also concerned that the trial would have distracted the nation from important business — read: his business.[15] Unfortunately, over the more than three decades since the pardon, Ford's justification has become more accepted by analysts and the public. When Ford died in late 2006, media coverage focused on his restoration of confidence in the U.S. government after the shenanigans of Vietnam and Watergate, which was far from the nation's impression of Ford's actions at the time.

Throughout American history, those in power have periodically done great harm and justified it as trying to protect the American people. The rule of law is the core of the American system, and if a long painful trial of a disgraced president was necessary to uphold it, then that should have trumped any feel-good actions to shield the public from the ugly proceedings.

And it turned out that the public didn't want to be shielded. Ford's popularity plummeted more than 20 percentage points after he pardoned Nixon.[16] The decision of clemency for Nixon hung over the rest of Ford's presidency and was a major factor in his 1976 defeat by Jimmy Carter.

Eight days after pardoning Nixon, Ford tried to take some heat off the episode by also offering amnesty to those who sidestepped the military draft to fight for "freedom" in the Vietnam War. The war resisters would get amnesty if they agreed to perform menial public service jobs for two years. Although conservatives thought this policy was too lenient, the protesters understandably thought they should have been given unconditional amnesty for opposing what they believed to be an immoral, unneeded, and disastrous war, so few took advantage of it.[17] Yet Ford didn't seem to think Nixon should have to do two years of menial work to earn his pardon for far greater crimes.

CONCLUSION

Ford's pardon of Nixon, his inconsistent and recession-inducing economic policy, and his attempt to get America reinvolved in helping South Vietnam qualify him for a poor ranking as president. The pardon was especially problematical, being both unconstitutional and devastating to the rule of law. Ford's spending restraint, continued détente with the communist powers, and signing of the Helsinki human rights accords were positive, but not great enough to move him up into the average category. Gerald R. Ford is ranked number sixteen here.

39

JAMES EARL CARTER, JR.

The Best Modern President

PP&L* RANKING: 8
Category: Good

Thirty-ninth president of the United States

Term: January 20, 1977, to January 20, 1981
Party: Democratic
Born: October 1, 1924, Plains, Georgia
Spouse: Rosalynn Smith Carter
Alma Mater: U.S. Naval Academy,
Georgia Southwestern College, Georgia Tech
Occupation: Politician, peanut farmer
Religion: Baptist

Although Jimmy Carter was naive and inexperienced about the meat grinder of Washington politics when he arrived in the city and was not very effective in dealings with his disparate and independent Democratic congressional majority, the policies that he formulated were, for the most part, based on his principles (whether good or bad), not politics. Initially, he refused to intimidate legislators or horse-trade to push through the legislation that he wanted.

The negative assessments that continue to haunt Carter are mostly a bum rap. If Richard Nixon was, contrary to his reputation, the last liberal president, Carter was surprisingly the first conservative chief executive since Calvin Coolidge. Carter was a transitional president at a time when the New Deal coalition, which had coalesced in the 1932 election, was being eclipsed by a growing conservative movement. He promoted individuals taking personal responsibility, opposed special interest groups feeding at the government trough, championed limiting the federal government and reducing the federal budget

---

*PP&L = Peace, Prosperity, and Liberty.

deficit, argued for greater local responsibility, advocated the deregulation of industries, and believed welfare eroded the family and the work ethic.

Carter also pursued a largely restrained foreign policy and reduced military spending for most of his term. Carter, however, was not one of the greatest presidents because he still suffered, to some extent, from the affliction of all recent presidents — that is, believing that the expanded role of the federal government adopted during the New Deal should not be repealed. In fairness, government programs are hard to eliminate once instituted, because the beneficiaries feel entitled to them and are usually politically powerful and well organized.

PEACE

Had a Restrained Foreign Policy

In foreign policy, more than any other recent president, Carter wisely set a less interventionist course. Like other presidents serving in the aftermath of questionable, unsuccessful, or excessively bloody wars, both Ford and Carter were less interventionist militarily overseas following the Vietnam War. Carter astutely believed that the Vietnam catastrophe demonstrated the limits of U.S. power and that the U.S. alone could not remedy the world's problems — something most other post–World War II presidents have missed.

In addition, Carter and Cyrus Vance, his secretary of state, were leery in principle of using force overseas to settle disagreements. Carter also attempted, sometimes successfully and sometimes not, to retract the overextended U.S. defense commitments overseas to more manageable proportions. He avoided war in the Horn of Africa, which was erroneously perceived to be strategic because of its proximity to the Middle East. When Somalia invaded Ethiopia in 1977 and claimed the Ogaden desert, the Soviet Union sided with Ethiopia and airlifted 12,000 Cuban troops and 1,500 Soviet advisors there to help the newly Marxist Ethiopian regime. Somalia, also a Soviet client state, turned to the United States for help, and Zbigniew Brzezinski, Carter's hawkish national security advisor, wanted to use U.S. air power to defend Somalia.

Instead, Carter took Vance's advice and refused to provide even defensive assistance to the Somalis until they withdrew from the Ogaden.[1] By refusing to support Somali aggression just because Somalia was fighting a Soviet-supported state, Carter avoided a confrontation with a nuclear-armed Soviet Union over a region that was dirt poor and hardly strategic to the United States.

In Latin America, Carter also avoided war with the Soviet Union over the existence of a Soviet combat brigade in Cuba, which Frank Church, the Democratic chairman of the Senate Foreign Relations Committee, made public to enhance his senatorial re-election campaign. Church put pressure on the administration to do something about a Soviet unit — only two thousand to three thousand men strong — that had been in Cuba since before the Cuban Missile Crisis and, according to many experts, posed no security threat to the United States. Carter defused the crisis by increasing surveillance and U.S. military presence in the Caribbean.[2] In 1980, when Fidel Castro said more than one hundred thousand Cubans could leave Cuba, Carter generously welcomed them to the United States, much to the chagrin of the residents of Florida, a critical state at election time.

Carter sensibly negotiated, and got Congress to ratify, an end to the neocolonial U.S. occupation of the Canal Zone on the sovereign territory of Panama, which took effect in the year 2000. Because U.S. aircraft carriers, the capital ships of the U.S. Navy, were too big to fit through the canal, the waterway's strategic significance had ebbed. In addition, Carter had been warned that if the canal were not transferred to the Panamanians, violent anti-U.S. protests might threaten the canal's security.

Carter criticized both sides in the Nicaraguan civil war and terminated U.S. military and economic aid to the brutal right-wing dictatorship of Anastasio Somoza Debayle, calling for mediation with Somoza's Sandinista opponents and eventually for his departure. Carter tried to cut back on U.S. meddling in the poor, backwater nation, unlike his successor, Ronald Reagan, who zealously supported a futile covert war by the thuggish Contras against the new Marxist Sandinista government.

In East Asia, Carter also commendably planned to pull the United States out of South Korea, but the proposal met a firestorm of criticism from Capitol Hill, including from Democrats. The legislators believed that a withdrawal of U.S. troops might encourage a second invasion of the south by North Korea. A phased U.S. withdrawal, however, would have likely forced the now-wealthy South Koreans to augment their own insufficient defenses, thus deterring a North Korean attack. Members of Congress who opposed the withdrawal never made a good argument about why even the worst-case invasion scenario was a direct threat to U.S. security. Nevertheless, they compelled Carter to defer implementation of the plan, which was eventually shelved. Unfortunately, even today, U.S. forces remain in South Korea — defending a now-rich country that should spend much more on its own defense against a poor enemy.

Carter finished the process of normalizing relations with China that the Nixon administration had begun. The two countries agreed to begin diplomatic relations after the United States agreed to terminate its defense alliance with Taiwan within a year. The United States, however, insisted on continuing some arms sales to the island after that time. A nuclear weapons state, China has regarded Taiwan as part of its territory and has been vehemently against any move by Taiwan to declare its independence. Carter was wise to terminate the formal U.S.-Taiwanese defense alliance because, ultimately, the United States would have been formally putting its own cities at risk of destruction to save Taiwan from a nuclear attack. Unfortunately, George W. Bush later made an informal pledge to defend Taiwan from a Chinese attack.

Inadvertently Helped Build a Future Conventional Threat to the U.S. Homeland

Unnerved by the Iranian fundamentalist Islamic revolution and fearing the same among its own Muslim populations — and anxious that a pro-Western regime change in Afghanistan would put U.S. spy technology on its borders — the Soviet Union invaded that country in late 1979. Carter saw the Soviet invasion of Afghanistan as a threat to the oil fields in unstable Iran and the Persian Gulf. He initiated the Carter Doctrine, which pledged to repel, using any means necessary, including force, any outside attempt to take over the Persian Gulf.

Although the United States had been interested in the security of Middle Eastern oil long before Carter took office, he was the first president to formally call for an ill-advised U.S. defense of the Persian Gulf and to create a military command structure to do so. Carter's Rapid Deployment Joint Task Force eventually morphed into the U.S. Central Command. Many economists would argue that even in the worst case, a Soviet-occupied Iran probably would have sold oil to get much-needed hard currency — making the U.S. defense of oil unnecessary.

Until the USSR's invasion of Afghanistan, Carter had downplayed ideological and geopolitical differences with the Soviet Union and adopted a policy of pragmatic negotiation on issues of mutual concern.[3] He successfully negotiated a Strategic Arms Limitation Talks II (SALT II) treaty with the Soviet Union that limited nuclear weapons. In an attempt to get Congress to ratify the treaty, Carter had to agree to deploy the unneeded MX missile — a missile that destabilized the U.S.-Soviet nuclear balance. In the end, after the

Soviet invasion of Afghanistan, Carter asked the Senate to suspend ratification of the treaty. Although the treaty was never congressionally approved, even the hard-line anticommunist Ronald Reagan informally observed the weapons limits Carter had negotiated with the Soviets.

Carter's holdup of the SALT II arms control treaty, boycott of the Olympic Games in Moscow, reinstatement of registration for the draft, and grain embargo against the Soviet Union were largely symbolic responses to the Soviet invasion of Afghanistan as alternatives for actions more punitive and dangerous against a nuclear-armed power. This in no way suggests that there were not at least some real ill effects from Carter's actions.

As a result of the Soviet invasion, Carter got NATO to agree to deploy the nuclear-tipped Pershing II and ground-launched cruise missiles in Europe and changed official U.S. nuclear targeting doctrine to hit Soviet military sites as well as cities. Both of these actions made nuclear war somewhat more likely. He also ordered the largest arms buildup in thirty years. Carter's response to the Soviet invasion, plus the decision to deploy the MX strategic missile, caused the Soviets to believe that instead of maintaining the existing nuclear parity between the superpowers, the United States was now attempting to achieve strategic primacy.[4] Furthermore, Carter allowed the Chinese to buy U.S. arms and civilian technologies that could be used for military purposes — all of which were prohibited from being exported to the Soviet Union — and gave the Chinese preferential trade treatment but did not do so for the Soviets.

Zbigniew Brzezinski's plan to begin funding the Afghan mujahideen (guerrilla fighters), to give the Soviet Union its own Vietnam, ultimately and inadvertently helped spawn the greatest conventional threat to the continental United States since the War of 1812 and was Carter's biggest foreign policy blunder. (Even worse, Reagan later drastically increased aid to the mujahideen to actually win this war as part of his own holy crusade against the Soviet Union.) A better strategy would have been to let the Soviets have Afghanistan without funding radical Islamists to oppose them. That U.S.-funded Islamist movement spawned al Qaeda, the organization that perpetrated the September 11 catastrophe. Afghanistan — like Korea, Vietnam, Cambodia, Laos, Angola, Nicaragua, and other Cold War battlegrounds in the developing world — wasn't worth fighting over, even by proxy. After World War II, the United States could have helped Western Europe and Japan (the only first world areas of technological and economic potential) with their defenses until they recovered economically, but let the Soviet Union overextend itself by assuming the costs of administering and aiding these economic basket cases in the developing world.

Failed in Iran

Carter's most visible foreign policy failure — his unsuccessful attempt to negotiate the release of the U.S. embassy personnel held hostage in Iran — probably
did not have negative long-term effects. U.S. policy in Iran had been headed
for failure even before Carter took office. Since the Nixon administration, the
United States had regarded Iran as the linchpin to maintain stability and security in the oil-rich Persian Gulf. Iran had influence in the OPEC (Organization
of the Petroleum Exporting Countries) cartel and exported oil to Israel; its military strength helped safeguard Western oil and acted as a roadblock to Soviet
expansion into the gulf. Therefore the United States sold the shah excessive
amounts of arms. Carter continued the policies of the Nixon and Ford administrations. Even though support for human rights was the cornerstone of Carter's
U.S. foreign policy, the administration hypocritically even sold the shah equipment to control crowds.[5] Yet because the shah had ruthlessly ruled Iran, there
was probably little Carter could have done to save him when the Iranian people
rose up, overthrew him, and ushered in the fundamentalist Islamic regime of
Ayatollah Khomeini.

Supported by Khomeini, radical Iranian students took over the U.S. embassy and held U.S. diplomats hostage. Although Carter probably had a right
to take military action against Khomeini's government — internationally, embassies are regarded as the soil of the home nation — the hostages might have
been killed. Carter's rescue mission was probably a better policy, but it was
eventually scrubbed because of equipment malfunctions, a lethal accident, and
U.S. military incompetence. The failed rescue mission and not winning the
hostages' release were hurting Carter's reelection chances, but he still refused
to unfreeze Iranian assets or sell Iran arms in exchange for a return of the
hostages, something Reagan didn't hesitate to do when hostages were taken by
the Iranian-sponsored Hezbollah group in Lebanon in the early 1980s.

Maintained an Evenhanded Middle East Policy

Strangely, Carter's only major accomplishment — in the eyes of analysts[6] —
might be one of his worst failures. On the plus side, his Middle East policy
was more evenhanded than the policies of most presidents, who usually have
been strongly in the Israeli camp for domestic political reasons. For example,
in 1980, ahead in the polls before the New York primary against Senator Edward Kennedy, Carter courageously authorized the United States to support a
U.N. resolution that called on Israel to dismantle settlements in occupied Arab

territories; this eventually contributed to his loss in the primary in a state with a significant Jewish population.

As a result of his more evenhanded approach, Carter was able to bring the Egyptians and the Israelis together to sign the Camp David peace accords and the Israeli–Egyptian peace treaty, but he had to pay both parties billions of dollars a year in aid — payments that continue to this day — to do what was in their own interest. Egypt got back the Sinai, and Israel got diplomatic recognition from the most populated and powerful Arab state. The agreements were possible only because the parties papered over differences on the fate of Gaza and the West Bank and other major issues. This outcome ensured that the United States would continue to be sucked into any dustup in the Middle East that might threaten the U.S.-mediated peace process. Carter was never able to complete a comprehensive peace settlement because of Israeli Prime Minister Menachem Begin's intransigence on Palestinian autonomy and his unwillingness to freeze the expansion of Jewish settlements in the Israeli-occupied territories.

Although it had a high visibility in the United States because of a powerful Jewish minority, the Israeli–Arab conflict was more a U.S. domestic issue than one of strategic importance. Israel is a U.S. ally, but alliances should be a means to security, not an end in themselves. The alliance with Israel is costly, could impede U.S. access to Arab oil, provides no tangible benefits to U.S. security, and threatens to drag the United States into brushfire wars in a nonstrategic region. At the same time that Carter was using taxpayer funds to pay for a Middle East peace, he was increasing the chances of a conflict in that region by selling jet fighters to both Israel and Saudi Arabia, thereby padding the wallets of U.S. arms merchants.

PROSPERITY

Appointed an Advocate of a Restrained Monetary Policy, Leading to Long-Term Prosperity

Carter was not reelected, in part, because of soaring oil prices and interest rates, sluggish or declining economic growth, and high inflation (stagflation) during the 1980 election year. But the Vietnam War and the bad economic policies of his predecessors in the early and mid-1970s — including expansive monetary policies — contributed heavily to most of these economic problems.

G. William Miller, chairman of the independent Federal Reserve Board and Carter's first appointment to that position, exacerbated the inflation problem for a time by mistakenly pushing the same easy-money policy as his predecessors. This was an attempt to ease the effect on the U.S. economy of the world oil price shocks emanating from the Iranian revolution. Even so, the economy performed well for most of Carter's term.

Carter then nominated Paul Volcker as Federal Reserve Board chairman, and Volcker's tight-money experiment led ultimately to the prosperity of the Reagan years and set the precedent for Alan Greenspan's similar tack, which led to good economic times under the Clinton administration and beyond. The poor economic ranking that Vedder and Gallaway gave Carter — thirty-sixth out of thirty-nine presidents — does not seem to reflect the all-important Volcker nomination or the fact that much of the stagflation during Carter's administration was inherited from his predecessors.

Volcker, who was undersecretary of the Treasury for President Nixon, had played a big part in that administration's disastrous devaluation of the dollar, elimination of the gold standard, and mandatory wage and price controls. In a turnabout, Volcker undertook a "monetarist experiment" after his appointment to the Federal Reserve leadership. Instead of directly regulating interest rates through raising or lowering the discount rate (the rate at which the Federal Reserve lent money to banks), he let the market set the rates and severely constricted the money supply, using open-market sales of federal securities. In an already slow economy, this policy meant higher interest rates and reduced economic growth,[7] which ultimately contributed to Carter's electoral defeat in 1980. A recession ensued during the early Reagan administration in 1981 and 1982 that was the worst since the 1930s, but it wrung the double-digit inflation out of the economy.[8]

Easy money and cheap credit during the 1970s, designed to reduce unemployment, had caused rampant inflation, which topped out at 13 percent in 1979. From 1969 to 1981, inflation caused four recessions, the worst being in 1981 and 1982. In the 1970s and early 1980s, people began to expect inflation, leading to a wage–price spiral and a self-fulfilling prophecy. Volcker and his successor, Greenspan, ran a tight-money policy and sucked the inflation out of the system. The Volcker-induced 1981–1982 recession caused inflation to drop to only 4 percent in 1983. Since 1982, there have only been two recessions. Under the tight-money policy that Volcker started, the U.S. economy performed better in the subsequent twenty years than in the prior twenty years.[9]

Carter's chief domestic advisor told him that no president had ever been reelected during a major recession for which he could be blamed. His economic advisors recommended federal spending increases and tax cuts to spur the economy to mollify Senator Edward Kennedy, preempt the Republicans, and bring the country out of the recession in time for the election. Carter rejected this idea, however, in favor of sticking to fiscal restraint to reduce the deficit.[10] Tax cuts without accompanying spending reduction are fake. Either taxes have to be raised later, the government has to borrow more money and thus raise interest rates, or it has to print money and thus generate inflation.

Volcker's policy of tight money and Carter's fiscal restraint reduced inflation and interest rates but exacerbated the recession, dooming Carter's reelection chances. As a result of improving inflation and interest rate numbers, fears of not being reelected got the best of Carter. He eventually supported a more modest tax cut than Republican candidate Reagan and pressured Volcker to increase the money supply.

Adopted Voluntary Wage and Price Controls

As inflation rose in early 1978, Carter adopted a system of voluntary wage and price controls, publicly berating business and labor for raising prices and wages, respectively. He also limited federal workers' pay increase to 5.5 percent and froze the salaries of his administration's political appointees. The latter two measures were merely symbolic, and the first measure has always been ineffectual because the real causes of inflation are excessive increases in the money supply and federal budget deficits. To his credit, Carter was trying to reduce the budget deficit by employing fiscal restraint.

Yet when the voluntary wage and price controls didn't stem the tide of inflation, Carter moved toward using more government coercion on businesses and unions. His Council on Wage and Price Stability set targets for wages and prices in major industries, then monitored prices, wages, and profits in those sectors, and finally took action if the actual increases surpassed the targets. For example, Carter threatened to withhold federal contracts from businesses that violated the wage and price standards. Despite price targets, corporate profits ballooned, spurring unions to demand wage hikes higher than the administration's guidelines. These developments prompted Alfred Kahn, Carter's chief inflation fighter, to deem the wage and price standards a "disaster."[11] Such government intrusion into what should be market decisions, even through voluntary controls, can only suppress prices and wages only in the short run, while distorting the economy in doing so.

Achieved Fiscal Restraint

Because Carter's top priority after he reached office was lowering inflation, not reducing unemployment, he was a budget hawk. For example, Carter enraged Congress by trying to terminate many pork-barrel water projects from the federal budget.[12] He was successful in eliminating some of them. He also proposed reducing agricultural price supports and reforming welfare without increasing the budget for it, but he ran into congressional opposition on both counts. He ran afoul of traditional Democratic constituencies that were instrumental in his election, especially organized labor, when he limited their efforts to increase the minimum wage and create new public works jobs.

Further alienating the constituencies that got him elected, Carter, in his urban program, bravely planned no additional federal funding for cities — relying instead on the private sector, state and local governments, and neighborhood and voluntary groups. Like John Tyler, Carter paid a price for his principled stands against expanding the federal government's responsibilities. His actions would cost him the support of enough people in his own party to be a major factor in his failure to get a second term.

Supported Social Programs Selectively

Because Carter generally put a higher priority on fighting inflation than on reducing unemployment, he was unenthusiastic about an effort to enact the Humphrey-Hawkins full employment bill, which dictated that the government should provide make-work jobs for people who couldn't find jobs anywhere else. Carter wanted some recognition from the bill that battling inflation was also important, which the Senate added when it watered down the bill. Government make-work employment is an artificial substitute for good government policies that allow the private sector to generate and sustain real private-sector jobs. In addition, because of Carter's fear of exacerbating inflation, he courageously refused to support an expensive proposal by Senator Edward Kennedy to provide federally funded national health insurance for all Americans.

Restrained Defense Spending

Carter's fiscal restraint also applied in the national security arena. He canceled the B-1 nuclear-capable bomber, a cost-ineffective flying white elephant designed to penetrate Soviet air defenses during the missile age. Carter was the first president to end a major weapon system so close to production. Reagan, who used the bomber as a symbol of his toughness on defense during the 1980 election campaign against Carter, brought back a modified version, the B-1B, which has been chronically plagued by problems and can be used only as an expensive flying truck to haul ordnance only after enemy air defenses have been eliminated. Carter also killed the low-blast neutron bomb, which was a nuclear weapon that saved buildings but killed people with radiation.

Finally, Carter terminated a proposed new aircraft carrier that he correctly said was not needed. The aircraft carrier is an inefficient way to deliver air power during a war because carrier-based aircraft cannot carry as much ordnance as land-based planes. Although Carter was a deficit hawk, he led each member country in the NATO alliance into a pledge to increase inflation-adjusted defense spending by 3 percent. This effort to prevent West European nations under the U.S. security umbrella from free riding actually did the opposite. The faraway United States, which should have been less alarmed about the Soviet threat to Western Europe than the Europeans were, fulfilled the goal of a 3 percent real increase, but many NATO allies did not. Thus the imbalance between U.S. and European defense efforts became even more pronounced.

Deregulated Industries

Carter's deregulation of important industries — transportation (airline and trucking), communication, energy (oil and natural gas), and financial services — allowed them to be more competitive and efficient and contributed to future economic prosperity. Although Carter's original energy policy proposals tried the misguided route of conservation through taxation, he eventually embraced deregulation of natural gas as a way to conserve the resource and distribute it more efficiently, and he played a crucial role in getting Congress's approval. He also was able to gradually decontrol oil prices. The deregulation of oil and natural gas were included in the most significant energy legislation in American history. Included in that plan, however, was an ill-advised tax for energy companies on windfall profits resulting from deregulation.[13] Such taxation reduced companies' incentives to produce more oil.

In areas that were not deregulated, Carter ordered that the Office of Management and Budget evaluate the cost of newly proposed agency regulations, identify alternatives, and choose the least burdensome and costly type of regulation.

Enlarged the Bureaucracy

To attempt to deal with the high oil prices that the nation faced during his term, Carter created the Department of Energy and the Synthetic Fuels Corporation.

The latter would publicly fund the development of synthetic fuels — expensive and nonviable solutions to dependence on foreign oil. He also proposed an Energy Mobilization Board to help cut through government red tape that inhibited new energy projects; imagine trying to increase efficiency by creating a new government bureaucracy to cut through the red tape from existing government bureaucracies. Congress correctly rejected this proposal as infringing on states' rights and environmental laws.

Carter fenced off vast areas from economic development to create new national parks, more than doubling the size of the national park system, and he almost tripled the size of wilderness preserves, including about one-third of Alaska. He also created a government superfund to clean up hazardous wastes at taxpayer expense. He should have simply relied on the court system to allow people and organizations to sue private companies for unlimited environmental damages caused by dumping their hazardous wastes. If companies had to pay for the cleanup instead of the taxpayers, it might better dissuade them from dumping such wastes in the first place.

Carter also created the Department of Education, marking a further federal intrusion into what had traditionally been a state and local responsibility. He would have liked to create a new Consumer Protection Agency as well, but opponents argued successfully that it would add another layer of federal regulation.[14] Instead, by executive order, he created a White House Consumer Affairs Council, which oversaw the consumer protection programs in forty-three federal agencies. Thus Carter added another layer of bureaucracy anyway to ride herd over existing agencies; this addition didn't make the government's efforts any better and actually made them less efficient.

Set Poor Domestic Policies

Insolvency existed in the Social Security system — with benefits increasing, revenues declining, and an aging population providing fewer workers to support more retirees. Carter tried to deal with such problems by raising payroll taxes and the wage ceiling above which payroll taxes were not collected.[15] The Social Security system is a government Ponzi scheme in which today's workers pay for today's retirees. A private individual or business would be arrested for concocting such a scheme. With an aging population, today's workers may not have enough of tomorrow's workers to support them when they retire. In addition, payroll taxes are regressive, meaning that poor people bear a disproportionate share of the burden of paying them. In contrast, Social Security benefits are mildly progressive — wealthier people get fewer benefits proportionally than less advantaged people. But then the wealthy don't really need to get anything from a government retirement program. Minorities are hurt by the Social Security system because many start paying into the system at an earlier age than whites — a larger proportion don't go to college — and get benefits for a shorter period than whites because of their shorter life expectancy.

Carter tried to offset the payroll tax increase with a $25 billion tax cut — a package that made the Social Security system more solvent but not the federal government. Instead, Carter should have tried to privatize the U.S. pension system, as many countries around the world have done, giving everyone his or her own retirement account to manage and invest. As a Democrat, Carter could have carried out this reform more easily than a Republican president could have done. Instead, Carter merely increased taxes and kicked the can down the road for future presidents to deal with. The problem is still with us.

In the face of coal shortages caused by a coal strike, Carter became the first president in more than twenty years to invoke — albeit reluctantly — the Taft-Hartley Act to force workers back to the job. Carter also threatened steel companies possessing mining subsidiaries that he would not help them with their trade problems until they were more flexible in their talks with the United Mine Workers. Carter's coercion of both sides in a private labor–management dispute showed excessive federal meddling in this arena.

Carter supported federal loan guarantees for the bankrupt city of New York, thus allowing the city to reenter public credit markets. This action rewarded irresponsible fiscal behavior on New York's part. He also supported the bailout of Chrysler Corporation, a government reward for business failure.

LIBERTY

Supported Human Rights

At home, Carter supported the Equal Rights Amendment, which had the goal of ensuring that women were treated equally in society, but the amendment ultimately failed. He also tried to heal the wounds of the Vietnam War by pardoning those who had avoided being drafted. He was better known, however, for promoting liberty outside U.S. boundaries.

Carter's outspoken policy on the promotion of human rights overseas was roundly criticized at the time for being too idealistic, but he was pragmatic about its implementation. He eschewed the United States' post–World War II tendency to support dictatorships that committed human rights violations, as long as they were anticommunist. Keeping watch on autocratic regimes' treatment of political opponents is good policy, lest the dissidents be forgotten by the world and mistreated even more. For the most part, Carter's policy was one of rhetorical protest rather than foolish punitive action against regimes that violated human rights. Even Carter's verbal criticism of other nations' human rights policies, however, was sometimes counterproductive. For example, although Carter banned the sale of spare parts for U.S. military exports already delivered to South Africa and civilian items that could be used for military purposes, these actions were mainly symbolic because that nation was getting large amounts of military aid from Israel and France. Carter's public criticism of South Africa's racist policies caused its white supremacist regime to repress black opposition more fiercely, and the resulting anger at Carter among the South African white community helped get apartheid-supporting Prime Minister John Vorster reelected.

Similarly, Carter's public rhetorical criticism of the Soviets over their human rights violations enraged them and caused them to crack down on dissidents. Carter, however, was against the Jackson-Vanik Amendment, which made free trade with the Soviet Union contingent on Jewish emigration, because it interfered in the internal affairs of a sovereign nation. Also, Carter's desire to complete normalizing relations with China inhibited him from pressuring the Chinese too hard about their human rights violations.

Keeping track of and challenging the treatment of foreign dissidents would have been better done through secret diplomatic channels rather than public U.S. protests. A more discreet U.S. policy would have avoided the resistance that public humiliation of foreign governments tended to generate.

CONCLUSION

Although it is frequently said that Carter was a better ex-president than president, Carter was a good chief executive. For a recent president, his policy achievements were greater than his policy failures and his occasional operational incompetence. Although Carter overreacted to the Soviet invasion of backwater Afghanistan, paid an exorbitant price for only partial peace in the Middle East, and instituted coercive "voluntary" wage and price controls, he generally exhibited restraint in foreign policy, gave back the Panama Canal to Panama, displayed fiscal discipline, had an admirable penchant for economic deregulation, and, most important, appointed Paul Volcker as chairman of the Federal Reserve Board.

Although some candidates run against the tide in Washington as outsiders, most become Washingtonians after they take office. Carter remained an outsider for all of his four years in office, frequently taking policy positions that angered the interest groups in the Democratic Party that were the key to his reelection. Like many presidents who take principled stands regardless of the political consequences — such as John Tyler, Martin Van Buren, and Chester Arthur — Carter was not allowed a second term. In August 1980, Carter had the lowest approval rating of any president in the history of polling — 21 percent — which was three percentage points lower than Richard Nixon's at the height of the Watergate scandal. With this low rating, it's amazing that Carter was able to come as close to Reagan as he did in the 1980 election.[16] Jimmy Carter is ranked number eight in this assessment.

40

RONALD REAGAN

Not Really That Conservative

PP&L* RANKING: 35

Category: Bad

Fortieth president of the United States

Term: January 20, 1981, to January 20, 1989
Party: Republican
Born: February 6, 1911, Tampico, Illinois
Died: June 5, 2004 (age ninety-three), Bel Air,
 Los Angeles, California
Spouse: Jane Wyman (first wife); Nancy Davis Reagan
 (second wife)
Alma Mater: Eureka College
Occupation: Actor, Politician
Religion: Presbyterian

Conservatives have enshrined Ronald Reagan as a demigod and, surprisingly, even liberals and moderates in the media have treated his presidency favorably. This excessively high esteem is largely due to his charisma and the perception that he single-handedly won the Cold War. The Berlin Wall fell less than a year after he left office. Although he wasted tens of billions of taxpayer dollars on his Star Wars fantasy of space-based missile defense, which has never fielded any space-based defenses, some analysts unbelievably credit the project with causing the collapse of the Soviet Union.[1] In reality, from 1981 until 1985, when Mikhail Gorbachev assumed power in the Soviet Union and dramatically sought to open the Soviet system and to better relations with the U.S., Reagan increased the existential nuclear threat to the republic by reversing Richard Nixon's policy of détente with the USSR and ratcheting up tensions.

---

*PP&L = Peace, Prosperity, and Liberty.

Also, largely because of his self-made image as a fiscal conservative, many analysts give Reagan much more credit than he deserves for reducing big government and generating the economic prosperity of the 1980s and 1990s. In fact, Reagan wasn't all that conservative. Reagan's war on entitlements was stillborn, and, in 1983, instead of trying to scrap and privatize Social Security, he helped save the failing system so that it could keep limping along. For all his antigovernment rhetoric, he doubled the size of government during his two terms. He was less economically conservative (limiting spending) and more protectionist on trade issues than Bill Clinton.[2] Reagan famously first cut taxes, but then retreated and raised income and payroll taxes. He paid lip service to the causes of evangelical Christians, but fortunately made no serious attack on women's reproductive rights.[3]

Traditional conservatives oppose executive usurpation of power at the expense of the checks and balances system enshrined in the Constitution. Reagan, however, sold arms to radical Iran, the sponsor of the Hezbollah and other terrorist groups, to try to ransom U.S. hostages held in Lebanon. He then secretly subverted Congress's most important remaining power under the Constitution — the power to fund the activities of the federal government — by taking the proceeds of the arms sales and giving them to the Nicaraguan Contra rebels in contravention of Congress's prohibition on assistance to the group.

Reagan's weakness in the face of terrorism didn't start with the Iran-Contra Affair. He withdrew from Lebanon with his tail between his legs after Hezbollah blew up the marine barracks and killed 241 U.S. service personnel. According to Osama bin Laden, this retreat provided the first evidence for the future al Qaeda leader that the United States would be weak in the face of terrorist attacks. To avoid this ignominious outcome and the initial taking of U.S. hostages, Reagan should have avoided intervening in nonstrategic Lebanon in the first place.

PEACE

Did Not Win the Cold War

Because even historians are suckers for charisma, they overrate Reagan's contribution in "winning" the Cold War. They focus on Reagan's macho and intimidating anticommunist rhetoric, i.e., calling the Soviet Union an "evil empire" and demanding, "Mr. Gorbachev, tear down this wall!" In fact, the latter speech was made to provide political cover for a "conservative" president who wanted to warm relations with the revolutionary Gorbachev and the Soviet Union. That warming eventually brought about a significant arms-control agreement on intermediate-range nuclear forces.[4] The truth be told, every president from Truman to George H. W. Bush had a role in prosecuting the forty-plus-year Cold War.

The reality was that the Soviet empire collapsed because of its own poor economic performance and consequent overextension. First, the centrally planned economy, which gave no one any incentive to produce anything of value, was nonviable and was eventually bound to fail, regardless of who the U.S. president was when it began to expire. Second, the Soviets were spending huge amounts on their own military and providing arms and assistance to many of the most economically backward or overly regulated economies in the world — something that their dysfunctional and teetering economy could not afford.

In March 1985, Mikhail Gorbachev, a reformist, took power and realized that the Soviet economy was in desperate need of economic restructuring, which would have happened with or without Reagan's U.S. military buildup. Although Reagan's profligate defense spending may have put some short-term pressure on the Soviet system, the dysfunctional communist economy, the overextension of the Soviet state, ethnic cleavages within the Soviet Union, and the geopolitical costs and logistics of its far-flung empire were the factors that, over time, caused the USSR to collapse.[5]

As president, Reagan justified his own military expansion as being a response to increasing Soviet military power. More recently, his boosters have argued that Reagan presciently saw that the Soviets were weaker than they appeared and increased U.S. defense spending to force the Soviets to spend more money on their own armed forces and supplies of arms and aid to their destitute allies — thus bankrupting the nation.

They have even made the far-fetched argument that the Reagan Star Wars missile defense program scared and bankrupted the Soviet Union into collapse, despite the fact that the budget for strategic nuclear weapons is only a small portion of any defense budget. Gorbachev correctly observed that even if U.S. missile defenses worked, he could build enough strategic warheads to overwhelm the expensive missile shield faster and more cheaply than the United States could build the defenses. The grandiose Star Wars program was so roundly ridiculed in the United States and the West that the Soviets would have been extremely gullible to quake in their boots over it.

Meanwhile, Reagan's military buildup cost U.S. taxpayers dearly. In fact, the huge Reagan defense budgets were merely a robust installment of a consistent military-heavy anti-Soviet containment policy by presidents of both parties during the Cold War.

An alternative and less costly U.S. policy after World War II would have been to try to overextend the Soviet empire more rapidly by allowing it to take over the backwater countries of little economic value that were the center of Cold War rivalry — for example, Korea, Vietnam, Laos, Cambodia, Angola, Mozambique, El Salvador, Nicaragua, and Afghanistan — while shoring up the defenses of the economic and technological powerhouses of Europe and Japan until they could stand on their own. The Soviets, in the interest of spreading international communism, would have had to assume the expensive administrative and aid costs for ruling all of these economic basket cases — straining their centrally planned economy even more.

After the Europeans and Japanese got back on their feet after World War II, the U.S. could have assumed a balancer-of-last-resort strategy, which would have allowed it to take a backup role for European and East Asian security, thus saving U.S. resources. As it was, the United States spent hundreds of billions of dollars doing what could have been done — because of the inherent economic weakness of the USSR — with a much lower expenditure of U.S. resources and lives. The Soviet Union was often called "the Upper Volta with missiles."

Intervened Abroad More Than His Immediate Predecessors

Even with the country's rival superpower declining on the world's chessboard, Reagan undertook some needless and counterproductive military adventures overseas. After the U.S. debacle in Vietnam, U.S. interventions decreased during the Ford and Carter administrations; but as the memory of the failed war faded, Reagan began to ramp up new military actions overseas. Without the Constitution's required congressional authorization, Reagan sent U.S. forces to Lebanon, invaded Grenada, and attacked Libya.

In the early 1980s, to provide indirect support for Israel's invasion of Lebanon to clear out Palestinian Liberation Organization fighters, Reagan provided marines for "peacekeeping" operations in that country after the war was over. As often happens during U.S. peacekeeping operations, the U.S. military began siding with one side in the Lebanese civil conflict: training, equipping, and patrolling with Christian forces against Muslim militias. As a result, in 1983, Hezbollah, a fundamentalist Shi'i Muslim group, blew up the marine barracks, which killed 241 American troops. Even though Reagan had a swaggering cowboy image, the bombing motivated him to withdraw U.S. forces — what would have been described as "cutting and running" had any other less macho president undertaken it. Even superpowers should exercise military restraint, because their prestige may be damaged if a failed armed intervention shows potential adversaries how to beat them using indirect or asymmetric means — for example, terrorism or guerrilla tactics. Osama bin Laden unfortunately learned this lesson all too well from Reagan's retreat.

To deflect attention from the unmitigated disaster in Lebanon and reestablish his tough-guy image, Reagan invaded the tiny island of Grenada under the guise of rescuing medical students and preventing Cubans from turning the island into a base. The invasion happened despite Reagan's promise to Britain, Grenada's former colonial overlord, that it would not be undertaken. The military escapade was poorly executed and featured such poor interservice communication compatibility that one U.S. serviceman used his commercial phone card to call the Pentagon to get a message through to the other services on the battlefield. The communist threat to the hemisphere was laughable because the vulnerable Grenadian airfield could have been immediately taken out in any war with only minimal U.S. air strikes.

Reagan also picked a fight with Muammar Gadhafi, the Libyan strongman who was focusing his terrorist attacks on European targets. Reagan believed him to be a Soviet pawn. Some analysts believe that Reagan, to help justify hefty U.S. defense spending increases, provocatively inserted the U.S. Navy into waters claimed by Gadhafi and sent naval aircraft to hit targets at sea and in Libya. When Gadhafi retaliated with anti-U.S. terrorism, the U.S. launched heavy bombing raids against Libya. The conventional wisdom was that those attacks cowed Gadhafi from any further acts of terrorism. In fact, Gadhafi merely went underground and began covertly focusing his attacks on numerous U.S. targets (striking some using proxies). Thus Reagan ended up generating a threat to U.S. citizens by his reckless and needless creation of a new active enemy.[6]

More important was Reagan's inadvertent aid to future U.S. enemies. Following Jimmy Carter's lead, he covertly aided Saddam Hussein's government in Iraq after it had attacked Iran — even providing valuable U.S. intelligence and military training and allowing U.S. war planners to plan some of Saddam's offensives. After defeating Iran with U.S. help, Iraq then became the dominant power in the region and later invaded Kuwait. From the Gulf War of 1991 to George W. Bush's invasion of Iraq in 2003, Carter's and Reagan's onetime covert ally became one of the U.S.'s foremost international foes.

The Carter administration also had begun supporting the fundamentalist mujahideen fighting the Soviets in Afghanistan — in order to try to ensnare the USSR in a Vietnam-like quagmire — but the Reagan administration took over this mission with zeal and vastly expanded the assistance. Out of this radical milieu stepped Osama bin Laden and the fundamentalist terrorists that were trained during that war. Reagan inadvertently contributed to what would become one of the greatest threats to the U.S. homeland in the country's history and the resultant killing of almost three thousand people on 9/11. The militaristic U.S. strategy of combating the Soviet Union in a nonstrategic backwater country seemed like a good idea at the time, but ended up creating a new threat to homeland security.

Exhibited Some Moderation Toward the Soviet Union

Reagan's supporters have never reconciled his supposed "start an arms race to exhaust the economically weak Soviet Union" thinking (harsh rhetoric and a military buildup that threatened the USSR and increased the existential nuclear threat to the United States) with his willingness to negotiate radical arms elimination — not just arms control — agreements with the Soviet Union. He negotiated the elimination of intermediate-range nuclear missiles in Europe and, to the consternation of his advisors, almost negotiated a ban on all nuclear ballistic missiles.[7] Reagan also ended the economic warfare of Jimmy Carter's ban on U.S. grain sales to the Soviet Union, but he honored the limits of the SALT II nuclear arms treaty that Carter had negotiated with the Soviets, even though the U.S. Senate had never ratified it. In 1981, when the Polish government, a Soviet client, used martial law to smash the Solidarity labor movement, Reagan did not risk war with the nuclear-armed USSR and wisely responded only rhetorically.

PROSPERITY

Let Federal Spending Rise

In 1981, his first year in office, Reagan made significant budget cuts; after that, federal spending rose. Reagan's massive peacetime military buildup and "roll-back" policy of supporting anticommunist insurgent groups in backwater nations — for example, Angola, Afghanistan, and Nicaragua — was expensive. This spending, plus Reagan's even greater increases in domestic spending, actually made federal government expand significantly. As a proportion of the GNP, federal spending increased from 21.6 percent in 1980 to 24.3 percent in 1986; federal expenditures as a proportion of net private product (output of the private sector) grew from 31.1 percent in 1980 to 34.3 percent in 1986. Furthermore, Reagan did not have the excuse that Congress added on to his funding requests because his proposed budgets and those that Congress eventually passed were fairly close in dollar total.[8]

Reagan had a tacit logrolling arrangement with congressional Democrats to accept their increased domestic spending if they accepted his big hikes in defense spending. Despite his small-government rhetoric, excessive defense spending trumped reducing government on Reagan's priority list. Federal spending nearly doubled during his watch. Federal spending was $590 billion in 1980, the last year of the Carter administration, but increased to $1.14 trillion by 1988, Reagan's last year.[9] During his two terms, only about $150 billion of this increase was added defense spending.[10] So Reagan traded off an increase of $400 billion in added domestic spending for only about $150 billion of extra defense spending. David Stockman, Reagan's budget director, who lost many fights over spending, later declared that the "Reagan revolution failed."[11]

Despite Reagan's conservative image, he was more liberal fiscally than Clinton. Even Vedder and Gallaway, who seem excessively sympathetic to the Reagan presidency, gave him a lower ranking than Clinton for policies promoting limited government and fighting inflation. Reagan, vaunted for his rhetorical love of limited government, earns a horrible ranking of thirty-second out of thirty-nine presidents, while Clinton placed twenty-seventh. As this study should have shown by now, party labels can be deceiving. It is striking that a president so revered by conservatives should have a limited government and inflation control ranking eighth from the worst among U.S. presidents.

Did Not Reduce Big Government

Despite his "small government" mantra, Reagan did not terminate a single government agency.[12] Also, his deregulation of the economy has been overblown. When first entering office, Reagan eliminated price controls on oil and suspended all new proposed regulations. But after reviewing 172 proposed rules that had been suspended, the administration approved 112 without change and rescinded only 18.[13]

Under the preceding Carter administration, deregulation had occurred at the Interstate Commerce Commission (the trucking industry), the Civil Aeronautics Board (the airline industry), and the Federal Reserve System (the financial industry).[14] (In addition to transportation and financial services, Carter deregulated the communications and energy industries, and he eased antitrust rules.) Reagan's few genuine regulatory accomplishments were to complete Carter's deregulation, enact some deregulation at the Federal Trade Commission, and deregulate unneeded workplace safety and health red tape at the Occupational Safety and Health Agency (OSHA).[15] Reagan stopped some new regulations at OSHA and the Environmental Protection Agency and formalized the cost-benefit analysis for new federal regulations that Carter had begun.

Carter had significantly reduced the number of antitrust cases brought against businesses; then Reagan reduced them further.[16] Initially under the Reagan administration, many antitrust cases against companies were dropped, and the Federal Trade Commission (FTC) shrunk by 30 percent.[17] FTC regulators were required to justify consumer safety regulations as being economical, and advertising guidelines for companies were loosened.[18] Later on, however, the administration became more stringent and began tightening up on antitrust enforcement and monitoring the Truth in Lending Act.[19] Under the Reagan administration, the number of laws under FTC purview actually increased from twenty-four to twenty-seven.[20]

Reagan failed to rein in the Environmental Protection Agency's excessive regulation and sold less public land to the private sector than Eisenhower, JFK, LBJ, or Nixon.[21] James Watt, Reagan's secretary of the interior, did open some government land for oil drilling and decreased the purchase of land for national parks.

Reagan also failed to return the government's welfare function to the states, as pledged, and he had no overall plan for desperately needed welfare reform. Thus it was left for the Clinton administration to successfully tackle at a later date. By the middle of his first term, Reagan had abandoned cuts to welfare and would occasionally approve welfare increases for political reasons. By the end of his second term, Reagan had given up opposition to the welfare state, and in 1988 he increased Aid to Families with Dependent Children (AFDC) by 10 percent.

Reagan lacked fiscal courage and generally protected the huge non-means-tested Medicare and Social Security programs (which are politically popular because they also benefit the wealthy and middle class), while at least initially cutting programs substantially for the poor — for example, Medicaid, Food Stamps, and AFDC.[22]

In 1981, Reagan proposed a cut in Social Security benefits for people who retired early at sixty-two, but he quickly backed off in the face of strong opposition. A presidential commission later suggested, and Reagan supported, compromise proposals that decreased Social Security benefits and raised payroll taxes — thus postponing Social Security's inevitable financial demise until after the turn of the twenty-first century.[23] Reagan made no attempt to create badly needed private accounts to replace the unfair government pension system.

Imposed Fake Tax Cuts

In 1981, Reagan presided over the largest tax cut in U.S. history up to that point, but his tax cuts were largely fake because without spending cuts, taxes have to be raised again at a later date (which they were), government borrowing has to be increased (raising interest rates and crowding out private borrowing), or the government has to print money (causing inflation). Turning John Hinckley's attempt to assassinate Reagan in March 1981 to political advantage, White House Chief of Staff James Baker III and media wizard Michael Deaver got much of Reagan's legislative agenda passed, including the tax cut. The tax cut included reduced personal income, capital gains, and business taxes.[24]

Reagan adopted the supply-side mantra[25] that the liberals had used during the 1960s, arguing that reducing tax rates would increase economic growth and thus actually recoup some of the lost tax revenue.[26] At its best, the supply-side argument merely figured out a different way to be a better tax collector for the welfare state. But tax revenues were less than expected, because economic growth was less than anticipated, and inflation was more than predicted.

As early as the latter part of 1981, Reagan began raising taxes surreptitiously by using euphemistic rhetoric — such as "revenue enhancements," "plugging loopholes," "raising fees," and "tightening tax enforcement" — to cover his tracks. In 1982, Reagan initiated the greatest tax increase, to date, in U.S. history. Two-thirds of the hike was an increase in business taxes, but new excise taxes on tobacco, communications, and airports were also added. Reagan's crafty method was to make cuts in taxes that were very visible to the taxpayer — income tax reductions and indexing tax brackets to avoid bracket creep — while increasing taxes in more obscure parts of the tax code. As noted earlier, in 1983, Reagan signed a reduction in Social Security benefits and accelerated a planned increase in the payroll tax, which funds the system. In 1984, Reagan signed a major tax increase that "closed loopholes."

In 1986, Reagan signed the Tax Reform Act, which didn't raise the overall level of taxation but shifted taxes from individuals toward corporations. Although this might seem like shifting taxes to those entities best able to pay them, corporate taxation is double taxation. The corporations' profits are taxed, and then the capital gains and dividend income of the company's stockholders are also taxed.

The act also was aimed at simplifying the tax code — reducing the number of tax brackets from fourteen to four — and lowering income tax rates across the board. The act also lowered the top corporate rate but eliminated corporate loopholes, tax shelters, and tax subsidies and raised taxes on capital gains. In addition, the act increased the earned income tax credit for low-income taxpayers — thus hiking the negative income tax for the disadvantaged — and took many poor people off the tax rolls entirely by raising personal exemptions and standard deductions. Some argued that the act did not simplify the tax code and, although helping tax fairness, did not realize its potential to increase savings and the labor supply.

Overall, from 1980 to 1986, taxes as a portion of the GNP fell only slightly from 18.9 percent to 18.35 percent, and as proportion of net private product from 27.2 percent to 26.6 percent.[27] But, as noted earlier, federal spending rose as a portion of the GNP and net private product during those years, rendering the slight reduction in taxes fake.

David Stockman promised spending cuts, but left them "to be determined." Powerful cabinet secretaries, especially Secretary of Defense Casper Weinberger, refused to let Stockman cut their budgets.[28] This episode shows that the Reagan administration — like recent Republican administrations, including that of George W. Bush — was more concerned with enacting fake tax cuts to win votes than in really shrinking the size of government.

The rich were more likely to benefit from these tax reductions than the average taxpayer. With bracket creep (inflation taking people into a higher tax bracket) and increases in Social Security taxes, the average taxpayer experienced a tax increase. Stockman later candidly admitted that supply-side economics didn't work as predicted and that it was just a maneuver to cut taxes for the wealthy. As a result of these government policies, the inequality of income distribution increased during the Reagan administration.[29]

Overall, Reagan's spending increases and slight net tax cuts created huge budget deficits, which his successors, up through Bill Clinton, had to work to eliminate. Reagan didn't care about deficits. The widening federal budget deficit — it hit a peacetime record of 5 percent of the GDP in 1984 — did, however, prevent the federal government from initiating new programs. From 1981, when Reagan took office, until 2003, when the George W. Bush administration added a prescription drug benefit to Medicare, no new major social or welfare programs were added to the federal budget. But that didn't stop federal spending on existing programs from increasing dramatically during those years.[30] Federal spending increased more during the Reagan years than during the Clinton years.

Reagan's greatest positive contribution was to long-term prosperity. But his fiscal policies — slightly cutting taxes as a portion of the GNP, profligate defense spending, and even greater increases in domestic spending — were not the causes of the extended period of prosperity.

Paul Volcker, whom Carter appointed as head of the Federal Reserve System, and Alan Greenspan, his successor, appointed by Reagan, ran a tight-money policy and sucked the inflation out of the system. The Volcker-induced 1981–1982 recession caused inflation to drop to only 4 percent in 1983. Since 1982, there have only been two recessions. Under the tight-money policy that Volcker started, the U.S. economy has performed better in the subsequent twenty years than in the prior twenty years.[31] Thus, Greenspan's continuation of this policy was largely responsible for the prosperity of the Clinton years and beyond.

LIBERTY

Instigated the Iran-Contra Affair, Which Was Worse Than Watergate

As bad as provoking blowback terrorism (from Libya), supporting a nation that sponsored terrorism (Iraq), and inadvertently helping to spawn terrorists (al Qaeda), the macho Reagan paid ransom, in the form of selling heavy weapons, to a state sponsor of terrorism for the return of U.S. hostages in Lebanon. Iran and the Hezbollah terrorists it sponsored, knowing a good source of revenue when they saw one, just kidnapped additional Americans for more ransom. In his book *Firewall: The Iran-Contra Conspiracy and Cover-Up*, Judge Lawrence Walsh, the Republican independent prosecutor for the Iran-Contra Affair, noted that Reagan clearly knew he was violating the arms embargo against Iran and the Arms Export Control Act, a statute with criminal penalties, when he authorized weapons sales to Iran in early 1986 without notifying Congress. In meetings, he joked about going to jail for the sales. The profits from sales of the arms, sold at inflated prices, were then transferred to the Nicaraguan Contras for their war against the Marxist Sandinista government.

By passing the Boland Amendment, the Congress had prohibited the president from using *any* funds for this Latin American brushfire war. Finding secret alternative ways to fund the Contras was unconstitutional and illegal. Yet in violation of the Constitution and this law, Reagan ordered his then–national security advisor Robert McFarlane to keep the Contras together. McFarlane illicitly solicited money for the Contras from Saudi Arabia, and Oliver North, McFarlane's zealous White House employee, illegally raised money from other sources. Almost on a daily basis, McFarlane kept Reagan informed on the growth of the Contra force and the military situation in Nicaragua.[32]

The most important remaining power possessed by Congress under the Constitution's checks and balances system (Congress's power to declare war has been moribund) is the power to appropriate money for government activities. Congressional approval of funding for federal undertakings is the legislative body's most effective, but already eroded, check on excessive executive power. The Reagan administration's attempt to completely nullify this power by developing secret and illicit alternative sources of funding for its brushfire war was a more serious violation of the Constitution than Nixon's obstruction of justice and misuse of security agencies during Watergate.

The only thing that saved Reagan from impeachment during Iran-Contra was Attorney General Edwin Meese's "discovery" of the diversion of profits from the Iran arms sales to the Contras. In the strange world of politics in the nation's capital, the more serious matter — violating the Constitution by funding the Contras contrary to Congress's wishes — was disclosed to hide the merely illegal matter of arms sales to Iran. (Unfortunately, this example shows that the U.S. Constitution has become less relevant over time.) Because the Reagan administration was the first to disclose the shenanigans before the press did, Reagan avoided Nixon's fate after Watergate, which was first uncovered by the media.

Enhanced Executive Power through Questionable Means

Although presidential signing statements, accompanying bills passed by Congress, had been around since George Washington, Reagan began to use these signing statements to contravene or nullify Congress's will without giving that body a chance to override a formal presidential veto. Edwin Meese, Reagan's attorney general, was able to have such statements included in the legislative history of laws so that courts could use the statements when interpreting the statutes' meanings. For example, Reagan declared in a signing statement that certain sections of the 1988 Veterans' Benefits Act would not be enforced. Successive presidents, such as George W. Bush, have made great use of Reagan's bad precedent, and courts have used such questionable signing statements to interpret the meaning of statutes.[33]

CONCLUSION

Reagan manipulated the media more than any recent president and set an unfortunate precedent for future executives. He consciously tried to imitate his hero, FDR, who also had been a dazzling media performer. Reagan exhibited FDR's jaunty optimism, and he, like FDR, was more popular than his policies. However, unlike Roosevelt, who had to content himself with radio, Reagan was an actor who could give a mesmerizing televised speech. Like FDR's staff, Reagan's staff meticulously prepared him for every public move. Although Reagan did not convert his party to majority status or have as extensive a legislative record as FDR did, he was moderately successful in making political gains for his party and getting his legislation through Congress. When Reagan left office, he had a 70 percent approval rating, the greatest ever for a retiring executive. His popularity recovered from the Iran-Contra Affair, but the scandal did make him a weak lame duck two years before his presidency ended.

Overall, Reagan's serious illegal and unconstitutional behavior during the Iran-Contra scandal — when combined with his profligate, unneeded increases in defense spending and even greater hikes in domestic spending, thus leading to a doubling of federal spending and record federal deficits as a portion of the GNP — more than offset his indirect role in the long-term prosperity generated primarily by the Federal Reserve's tight-money policy. Also, Reagan's rhetorically tough policy toward the Soviet Union and his fanciful Star Wars missile defense program get too much credit for the collapse of a country with a nonviable economic and social system. Early in his administration, Reagan's macho rhetoric and military buildup merely reversed Richard Nixon's policy of détente with the Soviet Union and increased the existential threat of nuclear war. Thus Reagan's image of being a small-government conservative and winner of the Cold War is largely a myth. In sum, Reagan's unconstitutional and bad policies were not offset by his very few major accomplishments. In this assessment, Ronald Reagan comes in at number thirty-four.

41

GEORGE H. W. BUSH
"Read My Lips," No Real Accomplishments

PP&L* RANKING: 33
Category: Bad

Forty-first president of the United States

Term: January 20, 1989, to January 20, 1993
Party: Republican
Born: June 12, 1924, Milton, Massachusetts
Spouse: Barbara Pierce Bush
Alma Mater: Yale University
Occupation: Businessman (oil)
Religion: Episcopalian

George H. W. Bush did much in his single term as president — largely in foreign policy and most of it bad. He continued the U.S. policy of attacking countries that had not directly threatened the United States — Panama and Iraq — and he involved the United States in nation-building in Somalia. Although Bush managed the Soviet breakup well, he didn't have the vision needed to see that a much more benign international environment might allow the United States to revert to its pre–Cold War, traditional foreign policy of military restraint.

Domestically, instead of letting the market work naturally, Bush undertook the largest and costliest industry bailout in U.S. history — that of the savings and loan banks. In addition, he raised taxes after pledging to avoid this outcome.

---

*PP&L = Peace, Prosperity, and Liberty.

PEACE

Was Not a "Wimp" in His Aggressive Foreign Policies

It's hard to imagine how Bush came to be perceived as a wimp, given his aggressive foreign policy, beginning in Panama. In 1989, not very long after taking office, for very little reason Bush invaded Panama and removed Panamanian dictator Manuel Noriega.[1] A grand jury had indicted Noriega on drug-trafficking charges, which had proved embarrassing to Bush, because Noriega was a CIA asset when Bush had been the director of the agency. Also, as vice president during the Reagan administration, Bush had served as head of a drug interdiction task force and was severely criticized when Noriega, surprisingly, was indicted and the United States abruptly had to terminate its support for the Noriega government.

Critics contended that Vice President Bush should have known about Noriega's illicit shenanigans sooner and acted to avert the abrupt calamity in relations with Panama.[2] In reality, the U.S. government was probably looking the other way with regard to a friendly dictator's drug running until it became publicly known via the indictment. After all, many senior leaders in Latin America have had connections to the drug trade.

When Noriega began stirring up anti-U.S. demonstrations and rigging elections, President Bush simply invaded and ousted the Noriega regime without congressional approval — a clearly impeachable violation of the Constitution. The Organization of American States and the United Nations both condemned the U.S. invasion of another sovereign nation.[3] Bush's action followed the precedent of Teddy Roosevelt's corollary to the Monroe Doctrine: the United States would intervene whenever instability anywhere in the Western Hemisphere might tempt an outside power. In other words, the United States could intervene in Latin America at any time to prevent any developments it found undesirable.

Initiated the First Iraq War

In August 1990, Saddam Hussein of Iraq invaded neighboring Kuwait. Iraqis had long considered Kuwait their nineteenth province, and the Kuwaitis had been stealing Iraqi oil by slant drilling across the border. Also, the Iraqis felt that they had fought the Iran-Iraq War on behalf of the Arabs, but Kuwait had declined to forgive their war debt or agree to raise OPEC's oil prices. Moreover, not having learned its lesson from the Korean War, the United States told Saddam Hussein's government that it would not get involved in inter-Arab territorial disputes and then wondered why Saddam took that as a green light to grab Kuwait. As in Korea, the United States should have either deterred the aggressor from invading in the first place or accepted that the nonstrategic victim had been overrun. The latter would have been preferable.

When grinding economic sanctions did not force Iraq's withdrawal from Kuwait, the United States asserted that it was worried about Saddam invading Saudi Arabia, home of the world's largest oil reserves. Yet there was no evidence that Saddam ever thought about taking such a drastic action, and a Saudi investigation of the Iraq–Saudi Arabia border area and Soviet satellite reconnaissance belied Bush administration claims that Saddam was massing his forces in Kuwait on the Saudi border.[4]

Bush used his diplomatic skills and good relations with many world leaders to assemble a massive force in the Saudi desert that would throw Saddam's forces out of Kuwait. To put pressure on a reluctant Congress to approve a buildup of 540,000 troops in the Persian Gulf under Operation Desert Shield, Bush first got U.N. Security Council approval to use force against Iraq. In a startling display of the imperial presidency and disregard for the Constitution's original intent, Bush claimed that he had the unilateral authority to wage a major ground and air war without congressional approval. In the face of congressional opposition to unilateral executive action, however, he elected, as a "courtesy," to ask for congressional legislation supporting the U.N. resolution just before the attack began in mid-January 1991. Bush insisted that he was not asking for congressional authorization to go to war, which he believed to be an executive decision.[5]

After a resounding, one-sided military victory, the elder Bush was criticized by neoconservatives for not having invaded Iraq and eliminated Saddam for good. Bush's son's invasion of that country in 2003 definitively showed those criticisms to have been unsound. The elder Bush and Brent Scowcroft, his national security advisor, correctly feared that a strengthened Iran would fill the power vacuum created by a vastly weakened Iraq and predicted the unruliness in Iraq that would ensue from toppling the iron rule that held the fractious country together. They also feared that unilaterally exceeding the international mandate to remove Saddam from Kuwait would ruin their hopeful precedent for international responses to aggression in the post–Cold War's new world order.[6]

Bush and Scowcroft, however, didn't mind causing Saddam trouble. Just after the Gulf War ended, they encouraged the oppressed Shi'a and Kurds to rise up against Saddam, implying that the United States would support their rebellion. Instead, the United States then watched as Saddam put down the uprisings and slaughtered the mutinous groups.

Had a Shaky Rationale for War

Although Bush managed both diplomacy and the military in extremely compe-tent fashion during the dazzling victory in the first Persian Gulf War, questions should have been raised about why the United States had to get involved in the first place. Bush gave two justifications for assembling the international coalition to eject Saddam from Kuwait: one idealistic and one realistic. Neither could survive closer examination. First, before the crisis Bush said, "This aggres-sion cannot stand." Yet throughout its history, the United States has allowed much aggression in the world to stand without response.

James Baker, Bush's secretary of state, provided the second justification dur-ing the crisis with the mantra "jobs, jobs, jobs." Baker was essentially saying that attacking another nation to foster American job growth was justified. What Baker really meant was "oil, oil, oil." Among policymakers in Washington, the conventional wisdom is that the United States needs to use military power to defend supplies of cheap oil for the U.S. economy. The idea of using the U.S. military to secure oil usually remains unstated, however, probably because of the similarity to Imperial Japanese policy that helped cause World War II. However, the great prize of Saudi Arabia, which has the largest oil reserves in the world, could have been defended without sending an offensive force to liberate Kuwait.

Yet neither the Japanese nor George H. W. Bush in 1990 and 1991 needed to use military force to secure oil. In fact, the oil market works so well that compared with war, it is cheaper and more efficient to just buy the oil — even if the price of oil goes up from time to time. Persian Gulf oil suppliers, who get between 65 and 95 percent of their export revenues from oil, have to sell oil as much or more as the United States needs to buy it. If they do something stupid, as they did in 1973, and try to cut off oil to America, the United States can just buy oil from someone else. But the oil embargo of 1973 was such a disaster for the Organization of the Petroleum Exporting Countries (OPEC) that they would probably not try it again.

Economists now believe that the economic damage that embargo allegedly did to the United States — the stagflation of the 1970s — had more to do with bad government monetary, fiscal, and regulatory polices, and less to do with high oil prices. In fact, modern economies have proved resilient to oil price increases. For example, from the fourth quarter of 1998 to the third quarter of 2000, Germany experienced a more than 200 percent increase in the price of oil, but its economy motored ahead. From 2006 through 2008, the United States has experienced high oil prices, but the economy hasn't collapsed.

David Henderson of the Naval Postgraduate School did an econometric analysis before the first Gulf War based on the hypothetical worst-case scenario that Saddam would invade and occupy Kuwait, the United Arab Emirates, and Saudi Arabia. The analysis showed that the lost economic output from higher oil prices caused by Saddam's increased market power would not have exceeded one half of 1 percent of the U.S.'s GDP.[7] Oil is valuable, and Saddam would have sold it into the market to gain badly needed revenues — after all, his financial straits after the Iran-Iraq War were part of the motivation for his invasion of Kuwait. In short, the U.S. spending hundreds of billions of dollars a year to defend something that doesn't need defending is a waste of lives and money.

Whereas Bush may have decided on his aggressive policy because of worry about oil, the policy made matters worse. Even before the war, the U.S. pressured other nations to boycott Iraqi oil, thus taking most of that oil off the world market and increasing the world petroleum price. This volume of unavailable oil was greater than the amount Henderson had calculated when estimating how much oil Saddam likely would have taken off the market if he had invaded Kuwait, the United Arab Emirates, and Saudi Arabia.[8] Even more oil was taken off the market when Iraqi troops torched Kuwaiti oil wells before retreating ahead of a U.S. invasion force retaking Kuwait. Thus the world lost more oil from sanctions and war against Iraq than it would have lost in the unlikelihood that Saddam had intended a more ambitious military agenda.

Instigated Other Negative Consequences of the First Persian Gulf War

Negative consequences of the war have piled up over the years. After the first Gulf War, the elder Bush left behind a permanent but unneeded U.S. military presence in the Persian Gulf. Even if the questionable need to defend oil is accepted, the U.S. did so in the war without a prior permanent ground presence in the Gulf. When Osama bin Laden went back to his home in Saudi Arabia after fighting Soviet "infidels" who had occupied Islamic Afghanistan, he became incensed that U.S. "infidels" were occupying soil that was home to the holiest shrines in Islam and were also present in other Muslim Persian Gulf nations. Bin Laden then decided to go to war with the United States, which ultimately resulted in one of the few threats to the U.S. homeland in the history of the republic.

In addition, the elder Bush's unnecessary meddling in the Persian Gulf area required building Saddam into a bigger threat than he was and putting U.S. prestige on the line to keep him contained. This policy eventually resulted in continued grinding sanctions that did little more than harm Iraqi civilians and led him, Bill Clinton, and George W. Bush to wage a low-level aerial bombing war — until the last president made the horrific mistake of trying to finish what his father had started. The invasion of Iraq then redoubled the ire of Islamist radicals against the United States.

The "victory" in the first Persian Gulf War just keeps on giving. Ironically, during the lead-up to the first Persian Gulf War, no one identified what legitimate threat Saddam — the former U.S. ally — ever posed *to the United States*. Saddam was never much of a threat to America, but putting him on the enemies list caused major problems for more than a decade and a half, and the meter is still running. Thus the first Bush has to be held responsible for initiating this chain of events.

Initiated the Intervention in Somalia

In December 1992, as a lame duck, Bush sent troops to Somalia to help guard food and medicine from attacks by Somali warlords, who were engaged in civil war. This use of force was the first time in about a century that U.S. troops had intervened in a genuinely humanitarian mode — with no U.S. national security objectives even remotely in sight. This humanitarian purpose was short-lived.

Bill Clinton usually gets criticized for the eighteen U.S. troops killed in Somalia — after U.S. forces had expanded their mission from guarding food and medicine into chasing around a particular warlord. Yet the mission creep in Somalia had started under George H. W. Bush and is endemic to such limited military operations.

Failed to Overhaul U.S. Foreign Policy after the Soviet Bloc's Collapse

During George H. W. Bush's term, the Eastern Bloc (1989) and the Soviet Union (1991) fell. Curiously, Ronald Reagan gets more credit for these developments than Bush, a perception that appears to arise from Reagan's defense buildup and anti-Soviet rhetoric — for example, calling the Soviet Union an "evil empire" and saying in Berlin, "Mr. Gorbachev, tear down this wall!" Actually, if the U.S. containment strategy worked, all presidents since Truman could take credit for the demise of Soviet power. In fact, the fall of the Soviet Union and its empire had less to do with any U.S. president's policy and more to do with the nonviability of the Soviet communist economic system.

Early in his presidency, Bush said the United States should move beyond containment of the Soviet Union,[9] and he did a credible job of managing the dangerous Soviet breakup. He didn't, however, go far enough in changing an outdated U.S. foreign policy after the Cold War was over.

The Soviets, in dire straits financially, pushed for arms control in chemical and strategic nuclear weapons, which Bush agreed to do. Bush and Soviet leader Mikhail Gorbachev signed the Strategic Arms Reduction Talks (START) I agreement, which was the first treaty to actually reduce (by a third), rather than just limit, strategic nuclear weapons. Nuclear weapons in former Soviet states were rounded up and safely returned to Russia. Bush and Gorbachev also signed an agreement to increase trade between the United States and Soviet Union.

In the summer of 1992, after the Soviet Union had collapsed, Bush and Boris Yeltsin, the president of Russia, signed the START II treaty to reduce strategic nuclear weapons still further, and Russia was given the most-favored, nation treatment in trade (providing low tariffs) with the United States.[10] Bush's arms-control agreements were a significant achievement, made possible primarily because the nonviable Soviet state and its Russian successor were exhausted financially, not because Reagan or Bush had built up the U.S. military or researched missile defenses.

As the Cold War ended, Bush came under pressure to reduce the deficit by lowering defense spending. Although somewhat reluctantly doing so, he actually reduced the defense budget more than his successor Bill Clinton did. Bush's Secretary of Defense Dick Cheney took the rare step of cutting some major weapon systems. Neither the elder Bush nor Clinton reduced defense spending enough, however, and the American people were denied the peace dividend that they so richly deserved after the long Cold War had ended.

Thus, Bush should face a major criticism for what he failed to do. There was no great power to take the Soviet Union's place. The time was ideal to return to the more traditional U.S. policy of military restraint, which originated with the country's founders and continued, with some notable exceptions, until the beginning of the Cold War created the perceived need for a large permanent peacetime military, far-flung overseas bases, armed alliances, and meddling around the world. Bush could have safely retracted this overextended U.S. empire and returned U.S. foreign policy to its more restrained roots, but instead chose to run a "Cold War Lite" policy.

Although he reduced the number of U.S. troops in West Germany and Europe, this was merely to get the Soviets to drop their opposition to a reunified Germany embedded in the retained NATO alliance. Also, Bush orally promised Soviet leader Gorbachev that NATO would not expand. NATO was set up to be a defensive alliance against the Warsaw Pact and should have gone out of business when the Pact collapsed, but Bush decided to keep it around and Bill Clinton and George W. Bush later expanded it and made its mission offensive. The elder Bush's presidency earns a major demerit for not returning to a more restrained traditional U.S. foreign policy when a great opportunity presented itself.

Achieved a Few Positive Results in Foreign Policy

More positively, Bush reacted properly to China's repression of student democracy activists in Tiananmen Square in 1989. Although Bush received a great deal of pressure to break relations and strengthen economic sanctions in solidarity with the students, he refused to do either. As Jimmy Carter learned, public scolding about human rights problems usually led the Chinese government to increase suppression of dissidents. Also, the way to get new ideas, such as democracy and respect for human rights, into China is not to isolate the nation with economic sanctions, but to have open trade, financial, and cultural relations with it. As a vindication of George H. W. Bush's policy, continued open commerce with China has gradually helped China to become freer politically.

After the Eastern Bloc broke apart, Bush avoided military action in the civil war engulfing Yugoslavia. He correctly realized that the United States had no vital interest in this backwater region of Europe. Bush astutely believed the Europeans had a greater interest in solving the problem. Unfortunately, Bill Clinton didn't follow Bush's policy and used U.S. military forces in the cases of both Bosnia and Kosovo.

Surprisingly, like Bill Clinton, "moderate" George H. W. Bush was more of a free-trade president than "conservatives" Ronald Reagan or George W. Bush. In 1989, the elder Bush signed an agreement to foster increased investment and trade with Mexico. In December 1992, he followed this up by signing the North American Free Trade Agreement with Mexico and Canada, creating a continental zone with no tariffs. Clinton then courageously got the treaty ratified over the objections of many in his own party. Bush also furthered the Uruguay Round of the General Agreement on Tariffs and Trade (GATT) negotiations by reaching a transatlantic compromise and supporting observer status for the Soviets in order to help open their economy to trade. Clinton would later finish negotiating the GATT treaty and sign it.

PROSPERITY

Pursued Government Intervention Domestically

Domestically, George H. W. Bush broke his "read my lips, no new taxes" pledge just at the wrong time — as the economy began to go into a recession in the summer of 1990. Vedder and Gallaway gave the elder Bush a very poor ranking on policies promoting limited government and fighting inflation — thirty-fourth out of thirty-nine presidents ranked.

Bush blamed the Democratic Congress's spending (he did veto some excessive spending) for the tax increase, but this excuse didn't wash with voters. After all, Bush had inherited the huge budget deficit from his free-spending predecessor, Ronald Reagan. The blunder of the tax increase and the continuing economic sluggishness ultimately cost Bush the 1992 election to Bill Clinton.

In another costly intervention, Bush chose not to take the free-market solution of letting savings and loans banks — which had lost billions of their depositors' money in fraudulent transactions and bad loans and investments — go broke. Instead, he approved the largest federal bailout in U.S. history, costing the federal government $300 billion over ten years[11] and ballooning the federal budget deficit.[12]

Like many recent presidents, Bush also wasted billions on a failed war on drugs at home and abroad; he doubled antidrug spending. Because of the high U.S. demand for illegal drugs, such profligate federal expenditure only allows the government to interdict 10 to 15 percent of such shipments coming into the United States, which the drug smugglers merely replace easily.

Also, Bush increased government regulation — this time by renewing the Clean Air Act in 1990 and the Americans with Disabilities Act.[13] The latter far-reaching law was difficult for businesses to comply with, required that state and local governments provide special facilities without receiving federal dollars (unfunded mandates), and hurt the people it was trying to help. Businesses were afraid to hire the disabled out of fear of getting sued for not having adequate facilities.

LIBERTY

During Bush's watch, the FBI covered up federal misconduct when residents were shot at the Ruby Ridge property in Idaho. A jury eventually acquitted the residents of all serious crimes. In contrast, FBI snipers had been given illegal shoot-to-kill orders, and FBI director Louis Freeh promoted one of the agents involved to the number-two job at the bureau.

In December 1992, just before leaving office, in a conflict of interest, Bush pardoned high-level Reagan administration officials who had been convicted in the Iran-Contra scandal. Bush, as vice president, had had a murky role in the affair and may have pardoned people to ensure their silence about his activities.

Unlike President Gerald Ford in pardoning former President Richard Nixon, however, Bush actually waited until former Secretary of Defense Caspar Weinberger, former National Security Advisor Robert "Bud" McFarlane, former Assistant Secretary of State Elliot Abrams, and three others had been charged, tried, and convicted of crimes before pardoning them. Yet his stated reasons for the clemency were questionable.

CONCLUSION

Although George H. W. Bush's military actions overseas tended to have more ill effects than Ronald Reagan's, Bush was a slightly better president; Reagan flouted, during the Iran-Contra Affair, a criminal statute and the core of the U.S. constitutional system of checks and balances — Congress's power to appropriate money for federal activities. Reagan also unnecessarily exacerbated the existential threat of nuclear war with harsh rhetoric toward the Soviet Union and a military buildup. Bush was responsible for interventionist actions in Panama, Somalia, and Iraq, the latter being a self-inflicted wound that continues to fester. After the Soviet Union fell, Bush failed to revert back to the traditional U.S. foreign policy of military restraint despite a major change in the international environment that permitted such a shift in strategy. Bush's few major accomplishments — including managing the Soviet breakup, signing arms control agreements with that nation, maintaining a moderate policy toward China when it was in upheaval, and cutting new multilateral trade deals — did not offset all of these negative actions. Thus, Bush earns a place in the category of bad presidents at number thirty-three.

42

WILLIAM J. CLINTON

More Fiscally Conservative
Than Reagan and the Bushes

PP&L* RANKING: 11
Category: Average

Forty-second president of the United States

Term: January 20, 1993, to January 20, 2001
Party: Democratic
Born: August 19, 1946, Hope, Arkansas
Spouse: Hillary Rodham Clinton
Alma Mater: Georgetown University;
University College, Oxford; Yale Law School

Occupation: Lawyer
Religion: Baptist

Bill Clinton — like Franklin Roosevelt, optimistic and charismatic by nature — was one of the best politicians of modern times. He, like FDR, could connect with the average citizen. Such skills allowed him to survive and recover politically from a 1994 Republican takeover of Congress and a 1998 impeachment. Clinton was not as good, however, at governing.

Over the balance of his two terms, Clinton's policies were middle of the road and fit aptly under his "New Democrat" campaign slogan. In economic and even some social policies, Clinton's actual policies were more conservative than those of George W. Bush, who billed himself as a "compassionate conservative." In contrast to Bush, who increased domestic spending at a faster rate than any president since Lyndon Johnson, Clinton actually slowed the increase in federal spending, with some help from Newt Gingrich's Republican Congress. Similarly,

---

*PP&L = Peace, Prosperity, and Liberty.

Reagan-friendly Vedder and Gallaway actually gave Clinton a better ranking for polices promoting limited government and fighting inflation than Ronald Reagan — Clinton was ranked twenty-seventh out of thirty-nine presidents rated, and Reagan only received an abysmal thirty-second ranking.

Besides putting the brakes on federal spending, Clinton's accomplishments included trade expansion, welfare reform, and deficit elimination. Set against those positives were a market-restricting health care proposal and many failed military interventions around the world. Most of the presidents in the average category are lackluster because their positive initiatives roughly balance their negative contributions. The top lackluster president, ranked eleventh overall, is Clinton.

Like Harding, whose presidency is associated with financial scandal, Clinton is often linked with sexual escapades and lying, which led to his unsuccessful impeachment. But Clinton probably has been overly pilloried for this episode.

Was Dishonest, but Probably Should Not Have Been Impeached

During the scandal over Clinton's relationship with White House intern Monica Lewinsky, the public showed maturity by distinguishing Clinton's private actions from his behavior as a public official — much more maturity than was displayed by the president's tawdry actions or by independent counsel Ken Starr's long partisan fishing expedition for Clinton misbehavior and his inclusion of unnecessarily salacious sexual details in a report designed to shock rather than inform the public. Clinton's critics were trying to use the criminal justice system for political ends, and the independent counsel was secretly coordinating with anti-Clinton groups.[1]

In the end, the House impeached Clinton, not for having sex with an intern, but for lying about this private matter to the grand jury investigating allegations of Clinton's alleged sexual harassment and for trying to obstruct that investigation. The old Washington cliché "It's the coverup that kills you" was certainly just as applicable in this case as it was for Nixon in Watergate. If Clinton had just promptly settled Paula Jones's sexual harassment suit against him, come clean about his affair with Monica Lewinsky, avoided lying in a legal deposition and to a grand jury, and refrained from encouraging others to go along with his lies, he would have experienced a scandal that quickly passed.

There can be legitimate debate about whether the founders intended to include such activities in the category of "high crimes and misdemeanors," which are the grounds in the Constitution for impeaching a president; the conclusion here is that they did not. Going back to the formulation of the Constitution casts doubt on whether Clinton should have been impeached for these offenses. When the Constitution was being created, the original phrase was "high crimes and misdemeanors against the state," but the "against the state" was removed by the committee on style, presumably not for substantive reasons. The founders probably wouldn't have included these offenses relating to a private matter as high crimes and misdemeanors against the state. Moreover, as we have learned, other presidents have committed far more dangerous, illegal, and unconstitutional acts and never faced impeachment — for example, running secret or overt wars without congressional knowledge or a declaration of war respectively, evading the congressional appropriations process, restricting constitutionally protected civil liberties, and undermining the checks and balances system in the Constitution.

Critics could make a reasonable argument, however, that when a president lies under oath and obstructs justice even concerning a private matter — as Clinton apparently did — these actions undermine the nation's judicial system. Of course, rather than facing the political process of impeachment, Clinton could have been prosecuted for these alleged crimes after he left office. In fact, after leaving office, Clinton had to face a threatened prosecution from a new independent counsel who had replaced the outgoing Starr. The new counsel, less partisan than Starr, made a deal with Clinton in which he could avoid prosecution by making a public confession that he lied under oath. Clinton also had to pay a fine and had his law license suspended for five years.

In any case, little doubt existed about the opinion of the American people. Clinton's job approval ratings remained fairly high during the scandal and actually increased after the impeachment.[2] Ironically, the voters punished the Republicans at the polls. The disastrous 1998 election results for the Republicans caused Speaker Gingrich — a driving force behind Clinton's impeachment — to resign, while Clinton easily survived the impeachment process — only the second Senate impeachment trial in U.S. history — and smiled through the rest of his presidency with fairly high approval ratings.

PEACE

Was the Post–World War II King of Overseas Military Interventions

Clinton is the post–World War II champion for getting the United States enmeshed in the greatest number of ill-advised foreign military adventures —

although Truman, LBJ, and George W. Bush share an even bigger trophy for entrapping the United States in the largest and most boneheaded military foreign quagmires using ground forces. Clinton usually kept U.S. military involvement within bounds and was astutely reluctant to commit large numbers of ground forces after his minor debacle in Somalia. Nevertheless, he used the military far too much, and often counterproductively, in areas of the world in which the United States had no strategic interest. Clinton intervened or threatened war in eight places around the world during his two terms: Somalia in 1993, Haiti in 1994, North Korea in 1994, Bosnia in 1995, Afghanistan and Sudan in 1998, Iraq in 1998, and Kosovo in 1999.

Clinton's foreign adventures began with an existing U.S. military presence in Somalia, left over from George H. W. Bush, who had sent troops to Somalia to guard relief convoys in that violent and anarchic nation. Thus Somalia may be the only legitimately humanitarian U.S. military intervention in the last century. Clinton's critics seem to excuse Bush's initial involvement and mission expansion and criticize Clinton for "mission creep." However, mission creep is inherent in most of the military's humanitarian or peacekeeping missions. Once on the ground, soldiers are usually sucked into the violence on one side or the other.

Clinton accelerated the existing mission creep by attempting to create peace in the anarchic country on behalf of the United Nations and then by attempting to kill or capture the warlord Mohammed Farah Aideed. The result was eighteen dead U.S. Army soldiers, some of whom were dragged through the streets in front of TV cameras. Clinton then withdrew U.S. forces. It was later learned that Osama bin Laden had some involvement in this attack; bin Laden said the lesson that he reaffirmed from this withdrawal under fire was that terror strikes resulting in significant casualties could make the United States pull out of a foreign occupation. Bin Laden had earlier learned this lesson from Reagan's withdrawal from Lebanon in the early 1980s after Hezbollah's bombing of the U.S. Marine barracks there, which killed 241 military people.

George W. Bush later focused on bin Laden's reaction to Clinton's withdrawal in Somalia to argue that the United States must not cut and run from Iraq or it would send the wrong message to bin Laden and al Qaeda. Of course, Bush conveniently omitted Reagan's original "cut and run" from Lebanon and its similar effect on bin Laden. In any case, Bush took the wrong lesson from the Lebanon and Somalia debacles. The lesson he should have taken is that U.S. leaders should not involve the nation's military in any faraway brushfire quagmires that are not vital to U.S. security — which the vast majority of them aren't — and are hard to "win." Even if there is initial public support in the United States for a particular intervention of choice, if things go wrong, the war lasts longer than expected, or U.S. casualties mount, then public support invariably evaporates.

Clinton partially learned his lesson after Somalia and was more reluctant to commit U.S. ground forces to humanitarian or peacekeeping missions, but this didn't stop him from intervening in foreign problem spots.

Intervened in Bosnia, Serbia, and Kosovo

After the Eastern Bloc fell, Yugoslavia erupted into a brutal civil war over secession of its constituent republics, with atrocities committed on all sides. The West focused on Serbia, its president, and his Bosnian Serb allies as the most powerful and dangerous players in the region. According to David Model, a professor of political science at Seneca College, NATO nations wanted to break up Yugoslavia, which was dominated by Serbia, because it was the last recalcitrant socialist nation in the region; he contends that the alliance used the humanitarian rationale of ending ethnic cleansing to do it. The CIA and the National Endowment for Democracy had backed conservative separatist groups in the Yugoslav republics with money, arms, and advice. The Yugoslav civil war might have been avoided if the West had refrained from recognizing Slovenia, Croatia, and Bosnia as independent from Yugoslavia.

Clinton was reluctant to put U.S. troops on the ground in the middle of a civil war; so to ensure fewer U.S. casualties, he allowed only the use of U.S. air power. However, the president did not get congressional approval for the air strikes. According to Model, the United States led NATO land- and sea-based aircraft in bombing Bosnian Serb military units and carpet-bombing Serb civilian enclaves in Bosnia — for example, the towns of Lukavica and Tuzia and the Serb suburbs of Sarajevo.[3] In any event, Clinton's bombing of the Serbs, when combined with a ground offensive by U.S.-trained Bosnian Muslim and Croat forces, caused the Serbs to capitulate. Clinton then coerced all the parties to sign the Dayton Peace Agreement in 1995 and sent U.S. soldiers to be part of a NATO peacekeeping mission, disingenuously saying that they would be there only a year. NATO troops are still in Bosnia today, and the society is an abysmal example of nation-building.

Although the U.S.'s justification for intervention in Bosnia was based on humanitarian grounds, there were hefty amounts of realpolitik involved. Reinvigorating NATO — so the United States could maintain and expand its influence in Europe in the post–Cold War era — was a major factor in the

Clinton interventions in Bosnia and later Kosovo. After the Cold War ended, the United States pushed its sphere of influence east into the countries of the former Eastern Bloc. This was done, not for U.S. security, but to enlarge the informal U.S. empire and to justify keeping U.S. forces in Europe after the main Soviet threat had gone away.

The United States wanted to retain NATO, an alliance that is very one-sided, with the United States providing security for European countries that are no longer poor and could and should bear more of the financial burden for their own defense. More important, as George Washington and Thomas Jefferson — opponents of permanent and entangling alliances — knew, alliances impede the flexibility of U.S. foreign and security policies. U.S. security guarantees for ever more countries under an expanding NATO, which Clinton began, will be on the books long after their usefulness has passed. In fact, those excessive commitments remaining on paper may drag the United States into future wars that it doesn't wish to be involved in — as the great powers of Europe were dragged into World War I by the European alliance systems of the day.

Clinton had been lukewarm about letting new countries into NATO until he saw the domestic political benefits of wooing Eastern European voters in key Northeast and Midwestern states, especially Ohio and Illinois. Not coincidentally, major steps toward admitting Poland, Hungary, and the Czech Republic into NATO were taken in the election years of 1994 and 1996. So NATO, originally a defensive organization, became an offensive alliance, which was used to attack Bosnia, Serbia, and Kosovo under Clinton and to attack and occupy Afghanistan under George W. Bush — countries outside the Western European NATO treaty area. These offensive missions were in violation of NATO's charter.

To see that perceived, rather than legitimate, realpolitik considerations trumped humanitarian considerations when deciding to go into Bosnia, one need only look as far as Rwanda. At about the same time that the smaller-scale killing of civilians was going on in Bosnia, as many as eight hundred thousand Rwandans were being massacred in a civil war. Knowing that the United States could realistically intervene in only a limited number of places at one time, the Clinton administration decided to intervene in Bosnia because Europe was regarded as more strategic than Africa.

The same objectives that led to the intervention in Bosnia in 1995 also resulted in the U.S.-led bombing of Serbia and Kosovo in 1999. The Clinton administration wanted to further weaken Serbia and Slobodan Milošević, its president. Now that the U.S.-dominated NATO had found a new offensive stabilization mission and had brought Bosnia into the U.S.'s orbit, the imperial "turbulent frontier" thesis took hold. To protect the U.S. investment in Bosnia, Serbia and its recalcitrant president had to be tamed.

When Milošević became president of Serbia in 1989, he began to take away the autonomy given to Kosovo, a largely Albanian province of Serbia, in 1974. The Serbs wanted to reassert more control over a province with cultural and religious shrines that make it the cradle of Serb history. The Kosovo Liberation Army (KLA) received covert support from the CIA and the German intelligence agency, despite the fact that Robert Gelbard, Clinton's special envoy to investigate the Kosovo crisis, had dubbed the KLA a terrorist group in 1998. By 1998, the KLA and the Serbian government were in a civil war, and, according to Henry Kissinger, the KLA committed 80 percent of the cease-fire violations.[4] The KLA began trying to provoke Milošević by attacking Serb law enforcement personnel and civilians. After the KLA attacks on Serbians, Milošević began a low-level campaign to remove Albanians from Kosovo, killing between 2,000 and 2,500 Albanians and throwing a few thousand others out of their homes.

The KLA used Milošević's overreaction to internationalize the conflict. NATO organized peace talks at Rambouillet in France, for show only, and made demands that Serbia, as a sovereign nation, could not possibly accept — for example, allowing NATO military forces to roam freely on Serbian territory and be exempt from Serb law. A senior State Department official even admitted as much. Not surprisingly, Milošević refused NATO's ultimatum. NATO, declaring that it wanted to stop Serbia's ethnic cleansing of Albanians, began bombing Kosovo and Serbia.

The Clinton administration went to war without a United Nations resolution or any advance approval from Congress, thus undermining the U.S. constitutional system of checks and balances — a far worse constitutional transgression than George W. Bush committed in invading Iraq.

To justify attacking Serbia, U.S. officials exaggerated Serb atrocities before the bombing began. Secretary of Defense William Cohen declared that one hundred thousand middle-aged Kosovar Albanian men were missing and were likely victims of Serb atrocities, and the State Department put the figure at five hundred thousand missing Kosovar Albanians. In fact, atrocities occurred on both the Serb and Albanian sides before NATO began its war, but only on a small scale. The level of Serb-committed atrocities was much higher after the NATO bombing commenced. After bombing began, the Serbs forcibly deported hundreds of thousands of Albanians from Kosovo. Clinton was warned of this likelihood before he commenced bombing, casting serious doubts about the humanitarian purpose of the NATO air strikes.[5] Having nothing to lose after the bombs began falling, Milošević predictably accelerated his violence against the Albanians.

To reduce U.S. military casualties and maintain support for the war in the United States, Clinton limited U.S. warplanes to bombing from an altitude of fifteen thousand feet or higher. Although such high-altitude bombing saved the lives of U.S. service personnel, it killed greater numbers of Albanians in Kosovo, people whom the United States was supposedly helping. In addition, the U.S. jets hit power plants, bridges, airports, railway stations, industrial factories, agricultural facilities, schools, hospitals, and other nonmilitary targets, including villages, in Serbia. At the end of the war, the Serbian military suffered only limited damage, but the Serb civilian infrastructure was in shambles.[6]

Clinton's counterproductive bombing was risky because Serbia's failure to immediately capitulate, which the administration had expected, could have required that U.S. ground forces be introduced. In the end, Clinton got lucky, and Milošević withdrew Serbian forces from Kosovo. Most likely this was caused, not by NATO bombing, but by the removal of Russian diplomatic support for Serbia. NATO sent fifty thousand troops to Kosovo to keep the peace, five thousand of them from the United States. In 2008, Kosovo finally declared its independence from Serbia, but Serbia protested vehemently because Kosovo is the cradle of Serb civilization (containing Serb cultural and religious shrines) and home to a minority of Serb inhabitants. The declaration of independence was marred by violence, and Kosovo is likely to remain a future flashpoint and a ward of the U.S. and Europe for its security and economic development.

Threatened War with North Korea

The most important intervention during the Clinton administration was a near miss. In March 1993, North Korea threatened to withdraw from the Nuclear Non-Proliferation Treaty and end international inspections of its nuclear program, thus implicitly threatening to make fissionable material for atomic weapons. Clinton — ignoring that the United States had the world's most potent nuclear arsenal for deterrence and that the despotic and paranoid North Korean regime might have some legitimate security concerns — had already declared that North Korean possession of nuclear weapons would not be tolerated.

William Perry, Clinton's soft-spoken new secretary of defense, threatened preventive war to end North Korea's nuclear program. The Department of Defense had studied the option of bombing North Korea's main nuclear facility but thought it might prompt an all-out North Korean invasion of South Korea.

Perry did not want war but was running a dangerous coercive bluff. Perry convinced Clinton to approve adding to the thirty-thousand-plus troops already in South Korea, which could have triggered an immediate North Korean invasion of the South.

Fortunately, former President Jimmy Carter had accepted an invitation by Kim Il Sung, North Korea's ruler, to visit North Korea, whether Clinton liked it or not. To give Kim a face-saving way to step back from the crisis, Clinton wisely blessed Carter's effort at mediation. Carter got Kim to freeze the North Korean nuclear program in exchange for direct negotiations with the United States, thus ending the crisis. North Korea agreed to halt its nuclear program in exchange for help in building civilian nuclear reactors and other assistance. Later North Korea cheated on the agreement, eventually pulled out of the Nuclear Non-Proliferation Treaty, and probably obtained a few nuclear weapons anyway, or at least the fissionable material to make them.[7] Thus Clinton's threat of war had little long-term effect and could have had horrendous short-term consequences.

Clinton's risky behavior mirrored John F. Kennedy's during the Cuban Missile Crisis. Clinton helped create the crisis in the first place, but then gave his opponent a face-saving way out. The risks in Clinton's case were much less than in JFK's because the Soviet Union, backing Cuba, had enough nuclear firepower to incinerate the United States, whereas North Korea was only an aspiring nuclear power. The acquisition of a few nuclear weapons by the autocratic North Korea would not have been a positive development. But North Korea, a Stalinist state, likely could have been deterred from attacking the United States, which has the most capable nuclear arsenal on the planet, without risking a large-scale regional war that could have killed tens or hundreds of thousands of people. The United States deterred an even more radical and dangerous Maoist China when it got nuclear weapons during the 1960s and backhandedly threatened nuclear war with the United States. If the United States could deter and contain the larger, more dangerous nuclear nations of the Soviet Union and China until they collapsed or moderated their behavior, it could certainly do the same with the smaller, weaker, and already unstable North Korea (as well as Iran).

Nearly Intervened in Haiti

Yet another unnecessary near-intervention was in Haiti. In 1991, elected leftist leader Jean-Bertrand Aristide was ousted from power in a coup. During the 1992 U.S. election campaign, Clinton had attacked the George H. W. Bush administration for refusing to allow Haitian refugees to come to the United States. This was good electoral politics in the U.S. black community. The Haitian people, however, heard of Clinton's words, and a hundred thousand of them planned to head for the United States as soon as he was inaugurated. Those refugees would need food, shelter, and medical attention. This flow would also cause Clinton a huge political problem on the Gulf Coast, especially in the key electoral state of Florida. In January 1993, even before he took office, Clinton was forced to rescind his pledge to take in Haitian refugees.[8] U.S. military vessels in the Caribbean ordered Haitians, escaping economic and political oppression in dangerous makeshift boats, to reverse course to Haiti.

In 1994, Clinton again modified his policy on Haitian refugees. Instead of being turned around, the refugees would get an onboard asylum hearing to see whether they qualified as political refugees. Again, an outpouring of refugees occurred, and this time they were held in the rapidly filling Guantanamo military base in Cuba. Clinton was eager to take a strong position on Haiti, and he moved forces to invade that island nation, ostensibly to reinstate Jean-Bertrand Aristide, the democratically elected president. In reality, Clinton needed to stop the refugee flow. So under the umbrella of a U.N. resolution, and despite congressional opposition (making the entire intervention unconstitutional), he assembled an armada off Haiti's coast. Such military intimidation caused Raoul Cédras, the nation's military leader, and his junta to leave the country at the last minute — after it was learned that the planes to drop U.S. paratroopers, who would begin the invasion, had already taken off from their bases. Then, not for the first time in U.S. history, U.S. forces occupied Haiti; when they left, Haiti was, as usual, every bit as poor and unstable as before they arrived.

Struck at Al Qaeda

In 1998, in retaliation for al Qaeda bombings of U.S. embassies in Kenya and Tanzania, Clinton used cruise missiles to strike al Qaeda training camps in Afghanistan and a pharmaceutical factory in Sudan. At the time, Clinton opponents cogently argued that the timing of the strikes was suspicious and that there was insufficient intelligence to target the pharmaceutical plant as being used by al Qaeda to make chemical weapons. In retrospect, however, the main criticism, only thinly justified, has become that Clinton should have done more than such strikes to capture or kill Osama bin Laden, al Qaeda's leader, before he attacked the United States on September 11, 2001.

The timing of the cruise missile attacks was suspicious — just after Clinton had waived executive privilege and testified before a grand jury in the Monica Lewinsky matter. Clinton's public rationale for launching the attacks then was that further terrorist strikes were imminent. Even if they were, the terrorists would have long been in place for any imminent attack. Hitting a training facility in Afghanistan might impair terrorist efforts in the long term, but they would not stop imminent attacks. Yet George Tenet, Clinton's CIA director, had told the president that U.S. intelligence expected bin Laden to be at the training camp in Afghanistan on a certain day in August. Perhaps this justification should have been the primary public one.

Clinton has argued since 9/11 that he took steps repeatedly to kill bin Laden, but the intelligence wasn't good or timely enough for an attack. After the Afghanistan episode, Clinton, by memoranda, tried to expand his authority to kill or capture bin Laden in a military assault or covert operation. Two submarines were stationed permanently off the coast of Pakistan, from which military personnel could send a cruise missile anywhere in Afghanistan within six hours of Clinton's command. Clinton also pressed the military to develop innovative contingency planning for U.S. commando strikes in Afghanistan to neutralize bin Laden, but the cautious U.S. military deflected these efforts.

The criticism after the failed cruise missile strike, that a beleaguered president was trying to divert attention away from the Lewinsky scandal, however, may have made Clinton less inclined to launch future strikes against bin Laden or to authorize local Afghan tribes to try to kill him. Clinton was also afraid that if he tried to kill bin Laden and failed, it would raise the terrorist's stature in the world of Islamic terrorists. Before 9/11, there was no support within the administration, Congress, the American people, or allied or Middle East nations for an invasion of Afghanistan to take out the al Qaeda–harboring Taliban regime.

In addition, Clinton was laboring with an FBI director who refused to cooperate or share information with the White House or other security agencies, something highlighted during investigations after the 9/11 intelligence failure. In mid-October of 2000, the USS *Cole* was bombed, but al Qaeda's involvement was not confirmed before Clinton left office, and the new George W. Bush administration did not retaliate even when the association was verified.[9]

In contrast, Clinton argues, quite correctly, that George W. Bush did even less during the first eight months of his presidency to get bin Laden than the Clinton administration had. Bush was more worried about missile defense. That said, before 9/11, both administrations probably could have done more to capture or kill bin Laden. But it is easier in hindsight to see the magnitude of the threat from al Qaeda. Al Qaeda's previous strikes had been conventional bombings of buildings, embassies, and ships — not credible attempts to kill massive numbers of people at one time using a unique, ingenious, and diabolical form of attack.

Ordered Bombing in Iraq

In 1998, Saddam Hussein refused to let U.S. weapons inspectors into Iraq to verify that he had scrapped his nuclear, biological, and chemical programs, as he had promised after the first Gulf War. In mid-December 1998, shortly after the House Judiciary Committee passed articles of impeachment against Clinton and while the full House was voting on them, Clinton ordered the bombing of Iraq to degrade sites for making such weapons. Like Clinton's threats of war over the North Korean nuclear program, the bombing of Iraq was a preventive action. Since U.S. intelligence didn't know where the sites were (there were none) and the bombing didn't cause Saddam to let the inspectors back in, the bombing was purely punitive and achieved nothing, except more Iraqi deaths and greater anti-U.S. animosity in Iraq.

PROSPERITY

Controlled Spending and Helped Create Economic Expansion

When Clinton took office, he faced a record federal budget deficit and national debt inherited from the Reagan and George H. W. Bush administrations, which liked to cut taxes for their wealthy Republican constituencies but were politically timid when finding offsetting spending cuts. In 1993, Clinton, with the support of Democratic-controlled legislative chambers, though none from the Republican side of the aisle, retained limits on government spending in order to make a brave attempt to cut the deficit. Later, free-market Republican Alan Greenspan, chairman of the Federal Reserve System under the Reagan, George H. W. Bush, Clinton, and George W. Bush administrations, called Clinton's deficit-cutting effort "an act of political courage" and compared it favorably with George W. Bush's profligate fiscal policies, which he criticized harshly. Clinton's effort was made before the Republicans took over Congress beginning in January 1995. Yet critics often understate Clinton's role in adopting a policy of fiscal austerity, while exaggerating the effect of Newt Gingrich's later ten-point Contract with America. Even though the ten initiatives advocated regulatory relief and fiscal austerity, the new Republican Congress only passed one item into law.

Although Clinton at times contested Republican budget cuts by vetoing spending bills — resulting in the temporary shutdown of the federal government — he generally adopted the Republican goals of balancing the budget, offering tax cuts, and restraining increases in Medicare. In short, the small-government message that voters sent in the 1994 elections, which allowed the Republican takeover of both houses of Congress, made Clinton adopt the even more fiscally conservative policies of his opponents. Even before this, however, Clinton had already restrained his liberal impulses to spend money on new initiatives in favor of deficit reduction. All in all, he and the Republican Congress slowed the rate of federal spending increases. In fact, according to Clinton biographer John F. Harris, Clinton governed much like an Eisenhower Republican.[10]

In addition, the longest economic boom in U.S. history helped Clinton take the budget from deficit to surplus; however, he also increased taxes on the wealthy and middle class, although his BTU energy tax failed to pass. Clinton and the Republicans couldn't agree on what to do with the emerging budgetary surplus, so it defaulted to reducing the national debt. In the modern era, it is difficult to lower government spending because much of the federal budget, in particular entitlement programs, is on autopilot to increase; powerful interest groups thwart any cuts to the remainder. Just restraining the growth of government expenditures below the growth of the GDP is considered an accomplishment. Thus Clinton did a reasonable job in holding the line on federal spending, given these severe constraints.

Clinton's slowing of federal spending increases and converting a government budget deficit into a surplus helped create the longest period of economic expansion in U.S. history. Years later, upon analysis, America's financial establishment came to this somewhat overstated conclusion: after years of risky deficit spending, Clinton's economic plan had been the catalyst to a decade of prosperity.[11] He certainly deserves some of the credit. Sustained growth rates of more than 4 percent per year had not been as good since the 1960s, inflation was low, productivity accelerated, exports boomed, the unemployment level was at only 3.9 percent, and the welfare rolls were the lowest in thirty years. The good economy helped to increase the median income of Hispanics and African Americans and to reduce crime, teenage pregnancy, and other social problems.[12]

Many conservatives, attributing all good developments to Ronald Reagan, argue that the groundwork for the Clinton prosperity was laid during the Reagan years. This is not true, as my discussion of Reagan explains. The long boom period during the Clinton administration was primarily a result of the Federal Reserve System's monetarist experiment, or tight-money policy, under Alan Greenspan. Greenspan was appointed by Reagan but learned his tricks from Jimmy Carter's Federal Reserve Board nominee, Paul Volcker. Volcker and Greenspan were the two persons — excluding all the entrepreneurs, businesspeople, and workers who really produced economic growth — who were most responsible for the prosperity during the Reagan and Clinton years.

Supported Welfare and Other Reforms

After the 1994 Republican election victory, Clinton decided to make good on his 1992 campaign pledge to "end welfare as we know it." He had been working on the issue since the 1980s and astutely believed that the welfare system was hurting those it intended to help. Clinton worked with the Republicans to pass legislation to devolve welfare programs to the states and convert a permanent underclass — with a perpetual dependency on government handouts, poor self-esteem, and no way toward advancement — into temporary aid recipients who were required to work while getting assistance.

These changes were the most important domestic initiative of Clinton's two terms, saved hefty amounts of federal dollars, and have been a fairly successful reform — much to the amazement of those who predicted a stark future for welfare recipients. Although not the perfect solution, welfare reform was an improvement to the then-abysmal status quo.[13]

One of the most significant things Clinton did was to expand the Earned Income Tax Credit, which reduced taxes for people just above the poverty line and encouraged them to keep working rather than go on welfare.[14] Reducing people's taxes is always a good incentive for them to work because they get to keep more of their earnings.[15]

Clinton, with support from both parties, decided to pass a financial reform bill in 1999 (the Gramm-Leach-Bliley Act), which scrapped the Glass-Steagall Act of 1933 and was the most important financial legislation in sixty years. The new law dramatically loosened regulations in the financial industry, allowing brokerage firms, banks, and insurance companies to merge.[16]

In 1998, Clinton unsuccessfully tried to get both parties to compromise and reform the costly entitlement programs of Medicare and Social Security, which are still on the road to insolvency. Clinton was being impeached that year, however, and needed every Democratic vote he could get. Democrats, usually priding themselves on their "compassion," never want to cut Medicare or Social Security, and Clinton didn't push them too hard to do so. Although trimming benefits would have made the existing system more solvent, it would not have changed the unfairness of the systems, in which today's workers support their elders — some of whom are society's richest people. The only fair system is to allow people to create their own medical savings and retirement accounts.

Advocated Free-Trade Initiatives

Clinton's international trade policies were more conservative and less protectionist than those of Ronald Reagan and George W. Bush. Although George H. W. Bush had negotiated the North American Free Trade Agreement (NAFTA) — which eliminated tariffs among the United States, Canada, and Mexico — Clinton, a rabid advocate of globalization and free trade, courageously assembled a coalition in Congress to ratify the measure against the wishes of the overwhelming majority of his own party. In 1994, Clinton created the World Trade Organization (WTO), under the auspices of the General Agreement on Tariffs and Trade (GATT), to lower tariffs and expand world trade. Although some have properly questioned the need for an additional international bureaucracy to do what governments could do on their own, the creation of the WTO, on balance, has beneficially increased world trade flows and globalization.

Later in his administration, Clinton unsuccessfully attempted to get the Congress to grant him fast-track authority to facilitate congressional approval of trade treaties with foreign nations. This was the first time since FDR's administration that Congress rejected a president's major proposal for more open trade. Although this authority would have made it easier to reduce government barriers to free trade in the world, legitimate concerns could be raised that it undermined the U.S. Constitution. Under a fast-track agreement, Congress, by law, would have agreed not to amend such treaties, thus allowing only an up-or-down vote on the pacts. Such a provision augments an imperial presidency and undermines Congress's constitutional role of giving its advice and consent to treaties.

Clinton also normalized relations with Vietnam, opened a U.S. embassy there, and lifted U.S. economic sanctions against that country — thus permitting long-overdue U.S. trade with and investment in Vietnam.

Was Afraid to Take On the Military

Because Clinton had to back off other issues early in his presidency, he allowed himself to be dragged into a fight over gays in the military.[17] He agreed with those who wanted to lift the ban on gays serving openly in the military.[18] Why should the government discriminate against gays in military service, since they already surreptitiously served in the armed forces? Chairman of the Joint Chiefs of Staff Colin Powell, along with Democratic Senator Sam Nunn, the powerful chairman of the Senate Committee on Armed Services, however, bitterly opposed Clinton's thinking on the basis that it would undermine the morale of the armed forces. These same arguments were used against Harry Truman's order to racially integrate the troops.

Clinton's stance was courageous, but he committed the tactical error of making it one of the first issues that he addressed. In the end, Clinton, the military, and Nunn compromised on the bizarre "Don't Ask, Don't Tell" policy. The policy prevented the military from interrogating and rooting out gays in the ranks, but it required gays in the military to remain in the closet about their sexual identity or face being kicked out. However disappointing to Clinton and the quest for gay rights, this compromise was an improvement for gays in the service.

Clinton's advocacy on this hot-button issue for the military and his evasion of the draft during the Vietnam War always made him wary of taking on the military thereafter. Early in his term, he continued George H. W. Bush's post–Cold War cuts in the defense budget, but he was reluctant to push the military hard enough on the issue. Thus his defense cuts were less than those of his predecessor, and later in his administration he began ramping up defense spending, even in the absence of new post–Cold War threats.

Was Conservative Only to a Point

Clinton's general budgetary restraint was tempered by the massive, complex, and bureaucratic health care proposal he put forth. Democrats had been trying to pass universal health care coverage since FDR's New Deal but had only succeeded in enacting it for the elderly (Medicare) and the poor (Medicaid). Meantime, about 20 percent of the American people remained without health coverage.

Clinton's health care plan was the most expansive social legislation since the New Deal. The proposal extended private health care coverage to all Americans through a system of government-regulated and managed competition, rather than taking advantage of more efficient unfettered market competition to provide medical services. In other words, health insurance companies could compete, but the benefits they offered and the returns they got would be highly regulated. In addition, insurance companies would charge everyone the same rate and thus could no longer adjust a premium based on the risk of insuring a specific patient. Even Donna Shalala, Clinton's secretary of health and human services, cautioned that the administration's plan was going down the wrong path toward an unmanageable bureaucracy.

Fortunately, Congress let Clinton's health care plan die because of its inordinate cost and complexity. Clinton could have compromised with Republicans and passed a milder plan with less government interference in the health marketplace — for example, one that merely increased subsidies to poor people who could not afford to buy health insurance. But Hillary Clinton, put in charge of the health care effort, would not take advice from Clinton's economic advisors and refused to compromise until it was too late.[19]

Another Clinton proposal was a program of national service for youth. Whether mandatory or voluntary, diverting youth from getting productive jobs in the private sector to do make-work jobs in the government is inefficient, unproductive, and actually retards economic growth. It is based on the false notion that young people need to pay their dues to society by doing public service. Doing a job that doesn't really need to be done or can be more efficiently accomplished by the private sector is not doing anyone any good. Young people working in the private sector usually pay their dues by working harder for lower pay than their bosses do. Why should older people, who may or may not have paid their dues in such a public program, encourage or require younger people to do so?

After the opposing party took over Congress in 1995, Clinton — like other presidents facing a hostile legislative body — attempted to enact his agenda via suspect executive orders. When Congress refused to pass Clinton's proposals on government regulation, affirmative action, the backing of organized labor, and environmental measures, Clinton got much of what he wanted by essentially ruling by decree. He issued more than thirty executive orders in the environmental area alone — some of which preserved land from economic development — after Congress failed to pass his program.[20] Clinton also issued executive orders altering Medicare, addressing global warming, creating new Food and Drug Administration regulations to reduce youth smoking, expanding federal authority over tobacco advertising, regulating meat inspection, and restricting mining in southern Utah by making the area a national monument.[21]

One such order, made when the then-Democratic Congress balked at passing legislation, approved a $43 billion bailout loan to Mexico to shore up the peso in the wake of the currency's collapse,[22] which had spooked foreign investors and threatened Mexico's economy. It is interesting that Clinton supported the free market in international trade but got cold feet when countries fell into financial trouble. Bailing out countries that are irresponsible financially merely leads other nations to follow their lead, and in this case the bailout publicly and unconstitutionally threatened Congress's all-important power of the purse.

Clinton also had a grand scheme to give the tobacco industry some immunity from class action lawsuits for damages in exchange for more stringent antismoking regulations in the future. This tradeoff is backward. Smoking is an individual decision — albeit a very bad one for personal health — so the government should minimize regulation of it. Tobacco companies, however, should face unlimited liability for the damage that their product does to people.

LIBERTY

Initiated Tragic Federal Raid

In 1993, in Waco, Texas, a flubbed raid by agents of the Bureau of Alcohol, Tobacco, and Firearms (ATF), which killed four federal agents and six civilians, led to a standoff with a well-armed Branch Davidian Christian religious cult. Federal authorities wanted David Koresh, head of the cult, for possession and manufacture of illegal weapons. Rather than surrender, Koresh engaged the authorities in a fifty-one-day standoff. Clinton and Attorney General Janet Reno ordered four hundred law enforcement agents to break down the walls of the Davidians' complex with government vehicular armor. As many as eighty-six more people died, including seventeen children, when a fire broke out in the compound.

Federal law enforcement agencies were properly put under the microscope for their actions, and Reno took full responsibility for the incident.[23] In 1995, to avenge the tragic federal raid against the Christian cult, terrorists Timothy McVeigh and Terry Nichols bombed a federal building in Oklahoma City, which killed at least 168 people, including 19 children.[24]

Assaulted Civil Liberties

Overall, the Clinton administration's record on civil liberties was not as bad as that of its successor, but it was not good and may very well have laid the groundwork for the broad expansion of executive power and horrendous abuses of the George W. Bush administration. Jim Bovard, a political commentator, quoted a 1998 report by the American Civil Liberties Union (ACLU) that said that the Clinton administration had "engaged in surreptitious surveillance, such as wiretapping, on a far greater scale than ever before.... The Administration is using scare tactics to acquire vast new powers to spy on all Americans."[25] For example, in reaction to the first World Trade Center bombing, the Oklahoma City bombing, and the gas attack on the Tokyo subway, the Antiterrorism and Effective Death Penalty Act was passed and signed in 1996, even though administration officials admitted that the added law enforcement powers in the new law would not have helped nab the perpetrators of such attacks in advance. The law, however, significantly increased government surveillance of Americans. Clinton left behind a significant increase in the government's policing powers and a substantial erosion of individual civil liberties.

CONCLUSION

Like other recent controversial presidents — Ronald Reagan and George W. Bush, for example — Clinton is difficult to evaluate dispassionately because analysts tend to be pulled into either the "love him" or "hate him" camp. Much of Clinton's love-him camp contains Democratic activists, and those who are smitten with his considerable charisma. Clinton's hate-him camp comprises conservative activists who are still bitter over Clinton's political strategies that successfully beat them at almost every turn, not over his actual middle-of-the-road policies.

While Clinton can be credited for important positive policies on international trade, fiscal austerity, and welfare reform, his record is tainted by his heavily interventionist foreign policy; his expansion of executive power; the administration's complicity in the tragic deaths in Waco, Texas, and other civil liberties violations; and his lying and obstructing justice in the Monica Lewinsky scandal. Adding to the black marks against his administration were Clinton's unsuccessful attempt to severely cripple any natural market forces remaining in the health care industry and his proposal for a national service program for youth. In short, he was an average president. William J. Clinton is number eleven in this assessment.

43

GEORGE W. BUSH

Interventionist Policies Undermined
the Republic at Home and Peace Abroad

PP&L* RANKING: 37
Category: Bad

Forty-third president of the United States

Term: January 20, 2001, to January 20, 2009
Party: Republican
Born: July 6, 1946, New Haven, Connecticut
Spouse: Laura Welch Bush
Alma Mater: Yale University, Harvard Business School
Occupation: Businessman (oil, baseball)
Religion: United Methodist

Bush's presidency was one of the worst of all time. The most obvious reason is that he invaded another country for no legitimate reason and enmeshed the U.S. in a costly militaristic quagmire and civil war. But that is not the most important reason. Worse, Bush tried to expand the powers of an already imperial presidency to a breathtaking extent—severely undermining the balance of power among the branches of government enshrined in the Constitution and riding roughshod over the civil liberties of American citizens and foreign nationals alike. In addition, the increase in domestic spending during his term was then the largest since Lyndon Johnson. Bush's disastrous economic policies triggered a severe recession, the worst since the Great Depression and one of the worst in U.S. history.

Although many active and former senior U.S. military officers were unenthusiastic about invading Iraq—and existing intelligence undermined virtually every rationale he proposed—Bush, trying to be a bold cowboy, invaded Iraq without cause. After the U.S. invasion, it became publicly obvious that Iraq did not restart

---

*PP&L = Peace, Prosperity, and Liberty

its nuclear, biological, and chemical weapons programs after the first Gulf War bombing and U.N. inspectors got rid of them in the early 1990s. Bush's failure to win a U.N. resolution approving the military action constituted one of the worst failures in U.S. diplomatic history. The largest antiwar protests in history erupted around the world[1]—later compelling even many normally staunch U.S. allies to let the United States swing in the wind when troops were needed for the eventual occupation of Iraq and money was needed for Iraqi reconstruction. But the greatest incompetence was exhibited when Bush tried to bring democracy to a fragmented, developing nation by way of a military invasion. Iraq is an artificial nation of three primary ethnic/religious groups and countless tribes—a fictitious state created by the British after World War I out of disparate pieces of the defunct Ottoman Empire. Prior to the U.S. invasion, the country had sunk to levels of economic development—through more than a decade of wars and economic isolation by stringent U.N. sanctions—that made sustaining any democracy problematical.

Some analysts have correctly characterized Bush's decision to invade Iraq as one of the most colossal foreign policy snafus in U.S. history. Retaining a U.S. military presence in Afghanistan after the fall of the Taliban may be close behind. Moreover, both of these actions likely increased the long-term terrorist threat to the United States.

PEACE

Invaded a Country for No Good Reason and Became Enmeshed in a Militaristic Quagmire

Toward the end of the Clinton administration, the Republican Congress had passed, and Clinton had signed, an act that made regime change the goal of U.S. policy toward Iraq, but Clinton was unenthusiastic about implementing it. George W. Bush was not. In his 2000 campaign, to contrast himself with the interventionist Clinton administration, Bush had promised a more humble foreign policy. As Bush's first days in office showed, this pledge was a lie that was a harbinger of many more to come.

According to Bush's Secretary of the Treasury Paul O'Neill, in January 2001, almost as soon as Bush assumed office and about eight months before the 9/11 attacks, the administration began serious talks about how to change the regime in Iraq. Similarly, according to James Risen, who reports on intelligence for the *New York Times*, officials from the CIA's Iraq Operations Group told an April

2002 gathering that Iraq had been on Bush's agenda from the very start of his administration and that 9/11 had delayed action. Whereas Bush's critics have correctly pointed out that the invasion of Iraq was a distraction from the more important task of counterattacking the 9/11 attackers, the Bush administration, obsessed with settling old scores with Saddam Hussein, believed the opposite: that 9/11 was a distraction from a Bush vendetta against Saddam.

As the Clinton administration became the Bush administration, there was no dramatic increase in the threat from Iraq. In fact, in the first Gulf War, the United States had drastically degraded Iraq's military force—halving its ground force strength and eliminating its air force. Since then, the most comprehensive multilateral embargo in history had impeded Iraq's military and economic resurgence. Thus by 2003, Iraq's military was probably not an offensive threat to its neighbors and was certainly not a threat to the faraway United States.

Stated the Grounds for War in Iraq Were "Weapons of Mass Destruction"

The Bush administration generally claimed that Iraqi leader Saddam Hussein had biological and chemical weapons and was rapidly getting nuclear weapons; it implied that Hussein might use such unconventional weapons imminently against the United States, directly or through terrorist proxies. For example, in June 2002, in a speech at West Point, Bush indirectly made the case for a preventive attack against Saddam Hussein by declaring:

> Containment is not possible when unbalanced dictators with weapons of mass destruction [unconventional weapons] can deliver those weapons on missiles or secretly provide them to terrorist allies.... If we wait for threats to fully materialize, we will have waited too long.[2]

In September 2002, taking advantage of the first anniversary of the 9/11 attacks to make the urgent case for an unrelated war against Iraq, Condoleezza Rice, Bush's then–National Security Advisor, said the United States might receive a "mushroom cloud" from an Iraqi nuclear attack if it did not act quickly against Iraq. Similarly, in a September 12, 2002, speech before the U.N. General Assembly, President Bush declared, falsely and with little hard evidence, that Iraq had nuclear weapons capacity.

At a joint news conference with British Prime Minister Tony Blair on September 7, 2002, Bush cited an International Atomic Energy Agency (IAEA) report estimating that Iraq was "six months away from developing a [nuclear] weapon."

That report was more than a decade old and came before Saddam's unconventional weapons programs were destroyed at the time of the first Gulf War.[3] More important, the last IAEA report in 1999 correctly indicated that Iraq had dismantled its nuclear weapons program.[4] All of the CIA's information pointed to Saddam's intention to suspend these programs until U.N. sanctions ended.

On August 26, 2002, Vice President Dick Cheney—one of the most powerful vice presidents in U.S. history—declared, "Many of us are convinced that Saddam Hussein will acquire nuclear weapons fairly soon."[5] Before the war, on NBC's *Meet the Press*, Cheney actually asserted that Saddam already had nuclear weapons—which no one in the U.S. intelligence community believed—and only reluctantly admitted this was untrue well after the fact.

But even in the worst case—if Saddam Hussein had obtained several nuclear weapons and had the long-range missiles to deliver them to the United States, which no one yet believed was the case—the United States could have deterred an Iraqi atomic attack using the thousands of nuclear warheads in the most potent nuclear arsenal on the planet. If Iraq had ever launched a nuclear attack on the United States with missiles, their home address could have been detected and incinerated. In this way, the United States had deterred the more radical Maoist China when it went nuclear in the 1960s and actually made an indirect nuclear threat against the United States.

Moreover, it was widely recognized that Iraq was behind North Korea and Iran in progress toward actually producing nuclear warheads and the long-range missiles that could deliver them to faraway America. If a preventive invasion were required to stop unconventional weapons proliferation, most analysts would have assumed that North Korea or Iran would have been higher on the list of possible target countries than Iraq.

The Bush administration may very well have chosen to make an example of Iraq because it was the weakest of the three members of Bush's fabricated and cartoon-like "axis of evil." The invasion of Iraq was likely designed to intimidate the two more potent members of the axis into better behavior. But this aggressive policy made the risk of weapons proliferation worse because Iran and North Korea raced to obtain or expand, respectively, nuclear arsenals to deter a similar U.S. invasion. North Korea renounced the Nuclear Non-Proliferation Treaty, unfroze its nuclear weapons program, and conducted an explosive nuclear test. Iran accelerated its uranium-enrichment program.

In addition, the threat of Iraq giving unconventional weapons to terrorist groups to use against the United States was remote, despite Bush's assertions. U.S. intelligence agencies had "low confidence" that Saddam would share such weapons with terrorists. They concluded that he would do so only if Iraq were under attack and "sufficiently desperate." This crucial point was omitted from the version of the intelligence document given to Congress and released to the public.[6] In a courageous act against the drumbeat to war, Bob Graham, chairman of the Senate Intelligence Committee, forced the intelligence community to declassify this passage, but it turned out to be a two-day media story. The U.S. media and public didn't seem to care that the conclusions of Bush's own intelligence agencies undermined his case for war. The march to war continued unhindered.

It is true that terrorists, with no home address to incinerate, are harder to deter from attacking than are rogue countries such as North Korea, Iran, and Saddam's Iraq. And that is why rogue states would probably not give or sell unconventional weapons to unpredictable terrorist groups. If after an unconventional terrorist attack on the United States, the weapons were traced back to a rogue state, that state would be in danger of nuclear incineration by the United States—a significant deterrent.

A summary memo of a meeting held at the end of January 2003 between Bush and Tony Blair, corroborated by the *New York Times*, indicated that Bush knew that Iraq had no unconventional weapons. Nevertheless, Bush told Blair that the war would start in March and then began exploring alternative justifications for it.[7]

Shortly before the invasion, Saddam allowed the International Atomic Energy Agency's inspectors to reenter Iraq, and they found no unconventional weapons or weapons programs. After the invasion, Bush and Secretary of Defense Donald Rumsfeld falsely claimed that Saddam would not let the weapons inspectors into his country. In fact, the inspectors had to leave only when Bush started the war. The IAEA issued two reports in the months and weeks before the invasion declaring that no evidence was found to show that Saddam was reconstituting a nuclear program. But Bush had told Blair that he was going to war even if the U.N. inspectors didn't find anything. Finally, in a vain attempt to forestall a U.S. attack, the Iraqis, through intermediaries, invited the Americans themselves in to see that they had no unconventional weapons. The CIA told the Iraqis that they would see them in Baghdad.[8]

Stated That Terrorism Was the Grounds for War in Iraq

The Bush administration repeatedly stated or implied that there was a connection between al Qaeda—and even the 9/11 attacks—and Saddam Hussein. On September 25, 2002, Bush claimed, "You can't distinguish between al Qaeda and

Saddam."[9] In his largely false speech to the U.N. Security Council on February 5, 2003, Colin Powell asserted that Saddam Hussein harbored al Qaeda terrorists, hosted training camps for the group, and provided its cells with information about chemical and biological weapons. In several speeches around this time, Bush echoed Powell's charges. In his May 2003 "mission accomplished" speech after the Iraq War appeared to be an initial success, Bush crowed, "We have removed an ally of al Qaeda."[10]

Yet just after the 9/11 attacks, Bush and his advisors were told that no connection existed between Saddam Hussein and al Qaeda or the 9/11 attacks. In a well-known incident, Richard Clarke, the White House's antiterrorism coordinator, reported that on the day after 9/11, even after he protested that there was no connection between Saddam Hussein and the 9/11 attacks, Bush personally insisted that he look for one. After gathering the CIA's and FBI's prominent terrorism specialists, Clarke wrote a memo to the president saying that no connection existed. The memo was returned to him by the office of Bush's National Security Advisor with the comment, "Wrong answer.... Do it again."

The 9/11 Commission, other investigative bodies, and captured senior al Qaeda operatives all have denied a connection between Saddam and al Qaeda or 9/11. In fact, the terrorist groups that Saddam Hussein supported were anti-Israeli groups and did not even focus their attacks on U.S. targets.

Stated that Saddam Being Evil Was the Grounds for War in Iraq

If Iraq was not much of a threat to the United States—conventionally or unconventionally—then what about the neoconservative argument that Saddam was a heinous despot and that overthrowing him would lead to a flowering of democracy in Iraq, which would serve as a model for the Middle East and the world? After no unconventional weapons were found and after Saddam's alleged links to al Qaeda or 9/11 were debunked, the refrain from the Bush administration and neoconservatives became "Are you saying that Iraq is not better off without Saddam Hussein?" The administration's goal to promote democracy in the Middle East and around the world was adopted only belatedly in his second term during the 2005 State of the Union address, in an attempt to show that invading Iraq was part of a larger strategic vision.

In reality, it appears that the Bush administration wanted a friendly, rather than a democratic, government in Iraq. Initial Pentagon planning wanted to decapitate the Iraqi leadership and install Iraqi exile Ahmed Chalabi and his colleagues in the highest positions of the Iraqi government, but Bush vetoed it, presumably because it looked bad. Then Paul Bremer, head of Bush's Coalition Provisional Authority (CPA) in Iraq and a man with little experience in Arab countries, was going to install a rather undemocratic caucus system. Under this system, the CPA and the Iraqi Governing Council (appointed by the CPA) would choose regional caucuses of friendly leaders, who would select local leaders and delegates to a constitutional convention, which would draft a new constitution. Bush only gave up this façade of democracy when the most powerful man in Iraq, Shi'i leader Ayatollah Ali al-Sistani, put tens of thousands of protesters in the streets demanding real democracy. Al-Sistani said that unelected people should not be writing the Iraqi constitution. Bush also canceled local Iraqi elections when the "wrong" people were expected to win.

The answer to the administration's question about whether Iraq was better off without Saddam Hussein wasn't as obvious as it first appeared. No doubt exists that Saddam was a vicious despot, but there were and are many other terrible leaders around the world. However, the U.S.-induced civil war in Iraq may have killed more Iraqis than Saddam ever did. Two studies that scientifically sampled Iraqis to see if they had had a relative killed in the U.S. invasion, occupation, and civil war estimated that either 151,000 or 601,000 additional Iraqis had been killed by violence since the U.S. invasion and occupation (there was also a 60 percent increase in nonviolent deaths not reflected in these numbers). The methodology used to come up with these numbers was widely used in estimating deaths in other wars.

The lower estimate sampled more respondents but may have understated the number of deaths because interviewees had to report family deaths to the Iraqi government, which might have proved dangerous if their relative was fighting against that government. The higher estimate was made by nongovernmental researchers.[11] If the higher number is correct, Saddam's rule, as bad as it was, may have been better for Iraq than the chaos, mayhem, and pervasive killing that had occurred during the U.S. invasion and occupation. If a divisive Iraq, no longer held together by the strong central government of a dictator or U.S. military occupation, falls into a larger sectarian civil war, the numbers of dead could even go much higher than 601,000. The violence continued, even after U.S. forces withdrew from the country at the end of 2011, and at this writing in early 2014, is escalating in intensity—adding many more Iraqi bodies to the cost of Bush's removal of Saddam Hussein from power.

In Saddam's Iraq, most citizens were safe if they stayed out of politics and played by Saddam's rules. In post-Saddam Iraq, uncertainty was pervasive, with no one safe from the prevalent insurgent violence, sectarian slaughter, and criminal carnage in a Wild West atmosphere, which included sporadic electricity and services and long gasoline lines.

Moreover, if the goal was merely to remove the authoritarian Saddam from power, this goal likely could have been achieved without going to war. According to journalist Bob Woodward, in early February 2003, more than a month before the U.S. invasion, Gamal Mubarak—the pro-American son of Egyptian President Hosni Mubarak—personally relayed a message to President Bush indicating that Saddam might be willing to go into exile. Bush, however, believed Saddam to be a terrorist and, in his secret meeting with Gamal, effectively nixed this idea by refusing to guarantee Saddam's protection once in exile; indeed, he said he would not look favorably on any country offering him protection. "If you are looking for assurances from me that we won't do something," Bush said, "you don't have those assurances."[12] According to the *Washington Post,* the Spanish newspaper *El País* obtained a transcript of a meeting between Bush and Spanish Prime Minister José María Aznar less than a month before the March 2003 invasion in which Bush confirmed that Saddam was talking to the Egyptians about going into exile. But Bush said that Saddam might be assassinated, an implied threat, and that Saddam's security would not be guaranteed. Bush also said at the same meeting that he expected U.S. forces to be in Baghdad by late March 2003. They were.[13]

Occupied Iraq

Bush administration officials ridiculed and effectively fired General Eric Shinseki, chief of the army, for estimating that hundreds of thousands of U.S. troops would be needed for a successful occupation, and then severely limited the number of U.S. forces inserted. They did the same to Larry Lindsey, the president's top economic advisor, for estimating that the Iraq War would cost between $100 and $200 billion—instead claiming that it would cost only $50 billion. The war ended up costing the United States more than $1 trillion.

The Bush administration's monumental blunders during the occupation included deploying inadequate numbers of U.S. forces, going to war with insufficient bulletproof vests and armor for vehicles, conducting insufficient postwar planning, disbanding the Iraqi security services, firing all Baath Party members from the

Iraqi government, underestimating the possibility that the Iraqis had preplanned a guerrilla insurgency, squandering funds to be used for economic development, and bungling the counterinsurgency war by using heavy-handed tactics.

The worst blunder, however, was to believe that democracy could currently take hold in that country. Unlike Japan and Germany after World War II, Iraq had no experience with democracy, little sense of national identity or unity, and fairly low levels of economic development. Furthermore, Iraq's history showed that only a strongman could hold together the artificial and fragmented country. When Saddam was removed by force and Iraq's social fabric was torn asunder with yet another war, Iraq predictably unraveled.

Experts on federal governance have concluded that to be successful, U.S.-style federations—the goal in remaking Iraq in the image of the United States—need high levels of societal cooperation. The experts say an informal cooperative and republican culture has to take hold naturally in a country before formal republican institutions can develop, not the other way around. Imposing republican institutions on a country from the top down by an outside power using military force leads to an even lower chance of success. Therefore, the fragmented Iraqi society was unlikely to be fertile soil from which a U.S.-style federation could grow. In fact, Iraq was one of the least likely countries in the Arab world to become a stable democracy.

The U.S. troop surge, a revised U.S. counter-insurgency strategy, ethnic cleansing that separated warring factions, and, most important, U.S. payoffs to Sunni guerrillas and some Shi'i militias reduced violence temporarily. But Iraq could still be on the precipice of a worst-case outcome—a multisided civil war in which the various factions don't have control over their fighters. This would make reaching a settlement difficult. Any full-blown civil war could escalate into a regional war—with Syria, Egypt, Jordan, and Saudi Arabia supporting the Sunnis and Iran supporting the Shi'a. At this writing, the civil wars in Syria and Iraq are merging. It is possible that Turkey could enter such a war directly to prevent its minority Kurds from separating and merging with Iraqi Kurdistan, virtually an independent country since the first Gulf War.

Even if the U.S.-imposed democracy ultimately succeeds in Iraq, it probably will not be a model for the rest of the Middle East. Arabs in other Middle Eastern countries probably will focus not on the benefits of republican government but on its imposition at gunpoint by a hated foreign power and the ensuing violence and chaos. If a unified, democratic, and peaceful Iraq is the eventual outcome—which is unlikely—the cost in blood and treasure has been enormous.

The U.S. intelligence community prognosticated in 2002, just before the invasion, that Iraq could remain unstable long after the United States took over the country. The community predicted a divided society, a significant probability of violence, an insurgency, sectarian violence, and a foreign occupying force that would be the target of attacks. U.S. intelligence doubted that democracy could be established in Iraq because the country lacked the level of socioeconomic development and political culture needed to sustain this cooperative form of government. The intelligence community was also skeptical that the invasion would affect the region positively—in fact, the intelligence agencies predicted that the U.S. war would likely spur increased strident Islamism and that Iraq would become a draw for radicals.[14] All such findings were ultimately proved correct, but were ignored at the time by an administration that was hellbent on war.

Hurt U.S. Antiterrorism Efforts by Invading Iraq

General William Odom, the conservative former head of the National Security Agency during the Reagan administration, said he was against the invasion of Iraq because he believed it would help the most dangerous enemy that the United States had in the Middle East—Iran. It did. By taking out Iran's chief neighboring rivals—Saddam Hussein in Iraq and the Taliban in Afghanistan— the United States allowed the more populous and economically powerful Iran to grow from a four-hundred-pound gorilla in the region to one of eight hundred pounds. As a result of U.S. policies, the Iranians accumulated great influence in Afghanistan and with the radical Shi'i groups now running Iraq. Furthermore, al Qaeda began to operate in Iraq only after the U.S. invasion, finding a safe haven for its activities and a training ground to give its operatives valuable combat experience.

The Bush administration bragged about the lack of major international terrorist incidents inside the United States since 9/11, but such attacks were rare even before 9/11, with the last occurring eight years before, in 1993, with the first World Trade Center bombing. Furthermore, for some time after 9/11, al Qaeda lessened its emphasis on attacking the U.S. directly and concentrated on driving a wedge between the United States and its allies by attacking the allies.

More important, between 9/11 and when the U.S. commenced a bombing campaign against Afghanistan in October 2001, the United States had intelligence on Osama bin Laden's whereabouts, but the military's strategy for Afghanistan was not flexible enough to take advantage of the intelligence. Bin Laden then escaped to the mountains of southeastern Afghanistan—where he was much harder to target. Even then, bin Laden was allowed to get away twice there because Afghan forces were used to corner him instead of U.S. ground forces. It is suspected that he was able to buy his way out of the predicament and thus to escape to Pakistan—keeping alive his threat to the U.S. homeland.

As in Iraq, then–Secretary of Defense Donald Rumsfeld, whose vision of future combat was small numbers of forces on the ground supporting air power, pressured commanders to limit the numbers of ground forces used. In Afghanistan, insufficient U.S. forces allowed bin Laden to escape. In Iraq, inadequate numbers of U.S. troops allowed a potent insurgency to arise and eventually hurl the country into a low-level civil war.

Although the Bush administration was initially successful in capturing or killing some of al Qaeda's top operatives and destroying al Qaeda's safe haven and training base in the Taliban's Afghanistan, the continued U.S. occupation of that country has caused a resurgence of the Taliban. U.S. policy in Afghanistan experienced familiar mission creep—shifting from killing or capturing bin Laden to nation building, counterinsurgency, and even drug interdiction (a mission at cross purposes with counterinsurgency because threatened poppy growers have thrown their financial power behind the Taliban). For a year after the 9/11 attacks, Pakistan's President Pervez Musharraf was willing to let the United States have free rein in his country to capture or kill bin Laden, but the Bush administration did not make good use of the time.

Michael Scheuer, a former CIA man in charge of tracking Osama bin Laden, has long alleged that the war in Afghanistan, like the conflict in Iraq, has been lost. Because the U.S. occupation of Afghanistan spurred a strong enough resurgence of al Qaeda and the Taliban in Afghanistan and Pakistan, another al Qaeda future safe haven and training area has arisen in Pakistan. The bulk of U.S. forces should have exited Afghanistan after it deposed the Taliban, threatening to return if any Afghan government became a future haven for al Qaeda. The absence of a foreign occupier likely would have reduced Afghan and Pakistani resentment, which is fueling a rekindled al Qaeda and Taliban insurgency. A small number of U.S. Special Forces could have been retained secretly in Afghanistan to go after bin Laden without trying to rebuild the entire nation.

Equally foolish, invading Iraq before neutralizing al Qaeda was a major blunder. The war in Iraq sucked away scarce policymaker attention, surveillance and human intelligence assets, and Special Forces troops from what should have been the primary mission after 9/11: neutralizing the real perpetrators of the attacks—bin Laden and al Qaeda. After 9/11, Bush virtually got a blank check from a congressional resolution, the American people, and the rest of the world to do what it took to take down bin Laden and al Qaeda, but he squandered the political capital on an unrelated invasion of Iraq.

Invading Iraq made the international terrorism problem worse. According to a database maintained by the Rand Corporation for the National Memorial Institute for the Prevention of Terrorism, the number of terrorism incidents worldwide increased 168 percent after 9/11. The number of fatalities from terrorist incidents since 9/11 increased 300 percent.[15] According to April 2006 reports from the Bush administration's own State Department and the National Counterterrorism Center, terrorist attacks worldwide tripled in 2005 to a record level of more than eleven thousand incidents.[16] The next year's State Department report noted another whopping increase of almost 28 percent to more than fourteen thousand incidents.[17] According to terrorism experts, the Iraq War was a significant cause.

The State Department noted that combat training in Iraq had become a pipeline for terrorists. Tactics learned in Iraq—suicide and roadside bombings—have been transplanted to Afghanistan and used against U.S. forces there. In addition to providing combat experience for terrorists, the non-Muslim United States occupying two Muslim nations—Iraq and Afghanistan—has inflamed the anger of radical Islamists all over the world. Although the Vietnam War killed fifty-eight thousand American troops overseas, Bush's invasion of Iraq—causing this inflammation and concomitant rise in terrorist attacks, some of which may trickle back to the formerly safe U.S. homeland—could prove to be a greater blunder in terms of national security.

The same phenomenon of a non-Muslim occupation of a Muslim nation generating Islamist fury occurred during the Soviet occupation of Afghanistan, the Russian occupation of Chechnya, and the Israeli occupation of Palestine. It should have been no surprise to the Bush administration that occupying Iraq and Afghanistan would stoke militant Muslims worldwide.

Many years after 9/11, bin Laden and his chief lieutenant, Ayman al Zawahiri, the seeming brains of al Qaeda, were still running free. The al Qaeda terrorist network had evolved into a more decentralized organization that may be more dangerous because it is harder to track and eliminate.

Perhaps bin Laden and Zawahiri would have been neutralized earlier if the Bush administration had focused all of its efforts on those who attacked the United States rather than committing naked aggression against an unrelated third party. If Bush had been president when the Japanese attacked Pearl Harbor and Hitler declared war on the United States, he probably would have gone to war against Argentina instead of Japan or Germany.

Undermined Israel's Long-Term Security with His Rabid Pro-Israel Stance

Bush was correctly critical of Bill Clinton's excessive emphasis on trying to achieve an Israeli–Palestinian peace settlement. When the peace process collapsed and violence ensued, Bush at first correctly distanced himself from getting involved. Later, however, he was dragged back into the process clutching his Middle East "road map" for peace.

Even worse, Bush slavishly supported Israel's aggressive policies, including its building a security fence, assassinating Palestinian leaders, bulldozing Palestinian houses, restricting Palestinian movement and commerce, and indiscriminately attacking Palestinians, which has killed more Palestinian civilians than Palestinian suicide bombers have killed Israeli civilians.

When Israel used the militant Shi'i Hezbollah group's kidnapping and killing of a few Israel soldiers as a pretext to pummel Lebanon with air strikes, killing many innocent Lebanese, Bush unquestioningly backed Israel rather than encouraging the Israelis to desist from attacking. Such unconditional U.S. support did nothing to help Israel's security—as Hezbollah rockets raining down on Israeli towns and cities showed. Hezbollah withstood Israeli attacks, thus immeasurably enhancing its prestige, and became so strong that it has severely undermined Lebanon's incipient move toward democracy.

Neither the Israelis nor the Palestinian Authority were ready to make peace, and the United States should have followed Bush's original instinct and stayed out of the matter. Palestine is not strategic to the United States, and the United States should not dole out billions in aid to get the parties to make peace, as it did under President Carter to get the 1978 Camp David Accords. In fact, the U.S. should terminate its expensive aid to Israel and Egypt.

PROSPERITY

Used War to Beget a More Bloated Welfare State

Stephen Moore, an antitax conservative, said of Bush, "He's the biggest spending president we've had in a generation."[18] According to conservative Fred Barnes, Bush was a big government Hamiltonian rather than a small-government Jeffersonian.19 This moniker means that Bush was willing to use the government to subsidize business, agriculture, religious, and other groups. Under the Bush administration, government spending saw the largest increase in decades, and the federal budget surplus Bush inherited from Bill Clinton exploded into deficits. Like Reagan, Bush increased federal spending as a percentage of GDP—only far worse.

Also, like Reagan, Bush loved enacting fraudulent tax cuts—that is, cutting taxes while allowing all-important federal spending to balloon. Vice President Cheney was famous for his belief that federal deficits didn't matter. Tell that to the capital markets when public borrowing crowds out private borrowing, increases interest rates, and drags down the economy.

Bush used the 9/11 attacks to drastically pump up the defense budget, even though most of the added money did not go to fight terrorism. Many defense programs tend to be welfare for those with political power. The military industrial-congressional complex has ensured that weapons systems designed during the Cold War or thereafter to fight a now-nonexistent great power threat needlessly remain under development or in production today. Terrorists are best countered with relatively cheap intelligence, unpiloted drones, law enforcement, CIA covert action specialists, and the military's elite Special Forces, not irrelevant gold-plated weapons systems, such as the stealthy supersonic F-22 fighter, the Virginia-class submarine, a new aircraft carrier, missile defense, or the army's future combat systems. Fighting brushfire wars against guerrillas, such as those in Afghanistan and Iraq, is best done with infantry forces, not with heavy firepower from futuristic weapons. The use of heavy firepower in Iraq and Afghanistan helped turn the indigenous population against the foreign occupier, the U.S.

Bush withdrew from the 1972 Anti-Ballistic Missile Treaty so that he could sink much money into building an unneeded missile defense system. With its vast arsenal of nuclear warheads, the U.S. can deter any atomic attack from rogue states, which would probably be delivered by a small aircraft or boat sailing into a U.S. port rather than by a missile. Likewise with such an unlikely nuclear attack from terrorist groups. Thus the expensive and rudimentary missile defense system doesn't address the major threats to the United States but does provide largesse for defense contractors.

After 9/11, Bush drastically increased and "consolidated" the federal bureaucracies. He combined twenty-two agencies into a new Department of Homeland Security and federalized airport security workers, in the largest government reshuffle since Truman's creation of the CIA and the Defense Department in 1947 and the largest expansion in federal bureaucracy since the New Deal in the 1930s.[20] The reorganization has already been deemed a failure, and the bureaucracy, like all government agencies, gives out contracts and federal money to the politically powerful, rather than to those most in need—in this case, states and localities that face the biggest threat from terrorists.

Bush also created a Director of National Intelligence to herd the nation's sixteen disparate intelligence agencies, adding another layer of bureaucracy on top of existing agencies rather than streamlining them to combat small, agile terrorist groups. In the lead-up to 9/11, the major problem was a lack of coordination among national security agencies in tracking al Qaeda. These two "reforms," by increasing the layers of bureaucracy, merely made the original problem of coordination worse.

Historically, war has increased domestic spending as well as defense spending and created new roles for the state in society. In his first six years as president, Bush increased domestic discretionary spending, with the help of Republican Congresses, an astounding average of 7 percent per year.[21] In those years domestic discretionary spending increased a total of 35 percent, the biggest increase since LBJ. It is significant that the two presidents are linked in this way, as both had a long war during their administration. Administrations in which domestic spending was more restrained—such as those of Carter, Reagan, George H. W. Bush, and Clinton—generally experienced only short wars or no conflicts at all. George W. Bush likes to compare himself to Ronald Reagan; however, the Bush administration most resembled LBJ's presidency—simultaneously pursuing guns and butter (foreign adventures and domestic largesse). Bush may have been a neoconservative in foreign policy and a conservative in social policy, but he was a liberal in domestic spending.

Bush masked this liberalism with the moniker "compassionate conservatism," but his massive federal spending gave him away. For example, the first major new domestic program since LBJ's Great Society was the irresponsible addition of a prescription drug benefit to the already insolvent Medicare entitlement program. This program merely gave added welfare to the demographic group in society with the highest average income and most political power—the elderly—at the expense of all other taxpayers.

Bush increased federal funding with attached mandates in traditionally state and local affairs. His No Child Left Behind Act imposed federal educational standards on local schools everywhere under penalty of losing federal funding. This caused teachers to teach only what was on the tests, eliminating the richness and diversity of curriculum usually decided at the local level. Thus, Bush further federalized education, which had traditionally been a state and locally led effort.

Bush also increased federal regulation of political campaigns by signing the McCain-Feingold bill, which did little to limit the effect of money on politics and actually made the U.S. political system less competitive. In the past, attempts at regulating campaigns merely eroded citizens' rights to free speech under the First Amendment, while allowing money to flow around the regulations. Campaign-funding restrictions usually help those making the laws—that is, incumbent politicians—at the expense of their challengers. Challengers usually need more funds to offset incumbent advantages.

After the Enron Corporation's phony accounting scandal, Bush signed new regulations on corporate governance that replaced intrinsic market pressures, which probably would have acted as their own more efficient constraint on company behavior.

Bush's faith-based welfare programs blurred the traditional barrier between church and state—a pillar of the founders' vision, American tradition, and the Constitution. Bush believed that the government should encourage certain services, without actually providing them, by steering federal money to religious groups. In some cases, a religious message accompanies the charity and religious discrimination in hiring service providers results. When Congress failed to pass Bush's faith-based initiative, he took the unconstitutional step of implementing a portion of it by executive order.

Also eroding the separation of church and state was Bush's signing of three bills that restricted abortions and advocacy of other such bills to mollify social conservatives, who were key Bush supporters. Although no right to privacy or to control your own body and its systems and functions is specifically mentioned in the Constitution's Bill of Rights, the Ninth Amendment implies that rights mentioned in the Bill of Rights are not the only ones guaranteed. Government control over women's reproductive systems does not seem to comport with the spirit of freedom celebrated at the nation's founding. Also, although the Constitution does not specifically give the federal government jurisdiction over a woman's womb, reproductive decisions, or even what constitutes human life, the federal government, under the Fourteenth Amendment, does have the power to prevent states from abusing citizens' rights. If state governments are violating women's rights by regulating their uteruses and reproductive choices, the federal government should stop this infringement of rights.

To help win reelection in 2004, Bush endorsed a constitutional amendment against gay marriage. Why should the government discriminate against some portion of its citizens just because others in a free society don't like their lifestyle?

Should the government discriminate against Republicans because Democrats don't like their politics or lifestyle?

Furthermore, Bush compensated for Washington's incompetent response to Hurricane Katrina's devastation of Mississippi and Louisiana by slathering the region with unduly large amounts of federal money for recovery. Fiscal conservatives in his party were disgusted at the more than $100 billion package. Conservatives pointed out that San Francisco had recovered from an earthquake in the early twentieth century with no federal aid at all.

In some cases, Bush subsidized corporations, sometimes at the expense of the poor. For example, in agricultural subsidies, Bush opened the funding spigot wide. Such U.S. subsidies allow U.S. agricultural producers to compete unfairly with poor farmers in the developing world, thus hurting the underprivileged. Foreign aid is usually wasted, distorts the target country's economy, or requires the recipient country to buy U.S. exports. If instead of increasing foreign aid, Bush had reduced, rather than increased, U.S. agricultural subsidies and had lowered tariffs on the exports from developing nations, the poor in the developing world would have been much better off.

Although Bush should not have rescued even the homeowners who took out loans they couldn't afford, his bailing out of financial institutions that should have known not to make bad loans is even more unbelievable. Such bailouts during the sub-prime mortgage crisis will merely result in future irresponsible behavior. Ben Bernanke, Bush's Federal Reserve chief, did not pursue the tight monetary policies of Paul Volcker, appointed by Carter, and for awhile of Alan Greenspan, appointed by Reagan. These wise policies had led to long-term prosperity and low inflation. Greenspan's and Bernanke's loose monetary policies led to the housing bubble, which burst, triggering the Great Recession and Bush's $700 billion bailout of large financial institutions. Also, Bush effectively nationalized the huge AIG insurance company and completed nationalization of the giant Fannie Mae and Freddie Mac mortgage lenders to save them all from financial ruin. Finally, Bush pushed and passed a Keynesian stimulus package to attempt to resuscitate the moribund economy using a counterproductive "sugar rush" strategy.

Was a Greater Protectionist on Trade Than Clinton

Bush was generally bad on tariffs and trade too. The large increases in subsidies for U.S. agriculture caused the collapse of the global trade negotiations in Cancun, Mexico, in 2003. Although supporting free trade in principle, George

W. Bush, like Ronald Reagan, proved to be more protectionist than Democrat Bill Clinton. To attempt to do well at election time in Pennsylvania and West Virginia, Bush imposed high tariffs on steel—the broadest protectionist measure in twenty years—which were removed only when the World Trade Organization (WTO) renounced them as illegal.

Bush did do a couple of useful things in the trade area. One was to support the entry of the rapidly growing China into the World Trade Organization. Although increased trade between countries does not guarantee that they will not go to war, high levels of U.S.-Chinese commerce builds a peace lobby in both countries. In 2001, a U.S. spy plane over international waters was forced by the Chinese to land in China. Significant U.S.-Chinese trade probably contributed to the peaceful resolution of the crisis. The other positive Bush action on trade was passing the Central America Free Trade Agreement (CAFTA).

Advocated a Few Enlightened Domestic Policies

On immigration, Bush took the approach that problems with illegal immigrants could be reduced if larger numbers were allowed to work in the U.S. legally. He realized that the U.S. economy needs the labor provided by immigrants. Unfortunately, Bush then caved in to the nativists in his party (who opposed immigration), and the immigration legislation that was passed focused on augmented border security.

One of the other few areas where Bush attempted to make a positive contribution was the partial privatization of the Social Security entitlement program. Even socialist Sweden has privatized its pension system. Social Security is a Ponzi scheme (which any private citizen would be arrested for running) that takes money from current workers and gives it to current retirees. The major problem is that demographic trends—an aging population that will lower the worker-to-retiree ratio—will soon make the system insolvent. Thus young people who have paid into the system will get little or nothing when they retire. Also, minorities are disadvantaged by the system. They go to college in lower percentages than whites and thus enter the workforce and pay into Social Security earlier; they also have lower life expectancies and thus get fewer payments than whites.

Bush's incremental proposal to reform the system was to set aside 2 percent of payroll taxes so each person could have a private retirement account. In turn, people would see a concomitant reduction in their Social Security benefits. Bush, however, was not that serious about such privatization because he waited until his second term to unsuccessfully push this agenda, while incongruously worsening the even more insolvent Medicare program by adding an expensive prescription drug benefit.

LIBERTY

Falsely Sold the War to the Public

The scariest part of Bush's push for war against Iraq was his ability to use the bully pulpit of the excessively powerful imperial presidency to stifle public debate on whether invading Iraq was a wise move. A great deal of information contradicting his claims was public before the invasion, but the U.S. media was cowed by the prospect of being called unpatriotic for forcefully bringing it out during the post-9/11 climate of fear.

Because hard-liners in the Bush administration thought the CIA was too soft on Saddam Hussein, Vice President Dick Cheney took the unprecedented step of repeatedly visiting CIA headquarters to ask CIA personnel tough questions about their analyses, and he also intervened directly in CIA field operations to obtain more robust action against Saddam's government.[22] The hard-liners at the Pentagon set up their own Counter-Terrorism Evaluation Group to find more damning evidence against Iraq than the CIA had produced. This group was easily manipulated by Israeli intelligence and Ahmed Chalabi—an Iraqi opposition figure deemed unreliable by the CIA and later exposed as a likely agent of the Iranians—who fed the Pentagon false intelligence about Iraq, including bad information on its alleged unconventional weapons. Despite Chalabi's revelation to the Iranians that the U.S. had broken their codes and was monitoring their secret communications, he was still welcomed back to Washington to meet with Cheney, Rumsfeld, and Rice.[23]

As noted earlier, administration officials repeatedly implied a false connection between Saddam and al Qaeda and even the 9/11 attacks. Despite overwhelming intelligence to the contrary and protests from CIA Director George Tenet, President Bush's 2003 State of the Union address falsely asserted that Iraq was seeking to buy uranium for its nuclear program from Niger. With little reliable information about the state of Iraq's nuclear program, the administration was hanging most of its claim that Iraq was reconstituting its nuclear weapons efforts on aluminum tubes Iraq had bought and was allegedly using to enrich fissionable material and also on the alleged uranium purchases from Niger—both of which had been previously debunked. Separately, inspectors had found some biological

growth medium that was no threat; but in his October 7, 2002, speech in Cincinnati, Bush distorted this finding and falsely claimed that Iraq had most probably
produced, using the medium, a huge amount of anthrax, a biological weapon.

Used War to Vastly Expand Executive Power

Bush's most dangerous acts may have involved the erosion of American civil
liberties, something that often happens during war—especially long wars like
the Cold War and the "War on Terror." It is ironic that Bush tried to spread
freedom abroad at gunpoint while simultaneously eroding freedom at home using
the same method. The erosion of civil liberties in the United States—caused by
wars—is part of the larger problem of an already imperial presidency continuing to expand. George W. Bush made grandiose claims about executive power
during wartime. Behind this dangerous assault on the Constitution's checks
and balances may have been powerful Vice President Cheney's belief that curbing the chief executive's power during Vietnam and Watergate had excessively
weakened the presidency. Cheney—and Bush by extension—believed in the
"unitary executive" theory, which included the view that in his role as wartime
commander in chief, the president was not subject to the constraints of the
constitutional separation of powers.[24] The founders would faint at this theory
invented out of whole cloth. Very few experts believe that the presidency is
currently weak by historical standards. Despite the slight retrenchment in the
1970s, the imperial presidency has continued to usurp power far past the intent
of the nation's founders.

Like his father prior to the Persian Gulf War of 1991, George W. Bush maintained that he had the authority, under his power as commander in chief, to
unilaterally invade Iraq without the approval of Congress. According to one
administration official, the White House did not "want to be in the legal position
of asking Congress to authorize the use of force when the president already has
that full authority." Bush, like his father, regarded congressional approval for
going to war as a desirable symbolic act that was not required.[25] The founders,
concerned with European monarchs conducting profligate wars at the expense
of their people's blood and treasure, would have been shocked at this presidential
disregard for Congress's critical constitutional power to declare war.

To demonstrate the original intent of the founders, one must go back to the
Quasi-War with France at the end of the eighteenth century. France, in its war
with Britain, was concerned that American goods were reaching British shores,
so it began to seize U.S. ships. In reaction, Congress gave the president the au-

thority to seize ships sailing *into* French ports. President John Adams, however, ordered the seizure of vessels going to and from French ports. When a U.S. ship seized a vessel coming out of a French port, the owners sued in the U.S. courts and won. The Supreme Court ruled that the U.S. captain was liable because Adams had gone beyond Congress's orders in carrying out his powers as commander in chief.[26] In other words, the founders believed that Congress had the war power and that the president's power as commander in chief was construed narrowly. Bush didn't care.

In addition, Bush ordered unconstitutional and illegal domestic spying on Americans and resident aliens. After 9/11, using as cover his own alleged "inherent" constitutional authority as commander in chief and the congressional resolution authorizing the war on al Qaeda, Bush claimed that he had the authority for secret warrantless wiretapping of people in the United States who were talking with foreigners overseas, if either party was suspected of being affiliated with terrorists. A Justice Department legal brief claimed that the Congress could not pass any law revoking the president's "inherent" constitutional authority.

The administration maintained that it was spying only on those people suspected of associating with terrorists, but independent bodies were not able to determine whom the secret program was actually monitoring. The surveillance program was so secretive that the public was unsure whether calls between domestic parties were being monitored as well. In February 6, 2006, testimony before the House Judiciary Committee, Alberto Gonzales, Bush's attorney general, would not rule out purely domestic warrantless surveillance. Caught doing unconstitutional and illegal wiretapping, Bush brazenly declared that he would continue to do it. It strains credulity to think that the nation's founders, recently having broken away from King George's tyrannical rule, would have endorsed Bush's wide interpretation of the commander in chief's role. In fact, the Tenth Amendment states that any powers not specifically given to the federal government—in this case the executive branch—fall to the people or the states.

In an alarming massive data-mining operation, the National Security Agency (NSA) got phone records from private U.S. communications companies so that the agency could keep track of ordinary phone calls made by millions of Americans. The agency also obtained access to most American e-mails in the U.S. communication network. The government determined who called or e-mailed whom to find "suspicious" patterns that could lead them to terrorists.

The congressional resolution authorizing the war on al Qaeda permitted actions overseas, not at home. Bush flagrantly violated the law by not getting warrants for domestic surveillance, effectively cutting the heart out of the Constitution's Fourth Amendment and its guarantee against unwarranted search and seizure. The amendment makes no exceptions for national emergency—times when citizens' rights especially need to be safeguarded.

Not surprisingly, a court ruled that the warrantless NSA domestic spying program was unconstitutional and illegal. In the face of the Democratic takeover of both houses of Congress, the administration, in early 2007, finally pledged to get court warrants for domestic spying, while still arguing that its warrantless program was legal.[27] Then the administration had the imperial chutzpah to demand that the newly Democratic-majority Congress make its illegal warrantless eavesdropping legal. Acting on its fear of being blamed for any future terrorist attacks, the legislative body not only legalized, but widened, the administration's power to conduct unconstitutional warrantless searches, watering down the judicial check on the executive branch.[28]

In the wake of 9/11, Bush and the Republican Congress had already endorsed the USA Patriot Act. The Patriot Act dramatically expanded the government's power to snoop on its citizens, while eroding the power of independent courts to oversee such spying. For example, the act unconstitutionally allowed the FBI to issue thousands of National Security Letters, without court approval, to get financial information on Americans from banks and financial organizations. The Justice Department's inspector general then found widespread illegalities and abuse on the part of the FBI in issuing the letters.

Assaulted Civil Liberties

According to historian David C. Whitney, after 9/11 and the anthrax attacks through the mail (also in September 2001):

> The U.S. adopted tactics usually associated with the world's most repressive governments. More than 1,000 immigrants and visitors were detained secretly and held without charge. The government held secret proceedings and thousands of people were secretly deported. None were accused of plots against the U.S. or of any criminal activity. The government increased the practice of holding people as material witnesses, a tactic that does not require that charges be filed.[29]

Such indefinite secret detentions without charge are unconstitutional. Furthermore, the Bush administration abused the "material witness" category to detain suspects without charges.

President Bush claimed—as an intrinsic power of the presidency and under the congressional authorization to go to war against al Qaeda—the right to seize and detain indefinitely Americans and others apprehended in the war on terror, including those captured at home, far from a foreign battlefield. As in totalitarian states, Bush claimed the power to "disappear" citizens without the need for an arrest warrant, notification of arrest, a list of charges, a trial, or access to a lawyer or civilian courts. Like Lincoln, Bush effectively and unconstitutionally suspended the Writ of Habeas Corpus—the right to challenge detention—for these individuals, a power the Constitution assigns only to Congress, and then only in times of rebellion or invasion. Even on 9/11, no rebellion or invasion occurred.

Such indefinite detention of Americans probably was the worst action of Bush's presidency. Bush believed that he could simply label anyone in the United States, or elsewhere in the world, an enemy combatant and seize and detain them indefinitely without regard for their constitutional rights—powers usually exercised by dictators. Fortunately, the United States Court of Appeals for the Fourth Circuit, in the *al-Marri v. Wright* case, ruled that Bush did not have the inherent power or authority from the congressional war resolution to do so. According to the court, validating such presidential authority "would have disastrous consequences for the Constitution—and for the country."[30]

In June 2004, the Supreme Court, in the *Rasul v. Bush* case, ruled that the U.S. military base at Guantanamo, Cuba, was under U.S. jurisdiction, thus entitling the prisoners held there to habeas corpus hearings.[31] Also in 2004, in the *Hamdi v. Rumsfeld* case, the Supreme Court ruled that the president could not hold people outside the reach of the justice system and that such prisoners had a right to contest their incarceration in court. Justice Sandra Day O'Connor wrote, "We have long since made clear that a state of war is not a blank check for the president when it comes to the rights of the nation's citizens." In 2006, Bush somehow managed to persuade a Republican Congress to deny, by legislation, Guantanamo prisoners the very right to challenge their detention that the Supreme Court had guaranteed.[32] This action is especially pernicious because many Guantanamo detainees were innocent, having been turned in by poor locals in Afghanistan just so they could collect U.S. reward money.

In the Hamdi case, however, the court shockingly validated the president's authority to declare any U.S. citizen an "enemy combatant" and try that person before a kangaroo military commission, with no presumption of innocence and insufficient guarantees of due process.

In a June 2006 ruling for *Hamdan v. Rumsfeld*, the Supreme Court struck a blow to Bush's dangerous attempt to grab vastly greater executive power. The ruling trashed Bush's plan to try detainees in military commissions established by executive order (kangaroo courts). The ruling was interpreted as a broad repudiation of Bush's newly claimed powers and left in doubt the constitutionality and legality of his other draconian, unneeded, and often counterproductive actions to fight terrorism.[33] Yet the Supreme Court, ignoring its own ruling in the 1866 *Ex parte Milligan* case—which stated that military commissions with lesser standards of justice could only be used in the theater of combat and only if civilian courts could not function—allowed military commissions as long as Congress authorized them or, if not, as long as they used the legal rules of courts-martial in the U.S. military and were consistent with the Geneva Conventions on the treatment of prisoners. Congress then meekly passed the Military Commissions Act of October 2006, which authorized military commissions with lesser standards of justice, including the use of evidence obtained by "aggressive interrogation methods"—read: torture.[34]

For the first time in U.S. history, President Bush simply directed that the internationally recognized Geneva Conventions on the treatment of prisoners of war did not apply, in all cases, to the war on terror—that is, at Guantanamo and in Afghanistan. Only much later, the Supreme Court ruled that the president couldn't flout the Geneva Conventions, which demands that a panel review the status of prisoners.

Saying that the Geneva Conventions did not apply was designed to shield U.S. personnel from prosecution under the U.S. War Crimes Act. This directive was interpreted down the chain of command to authorize questionable interrogation techniques at Guantanamo, in Afghanistan, and at Abu Ghraib prison and elsewhere in Iraq. For example, inmates were stripped, had to assume stress positions for long periods of time, were intimidated by attack dogs, were subjected to sleep and light deprivation, and underwent simulated drowning. Former senior military legal officers condemned such tactics, because the precedent could cause the same to be done to U.S. troops during a conflict and because most experts say torture usually produces bad information. Also, in any future war, if the U.S. has a reputation for torturing prisoners, enemy soldiers will be more likely to fight than surrender.

According to a report by Human Rights First, a human rights watchdog group, nearly one hundred prisoners died in U.S. prisons—forty-five of whom were suspected or confirmed homicides resulting from physical mistreatment or draconian conditions of confinement. The International Red Cross actually concluded that "systematic mistreatment" of Iraqi detainees was occurring and saw and recorded "physical and psychological coercion" as "standard operating procedures by military intelligence." In April 2004, a commission headed by former Secretary of Defense James Schlesinger noted that abuses were "widespread" and concluded that there was both "institutional and personal responsibility at higher levels."[35] Since then, more evidence arose to show high-level involvement in approving torture of prisoners.

The CIA kidnapped suspected terrorists off the streets of foreign countries and spirited them away to CIA secret prisons or indigenous jails in countries around the world—some of which practiced torture. Establishing the military prison at Guantanamo and the CIA's secret prisons overseas was designed to keep the detainees away from the American judicial system and the rights it guarantees to suspects. The CIA kept the identities of some prisoners—called "ghost detainees"—from the International Red Cross.

The scandalous photos of the mistreatment of inmates at Abu Ghraib prison and other reports of U.S. torture, along with Bush's refusal to demand full accountability for such episodes, greatly harmed the U.S. war on terror and war in Iraq—by undermining the effort to win Iraqi hearts and minds and further stoking the flames of anti-Americanism in Islamic nations and around the world.

In sum, although the Clinton administration restricted civil liberties after the 1993 World Trade Center bombing and the 1995 Oklahoma City bombing by signing the Antiterrorism and Effective Death Penalty Act of 1996, these strictures were far milder than the measures imposed during the George W. Bush administration by law and executive order.

Used Presidential Signing Statements to Increase His Power

Although Ronald Reagan set the precedent of using presidential signing statements, accompanying congressionally passed bills, to contravene or nullify the will of Congress, George W. Bush dramatically increased the practice. Reagan used the statements to undermine 71 legislative provisions, Clinton used them to attack 105 items, and George W. Bush, in only the first five years of an eight-year presidency, used them 500 times. For example, in 2003, Congress created an inspector general to oversee the new U.S. occupation of Iraq. Without any mention in the legislation, Bush's signing statement ordered the inspector general not to investigate intelligence and counterintelligence activities in Iraq.

CONCLUSION

Some presidents who have run less than perfect administrations operationally have been saved by some of the policies that they undertook or got enacted—for example, Jimmy Carter. George W. Bush was not one of them—he advocated bad policies and demonstrated horrendous operational incompetence. The disastrous and expensive (in casualties and money) nation-building projects in Iraq and Afghanistan were only exceeded in catastrophic results by Bush's expansion of executive power and theft of the civil liberties that make the United States unique. Bush had almost no accomplishments to offset such policy foibles. Bush was thus one of the nation's worst presidents. But he was not the worst president the United States has ever had because James Polk, William McKinley, Harry Truman, and Woodrow Wilson presided over wars or Cold Wars with even more pernicious and dangerous effects. In this assessment, George W. Bush is number thirty-seven.

The long-term consequences of Bush's gargantuan bailout of the financial industry were significant. The bailout entailed unprecedented government intervention in the country's financial system and another expansion of executive power. It brought the U.S. closer to socialism—the nationalization of private companies during peace time—and Mussolini-style corporatism—with the government owning shares in the troubled firms. Lastly, the bailout involved welfare for the rich, as the government acquired the authority to buy bad debt en masse. Like Herbert Hoover, Bush and Bernanke flooded a market replete with credit with even more credit. This move likely exacerbated and deepened the global financial meltdown that was caused by many financial institutions' risky loans, which were encouraged by, among other factors, earlier bailouts.

Instead, Bush should have let large financial institutions fail, removing the deadwood from the economy, and should have allowed the market to re-establish equilibrium naturally. However, he and his successor, Barack Obama, tried to artificially prop up the economy to avoid short-term pain, only to ensure longer-term economic malaise.

44

BARACK OBAMA

Only a Slightly Improved
Version of George W. Bush

PP&L* Ranking: 34
Category: Bad

Forty-fourth president of the United States

Term: January 20, 2009, to the present
Party: Democratic
Born: August 4, 1961
Spouse: Michelle Robinson Obama
Alma Mater: Columbia University, Harvard Law School
Occupation: Law professor, civil rights lawyer, community organizer
Religion: Christian

In many ways, despite their divergent party and ideological labels, the presidencies of Barack Obama (labeled a liberal Democrat) and, his predecessor, George W. Bush (labeled a conservative Republican) were similarly bad. If their major policies are tabulated across from each other under the categories of peace, prosperity, and liberty, they are surprisingly similar.

In both administrations, peace was elusive. Both men attacked countries for no legitimate reason, escalated needless wars that should have been de-escalated, got many U.S. soldiers and indigenous people killed for little gain, and ended up leaving all affected countries in shambles.

Prosperity was also elusive during both administrations. Bush's fraudulent tax cuts (cutting taxes while massively increasing spending converted surpluses in

---

*PP&L = Peace, Prosperity, and Liberty. One major caveat to this analysis is that it was done in mid-2014, only five-and-a-half years into a two-term, eight-year presidency.

the unified federal budget inherited from Bill Clinton into huge fiscal deficits), massive war spending, vast new domestic expenditures (including Medicare prescription drug coverage for senior citizens), and increases in the money supply overheated the economy into a bubble, which burst and led to the greatest recession since the Great Depression. In response, Bush provided a $168 billion Keynesian stimulus, bailed out the nation's biggest banks and Wall Street with the $700 billion Troubled Asset Relief Program (TARP), provided the first bailout for auto companies, nationalized the AIG Insurance giant, and finished nationalizing Freddie Mac and Fannie Mae mortgage lenders. Obama—continuing Bush's Keynesian intervention in the economy in a vain attempt to jumpstart it out of the doldrums—produced only an elongated anemic "recovery" by effectively nationalizing two of the three U.S. carmakers, imposing new regulations on the financial industry in a misguided attempt to prevent future financial declines, and continuing Bush's massive federal domestic largesse by launching a massive, ineffective "stimulus" spending effort costing well over $1 trillion. Also, Obama continued Bush's federalization of education, which began with the excessively rigid national education standards in Bush's "No Child Left Behind."

Although during his campaign, Obama decried Bush's taking advantage of wars to drastically expand executive power and erode the nation's unique civil liberties, he wielded most of Bush's enlarged powers and continued most of his objectionable infringements on liberty—for example, killing people overseas without congressional approval of hostilities, detention without trial, kangaroo military tribunals for terrorism suspects, and unconstitutional domestic spying. Obama expanded Bush's largely illegal anti-terrorist drone wars, which in most countries, continued to violate the Constitution's requirement for congressional approval of military action.

Even their use of dubious methods was similar. Bush took advantage of the horrendous tragedy on September 11, 2001 to conduct an unrelated invasion of Iraq. The Obama administration took advantage of the economic collapse to enact health care "reform" and also massive increases in long-term spending on health care, education, energy, and infrastructure in his stimulus initiative. Obamacare deepened government interference in the health care market. In switching priority to passing Obamacare, the president ignored advice that he focus like a laser on the collapsing economy, thus contributing to his eroding popularity.

Both Obama and Bush were in the bottom half of the "bad" presidents category. Obama earned a slightly better ranking, however, at number 34, than

George W. Bush at number 37, because he did one or two significant things right, whereas Bush joined the club of presidents, beginning with Ronald Reagan at number 35 and John F. Kennedy at number 36, who did almost everything wrong. Also, Obama inherited a bad situation from Bush, one of the worst for a new president in U.S. history: two wars that were already unwinnable quagmires, an economic collapse that had not yet shown its worst effects, and huge budget deficits and rapidly accumulating debt caused by such wars, the economic plunge, and Bush's profligate domestic spending. Although George H. W. Bush, George W. Bush's father, was also a bad president, he ranks just ahead of Obama at number 33 because of his two monumental agreements with Russia to actually reduce numbers of strategic nuclear warheads (prior treaties had just limited increasing arsenals), thus reducing the threat of nuclear Armageddon.

George W. Bush allowed U.S. military resources to be diverted to the unrelated and unneeded war in Iraq, while Osama bin Laden, the perpetrator of the 9/11 attacks, went free for ten years until Obama killed him within the confines of a congressionally approved effort to do so. Obama also withdrew U.S. ground troops from Iraq (despite his renewed bombing campaign that began in August 2014) and is in the process of withdrawing at least the vast majority of them from Afghanistan (after his ill-advised escalation of that conflict). Although Obama increased federal spending in a failed Keynesian attempt to stimulate the economy out of a Bush-induced economic collapse, he had always planned to reverse course and reduce the federal deficit in the longer term. Helped by pressure from congressional Tea Party Republicans and Washington budget gridlock, he did so—from fiscal year 2009 to fiscal year 2014, federal spending actually decreased about 2.5 percent in real terms, the first time such expenditures have decreased since the Korean War in the early 1950s. During the same period, federal spending as a percentage of GDP declined by three percentage points from 25.2 percent to 22.2 percent.[1] The only areas of civil liberties in which Obama reversed Bush's transgressions came in stopping secret detention of suspected terrorists in CIA prisons overseas, ending torture of them as an interrogation tactic, and preferring civilian courts over unconstitutional military tribunals in prosecuting them. At this writing, Obama may also roll back and judicially constrain George W. Bush's unconstitutional widespread collection of Americans' phone records and renew his attempt to close Guantanamo prison.

PEACE

Eventually De-escalated Needless Inherited "Nation-Building" Wars

Obama won the 2008 election, in part, by promising to withdraw U.S. forces from Iraq, which is one of the many unpleasant gifts that George W. Bush bequeathed him when leaving office. Obama slowly did reduce American troops, only finishing the job at the end of 2011. At first, he said he was going to withdraw all "combat forces," an elastic term that would have allowed some U.S. forces to remain to conduct missions seeming strangely similar to combat and to continue to train the sub-par Iraq security forces, which had been foolishly disbanded and re-created years before under Bush. Fortunately, even those residual U.S. forces were pulled out, largely because the government of Iraq refused the rather imperial demand that U.S. troops would be exempt from Iraqi criminal law. Given the resurgence of violence in that country at this writing (early 2014), such a small force would have been very vulnerable to attack. However, a large U.S. embassy and a reduced number of State and Defense Department contract personnel remain and are vulnerable to the increasing violence.

The ethno-sectarian forces unleashed by toppling Iraqi strongman Saddam Hussein were bound to recur at some point in this artificial country. Nine years of U.S. military occupation and nation building could only temporarily and partially suppress these powerful societal forces, and Obama should be credited with saving some American lives by eventually getting U.S. forces out. Of course, he could have saved more lives had he withdrawn U.S. forces faster.

Afghanistan was another matter. Running as a Democratic anti-war candidate in the early twenty-first century in neo-imperial America, Obama did not feel he could be against all questionable wars. So unlike the Iraq War, in Afghanistan, he did not pledge to immediately withdraw U.S. forces—essentially declaring this nation-building conflict to be the "good war," which responded to the 9/11 attacks and which would require more military resources to succeed.

Bush had not been able to resist the imperial American urge to conduct an extended nation-building occupation to "drain the swamp" of terrorists by defeating the Afghan Taliban and remodeling Afghanistan and its government— rather than simply degrading al Qaeda using Special Forces raids, piloted aircraft, or unpiloted drones. Obama—continuing Bush's troop surge in Afghanistan and imitating Bush's even bigger surge in Iraq, which temporarily quieted the violence there mostly by bribing non–al Qaeda Sunni insurgents to fight al Qaeda instead of the U.S. occupiers—upped the ante in Afghanistan, more than doubling U.S. forces to almost 100,000.[2] In his memoir, *Duty: Memoirs of a Secretary at War*, former Secretary of Defense Robert Gates excoriated Obama, because by early 2010, only a year into Obama's presidency, Gates concluded that the president "doesn't believe in his own strategy, and doesn't consider the war to be his. For him, it's all about getting out." He continued that the president was "skeptical if not outright convinced it [the strategy] would fail."[3] Similarly, Bob Woodward, in *Obama's Wars*, reported that Obama approved the troop surge in Afghanistan, not because he thought it would work, but to appease the military as a powerful interest group pressuring a new, anti-war Democratic president.[4] Not being able to bribe the radical Islamist Afghan Taliban as it did the more secular, non–al Qaeda Sunni insurgents in Iraq, the U.S. troop surge failed to stabilize Afghanistan, even temporarily. But the surge did allow Obama to say he gave it the old college try and announce a withdrawal of all "combat" troops from Afghanistan by the end of 2014. Yet additional Americans (and Afghans) apparently died just to give Obama political cover for troop withdrawal.

At this writing Obama is still trying to pressure the Afghan Taliban and their chief backers in Pakistani intelligence to negotiate peace, but he is likely to have little luck since the U.S. military is losing the Afghan War and he has announced that the United States is a lame duck in Afghanistan. He is also again trying to negotiate with a client government—this time, that of Afghan President Hamid Karzai—to allow a residual U.S. force, after all American "combat" troops are withdrawn at the end of 2014, to train the still creaky Afghan security forces and to conduct "counterterrorism missions" (which again seems very similar to combat). The ever-mercurial Karzai, even in the face of a probable post-U.S. Taliban resurgence, is trying to wring every concession from the United States before the residual U.S. force is allowed to defend the Afghan government. Hopefully, Karzai, like the Iraqi government, will be successful in scuttling a residual deployment, because a small American force will merely take casualties in a likely escalating future Afghan civil war.

U.S. intelligence believes that only about 50 to 100 al Qaeda fighters remain in Afghanistan[5] and those could be handled by using air power (drones or piloted aircraft) or Special Forces insertions from the air or from neighboring countries.

Obama, shortly after taking office, should have defied the generals and pulled the plug immediately on what everyone but the U.S. military knew was a lost war (even in the military, many questioned the escalation), instead of ramping up U.S. involvement. Many U.S soldiers who died for a lost cause would still be alive today and many taxpayer dollars could have been saved. As in Vietnam and Iraq, however, once the United States gets into a quagmire, it is psychologically, institutionally, and politically hard to get out unless the president shows courageous leadership. Obama's leadership in both Iraq and Afghanistan was tepid and fearful of the U.S. military.

Left Libya in Chaos

Obama was also timid in the face of pressure from France, Libya's former colonial master, to take advantage of the Arab Spring uprising in Libya in order to use a military attack to get rid of dictator Muammar Gaddafi. Ostensibly, Western armed intervention was rationalized by the alleged need to protect Libyan rebels and civilians from Gaddafi's threats, and that is what the United Nations Security Council resolution authorized when it allowed an allied "no-fly" zone over Libya. After the fact, the Russians felt double-crossed when the Western allies used the resolution as a cover to use air power, combined with indigenous rebel forces on the ground, to remove Gaddafi from power. American hawks criticized Obama for "leading from behind," because they believed that no military attack or invasion in the world should be absent triumphalist public U.S. leadership. Yet despite France's aircraft leading many of the strike missions, the United States remains the only superpower, principally because only it can provide the behind-the-scenes the logistics, transport, and command, control, communications, and intelligence needed to project power internationally in potent doses. Without this hidden critical U.S. support, NATO likely could not have successfully overthrown Gaddafi.

The real question is whether the West should have overthrown Gaddafi in the first place. Granted, he was a dictator with a history of human rights abuses and sponsorship of terrorism, but in recent years he had made nice with the West by giving up terrorism and dismantling his nuclear weapons program. Especially given this improved trajectory, overthrowing Gaddafi sent a really bad message to nuclear aspirants, such as Iran, about what happens when countries voluntarily give up their nuclear weapons programs, reinforcing the same message sent by the U.S. invasion of non-nuclear Iraq to overthrow Saddam Hussein. In contrast, the United States behaves gingerly around the likely nuclear North Korea. Such disparity in treatment buttresses the view of many nuclear aspirants, such as Iran, that getting atomic weapons may be the only way to deter a U.S. or Western attack or invasion.

More immediately, as in Iraq, removing the autocratic glue that held a fractious country together left Libya in chaos. In Libya, the divisions are tribal rather than the ethno-sectarian fissures found in Iraq, but the result was the same. At this writing, a weak central government is at the mercy of feuding tribal militias, leading to violence of the kind that engulfed the American consulate in Benghazi and killed four U.S. diplomats, including the ambassador. Regrettably, Obama's State Department, and even the ambassador himself, arranged too little security for American personnel in this new hazardous environment.

And the chaos from this U.S.-backed military intervention led to regional instability, as jihadist fighters from Libya and the weapons from Gaddafi's plentiful arms stockpiles migrated into Mali, precipitating a French military intervention there to beat back the militants. Worry had existed in the CIA that removing Gaddafi would strengthen radical Islamists within Libya and that they would use the country as a base for attacking targets in northern Africa. That worry is now reality. All told, the United States has left Libya, Afghanistan, Iraq, and the regions surrounding them in turmoil by its recent military interventions.

Furthermore, in violation of the Constitution and the War Powers Act of 1973, Obama went to war in Libya without any congressional approval. In Afghanistan and Iraq, George W. Bush at least got some form of congressional consent.

Obama Expands Bush's Illegal Drone Wars

Using the congressional resolution authorizing the use of U.S. military force after the 9/11 attacks, a drone war was legally permissible in Afghanistan and Pakistan, as long as it was directed against the perpetrators of those attacks (the main al Qaeda group) or those harboring them (the Afghan Taliban in Afghanistan and Pakistan). However, George W. Bush, in his unconstitutional and counterproductive "war on terror," began using drones in Pakistan against the Pakistani Taliban and in Yemen and Somalia (and maybe other countries unbeknownst to the American people) against franchise groups only loosely affiliated with the main al Qaeda group—none of which had any part in the 9/11 attacks. But this policy fit with the pattern of George W. Bush often diverting precious national security resources and assets to flail away by attacking everyone except those who actually struck the United States on 9/11.

Obama then took Bush's "unrelated-to-9/11" drone wars and unfortunately expanded them, further riling up anti-Americanism unnecessarily in Pakistan, Yemen, and Somalia. Thus, destabilizing these nations created more anti-U.S. terrorists (most meticulously documented in Yemen) and even motivated them to launch "blowback" attempts at retaliatory terrorism on U.S. soil—carried out by groups that had theretofore not focused their efforts on attacking U.S. targets (for example, a Yemeni group's sponsorship of the underwear bombing attempts on U.S. flights and the Pakistani Taliban's attempted Times Square bombing). To his credit, in early 2013, Obama eventually seems to have realized that bombing rubble for lack of real terrorist targets—and sometimes inadvertently killing civilians—in these places was becoming counterproductive. He pledged to limit the war on terror, but such problematical drone attacks continue in all of these locations. A place exists for drone attacks in counterterrorism, but they must be used only sparingly in the most critical situations—to reduce the anti-Americanism and consequent retaliatory blowback terrorism that can accompany them—and be constitutionally approved by Congress. Neither Bush nor Obama have met these two criteria in their use.

Obama's attorney general has even claimed the presidential power to use lethal military force against an American within the United States under "extraordinary circumstances," such as attacks similar to those on 9/11. "The president could conceivably have no choice but to authorize the military to use such force if necessary to protect the homeland," Eric Holder said in testimony before Congress.[6] Unfortunately, the loosely worded 2001 congressional resolution might actually allow this action if the attack emanates from the main al Qaeda group (much as the overly broad congressional Gulf of Tonkin Resolution allowed LBJ to escalate the Vietnam War), and bad precedents, beginning with George Washington's repression of the Whiskey Rebellion using the militia at the dawn of the republic in 1794, didn't help here either.

Killed Perpetrator of the 9/11 Attacks

More positively, as soon as he entered office, Obama began to de-escalate the unrelated-to-9/11 war in Iraq (although it took him too long), thus allowing a priority to be placed on devoting attention and resources to the Afghanistan War (even this was a distraction) and finding and neutralizing al Qaeda leaders in neighboring Pakistan (this had been the real prize in plain sight all along). Staying within the constitutional limits of the congressional resolution passed after the 9/11 attacks, Obama killed Osama bin Laden, the force behind the 9/11 attacks, using a U.S. Special Forces raid in Abbottabad, Pakistan on May 2, 2011—nearly ten years after bin Laden perpetrated those strikes. With all its expensive intelligence capabilities and military power, taking almost ten years for the world's superpower to locate and neutralize one man was a national disgrace.

However, after achieving what his predecessor never did, Obama should have categorically declared the war on terror to be over, conclusively ended the drone wars, and shepherded a return to "normalcy" by restoring all of the civil liberties that Bush had stolen from the American people after 9/11. Unfortunately, Obama did none of these things.

Showed Some Restraint in the Middle East

Hawks in the United States pressured Obama to intervene on the side of the rebels in the Arab Spring-induced civil war in Syria and to bomb Iran's nuclear facilities. Obama severely limited the former and, at this writing, has been able to avoid the latter.

To relieve the political pressure, a reluctant Obama did provide some low-level lethal and non-lethal aid to the fragmented Syrian rebels. He was correctly unenthusiastic about it though because of fears that such aid would fall into the hands of rebel groups associated with al Qaeda, which are the most ruthless and best fighters on the rebel side. Apparently, the lesson of U.S. aid to Afghan Islamist fighters against the Soviet invaders of Afghanistan in the late 1970s and 1980s didn't teach the hawks that U.S. assistance helped spawn al Qaeda.

Curiously, Obama drew a "red line" on any large-scale use of chemical weapons by the Syrian regime (although some indications exist that the rebels also used chemical weapons), even though, as in most wars, such weapons in the Syrian conflict have only accounted for only about one percent of the deaths—with conventional bullets, shells, and bombs generating the rest. He probably regretted drawing this line when a large-scale chemical weapons attack actually occurred. Yet he was able to negotiate an improbable agreement with the Syrian regime and its Russian backers to destroy all Syrian chemical weapons. Unlike Obama, President Bashar al-Assad probably knew the statistics on deaths from chemical weapons and decided that they wouldn't really be decisive in winning his civil war but could catastrophically (for him) bring the United States into the conflict. At any rate, it was an achievement—although one shouldn't get carried away with its significance—that Assad agreed to the destruction of his chemical weapons stockpile.

American hawks were not pleased about the agreement because it at least delayed any U.S. attack on Syria, which would weaken a regional rival of U.S. ally Israel. In Israel, however, as in the United States, debate existed about the wisdom of overthrowing the unfriendly and dictatorial Assad regime—the thought by some was that an Islamist takeover or the chaos of a fragmented Syria might be worse than a familiar autocrat who could keep some semblance of order. Because neither the rebels nor the regime is probably strong enough to control the entire country, a splintering of Syria probably will be the likely outcome.

Obama was right to resist ensnaring the United States in yet another Middle East bog, especially given the war weariness among the American people in the wake of the long war on terror and the quagmires in Iraq and Afghanistan. Such U.S. military interventions, with the armed meddling in Libya thrown in for good measure, have all been counterproductive and have destabilized these three countries, as well as Pakistan, Yemen, and Somalia. And although Israel might have a vital interest in the outcome of the Syrian civil war, the United States doesn't. The Cold War is over and America does not need to reflexively take the side opposite of the Russians and the Iranians. Although Assad has had a poor human rights record, al Qaeda-linked rebel groups, if they took over Syria, may make him look like a moderate.

Besides, Obama has not been consistent in his treatment of the Arab Spring revolts. In Libya and Yemen, he got rid of dictators, either by using direct military action to help rebels or by easing out the autocrat but retaining the regime, respectively. In Syria, he has provided only limited assistance to rebels but somehow managed to get the Syrian dictator, Bashar al-Assad, to agree to eliminate his chemical weapons arsenal without using force. In contrast, in Bahrain, because of the U.S. Fifth Fleet base there, the United States allowed the Saudi Arabia-backed government to crush the Arab Spring uprising there.

In Egypt, one of the most important Arab countries, Obama administration policy was muddled. Initially, the administration was reluctant to see long-time dictator Hosni Mubarak overthrown. After Mohammed Morsi of the fundamentalist Muslim Brotherhood was legitimately elected subsequent to the long-time dictator Hosni Mubarak being deposed, the United States gave Egypt $1 billion, in addition to the normal $2 billion in annual aid, to facilitate transition to democracy. Nevertheless, the United States, suspicious of Morsi's Islamic fundamentalism, took a wait-and-see attitude. In the end, the Obama administration, with only mild protest and suspension of some non-critical aid, acquiesced to a military coup that overthrew the elected Morsi government.

Democratic rhetoric aside, of all possible outcomes in Egypt, the United States actually prefers military-related dictators to democracy because Israel does. The United States has been providing large amounts of aid to the Egyptian military since the late 1970s to pay it for upholding the Camp David peace accords with Israel. In reality, the U.S. government believes that rule by Egyptian military-related dictators best guarantees that those agreements by Israel's strongest potential enemy will continue to be honored. So despite its pluralistic rhetoric, the U.S. government, the Obama administration included, often prefers stability to democracy. Of course, this makes U.S. policy appear hypocritical in the Middle East. To rectify this problem, the United States could end its military and financial interventions in the region and restrict its backing of any emerging democracy to moral support.

The American hawks also wanted the Obama administration to attack Iran. However, even many U.S. military officers believe that no good military option exists to eliminate Iran's nuclear program—air strikes would likely only set the program back and motivate Iran to go full steam ahead to get the bomb. At this writing, even U.S. intelligence believes Iran has not made the decision to create a nuclear weapon. Thus, the hawks, as in the case of Syria, appear to want a U.S. or Israeli attack to weaken a regional rival of Israel.

Fortunately, Obama, at this time, has not taken the bait and actually negotiated an interim deal with the new more moderate Iranian prime minister that freezes, and in some cases rolls back, the Iranian nuclear program. Better U.S.-Iranian relations would not be good for Israel, a rival of Iran.

Saudi Arabia, another U.S. ally in the region, is furious with Obama for "weakness" on the allied nations of Syria and Iran. The Sunni Saudis support the Sunni rebels in Syria against the Shi'ite-affiliated Alawite Assad regime and are also a regional rival with Shi'ite Iran. In the book, *No War for Oil: U.S. Dependency and the Middle East*, this author busted the myths that oil is a strategic commodity and that it is necessary to coddle Saudi Arabia, the biggest Middle Eastern producer. The market is the best conveyor of oil to the American economy. Recent gains in U.S. oil production have made the United States even less dependent on Middle Eastern oil and thus should make U.S. policy in the region even less dependent on oil considerations.

So although Saudi Arabia, the American hawks, and Israel have pressured Obama for more aggressive policies in the Middle East, sensing the war weariness of the American public, he has wisely chosen peace. Peace is not weakness.

Reducing Nuclear Weapons and Missile Defense

In April 2010, Obama signed with Russia the New START Treaty, which reduced strategic nuclear missile launchers by half and created a new verification and inspection regime to ensure compliance. The treaty was ratified in late 2010 and entered into force in early 2011. However, the treaty didn't restrict the operationally inactive stockpiles of nuclear warheads that number in the high thousands in both atomic arsenals. Although the nuclear danger has been largely forgotten after the Cold War ended, any reduction of these still massive arsenals, capable of launching Armageddon, is a very good thing.

The Bush administration had committed to build a missile defense system in Poland and the Czech Republic, which it argued was meant to protect U.S. European allies from any Iranian missiles that that could reach Europe. Although not really a threat to reduce the potency of Russian long-range nuclear deterrent, the system, to Russia, represented further expansion of the Cold War NATO alliance near Russia long after the Cold War era was over. (Russia's aggressive behavior in Ukraine, one of Russia's last remaining buffer states against the encroaching alliance, is a direct reaction to such expansion, and Obama's restraint during this crisis was laudable.) Wisely, Obama decided to scale the missile defense system back. He should have killed it; the Cold War is over, and if wealthy European countries want a missile defense against Iran, they can build it with their own money.

Obama Is a Foreign Policy Realist

Over all, Obama—like Dwight Eisenhower, Richard Nixon, and George H. W. Bush—is of the realist foreign policy school. This school of thought believes that despite countries' soaring foreign policy rhetoric, they—including the United States—really behave to secure their underlying interests. This school tends to be more restrained and pragmatic in their foreign policy dealings than those of the ideologically driven neo-conservative school—for example, Ronald Reagan or George W. Bush—or the idealistic liberal interventionist school—for example, Harry Truman, John F. Kennedy, Lyndon Johnson, or Bill Clinton. It doesn't mean that realist presidents will not take military action, but they exhibit some caution about doing so. When stacked up against the foreign policies of other post–World War II presidents, although the foreign policies of Eisenhower and Obama weren't quite as humble as those of post-Vietnam War presidents Gerald Ford and Jimmy Carter, they were laudably restrained.

PROSPERITY

Obama Continued Bush's Massive Government Intervention to Try to Right the Sagging Economy

In fairness to Obama, the situation confronting him when taking office rivaled the worst in American history, with only perhaps those of George Washington, Abraham Lincoln, Andrew Johnson, and Franklin Delano Roosevelt being more daunting. George W. Bush left Obama with U.S. troops in two ground quagmires in Afghanistan and Iraq; Osama bin Laden of al Qaeda still on the loose after seven-and-a-half years; profligate federal spending, a greater than $1 trillion annual federal budget deficit and soaring national debt accumulation; and the greatest economic calamity since the Great Depression. Credit was frozen, consumer confidence was at an all-time low, and the economy was contracting at an unprecedented 8.9 percent rate.[7] The thinking was that it couldn't get much worse. In some ways Obama improved the situation, but not by much, and he may have made other situations worse.

The Great Recession, as it has become known, was the second of two economic bubbles that popped. To re-inflate the economy after the dot.com bubble burst during the late Clinton administration, Alan Greenspan, Chairman of the Federal Reserve, began printing money and continued through the 9/11 attacks to insure that the economy would not tank because of that tragedy. His successor, Ben Bernanke, kept the printing presses rolling. When money is printed it ultimately flows into sectors of the economy that are perceived to be hot. In the 1990s, the money flowed into the stocks of dot.com companies. In the mid-2000s, it flowed into a real estate sector that benefited from the government's desire to allow people who really couldn't afford them to own homes. As in the unsustainable dot.com bubble funded by freshly printed cash, people eventually saw that the demand for housing was artificial and the bubble popped in late 2008.

Instead of letting the economy right itself by restoring the natural balance between supply and demand, George W. Bush, following the precedent of his fellow Republican Herbert Hoover, tried to alleviate the immediate pain by using government intervention in the marketplace. At a cost of a whopping $700 billion, Bush set a bad precedent by bailing out financial institutions that were deemed "too big to fail," thus creating an incentive in the future for more reckless behavior by these organizations, which know the government will again bail them out if they take heavy losses. AIG, a huge insurance company, was also deemed "too big to fail" and was effectively nationalized by the supposedly conservative Bush. Bush also finished effectively nationalizing the giant Freddie Mac and Fannie Mae mortgage lenders and arranged a bailout of Bear Stearns and U.S. car companies. Bush, however, did play favorites and let the Lehman Brothers financial house go under. Finally, Bush adopted a Keynesian "stimulus" bill, which cost $168 billion and attempted to increase demand in the economy by sending checks to poor and middle class families.[8]

Obama continued Bush's Keynesian "rescue" of the still plummeting economy by enacting an even bigger stimulus costing over $1 trillion (in two tranches, costing $831 billion in early 2009 and more than $700 billion later). (Even the Republican alternative bills to the Obama first tranche were huge—$478 billion and $715 billion.) Just the first tranche of $831 billion, in constant dollars, was more than 50 percent larger than Franklin D. Roosevelt's (FDR's) entire New Deal and twice as big as the Louisiana Purchase and Marshall Plan combined. The first Obama tranche of about $800 billion was about 5 percent of GDP; in FDR's most aggressive year during Great Depression, the New Deal's stimulus was only about 1.5 percent of GDP.

Specifics of Obama's Huge Stimulus Program

Keynesian economic theory did not justify the end dollar amount for the Obama stimulus; it was chosen on how it likely would be received by the voting public. "It was all driven by Washington stupidity—not what the economy needed, just this arbitrary number of 800," Rahm Emanuel, Obama's chief of staff, bluntly admitted. The stimulus's well-deserved reputation of arbitrary spending on everything under the sun eventually resulted in it being very unpopular with the public. Obama wanted to think big and desired a large iconic initiative that was experimental, essentially an updated New Deal. The $831 billion in the first tranche of the stimulus included about $300 billion in progressive tax cuts for the middle class and working poor, about $165 billion for aid to the states through increases in Medicaid and education funding, and about $140 billion for the largest expansion of social safety net spending ever. In all, about 37 percent of the first tranche of stimulus was tax cuts, 18 percent was increased aid to the states, and 45 percent was hiked federal spending.

Obama had blamed the economic meltdown on Wall Street leveraging cash it didn't have and homeowners taking out mortgages they couldn't afford, yet he was trying to solve the problem by having the government spend about $800 billion in borrowed money. So Keynes's and Obama's prescription for solving an economic crisis caused by profligate borrowing, confidence, and spending is more borrowing, confidence, and spending. For example, despite the origin of the economic meltdown being irresponsible mortgage borrowing, Obama approved a plan to prevent bank foreclosures of bad loans (giving home owners a disincentive to pay their mortgages), and the stimulus bill offered an $8,000 credit for first time homebuyers to encourage more of the same! And the Obama administration struggled to find ways to spend the more than $1 trillion in stimulus money.[9]

The stimulus tried to goose aggregate spending in the economy in the short-term by increasing funding for food stamps (the number of recipients increased 66 percent); child care; Head Start; public housing; rental assistance; unemployment benefits; the Earned Income Tax credit for low-income workers; a very limited universe of truly "shovel-ready" infrastructure projects, and aid to state governments (including increases in Medicaid) to prevent the firing of police, teachers, and other public employees due to state budget cuts. However, the stimulus also surreptitiously funded Obama's long-term agenda in health care, education, and green energy, and the much larger universe of non-shovel-ready infrastructure initiatives.[10]

Thus, one of the most sweeping laws in modern history passed mostly under the radar. And like Ronald Reagan's Strategic Defense Initiative (the "Star Wars" missile defense program) in the 1980s, so much money was rapidly thrown at all these programs that much doubt exists about whether it was absorbed efficiently. According to one Obama team member, "Some people think we were just trying to spend as much as possible. Well, they're right! You'd find this great program that needed $1 billion. Then someone would ask: Can you do it for $10 billion?"[11]

About 16 to18 percent of the $831 billion in initial stimulus spending went to Obama's long-term agenda. The Obama "recovery package" was the biggest stimulus bill in U.S. history. It was also the largest energy bill in U.S. history: a staggering $90 billion alone was spent on green energy projects (increasing spending on such boondoggles by ten-fold over the previous few billion a year)— such as high-speed rail and research into wind, solar, biofuel, clean coal, geo-thermal, electric car, and smart electrical grid technologies—none of which probably would have been otherwise viable in the market. (Remember all the wasted billions on Jimmy Carter's synthetic fuels program?) The high-speed rail project—not loved by Obama's economists but needed for the stimulus to have a marquee project after school construction was quashed—was the biggest new transportation program since Dwight Eisenhower's interstate highway initiative but is now projected to connect only the small cities of Fresno and Bakersfield in California. All of the green energy projects were designed to reduce U.S. dependence on foreign oil and to guide the United States toward conformity with the international effort to reduce global warming.

The stimulus also contained the largest education "reform" bill since Lyndon B. Johnson's (LBJ's) Great Society, funding Obama's "Race to the Top" initiative that continued Bush's effort to nationalize education standards, testing, and cur-riculum ("No Child Left Behind"), traditionally a state and local responsibility. The stimulus was a big health care bill too, for example funding the comput-erization of patients' health records, which set the stage for Obamacare a year later. Finally, the bill included the biggest excursion into industrial policy since FDR (providing funds for the government to create new advanced battery, ultra-high-speed Internet, and green home weatherization industries from scratch), the largest expansion of anti-poverty programs since LBJ, the biggest fraudulent middle class tax cut since Ronald Reagan (neither Reagan nor Obama cut government spending, thus exacerbating the federal deficit), and the largest infusion of money into government research in U.S. history. For Obama's tax cut for the middle class in the stimulus, in contrast to that found in Bush's smaller stimulus, taxpayers found that the government withheld less from their paychecks rather than gave them a rebate check.[12]

Obama's liberal economic advisers just wanted to spend to goose the economy without caring too much about what the money was spent on. Hence, almost every sector of the society got some money. Some of his more moderate advisers, who got the best economic jobs in the administration, and Obama himself, expressed concern about the long-term deficits caused by Bush's and Obama's massive cumulative spending, but believed in Keynesian stimulation of the economy by government spending in the shorter term. Yet a substantial portion of the projects in the stimulus bill instead discreetly funded Obama's long-term policy agenda. Rahm Emanuel, then-Obama's chief of staff, best summarized Obama's strategy, "You never let a serious crisis go to waste. And what I mean by that it's an opportunity to do things you think you could not do before."[13]

More Government Intervention

Ben Bernanke, the Fed chairman, who was appointed by George W. Bush but later reappointed by Obama, brought monetary policy into alignment with the Bush and Obama administrations' expansive fiscal policy by conducting the greatest expansion of credit in the nation's history—essentially printing $3 trillion in new money. The Fed effectively printed so much money using traditional means—with so little impact on the stagnant economy, it was like pushing on a string—that it had to get creative with new ways to do so. Bernanke effectively lent trillions of dollars to investment banks, hedge funds, manufacturers, and other borrowers who never expected to get such handouts from the federal government.[14] This massive monetary expansion made it likely that all the new money would overheat some other economic sector in the future and create yet another artificial economic bubble. And like the dot.com and the mortgage bubbles, at some future time, this bubble will likely burst and send the economy into another tailspin. Also, the huge credit expansion kept short-term interest rates near zero percent, which has, among other things, hurt savers and people living on fixed incomes and purposefully distorted investment decisions in the economy toward a red hot stock market.

U.S. car companies, despite Bush's earlier bail out, had begun to falter again. In another "too big to fail" move, Obama effectively nationalized two out of the three major producers—General Motors and Chrysler. The government eventually sold its stock in the companies but the taxpayers lost billions bailing out companies that should have been allowed to go under. Obama also started the "Cash for Clunkers" initiative that gave motorists a subsidized incentive to send their old gas-guzzlers to the junkyard and buy more fuel-efficient vehicles. It is a very expensive way to reduce fuel use.[15] Although this effort may have stimulated some slight added demand for new cars, it mostly just sped up auto purchases that would have occurred later anyway, thus merely displacing future demand forward.

As noted earlier, because Bush had bailed out the "too-big-to-fail" financial institutions—thus creating the risk that they would engage in future reckless behavior, given the government safety net under them—pressure then occurred to regulate them to constrain this risk. This is an example of one dubious government intervention spawning others.[16] Thus, under the Obama administration, excessive new regulation of the financial sector was legislated under Dodd-Frank, which later spawned the so-called "Volcker rule." The Volcker rule tried to mitigate excessive risk-taking by banks by allowing them to do market trading for their clients but not for themselves. In general, Dodd-Frank ushered in the most extensive increase in the regulation of Wall Street (for example, on hedge funds, derivatives, and insurance companies) since the Great Depression and created a consumer financial protection agency that would further regulate mortgage and credit card lending.[17] Although Obama didn't nationalize banks, as he effectively did with auto companies, he conducted stress tests on their books to "stabilize" the financial industry.

Counterintuitively, a better outcome would have been to let even big banks that misbehaved or were excessively reckless with mortgage lending just go out of business. The economy would have been temporarily shocked at the demise of a few large financial institutions, but the vast majority of smaller community banks across the country were sound. After all, they had not benefited as much from a history of federal government favor and bailouts that the "too-big-to-fail" financial institutions have enjoyed since the beginning of the republic. Thus, the market itself, after some pain, would have cleared the dead wood out of the system.

III Effects of Bush and Obama Economic Policies

Bailouts, huge fiscal stimuli, large federal deficits, the rapid accumulation of humongous public debt, and the massive printing of money simply delay the day of reckoning by creating another unsustainable bubble. With repeated and growing government intervention in the economy, the economy has gone from one bubble to another to still another—ever on an artificial sugar high.

Although George W. Bush added $4 trillion dollars to the national debt during his presidency and Obama added about $6 trillion in only his first four years,[18] Obama argued that most of the budget deficit increases during his administration were caused by policies put into the pipeline by Bush—that is, for the following unpaid for items: wars (two), huge tax cuts, and an expensive new entitlement for senior citizens covering their prescription drugs under Medicare and other profligate domestic spending. In addition, Obama implicitly blamed Bush for causing the greatest economic calamity since the Great Depression, which ballooned the deficits. Thus, he claimed that his stimulus package only made up 10 percent of the increased deficits.[19] In his fact checking column for the *Washington Post*, Glenn Kessler tried to debunk this Obama claim, estimating that the severe economic recession (and technical estimation errors) caused about 50 percent of the deficits from fiscal years 2009 to 2011 (the downturn caused lower tax revenues and automatic increases in government benefits, such as unemployment compensation and welfare payments) and that policies of both the Bush and Obama administrations shared responsibility for the other 50 percent.[20]

On the other hand, graphs by the Congressional Budget Office and the Center for Budget and Policy Priorities seem to be closer to Obama's claim, showing that the first tranche of the Obama stimulus (the Recovery Act) made up only a small part of the deficit, even during fiscal years 2009 to 2011, and dissipated to almost negligibility after that. The chart by the Center for Budget and Policy Priorities shows that all recovery measures, including the Recovery Act and Bush's TARP bank bailout, began to dissipate in their effects on the deficit after fiscal year 2011. In that graph, the biggest drivers of the long-term deficits were the Bush/Obama tax cuts, the continuing effects of the Great Recession, and the wars;[21] Obama must share the blame for all of these with Bush.

Obama eventually wound down both the Iraq and Afghanistan wars, but he could have saved more dollars and lives by doing so immediately after entering office. Instead he lollygagged in Iraq and escalated in Afghanistan before eventually throwing in the towel. Bush tax cuts were largely fraudulent, because he not only failed to reduce spending, but he actually spent like a drunken sailor both militarily and domestically. Future generations will need to pay for Bush's profligacy. Of course, Obama first extended all Bush's fraudulent tax cuts and then later further extended them again, except for earners of the highest incomes. Obama also instituted a temporary cut in the regressive payroll tax and reduced the estate tax for heirs of the well-off, which had failed to pass during the Bush administration.

Instead of Obama cutting spending to match Bush's lower revenues, he spent more than $1 trillion just to be spending it in a Keynesian attempt to jumpstart the economy. And the annual federal budget deficits were an even bigger stimulus yet. For all that "stimulus," he still got a slow, anemic economic recovery. Obama has had the weakest economic recovery from a recession of any post-World War II president. Obama should have known that most past fiscal stimuli have failed. In fact, as during Herbert Hoover's presidency, trying to keep the private economy artificially inflated through government action probably worsened the economic downturn—somewhat like a sugar rush followed by lethargy.

Obama was trying to reignite the housing market and bank lending, which caused the economic bubble in the first place and helped lead to the excessive debt dragging the economy (as did Obama's spending to attempt to goose the economy with massive stimulus spending). During the Great Recession, 8 trillion dollars in housing wealth evaporated, and people could no longer use their homes as cash machines to fund excessive consumption that contributed to the bubble that burst; a market clearing was needed, and thus a retrenchment in consumption, although painful, was required for those who had been living beyond their means. Also, rising government debt crowded out the private borrowing and investment needed for a healthy economy. The problem was not liquidity in the economy but instead was fear of Bush's and Obama's profligate spending, budget deficits, and rising debt. To pay for any government stimulus (regardless of whether it originated under Bush or Obama), either the government has to remove scarce resources from the much more efficient private sector by increasing taxes; or it has to borrow money, pay interest, and still raise taxes later to pay back the loans; or it has to print money—none is good for the medium-term and long-term economy. As Obama even admitted, "Look, I get the Keynesian thing. But it's not where the electorate is."[22] The public wisely refused to believe the dubious Keynesian concept that public spending is needed when private demand has evaporated. Instead, the government needs to avoid impeding the natural market clearing of dead wood from the economy.

After the Binge of Government Intervention, Reduced Federal Spending and Deficits

After Obama's Recovery Act passed, he had the chance to veto a pork-infested budget left over from the Bush administration. The budget bill contained more than 8,000 earmarks—special pork projects to satisfy members of Congress. Unfortunately, Obama reluctantly signed the bill. More positively, an embarrassed

Obama refused to support a $450 billion bipartisan transportation bill (Republicans love concrete too) that would have funded some of the long-term highway pork that couldn't be included in the $1 trillion dollar stimulus package because the projects were not shovel-ready.[23]

Yet overall, under Obama, from fiscal year 2009 through fiscal year 2014 (est.), real federal spending (outlays) shrunk about 2.5 percent, something that hasn't happened since the end of the Korean War. Also, federal spending as a portion of GDP declined three percentage points from 25.2 percent to 22.2 percent during that same period. Annual real federal budget deficits (in constant 2005 dollars) were gradually cut from more than almost $1.3 trillion per year that Obama inherited from Bush in fiscal year 2009 to less than half that—$610 billion in fiscal year 2014 (est.). As a portion of GDP during that same period, the federal deficit went from 10.1 percent of GDP to less than half that at 4.4 percent.[24] Those favorable outcomes happened because Obama eventually ended the Iraq War, budget stalemate in Washington was the order of the day, and that gridlock ultimately required the imposition of automatic across-the-board (except for entitlements) "sequestration" budget cuts that Obama had proposed and both he and congressional Republicans had approved. At this writing, however, Obama and Congress unfortunately eased the sequestration cuts for fiscal years 2014 and 2015.

Finally, although repealing entitlements is difficult once they are legislated, especially when going against the powerful senior citizens lobby, Obama made no attempt at all to repeal Bush's new Medicare prescription drug benefit and probably added to the long-term deficits and debt by passing the Affordable Care Act (Obamacare health "reform").

Downgrading U.S. Credit Rating and Government Shutdown

After the Republicans obtained a majority in the House of Representatives in early 2011 after the 2010 election, a budget stalemate resulted in Washington from the Democrats' desire to spend in a Keynesian frenzy to try to shore up the sagging Obama economic recovery and the Republicans, in opposition, discovering fiscal rectitude after years of profligate security and domestic spending when they controlled the government under George W. Bush. Although the Republicans refused to raise the nation's debt ceiling (a legal limit governing how much the U.S. government can borrow to pay bills already incurred) in a laudable attempt to get more budget cuts, the dispute caused the U.S. credit rating to be downgraded. Obama did agree to the budget cuts, and the downgrading didn't seem to have had much ill effect in the real world. On another occasion of budget impasse, the Republicans chose to shut down the federal government for a few days; although unpopular with the public and poaching their own message on the implementation failures of Obamacare, the shutdown also seemed not to have had the catastrophic effects predicted.

Driving Federal Tentacles Further into the Health Care Market

Like George W. Bush, Obama took advantage of a crisis to pass a largely unrelated item. Although health care does affect the economy, it was not the primary cause of the economic meltdown that occurred. Yet Obama used the severe economic downturn to ram Obamacare through Congress.

Although the Congressional Budget Office (CBO) projected that Obamacare would reduce deficits and debt, that outcome is unlikely. This favorable result would allegedly be achieved by driving health care costs down, as if that can be effectively legislated or regulated by government. Government efforts at controlling costs and prices usually fail. Already CBO is hiking cost estimates for the program, increasing projections of taxation required to fund it, and reducing its estimates of the program's deficit reduction.[25] Another notable analyst, Chuck Blahous, who was appointed by Obama to be a trustee of the Social Security and Medicare programs, estimated, in his peer-reviewed study, that Obamacare would add between $340 to $530 billion to federal deficits while ballooning federal spending by more than $1.15 trillion. Also, the ambit of the program is so wide that Congress could expand any part of it in the future, as it has with Medicare over the years.[26]

Obama sold his health care program as insuring the uninsured and moving toward the progressive goal since President Harry Truman of providing universal health care coverage for all Americans. For the poor, Obama is providing health care benefits by expanding Medicaid. For the near poor and up, however, Obama adopted a plan patterned after one originally proposed by the conservative Heritage Foundation, which required people to buy coverage in government created health insurance markets or be fined by the government. (Yet conservatives, including the lobbying arm of that organization, Heritage Action, virulently opposed the plan once Obama proposed it.) Republican presidential candidate Mitt Romney had instituted a similar plan as governor of Massachusetts, but he didn't seem to like Obama's plan either.

Obama made it seem like he was doing the near poor a favor by providing them health insurance, but he required them to buy it (unbelievably, the conservative-dominated Supreme Court declared this to be constitutional) and then didn't subsidize the full cost of the policies. If a near poor person struggles to buy food and shelter, not having health insurance, although not desirable, may be rational for some people, especially if they are young and healthy. The Obama administration was fairly bald in its attempt to get many young healthy people signed up so that they would pay insurance premiums but not use many health services, essentially paying for older, less healthy people. Also, restrictions exist on how much older people can be charged for health care premiums. However, in general, older people tend to be better off financially than younger people, because they have had many more years to accumulate wealth. Thus, as in the Social Security system, the young are sacrificing for the old, and the progressives backing these programs seem to be actually transferring wealth from the better off to the less well off.

Essentially the health insurance industry bought Obama's concept, and their lobbyists wrote the law. After all, what industry wouldn't want the government to require customers to buy their product—thereby increasing the number of buyers, sales, and profits? Thus, insurance stock prices went up when the law was passed.

If Obama wanted to expand health insurance coverage and cut health care costs, he could have achieved economies of scale by deregulating the 51 oligopolistic state health care markets into one national market and then just have given poor and near poor people vouchers to buy coverage in that market. The insurance industry would not have liked that outcome, however, because regulations often shield companies from cost-cutting competition. And certainly Obama should not coerce people into buying health care coverage if it makes little sense for them to do so in their situations.

In short, Obamacare is inefficient, will likely be more costly than expected, and erodes liberty by its government requirement to purchase insurance (which should have been ruled unconstitutional).

In so-called S-CHIP legislation, Obama also expanded children's health insurance.

Annulling Bill Clinton's Welfare Reform

Obama rescinded a key aspect of President Bill Clinton's welfare reform of 1996—imperfect but one of the most successful bipartisan reform efforts in modern American history. At the time it passed, Clinton noted that his goal was to "make welfare what it was meant to be, a second chance, not a way of life." For four years after the reform's enactment, welfare caseloads fell by more than half. Most of the former welfare beneficiaries found jobs. After that period, caseloads continued to drop during the George W. Bush administration and first Obama administration but at a slower rate.

However, in July 2012, the Obama administration's Department of Health and Human Services—in violation of the Clinton-era law, which explicitly prohibited waivers of the work requirement—waived the requirement that had moved so many people from the welfare dole into jobs. A drafter of the original law and the U.S. Government Accountability Office both said that the administration had exceeded its authority under the law. The administration also did so by beginning to measure success in welfare programs by increasing caseloads, which the welfare reform statute prohibited.[27]

Obama's different approach to welfare compared to that of Clinton can be seen in such rising caseloads. In the 1990s, an average of about 35 percent of Americans lived in a household that received some type of welfare[28]; in the Obama period, almost 50 percent of Americans do.[29] Of course, part of this increase is undoubtedly due to the poorer economic conditions during the Obama period than during the Clinton era, but part of the result is also the difference in the waiver of the work requirement and its effect on welfare caseloads. Contrary to the Obama methodological approach to measuring success, these rising caseloads can hardly be called an accomplishment—quite the opposite. Moreover, better policies concerning deficits and debt during the Clinton administration, as compared to those of the Obama administration, likely helped create a much more favorable economic climate.

Although Obama did not propose doling out government make-work jobs, as did FDR's Work Progress Administration (WPA) during the New Deal, his stimulus bill gave states money to subsidize 260,000 jobs in the private sector.[30]

As for public sector jobs, ironically, nationwide, governments shed more than 500,000 jobs during the Obama presidency—almost two-thirds of the government jobs added during the Bush administration. Most of the public jobs lost were at state and local levels, and the loss would have been greater if the Obama stimulus had not attempted to stem that tide by providing aid to states—so that they could retain police, teachers, and other employees who might have otherwise been laid off.

Encouraging Irresponsibility with Student Loans

In his re-election bid in 2012, Obama tried to motivate young people, one of his key constituency groups, to vote by promulgating an executive order that allowed student borrowers with government loans and government-backed private loans to consolidate loan balances, limit loan payments to 10 percent of a graduate's income, and have debt forgiven that was still outstanding after 20 years. Although he essentially punished, and thus angered, responsible borrowers who had already paid off their student loans and only saved current borrowers $10 per month, he created expectations among such student borrowers that the government would ease their burden, thus potentially encouraging future irresponsibility.[31]

LIBERTY

Obama Not Much Better than Bush on Civil Liberties

Almost immediately after Obama took office, he pledged to close Guantanamo prison in Cuba, which had become a giant smudge on the U.S. human rights record. Yet five years later, it remains open. Obama can fairly blame Congress, and Republicans in particular, for legislation preventing him from transferring inmates from that prison. Obama is renewing his effort to close the prison.

Outrageously, many of the remaining inmates at Guantanamo have been cleared of guilt after many years of being locked up without trials, but they have been kept incarcerated there anyway, because their home countries wouldn't take them or would likely abuse them; Congress prevented their transfer to the United States. One would think that after the United States had done these people wrong, the government would feel so guilty that it would quickly welcome them into the United States to start a new life. But members of Congress are afraid of voting to "allow terrorists to come to America's shores." Bush and Obama could have done more to release unfairly held detainees from there. However, being the government evidently means that you never have to say you're sorry.

However, even if, by some miracle, Guantanamo were closed, the problem of civil liberties erosion would continue. In general, Obama has continued most of the objectionable policies of George W. Bush: indefinite detentions without trial, kangaroo military commissions (albeit with a few more defendant safeguards and a greater preference for the use of alternative civilian courts), killing of people overseas (including Americans) without congressional approval of hostilities, and domestic surveillance of Americans without warrants issued on probable cause that a crime has been committed—all unconstitutional. In stopping torture and in ending secret detentions overseas in CIA-run clandestine prisons Obama has significantly improved on Bush's horrid record on civil liberties for terror suspects. Yet Obama refused to prosecute Bush administration people for illegal torture and other abuses—which went to the heart of what the republic stands for—because it would have taken the focus off his own policy agenda (this was similar to Gerald Ford's unconstitutional pardoning of Nixon before any criminal conviction in order to get the issue out of the way for his own agenda).

On the domestic spying issue, Bush's illegal and unconstitutional spying was rendered only unconstitutional by the eventual legalization by Congress, late in his second term, of warrantless spying on the contents of Americans' communications—as long as they were communicating with foreign terror suspects overseas. Previously, the Bush administration had been illegally failing to get a warrant for such spying from the secret Foreign Surveillance and Intelligence Court. Yet all three branches of government agreeing on something doesn't make it constitutional. The Fourth Amendment's requirement that judicially approved warrants are required for specific domestic spying, based on probable cause that a crime has been committed, doesn't have an exemption for national security.

Similarly, during the Obama administration, Edward Snowden, a contractor for the National Security Agency, revealed that the agency, since the Bush administration, has been vacuuming up data on all e-mails and phone calls of every American (the e-mail program was eventually terminated but the phone program remained). The phone "metadata" program has had congressional oversight and has been approved by the secret surveillance court, yet clearly violates the Fourth Amendment's implied ban on general searches (all Americans cannot be terrorism suspects) and its requirement that searches be conducted only when evidence exists of "probable cause" that a crime had been committed (the records of calls are examined when a lower standard of "reasonable articulable suspicion" of terrorism is fulfilled). So again, the agreement of all branches doesn't ensure constitutionality. At this writing, Obama seemingly has accepted requiring court approval for the government's specific examination of certain phone records, but the constitutionality of the program is still in question because a standard lower than "probable cause" for such examination will remain, and even just the government's collecting of the phone data still runs afoul of the Fourth Amendment's ban on general searches. However, Obama may roll back government collection of the data, thus leaving it with private phone companies. Moreover, evidence has shown that the phone "metadata" program has had little effect on stopping, or even finding, terrorism-related activities.

Substituting illegal unconstitutional domestic spying programs for merely unconstitutional ones should give no American peace of mind. Tyrannies spy on their own citizens, not republics. The government is destroying the republic and its freedoms in order to save it from low-probability and low-impact threats.

452   Barack Obama

In the wake of the secretive Bush administration, Obama promised to have a transparent administration, but his administration also has been very opaque to the public. Obama has directly or indirectly pursued journalists criminally for merely revealing embarrassing government secrets and is over charging Edward Snowden, who was almost certainly not spying for a foreign country and was mainly a whistleblower disclosing unconstitutional government spying on Americans.

The average citizen might ask why the country should be so concerned with the rights of suspected terrorists, but the government can be wrong in its suspicion, jailing, and harsh treatment of those accused of even the most heinous crimes. Such error is demonstrated by the large percentage of innocents apparently swept up in Afghanistan, because of U.S. bounties for suspected terrorists in a very poor country, and taken to Guantanamo for mistreatment and indefinite detention without trial. In fact, when the rights of the accused are upheld, the rights of everyone are safeguarded.

Obama did a little better in safeguarding rights of societal groups not suspected of terrorism. He got Congress to scrap the ludicrous "Don't Ask Don't Tell" policy, whereby gays and lesbians could be in the U.S. military if they didn't tell anyone their sexual orientation. Subsequently, gays could finally serve openly in the military. Also, Obama ordered Justice Department lawyers to stop defending the Defense of Marriage Act in the courts. Both Don't Ask Don't Tell and the Defense of Marriage Act treat gays and lesbians as second-class citizens in seeming violation of the equal protection clause of the Constitution's fourteenth amendment. That clause prevents denial of "equal protection of the laws."

Conclusion

Barack Obama is rated 34 out of 41 presidents, because he has not been very good but at least had one or two significant accomplishments, which those below him— such as Ronald Reagan (number 35), John F. Kennedy (number 36), and George W. Bush (number 37)—did not. He eventually withdrew the bulk of U.S. ground forces from the Bush-initiated Iraq and Afghanistan quagmires, found and killed Osama bin Laden within the confines of a congressionally approved resolution, reached a deal with Russia to further reduce strategic nuclear launchers, cut real federal spending in absolute terms and as a portion of GDP, and ended U.S. torture and secret CIA prisons overseas. Also, he preferred using civilian courts to prosecute terrorists rather than employing unconstitutional, kangaroo military tribunals.

However, Obama attacked Libya to overthrow a dictator the United States never liked and continued Bush's illegal drone wars, all without seeking constitutionally required congressional approval. Taking advantage of the Bush-induced severe recession, Obama had one of the most productive legislative periods since the New Deal and Great Society—passing the massive stimulus, Obamacare, the auto bailout, Dodd-Frank financial regulation, and other legislation that followed Bush's precedent of massive federal intervention to shore up the economy.[32] Yet, as in the New Deal and Great Society eras, much of the legislation passed was of questionable value and was likely responsible for the sluggish economic recovery. Other than his laudable ending of torture and secret CIA detentions overseas and his preference for civilian courts over military commissions, as well as ending the ridiculous "Don't Ask Don't Tell" policy preventing gays and lesbians from having equal rights in the military, Obama's record on civil liberties wasn't much better than Bush's.

Bush's father, George H.W. Bush, scored slightly better than Obama at number 33, because his START treaties actually set the precedent for reducing, rather than just limiting increases in, strategic nuclear weapons—the only existential threat to the United States and the world. Obama did follow the elder Bush's precedent by further reducing strategic arsenals.

In short, however, Obama's bad policy choices vastly overshadowed the few substantially good things that he has done.

Conclusion

The real story in this assessment is that many presidents who are ranked highly by historians, journalists, law professors, and the public were not very good at all when we look at how well they stayed within the presidential portfolio, as intended by the Constitution, and how well they did promulgating policies that promoted peace, prosperity, and liberty. In other words, the framers would not have rated them highly.

Abraham Lincoln, regularly ranked by analysts as one of the three greatest presidents in U.S. history, helped to provoke a massive civil war—his predecessors certainly did their share to make it happen—and then pursued it ineptly and brutally. Although this war saved the union, it is still the bloodiest war America ever fought, and it left scars on the country's social fabric that remain today. The war nominally ended slavery, but for many decades African Americans experienced only marginally more freedom from bitter white southerners than before their emancipation. Peaceful alternatives might have achieved a better outcome more quickly and without as much retribution against African Americans.

Thomas Jefferson, although a proponent of small government, imposed an embargo of U.S. trade that led to starvation in America and instituted measures to enforce it that severely limited the liberty that he championed rhetorically. He also set bad precedents for acquiring new territory by purchasing the Louisiana Territory in an unconstitutional manner and for ethnically cleansing Native Americans by forcing them to emigrate to less desirable land farther west.

The charismatic Teddy Roosevelt was a less consequential president than his dull predecessor, William McKinley, was excessively belligerent in foreign policy, and was a champion of "progressive" policies that actually harmed the people he was allegedly trying to help.

George Washington, also considered by analysts to be one of the three greatest presidents, grabbed more presidential power and made the federal government more active than most of the framers of the Constitution had envisioned. He also set some other bad precedents, including unconstitutionally crushing the Whiskey Rebellion in 1793. This assessment, however, ranks him a respectable seventh because he had republican intentions, shunned being a king or dictator, and set a most valuable precedent by leaving office after two terms. So much for the standard reverence given to the presidents enshrined on Mount Rushmore.

Several other presidents are often acclaimed to have been successful, or even great, when in actuality they harmed the peace, prosperity, and liberty of American citizens.

Although Franklin Delano Roosevelt's likeness is not on that mountain, most analysts regard him as one of the three greatest presidents. He is credited with helping to alleviate the suffering of the Great Depression and orchestrating the great military victories against dark authoritarian enemies in World War II. But FDR's New Deal had no coherent philosophy, wasted hundreds of billions of taxpayer dollars, and cemented the expectation of permanent big government in the minds of the American public. He actually deepened and prolonged the Great Depression by pursuing such activist government policies rather than letting natural market forces correct the economic slowdown. Also, FDR lied the United States into a massive war that he intentionally helped to provoke and allied himself with a dictator, Joseph Stalin, who killed more people than Adolf Hitler. After U.S. entry into World War II, however, FDR managed the massive conflict much more competently than Abraham Lincoln had handled the Civil War, but he committed war crimes by intentionally bombing enemy cities.

Harry Truman, FDR's successor, continued FDR's bombing of civilians, institutionalized the expansion of executive power into an imperial presidency, stole the constitutional power to make war from Congress, took actions that led to the creation of the military-industrial complex and the first large peacetime standing army in U.S. history, and initiated a permanent informal U.S. empire abroad and a nontraditional interventionist foreign policy to police it.

John F. Kennedy, always ranked highly by the public because of his charisma and because he died before his time, may well be the most overrated person in U.S. history, as many analysts argue. By this book's criteria, Kennedy was one of the worst presidents ever. He took rash actions that led to the Cuban Missile Crisis, which almost incinerated the world, and he was reluctant to push civil rights for African Americans.

Andrew Jackson, although theoretically a proponent of small government, used excessive coercion to keep South Carolina in the Union during the nullification crisis of 1832—thus setting a bad precedent for Abraham Lincoln during the Civil War. Also, Jackson had dishonest and unduly aggressive policies toward Native Americans.

Ronald Reagan, adored by conservatives, was not all that conservative and did not "win" the Cold War. His harsh anti-Soviet policies and massive defense buildup wasted money, reversed Richard Nixon's policy of détente with the USSR, and unnecessarily raised the existential threat of nuclear war. His tax cuts were fake because they weren't accompanied by cuts in spending. To win congressional support for his military expansion, he allowed domestic expenditures to be increased much more than defense spending. Thus the federal government doubled in size under Reagan's watch. The American public ultimately had to pay for all this defense and non-defense spending in some manner. Even worse, in the Iran-Contra Affair, he authorized illegal arms shipments to state sponsors of terrorism in order to secretly generate funds for the Contra army in Nicaragua; this secretly undermined Congress's most important remaining role under the Constitution—holding the power of the purse.

James Madison was one of the worst presidents because he started a war with Britain that didn't solve anything, led to the only foreign invasion in U.S. history, got the U.S. capital city burned, and opened the way for whites to steal Native American land as they pushed toward the West Coast.

Many analysts today admire Woodrow Wilson for inventing the nontraditional interventionist U.S. foreign policy that Harry Truman resurrected and made permanent after World War II. However, Wilson inadvertently caused most of the violence in the bloody twentieth century by unnecessarily involving the United States in tipping the balance toward Britain and France in World War I. World War II, the Bolshevik Revolution, and the ensuing Cold War, as well as the most severe restrictions on civil liberties in U.S. history, originated from the U.S.'s needless intervention in World War I.

In addition to describing why and how many popularly revered presidents did not serve the people well on the issues of peace, prosperity, and liberty, this narrative continues by identifying those who did. They were not necessarily charismatic, and they certainly crossed party lines.

As for party affiliation, the rankings here indicate that the Democratic Party (including its original Republican Party and Democratic-Republican Party antecedents) had most of the very best and worst presidents, while modern-day (Civil War and after) Republican Party presidents tend to be more numerous in the mid-ranges. For recent presidents, the same conclusion holds.

Yet history shows that party affiliation is not necessarily a good indicator of what a particular president's policies will be. Until Woodrow Wilson, the worst president ever, the Democrats were the party of small government and the Republicans were the party of big government. During Wilson's two terms and after, the Democrats permanently joined the Republicans in the big government camp.

If the list of overrated presidents (many in the "bad" category) is top-heavy with Democrats, so is the list of the underrated chief executives (some being ranked "excellent" here). John Tyler, earning the number one ranking, was a former Democrat turned Whig. Remaining a nineteenth-century Democrat in philosophy, he ran afoul of his new party by courageously blocking much of its big government program and did not get a second term. Grover Cleveland and Martin Van Buren, numbers two and three in this assessment, were Democrats who also followed the party's nineteenth-century philosophy of small government, restrained executive power, and a humble foreign policy. Rutherford B. Hayes, the lone Republican in the excellent category, was like John Tyler — fiscally responsible in the face of his party's nineteenth-century bent toward activist government.

Most of the "excellent" presidents are remembered as bland men with rather gray personalities, but they largely respected the Constitution's intention of limiting government and restraining executive power, especially in regard to making war. They realized that America is great not because of its government's activism at home and abroad, but because of the hard work and great ideas of private American citizens living in freedom. In other words, they realized that peace, prosperity, and liberty are best achieved by the framers' notion of restricting government power. The framers would have rated them highly. Also, most of the best presidents paid a high price for upholding the principle of limiting governmental activism: they did not serve a second term.

Boring can be beautiful. Perhaps a new mountain should be chiseled with likenesses of John Tyler, Grover Cleveland, Martin Van Buren, and Rutherford B. Hayes. In tribute to their lack of flair, Grays Peak in Colorado might be a nice location.

Notes

Introduction

1. Anaïs Nin, quoted in James W. Loewen, *Lies My Teacher Told Me: Everything Your American History Textbook Got Wrong* (New York: Simon and Schuster, 1995), 239.

2. Ibid., 215–216.

3. Stephen E. Ambrose, *Eisenhower: Soldier and President* (New York: Simon and Schuster, 1990), 541.

4. Siena Research Institute, Siena College, press release, "FDR America's Greatest President; Lincoln, Teddy Roosevelt, Washington, and Jefferson Round Out Top Five; Andrew Johnson, Buchanan, Harding Bring Up the Rear," August 19, 2002, *www.lw.siena.edu/sri/results/2002/02AugPresidentsSurvey.htm*.

5. Fred Greenstein cited in Fred Barnes, *Rebel-in-Chief: Inside the Bold and Controversial Presidency of George W. Bush* (New York: Three Rivers Press, 2006), 203.

6. Patrick J. Maney, *The Roosevelt Presence: The Life and Legacy of FDR* (Berkeley: University of California Press, 1992), 70, 72–73, 76, 78.

7. Cited in David C. Whitney, *The American Presidents: Biographies of Our Chief Executives*, 10th ed. (New York: GuildAmerica Books, 2005), 325.

8. Robert Dallek, *An Unfinished Life: John F. Kennedy 1917–1963* (Boston: Little, Brown, 2003), 700.

9. Wilson Sullivan and Hans L. Trefousse, "Abraham Lincoln: The Great Emancipator," in *The Presidents: Every Leader from Washington to Bush*, ed. Michael Beschloss (New York: Simon and Schuster, 2003), 203.

10. David Jacobs (rev. Lewis L. Gould), "Harry S. Truman: The Buck Stopped Here," in *The Presidents*, ed. Beschloss, 375.

11. H. W. Brands, *Andrew Jackson: His Life and Times* (New York: Doubleday, 2005), 485.

12. Chris Wallace, *Character: Profiles in Presidential Courage* (New York: Rugged Land, 2004), 141.

13. Zachary Karabell, *Chester Alan Arthur* (New York: Times Books, 2004), 142.

14. John Seigenthaler, *James K. Polk* (New York: Times Books, 2003), 154.

15. Robert H. Bork, "Franklin Delano Roosevelt (1933–1945)," in *Presidential Leadership: Rating the Best and the Worst in the White House*, ed. James Taranto and Leonard Leo (New York: Wall Street Journal, 2004), 156.

16. Fred Greenstein cited in Jay Tolson, "The Worst Presidents: It's Too Soon to Judge the Current One, but for Past Leaders the Verdict Is In," *U.S. News and World Report*, February 18, 2007.

17. Allan Peskin, "James Abram Garfield," in *Presidential Leadership*, ed. Taranto and Leo, 105.

18. John O. McGinnis, "John Calvin Coolidge," in *Presidential Leadership*, ed. Taranto and Leo, 149.

19. Taranto and Leo, *Presidential Leadership*, reproduced poll, 11–12.

20. "Presidential Leadership: The Rankings," OpinionJournal, *Wall Street Journal*, Editorial Page, September 12, 2005, *www.opinionjournal.com/extra/?id=110007243*.

21. Siena Research Institute, press release.

22. Richard Vedder and Lowell Gallaway, "Rating Presidential Performance," in *Reassessing the Presidency: The Rise of the Executive State and the Decline of Freedom*, ed. John V. Denson (Auburn, AL: Ludwig Von Mises Institute, 2001), 1–32. Vedder and Gallaway generate several rankings of presidential economic performance, but the best is a composite ranking based on the change of the federal government as a portion of the GDP and the rate of inflation (left column on table 4 on page 19 of Denson's book), which is reproduced in table 2 in this volume (page 16). This composite ranking will be cited in almost all of this book's chapters on individual presidents, but will not be further endnoted.

Notes to George Washington

1. James MacGregor Burns and Susan Dunn, *George Washington* (New York: Times Books, 2004) 55, 57, 65–67, 128.

2. Richard Brookhiser, "George Washington," in *Presidential Leadership*, ed. Taranto and Leo, 15–19; and Burns and Dunn, *George Washington*, 99–103.

3. Loewen, *Lies My Teacher Told Me*, 116, 125.

4. Matthew Crenson and Benjamin Ginsberg, *Presidential Power: Unchecked and Unbalanced* (New York: W. W. Norton and Company, 2007), 325.

5. Ibid., 216.

6. For more on this exaggeration, see Raoul Berger, *Executive Privilege: A Constitutional Myth* (Cambridge, MA: Harvard University Press, 1974), 163–176.

7. Wilson Sullivan and Robert A. Rutland, "George Washington: Father of His Country," in *The Presidents*, ed. Beschloss, 17–33.

8. Burns and Dunn, *George Washington*, 64–65, 68–69, 73, 77–78, 97, 138, 139–140, 142–143, 147–149.

9. Ibid., 79–84.

10. Sullivan and Rutland, "George Washington," in *The Presidents*, ed. Beschloss, 17–33; and Burns and Dunn, *George Washington*, 110–111.

11. Burns and Dunn, *George Washington*, 66, 72.

12. Brookhiser in *Presidential Leadership*, ed. Taranto and Leo, 15–19; and Burns and Dunn, *George Washington*, 55, 57, 65–67, 128.

13. Burns and Dunn, *George Washington*, 133.

Notes to John Adams

1. Crenson and Ginsberg, *Presidential Power*, 324–325.

2. David McCullough, *John Adams* (New York: Simon and Schuster, 2001), 484.

3. Matthew Spalding, "John Adams," in *Presidential Leadership*, ed. Taranto and Leo, 23; and McCullough, *John Adams*, 491, 499, 504, 507, 510–513, 515–517, 522, 525, 531, 539, 554, 555, 557, 566.

4. David Jacobs and Robert Rutland, "John Adams: Following in the Footsteps," in *The Presidents*, ed. Beschloss, 45–46.

5. Michael Farquhar, *A Treasury of Great American Scandals* (New York: Penguin Books, 2003), 156.

Notes to Thomas Jefferson

1. Noble E. Cunningham, *In Pursuit of Reason: The Life of Thomas Jefferson* (New York: Random House, 1987), 240, 247–248, 278, 313–314, 320–321.

2. Cunningham, *In Pursuit of Reason*, 259–265, 267; and Whitney, *American Presidents*, 40.

3. Crenson and Ginsberg, *Presidential Power*, 70.

4. Ibid., 217.

5. Whitney, *American Presidents*, 40.

6. Crenson and Ginsberg, *Presidential Power*, 318.

7. Loewen, *Lies My Teacher Told Me*, 122–123.

8. Wilson Sullivan and Robert A. Rutland, "Thomas Jefferson: Renaissance Leader," in *The Presidents*, ed. Beschloss, 63.

9. For more on this point, see Norman K. Risjord, *The Old Republicans: Southern Conservativism in the Age of Jefferson* (New York: Columbia University, 1965); Arthur A. Ekirch, Jr., *The Decline of American Liberalism* (New York: Atheneum, 1969); Cunningham, *In Pursuit of Reason*, 246, 249–251.

10. Wallace, *Character*, 246–248.

11. Ibid., 244–248.

12. Forrest McDonald, "Thomas Jefferson," in *Presidential Leadership*, ed. Taranto and Leo, 28–29.

13. Wallace, *Character*, 244–246.

14. Cunningham, *In Pursuit of Reason*, 315–316.

15. Leonard Levy quoted in Sullivan and Rutland, "Thomas Jefferson," in *The Presidents*, ed. Beschloss, 60.

16. Cunningham, *In Pursuit of Reason*, 270, 277.

17. Ibid., 272–274.

18. For more on Jefferson's mistreatment of Native Americans, see Walter C. Fleming, *Native American History* (New York: Alpha Books, 2003), 118; and Roger G. Kennedy, *Mr. Jefferson's Lost Cause: Land, Farmers, Slavery, and the Louisiana Purchase* (New York: Oxford University Press, 2003).

19. Ray Raphael, *Founding Myths: Stories That Hide Our Patriotic Past* (New York: The New Press, 2004), 107–108, 111–113.

Notes to James Madison

1. Lynne Cheney, "James Madison," in *Presidential Leadership*, ed. Taranto and Leo, 32.

2. Loewen, *Lies My Teacher Told Me*, 123–124.

3. Whitney, *American Presidents*, 47.

4. For more on Madison's mercantilist view that embargoes could work, see Drew R. McCoy, "Republicanism and American Foreign Policy: James Madison and the Political Economy of Commercial Discrimination, 1789–1794," *William and Mary Quarterly*, 3rd ser., 31, 4 (October 1974), 633–646; and J. C. A. Stagg, "James Madison and the Coercion of Great Britain: Canada, the West Indies, and the War of 1812," *William and Mary Quarterly*, 3rd ser., 38, 1 (January 1981), 3–34.

5. Ralph Ketcham, *James Madison* (Charlottesville: University of Virginia Press, 1990), 492–493.

6. Ibid., 535, 540, 547.

7. Ibid., 536.

8. Ibid., 514–515, 522.

9. Ibid., 498, 506, 531–532.

10. Vincent Buranelli and Robert A. Rutland, "James Madison: The Nation Builder," in *The Presidents*, ed. Beschloss, 72–73.

11. Loewen, *Lies My Teacher Told Me*, 124.

12. For more on the deterioration of republican ideology and advocacy of a standing army at the expense of the militia, see Ekirch, *Decline of American Liberalism*, chapter 5.

13. Gary Hart, *James Monroe* (New York: Henry Holt and Company, 2005), 78.

14. For more on U.S. covert operations in Florida, see Roger G. Kennedy, *Mr. Jefferson's Lost Cause: Land, Farmers, Slavery, and the Louisiana Purchase* (New York: Oxford University Press, 2003); and William Earl Weeks, *John Quincy Adams and American Global Empire* (Louisville: University Press of Kentucky, 1992).

15. Ketcham, *James Madison*, 500–502.

Notes to James Monroe

1. Hart, *James Monroe*, 104–105.

2. David B. Rivkin, Jr., and Mark Wendell DeLaquil, "James Monroe," in *Presidential Leadership*, ed. Taranto and Leo, 35–38.

3. Hart, *James Monroe*, 61–63, 69–70, 76–78, 80–82, 85–86.

4. Ibid., 76–78.

5. For more on the empire building of these times, see Weeks, *John Quincy Adams*.

6. Rivkin and DeLaquil, "James Monroe," in *Presidential Leadership*, ed. Taranto and Leo, 37.

7. For more on such covert operations, see Kennedy, *Mr. Jefferson's Lost Cause*.

8. Crenson and Ginsberg, *Presidential Power*, 219–220.

9. The authoritative source on the economic downturn of 1819 is Murray N. Rothbard, *The Panic of 1819* (New York: Columbia University Press, 1963).

10. Rivkin and DeLaquil, "James Monroe," in *Presidential Leadership*, ed. Taranto and Leo, 35.

11. David Jacobs and Robert A. Rutland, "James Monroe: The Era of Good Feelings," in *The Presidents*, ed. Beschloss, 83–85.

12. For more on the residual mercantilism of the founders, see William Appleman Williams, *The Contours of American History* (New York: New Viewpoints, 1973), part I.

Notes to John Quincy Adams

1. Whitney, *American Presidents*, 59.

2. Robert V. Remini, *John Quincy Adams* (New York: Henry Holt and Company, 2002), 82; and Paul E. Teed, *John Quincy Adams: Yankee Nationalist* (New York: Nova Science Publishers, 2006), 101, 107–108.

3. Richard Norton Smith, "John Quincy Adams," in *Presidential Leadership*, ed. Taranto and Leo, 42.

4. Remini, *John Quincy Adams*, 85–86. For more on the significance of the National Road, see Marc Egnal, "The Beards Were Right," *Civil War History*, 47, 1 (2002), 30–56.

5. Teed, *John Quincy Adams: Yankee Nationalist*, 118.

6. David Jacobs and Robert A. Rutland, "John Quincy Adams: Born to Lead," in *The Presidents*, ed. Beschloss, 97.

7. Remini, *John Quincy Adams*, 107–108; and Teed, *John Quincy Adams: Yankee Nationalist*, 113.

8. Remini, *John Quincy Adams*, 90–91, 94–95, 97, 99; and Teed, *John Quincy Adams: Yankee Nationalist*, 103–105.

9. Smith, "John Quincy Adams," in *Presidential Leadership*, ed. Taranto and Leo, 41–42.

Notes to Andrew Jackson

1. Saul Braun and Robert A. Rutland, "Andrew Jackson: Old Hickory," in *The Presidents*, ed. Beschloss, 113.

2. For more on Jackson's aggressive nature, see Ronald Takaki, *Iron Cages: Race and Culture in Nineteenth-Century America* (New York: Oxford University Press, 1990), 94–96; and Richard Drinnon, *Facing West: The Metaphysics of Indian-Hating and Empire-Building* (New York: Schocken Books, 1990), 107.

3. H. W. Brands, *Andrew Jackson: His Life and Times* (New York: Doubleday, 2005), 434, 447, 475–481; Braun and Rutland, "Andrew Jackson: Old Hickory," in *The Presidents*, ed. Beschloss, 110; and H. W. Brands, "Andrew Jackson," in *Presidential Leadership*, ed. Taranto and Leo, 46.

4. H. W. Brands, *Andrew Jackson: His Life and Times*, 88.

5. Daniel Farber, *Lincoln's Constitution* (Chicago: University of Chicago Press, 2003), 37–38, 40.

6. Ibid., 90–91.

7. Brands, *Andrew Jackson: His Life and Times*, 521–522, 524, 525–526.

8. Whitney, *American Presidents*, 81.

9. Ibid., 82.

10. Crenson and Ginsberg, *Presidential Power*, 78.

11. Ibid., 79–81, 91.

12. Brands, *Andrew Jackson: His Life and Times*, 469–470.

13. Wallace, *Character*, 61–62. For more on the bank's corruption, see Sean Wilentz, *The Rise of American Democracy: Jefferson to Lincoln* (New York: W. W. Norton and Company, 2005), 214–216 and 843–844, notes.

14. Brands, *Andrew Jackson: His Life and Times*, 460, 466.

15. Wallace, *Character*, 66–70.

16. Brands, *Andrew Jackson: His Life and Times*, 436–437.

17. Whitney, *American Presidents*, 81.

18. Wallace, *Character*, 71.

19. Ted Widmer, *Martin Van Buren* (New York: Times Books, 2005), 100–101.

20. Walter C. Fleming, *Native American History* (New York: Alpha Books, 2003), 126.

21. Brands, *Andrew Jackson: His Life and Times*, 489.

22. Brands, "Andrew Jackson," in *Presidential Leadership*, ed. Taranto and Leo, 46–47.

23. Brands, *Andrew Jackson: His Life and Times*, 491–493.

24. Ed Rayner and Ron Stapley, *Debunking History: 152 Popular Myths Exploded* (London: Sutton Publishing, 2006), 11.

25. Fleming, *Native American History*, 122–129.

26. Whitney, *American Presidents*, 81.

Notes to Martin Van Buren

1. Jeffrey Rogers Hummel, "The Greatest American President," *The Independent Review*, vol. 4, no. 2 (Fall 1999), 260–261.
2. Wilson Sullivan and Robert A. Rutland, "Martin Van Buren: The Red Fox," in *The Presidents*, ed. Beschloss, 119–123.
3. Hummel, "Greatest American President," 258–261.
4. Ted Widmer, *Martin Van Buren* (New York: Times Books, 2005), 129–130.
5. Ibid., 118.
6. Hummel, "Greatest American President," 271–272; and Fleming, *Native American History*, 122, 127–129.
7. Hummel, "Greatest American President," 261–269.
8. Widmer, *Martin Van Buren*, 141.
9. Ibid., 102.
10. Ibid., 106, 131.
11. Ibid., 121–123.

Notes to John Tyler

1. Ratified in 1967, the Twenty-fifth Amendment states that if the president can no longer serve, the vice president becomes the chief executive.
2. Crenson and Ginsberg, *Presidential Power*, 89–90.
3. Norma Lois Paterson, *The Presidencies of William Henry Harrison and John Tyler* (Lawrence: University Press of Kansas, 1989), 157.
4. For more on the Dorr War, see George M. Dennison, "Martial Law: The Development of a Theory of Emergency Powers," *American Journal of Legal History*, 18, 1 (January 1974), 52–79; and George M. Dennison, *The Dorr War: Republicanism on Trial, 1831–1861* (Lexington: University of Kentucky Press, 1976).
5. Paterson, *The Presidencies*, 108–111.
6. Ibid., 126–130.
7. John S. Baker, Jr., "John Tyler," in *Presidential Leadership*, ed. Taranto and Leo, 56–59.
8. Michael Harwood and Robert A. Rutland, "Zachary Taylor: Old Rough-and-Ready," in *The Presidents*, ed. Beschloss, 154.
9. Paterson, *The Presidencies*, 98–108, 170–172.

Notes to James K. Polk

1. Crenson and Ginsberg, *Presidential Power*, 93.
2. Seigenthaler, *James K. Polk*, 154–156.
3. Douglas G. Brinkley, "James Knox Polk," in *Presidential Leadership*, ed. Taranto and Leo, 62; and Saul Braun and Robert A. Rutland, "James Knox Polk: The Dark Horse," in *The Presidents*, ed. Beschloss, 148.
4. Harwood and Rutland, "Zachary Taylor: Old Rough-and-Ready," in *The Presidents*, ed. Beschloss, 154–155.
5. Whitney, *American Presidents*, 105.
6. Irving W. Levinson, *Wars within Wars: Mexican Guerillas, Domestic Elites, and the United States of America, 1846–1848* (Fort Worth: Texas Christian University Press, 2005), 57–64.

7. Seigenthaler, *James K. Polk*, 135–141.

8. Otis A. Singletary, *The Mexican War* (Chicago: University of Chicago Press, 1960), 3.

9. Crenson and Ginsberg, *Presidential Power*, 16–18.

10. Seigenthaler, *James K. Polk*, 143–147, 151–152.

11. Charles A. McCoy, *Polk and the Presidency* (Austin: University of Texas Press, 1960), 3.

12. Braun and Rutland, "James Knox Polk," in *The Presidents*, ed. Beschloss, 146.

13. Sam W. Haynes, *James K. Polk and the Expansionist Impulse* (New York: Addison Wesley Longman, 1997), 140.

14. Ibid., 122–128.

15. Whitney, *American Presidents*, 106.

16. Haynes, *James K. Polk and the Expansionist Impulse*, 151.

17. Seigenthaler, *James K. Polk*, 102, 113, 116.

18. Braun and Rutland, "James Knox Polk," in *The Presidents*, ed. Beschloss, 150.

19. Paul H. Bergeron, *The Presidency of James K. Polk* (Lawrence: University Press of Kansas, 1987), 191.

20. Seigenthaler, *James K. Polk*, pp, 102–103, 122.

21. William Dusinberre, *Slavemaster President: The Double Career of James Polk* (New York: Oxford University Press, 2003), 143–146.

22. Ibid., 148–150.

Notes to Zachary Taylor

1. Farquhar, *A Treasury of Great American Scandals*, 115.

2. U.S. Constitution, art. 4, sec. 3.

3. Brendan Miniter, "Zachary Taylor," in *Presidential Leadership*, ed. Taranto and Leo, 65–66.

4. Harwood and Rutland, "Zachary Taylor: Old Rough-and-Ready," in *The Presidents*, ed. Beschloss, 158–159.

5. Whitney, *American Presidents*, 113.

6. Harwood and Rutland, "Zachary Taylor: Old Rough-and-Ready," in *The Presidents*, ed. Beschloss, 159.

7. Ibid., 111–112.

8. Fleming, *Native American History*, 136.

Notes to Millard Fillmore

1. David Jacobs and Robert A. Rutland, "Millard Fillmore: Forgotten Leader," in *The Presidents*, ed. Beschloss, 166–167.

2. U.S. Constitution, art. 4, sec. 3.

3. Melanie Kirkpatrick, "Millard Fillmore," in *Presidential Leadership*, ed. Taranto and Leo, 68–69.

4. Whitney, *American Presidents*, 117.

Notes to Franklin Pierce

1. Cynthia Crossen, "Franklin Pierce," in *Presidential Leadership*, ed. Taranto and Leo, 73.

2. Martin Luray and Robert A. Rutland, "Franklin Pierce: Overwhelmed by Events," in *The Presidents*, ed. Beschloss, 175–176.

3. *A Compilation of the Messages and Papers of the Presidents, 1779–1897* (Washington, D.C.: U.S. Government Printing Office, 1897), 273ff.

4. U.S. Constitution, art. 4, sec. 3.

5. Whitney, *American Presidents*, 123.

6. Crossen, "Franklin Pierce," in *Presidential Leadership*, Taranto and Leo, 72–74.

7. See William R. Leslie, "The Influence of Joseph Story's Theory of the Conflict of Laws on Constitutional Nationalism," *Mississippi Valley Historical Review*, 35, 2 (September 1948), 214–215.

8. Fleming, *Native American History*, 138.

Notes to James Buchanan

1. Michael Harwood and Robert Rutland, "James Buchanan: An American Nero," in *The Presidents*, ed. Beschloss, 179, 180.

2. Jean H. Baker, *James Buchanan* (New York: Times Books, 2004), 84–86.

3. Alfred W. Blumrosen and Ruth G. Blumrosen, *Slave Nation: How Slavery United the Colonies and Sparked the American Revolution* (Naperville, IL: Sourcebooks, 2005), 171–224.

4. U.S. Constitution, art. 4, sec. 3.

5. Baker, *James Buchanan*, 79–80, 87.

6. Ibid., 93–104, 114.

7. Whitney, *American Presidents*, 127.

8. Harwood and Rutland, "James Buchanan," in *The Presidents*, ed. Beschloss, 185.

9. Baker, *James Buchanan*, 125.

10. Ibid., 117, 121, 123.

11. For more on the political economy of slavery, see William Freehling, *Road to Disunion: Volume II: Secessionists Triumphant, 1854–1861* (New York: Oxford University Press, 2007).

12. Freehling, *Road to Disunion*, 107–110.

13. Ibid., 114, 115.

14. Ibid., 89–90, 117–118.

15. Poll replicated in *Presidential Leadership*, ed. Taranto and Leo, 11–12.

Notes to Abraham Lincoln

1. Jay Winik, "Abraham Lincoln," in *Presidential Leadership*, ed. Taranto and Leo, 82.

2. Crenson and Ginsberg, *Presidential Power*, 97–98.

3. Ibid.

4. Farber, *Lincoln's Constitution*, 14, 111–112; Thomas J. DiLorenzo, *The Real Lincoln: A New Look at Abraham Lincoln, His Agenda, and an Unnecessary War* (New York: Three Rivers Press, 2003), 20–21, 257; and Sullivan and Trefousse, "Abraham Lincoln: The Great Emancipator," in *The Presidents*, ed. Beschloss, 197–198.

5. Winik, "Abraham Lincoln," in *Presidential Leadership*, ed. Taranto and Leo, 80–81.

6. Sullivan and Trefousse, "Abraham Lincoln: The Great Emancipator," in *The Presidents*, ed. Beschloss, 197.

7. DiLorenzo, *The Real Lincoln*, 121.

8. Ibid., 119–120, 121.

9. Winik, "Abraham Lincoln," in *Presidential Leadership*, ed. Taranto and Leo, 81.

10. DiLorenzo, *The Real Lincoln*, 123.

11. Ibid., 85; William Appleman Williams, *America Confronts a Revolutionary World, 1776–1976* (New York: Morrow, 1976), 111; and Farber, *Lincoln's Constitution*, 106.

12. Dwight L. Durmond, *The Secession Movement, 1860–1861* (New York: Macmillan, 1831), 120–121.

13. Widmer, *Martin Van Buren*, 114.

14. Walter Williams in a foreword to DiLorenzo, *The Real Lincoln*, ix–x.

15. DiLorenzo, *The Real Lincoln*, 4, 9, 47–48, 49, 50–51, 52, 277, 294–297.

16. Josiah Bunting III, *Ulysses S. Grant* (New York: Times Books, 2004), 123.

17. Bevin Alexander, *How the South Could Have Won the Civil War: The Fatal Errors That Led to Confederate Defeat* (New York: Crown Publishers, 2007), 186–187.

18. For more on the North's total war strategy, see Edward Hagerman, "Union Generalship and Total War Strategy," in *On the Road to Total War*, ed. Stig Forster and Jorg Nagler (Cambridge, UK: Cambridge University Press, 1997), 141–169.

19. DiLorenzo, *The Real Lincoln*, 6–7, 172–173, 177, 180–182, 184, 186–187, 190.

20. Ibid., 6.

21. For more on Lincoln's view of his presidential and war powers, see Peter Irons, *War Powers: How the Imperial Presidency Hijacked the Constitution* (New York: Henry Holt and Company, 2005), chapter 4; and Edward S. Corwin, *Total War and the Constitution* (New York: Alfred A. Knopf, 1947), 16–21.

22. Sullivan and Trefousse, "Abraham Lincoln: The Great Emancipator," in *The Presidents*, ed. Beschloss, 201–202.

23. Farber, *Lincoln's Constitution*, 17–18, 20, 118, 136–138.

24. DiLorenzo, *The Real Lincoln*, 134.

25. Crenson and Ginsberg, *Presidential Power*, 326–327.

26. Alexander, *How the South Could Have Won the Civil War*, 187.

27. Ibid., 3, 4–5, 57–60, 82, 83, 227–228, 245, 252–255, 304–305.

28. Ibid., 78–79.

29. For more on this point, see *The Myth of the Lost Cause and the Civil War*, ed. Gary Gallagher and Alan T. Nolan (Bloomington: Indiana University Press, 2000).

30. Loewen, *Lies My Teacher Told Me*, 190.

31. Crenson and Ginsberg, *Presidential Power*, 326–327.

Notes to Andrew Johnson

1. Poll cited in *Presidential Leadership*, ed. Taranto and Leo, 11–12.

2. For more on the political economy of slavery, see William Freehling, *Road to Disunion: Volume II: Secessionists Triumphant, 1854–1861*.

3. Whitney, *American Presidents*, 152.

4. David Jacobs and Hans L. Trefousse, "Andrew Johnson: Between North and South," in *The Presidents*, ed. Beschloss, 213.

5. James E. Sefton, *Andrew Johnson and the Uses of Constitutional Power* (Boston: Little, Brown, 1980) 146–147.

6. Ibid., 148–149.

7. Wallace, *Character*, 92–93.

8. Whitney, *American Presidents*, 155–157; and Tulis, "Andrew Johnson," in *Presidential Leadership*, ed. Taranto and Leo, 92–93.

9. For more on the post–Civil War use of military tribunals, see Mark E. Neely, Jr., *The Fate of Liberty: Abraham Lincoln and Civil Liberties* (New York: Oxford University Press, 1991), 167–179.

10. Whitney, *American Presidents*, 155.

Notes to Ulysses S. Grant

1. Josiah Bunting III, *Ulysses S. Grant* (New York: Henry Holt, 2004), 10.

2. Wallace, *Character*, 127, 128–131, 139–141; and Bunting, *Ulysses S. Grant*, 99, 101, 102, 106.

3. Bunting, *Ulysses S. Grant*, 103–105; and Sullivan and Trefousse, "Ulysses Simpson Grant: The Hero as Politician," in *The Presidents*, ed. Beschloss, 229.

4. Whitney, *American Presidents*, 164.

5. For more on southern resistance to Reconstruction as low-level guerrilla warfare, see Richard E. Rubinstein, *Rebels in Eden: Mass Political Violence in the United States* (Boston: Little, Brown, 1970), 69–70.

6. Sullivan and Trefousse, "Ulysses Simpson Grant: The Hero," in *The Presidents*, ed. Beschloss, 229–230.

7. Michael Barone, "Ulysses Simpson Grant," in *Presidential Leadership*, ed. Taranto and Leo, 96.

8. Bunting, *Ulysses S. Grant*, 108–110.

9. Ibid., 120–121.

10. Barone, "Ulysses Simpson Grant," in *Presidential Leadership*, ed. Taranto and Leo, 97; and Bunting, *Ulysses S. Grant*, 87, 94–95, 141–142.

11. Bunting, *Ulysses S. Grant*, 135–136; and Sullivan and Trefousse, "Ulysses Simpson Grant," in *The Presidents*, ed. Beschloss, 232.

12. Bunting, *Ulysses S. Grant*, 133–134.

13. Whitney, *American Presidents*, 164–165.

14. Bunting, *Ulysses S. Grant*, 145.

15. Whitney, *American Presidents*, 164.

16. Bunting, *Ulysses S. Grant*, 119–120; and Barone, "Ulysses Simpson Grant," in *Presidential Leadership*, ed. Taranto and Leo, 97.

17. Poll cited in *Presidential Leadership*, ed. Taranto and Leo, 11–12.

18. Poll cited in Tolson, "The 10 Worst Presidents," *U.S. News and World Report*, February 18, 2007.

Notes to Rutherford B. Hayes

1. Kenneth E. Davison, "The Presidency of Rutherford B. Hayes," in *Contributions in American Studies*, no. 3, ed. Robert H. Walker (Westport, CT: Greenwood Press, 1972), 157.

2. Ari Hoogenboom, *The Presidency of Rutherford B. Hayes* (Lawrence: University Press of Kansas, 1988), 101–102, 130, 139, 144–145, 147, 149–151, 160–161, 174–177.

3. Louis W. Koenig, "Rutherford Birchard Hayes: Striving for a Fresh Start," in *The Presidents*, ed. Beschloss, 244; and Hans L. Trefousse, *Rutherford B. Hayes* (New York: Henry Holt and Company, 2002), 124–125.

4. Trefousse, *Rutherford B. Hayes*, 109; and Hoogenboom, "Rutherford Birchard Hayes," in *Presidential Leadership*, ed. Taranto and Leo, 102.

5. Koenig, "Rutherford Birchard Hayes: Striving for a Fresh Start," in *The Presidents*, ed. Beschloss, 244–245.

6. For more on the history and benefits of immigration, see Lowell E. Galloway, Stephen Moore, and Richard K. Vedder, "The Immigration Problem: Then and Now," *The Independent Review*, vol. 4, no. 3 (Winter 2000), 347–364.

7. Hoogenboom, *The Presidency of Rutherford B. Hayes*, 60–61.

8. Trefousse, *Rutherford B. Hayes*, 109, 123

9. For more on flaws in Indian policy, see *Property Rights and Indian Economies*, ed. Terry L. Anderson (Lanham, MD: Rowman & Littlefield Publishers, 1992).

10. Fleming, *Native American History*, 172–183; and Hoogenboom, *The Presidency of Rutherford B. Hayes*, 155–167, 187–192.

Notes to Chester A. Arthur

1. Anthony S. Pitch, *Exclusively Presidential Trivia* (Potomac, MD: Mino Publications, 2005), 25, 33.

2. Zachary Karabell, *Chester Alan Arthur* (New York: Times Books, 2004), 116–119.

3. Crenson and Ginsberg, *Presidential Power*, 108–109.

4. For more on the unresponsive bureaucratic state, see Murray N. Rothbard, "Bureaucracy and the Civil Service in the United States," *Journal of Libertarian Studies*, 11, 2 (Summer 1995), 3–75; and John C. Calhoun, "Speech on the President's Power of Removal, 20 February 1835," in *John C. Calhoun: Selected Writings and Speeches*, ed. H. Lee Cheek, Jr. (Washington, D.C.: Regnery Publishing, 2003), 464–477.

5. Karabell, *Chester Alan Arthur*, 69–70, 74, 81, 102–110; and Louis Koenig, "Chester Alan Arthur: The Self-Reformer," in *The Presidents*, ed. Beschloss, 260–261, 263.

6. Justus D. Doenecke, *The Presidencies of James A. Garfield and Chester Arthur* (Lawrence: The Regents Press of Kansas, 1981), 77, 83–84, 90–91.

Notes to Grover Cleveland

1. Crenson and Ginsberg, *Presidential Power*, 112–113.

2. Henry F. Graff, *Grover Cleveland* (New York: Henry Holt and Company, 2002), 85.

3. Crenson and Ginsberg, *Presidential Power*, 111–112.

4. Richard E. Welch, Jr., *The Presidencies of Grover Cleveland* (Lawrence: University Press of Kansas, 1988), 53–54.

5. H. Paul Jeffers, *An Honest President: The Life and Presidencies of Grover Cleveland* (New York: HarperCollins, 2000), 144–145.

6. Whitney, *American Presidents*, 188, 192–193.

7. Louis Koenig, "Grover Cleveland: The Law Man," in *The Presidents*, ed. Beschloss, 273; and Whitney, *American Presidents*, 197.

8. Welch, *The Presidencies of Grover Cleveland*, 159, 162–163.

9. Ibid., 160, 192–193.

10. Jeffers, *An Honest President*, 157–160.

11. Robert Higgs, *Crisis and Leviathan: Critical Episodes in the Growth of American Government* (New York: Oxford University Press, 1987), 77–79, 89.

12. Jeffers, *An Honest President*, 199–201, 286, 289; and Welch, *The Presidencies of Grover Cleveland*, 83, 85, 87–88, 133, 136–137.

13. Grover Cleveland, quoted in Jeffers, *An Honest President*, 193–194, 359.

14. U.S. Constitution, art. 1, sec. 8 and art. 4, sec. 4.

15. Fleming, *Native American History*, 196–199.

16. Kevin Phillips, *William McKinley* (New York: Times Books, 2003), 149.

17. Graff, *Grover Cleveland*, 85.

18. For more on the regulatory expansion of government from the 1880s to the 1930s, see William J. Novak, "Police Power and the Transformation of the American State," *www.abf-sociolegal.org/novakpaper.pdf*.

19. Farquhar, *A Treasury of Great American Scandals*, 123.

Notes to Benjamin Harrison

1. Jessica King, "Benjamin Harrison," in *Presidential Leadership*, ed. Taranto and Leo, 116–118.

2. Louis W. Koenig, "Benjamin Harrison: Presidential Grandson," in *The Presidents*, ed. Beschloss, 285.

3. Whitney, *American Presidents*, 205–206, 208.

4. Fleming, *Native American History*, 185–187.

5. Ibid., 206, 208.

6. Koenig, "Benjamin Harrison: Presidential Grandson," in *The Presidents*, ed. Beschloss, 284.

7. Ibid., 287.

Notes to William McKinley

1. Tolson, "The 10 Worst Presidents," *U.S. News and World Report*, February 18, 2007.

2. Farquhar, *A Treasury of Great American Scandals*, 125.

3. Donald Young and John Milton Cooper, Jr., "William McKinley: Bridge to a New Century," in *The Presidents*, ed. Beschloss, 292.

4. Young and Cooper, "William McKinley: Bridge," in *The Presidents*, ed. Beschloss, 293; Fred Barnes, "William McKinley," in *Presidential Leadership*, ed. Taranto and Leo, 122; and Whitney, *American Presidents*, 214.

5. Phillips, *William McKinley*,, 90–91; and Whitney, *American Presidents*, 215.

6. Phillips, *William McKinley*, 94.

7. Ibid., 95; Whitney, *American Presidents*, 215; and Young and Cooper, "William McKinley," 293.

8. Phillips, *William McKinley*, 103–104.

9. For more on the problems with tariffs, see Joseph Schumpeter, *Imperialism, Social Classes: Two Essays* (New York: Meridian Books, 1955).

10. Crenson and Ginsberg, *Presidential Power*, 34–35.

11. Ibid., 286.

12. Ibid., 247.

13. Ibid., 121–122.

14. Phillips, *William McKinley*, 110.

15. Schumpeter, *Imperialism, Social Classes*, 87, 90, 109–110, 115, 116, 143, 152; and Whitney, *American Presidents*, 210, 214, 217

16. Phillips, *William McKinley*, 109–110, 113–114, 151.

17. Barnes, "William McKinley," in *Presidential Leadership*, ed. Taranto and Leo, 122.

18. Young and Cooper, "William McKinley," in *The Presidents*, ed. Beschloss, 294.

19. Phillips, *William McKinley,* 104–106.

20. Ibid., 89–90, 105–106.

21. Whitney, *American Presidents,* 210.

Notes to Theodore Roosevelt

1. Wallace, *Character,* 150–151.

2. Tolson, "The 10 Worst Presidents," *U.S. News and World Report.* For the wider context of how civilian machismo and militarism helped cause the Spanish-American and Philippine-American wars, see Kristin L. Hoganson, *Fighting for American Manhood: How Gender Politics Provoked the Spanish-American and Philippine-American Wars* (New Haven, CT: Yale University Press, 1998). A similar phenomenon recurred with the "chicken hawks" inside and outside the George W. Bush administration — for example, the president, Vice President Dick Cheney, and Deputy Secretary of Defense Paul Wolfowitz — who, in one way or another, evaded the draft during the Vietnam War, but were the main architects and advocates of an invasion of Iraq.

3. Edmund Morris, *Theodore Rex* (New York: Modern Library, 2001), 482–485, 492–495, 502–503, 534.

4. Ibid., 251, 254–255, 262–265, 268, 273–283, 289–298, 300–302, 312.

5. Russell Mokhiber and Robert Weissman, "How Wall Street Created a Nation," NewsCenter, CommonDreams.org, October 27, 2001, *www.commondreams.org/views01/1027-03.htm.*

6. For more on the Raisuli episode, see Charles A. Beard, *A Foreign Policy for America* (New York: Alfred A. Knopf, 1940), 58–59.

7. Morris, *Theodore Rex,* 214, 219, 456–457, 459, 461, 464; and Wilson Sullivan and John Milton Cooper, Jr., "Theodore Roosevelt: The Giant in the Bully Pulpit," in *The Presidents,* ed. Beschloss, 310.

8. Morris, *Theodore Rex,* 24–25.

9. For the view of John Bigelow, a classical liberal diplomat, about the downside of Roosevelt's mediation effort, see Margaret Clapp, *Forgotten First Citizen: John Bigelow* (Boston: Little, Brown, 1947).

10. Lewis L. Gould, *The Presidency of Theodore Roosevelt* (Lawrence: University Press of Kansas, 1991), 186, 188.

11. Morris, *Theodore Rex,* 378–379, 381, 440–441.

12. Ibid., 207, 554.

13. Sullivan and Cooper, "Theodore Roosevelt: The Giant in the Bully Pulpit," in *The Presidents,* ed. Beschloss, 306.

14. Gabriel Kolko, *The Triumph of Conservatism: A Reinterpretation of American History, 1900–1916* (London: Free Press of Glencoe, Collier-Macmillan Limited, 1963), 112.

15. Roosevelt's autobiography indicates that he thought he was curbing the power of big business, rhetoric that might be self-serving. See Theodore Roosevelt, *An Autobiography* (New York: Charles Scribner's Sons, 1921), 423.

16. For more on the public choice arguments surrounding the Pure Food and Drug Act, see Jack High and Clayton Coppin, "Wiley and the Whiskey Industry: Strategic Behavior and Passage of the Pure Food Act," *Business History Review* 62 (Summer 1988): 286–309; and Gabriel Kolko, *The Triumph of Conservatism.*

17. Kolko, *Triumph of Conservatism,* 68–70, 72, 77–78.

18. Thomas E. Woods, Jr., "Theodore Roosevelt and the Modern Presidency," in *Reassessing the Presidency: The Rise of the Executive State and the Decline of Freedom*, ed. John V. Denson (Auburn, AL: Ludwig Von Mises Institute, 2001), 349.

19. For more on the Hepburn Act, see George E. Mowry, *Theodore Roosevelt and the Progressive Movement* (Madison: University of Wisconsin Press, 1946), 26.

20. Morris, *Theodore Rex*, 507.

21. John S. McCain, "Theodore Roosevelt," in *Presidential Leadership*, ed. Taranto and Leo, 128; and Morris, *Theodore Rex*, 485–487, 501.

22. Crenson and Ginsberg, *Presidential Power*, 130–131.

23. Donald Worster, *Rivers of Empire: Water, Aridity, and the Growth of the American West* (New York: Pantheon Books, 1985), 156–169; and Morris, *Theodore Rex*, 114–115.

24. Worster, *Rivers of Empire*, 131–135, 150–161, 163–164, 165–167.

25. Morris, *Theodore Rex*, 48, 49–50, 52–53, 55–56, 58, 198–200, 202–203, 213, 301, 351, 455, 462, 464–467, 470–474, 477, 479–482, 511.

Notes to William Howard Taft

1. Farquhar, *A Treasury of Great American Scandals*, 127–128.

2. Michael Harwood and John Milton Cooper, Jr., "William Howard Taft: Reluctant Leader," in *The Presidents*, ed. Beschloss, 318.

3. Ibid.

4. Oscar M. Alfonso, *Theodore Roosevelt and the Philippines: 1897–1909* (New York: Oriole Editions, 1970), 137–141.

5. Paolo E. Coletta, *The Presidency of William Howard Taft* (Lawrence: University Press of Kansas, 1973), 53–75.

6. For more information on withdrawal of land for conservation, see William Harbaugh, *Lawyer's Lawyer: The Life of John W. Davis* (Charlottesville: University Press of Virginia, 1990 [1973]), 98–101.

7. Theodore B. Olsen, "William Howard Taft," in *Presidential Leadership*, ed. Taranto and Leo, 131–133.

8. Whitney, *American Presidents*, 238.

Notes to Woodrow Wilson

1. For more on this pyrrhic victory, see Thomas Fleming, *The Illusion of Victory: America in World War I* (New York: Basic Books, 2003).

2. William Appleman Williams, *America Confronts a Revolutionary World, 1776–1976* (New York: Morrow, 1976), 144.

3. For more on the implications of World War I, see Murray N. Rothbard, "World War I as Fulfillment: Power and the Intellectuals," *Journal of Libertarian Studies*, 9, 1 (Winter 1989) 81–125.

4. For more on the origins of permanent big government during World War I, see Ronald Schaffer, *America in the Great War: The Rise of the War Welfare State* (New York: Oxford University Press, 1991).

5. Max Boot, "Thomas Woodrow Wilson," in *Presidential Leadership*, ed. Taranto and Leo, 136.

6. Ibid., 138.

7. Alexander L. George and Juliette L. George, *Woodrow Wilson and Colonel House: A Personality Study* (Mineola, NY: Dover Publications, 1956), 158.

8. Niall Ferguson, *The Pity of War* (New York: Basic Books, 1999), 458.

9. Jim Powell, *Wilson's War: How Woodrow Wilson's Great Blunder Led to Hitler, Lenin, Stalin, and World War II* (New York: Crown Forum, 2005), 1–2, 290, 292, 294.

10. Howard Zinn, *A People's History of the United States* (New York: Harper Perennial, 2003), 353.

11. Joseph L. Gardner and John Milton Cooper, Jr., "Woodrow Wilson: Prophet without Honor," in *The Presidents*, ed. Beschloss, 328.

12. Powell, *Wilson's War*, 13–14.

13. Wallace, *Character*, 270–271.

14. Whitney, *American Presidents*, 253.

15. Ralph Raico cites international lawyer John Bassett Moore and others on such rights in Ralph Raico, "World War I: The Turning Point," in John V. Denson, *The Costs of War: America's Pyrrhic Victories* (New Brunswick, NJ: Transaction Publishers, 1999), 223.

16. For more on the British hunger blockade, see Ralph Raico, "The Politics of Hunger: A Review," *Review of Austrian Economics*, 3 (1989), 253–259.

17. Powell, *Wilson's War*, 95, 98.

18. Gardner and Cooper, "Woodrow Wilson: Prophet without Honor," in *The Presidents*, ed. Beschloss, 329.

19. Boot, "Thomas Woodrow Wilson," in *Presidential Leadership*, ed. Taranto and Leo, 138.

20. Ibid., 139.

21. Whitney, *American Presidents*, 253–254.

22. William Appleman Williams, *The Tragedy of American Diplomacy* (New York: W. W. Norton and Company, 1988), 100–101.

23. For more on the roots in World War I of modern problems in the Middle East, see David Fromkin, *A Peace to End All Peace: Creating the Modern Middle East, 1914–1922* (New York: Henry Holt and Company, 1987).

24. Whitney, *American Presidents*, 255.

25. Ibid., 1, 93–95, 98, 291, 292.

26. Powell, *Wilson's War*, 8–9.

27. Loewen, *Lies My Teacher Told Me*, 250.

28. Boot, "Thomas Woodrow Wilson," in *Presidential Leadership*, ed. Leo and Taranto, 138–139.

29. Powell, *Wilson's War*, 83–87.

30. Ibid., 88.

31. Loewen, *Lies My Teacher Told Me*, 220.

32. Ibid., 24–26, 34.

33. For more on this point, see Richard Gamble, *The War for Righteousness: Progressive Christianity, the Great War, and the Rise of the Messianic Nation* (Wilmington, DE: Intercollegiate Studies Books, 2003).

34. For more on the private bank clearinghouse mechanism, see Richard Timberlake, "The Central Banking Role of Clearinghouse Associations," in *Financial Crisis, Contagion, and the Lender of Last Resort*, ed. Charles Goodhart and Gerhard Illing (New York: Oxford University Press, 2002).

35. Gardner and Cooper, "Woodrow Wilson," in *The Presidents*, ed. Beschloss, 325.

36. Whitney, *American Presidents*, 250.

37. For more on the creation of the Federal Reserve System, see Murray N. Rothbard, "The Origins of the Federal Reserve," in *A History of Money and Banking in the United States* (Auburn, AL: Ludwig Von Mises Institute, 2002), 183–258.

38. Gabriel Kolko, *The Triumph of Conservatism* (New York: Free Press, 1977), 256, 260, 267; and Gardner and Cooper, "Woodrow Wilson," in *The Presidents*, ed. Beschloss, 325–326; and Whitney, *American Presidents*, 251.

39. Murray N. Rothbard, "World War I as Fulfillment: Power and the Intellectuals," *The Journal of Libertarian Studies*, vol. 9, no. 1 (Winter 1989), 85–86.

40. Gardner and Cooper, "Woodrow Wilson," in *The Presidents*, ed. Beschloss, 329.

41. Crenson and Ginsberg, *Presidential Power*, 19–20.

42. Ibid., 340.

43. James Weinstein, *The Corporate Ideal in the Liberal State 1900–1918* (Boston: Beacon Press, 1985), 222–223; and Crenson and Ginsberg, *Presidential Power*, 221–223.

44. Crenson and Ginsberg, *Presidential Power*, 247.

45. Loewen, *Lies My Teacher Told Me*, 29–31.

46. For more on the Goldstein affair, see *Robert Goldstein and "The Spirit of '76,"* ed. Anthony Slide (Lanham, MD: Scarecrow Press, 1993).

47. Fleming, *The Illusion of Victory*, 251.

48. For a critique of the Espionage Act, see John W. Burgess, *Recent Changes in American Constitutional Theory* (New York: Columbia University Press, 1923).

49. Farquhar, *A Treasury of Great American Scandals*, 196–202.

50. Gardner and Cooper, "Woodrow Wilson," in *The Presidents*, ed. Beschloss, 326.

51. Loewen, *Lies My Teacher Told Me*, 26–28, 230.

52. For more on Edith Wilson's "presidency," see Phyllis Lee Levin, *Edith and Woodrow: The Wilson White House* (New York: Scribner Books, 2001).

Notes to Warren G. Harding

1. For more details on this cogent perspective, see Robert H. Ferrell, *The Strange Deaths of President Harding* (Columbia: University of Missouri Press, 1998).

2. Tolson, "The 10 Worst Presidents," *U.S. News and World Report*, February 18, 2007.

3. For more on this overblown scandal, see David H. Stratton, *Tempest Over Teapot Dome: The Story of Albert B. Fall* (Norman: University of Oklahoma Press, 1998).

4. Farquhar, *A Treasury of Great American Scandals*, 203–206.

5. Tolson, "The 10 Worst Presidents," *U.S. News and World Report*, February 18, 2007.

6. Jeremy Rabkin, "Warren Gamaliel Harding," in *Presidential Leadership*, ed. Taranto and Leo, 142.

7. Ibid.

8. John W. Dean, *Warren G. Harding* (New York: Henry Holt and Company, 2004), 107–111.

9. Murray N. Rothbard, *America's Great Depression*, 5th ed. (Auburn, AL: Ludwig von Mises Institute, 2000), 4, 6–7, 9, 12, 14, 92–93, 95. Rothbard includes the surrender value of life insurance policies as part of the money supply, an addition with which some economists would disagree. Nevertheless, even taking a more restricted view of the money supply and omitting this category, during the eight-year period from mid-1921 to mid-1929, the money supply increased by a still whopping 54.3 percent, or a 6.8 percent average annual increase. This change, however, does make Coolidge look a little better

and Harding look a little worse in terms of money supply growth, but my underlying conclusions about their presidencies would remain much the same.

10. Crenson and Ginsberg, *Presidential Power*, 20–22.

11. Dean, *Warren G. Harding*, 101–102, 103–104, 111–113, 115–121.

12. For more on Harding's civil rights record, see David Bernstein, *Only One Place of Redress: African Americans, Labor Regulations, and the Court, from Reconstruction to the New Deal* (Durham, NC: Duke University Press, 2001).

13. Poll cited in Tolson, "The 10 Worst Presidents," *U.S. News and World Report*, February 18, 2007.

14. Taranto and Leo, *Presidential Leadership*, 11–12.

15. Paul Johnson, *Modern Times: The World from the Twenties to the Eighties* (New York: Harper & Row, 1983), chapter 6.

Notes to Calvin Coolidge

1. Crenson and Ginsberg, *Presidential Power*, 145.

2. Ibid., 147.

3. Michael Harwood and Lewis L. Gould, "Calvin Coolidge: The New Englander," in *The Presidents*, ed. Beschloss, 347–348.

4. Whitney, *American Presidents*, 272, 274.

5. Harwood and Gould, "Calvin Coolidge: The New Englander," in *The Presidents*, ed. Beschloss, 346.

6. Whitney, *American Presidents*, 272.

7. Rothbard, *America's Great Depression*, 4, 6–7, 9, 12, 14, 92–93, 95. Rothbard includes the surrender value of life insurance policies as part of the money supply, an addition with which some economists would disagree. Nevertheless, even taking a more restricted view of the money supply and omitting this category, during the eight-year period from mid-1921 to mid-1929, the money supply increased by a still whopping 54.3 percent, or a 6.8 percent average annual increase. This change, however, does make Coolidge look a little better and Harding look a little worse in terms of money supply growth, but my underlying conclusions about their presidencies would remain much the same.

8. John O. McGinnis, "John Calvin Coolidge," in *Presidential Leadership*, ed. Taranto and Leo, 150.

9. Ibid., 148, and Harwood and Gould, "Calvin Coolidge: The New Englander," in *The Presidents*, ed. Beschloss, 345–346.

10. McGinnis, "John Calvin Coolidge," in *Presidential Leadership*, ed. Taranto and Leo, 146–147.

11. Johnson, *Modern Times*, chapter 6; and Thomas B. Silver, *Coolidge and the Historians* (Durham, NC: Carolina Academic Press, 1982).

Notes to Herbert Hoover

1. Whitney, *American Presidents*, 277, 282.

2. Crenson and Ginsberg, *Presidential Power*, 160–162.

3. Robert H. Ferrell, "Herbert Clark Hoover," in *Presidential Leadership*, ed. Taranto and Leo, 152–153.

4. Crenson and Ginsberg, *Presidential Power*, 149; *Herbert Hoover and the Crisis of American Capitalism* (Cambridge, MA: Schenkman Publishing Co., 1973) with essays by

Murray Rothbard, Robert Himmelberg, Gerald Nash, and Ellis W. Hawley; and Ellis W. Hawley, "Herbert Hoover, the Commerce Secretariat, and the Vision of an 'Associative State,'" *Journal of American History*, 61, 1 (June 1974), 116–140.

5. Robert Higgs, *Crisis and Leviathan* (New York: Oxford University Press, 1987), 165.

6. Patrick J. Maney, *The Roosevelt Presence: The Life and Legacy of FDR* (Berkeley: University of California Press, 1992), 52.

7. Rothbard, *America's Great Depression*, 4, 6–7, 9, 12, 14, 92–93, 95, 191, 210–212, 215–217, 228–234, 241, 243, 264–265, 286–287; and Higgs, *Crisis and Leviathan*, 164.

8. Saul Braun and Lewis L. Gould, "Herbert Clark Hoover: The Great Engineer," in *The Presidents*, ed. Beschloss, 355.

9. Whitney, *American Presidents*, 282.

Notes to Franklin D. Roosevelt

1. Anthony S. Pitch, *Exclusively Presidential Trivia* (Potomac, MD: Mino Publications, 2005), 145.

2. Eric Alterman, *When Presidents Lie: A History of Official Deception and Its Consequences* (New York: Viking, 2004), 26.

3. Maney, *The Roosevelt Presence*, 112–113, 118–121.

4. Crenson and Ginsberg, *Presidential Power*, 220.

5. James J. Martin, "A Look at Conscription, Then and Now," in James J. Martin, *Revisionist Viewpoints: Essays in a Dissident Historical Tradition* (Colorado Springs, CO: Ralph Myles, 1971), 10, http://tmh.floonet.net/articles/conscrpt.shtml.

6. Robert Higgs, "Regime Uncertainty: Why the Great Depression Lasted So Long and Why Prosperity Returned after the War," *The Independent Review*, vol. 1 (Spring 1997), 562–563, and Wallace, *Character*, 267–268.

7. Wallace, *Character*, 271–272.

8. Michael Barone, "Presidents at War," *U.S. News and World Report*, January 30–February 6, 2006, 46.

9. Maney, *The Roosevelt Presence*, 136–137, 144–145.

10. Ibid., 126–129.

11. Ibid., 120–121.

12. Ibid., 127–129.

13. For more on FDR's behavior prior to World War II, see Charles A. Beard, *President Roosevelt and the Coming of the War, 1941* (New Haven, CT: Yale University Press, 1948), epilogue, 573–598.

14. A. C. Grayling, *Among the Dead Cities: The History and Moral Legacy of the WWII Bombing of Civilians in Germany and Japan* (New York: Walker & Company, 2006), 5–6.

15. For more on FDR's Mussolini-style corporatism and expanding of presidential power, see Thomas Fleming, *The New Dealer's War: F.D.R. and the War within World War II* (New York: Basic Books, 2001); John T. Flynn, *As We Go Marching* (Garden City, NY: Doubleday, Doran & Co., 1944); and John T. Flynn, *The Roosevelt Myth* (San Francisco: Fox & Wilkes, 1998 [1948]), 39.

16. Robert Higgs, "War and Leviathan in Twentieth-Century America: Conscription as the Keystone," in *The Costs of War: America's Pyrrhic Victories,* ed. John V. Denson (New Brunswick, NJ: Transaction Publishers, 1999).

17. Crenson and Ginsberg, *Presidential Power,* 340. For more detail on the bank closure, see Ralph Raico, *Fascism Comes to America,* chapter 9: "First Inaugural Address; He Closes the Banks," *www.lewrockwell.com/raico/fdr-toc.html.*

18. Thomas DiLorenzo, "Franklin Delano Roosevelt's New Deal," in John V. Denson, *Reassessing the Presidency: The Rise of the Executive State and the Decline of Freedom* (Auburn, AL: Ludwig Von Mises Institute, 2001), 431.

19. Flynn, *The Roosevelt Myth,* 39.

20. Maney, *The Roosevelt Presence,* 54, 67–68.

21. Robert H. Ferrell, "Herbert Clark Hoover," in *Presidential Leadership,* ed. Taranto and Leo, 154.

22. Crenson and Ginsberg, *Presidential Power,* 162.

23. Ibid., 291–292.

24. Maney, *The Roosevelt Presence,* 52.

25. Whitney, *American Presidents,* 292.

26. For more details on the Wagner Act, see Morgan O. Reynolds, "An Economic Analysis of the Norris-LaGuardia Act, the Wagner Act, and the Labor Representation Industry," *Journal of Libertarian Studies,* VI (Summer/Fall, 1982), 238.

27. For more on FDR's abandonment of the gold standard, see Raico, *Fascism Comes to America,* chapter 10: "Roosevelt Seizes the Country's Gold; NRA and Fascism," *www.lewrockwell.com/raico/fdr-toc.html;* and Rothbard, *America's Great Depression,* 97.

28. Robert H. Bork, "Franklin Delano Roosevelt," in *Presidential Leadership,* ed. Taranto and Leo, 156.

29. Crenson and Ginsberg, *Presidential Power,* 224–228.

30. Higgs, *Crisis and Leviathan,* 205–209.

31. Crenson and Ginsberg, 194–195.

32. Ibid., 179–180, 182.

33. Ibid., 224–228.

34. Maney, *The Roosevelt Presence,* 117–118, 186–187.

35. For more on the imprisonment of Japanese Americans, see Richard Drinnon, *Keeper of Concentration Camps: Dillon S. Meyer and American Racism* (Berkeley: University of California Press, 1987); Jacobus tenBroek, Edward N. Barnhart, and Floyd M. Matson, *Prejudice, War and the Constitution* (Berkeley: University of California Press, 1975 [1954]); and Peter Irons, *Justice at War: The Story of Japanese American Internment Cases* (Berkeley: University of California Press, 1993 [1983]).

36. Greg Robinson, *By Order of the President: FDR and the Internment of Japanese Americans* (Cambridge, MA, and London, UK: Harvard University Press, 2001), 74–76.

37. Crenson and Ginsberg, *Presidential Power,* 332.

38. Ibid., 331.

39. Ralph Raico, "Rethinking Churchill," in *The Costs of War,* ed. Denson, 274.

40. Geoffrey Stone, *Perilous Times: Free Speech in Wartime from the Sedition Act of 1798 to the War on Terrorism* (New York and London: W. W. Norton and Company, 2004), 248–249, 251, 256–257.

Notes to Harry S Truman

1. Alterman, *When Presidents Lie*, 66.

2. For more information on the Marshall Plan, see Michael J. Hogan, *The Marshall Plan: America, Britain, and the Reconstruction of Western Europe, 1947–1952* (New York: Cambridge University Press, 1987).

3. For more on the exaggerated effects of the Marshall Plan, see Tyler Cohen, "The Marshall Plan: Myths and Realities," in *U.S. Aid to the Developing World: A Free Market Agenda*, ed. Doug Bandow (Washington, D.C.: Heritage Foundation, 1985), 61–74 (chapter 5), *www.gmu.edu/jbc/Tyler/Marshall_Plan.pdf*.

4. For more on U.S. assistance to Greece, see Lawrence S. Wittner, *American Intervention in Greece, 1943–1949* (New York: Columbia University Press, 1982); and Constantine Tsoucalas, *The Greek Tragedy* (London: Penguin Books, 1969).

5. Howard Zinn, *A People's History of the United States: 1492–Present* (New York: Harper Perennial, 2003), 417.

6. David McCullough, *Truman* (New York: Simon and Schuster, 1992), 545–546.

7. Geoffrey Perret, *Commander in Chief: How Truman, Johnson, and Bush Turned a Presidential Power into a Threat to America's Future* (New York: Farrar, Straus, and Giroux, 2007), 8–9.

8. Crenson and Ginsberg, *Presidential Power*, 254–256.

9. Ibid., 274.

10. McCullough, *Truman*, 791–792, 833.

11. Crenson and Ginsberg, *Presidential Power*, 257.

12. Ibid., 252–253.

13. For more on the post-atomic-attack Japanese conditional surrender, see Fleming, *The New Dealer's War*, 546–547.

14. For more on the Strategic Bombing Survey, see Zinn, *A People's History*, 414.

15. For an example of an author who thinks the real target of the bomb was the USSR, see ibid., 415.

16. Alterman, *When Presidents Lie*, 55.

17. McCullough, *Truman*, 439.

18. Bruce Cumings, "Nuclear Threats Against North Korea: Consequences of the 'Forgotten' War," *Le Monde Diplomatique*, December 20, 2004, *www.zmag.org/content/showarticle.cfm?ItemID=6901*.

19. Alterman, *When Presidents Lie*, 43, 51–52, 54–59, 63.

20. McCullough, *Truman*, 449–451.

21. Alterman, *When Presidents Lie*, 55–57, 65–66.

22. McCullough, *Truman*, 490–491, 543–545.

23. Ibid., 287–288, 290–291.

24. Wallace, *Character*, 294, 297.

25. For more on the U.S. role in creating Israel, see Justus D. Doenecke, "Principle and Expediency: The State Department and Palestine, 1948," *Journal of Libertarian Studies*, 2, 4 (Winter 1978), 343–356.

26. McCullough, *Truman*, 595–605, 612, 615–620.

27. Stephan P. Halbrook, "The Alienation of a Homeland: How Palestine Became Israel," *Journal of Libertarian Studies*, vol. 5, no. 4 (Fall 1981), 365–369.

28. McCullough, *Truman*, 468–469, 473–474, 476, 485, 532, 586, 632–633, 642–643, 726, 915.

29. Whitney, *American Presidents*, 305; and Jacobs and Gould, "Harry S. Truman: The Buck Stopped Here," in *The Presidents*, ed. Beschloss, 378.

30. McCullough, *Truman*, 494–501, 503–506.

31. Zinn, *A People's History*, 416–417, 424, 427.

32. For more on Truman's loyalty program that helped fuel McCarthyism, see Athan Theoharis, *Seeds of Repression* (Chicago: Quandrangle, 1971); and Richard M. Freeland, *The Truman Doctrine and the Origins of McCarthyism: Foreign Policy, Domestic Politics, and Internal Security, 1946–1948* (New York: Schocken Books, 1974).

Notes to Dwight D. Eisenhower

1. Stephen E. Ambrose, *Eisenhower: Soldier and President* (New York: Simon and Schuster, 1990), 526.

2. Ibid., 481–487.

3. Ibid., 294–295, 327–331.

4. Ibid., 303; and Charles L. Mee, Jr., and Lewis L. Gould, "Dwight David Eisenhower: I Like Ike," in *The Presidents*, ed. Beschloss, 393.

5. Ambrose, *Eisenhower*, 301–302.

6. Ibid., 422–423, 434.

7. For more on Ike's reliance on nuclear weapons, see John Lewis Gaddis, *Strategies of Containment: A Critical Appraisal of Postwar American National Security Policy* (New York: Oxford University Press, 1982), 127–163. For more on the ideology of the use of strategic air power, see Michael H. Gorn, *Harnessing the Genie: Science and Technology Forecasting for the Air Force, 1944–1986* (Washington, D.C.: Office of Air Force History, USAF, 1988); *The Paths of Heaven: The Evolution of Airpower Theory*, ed. Col. Phillip S. Meilinger (Maxwell Air Force Base, AL: Air University Press, 1997); and Fred Kaplan, *The Wizards of Armageddon* (New York: Simon and Schuster, 1983). And for more on the economic savings of emphasizing nuclear air power, see Blanche Wiesen Cook, *The Declassified Eisenhower* (New York: Penguin Books, 1984), 293–346.

8. Ambrose, *Eisenhower*, 547–548.

9. Mee and Gould, "Dwight David Eisenhower," in *The Presidents*, ed. Beschloss, 398.

10. Ambrose, *Eisenhower*, 465–469.

11. Ibid., 332–333.

12. Loewen, *Lies My Teacher Told Me*, 363, 370–371.

13. Ibid., 373–385.

14. Ambrose, *Eisenhower*, 311–312.

15. Ibid., 324–326.

16. For more on Ike and the military-industrial complex, see H. W. Brands, "The Age of Vulnerability: Eisenhower and the National Insecurity States," *American Historical Review*, 94, 4 (October 1989), 963–989.

17. Mee and Gould, "Dwight David Eisenhower," in *The Presidents*, ed. Beschloss, 395.

18. Ambrose, *Eisenhower*, 386–387.

19. Ibid., 394–395; and Edwin Meese III, "Dwight David Eisenhower," in *Presidential Leadership*, ed. Taranto and Leo, 167.

20. Raoul Berger, *Executive Privilege: A Constitutional Myth* (Cambridge, MA: Harvard University Press, 1974), 234–241.

Notes to John F. Kennedy

1. Robert Dallek, *An Unfinished Life: John F. Kennedy, 1917–1963* (Boston: Little, Brown, 2003), 699–701.
2. Wallace, *Character,* 312–315, 317.
3. Dallek, *An Unfinished Life,* 361.
4. Ibid., 362–365.
5. Alterman, *When Presidents Lie,* 112–114; and David Ruppe, "U.S. Military Wanted to Provoke War with Cuba — Book: U.S. Military Drafted Plans to Terrorize U.S. Cities to Provoke War with Cuba," ABC News, May 1, 2001, *http://abcnews.go.com/US/story?id=92662.*
6. Dallek, *An Unfinished Life,* 418–419, 421, 423, 427–434, 482.
7. Alterman, *When Presidents Lie,* 123–124, 125; and Dallek, *An Unfinished Life,* 538–541.
8. Dallek, *An Unfinished Life,* 538–539, 546–547, 548.
9. Alterman, *When Presidents Lie,* 94.
10. Ibid., 122.
11. Ibid., 123–124, 125.
12. Tolson, "The 10 Worst Presidents," *U.S. News and World Report,* February 18, 2007.
13. Dallek, *An Unfinished Life,* 532–538, 545.
14. Ibid., 573–574.
15. Alterman, *When Presidents Lie,* 132–133.
16. Ibid., 88–89.
17. Michael Barone, "Presidents at War," *U.S. News and World Report,* January 30–February 6, 2006, 47–48.
18. Dallek, *An Unfinished Life,* 331–332, 381, 385–388, 493–495, 580, 641–646.
19. Loewen, *Lies My Teacher Told Me,* 234–235.

Notes to Lyndon B. Johnson

1. William R. Polk, *Violent Politics: A History of Insurgency, Terrorism, and Guerrilla War, from the American Revolution to Iraq* (New York: HarperCollins, 2007), 167–168.
2. Lewis L. Gould, "Lyndon Baines Johnson: So Close to Greatness," in *The Presidents,* ed. Beschloss, 420–421.
3. Alterman, *When Presidents Lie,* 149.
4. Robert Dallek, *Lyndon B. Johnson: Portrait of a President* (New York: Oxford University Press, 2004), 220–223.
5. Gould, "Lyndon Baines Johnson," in *The Presidents,* ed. Beschloss, 421.
6. Alterman, *When Presidents Lie,* 219, 220.
7. Dallek, *Lyndon B. Johnson,* 300–302, 304, 309, 318–319.
8. Loewen, *Lies My Teacher Told Me,* 215.
9. Dallek, *Lyndon B. Johnson,* 215–217.
10. Ibid., 289–290.
11. Gould, "Lyndon Baines Johnson," in *The Presidents,* ed. Beschloss, 420, 425.
12. Dallek, *Lyndon B. Johnson,* 153–155.
13. Ibid., 242–243.
14. Ibid., 193–195, 273.
15. Ibid.
16. Ibid., 200–201.
17. Ibid., 279–280, 351.

Notes to Richard M. Nixon

1. Farquhar, A Treasury of Great American Scandals, 222.

2. Richard Reeves, President Nixon: Alone in the White House (New York: Simon and Schuster, 2001), 288.

3. Ibid., 564.

4. For more on Nixon's conception of the war power and a refutation, see Francis D. Wormuth, "The Nixon Theory of the War Power: A Critique," California Law Review, 60, 3 (May 1972), 623–703.

5. Ibid., 605.

6. Ibid., 392–393, 607.

7. Greg Kaza, "A Future for Gold," Ludwig Von Mises Institute, October 5, 2000, www.gold-eagle.com/editorials_00/kaza100500.html.

8. Roger Leroy Miller and Raburn M. Williams, The New Economics of Richard Nixon: Freezes, Floats, and Fiscal Policy (San Francisco: Canfield Press, 1972), 1–2.

9. For more on Nixon's abandoning the gold standard, see Murray N. Rothbard, What Has the Government Done to Our Money? (Auburn, AL: Ludwig Von Mises Institute, [1963], 1990), 105–107.

10. Reeves, President Nixon, 295–297.

11. Ibid., 44, 294–295.

12. For more on Nixon being the last Cold War liberal, see H. W. Brands, The Strange Death of American Liberalism (New Haven, CT: Yale University Press, 2001).

13. Allen J. Matusow, Nixon's Economy: Booms, Busts, Dollars, and Votes (Lawrence: University Press of Kansas, 1998), 119–121.

14. Robert Mason, Richard Nixon and the Quest for a New Majority (Chapel Hill and London: University of North Carolina Press, 2004), 93. For more details on Nixon's aggressive antidrug policies, see Confronting Drug Policy: Illicit Drugs in a Free Society, ed. Ronald Bayer and Gerald M. Oppenheimer (Cambridge, UK: Cambridge University Press, 1993), 148.

15. Melvin Small, The Presidency of Richard Nixon (Lawrence: University Press of Kansas, 1999), 153, 198.

16. Reeves, President Nixon, 131, 513.

17. Thomas F. Schaller, Whistling Past Dixie: How Democrats Can Win without the South (New York: Simon and Schuster, 2006), 41.

18. Ibid., 112, 566.

19. Lewis L. Gould, "Richard Milhous Nixon: The Road to Watergate," in The Presidents, ed. Beschloss, 429.

20. Whitney, The American Presidents, 386–387.

21. Ibid., 354.

22. Reeves, President Nixon, 608.

23. Ibid., 541.

Notes to Gerald R. Ford

1. Thomas J. Bray, "Gerald Rudolph Ford, Jr.," in Presidential Leadership, ed. Taranto and Leo, 185.

2. "Capture and Release of SS Mayaguez by Khmer Rouge Forces in May 1975," U.S. Merchant Marine Web site, www.usmm.org/mayaguez.html.

3. Whitney, American Presidents, 405–406.

4. Crenson and Ginsberg, *Presidential Power*, 272.

5. John Robert Greene, *The Presidency of Gerald R. Ford* (Lawrence: University Press of Kansas, 1995), 79.

6. Bray, "Gerald Rudolph Ford, Jr.," in *Presidential Leadership*, ed. Taranto and Leo, 186.

7. Whitney, *American Presidents*, 391, 402–403.

8. Don Losman, "Economic Security: A National Security Folly," Cato Institute Policy Analysis no. 409, August 1, 2001, 7.

9. Whitney, *American Presidents*, 391, 400–401.

10. Evan Thomas, "More Than Met the Eye: The 38th President," *Newsweek*, January 8, 2007, 38.

11. Ibid.

12. Ibid., 36.

13. Quoted in a previously unpublished Ford interview with historian Michael Beschloss done in September 1995, in Michael Beschloss, "Ford's Long Shadow," *Newsweek*, January 8, 2007, 32.

14. Greene, *The Presidency of Gerald R. Ford*, 37–42.

15. Bray, "Gerald Rudolph Ford, Jr.," in *Presidential Leadership*, ed. Taranto and Leo, 184.

16. Louis L. Gould, "Gerald Rudolph Ford: A Time for Healing," in *The Presidents*, ed. Beschloss, 442.

17. Whitney, *American Presidents*, 401.

Notes to James Earl Carter, Jr.

1. Burton I. Kaufman and Scott Kaufman, *The Presidency of James Earl Carter, Jr.*, 2nd ed. (Lawrence: University Press of Kansas, 2006), 110–112.

2. Ibid., 189–191.

3. Ibid., 45.

4. Ibid., 230–231.

5. Ibid., 156.

6. For an example of this view, see Joshua Muravchick, "James Earl Carter, Jr.," in *Presidential Leadership*, ed. Taranto and Leo, 192.

7. Kaufman and Kaufman, *The Presidency of James Earl Carter, Jr.*, 175.

8. Robert J. Samuelson, "Friedman's Large Legacy," *Washington Post*, January 20, 2007, A17.

9. Robert J. Samuelson, "A Big Story, Missed," *Washington Post*, August 3, 2005, A19.

10. Kaufman and Kaufman, *The Presidency*, 217.

11. Ibid., 168, 172.

12. Lewis L. Gould, "Jimmy Carter: Not a Politician," in *The Presidents*, ed. Beschloss, 449, 452–453.

13. Kaufman and Kaufman, *The Presidency of James Earl Carter, Jr.*, 129–131, 214.

14. Ibid., 84–85.

15. Ibid., 91.

16. Ibid., 323, 235.

Notes to Ronald Reagan

1. Harvey Mansfield, "Ronald Wilson Reagan," in *Presidential Leadership* ed. Taranto and Leo, 196; and Lewis L. Gould, "Ronald Wilson Reagan: The Great Communicator," in *The Presidents*, ed. Beschloss, 468.

2. For the details on Reagan's protectionism, see Sheldon Richman, "Ronald Reagan: Protectionist," *The Free Market*, vol. 6, no. 5 (May 1988), *www.mises.org/freemarket_detail .asp?control=489* and Lloyd R. Cohen, "Deregulation of the U.S. International Trade Commission," in *Regulation and the Reagan Era: Politics, Bureaucracy, and the Public Interest,* ed. Roger E. Meiners and Bruce Y. Yandle (San Francisco: The Independent Institute, 1989), 169.

3. Schaller, *Whistling Past Dixie,* 42–43.

4. James Mann, "Tear Down That Myth," *New York Times,* June 10, 2007, 4–14.

5. For more on the real underlying causes of the Soviet collapse, see Randall Collins, "Prediction in Macrosociology: The Case of the Soviet Collapse," *American Journal of Sociology,* 100, 6 (May 1995), 1552–1593; and Ned Lebow and Janice Grosstein, *We All Lost the Cold War* (Princeton, NJ: Princeton University Press, 1994), 371–375.

6. For more on the exact sequence of attacks, showing that Reagan provoked Gadhafi and not vice versa, see Ivan Eland, "Does U.S. Intervention Overseas Breed Terrorism?: The Historical Record," Cato Institute Foreign Policy Briefing no. 50, December 17, 1998, 12–13; and Michael Oren, *Power, Faith, and Fantasy: America in the Middle East, 1776 to the Present* (New York: W. W. Norton & Company, 2007), 557.

7. Lou Cannon, "Reagan-Gorbachev Summit Talks Collapse as Deadlock on SDI Wipes Out Other Gains," *Washington Post,* October 13, 1986, A1.

8. Murray N. Rothbard, "The Myths of Reaganomics," in *The Free Market Reader,* ed. L. H. Rockwell (1988), *www.mises.org/fullstory.axpx?control=1544,* 3342–3362.

9. Anthony Gregory, "Government Growth, the Party of Lincoln, and George W. Bush," *www.lewrockwell.com/gregory/gregory40.html.*

10. Office of Management and Budget, Historical Tables: Budget of the United States Government, 2007, *www.whitehouse.gov/omb/budget/FY2007/pdf/hist.pdf,* 75, 76.

11. Fred Barnes, *Rebel-in-Chief: Inside the Bold and Controversial Presidency of George W. Bush* (New York: Three Rivers Press, 2006), 167.

12. Roger E. Meiners and Bruce Yandle, "Refulatory Lessons from the Reagan Era: Introduction," *Regulation and the Reagan Era,* ed. Meiners and Yandle, 4.

13. William A. Niskanen, *Reaganomics: An Insider's Account of the Policies and the People* (New York: Oxford University Press, 1988), 117–118.

14. Meiners and Yandle, "Regulatory Lessons," in *Regulation and the Reagan Era,* ed. Meiners and Yandle, 7.

15. Thomas F. Walton and James Langenfeld, "Regulatory Reform under Reagan — The Right Way and the Wrong Way," in *Regulation and the Reagan Era,* ed. Meiners and Yandle, 41.

16. William F. Shughard, II, "Antitrust Policy in the Reagan Administration: Pyrrhic Victories?," in *Regulation and the Reagan Era,* ed. Meiners and Yandle, 99.

17. Ibid., 93.

18. Walton and Langenfeld, "Regulatory Reform Under Reagan," in *Regulation and the Reagan Era,* ed. Meiners and Yandle, 45–47.

19. Ibid., 47, 49.

20. William C. MacLeod and Robert A. Rogowsky, "Consumer Protection at the FTC during the Reagan Administration," in *Regulation and the Reagan Era,* ed. Meiners and Yandle, 74.

21. Robert H. Nelson, "Privatization of Federal Lands: What Did Not Happen," in *Regulation and the Reagan Era,* ed. Meiners and Yandle, 144–145, 147, 159.

22. Gareth Davis, "The Welfare State," in *The Reagan Presidency: Pragmatic Conservatism and Its Legacies*, ed. W. Elliot Brownlee and Hugh Davis Graham (Lawrence: University Press of Kansas, 2003), 211, 221.

23. Martha Dethick and Steven M. Teles, "Riding the Third Rail: Social Security Reform," in *The Reagan Presidency*, ed. Brownlee and Graham, 187–196, 199–200; and Gould, "Ronald Wilson Reagan," in *The Presidents*, ed. Beschloss, 467.

24. Paul E. Peterson and Mark Rom, "Lower Taxes, More Spending, and Budget Deficits," in *The Reagan Legacy: Promise and Performance*, ed. Charles O. Jones (Chatham, NJ: Chatham House Publishers, 1988), 218–219.

25. For more on Reagan's supply-side views, see W. Elliot Brownlee and C. Eugene Steuerle, "Taxation," in *The Reagan Presidency*, ed. Brownlee and Graham, 155–160.

26. Bruce Bartlett, "How Supply-Side Economics Trickled Down," *New York Times*, April 6, 2007, 21.

27. Rothbard, "Myths of Reaganomics," in *The Free Market Reader*, ed. L. H. Rockwell, *www.mises.org/fullstory.axpx?control=1544*, 3342–3362.

28. John Ehrman, *The Eighties: America in the Age of Reagan* (New Haven: Yale University Press, 2005), 56.

29. Ibid., 59, 63.

30. Ibid., 62, 66.

31. Samuelson, "A Big Story, Missed," *Washington Post*, A19.

32. Lawrence E. Walsh, *Firewall: The Iran-Contra Conspiracy and Cover-up* (New York: W. W. Norton and Company, 1997), 6–7, 19–20.

33. Crenson and Ginsberg, *Presidential Power*, 197–199.

Notes to George H. W. Bush

1. For a good summary of the entire Panama episode, see R. M. Koster and Guillermo Sanchez, *In the Time of Tyrants, Panama: 1968–1990* (New York: W. W. Norton and Company, 1990).

2. Whitney, *American Presidents*, 468.

3. David Mervin, *George Bush and the Guardianship Presidency* (New York: St. Martin's Press, 1996), 167–169.

4. David Model, *Lying for Empire: How to Commit War Crimes with a Straight Face* (Monroe, ME: Common Courage Press, 2005), 211–212.

5. Crenson and Ginsberg, *Presidential Power*, 273–274.

6. Pete du Pont, "George Herbert Walker Bush," in *Presidential Leadership*, ed. Taranto and Leo, 200.

7. David Henderson, "Do We Need to Go to War for Oil?" Cato Institute Foreign Policy Briefing no. 4, October 24, 1990, *www.cato.org/pub_display.php?pub_id=1529&full=1*, 3.

8. Ibid.

9. Ryan J. Barilleaux and Mark J. Rozell, *Power and Prudence: The Presidency of George H. W. Bush* (College Station: Texas A&M University Press, 2004), 123.

10. Whitney, *American Presidents*, 482–484, 487.

11. Ibid., 485.

12. Paul J. Quirk, "Domestic Policy: Divided Government and Cooperative Presidential Leadership," in *The Bush Presidency: First Appraisals*, ed. Colin Campbell, S.J. Rockman, and Bert A. Rockman (Chatham, NJ: Chatham House Publishers, 1991), 79–80.

13. Louis L. Gould, "George Herbert Walker Bush: The Last Cold Warrior," in *The Presidents*, ed. Beschloss, 478.

Notes to William J. Clinton

1. John F. Harris, *The Survivor: Bill Clinton in the White House* (New York: Random House, 2006), 312.
2. "The Clintons' Ups and Downs," *USA Today*, March 29, 2007.
3. Model, *Lying for Empire*, 253–254, 256.
4. James Bovard, *Feeling Your Pain: The Explosion and Abuse of Government Power in the Clinton-Gore Years* (New York: St. Martin's Press, 2000), 326.
5. Model, *Lying for Empire*, 258–266, 270–271, 272.
6. Bovard, *Feeling Your Pain*, 335–336.
7. Harris, *The Survivor*, 128–132.
8. Ibid., 6–7.
9. Ibid., 403–409, 414–415.
10. Ibid., 85.
11. Ibid., 92.
12. Ibid., 521–522.
13. Robert Samuelson, "A Reform That Worked," *Washington Post*, August 3, 2006, *www.washingtonpost.com/wp-dyn/content/article/2006/08/02/AR2006080201387.html*.
14. Harris, *The Survivor*, 84.
15. Curiously, some conservatives, who normally champion tax cuts, regard the Earned Income Tax Credit as merely redistributing the tax burden to other economic classes (including theirs). Yet this redistribution is needed only because the government has not been shrunk proportionally to the tax cuts in the Earned Income Tax Credit. In this sense, economy-wide, the tax credit can be seen as a fake tax cut — much like those of the free-spending Reagan and George W. Bush administrations. Yet this fact did not seem to impede conservatives' support for Reagan's and Bush's tax cuts, which benefited wealthier groups. At least the Earned Income Tax Credit is a tax cut for the poor.
16. Whitney, *American Presidents*, 520.
17. Mark Halperin and John F. Harris, *The Way to Win: Taking the White House in 2008* (New York: Random House, 2006), 87.
18. Lewis L. Gould, "William Jefferson Clinton: Prosperity and Turmoil," in *The Presidents*, ed. Beschloss, 487.
19. Harris, *The Survivor*, 112–116.
20. Crenson and Ginsberg, *Presidential Power*, 200–201.
21. Bovard, *Feeling Your Pain*, 342.
22. Crenson and Ginsberg, *Presidential Power*, 217.
23. Harris, *The Survivor*, 57.
24. Whitney, *American Presidents*, 497–498.
25. Bovard, *Feeling Your Pain*, 122.

Notes to George W. Bush

1. Whitney, *American Presidents*, 550.
2. Ibid., 87.
3. Alterman, *When Presidents Lie*, 297.

4. Elizabeth Holtzman and Cynthia L. Cooper, *Impeachment of George W. Bush: A Practical Guide for Concerned Citizens* (New York: Nation Books, 2007), 65–66.

5. Ibid., 59–60.

6. Ibid., 63; and Alterman, *When Presidents Lie*, 298.

7. Ibid, 66–67.

8. James Risen, *State of War: The Secret History of the CIA and the Bush Administration* (New York: Free Press, 2006), 123.

9. Holtzman and Cooper, *Impeachment of George W. Bush*, 58.

10. Ibid., 64.

11. David Brown and Joshua Partlow, "New Estimate of Violent Deaths among Iraqis Is Lower," *Washington Post*, January 10, 2008, A18.

12. Bob Woodward, *Plan of Attack* (New York: Simon and Schuster, 2004), 314.

13. Karen DeYoung and Michael Abramowitz, "Report Says Hussein Was Open to Exile before 2003 Invasion," *Washington Post*, September 27, 2007, A17.

14. Holtzman and Cooper, *Impeachment of George W. Bush*, 81–82, 177.

15. Rand-National Memorial Institute for the Prevention of Terrorism data cited in Carl Conetta, "War and Consequences: Global Terrorism Has Increased since 9/11 Attacks," Project for Defense Alternatives Briefing Memo no. 38, September 25, 2006, *www.comw.org/pda/0609bm38.html*.

16. Holtzman and Cooper, *Impeachment of George W. Bush*, 179–180.

17. Scott Shane, "Terrorist Attacks in Iraq and Afghanistan Rose Sharply Last Year, State Department Says," *New York Times*, May 1, 2007, A10.

18. Schaller, *Whistling Past Dixie*, 249.

19. Barnes, *Rebel-in-Chief*, 51.

20. Whitney, *American Presidents*, 548.

21. Jonathan Weisman, "Bush's Budget Win May Cost Him: Victories over Democrats Could Increase Debt and Impede His Own Agenda," *Washington Post*, December 15, 2007.

22. Risen, *State of War*, 78.

23. Ibid., 129.

24. Perret, *Commander in Chief*, 391–392.

25. Crenson and Ginsberg, *Presidential Power*, 15.

26. Ibid., 324–325.

27. James Risen, "Administration Pulls Back on Surveillance Agreement," *New York Times*, May 2, 2007, A16; and James Vicini, "Bush Won't Reauthorize Eavesdropping," *Reuters*, January 17, 2007, 1.

28. James Risen, "Bush Signs Law to Widen Reach for Wiretapping; Restrictions Are Eased: Rules on Eavesdropping Are Altered to Match Program in Use," *New York Times*, August 6, 2007, A1.

29. Whitney, *American Presidents*, 540.

30. "A Ruling for Justice," *New York Times*, June 12, 2007, A22.

31. Crenson and Ginsberg, *Presidential Power*, 337–338.

32. Scott Shane, "White House Retreats Under Pressure," *Washington Post*, January 17, 2007.

33. Crenson and Ginsberg, *Presidential Power*, 228–229.

34. Ibid., 338–339.

35. Holtzman and Cooper, *Impeachment of George W. Bush*, 119–120, 134–135.

Notes to Barack Obama

1. Calculations derived from data from the Office of Management and Budget (OMB), "Table 1.3: Summary of Receipts, Outlays, Surpluses or Deficits in Current Dollars, Constant (FY 2005) Dollars, and as a Percentage of GDP (1940–2018) in OMB, *Historical Tables,* www.whitehouse.gov/omb/budget/historicals

2. Reuters, Graph compiled from Congressional Research Service and media reports using Department of Defense data on U.S. troop levels in Afghanistan, http://www.policymic .com/articles/74241/a-new-security-deal-may-keep-america-in-afghanistan-indefinitely

3. Robert Gates, *Duty: Memoirs of a Secretary at War* (New York: Knopf Doubleday Publishing Group, 2014) as reviewed in Bob Woodward, "Robert Gates, Former Defense Secretary, Offers Harsh Critique of Obama's Leadership in 'Duty'," *Washington Post,* January 7, 2014, www.washingtonpost.com/world/national-security/robert-gates-former-defense -secretary-offers-harsh-critique-of-obamas-leadership-in-duty/2014/01/076a6915b2-77cb -11e3-b1c5-739e63e9c9a7_story.html. At the time of this writing, Woodward's review was written from an advance copy of the book, but the book was not yet publicly available.

4. Bob Woodward, *Obama's Wars* (New York: Simon & Schuster, 2010), electronic version.

5. Bill Roggio, "The Taliban on U.S. Estimates of al Qaeda Strength in Afghanistan," *The Threat Matrix: A Blog of the Long War Journal,* May 20, 2012, http://www.longwarjournal. org/threat-matrix/archives/2012/05/the_taliban_on_us_estimates_on.php

6. Jon Swaine, "Barack Obama 'Has Authority to Use Drone Strikes on U.S. Soil,'" *The Telegraph,* March 6, 2013, www.telegraph.co.uk/news/barackobama/9913615/Barack -Obama-has-authority-to-use-drone-strikes-on-US-soil.html.

7. Michael Grunwald, *The New New Deal: The Hidden Story of Change in the Obama Era* (New York: Simon & Schuster, 2013), 13.

8. Ibid., 66–67.

9. Ibid., 10, 115, 120–121, 128, 198, 219–220, 222, 230–231, 238, 345, 432–433, 434, photo insert 10.

10. Ibid., 10–11, 18–19, 39, 126, 162, 179, 195, 197

11. Quoted in Ibid., 165.

12. Ibid., 10–11, 18–19, 39, 126, 162, 179, 195, 228–229, 237, 242–243, 267–268, 305, 325–326, 409–412.

13. http://www.brainyquote.com/quotes/quotes/r/rahmemanue409199.html

14. Grunwald, *The New New Deal,* 298.

15. Ibid., 121–122.

16. For a history of how one dubious government intervention leads to others, including the government's ill-fated actions in the most recent financial crisis, see Vern McKinley, *Financing Failure: A Century of Bailouts* (Oakland, California: The Independent Institute, 2011).

17. Ibid., 392.

18. www.brillig.com/debt_clock) and the calculations for debt accumulations during the two Bush terms and the Obama administration (for the first four years) were made in David Harsanyi, *Obama's Four Horsemen: The Disasters Unleashed by Obama's Reelection* (Washington: Regnery, 2013), 52, 56 (electronic version). Debt accumulation slowed in Obama's fifth year after Harsanyi's calculation because of budget gridlock in Washington and consequent across-the-board budget cuts through "sequestration." But Congress and the president subsequently eased that sequestration for 2014 and 2015.

19. President Obama interviewed on CBS's 60 Minutes, Broadcast on September 23, 2012.

20. Glenn Kessler, "The Fact Checker: Obama's Claim that '90 Percent' of the Current Deficit Is Due to Bush Policies," The Washington Post, September 26, 2012, http://www .washingtonpost.com/blogs/fact-checker/post/obamas-claim-that-90-percent-of-the-current -deficit-is-due-to-bush-policies/2012/09/26/e9bfbcd0-077e-11e2-a10c-fa5a255a9258_blog .html.

21. Graphs by the Congressional Budget Office and Center for Budget and Policy Priorities in Grunwald, The New New Deal, Photo insert 17.

22. Grunwald, The New New Deal, 338, 427.

23. Ibid., 246.

24. Calculations from data from the Office of Management and Budget (OMB), "Table 1.3: Summary of Receipts, Outlays, Surpluses or Deficits in Current Dollars, Constant (FY 2005) Dollars, and as a Percentage of GDP (1940–2018) in OMB, Historical Tables, www .whitehouse.gov/omb/budget/historicals

25. Avik Roy, "CBO: Obamacare Will Spend More, Tax More, and Reduce the Deficit Less Than We Previously Thought," Forbes, July 27, 2012, http://www.forbes.com/sites /aroy/2012/07/27/cbo-obamacare-will-spend-more-tax-more-and-reduce-the-deficit-less -than-we-previously-thought/

26. Harsanyi, Obama's Four Horsemen, 55–56.

27. Ibid., 25–26.

28. Nicholas Eberstadt, A Nation of Takers: America's Entitlement Epidemic (West Conshohocken, Pennsylvania: Templeton Press, 2012), 31.

29. Phil Izzo, "Number of the Week: Half of U.S. Lives in Households Getting Benefits," Wall Street Journal, May 26, 2012, http://blogs.wsj.com/economics/2012/05/26/number-of -the-week-half-of-u-s-lives-in-household-getting-benefits/

30. Grunwald, The New New Deal, 331–332.

31. Harsanyi, Obama's Four Horsemen, 19–20.

32 Grunwald, The New New Deal, 109, 205–206, 349, 392.

Index

ABM defense system, 317

Abu Ghraib, Iraq, 425

Acheson, Dean, 269, 270

ACLU (American Civil Liberties Union), 399–400

actions of the presidents: evaluation criteria for this book, 7, 9–13; historical overemphasis on, 1–2. *See also* analyzing presidents; specific presidents

activism bias, 8–9, 170, 176, 230–31

activist government, 2, 242, 243–44, 261, 281, 296–97

Adams, John, 25–29

Adams, John, actions of: Alien and Sedition acts, 25, 28; exceeding authority, 26, 28; Marshall appointment, 27–28; peace initiative to France, 26; Quasi-War with France, 7, 21, 26, 420

Adams, John Quincy, 55–59

Adams, John Quincy, actions of: antebellum New Deal, 56–57; big government, 56–57; Clay as secretary of state, 56; "failed state" argument, 52–53; Panama Congress, 56; serving in House after presidency, 59; spending plans of, 57; won freedom of *Amistad* slaves, 75

Adams-Otis Treaty, 53

AFDC (Aid to Families with Dependent Children), 331, 366

Afghanistan: alternative to occupation, 411; and bin Laden's whereabouts, 410; Clinton targets al Qaeda in, 391–92; enemy combatants from, 422–25; Obama's policies, 430–31; Soviet invasion of, 347–48; Taliban resurgence in, 411; U.S. and radical Islamists, 348, 363–64

African Americans: backlash post–Civil War, 128, 133–34, 137–38, 142–43; civil rights bills, 137, 147–48, 284, 297, 310, 321, 322; civil rights opponents, 203–4, 240, 264, 297–98; desegregation of, 284, 297, 310, 321, 322; FDR's racism, 264–65; federal protection for, 127; Grant's hope to deport, 141;

Lincoln's racism, 127; presidents supporting civil rights, 147–48, 284; segregation of, 138, 170, 227, 264, 284, 297; voting rights of, 147, 155–56, 170, 175, 321–22. *See also* slavery

Affordable Care Act (Obamacare), 446–49

Agnew, Spiro, 335

Agricultural Adjustment Act (1933), 244, 258

agriculture industry: Coolidge's veto of relief for, 238; Department of Agriculture, 116, 168, 169; Eisenhower's veto of farm bill, 296; food stamp program, 320, 331, 366; Hoover's support for, 244, 245; regulation of, 257; subsidies for, 95, 413, 417

Aideed, Mohammed Farah, 385

Aid to Families with Dependent Children (AFDC), 331, 366

airline industry, 365

Alabama, 310, 322

Alabama (Confederate warship), 140–41

Alaska, 113, 136–37

Alien Act (1798), 25, 28, 35, 226

Alien Registration Act (1940), 266

Allende, Salvador, 328

Alterman, Eric, 276–77, 303

Ambrose, Steve, 2–3, 287

America First Committee, 336

American Civil Liberties Union (ACLU), 399–400

American Revolution, 6–7, 12

Americans with Disabilities Act (1990), 380

American System of Henry Clay, 56–57, 66, 87–88, 125, 342–43

America's Great Depression (Rothbard), 474n9, 475n7

Amistad (Spanish slave ship), 75

amnesty, 137, 343

Amtrak, 330

analyzing presidents: on ability to dominate, 83; based on founders' original intent, 9–13; overview, 1, 454–57; PP&L rankings vs. short-term economic performance, 15–17, 486n22; "Rankings of Presidential Success,"

About the Author

 Ivan Eland is Senior Fellow and Director of the Center on Peace & Liberty at the Independent Institute. Dr. Eland is a graduate of Iowa State University and received an M.B.A. in applied economics and a Ph.D. in Public Policy from George Washington University. He has been Director of Defense Policy Studies at the Cato Institute, and he spent 15 years working for Congress on national security issues, including stints as an investigator for the House Foreign Affairs Committee and Principal Defense Analyst at the Congressional Budget Office. He also has served as Evaluator-in-Charge (national security and intelligence) for the U.S. General Accounting Office (now the Government Accountability Office), and has testified on the military and financial aspects of NATO expansion before the Senate Foreign Relations Committee, on CIA oversight before the House Government Reform Committee, and on the creation of the Department of Homeland Security before the Senate Judiciary Committee. Dr. Eland is the author of *The Empire Has No Clothes: U.S. Foreign Policy Exposed, Partitioning for Peace: An Exit Strategy for Iraq, No War for Oil: U.S. Dependency and the Middle East,* and *Putting "Defense" Back into U.S. Defense Policy,* as well as *The Efficacy of Economic Sanctions as a Foreign Policy Tool.* He is a contributor to numerous volumes and the author of 45 in-depth studies on national security issues.

His articles have appeared in *American Prospect, Arms Control Today, Bulletin of the Atomic Scientists, Emory Law Journal, The Independent Review, Issues in Science and Technology* (National Academy of Sciences), *Mediterranean Quarterly, Middle East and International Review, Middle East Policy, Nexus, Chronicle of Higher Education, American Conservative, International Journal of World Peace,* and *Northwestern Journal of International Affairs.* Dr. Eland's popular writings have appeared in such publications as the *Los Angeles Times, San Francisco Chronicle, USA Today, Houston Chronicle, Dallas Morning News, New York Times, Chicago Sun-Times, San Diego Union-Tribune, Miami Herald, St. Louis Post-Dispatch, Newsday, Sacramento Bee, Orange County Register, Washington Times, Providence Journal, The Hill,* and *Defense News.* He has also appeared on ABC's "World News Tonight," NPR's "Talk of the Nation," PBS, Fox News Channel, CNBC, Bloomberg TV, CNN, CNN "Crossfire," CNN-fn, C-SPAN, MSNBC, Canadian Broadcasting Corp. (CBC), Canadian TV (CTV), Radio Free Europe, Voice of America, BBC, and other local, national, and international TV and radio programs.

Independent Studies in Political Economy